Century of Genocide

D0380606

Garland Reference Library of Social Science
(Vol. 772)

Century of Genocide
Eyewitness Accounts and Critical Views

Edited by
Samuel Totten
William S. Parsons
Israel W. Charny

GARLAND PUBLISHING, INC.
New York & London
1997

Library of Congress Cataloging-in-Publication Data

Century of genocide : eyewitness accounts and critical views / edited by Samuel
Totten, William S. Parsons, Israel W. Charny.
    p. cm. — (Garland reference library of social science ; vol. 772)
    Includes bibliographical references and index.
    ISBN 0-8153-2353-0 (alk. paper)
    1. Genocide—History—20th century. 2. Crimes against humanity—
History—20th century. I. Totten, Samuel. II. Parsons, William S.
III. Charny, Israel W. IV. Series: Garland reference library of social science ; v. 772.
HV6322.7.C46   1997
909.82—dc20   96–44156
                                        CIP

Cover: Two Romani children on the outskirts of Warsaw, February 1941. Photographer:
Joe J. Heydecker, courtesy of Bildarchiv Preussischer Kulturbesitz, Berlin.
Paperback cover design by Lawrence Wolfson Design, N.Y.

Printed on acid-free, 250-year-life paper
Manufactured in the United States of America

To Leo Kuper, whose lifelong dedication and passion for justice resulted in noble actions and exemplary scholarship in the field of genocide studies.

Contents

Acknowledgments

Above all, we wish to sincerely thank all of the contributors to this book. All are extremely busy and dedicated scholars, and we greatly appreciate their contributions. At Garland Publishing, we wish to thank our editor, Ms. Marie Ellen Larcada, for her support, patience and guidance. We are also indebted to Ms. Chuck Bartelt of Garland for her gracious, quick, and outstanding computer and conversion work. Ms. Kristy L. Brosius and Dr. Sybil Milton deserve a special thank you for their excellent work in translating court testimonies that appear in the chapter entitled "Holocaust: Disabled Peoples." Along with Sybil Milton, we also wish to sincerely thank Dr. Michael Krausnick for providing insight into additional source material on Gypsy eyewitness accounts. With Dr. Rouben Adalian, we offer a heartfelt thanks to Dr. Donald E. Miller and Lorna Touryan Miller for granting us permission to publish several of the accounts they conducted with survivors of the Armenian genocide. Dr. René Lemarchand and the editors also wish to acknowledge and sincerely thank Dr. Liisa Malkki for granting us the right to reproduce the accounts of the Burundi genocide from her doctoral dissertation, *Purity and Exile: Transformations in Historical-National Consciousness among Hutu Refugees in Tanzania*. Finally, we greatly appreciate, too, all of the publishers and organizations that provided us with permission to use excerpts of various eyewitness accounts that previously appeared in their publications.

Foreword
Which Genocide Matters More?
Learning to Care about Humanity

Israel W. Charny

He was all alone after the inferno had ended. He had lost his wife and six children, also his parents, three brothers, and two sisters.

This is the vignette I begin with when I speak to audiences on "uniqueness versus universality of genocide," a subject I have been invited to talk about not only in professional settings but also on several occasions before both specifically Jewish and Armenian audiences.

In each case of a specific ethnic audience, the living survivors of the tragic hell of their respective genocide have no doubt in their minds that *their* genocide, the Holocaust or the Armenian genocide, was unique. I never argue with the survivors, for I have no question that on an experiential level, the staggering suffering endured in any genocidal event is in the eyes and hearts of those who undergo it "beyond belief," and beyond anything that any other civilized people could have endured.

In the small events of our everyday lives, too, each of us tends naturally to speak excitedly about our own individual experience of events—"I shook the hand of the president," "I was at the scene of the fire," "I heard the shot a block away," and so on. Certainly each survivor of a forced march to a death camp is entitled to speak of his/her personal horror as overwhelmingly unique in much the same way, and collective groups of peoples who have suffered genocide quite naturally frame the tragedy and suffering they have endured as unique.

I then turn to my audience and say, in each case according to the audience's collective ethnic identity:

I am aware of the pain you felt for this survivor, but I have to point out to you that I did not actually say to you that this 52-year-old-man and his family were (Jewish/Armenian). How would you feel if I now told you that, in fact, they were an (Armenian/Jewish) family?

and I then reverse the identity from that of the audience. The feeling in the audience seems to change immediately. Something of the terrible heaviness of shock and mourning that had been filling the room seems to lift the moment I suggest the victims are not of the people of the audience.

Now I comment on this phenomenon:

I have the feeling that the pain in the room has lessened now, but why have your feelings changed?

You seem now to feel less deeply for the victims than when you thought they were of your people. Of course, I believe that it is entirely natural to feel more deeply about one's own people, and less for another people, and I don't think that is wrong in any way. But you and I nonetheless need to ask ourselves whether we feel sufficiently involved and caring for this other people. How much do you as a (Jew/Armenian) *want* to care about this other people?

A discussion then generally ensues in which some members of the audience acknowledge that, of course, they feel more intensely about their own people, but that they also do care about the (Holocaust/Armenian genocide). Typically, some will add that they know many (Jews/Armenians); they have learned a good deal about their history; and, in fact, that there are historical connections between the Armenian genocide and the Holocaust because in the opinions of many scholars, the "successful" completion of the Armenian genocide paved the way for the Holocaust twenty years later.

Obviously, it is the simple nature of humans that we care more about ourselves first of all. Each of us cares selfishly about our own survival first, next for our loved ones, and then for our people, but we also should not be indifferent to the plight of others and the tragedies of their losses of life. In any case, it is also a matter of self-interest to care about the genocide of others. In cases of genocide of peoples other than our own, it should be obvious to us that any and every event of mass murder, to any and every people, also opens the door to greater possibilities of further genocidal massacres of additional peoples, perhaps, again, including our own people.

I turn to the audience once again and now add as follows:

The truth that I haven't told you is that the family I have described was neither Jewish nor Armenian. Please see now how you feel if I tell you that, in fact, the family that I described was Cambodian.

Now the mood in the room changes once again. It is evident that, unwittingly, some lesser degree of caring than before settles on the majority of the members of the audience; in both cases, Jews and Armenians tend to feel less familiar with and less involved with the much more different and faraway Asiatics.

Again I comment on the naturalness of the phenomenon:

As I said earlier, I believe it is proper to accept the naturalness of the fact that we all tend to care less about other people the further away we feel from them. In this case, these are people who live on the other side of the world, look very different from us, speak a more unfamiliar language, practice a religion with which we have less historic connection, and so on, but again the question has to be, how much genuine empathy do we want to feel for this other people?

How much do we want to expect of ourselves to feel towards a "strange" people who have suffered a horrifying extermination of their innocent men, women, and children?

In Western consciousness, there is generally widespread acceptance of the Holocaust as the single most terrible event of genocide to date in human history, to such an extent that it has become the *archetypal* or generic statement of mass murder, referring not only to its own incredible events, but now also standing as a reminder of other instances of genocide to other people.

Consciousness of the Holocaust has become not only a memorial to the terrible Jewish tragedy but a reminder of all mass murders, with the welcome result that, ideally, humankind can never again be as indifferent to or unaware of the dangers of genocide in the future history of our species.

The Holocaust is unique in a number of ways, but these actually underscore that much more how capable human beings and society have been— and still are—of destroying different peoples en masse.

Never was there a society so totally committed to an ideology of the total destruction of another people; never were the near-total resources and the organizational genius of a modern society devoted toward creating an actual "industry of death"; never were the tools of science and engineering harnessed so extensively for making more efficient deaths of civilians in assembly-line machinery that transformed people into disposable refuse to be burned in ovens; and never were a people persecuted so relentlessly as subhuman, degraded, and tortured cruelly and systematically for long periods of time on their way to their tormented "appointments" with death.

The Holocaust was a decidedly unique event which is superimposed on a pattern of genocidal killing long familiar in human history, and this is the reason it has forced us into a new stage of awareness of the dangers of mass murder in the evolution of human society.

Caring about Oneself and Others

There should be a scale along which one should be able to judge both the extent of devotion to one's own people and then *also* the extent to which one sincerely and maturely feels a kinship to the plights of other human beings.

Learning to care about human life is, of course, a psychological developmental process. It begins with an infant caring about itself and the unfolding of its natural narcissism of healthy *self*-ness. Disturbances of this vital foundation for life are seen in later years either when people *under*value themselves or when they overcompensate with *over*valuation of themselves (pathological narcissism, which might be defined much more as selfishness than healthy self-ness).

As the child grows in warm self-regard and as a secure human being, the child's caring extends through a natural progression to take in mother, father, and siblings, then extends to and becomes a basic loyalty to one's entire family.

From the connection to family grows a sense of connection to one's extended family, and then also a sense of inner loyalty to one's tribe, religion, ethnic identification, and nation. There are also other important focuses for one's identification and loyalty such as pride and acceptance of one's gender as male or female, and pride and loyalty to one's occupational group—profession, guild, or union—and place of employment. However, one must note that these natural loyalties also show up at times as obligatory and forced loyalties to one's "kinfolk" when, in fact, the person does not have a healthy foundation of self-love and there is no genuine love of one's family or people. Unfortunately, as in many other aspects of human nature, people can force an approximation of the subsequent stages of development. Many times people even make understandable unconscious efforts to continue growing, or at least to simulate growth and convince themselves that they are OK, even though, sadly, they are not really developing inside themselves. An example is how many people get married when they really are not ready for a marriage relationship. People who are pretending to feel loyalty to their family or nation, even if for understandable and decent reasons of wanting to be connected to their worlds, will, nonetheless, not be able to move easily to still higher levels of development of caring about and for other peoples and nations.

Along the way, any of one's natural reference groups—family, tribe, religion, etc.—can, and often does, betray or so insult the feelings and values of a person that the loyalty and identification with that reference group lessen. However, for a psychologically healthy person, even reduced identification, say, with a relative who has greatly disappointed us, or with one's nation when it has gone into a war that we do not believe is just, does not cause a final rupture in the more basic sense of *belonging* to the group identity. There may be mourning and sadness over not being able to enjoy fully our connection to those who have betrayed us, but the deepest connection to whom we are and come from persists.

For fully alive people, the range of belonging and identification continues to expand steadily with the unfolding of their lives and becomes part of an overall love of life. Slowly but surely, the developing personality becomes aware of new connections that go far beyond the concrete personal connections, to which one was born by chance, of one's specific family, tribe, or nation, and one becomes aware of many other human beings and their families, tribes, and nations.

A sense of kinship with all other peoples begins to take form, and a notion of a common humanity begins to transcend identifications with any specific sector of that humanity. One's sense of connection with one's own personal territory expands to a sense of larger geographic regions and of the common destinies of peoples who share oceans, forests, skies, and weather zones that go beyond artificial political territorial boundaries. There then develops further even a sense of being part of our entire planet Earth together with all the peoples who inhabit our one planet. Moreover, as mankind grasps dimly the enormous vastness of the universe and then other universes far beyond the territory of our own planet, the fully developing human being will also feel a tug toward a nameless, not understandable identification with a larger cosmos and its infinite history and future.

Within the context of such optimal psychological development, there grows an appreciation of the *holiness* of all life, and there develops a value-commitment to opposing the mass destruction of *any* people, religion, ethnicity, or nation.

Real and False Caring about Others

As indicated earlier, along the way people can fool themselves and others by adopting later stages of development that they have not really reached inwardly. Thus, many people can look like they care or talk about their apparent caring for other people, but not really feel caring.

Some of the most familiar examples of such false development of people and groups who take on appearances of connection and caring to others but do not really experience genuine respect and caring are found in connection with religious orders who preach "tolerance" but do not practice it toward the minorities in their midst. Many religious leaders, of many faiths, have risen high in their organizational hierarchies but do not really have in their hearts a spiritual connection with their Creator as having created the many different peoples of our planet "in the image of God." Moreover, as overall organizations, any number of religious movements have failed abysmally to fight against genocide. Many religions have not taken a stand against the genocides perpetrated by their own societies and nations; and many religions have themselves supported and themselves committed genocide in the very names of their gods.

Similarly, there are political leaders and movements that ostensibly call for "freedom" and "democracy" and "justice" but in the process allow themselves to murder masses of people in the name of these values. In the names of *liberté, egalité,* and all manner of idealistic values, people have gone into orgies of murdering. Self-righteousness is often the basis for arrogant self-entitlement to create ever-expanding definitions of who "deserves" to die as the "enemy" of whatever grand idealistic values.

Tragically, many times in history even previously oppressed groups and minorities who justifiably turn to revolution and battle against their cruel and exploitative rulers will adopt in the course of their battle a use of force that includes torture, cruelty, and mass murder of others. Then, like everyone else, the previous victims enter into a progressively expanding lust for killing. Once having gained power, the revolutionaries are transformed into new versions of preening narcissists and ugly dictators, for example, the bizarre megalomanic mass murders by Stalin and the Communists, Idi Amin in Uganda, or Ceausescu in Romania, all of whom cultivated bizarre forms and degrees of idolatry to their images and all of whom oppressed and brought about mass deaths of their "opponents."

It is entirely natural to care the most deeply about one's self and one's own people, and to care more intensely for some other peoples with whom one feels a more immediate kinship, but ultimately the challenge of human development, both for the benefit of individual mental health and happiness and for the benefit of humanity, is for more people to care about all human life.

Introduction

Samuel Totten
William S. Parsons

Will the killing ever stop? Will the scourge of genocide ever be eradicated? Will humanity ever be wise enough to prevent the deaths of potential genocidal victims *before* they "become yet another set of statistics in the welter of statistics" (Totten, 1987, p. 63)?

These and similar thoughts weigh heavily on our minds as we write this introductory essay to *Century of Genocide: Eyewitness Accounts and Critical Views*. How could they not? Daily broadcasts and reams of print journalism issue terrible news about the "ethnic cleansing" that took place in Bosnia-Herzegovina; the recent slaughter of hundreds of thousands of Tutsis and Tutsi sympathizers by Rwandan government forces and paramilitary extremists; the mass killings perpetrated in Burundi; the intransigence and resurgence of the Khmer Rouge in Cambodia; the hateful epithets and actions of neo-Nazis in Germany, the United States, and elsewhere; the incremental and insidious destruction of indigenous peoples' ways of life across the globe; and the ubiquitous deprivation of various peoples' human rights (which, at times, explode into genocidal actions).

It is also, to say the least, disconcerting that we live in a world in which certain parties and nations perpetuate the denial of certain genocides that have occurred. Such denial runs the gamut from those who refuse to acknowledge the issue of genocide due to the discomfort the subject causes them, to those who distort history for personal or political gain, to those who deny and distort out of sheer ignorance and/or hate. Scholars often arrive at different historical interpretations, but those who purposely distort the historical record and disregard vast amounts of historical documentation know exactly the game they play. As every attorney knows, it is often easier to create doubt and win than it is to prove what actually took place. Indeed, such deniers, minimizers, and obfuscators (Hawk, 1988, p. 151) seem to gain a satisfaction from the fact that they drain the energy and limited resources of legitimate scholars in genocide studies who are compelled to repudiate the distortions in order to keep the historical record intact.

By minimizing or distorting a particular genocide, deniers assault survivors one more time. In fact, one of the key rationales for including accounts by survivors and other eyewitnesses in this volume is to send a message to all doubters that no matter how hard the deniers try to manipulate history, accounts of the genocide will be heard *and* remembered.

The essays in this book also reveal, time and again, the attempts by governments to cover up genocides and/or to minimize the destruction of such acts. In essay after essay we read about the efforts of governments to rationalize mass killings; and thus we hear about "security zones," "enemies of the state," and "regrettable losses of life." We also read about the excuses and compromises offered by governments as to why they *choose not* to intervene in order to prevent acts of genocide from being perpetrated.

At times it is difficult not to be disheartened, especially when governments deny and distort the historical record of genocide and/or do too little or nothing at all when new genocides erupt across the globe. Indeed, at times it is difficult not to wonder whether all the scholarship, all the words, and all the pledges to "Never Forget" are simply an anodyne to ease the pain of the survivors and soothe the consciences of those who deeply care about such tragedies but feel impotent to stanch the deadly violence now referred to as genocide. And at times it is difficult not to wonder whether those of us who hold out hope that genocide can, at a minimum, be halted early on are doing so more out of desperation than any sense of objectivity or reality. This is especially so in this century that some have deemed the "century of genocide" (Smith, 1987; Charny, 1988b, p. 7).

We recognize that these are terribly bleak words and thoughts with which to introduce this volume; but then again, it is our sense that the situation cries out for bluntness and *anger.* That said, and despite the ostensible ludicrousness of it, we do hold out hope—no matter how slim—that somehow, some way, some day, this bleak situation will be changed.

Certainly a primary reason why we harbor such optimism is due to the fact that we see glimmers of hope on the horizon in regard to combatting genocide. Certainly the fact that the incipient field of genocide studies is growing, that there has been an increase in the number of activist and other nongovernmental organizations whose focus is the intervention in and/or prevention of genocide, that there is increasing interest in the concept of the development of a genocide early warning system, that there is talk of bringing perpetrators of current genocidal policies to trial, that an increasing number of scholars and activists are becoming more vocal about the need to break the stranglehold that realpolitik has on efforts to put a quick end to genocidal actions, and that there has been an increased focus on educating about genocide in universities, colleges, and secondary schools, all merit some type of hope.

Finally, we should note that when all is said and done, a key reason we are coediting this book is to inform, educate, cajole, prod, and encourage people to break out of their mold of silence, to collectively reach out to the victims and the voiceless, and to demand that such atrocities be halted before the tally of deaths becomes, once again, nothing more than another welter of statistics.

Issues in the Definition of the Term "Genocide"
Ever since Raphael Lemkin, a Polish Jewish émigré and noted scholar who taught law at Yale and Duke universities, coined the term *genocide* in 1944, there has been an ongoing, and often heated, debate about what constitutes the most "exact" and "useful" definition of genocide. To form the new term, Lemkin (1944) combined the Greek *genos* (race, tribe), and *cide* (killing). He went on to define genocide as

> . . . the coordinated plan of different actions aiming at the destruction of essential foundations of the life of national groups with the aim of annihilating the groups themselves. The objectives of such a plan would be the disintegration of the political and social institutions of culture, language, national feelings, religion, economic existence, of national groups and the destruction of the personal security, liberty, health, dignity, and even the lives of the individuals belonging to such groups. Genocide is directed against the national group as an entity, and the actions involved are directed against individuals, not in their individual capacity, but as members of the national group. (p. 79)

As one can readily ascertain, Lemkin's definition is extremely broad and even includes "nonlethal acts" (Chalk and Jonassohn, 1990, p. 9). After lengthy debate and ample compromise, on December 9, 1948, the United Nations adopted the Genocide Convention and in doing so defined genocide in the following manner:

In the present Convention, genocide means any of the following acts committed with the intent to destroy, in whole or in part, a national, ethnical, racial, or religious group, as such:

a. Killing members of the group;
b. Causing serious bodily or mental harm to members of the group;
c. Deliberately inflicting on the group conditions of life calculated to bring about its physical destruction in whole or in part;
d. Imposing measures intended to prevent births within the group;
e. Forcibly transferring children of the group to another group.

Quite obviously, this definition is, at one and the same time, extremely broad *and* extremely narrow. As a result, it is not surprising that over the years many scholars have proposed alternative definitions of genocide (Chalk and Jonassohn, 1990, p. 23; Charny, 1984, p. 65; Dadrian, 1975, p. 123; Drost, 1959; Fein, 1990, pp. 23–25; Horowitz, 1980). As of yet, "no generally accepted definition of genocide is available in the literature" (Chalk and Jonassohn, 1990, p. xvii). This, of course, constitutes a serious problem, especially as it relates to the intervention in and prevention of genocide as well as the prosecution of cases that involve genocidal-like actions. It also complicates the work of scholars as they undertake the study of the preconditions, processes, and ramifications of genocide.*

It should be noted that we, along with many other scholars (Charny, 1988a, 1988b; Drost, 1959; Kuper, 1981, 1985; Whitaker, 1985), believe that both political and social groups should be included in any definition of genocide. In light of that, we have chosen to include certain cases of mass destruction of political and social groups in this book.

Focus of the Book

The contents of this volume comprise two main types of work. First, there are critical essays by some of the most noted scholars in the field of genocide about various genocidal acts committed in this century. Second, each essay on a specific genocide is accompanied by eyewitness accounts regarding that particular genocide.

The genocidal acts addressed herein are as follows: genocide of the Hereros; the Armenian genocide; the Soviet man-made famine in Ukraine; the Soviet deportation of whole nations; the Nazi genocide of Jews, Gypsies, and dis-

abled peoples; the Indonesian massacre of suspected "communists"; the genocide in East Timor; the Bangladesh genocide; the genocide of the Hutu in
Burundi; the Cambodian genocide; the physical and cultural genocide of various indigenous peoples; and the Rwandan genocide.

Determining whether or not a contemporary case of mass destruction
is genocide is often difficult due to the lack of a historical record. A case in
point is the recent situation in Bosnia-Herzegovina. That said, and despite
the fact that new evidence is flowing out of Bosnia-Herzegovina every day,
the editors have decided that an examination of genocide in this century
should include a discussion of the events in Bosnia; thus a short but detailed
piece on the state of affairs in that part of the world is included in this book.

The cases presented in this book were chosen because the editors believe that each one constitutes an act of genocide or, at the very least, constitutes an action which involved a genocidal process. Decisions as to which
cases to include in this book also depended, at least to a certain extent, upon
the availability of leading scholars who were willing to contribute an essay.
Another factor that was taken into consideration was whether or not eyewitness accounts were available on a particular genocidal act. If no such
documentation was available, then the genocide was not included.

In order to assure some semblance of continuity, each author was asked
to address a series of questions posed by the editors: Who committed the
genocide? How was the genocide committed? Why was the genocide committed? Who were the victims? Who was involved (e.g., state, societal institutions, various peoples—ethnic groups, individuals with certain job roles/
professions, bystanders, etc.)? What were the outstanding historical forces/
trends at work that led to the genocide? What was the long-range impact of
the genocide on the victim group? What have been the responses of individuals, groups, and nations to this particular genocide? Is there agreement
or disagreement among "legitimate scholars" as to the interpretation of this
particular genocide (e.g., preconditions, implementation, ramifications)? Do
people care about this genocide today? If so, how is that concern manifested? and, what does a study of this genocide contribute to the field of
genocide studies?

Since the intent of this book is to highlight a range of genocides in
the twentieth century, readers need to keep in mind that each essay simply provides a *basic overview* of the various historical events, detailed though
they are.

Each of the contributing authors was also asked to select one to four of

the most informative eyewitness accounts that could be located of the genocide discussed in his or her essay. As the reader will ascertain, some of the
authors were hard-pressed to locate much at all in the way of eyewitness
accounts. This is an acute problem, and one which will be discussed in
more detail elsewhere in this introduction.

Value and Limitations of Eyewitness Accounts

Time and again, scholars have noted the unique contribution eyewitness
accounts make in providing a more thorough understanding of the genocidal process. In speaking about eyewitness accounts of the Armenian genocide, Richard Hovannisian (1973), professor of history and director of the
Near Eastern Center at the University of California at Los Angeles, has
stated: "Eyewitness accounts of decisive events may be as valuable as official
dispatches and reports. It is in such versions especially that the human element becomes manifest, affording insights not to be found in documents"
(p. xxiii).

Totten (1991c) has noted: "First-person accounts by victims and others are capable of breaking through the numbing mass of numbers in that
they provide the thoughts, the passions and the voices of those who experienced and/or witnessed the terrible calamity now referred to as genocide.
And, while first-person accounts serve many purposes, among the most significant is the fact that authentic accounts constitute valuable testimony as
to what it means to be caught up in the maelstrom of hatred and savagery
that is genocide" (p. xi).

Oral accounts remind scholars, educators, and students who record
and/or study statistics, examine documents, and argue over definitions of
genocide and interpretations of genocidal actions that innocent children,
women, and men perish as the result of genocidal actions.

At the same time, it needs to be noted that although eyewitness accounts are a valuable means of documenting historical events, their validity
as a primary source is only as good as the procedures by which they are
collected as well as the accuracy of the witnesses whose account is being
documented. The same research standards used to develop historical works
need to be applied to gathering, recording, authenticating, and interpreting
eyewitness accounts.

Dearth of Oral Testimony

Just as the documentation and scholarship is much richer for certain genocides and genocidal processes than others, the availability of eyewitness accounts of certain genocidal situations varies greatly.

Totten (1991c) has noted:

> The greatest number of [first-person testimonies] is available on the Holocaust. Compared with the number of accounts on other genocidal acts, the number on the Holocaust is massive. There are literally tens of thousands of such accounts in English, German, Yiddish, Hebrew, and other languages. [As of 1990, the Yad Vashem Archive in Jerusalem, Israel, had amassed over 50,000 accounts alone.] A much smaller but still relatively large amount (when compared with what has been collected on other acts) is available in English on the Armenian genocide and the Soviet man-made famine in Ukraine. An even smaller number of accounts exists on the Soviet deportation of whole nations, the Bangladesh genocide, and the Cambodian genocide. Finally, a minute number of accounts (again, in English) is available on the genocidal slaughter of the Hereros, the over 2,000 pogroms carried out in 1919 by the Ukrainians, the genocide of the Gypsies during the Holocaust years, the genocide of the Ibos in Nigeria, the genocidal massacres in Uganda under Idi Amin and Milton Obote, the genocidal massacre of suspected "Communists" marked for slaughter by the Indonesian government, the genocides of the East Timorese, the Guatemalan Indians, the Ache Indians in Paraguay, [and] the Brazilian Indians. (pp. xliii–xliv, xlvii)

There are numerous reasons for the dearth of first-person accounts of various genocidal acts, but among the main ones are the following: the survivors may not have been literate, and thus did not have the means to develop a written record; in the aftermath of the genocide the survivors may have had to struggle simply to survive, thus documenting their tragedy was not foremost on their minds; the survivors may not have had the financial means to take the time to record and collect testimony; the survivors may not have had a constituency that was interested in their plight and thus no one collected or supported documentation of their tragedy; the survivors may have been (and/or continue to be) leery of people who question them about their plight; and, some survivors may have continued to live under the very regime that perpetrated the genocide which, in turn, prevented (through censorship, coercion, or threats of violence) the survivors or others from documenting the atrocities.

The Gypsies provide a case in point in regard to a number of the afore-mentioned concerns. Gabrielle Tyrnauer (1986) has noted three major reasons why there are so few first-person accounts by Gypsy survivors of the Holocaust. First, Gypsies, for the most part, "lack a literate or historical tradition" (p. 158); second, owing to the horrific experiences Gypsies faced under the "racial researchers" of the Third Reich, they still do not trust outside researchers and thus frequently refuse to speak with them (p. 158); and third, "Gypsies remain invisible and forgotten when they are not pounding on the door" (p. 159).

In their introductions to the oral testimony that accompany their essays in this volume, a number of contributing authors address the dearth of first-person accounts. For example, in his introduction to the eyewitness accounts on the Burundi genocide, René Lemarchand notes that "oral witness accounts of the events surrounding the 1972 genocide are extremely scarce, in part because of the restrictions placed by the Burundi authorities on unaccompanied travel through the countryside—especially when the aim is to interview survivors of the genocide—and in part because of the logistical, administrative and political difficulties involved in gaining access to refugee camps in neighbouring states."

Speaking about the dearth of eyewitness accounts of the Indonesian genocide of suspected "communists," Robert Cribb reports:

The Indonesian killings have produced remarkably few direct testimonies by survivors or participants. . . . [In fact,] few records of any kind were made or kept of the killings as they took place. The few foreign journalists who were in the country found access to the countryside very difficult and were in any case kept busy reporting the complex political changes taking place in national politics. Indonesians on the whole have remained reluctant to speak about the killings, except in very general terms. This reluctance probably stems both from a sense of shame at the magnitude of the massacres and an unwillingness to discuss what is still a sensitive topic in a country dominated by the military who presided over the killings in the first place.

As for the dearth of eyewitness accounts of the genocidal actions perpetrated against indigenous peoples, Robert K. Hitchcock and Tara M. Twedt note:

It is extremely difficult to obtain reliable information on genocides of indigenous peoples. This is particularly true when it comes to finding first-person accounts of genocidal actions against indigenous groups. There are several reasons for this. First of all, most contemporary indigenous groups that are victimized tend to be located in remote places or in conflict zones which are difficult to gain access to or are dangerous. Secondly, many indigenous groups have members who do not read or write; as a consequence, written records of what happened to them are rare. Moreover, indigenous peoples frequently speak their own languages, not necessarily national languages which investigators tend to speak. The result is that translation becomes something of a problem. . . .

Gathering data on genocides of indigenous peoples is also difficult because in many cases the gross violations of human rights are ongoing. Individuals are reluctant to talk for fear of reprisals. It is not uncommon for people to express deep concern that those responsible for the genocidal acts would retaliate against them and their families for their having revealed what transpired.

Despite the aforementioned impediments and difficulties that scholars, activists, and others face in collecting eyewitness accounts of certain genocidal acts, it is still extremely disturbing that there has not been a concerted and collective effort by both the scholarly and activist communities to collect as many accounts as possible of the least-documented genocides in this century. While not wishing to appear cynical, it seems that by not assisting those who have largely remained voiceless, we—the scholars and the activists—have contributed to, rather than ameliorated, the problem. Instead of locating the survivors and other witnesses in order to "return" the voices to the voiceless, we have remained on the sidelines. Cliché though it is, it seems that if there were a will, a way could certainly be found in order to overcome many of the aforementioned problems. Certainly a place to begin the collection of such testimony would be in many of the refugee camps located across the globe. Other places are those communities and enclaves in various parts of the world where relatively large numbers of survivors of the same genocide now reside and where censorship and political constraints do not pose a problem to the witnesses or the researchers. We, of course, commend the efforts of many of the contributors to this volume for their Herculean efforts to collect eyewitness accounts under extremely difficult conditions.

Indeed, when survivors and witnesses to the genocide are still alive, it is incumbent upon scholars and activists to collect as many accounts as possible. Not to do so leaves the historical record bereft of what could prove to be invaluable information. It also constitutes a further injustice to the victims.

Scholarly Activity: Need for Intensified Study of Genocide, Its Preconditions, and Methods of Intervention and Prevention

The amount and quality of scholarly study of different genocidal acts has varied greatly over the years. More specifically, while the Holocaust is the most heavily documented and studied genocide in the history of humanity, other genocidal events suffer from a serious lack of scholarly examination.

There is a great need to continue the scholarly work that has been done in order to understand the processes that lead up to and eventuate in acts of genocide. As recently as 1990, sociologist Helen Fein bemoaned the fact, and understandably so, that

no stream of sociology or major theorist since 1945 has considered genocide focally, either to explain genocide or to consider its implications for theories of the state, of development, and of community and society. Few sociologists have studied genocide and even fewer attempted a general explanation: *this is also true of anthropologists, political scientists, and psychologists* [italics added]. There is a similar paucity of social scientists who consider state violence, terror and repression or the development of human rights: social science most often glosses over blood and victims in an antiseptic abstraction, masking the nature of the state, McCamanat observes (1983). (p. 32)

That said, as previously mentioned, it is also true that over the past several years a new field now referred to as "genocide studies" has begun to emerge. As Israel Charny (1988b) has written:

Like many catastrophic natural events and incurable terminal illnesses, genocide for many years has simply been an event that happened, with little to no warning, for reasons unknown. Even many of the peoples who themselves suffered genocide did not seek much beyond a "Bad man" or prejudice-discrimination explanation of how an enemy did them in.

Today, however, one can look with some satisfaction on the increasing emergence of scholarship and scientific study of genocide as a process whose origins and lawful development can be tracked with some measure of understanding and also predictability, and therefore one may also dare begin to think of possibilities for some day preventing genocide. (p. 1)

Certain scholars *and* activists seem to have come to the conclusion that, if there is ever going to be any hope at all of stanching genocidal actions, then they (and not governments) are going to have to be the catalyst behind such hope. And rightly so. Numerous times throughout this century no government (either individually or collectively) has taken it upon itself to address this issue nor to be proactive in this regard. Furthermore, as Leo Kuper (1985) has trenchantly commented, "I assume that realistically, only a small contribution can be expected from the United Nations, at any rate in the immediate future" (p. 21). He goes on to say: "The performance of the United Nations in response to genocide is as negative as its performance on charges of political mass murder. There are the same evasions of responsibility and protection of offending governments and the same overriding concern for state interests and preoccupation with ideological and regional alliances" (Kuper, 1985, p. 160).

We believe that a concerted effort needs to be made by as many scholars, activists, and nongovernmental bodies as possible to continue to study all aspects of genocide and human rights violations with an eye toward developing, as soon as possible, a genocide early warning system. It goes without saying that such a system will, at least at the outset and possibly for a good number of years, be quite rudimentary. So be it. Over time, it can be updated, overhauled, and strengthened with the aim of making it a more sophisticated and effective system.

The Need for a Well-Organized, Collective, and Concerted Effort to Intervene in and/or Prevent Genocide

Individually a person can only do so much to protest genocidal actions or to work on the behalf of oppressed individuals. Collectively, people have a much better chance of effecting positive change. Interestingly, it is estimated that today there are over 2,000 nongovernmental organizations working on various issues in the protection of international human rights (Wiseberg and Scoble, 1981). A small number of these organizations are working, in one way or another, on the issue of genocide. Many of them face a constant struggle to remain in existence; and this is due, in large part, to the limited resources they have at their disposal. As a result of this situation, both the focus of their efforts as well as their influence is limited. Certainly one key way for these organizations to gain more clout is to band together in order to complement and supplement one another's strengths as well as to act as a single body and to speak in one voice when addressing issues that they hold in common.

It is encouraging to note that the work of such nongovernmental organizations in the field of international human rights has been, on the whole, positive. As Kuper (1985) states:

> Given the poor record of intergovernmental organizations and of states in the punishment of genocide and mass murder and the paucity of formal interstate complaints, the major initiative rests with individuals and nongovernmental organizations. And they have been taking this initiative with increasing impact on international public opinion and on intergovernmental organizations, as notably in the campaigns against disappearances and torture. They act in both the international and domestic spheres. In the international organizations they are the main source of charges of gross violations of human rights. Nongovernmental organizations, in particular, carry out the important task of investigating and publishing the facts, and the reports of such bodies as Amnesty International have high credibility in international circles. Domestically, these organizations, and individuals, may be able to exert pressure on their own governments to take some action against offending states by diplomacy and by the more positive restraints of trade sanctions and the denial of aid. They themselves may organize boycotts and protests. (p. 188)

Those working on the issue of genocide need to begin to undertake similar efforts against the crime of genocide. More specifically, they need to begin to initiate campaigns against genocide with an eye toward influencing international public opinion as well as the decisions and actions of governmental organizations. They also need to establish themselves as a main source of documentation for investigating the perpetration of genocide. As it now stands, most individuals and organizations dealing with the issue of genocide are putting more time into working on the scholarly examination of genocide (including issues of intervention and prevention) rather than the actual intervention or prevention of genocide. There are, though, several major exceptions to this rule, and among the most notable are the German-based Gesellschaft für Bedrohte Völker (Society for Threatened Peoples), the London-based International Alert: Standing International Forum on Ethnic Conflict, Genocide and Human Rights (IA), the Denmark-based International Work Group for Indigenous Affairs (IWGIA), and the Washington, D.C.-based Refugees International (RI).

Gesellschaft für Bedrohte Völker, for example, conducts research and documents and disseminates information about genocide with an eye toward preventing its occurrence. Two of its major areas of focus are the plight of indigenous peoples and those of other minorities.

International Alert (IA) has two primary goals: conflict resolution and conflict avoidance in accordance with international standards. IA aims at promoting internal peace and conciliation through dialogue; and it works to draw international attention to situations of ethnic violence which may be moving in the direction of genocide. The focus and work of IA is certainly a start in the right direction.

A key focus of the work of the International Work Group for Indigenous Affairs (IWGIA) is the organization of campaigns to put pressure on governments and international organizations as well as the mobilization of public opinion to protest against suppression and violation of indigenous peoples' human rights. These efforts are often coordinated with human rights organizations in other countries.

Refugees International (RI) monitors and analyzes refugee crises around the globe in order to develop and promote strategies and solutions that address specific refugee needs. Using both quiet diplomacy and the power of public opinion, RI presses governments and international organizations to improve protection for refugees. In doing so, it "attempts to anticipate life-threatening situations, assess and recommend key protection and care remedies, and influence the relevant governments and international organizations to adopt these solutions" (correspondence between RI and Totten).

The need for a collective and well-structured effort by various organizations has been underscored by Julian Berger (1987), author of *Report from the Frontier: The State of the World's Indigenous Peoples*. More specifically, he states that "the proliferation of nongovernmental organizations working for the human rights of indigenous peoples has . . . brought its difficulties. There continues to be great duplication of research and publications, and there is as yet little pooling of resources and coordination of action" (p. 278). Though he was commenting specifically on the organizations that work on behalf of indigenous peoples, his comments are equally apropos of the efforts of those organizations working on issues related to genocide.

It seems as if it would not only behoove the international community of scholars and activists working on the issue of genocide to support the efforts of the aforementioned organizations, but that it would also behoove them, along with interested scholars and activists, to forge a working relationship, in which their work and the work of other nongovernmental organizations resulted in a strong and well-structured network which enabled them to combine forces in order to intervene and prevent genocide from taking place. Such an effort would constitute the inception of a strong, united critical mass working in concert toward the common goals of intervention and prevention. Ideally, such an effort would avoid the duplication of efforts as well as the lack of coordination that Berger addresses.

One of the key goals of such a network should be the development of a genocide early warning system whose purpose would be the early detection, intervention and, ultimately, prevention of genocide.

Genocide Early Warning System

For over a decade numerous individuals have called for, studied the possibility of, and worked on the development of a genocide early warning system (Charny, 1982; Charny, 1988a, pp. 20–38; Kuper, 1981, 1985, pp. 218–228; Howard and Howard, 1984, pp. 324–329; Rupesinghe and Kuroda, 1992; Totten, 1991c, pp. lviii–lix; and Whitaker, 1985, pp. 41–45). The express purpose of such efforts is to identify criteria for detecting conditions which are likely to result in the occurrence of genocide. The ultimate goal is to develop a system whose purpose would be to detect genocidal situations, disseminate information about genocidal actions, and apply pressure on objective, international bodies to intervene and prevent the genocide from taking place.

Speaking about the significance and value of such a system, Kuper (1985) states that "the setting up of an early warning system with related monitoring is immediately practical. [For example,] [i]n the past, the destruction of the way of life of indigenous groups was usually well advanced before information surfaced in the outside world. But this is now less likely, with the contemporary mobilization of indigenous groups and of organizations devoted to their interests" (p. 219).

In his report to the United Nations, Whitaker (1985) delineated a number of the components and processes needed for an effective genocide early warning system:

> In cases where evidence appears of an impending genocidal conflict, mounting repression, increasing polarization or the first indications of any unexpected case, an effective early warning system could help save several thousands of lives. This requires an efficient coordinating network, maintained in a state of permanent readiness, which should possibly also watch for early indications of mass famine and exoduses of refugees in conjunction with bodies such as the Office of the United Nations Disaster Relief Coordinator and the International Committee of the Red Cross. On an early warning alert being received, the steps to be taken could include: the investigation of allegations; activating different organs of the United Nations and related organizations, both directly and through national delegations, and making representations to national Governments and to interregional organizations for active involvement; seeking support of the international press in providing information; enlisting the aid of other media to call public attention to the threat, or actuality, of genocidal massacre; asking relevant racial, communal and religious leaders, in appropriate cases, to intercede; and arranging the immediate involvement of suitable mediators and conciliators at the outset. Finally, there are the possibility of sanctions which could be applied with public support, by means of economic boycotts, the refusal to handle goods to or from offending States, and selective exclusion from participation in international activities and events. Representations would also be made to Governments to enlist their support in the application of sanctions." (pp. 43–44)

Totten (1991c) has asserted that a key component of any early warning system should be the collection and analysis of eyewitness accounts of events that might be leading up to genocide or of particular genocidal acts themselves. As he has stated: "Time and again throughout this [the twentieth] century, some of the first warnings that a genocidal act was taking place were the appearance of first-person accounts by members of the victim group who either managed to escape or smuggle out reports, or accounts by other witnesses (e.g., journalists, consular officials, relief workers)" (Totten, 1991c, p. lvii).

While a completely operational genocide early warning system has yet to be developed, various components have been designed and implemented. For example, the work of International Alert is certainly in line with what needs to be done in order to detect and defuse possible situations that might culminate in genocide. On another note, Israel W. Charny, Director of the Institute on the Holocaust and Genocide (Jerusalem, Israel), has developed a major data base on all aspects (including preconditions) of genocide. Charny eventually wants to incorporate this data into a genocide early warning system.

Some of those who are dubious about the efficacy of such a system are concerned that unless the criteria for identifying the preconditions of genocide are clearly and exactly delineated early on the system might sound the alarm too often and consequently be disregarded due to its unreliability. It is our sense, though, that while an initial system may not work as well as anyone would like, to wait until such a system is totally reliable, or even, for example, just 50 percent reliable, is ludicrous. That said, we fully agree that there should be a genuine effort by those who develop and implement such a system to attempt to avoid "crying wolf" (i.e., claiming genocide) without ample research (which, especially in the age of information, can be accomplished fairly quickly); however, one of the most valuable contributions of a genocide early warning system will be to stave off situations that are moving toward genocide. Thus, even if a situation never explodes into genocide, the very fact, for example, that a team of conflict resolution specialists was sent to a trouble spot and managed to head off a massacre constitutes real progress.

Educating about Genocide

In his hard-hitting and perceptive report entitled *Revised and Updated Report on the Question of the Prevention and Punishment of the Crime of Genocide,* Ben Whitaker (1985) argues that

> the results of research [on the causes of genocide] could help form one part of a wide educational programme throughout the world against such aberrations, starting at an early age in schools. Without a strong basis of international public support, even the most perfectly redrafted [U.N.] Convention [on Genocide] will be of little value. Conventions and good Governments can give a lead, but the mobilization of public

awareness and vigilance is essential to guard against any recurrence of genocide and other crimes against humanity and human rights. . . . As a further safeguard, public awareness should be developed internationally to reinforce the individual's responsibility, based on the knowledge that it is illegal to obey a superior order or law that violates human rights. (p. 42)

We agree with Whitaker that it is crucial for schools at all levels across the globe to teach their students about the causes and ramifications of genocide *as well as* each person's responsibility for acting in a moral manner when human rights infractions (including genocide) rear their ugly heads. As for the goal of Holocaust and genocide education, Israel Charny (1993) makes the perspicacious point that the goal "must be to make awareness of Holocaust and genocide part of human culture, so that more and more people are helped to grow out of killing and from being accomplices to killers, or from being bystanders who allow the torture and killing of others" (p. 3).

In essence, the sort of study that we advocate is one that is immersed in both the cognitive and the affective (beliefs, values, and feelings) domains. More specifically, it is one that (1) engages the students in a study of accurate and in-depth information, ideas, and concepts, (2) contextualizes the history, (3) avoids simple answers to complex history, (4) and addresses issues of personal and societal responsibility both from a historical as well as a contemporary perspective. (For a more in-depth discussion of such concerns, see Parsons and Totten's (1991) "Teaching and Learning about Genocide: Questions of Content, Rationale, and Methodology," and Totten's (1991a) "Educating about Genocide: Curricula and Inservice Training.")

Indeed, an all-out educational effort by scholars, activist organizations, and educators is needed. Working together, these three groups could produce outstanding curricular materials and reach students in a way that has not been attempted thus far, at least, in regard to the issue of genocide. While such organizations could approach such educational endeavors in a host of ways, we think the following avenues would certainly prove to be a good starting point: (1) Develop engaging and highly readable resource books on genocide; (2) develop accurate, informative, and engaging films and videos on various aspects of genocide; (3) develop state of the art computer software on various aspects of genocide; (4) develop teacher manuals and curriculum guides that help integrate the study of genocide into existing courses such as social studies, history, geography, economics, anthropology, humanities, government studies, contemporary issues, English, and art; (5) establish international computer conferences specifically for secondary and university students. Such conferences could lead to a global network of people engaged in thought-provoking discussion about genocide, its causes and ramifications, the ways individuals and groups are working to intervene in current crises and to prevent future genocides, and other similar topics; (6) establish international "community service projects" where students in different nations work on similar problems to do with genocide in an effort to provide support for organizations whose specific focus is genocide; (7) organize an efficacious system for disseminating information to educators across the globe about genocide and ways to teach about it; (8) work with textbook companies to encourage inclusion of genocidal issues in their products; (9) collect video testimonies of survivors and eyewitness accounts, and edit the collection for use in elementary, secondary, and college classrooms; and (10) conduct research into the efficacy of current efforts to teach about the Holocaust and genocide.

Conclusion

The scholars who have contributed essays to this book are doing vitally significant, and, in many cases, groundbreaking work in assisting humanity to gain a clearer understanding as to how, why, and when genocide is perpetrated. They, and others like them, are to be warmly commended. Their efforts provide a badly needed and outstanding service. At the same time, however, and as we have repeatedly stated herein, what is still needed is the development of a critical mass of humanity across the globe to work for the intervention in and prevention of genocide. To develop such a critical mass, individuals, communities, and states need to undertake an effort to educate themselves and their children about genocide; speak out against injustices anywhere against anybody; remain vigilant; and finally, encourage, even prod, family, friends, community, and nation to be vigilant.

In that vein, we agree with our coeditor, Israel Charny (1988a), when he argues:

There needs to be a growing consensus on the part of human beings and organized society that penetrates the very basis of human culture that mass killing is unacceptable to civilized peoples, otherwise the prevailing momentum of historical experience will continue to confirm for generation after generation that genocide is a phenomenon of nature, like other disasters, and this view of the inevitability of genocide as an almost natural event will continue to justify it in the sense of convincing people that nothing can be done. (p. 23)

Finally,

> . . . it is easy to call for the prevention of genocide. In fact, far too often in [books] of this sort, as well as at commemorative ceremonies for the victims and survivors, well-intentioned people almost perfunctorily recall Santayana's admonition, "Those who do not remember the past are condemned to repeat it." Through its repeated use, this finely wrought and powerful notion has become not much more than a cliché. The past must be remembered, yes; but humanity must go beyond merely remembering a particular genocidal act. Inherent in authentic remembrance is vigilance and action. More often than not, remembrance has been bereft of such crucial components. As Elie Wiesel has eloquently and powerfully stated: "Memory can be a graveyard, but it also can be the true kingdom of man." The choice is before humanity. (Totten, 1991b, pp. 334–335)

Century of Genocide

Chapter One
Genocide of the Hereros

Jon Bridgman
Leslie J. Worley

In January 1904, a revolt broke out in German South-West Africa. The Hereros, who inhabited most of the best grazing land in the colony, rose against the Germans. Two years later, when the German Army finally succeeded in stamping out the last embers of the revolt, the Hereros all but ceased to exist as a cultural entity. Of the original 80,000 Hereros, only 20,000 remained alive and the survivors were so shaken by the catastrophe that they lapsed into a terrible lethargy which lasted for decades.[1]

On the face of it, the destruction of the Hereros might appear a paradigm of genocide, but there are some complications. By definition, genocide usually refers to the deliberate policy of a government as opposed to a random massacre by a local commander. To a large extent, the destruction of the Hereros was not the deliberate policy of the German government in Berlin, but rather the decision of the local commander. This is not to say that the German actions during the revolt were not morally repulsive, but whether they should be subsumed under the rubric of "genocide" is another matter. When the Nazi regime and its collaborators set out to annihilate the Jews of Europe, the whole administrative structure of the government was pressed into service to carry out this diabolical policy, and the few voices of protest that were heard were in vain. When the Germans began the annihilation of the Hereros, loud and insistent protests were raised in Germany and many agencies of the German government refused to be involved in what they considered an immoral act. These protests were not totally in vain. Eventually, the German forces in South-West Africa were forced to halt the overt slaughter of the Hereros before the entire tribe had perished. And yet, this was genocide because it was an attempt by representatives of the German government to destroy a whole people with the knowledge and the tacit approval of the Kaiser and the General Staff, the two most important elements of the government.

The Victims

The Hereros were part of the Bantu tribal peoples, and related to the Ovambo, a tribe so fierce and warlike that the Germans for the most part left it alone. Early European travelers among the Hereros were impressed by their physical, handsome appearance. Charles John Andersson (1856), a Swedish explorer, wrote, "The Damara (the Hottentot name for the Hereros), speaking generally, are an exceeding fine race of men. . . . Indeed, it is by no means unusual to meet individuals six feet and some inches in height, and symmetrically proportioned withal. Their features are, besides, good and regular; and many might serve as models of the human figure" (p. 49). Andersson was less impressed with the personal hygiene of the Hereros. "Both sexes are exceedingly filthy in their habits. Dirt often accumulates to such a degree on their persons, as to make the colour of their skin totally indistinguishable; while to complete the disguise, they smear themselves with a profusion of red ochre and grease. Hence the exhalation hovering about them is disgusting" (Andersson, 1856, p. 50).

Traditionally, the social and political organization of the Hereros was fairly complex, and centered around paternal and maternal groupings. The nation was divided into almost 20 different *oruzo* or paternal groups. Each had a chief, who generally acquired his position through inheritance, a herd of sacred cattle, which was inalienable, and lived in a *werft* or village of mud and dung huts. If a *werft* became too large, the chief usually permitted the founding of a new and separate village, but this had to remain dependent on and subordinate to the *oruzo* chief. Parallel to the *oruzo* groups were the *eanda* groups, which were maternal. The cattle of these were used to pay debts and at times loaned to poor members of the group. *Eanda* members were generally not allowed to live in the same *oruzo*. Thus the *eanda* organization formed a network which bond the Herero people as a whole together. All land was held to be common property of the tribe and could not be alienated except for temporary purposes.

By 1903, this traditional organization had deteriorated and altered somewhat in large part due to the increased presence of the Germans and other Europeans, and their influence. As the possibility of selling cattle for cash expanded, some Hereros became cattle ranchers. This caused social distinctions to appear between the poor "field Hereros," who owned few or no cattle and were obliged to work, and the richer Hereros, mainly chiefs, who had acquired large herds by means fair and foul. The Herero nation was divided into nine tribes. The largest of these was centered on Okahandja and was estimated to have some 23,000 members living in about 150 villages. Other large tribes existed near Omaruru, Otijimbingwe, and Waterberg, while the five tribes of eastern Hereroland were all fairly small. The total Herero population was estimated to be roughly 80,000 men, women, and children.[2]

While each tribe had a chief who was its nominal leader, even the richest chief was no more than a *primus inter pares* since all the cattleowners in the tribe shared in the decision-making process. Samuel Maherero held the position of Paramount Chief, a fairly new office, because he was chief of the tribe located in the Okahandja area, the largest single grouping of Hereros, and was supported by the German colonial authorities and the Rhenish Missionaries, since he was a Christian. In actual practice intertribal authority was almost non-existent as each chief ruled his own tribe, and the agreement of all the chiefs was needed for common action.

Even in 1903, the Hereros longed for and sought to preserve their traditional way of life. They were a pastoral people whose entire way of life centered on their cattle. The Herero language, while limited in its vocabulary for most areas, contained over a thousand words for the colors and markings of cattle. Herero myths extolled the fact that the creator gave them the cow and the bull, while the rest of mankind suffered with lesser gifts. So much did the Herero love his animals that he rarely slaughtered them. The basis of his diet was sour milk mixed with blood drawn from the cattle and the wild fruits and berries that he found in the bush. The Hereros were content to live in peace as long as their cattle were safe and well-pastured; but when their cattle were threatened, the peaceful Hereros became formidable warriors.[3]

The Perpetrators

In the early 1880s German influence in South-West Africa was stronger than that of any other European power, but for all that it was still minuscule. Furthermore, the government in Berlin, under Chancellor Bismarck, had no interest in imperial expansion. Bismarck modified his position somewhat in 1882 when he gave Adolf Lüderitz, a German trader, a guarantee of imperial protection for such lands as he might acquire in Africa, providing Lüderitz acquired a harbor and "clear title." Subsequently, Lüderitz purchased several large parcels of land and the harbor of Angra Pequena in South-West Africa from the Orlam tribe, and asked the German government for official recognition and protection. After a two-year period of inquiries to Whitehall and the Cape Government concerning the British position on South-West Africa, which resulted in no clear statement or policy, Bismarck in April 1884 had all parties notified that Lüderitz and his property were under the protection of the Reich.

In April 1885, Dr. Goering, the father of Hermann Goering, the future Reichsfeldmarschall of the Third Reich, arrived in South-West Africa as Imperial Commissioner. Goering's main task was to extend German control and influence beyond Lüderitz's holdings by persuading the various tribal chiefs to sign treaties of protection. Kamaherero, the Herero chief, signed such a treaty on October 21, 1885. Within four years, the Herero leader repudiated this treaty. Kamaherero felt the treaty was utterly useless since it provided him with neither men, money, nor arms and equipment to protect the Herero cattle and to fight the Orlam, a neighboring tribe with whom the Herero had cattle wars. To add insult to injury, Kamaherero told Goering that he was giving Robert Lewis, an English adventurer, power of attorney to exercise control and authority over the territory. The threat of English intervention along with the collapse of the Deutsche Kolonialgesellschaft für Südwestafrika forced Bismarck to dispatch Captain Curt von François with a small detachment of soldiers to South-West Africa. For better or worse, South-West Africa now became a German colony and the direct responsibility of the German government. The people of this colony were to obey the Germans not because they had agreed to, but because the Germans had the force to coerce them.

Why the Genocide Was Committed

In the autumn of 1903, the German administrators and officials in South-West Africa were quietly confident that the colony was advancing in an orderly way along the path that led to "civilization."[4] Since the last "native" uprising in 1896, law and order had, for the most part, prevailed. Year after year the governor, Major Theodor Leutwein, had traveled throughout the colony visiting the chiefs and dispensing justice. In the summer of 1903 he had demanded that the old Herero chief Tjetjo and his tribe turn in all their weapons. Backed by the support of the principal Herero chief, Samuel Maherero, who had been a longtime enemy of Tjetjo, Leutwein was able to enforce compliance without recourse to arms (Schwabe, 1904, p. 67). The whole incident seemed to prove to Leutwein that the Hereros had lost the will to resist the white man. Therefore, in the autumn of 1903, he withdrew over half of the troops stationed in Hereroland for duty in the extreme south of the colony.

Yet beneath the tranquil surface there was growing bitterness among the Hereros, and indeed most of the other tribes as well, at the treatment they received at the hands of the German settlers and traders. On the eve of the rebellion, a Herero told a German officer that "if the Herero is angry and storms at you there is nothing to fear, but when he laughs and is friendly be on your guard. . . . Sir, they are so crafty that (even) if you understand their speech and sit with them at the fire, they can be deciding your death whilst you think they are talking about flowers" (Wellington, 1967, p. 67). And so it was in the last days of 1903; the Germans deluded themselves into thinking their subjects were quiescent when in reality they were planning an uprising that would shake the German rule to its foundations.

By 1904, the Hereros had so many reasons for rebelling that it might be more profitable to ask why they had not acted sooner, rather than why they revolted when they did. First, every Herero was alarmed at the progressive loss of land. Up to 1900, only a minor portion of the Herero hereditary lands had been alienated, but with the completion of the railroad from the coast to the capital of the colony, Windhoek, the pace of alienation accelerated rapidly, so that by the end of 1903, three and one-half million hectares out of a total of thirteen million had been lost, and the day when the Hereros would not have enough land to continue their traditional way of life was fast approaching. The loss of land, frightening as it was to any Herero who looked only a few years into the future, did not yet in 1903 affect the daily life of the Hereros.

The problem of debt was another matter. For many years, Hereros had fallen into the habit of borrowing money from the white traders at usurious rates of interest. Leutwein had long been concerned about this practice, which he considered not only immoral, but also politically explosive; however, all his attempts to find a solution had been frustrated by the powerful colonial interests which grew rich on the profits. Finally, on July 23, 1903, Leutwein grasped the nettle and issued an ordinance which provided that all outstanding debts which were not collected within a year would be null and void.[5] The ordinance went into effect on November 1, 1903. This law, whose sole purpose was to wipe the slate clean after a reasonable period of time and then discourage further abuse of the credit system, had—in the short run—the opposite effect. The German traders, knowing that if they did not collect all outstanding debts within a year would lose them forever, not unnaturally began recalling their loans as quickly as possible. To facilitate the collection process, government officials, and on some occasions even soldiers, were pressed into service to aid traders. In some cases, traders turned over lists of their debtors to local officials; in others, the traders themselves expropriated as many cattle as they thought necessary to cover claims—and, as one trader remarked, a few extra to cover any future claims.[6] Moderate German newspapers were almost unanimous in citing the credit ordinance as the principal reason for the uprising. On January 25, 1904, the *Kölnische Zeitung* editorialized: "The credit ordinance . . . is one of the direct causes of dissatisfaction among the Hereros. The dubious past of the traders in Europe is quite often the reason for their being down there in the first place" (Bridgman, 1981, p. 60).

The Outstanding Historical Forces and Trends at Work That Led to the Genocide

The naked economic exploitation of the natives was a major reason for the rebellion, but a purely economic explanation is too simple. Racial tension, also a major factor, was real and very intense by 1903. Every year saw more and more white settlers coming into the colony "as conquerors, in a land which had not been conquered," as Leutwein put it.[7] Typically these new settlers were ne'er-do-wells, and not a few of them were criminally inclined younger sons of the aristocracy, packed off to "darkest" Africa to prevent them from disgracing the family name at home. The old colonial hands like Leutwein had a real respect for Africans as men, because they knew them as soldiers and because they had fought against them. The newer arrivals saw the black African as nothing but a potential source of cheap labor at best, and some even raised the question whether the colony would not be better off if the black population were completely eliminated. Indeed, when the rebellion broke out, a number of settlers voiced the opinion that the uprising was a positive advantage because it gave the Germans a chance to annihilate the natives. This prompted one missionary to exclaim in horror: "The Germans are consumed with inexpiable hatred and a terrible thirst for revenge, one might even say they are thirsting for the blood of the Hereros. All you hear these days is words like 'make a clean sweep, hang them, shoot them to the last man, give no quarter.' I shudder to think of what may happen in the months ahead. The Germans will doubtless exact a grim vengeance" (Imperial Colonial Office, File No. 2114, pp. 80–82).[8]

The consciousness of being white, which had no doubt played a major role in German actions from the very beginning, became a dominant factor for many colonists. White settlers normally referred to black Africans as "baboons" and treated them accordingly. As one missionary reported: "The real cause of the bitterness among the Hereros toward the Germans is without question the fact that the average German looks down upon the natives as being about on the same level as the higher primates ('baboon' being their favorite term for the natives) and treats them like animals. The settler holds that the native has a right to exist only in so far as he is useful to the white man. It follows that the whites value their horses and even their oxen more than they value the natives" (Drechsler, 1980, p. 133, no. 6). Among other things, this attitude manifested itself in the mistreatment of native women. In 1903, there were about 4,000 white males in South-West Africa and only 700 white women. The inevitable result of this imbalance was what the Germans referred to as "Verkafferung" or "Schmutzwirtschaft." From the perspective of the natives, "Verkafferung" meant that the German men took their women, peacefully if possible, but otherwise by force.

This contempt for the black African was held to be the reason for many acts of violence that whites perpetrated on the Hereros. Indeed, settlers were wont to explain such behavior in quasi-medical terms, inventing a disease called "tropical frenzy," which was said to overtake white men in the tropics. A German doctor writing in 1902, however, rejected such an explanation: "I have never found anywhere any evidence of the disease which in the accounts of murders in the daily newspapers from the colonies plays such a role, that is 'tropical frenzy.' . . . There are a relatively large number of men of a passionate temperament among the Europeans in the colonies because the average man of mild temperament would rather remain in his homeland. For a man of weak character there are, out under the palms, opportunities greater than in Europe to avoid the moral imperatives" (Drechsler, 1980, p. 133, no. 8). This contemptuous attitude was not confined to settlers. The Kaiser, and his Chief of Staff Count von Schlieffen, displayed attitudes hardly different from those of the average settler in South-West Africa; the Kaiser was known to have said that Christian precepts were not applicable to heathens and savages (von Bülow, 1930–1931, 1:24). And when Matthias Erzberger, speaking in the Reichstag, pointed out that the black men had immortal souls just as the Germans did, he was hooted down by the whole right side of the house (Epstein, 1959, p. 637).

Such, then, was the temper of the whites and blacks in Hereroland on the eve of the rebellion. The Hereros, or at least a large portion of them, had decided that German rule meant not only personal humiliation and economic ruin, but the end of their traditional way of life. Given this conviction, they saw little reason to wait and see if conditions would improve. By 1903, the tinder was ready and only a spark was needed to set Hereroland aflame. That spark was provided in an unexpected way and from an unexpected quarter. Almost 500 miles to the south of Windhoek lived a Hottentot tribe called the Bondelzwarts. (See Kriegsgeschichtliche Abteilung, Grosser Generalstab, for a detailed account.) Their land, which lay between the Karras Hills and the Orange River, was bleak and arid. Just how many Bondelzwarts there were was not known; the Germans, however, estimated that the tribe could muster somewhere between 300 and 700 warriors. A total of 161 white men lived in the area; included in this number were the military force, which consisted of one officer, three non-commissioned officers, twelve men, and two civilian policemen. Since 1890, the Bondelzwarts had lived in peace with the Germans.

Then, in 1903, the local German authorities ordered the Bondelzwarts to register their guns. This demand, which the Bondelzwarts correctly interpreted as a prelude to total disarmament, was rejected by their chief, Willem Christian. To enforce compliance, the district chief, accompanied by five men, rode into Willem Christian's encampment. A firefight ensued in which three Germans were killed and a fourth wounded. Four days later (October 29, 1903) Leutwein in Windhoek received news of the affair. He at once dispatched two companies of regulars to restore order in the south. After a month of desultory fighting, the situation had not improved, but had actually deteriorated. The Bondelzwarts were by then cooperating with small bands of robbers who infested the Karras Hills and Leutwein himself went to the south to take personal command, leaving almost no troops in the north.

The Hereros sensed at once that they had an opportunity that might not come again. However, the absence of the soldiers and Leutwein was also a danger to them. No sooner was the restraining hand of Leutwein removed than the settlers began pushing the natives, hoping to drive them to some desperate act which would permit a final solution of the "black problem." The Hereros trusted Leutwein (whom they called "Majora," with a mixture of deference and affection), but to the whites he was a traitor to his race. One German apologist stated, "Leniency toward blacks is cruelty toward whites."[9] And the German Colonial League produced a pamphlet which demanded that "the policy pursued so far towards the natives be changed in favor of our race" (Imperial Colonial Office, File No. 2111, p. 26). Shortly after his departure, rumors were abroad in the land that the Germans had suffered a major military defeat in the south. Some said that Leutwein and seventy-five men had been killed; according to another version, Leutwein had been driven across the frontier and interned by the British. In a letter to Leutwein, Samuel Maherero described the situation in Hereroland at the time:

> And now in those days the white people said to us that you (Leutwein) who were at peace with us and loved us, were gone, and they said to us: The governor who loved you has gone to fight a difficult war; he is dead and because he is dead you (Hereros) must die also. They went so far as to kill two men of Chief Tjetjo's tribe. Even Lieutenant N began to kill my people in jail. Ten died and it was said they died of sickness, but they died at the hands of the labor overseer and by the lash. Eventually Lieutenant N began to treat me so badly and to look for a reason for killing me, so he said: the people of Kambasembi and Uanja are making war. Then he called me to question me, I answered truthfully 'No,' but he did not believe me. I did not go; I saw his intentions and so I fled. . . . Because of these things I became angry and said "Now I must kill the white people even if I die." (Leutwein, 1908, p. 512)

During the last days of 1903 and the first of 1904, the Hereros made their final plans for a concerted attack which, they hoped, would undermine the sources of German power in their land. Their greatest single advantage was the element of surprise and they exploited it to the utmost. Leutwein knew Samuel Maherero very well and was absolutely convinced that the old chief was far too fond of the good life, particularly of alcohol and women, to take up arms against his friends and patrons the Germans who, after all, supplied him with the wherewithal to sustain his pleasures. Leutwein said of Samuel that he was "a large man, imposing and of proud mien, a man not without spirit and understanding"; but he added that Samuel was "lacking in character" and sacrificed the duties of his office as Paramount Chief to pleasure. Leutwein was convinced that without Samuel's name and authority, no common action on the part of the Hereros was possible.

The ultimate objective of the revolt was, of course, to drive the Germans out of Hereroland. This goal was to be achieved by undermining the German power structure from two different angles. First, an attack was to be made on German outposts and garrisons as well as on the transportation and communication system, with the objective of crippling German military power so that the German government would lose the ability to protect the colony. Second, an all-out attack was to be made on German farmers. They offered a tempting target, controlling as they did hundreds of thousands of acres of land and having 42,000 cattle, 3,000 horses, and 210,000 sheep and goats. The farms all tended to be very large and isolated, and were thus hardly defensible. In all, there were only 267 farms in the northern part of the colony. The Hereros reasoned that since the colonial government existed largely for the sake of those farms; and thus, if the settlers became discouraged and left the land, then the rest of the Germans would also pack up and leave.

While male Germans, both military personnel and farmers, were targets of the Hereros, Samuel feared that a general attack on defenseless civilians might easily lead to an orgy of wanton killing, and this he wanted to avoid at all costs. Therefore, on the eve of the revolt, he issued a strikingly unequivocal manifesto in which he declared: "I am the principal chief of the Hereros. I have proclaimed the law and the just word, and I mean for all my people. They should not lay hands on any of the following: Englishmen, Basters, Berg Damaras, Namas, and Boers. On none of these shall hands be laid. I have pledged my honor that this thing shall not take place. Nor shall missionaries be harmed. Enough!" (Great Britain, 1918, p. 57)[10]

While the Germans found this unexpected streak of humanity hard to understand, from Samuel's point of view there were several good reasons for this manifesto. Militarily, the Herero chief wanted to reduce the number of his enemies, and obtain, if possible, allies in the struggle against the Germans. The Basters, Berg Damaras, and the Namas were all traditional enemies of the Hereros. However, if the latter refrained from attacking these other tribes, they probably would not join the Germans, and might be persuaded to cooperate with the Herero against the common oppressor.[11] This same logic held true for the British and the Boers; by not attacking them, Samuel held open the possibility of British assistance in the event the rebellion sparked a colonial war (Drechsler, 1980, p. 144). Politically, Samuel also needed an ally or allies, someone to plead the Herero cause, particularly in Germany. The most obvious choice was the Rhenish Missionary Society. The missionaries in the past had supported Samuel and he owed his position as Paramount Chief to their influence. There was no reason to believe that if the missionaries were left unhurt and unmolested in this rebellion, that the Rhenish Missionary Society would not use its influence in Germany and argue for justice and the just cause of the Herero.[12] And finally, Samuel seems to have had a sense of destiny. From the missionaries and colonial officials, he had been taught that he was a "barbarian" and that they were "civilized." One of the most commonly cited proofs of the barbarism of the natives was their manner of making war—with indiscriminate slaughters of prisoners, massacres of women and children, torture, cruelty, and unrestrained sadism.[13] Samuel seemed to realize that he and his people at this moment in history had to surpass the standards of civilization as defined by their enemy.

On January 12, 1904, the Hereros launched their first attacks. During the next ten days almost every farm, village, and fort in Hereroland was attacked or, at least, threatened by marauding bands. The majority of the German farms were destroyed during those hectic days. By January 20, in the Windhoek area alone civilian casualties had reached thirteen: six farmers, one farmhand, two surveyors, two merchants, one policeman, and one 14-year-old boy. No women or children had been killed. Of those farmers who survived, all fled to Windhoek and, in most cases, they had lost everything: their livestock had been stolen, their possessions looted and their buildings burned. In addition, all the major fortified places in Hereroland were loosely besieged, though no fortified place had fallen.

Leutwein called the first days of the uprising "nerve-shattering," but despite the initial success of the Hereros, by late spring of 1904 German troops were pouring into the colony and the defeat of the Hereros was only a matter of time. In August, the day of reckoning arrived when the main Herero forces were surrounded and crushed at the Battle of Waterberg.

How the Genocide Was Committed and Those Who Were Involved

General Lothar von Trotha, the newly arrived commander of German forces in South-West Africa, had one aim, to utterly destroy the Hereros. With this in mind, he deployed his strongest units on three sides of Waterberg, while placing a weak force on the southeast. Thus, the Hereros could either stay trapped in a killing zone, or fight their way out to the southeast and into the vast wastes of the Omaheke Desert. In fact, von Trotha was following the results of a study prepared by the German General Staff: "If, however, the Hereros were to break through, such an outcome of the battle could only be even more desirable in the eyes of the German Command because the enemy would seal his own fate, being doomed to die of thirst in the arid sandveld" (Grosser Generalstab, 1906–1907, 1:132). After two days of fierce fighting, Samuel and the other Herero chiefs were forced to recognize the uselessness of facing the superior firepower of the German forces, equipped with thirty pieces of artillery and twelve machine guns. The Hereros broke through the German lines in the southeast and fled toward the desert.

Von Trotha pursued and kept constant pressure on the fleeing tribe, driving it southeast. When groups of Hereros broke off from the main body and tried to flee north or south, in either case away from the line-of-march and the desert, German units made sweeping, flanking movements to force the natives back into the main body and toward the sandveld. As this march continued, exhausted Hereros lagged behind and fell to the ground unable to move. The pursuing Germans, acting on orders, took no prisoners, but instead killed men, women, and children indiscriminately. Jan Cloete from Omaruru, who acted as a guide/scout for the Germans, later testified: "I was present when the Hereros were defeated in the battle at Hamakiri in the vicinity of Waterberg. After the battle all men, women and children who fell into German hands, wounded or otherwise, were mercilessly put to death. Then the Germans set off in pursuit of the rest, and all those found by the wayside and in the sandveld were shot down or bayoneted to death. The mass of the Herero men were unarmed and thus unable to offer resistance. They were just trying to get away with their cattle" (Great Britain, 1918, p. 64).

By the end of August, the Hereros had been forced into the Omaheke. Now the tactics changed from direct contact and conflict with the natives to the elimination of their water. Von Trotha had German units patrol the water holes, and drive away or kill any natives attempting to obtain water. The German commander defended his orders as necessary in the *Berliner Neueste Nachrichten* on February 3, 1909: "My force was on the verge of disaster. If I had made the small water-holes accessible to the womenfolk, I would have run the risk of an African catastrophe comparable to the Battle of Beresonia" (Drechsler, 1980, p. 158). At some point, the Germans poisoned these water-holes; now, the choice for the Hereros was to die from poison or to die from thirst.[14] German patrols subsequently found hand-dug holes forty feet deep, grim evidence of the Hereros' futile attempts to find water in the Omaheke Desert.

To prevent the Hereros from returning to German South-West Africa, von Trotha sealed off the western rim of the desert with a series of forts and fortified positions stretching for several hundred miles. On September 28,

1904, a small band of Hereros tried to break through the German lines; they were repulsed almost without a fight. "All contacts with the enemy since the Battle of Waterberg have demonstrated [that] strength of will, unity of command, and the last remnants of resistance have been lost," wrote von Trotha (Grosser Generalstab, 1906–1907, 1:206). The trails through the desert were littered with hundreds of carcasses. Prisoners reported that people were weary of the war and willing to surrender. They also stated that Samuel and several other leaders had crossed the desert and found refuge in British territory.

On October 2, 1904, von Trotha promulgated his infamous "Schrecklichkeit" (Atrocity or Extermination) order in an attempt to stamp out the last embers of the revolt before the end of the year. The order read as follows:

Osombo-Windimbe October 2, 1904

I, the great general of the German troops, send this letter to the Herero people. Hereros are no longer German subjects. They have murdered, stolen, they have cut off the noses, ears, and other bodily parts of wounded soldiers and now, because of cowardice, they will fight no more. I say to the people: anyone who delivers one of the Herero captains to my station as a prisoner will receive 1000 marks. He who brings in Samuel Maherero will receive 5000 marks. All the Hereros must leave the land. If the people do not do this, then I will force them to do it with the great guns. Any Herero found within the German borders with or without a gun, with or without cattle, will be shot. I shall no longer receive any women or children. I will drive them back to their people or I will shoot them. This is my decision for the Herero people.

Signed: The Great General of the Mighty Kaiser, von Trotha

This order is to be read to the troops at quarters with the additional statement that even if a trooper captures a captain of the Hereros he will receive the reward, and the shooting of women and children is to be understood to mean that one can shoot over them to force them to run faster. I definitely mean that this order will be carried out and that no male prisoners will be taken, but it should not degenerate into killing women and children. This will be accomplished if one shoots over

their heads a couple of times. The soldiers will remain conscious of the
good reputation of German soldiers.

The General Command
Signed: Lieutenant-General von Trotha
(Drechsler, 1980, p. 156)

Two days later von Trotha explained his order to General von Schlieffen,
Chief of the General Staff:

There is only one question to me: how to end the war? The ideas of the
governor and the other old African hands and my ideas are diametri-
cally opposed. For a long time they have wanted to negotiate and have
insisted that the Hereros are a necessary raw material for the future of
the land. I totally oppose this view. I believe that the nation as such
must be annihilated or if this is not possible from a military standpoint
then they must be driven from the land. It is possible by occupying the
waterholes from Grootfontein to Gobabis and by vigorous patrol activity to stop those trying to move to the west and gradually wipe them
out. . . . My knowledge of many central African peoples, Bantu and
others, convinces me that the Negro will never submit to a treaty but
only to naked force. Yesterday before my departure I ordered the execution of those prisoners captured and condemned in the last few days
and I have also driven all the women and children back to the desert to
carry the news of my proclamation. . . . The receiving of women and
children is a definite danger for our troops, to take care of them is an
impossibility. . . . This uprising is and remains the beginning of a racial
war. (Drechsler, 1980, p. 161)

The immediate impact of von Trotha's decision to annihilate the Hereros
was unfavorable. Leutwein cabled the Foreign Office: "According to reliable
reports the Hereros have asked for terms. Up to now the question of nego-
tiation has been decided without consulting me. Therefore I ask for clarifi-
cation: how far does my authority extend?" (Drechsler, 1980, pp. 161ff.)
When the Foreign Office answered that von Trotha alone had authority to
deal with the natives, Leutwein asked to be relieved of his duties (Drechsler,
1980, p. 162). Nor was Leutwein the only German disturbed by von Trotha's
modus operandi. The highest civilian in the colony after the dismissal of

Leutwein, Regierungsrat Tecklenburg, said that, in his opinion, German prestige with the natives was "lost beyond recall" by von Trotha's actions (Bridgman, 1981, p. 129). Also from the colony the self-interested voices of the Rhenish Missionary Society and some of the settlers complained; the former feared that if the slaughter continued, the discontinuation of all missionary work was only a matter of time, and the latter feared the complete loss of the native labor needed on the farms. In Berlin, dissent was heard in the Reichstag where liberal Social Democrats criticized the von Trotha policy (Drechsler, 1980, p. 151; Swan, 1991, p. 51). Even the government in Berlin was alarmed by the bad press that the military action in South-West Africa was receiving. On November 23, 1904, von Schlieffen informed the Chancellor, Bernard von Bülow, of the army's position:

According to all appearances our troops will be forced to stop the enemy from returning to the west by a system of extended posts and will have to carry on a war of attrition with all its horrors such as typhus, malaria, and heart attacks. . . . It is conceivable that in such circumstances the call for a quick peace will be raised. With rebels, however, a peace can only be concluded on the basis of unconditional surrender. Up to now neither the whole Herero nation nor even part of it is amenable to such conditions. Prisoners whom Major von Estorff had captured were released after good treatment in order to win their fellow countrymen over to the idea of accepting German protection, but they have not been seen since. If the Hereros will not come in freely then they must be forced and encouraged to give up. To enter into negotiations with the Herero captains for this purpose is out of the question. They have forfeited their lives and in order to create acceptable conditions in the protectorate, they must be removed from office. If General von Trotha has put a price on the heads of the captains, then he adopted the customary way of getting rid of them. The sums which he offered are, however, clearly too low and must be expressed not in terms of money but rather in terms of head of cattle. When the influence of the captains is broken, then one can hope for the surrender of Hereros in meaningful numbers.

The measures which von Trotha has taken . . . are prejudicial to such an outcome. One can agree with his plan of annihilating the whole people or driving them from the land. The possibility of whites living peacefully together with blacks after what has happened is very slight unless at first the blacks are reduced to forced labor, that is, a sort of slavery. An enflamed racial war can be ended only through the annihilation or complete subjugation of one of the parties. The latter course is, however, not feasible considering the present estimate of the length of the struggle. The intention of General von Trotha can therefore be approved. The only problem is that he does not have the power to carry it out. He must remain on the western edge of the Omaheke and cannot force the Hereros to leave it. If they should voluntarily leave the land we would not have gained much. They would present a constant threat in Bechuanaland in the event that the Cape Government would not or could not render them harmless.

There is therefore scarcely any other alternative but to try to persuade the Hereros to give up. That is made more difficult by the proclamation of General von Trotha which states that any Herero who tries to give up will be shot. If a new proclamation is issued which states that any Herero who gives up will be spared, they will scarcely trust this statement. Yet it must be tried. I believe therefore that it must be proposed to General von Trotha that (1) a higher price be put on the heads of the captains and the leaders; (2) by means of a new proclamation or in some other suitable way we spare the lives of those Hereros who give themselves up. (Drechsler, 1980, pp. 162ff.)

Put another way, von Schlieffen did not suggest that he was offended by von Trotha's way of making war, but he was convinced that it would not be successful. On the strength of this letter, von Bülow asked the Kaiser to lift the "Schrecklichkeit" order. He gave four reasons for doing so: (1) a policy of total annihilation was un-Christian; (2) it was not feasible; (3) it was economically senseless; and (4) such a way of making war would give the Germans a bad reputation among civilized people. The Kaiser, even when pressured by his Chancellor and Chief of the General Staff, was reluctant to command von Trotha to lift the order. For over three weeks he delayed, despite pressure from von Bülow, until finally in late December he gave in. Von Trotha was equally reluctant and when he finally bowed to the inevitable, he did it with as little grace as possible. Those Hereros who surrendered would not be shot, that much he conceded, but they were to be chained, used for forced labor, and branded with the letters GH (*gefangene* [captured] *Herero*), and any who refused to reveal the whereabouts of weapons caches were to be shot out of hand.

When the new policy went into effect in the beginning of 1905, the Herero revolt, or what was left of it, quickly flickered out. The surviving Hereros either voluntarily presented themselves at collecting stations or were driven there by German patrols. This once proud tribe which had numbered about 80,000 people had apparently suffered 20,000 to 30,000 dead in the period from the start of the rebellion to the conclusion of the Battle of Waterberg, most of these no doubt the result of the one major confrontation. While there is no way of knowing how many Hereros were killed outright, since the Germans did not do a body count, in modern combat (combat employing the machinegun and artillery), there are usually three or four wounded for every individual killed in action. With this in mind, the Hereros had 5,000 to 6,000 KIA (killed-in-action) while the remainder of the casualties had initially been wounded and fell victim to von Trotha's no prisoner policy. These numbers included men, women, and children because the entire tribe, or most of it, was in a single locale at the time. Between 50,000 and 60,000 Hereros survived the Battle of Waterberg and went to the Omaheke. Of these, about 1,000 reached British territory; rather less than 1,000 found refuge in Ovamboland; and perhaps the same number escaped to Namaland. An undetermined number filtered back through the German lines to their old homeland where they scratched out a living stealing cattle.

In September 1905, a sweep was made through Hereroland which netted 260 prisoners and 86 guns. During this operation, about 1,000 Hereros were killed. After September, there could hardly have been more than a few dozen free Hereros in all of Hereroland. In the German prison labor camps there were 10,632 women and children, and 4,137 men (Imperial Colonial Office, File No. 2119, p. 44; Drechsler, 1980, p. 208; Bridgman, 1981, p. 131). Subsequently, in the next year, 7,682 of the imprisoned natives died as a result of forced labor and harsh treatment (Imperial Colonial File, No. 2140, p. 161; Drechsler, 1980, p. 213; Swan, 1991, p. 53). It should be noted that this number includes some natives from other tribes, but the vast majority were Hereros. In 1911, the official census taken by colonial officials showed that there were a mere 15,130 Hereros in South-West Africa. Thus, out of the original 80,000 people, the Herero population had been reduced by 81 percent (Great Britain, 1916, p. 35; Drechsler, 1980, p. 214). Truly a genocide had taken place.

The Long-Range Impact of the Genocide on the Victim Group

"The death-rattle of the dying and the shrieks of the mad . . . they echo in

the sublime stillness of infinity!" (Grosser Generalstab, 1906–1907, 1:214)
So one German soldier described the end of the Hereros. The German official historians were blunter: "The Hereros ceased to exist as a tribe" (Grosser
Generalstab, 1906–1907, 1:214). In fact, the German official historians
recorded the truth. The Herero tribe ceased to exist as a functioning social,
political, and cultural entity. Further, the German colonial authorities took
definite steps to ensure that the tribe would not be a phoenix, and rise again
from the ashes of war and genocide.

In August 1906, the labor camps were closed and the surviving Hereros
were divided up into small groups and shipped off to work on the farms and
ranches of the German settlers. This move, in part, was motivated out of
fear that the concentration of large numbers of Hereros in camps might
possibly lead to a reorganization of the tribe, and another uprising (Drechsler,
1980, p. 208). With small groups of Herero dispersed on hundreds of ranches
and farms spread over thousands of square miles, there was little chance of a
tribal reorganization, let alone a renewed rebellion.

To ensure that the traditional Herero lifestyle ceased, Hereroland was
confiscated by the Germans. Hans Tecklenberg, Deputy Governor of South-
West Africa, outlined the Colonial Administration's policy in a report: "The
tribal property of the tribes fully or partly involved in the rebellion will be
subject to confiscation. Whether they have carried out, or aided and abet-
ted, warlike acts will make no difference. It would be a sign of weakness, for
which we would have to pay dearly, if we allowed the present opportunity
of declaring all native lands to be Crown territory to slip by. . . . With the
confiscation of their land, the natives will be deprived of the possibility of
raising cattle. All objections notwithstanding, they must not, as a matter of
principle, be allowed to own cattle because they cannot be conceded the
grazing land required for this purpose" (Imperial Colonial Office File No.
2140, pp. 28–35).[15]

This policy was formalized on August 18, 1907, with the issuance of
three orders. First, no native could own land or cattle. Second, all males
over seventeen had to carry passes. And third, any native unable to prove
the source of his/her livelihood was subject to prosecution for "vagrancy"
(Bridgman, 1981, p. 165; Drechsler, 1980, p. 231).

Now the remnants of the Herero people were reduced to a permanent
class of forced labor for German masters. Natives whose work was deemed
unsatisfactory by their masters were turned over to the local authorities for
punishment, which usually took the form of floggings. During 1911, 1,655

cases of official floggings of natives were recorded. Yet, without a doubt, this number is nowhere near the actual number of floggings that occurred in South-West Africa in that year since most white masters administered their own punishments. A farmer named Kramer, for instance, was charged with abusing seven women and one man. It was revealed that he flogged the man all afternoon, and one woman all evening. Two pregnant women had been so brutally whipped on two successive days that they miscarried, and two others had died from their punishments. Virtually all of Kramer's native laborers were found to have festered, whip-inflicted wounds. For his crimes, Kramer was sentenced to twenty-one months in prison, but on appeal his sentence was reduced to three months in prison and a fine of 2,700 marks (Bridgman, 1981, pp. 165ff; Drechsler, 1980, p. 235).

Although the Germans lost South-West Africa to a British invasion in 1915, the plight of the Hereros remained the same. They soon learned that while the colonial imperialists would wage war on one another, in the end the Europeans would come to terms in order to continue the oppression of the native labor force. Even the end of British colonial rule did not end the struggle for existence of the Herero. Only the administrative officials changed. Just as British officials had taken over from the Germans, South African officials replaced the British. But the Germans still ran the farms and the ranches, and life for the native laborer changed not at all. Now that South-West Africa has become the independent nation of Namibia, only time will tell the fate of the descendants of the Herero.

The Response of Individuals, Groups, and Nations to This Particular Genocide

The decimation of the Hereros was largely ignored by most of Europe and the world. For some, particularly the imperialistic segments of German society and government, including the Colonial Office, complacency was a form of expediency. The colonial officials saw in the elimination of the natives the quickest and most efficient solution to the problem of ruling South-West Africa. Without the natives the land could be settled by Germans and ruled as a German territory. It seemed to them a sensible solution for a knotty problem. When two minor officials in the Colonial Office brought forward to their superiors evidence of widespread misconduct by German officials in South-West Africa, the reports were quickly filed and no action taken, except to force the retirement of the two officials on the grounds of "mental incapacity." Ultimately this information was leaked to a member of the Reichstag who presented it to Chancellor von Bülow. The Chancellor's only concern was that confidentiality and secrecy had been violated (Epstein, 1959, pp. 647ff.).

For two years, from 1904 to 1906, the anti-colonial parties—the Socialists, the Center, and the Radicals—in the Reichstag time and again protested the misconduct in South-West Africa by, among other things, voting down budgetary requests. Then in December 1906 von Bülow dissolved the house and went to the German people asking for a mandate to carry on colonial affairs. In the only election in European history fought exclusively on imperial and colonial issues, the anti-colonial coalition suffered a severe setback. The German voters gave those parties and politicians favoring colonial expansion a massive mandate. Von Bülow took a record of inhumane cruelty and military failure to the people, and the people chose imperialism by a great majority.[16]

For Europeans as a whole, the revolt of the Hereros, and its subsequent consequences, was an all too familiar occurrence for all colonial powers, and thus easy to ignore or rationalize. While by European standards the behavior of the Germans in South-West Africa could be described as at best harsh and at worst sadistic, the Germans were not the only Europeans, let alone the only colonial power, to use and/or treat their subject peoples cruelly. The French—in Madagascar, in Equatorial Africa, and in Indochina—had suppressed uprisings with methods not much different from the Germans. The Belgians in the Congo, the Americans in the Philippines, the Dutch in the East Indies, and the Japanese in Korea had all used the machine gun, the whip, and forced labor to bring their subjects to heel. Even the British could be ruthless when they thought it served their interests.

The general European attitude can find no more eloquent expression than in "The Report of the Commissioners into the Administration of the Congo State." King Leopold appointed this commission in 1904, after intense international pressure, to investigate the allegations that Belgians had employed means repugnant to civilized men in order to control the Congo Free State. After cataloguing repeated instances of shocking treatment of the native population, the commissioners concluded that although such behavior was not exemplary, it was absolutely necessary to rule inferior races and bring them along the road to civilization. "In a word, it is by this basis alone that the Congo can enter into the pathway of modern civilization and the population be reclaimed from its natural state of barbarism" (Bridgman, 1981, p. 167).

After South-West Africa was occupied by British forces in 1915, an attempt was made to document the German atrocities against the natives. Two officers were assigned the task of investigating and drawing up a report detailing the treatment of the South-West Africans by German colonial authorities. This report was submitted in 1918 and provided an explicit, unbiased account of the German domination of the region and its consequences. While this could have brought the Herero genocide out of the shadows and into the light for all to see, the apparent purpose of the report was not humanitarian but political, namely to document the incompetence of the Germans as colonial administrators and thus rule out a possible return of South-West Africa to Germany after World War I. In fact, the League of Nations mandated South-West Africa to the Union of South Africa. This move placed British–South African officials and German farmers on the same side, one desiring a peaceful and prosperous region. At a session of the South-West African Legislative Assembly on July 19, 1926, a resolution was adopted which: (1) labeled the report an "instrument of war," and said it was time for all such instruments to be set aside; (2) asked for the removal of the report from the official files of the Government of the Union and the British Government; and (3) requested the removal and destruction of all copies of the report found in public libraries and official bookstores (Drechsler, 1980, p. 10). This relegated the most damning record of the German genocide of the Hereros to virtual oblivion, instead of placing it before the world as a possible warning of things to come.

Scholars' Interpretations of This Particular Genocide

It is possible that the general public and the world might become more conscious of and knowledgeable about the genocide of the Hereros if scholars were more united in their evaluations and interpretations of German conduct in South-West Africa. This is unlikely to occur, and thus for the present, at least, two distinct schools of thought exist and oppose one another.

The first, or what can be called the "genocide school," believes that the German authorities committed genocide in South-West Africa. Obviously, this essay supports this belief. Two of the leading scholars of this school are Horst Drechsler and Jon Bridgman. Drechsler's *Südwestafrika unter deutschen Kolonialherrschaft,* which appeared in 1966, is the most complete and carefully documented work to date dealing with the German colonial activity and the natives of South-West Africa. Bridgman's *The Revolt of the Hereros,* published in 1981, is the first work in English to detail the struggle of the Hereros and their destruction. Jon Swan (1991) has recently added his voice and pen to the "genocide school" with an article entitled "The Final Solution in South-West Africa," and has a forthcoming book which links the German colonial experience and the Holocaust.

On the other side, the "non-genocide school," the opposing view is set forth mostly by West German ethnologists. Katesa Schlosser in "Der Herero im Britisch-Betschuanaland-Protektorat und ein Besuch in einer ihrer Siedlunger: Newe-le-tau" recounts her visit to a Herero settlement in Bechuanaland, and plays down the consequences of the Herero Revolt.[17] The logic of her argument is that since 5,000 Hereros were in Bechuanaland in 1936, the number of Hereros who escaped the Germans and successfully crossed the desert must have been greater than previously thought. Thus, the number of dead was less than 60,000, and genocide did not occur.

More recently Karla Poewe has taken up the non-genocide cause. In *The Namibian Herero: A History of Their Psychosocial Disintegration and Survival,* Poewe (1985), who also questions the accuracy of the numbers regarding the Herero dead, explains von Trotha's "extermination order" as attempted psychological warfare. "The intent was to keep small guerilla bands away from the German troops. The former shot upon the latter unexpectedly and cruelly mutilated dead German soldiers" (Poewe, 1985, p. 65). She also denies that von Trotha's order really called for extermination. "The use of the word 'vernichten' which unknowledgeable people translate as 'extermination,' in fact, meant, in the usage of the time, breaking the military, national, or economic resistance" (Poewe, 1985, p. 60). Thus, she argues, no genocide was intended.

With two such schools of thought in existence, the stage is set for the debate to continue for some time to come.

What This Genocide Can Teach Us in Regard to Our Effort to Protect Others from Such a Tragedy

The study of and discussion about the genocide of the Hereros must continue for the valuable lesson, or lessons, it offers concerning genocide in general. Genocide is not a random, unconscious, or unplanned act. Genocide is always initiated and committed by deliberate, calculating, and thinking men. While a few of these may be irrational or insane, the majority are not. The majority are generally followers who see nothing wrong in their actions. The rational participants in genocide have, unfortunately, developed an irrational attitude or mind-set which allows them to kill thousands, or even millions, without remorse. Often these attitudes are culturally or nationally inspired and concern the superiority of one group and the inferiority of the other. Such attitudes and their development can be identified by the study of the Herero genocide, and in fact all genocides, and serve as a lesson or warning for future generations. With such lessons from the past, hopefully future generations will be able to identify possible targeted cultural groups, tribes, or races and prevent new genocides.

The overriding lesson from the genocide of the Hereros is that dehumanization or degradation of a people or peoples can lead to atrocities and genocide. It is easy to kill "subhumans" or "non-humans." Too many German settlers and officials of South-West Africa thought of the natives as "baboons." "Baboons" were not human and therefore did not have the same feelings and emotions, let alone rights, as humans. "Baboons" were wild animals. This labeling not only dehumanized the labeled but desensitized the labelers. There was no moral or ethical penalty to be considered in the treatment of "baboons" or wild animals, particularly when those wild animals bared their fangs and demonstrated their basic beastial nature. In fact, it was only prudent to destroy all such animals in the vicinity in order to protect peaceful, civilized white people from future attacks. Thus, the Herero were exterminated.

This same practice of dehumanization was employed against the Jews and others by the Germans several decades later. Hitler's propaganda labeled the Jews a "lower form of life" and the Slavs "untermenschen" or "subhumans." This resulted in the slaughter of millions in the Holocaust.

Unfortunately, even as this is being written history repeats itself as Serbian forces engage in "ethnic cleansing" of "inferior" peoples in the now fragmented region that once was Yugoslavia.

Eyewitness Accounts
Genocide of the Hereros

Firsthand accounts of the events in South-West Africa during the native uprisings are fairly numerous but vary dramatically in style, factuality, and perspective. Generally, these fall into three categories.

The first of these are the memoirs and journals of a popular nature. As one would expect, these were almost exclusively written by German soldiers and officials who served in the colony. Obviously, these were written from the perspective of the victors and treat favorably the Imperial colonial policy and the conduct of the war.

The second source, also German, is the files of the Imperial Colonial Office. Until 1955 these records were unavailable to scholars and other interested parties. In the Kaiser's day, these documents were held in strict confidentiality. During the Weimar Republic and the Third Reich, the Imperial Colonial Office files were suppressed for fear they might damage Germany's image and interests. And after World War II, all German government records were seized by the allies with those of the Imperial Colonial Office falling into Soviet hands. These files were returned in 1955 and placed in the Deutsches Zentralarchiv Potsdam. While East Germany gradually allowed more and more access to these files, restrictions continued to apply until the fall of East Germany. Thus even today only a very small portion of the Imperial Colonial Office files have been published, and a trip to the archives is often necessary. Interestingly, such a trip usually reveals that the German colonists and authorities, knowing that their reports were not intended for publication, submitted fairly accurate and straightforward accounts of the conditions in the colony.

The only account from the native viewpoint and in English, and the one used in this "Eyewitness Accounts" section, is the *The Report on the Natives of South West Africa and Their Treatment by Germany,* which can be found in *The Sessional Papers of the House of Lords* (vol. 13, 1918). Although the report in its narrative is anti-German, and at times quite dramatic and defamatory—von Trotha is called "no more worthy son of Attila," which of course is a reference to the great leader of the Huns, their barbaric warfare, and the derogatory name applied to the Germans during World War I—it does contain an extensive body of testimony from survivors of and witnesses to the Herero Revolt and the genocidal nature of the warfare.

What follows are a number of excerpts from the *Report* using the headings found in it:

The Outbreak of the Herero Rising and the Humanity of the Herero

Under-Chief Daniel Kariko, who is noted as a bitter lifelong enemy of the Germans, stated:

> We decided that we should wage war in a humane manner and would kill only the German men who were soldiers, or who would become

soldiers. We met at secret councils and there our chiefs decided that we should spare the lives of all German women and children. The missionaries, too, were to be spared, and they, their wives and families and possessions were to be protected by our people from all harm. We also decided to protect all British and Dutch farmers and settlers and their wives and children and property as they had always been good to us. Only German males were regarded as our enemies, and then not young boys who could not fight—these also we spared: We gave the Germans and all others notice that we had declared war. (p. 57)

An unidentified Dutch housewife, who was alone at the time the rebellion started, reported on a visit by Michael Tysesita in which he said:

I have come to assure you that you and your children will be quite safe in your own home. You are under my protection. Do not go into the German fort. The Germans are foolish to take their women and children there, as they may be killed by our bullets, and we are not making war on women and children. Keep calm and stay indoors when there is fighting, I assure you my people will do you no harm. [In reply to a question about her husband, Tysesita responded:] We are not barbarians. Your husband is our friend; he is not a German. I have already sent a special messenger to him, to tell him he is under my protection as long as he remains quietly on his farm. His cattle and sheep are safe also. In order not to inconvenience your husband, I have specially ordered my people who are working for him to remain there and do their work loyally until I send further instructions. (p. 57)

Barmenias Zerua, son of Chief Zacharias Zerus of Otjimbingwe, testified on the conditions of armament:

He (our chief) knew that if we rose we would be crushed in battle, as our people were nearly all unarmed and without ammunition. We were driven to desperation by the cruelty and injustice of the Germans, and our chiefs and people felt that death would be less terrible than the conditions under which we lived. (p. 58)

Preliminary Steps and Treachery of the Germans

Gottlob Kamatoto, a servant to one of the German officers, stated:

> I accompanied the troops to Ombakaha above Gobabis and near Epikiro in the sandveld. At a farm called Otjihaenena the Germans sent out messages to the Hereros that the war was now over and they were to come in and make peace. As a result of this message seven Herero leaders came into the German camp to discuss peace terms. As soon as they came in they were asked where Samuel Maherero the chief was. They said he had gone towards the desert on his way to British Bechuanaland. That evening at sunset the seven peace envoys were caught and tied with ropes. They were led aside and shot. Before being shot they protested bitterly; but seeing that they were doomed they accepted their fate. (p. 59)

Gerard Kamaheke, a former leader of the Hereros in the uprising and at the time he testified a Headman at Windhoek, recalled:

> The Chiefs Saul, Joel, and I with a number of our followers were camped in the veld at Ombuyonungondo, about 30 kilos. from Ombakaha. This was in September. A messenger, a German soldier, came to our camp on horseback. He said he had come from the German commander at Ombakaha, who had sent him to tell us to come to Ombakaha and make peace. Joel then sent the schoolmaster Traugott Tjongarero personally to Ombakaha to confirm the truth of the soldier's message and to inquire if peace were intended, whether the Herero leaders would be given safe conduct and protection if they went to Ombakaha. Traugott came back a few days later and said he had seen the German commander, who confirmed the message brought by the soldier. Traugott said that the German commander had invited us all to come in and make peace; that our lives would all be spared; that we would be allowed to retain our cattle and other possessions; and that we would be allowed to go to Okahandja to live. I fell in with the wishes of the majority and we left for Ombakaha in the evening, and arrived at the German camp at noon the next day. With me were the Chiefs Saul and Joel, and the under-chiefs Traugott, Elephas, Albanus, Johannes Munqunda, Elephas Munpurua and two others whose names I now forget. We had with us 70 Herero soldiers. The wives and children we had left at our camp. On arrival at Ombakaha the 70 men who were

under my command were halted near the German camp under some trees, as the sun was hot and we were very tired. Joel and the other leaders went on to the German commander's quarters about 100 yards away; they left their arms with us. The Germans then came to me and said we were to hand over our arms. I said, "I cannot do so until I know that Joel and the other leaders who are now in the camp have made peace." I sat there waiting, when suddenly the Germans opened fire on us. We were nearly surrounded, and my people tried to make their escape. I tried to fight my way through, but was shot in the right shoulder and fell to the ground (I show the wound), and I lay quite still and pretended to be dead. I was covered with blood. The German soldiers came along bayoneting the wounded; and as I did not move they thought I was dead already and left me. The Chiefs Saul and Joel and all other headmen were killed. I got up in the night and fled back to our camp, where I found our women and children still safe and also some survivors of my 70 men. We then fled further towards the Sandveld and scattered in all directions. (pp. 59ff.)

How the Hereros Were Exterminated
Daniel Kariko, Under-Chief of Omaruru, recalled:

The result of the war is known to everyone. Our people, men, women and children were shot like dogs and wild animals. Our people have disappeared now. I see only a few left; their cattle and sheep are gone too, and all our land is owned by the Germans. . . . After the fight at Waterberg we asked for peace; but von Trotha said there would only be peace when we were all dead, as he intended to exterminate us. I fled to the desert with a few remnants of my stock and managed more dead than alive to get away far north. I turned to the west and placed myself under the protection of the Ovambo chief Uejulu, who knew that I was a big man among the Hereros. . . . [I]n 1915 they told me that the British were in Hereroland, and I hurried down to meet them. . . . I was allowed to return to Hereroland after 10 years of exile. (p. 63)

Hosea Mungunda, Headman of the Hereros at Windhoek, stated:

We were crushed and well-nigh exterminated by the Germans in the rising. With the exception of Samuel Maherero, Mutati, Traugott,

Tjetjoo, Hosea and Kaijata (who fled to British territory) all our big chiefs and leaders died or were killed in the rising, and also the great majority of our people. All our cattle were lost and all other possessions such as wagons and sheep. At first the Germans took prisoners, but when General von Trotha took command no prisoners were taken. General von Trotha said, "No one is to live; men, women and children must all die." We can't say how many were killed. (p. 63)

Samuel Kariko, son of Daniel Kariko and former secretary to the Omaruru Chief, testified:

A new general named von Trotha came, and he ordered that all Hereros were to be exterminated, regardless of age or sex. It was then that the wholesale slaughter of our people began. That was towards the end of 1904. Our people had already been defeated in battle, and we had no more ammunition . . . we saw we were beaten and asked for peace, but the German General refused peace and said all should die. We then fled towards the Sandveld of the Kalahari Desert. Those of our people who escaped the bullets and bayonets died miserably of hunger and thirst in the desert. A few thousand managed to turn back and sneak through the German lines to where there were water and roots and berries to live on. (p. 63)

Manuel Timbu, a Cape Bastard and Court Interpreter in native languages at Omaruru, described his experiences with the Germans:

I was sent to Okahandja and appointed groom to the German commander, General von Trotha. I had to look after his horses and to do odd jobs at his headquarters. We followed the retreating Hereros from Okahandja to Waterberg, and from there to the borders of the Kalahari Desert. When leaving Okahandja, General von Trotha issued orders to his troops that no quarter was to be given to the enemy. No prisoners were to be taken, but all, regardless of age or sex, were to be killed. General von Trotha said, "We must exterminate them, so that we won't be bothered with rebellions in the future." As a result of this order the soldiers shot all natives we came across. It did not matter who they were. Some were peaceful people who had not gone into rebellion; others, such as old men and old women, had never left their homes; yet they were all shot. I often saw this done. Once while on the march near Hamakari beyond Waterberg, we came to some water-holes. It was winter time and very cold. We came on two very old Herero women. They had made a small fire and were warming themselves. They had dropped back from the main body of Hereros owing to exhaustion. Von Trotha and his staff were present. A German soldier dismounted, walked up to the old women and shot them both as they lay there. Riding along we got to a vlei, where we camped. While we were there a Herero woman came walking up to us from the bush. I was the Herero interpreter. I was told to take the woman to the General to see if she could give information as to the whereabouts of the enemy. I took her to General von Trotha; she was quite a young woman and looked tired and hungry. Von Trotha asked her several questions, but she did not seem inclined to give information. She said her people had all gone toward the east, but as she was a weak woman she could not keep up with them. Von Trotha then ordered that she should be taken aside and bayoneted. I took the woman away and a soldier came up with his bayonet in his hand. He offered it to me and said I had better stab the woman. I said I would never dream of doing such a thing and asked why the poor woman could not be allowed to live. The soldier laughed, and said, "If you won't do it, I will show you what a German soldier can do." He took the woman aside a few paces and drove the bayonet through her body. He then withdrew the bayonet and brought it all dripping with blood and poked it under my nose in a jeering way, saying, "You see, I have done it." Officers and soldiers were standing around looking on, but no one interfered to save the woman. Her body was not buried, but, like all others they killed, simply allowed to lie and rot and be eaten by wild animals.

A little further ahead we came to a place where the Hereros had abandoned some goats which were too weak to go further. There was no water to be had for miles around. There we found a young Herero, a boy of about 10 years of age. He apparently lost his people. As we passed he called out to us that he was hungry and thirsty. I would have given him something, but was forbidden to do so. The Germans discussed the advisability of killing him, and someone said that he would die of thirst in a day or so and it was not worthwhile bothering, so they passed on and left him there. On our return journey we again halted at Hamakari. There, near a hut, we saw an old Herero

woman of about 50 or 60 years digging in the ground for wild onions. Von Trotha and his staff were present. A soldier named Konig
jumped off his horse and shot the woman through the forehead at
point blank range. Before he shot her, he said, "I am going to kill
you." She simply looked up and said, "I thank you." That night we
slept at Hamakari. The next day we moved off again and came across
another woman of about 30. She was also busy digging wild onions
and took no notice of us. A soldier named Schilling walked up behind her and shot her through the back. I was an eyewitness of everything I related. In addition I saw the bleeding bodies of hundreds of
men, women and children, old and young, lying along the road as we
passed. They had all been killed by our advanced guards. I was for
nearly two years with the German troops and always with General
von Trotha. I know of no instance in which prisoners were spared.
(pp. 63ff.)

Jan Cloete, a Bastard of Omaruru, stated:

I was in Omaruru in 1904. I was commandeered by the Germans to
act as a guide for them to the Waterberg district, as I knew the country
well. I was with the 4th Field Company under Hauptmann Richardt.
The commander of the troops was General von Trotha. I was present at
Hamakari, near Waterberg when the Hereros were defeated in battle.
After the battle, all men, women and children, wounded and un-
.wounded, who fell into the hands of the Germans were killed without
mercy. The Germans then pursued the others, and all stragglers on the
roadside and in the veld were shot down and bayoneted. The great
majority of the Herero men were unarmed and could make no fight.
They were merely trying to get away with their cattle. Some distance
beyond Hamakari we camped at a water-hole. While there, a German
soldier found a little Herero baby boy about nine months old lying in
the bush. The child was crying. He brought it into the camp where I
was. The soldiers formed a ring and started throwing the child to one
another and catching it as if it were a ball. The child was terrified and
hurt and was crying very much. After a time they got tired of this and
one of the soldiers fixed his bayonet on his rifle and said he would catch
the boy. The child was tossed into the air towards him and as it fell he
caught it and transfixed the body with the bayonet. The child died in a

few minutes and the incident was greeted with roars of laughter by the Germans, who seemed to think it was a great joke. I felt quite ill and turned away in disgust because, although I knew they had orders to kill all, I thought they would have pity on the child. I decided to go no further, as the horrible things I saw upset me, so I pretended that I was ill, and as the Captain got ill too and had to return, I was ordered to go back with him as guide. After I got home I flatly refused to go out with the soldiers again. (pp. 64ff.)

Johannes Kruger, a bastard of Ghaub, was appointed by Leutwein as "Chief" of the Bushmen and Berg-Damaras of the Gootfontein area. Kruger testified:

I went with the German troops right through the Herero rebellion. The Afrikaner Hottentots of my werft were with me. We refused to kill Herero women and children, but the Germans spared none. They killed thousands and thousands. I saw this bloody work for days and days and every day. Often, and especially at Waterberg, the young Herero women and girls were violated by the German soldiers before being killed. Two of my Hottentots, Jan Wint and David Swartbooi (who is now dead) were invited by the German soldiers to join them in violating Herero girls. The two Hottentots refused to do so. (p. 65)

Jan Kubas, a Griqua living at Gootfontein, stated:

I went with the German troops to Hamakari and beyond. . . . The Germans took no prisoners. They killed thousands and thousands of women and children along the roadsides. They bayoneted them and hit them to death with the butt ends of their guns. Words cannot be found to relate what happened; it was too terrible. They were lying exhausted and harmless along the roads, and as the soldiers passed they simply slaughtered them in cold blood. Mothers holding babies at their breasts, little boys and little girls; old people too old to fight and old grandmothers, none received mercy; they were killed, all of them, and left to lie and rot on the veld for the vultures and wild animals to eat. They slaughtered until there were no more Hereros left to kill. I saw this every day; I was with them. A few Hereros managed to escape in the bush and wandered about, living on roots and wild fruits. Von Trotha was the German General in charge. (p. 65)

Hendrik Campbell, War Commandant of the Bastard tribe of Rehoboth and Commander of the Bastard Contingent called out by the Germans to help them, testified:

> At Katjura we had a fight with the Hereros, and drove them from their position. After the fight was over, we discovered eight or nine sick Herero women who had been left behind. Some of them were blind. Water and food had been left with them. The German soldiers burnt them alive in the hut in which they were living. The Bastard soldiers intervened and tried to prevent this, but when they failed, Hendrik van Wyk reported the matter to me. I immediately went to the German commander and complained. He said to me "that does not matter, they might have infected us with some disease." . . . Afterward at Otjimbende we (the Bastards) captured 70 Hereros. I handed them over to Ober-Leutenants Volkmann and Zelow. I then went on patrol, and returned two days later, to find the Hereros lying dead in a kraal. My men reported to me that they had all been shot and bayoneted by German soldiers. Shortly afterwards, General von Trotha and his staff accompanied by two missionaries, visited the camp. He said to me, "You look dissatisfied. Do you already wish to go home?"
>
> "No," I replied, "the German Government has an agreement with us and I want to have no misunderstandings on the part of the Bastard Government, otherwise the same may happen to us weak people as has happened to those lying in the kraal yonder."
>
> Lieut. Zelow gave answer: "The Hereros also do so." I said, "But, Lieutenant, as a civilized people you should give us a better example." To this von Trotha remarked, "The entire Herero people must be exterminated." (p. 65)

Daniel Esma, a European who lived at Omaruru and drove transport wagons for the Germans, stated:

> I was present at the fight at Gross Barmen, near Okahandja, in 1904. After the fight the soldiers (marines from the warship "Habicht") were searching the bush. I went with them out of curiosity. We came across a wounded Herero lying in the shade of a tree. He was a very tall, powerful man and looked like one of their headmen. He had his Bible next to his head and his hat over his face. I walked up to him and saw

that he was wounded high up in the left hip. I took the hat off his face and asked him if he felt bad. He replied to me in Herero, "Yes, I feel I am going to die." The German marines, whose bayonets were fixed, were looking on. One of them said to me, "What does he reply?" I told him. "Well," remarked the soldier, "if he is keen on dying he had better have this also." With that he stooped down and drove his bayonet into the body of the prostrate Herero, ripping up his stomach and chest and exposing the intestines. I was so horrified that I returned to my wagons at once.

In August 1904, I was taking a convoy of provisions to the troops at the front line. At a place called Ouparakane, in the Waterberg district, we were outspanned for breakfast when two Hereros, a man and his wife, came walking to us out of of the bush. Under-Officer Wolff and a few German soldiers were escort to the wagons and were with me. The Herero man was a cripple, and walked with difficulty, leaning on a stick and on his wife's arm. He had a bullet wound through the leg. They came to my wagon, and I spoke to them in Herero. The man said he had decided to return to Omaruru and surrender to the authorities, as he could not possibly keep up with his people who were retreating to the desert, and that his wife had decided to accompany him. He was quite unarmed and famished. I gave them some food and coffee and they sat there for over an hour telling me of their hardships and privations. The German soldiers looked on, but did not interfere. I then gave the two natives a little food for their journey. They thanked me and then started to walk along the road slowly to Omaruru. When they had gone about 60 yards away from us I saw Wolff, the Under-Officer, and a soldier taking aim at them. I called out, but it was too late. They shot both of them. I said to Wolff, "How on earth did you have the heart to do such a thing? It is nothing but cruel murder." He merely laughed, and said, "Oh! These swine must all be killed; we are not going to spare a single one."

I spent a great part of my time during the rebellion at Okahandja, loading stores at the depot. There the hanging of natives was a common occurrence. A German officer had the right to order a native to be hanged. No trial or court was necessary. Many were hanged merely on suspicion. One day alone I saw seven Hereros hanged in a row, and on other days twos and threes. The Germans did not worry about rope. They used ordinary fencing wire, and the unfortunate native was hoisted up by the neck and allowed to die of slow strangulation. This was all done in public, and the bodies were allowed to hang a day or so as an example to the other natives. Natives who were placed in gaol at the time never came out alive. Many died of sheer starvation and brutal treatment. . . . The Hereros were far more humane in the field than the Germans. They were once a fine race. Now we have only a miserable remnant left. (p. 66)

Johann Noothout, a Hollander and naturalized British subject, testified:

I left Cape Town during the year 1906, and signed on with the Protectorate troops in South-West Africa. I arrived at Luderitzbucht, and after staying there a few minutes I perceived nearly 500 native women lying on the beach, all bearing indications of being slowly starved to death. Every morning and towards evening four women carried a stretcher containing about four or five corpses, and they had also to dig the graves and bury them. I then started to trek to Kubub and Aus, and on the road I discovered bodies of native women lying between stones and devoured by birds of prey. Some bore signs of having been beaten to death. . . . If a prisoner were found outside the Herero prisoners' camp, he would be brought before the Lieutenant and flogged with a sjambok. Fifty lashes were generally imposed. The manner in which the flogging was carried out was the most cruel imaginable . . . pieces of flesh would fly from the victim's body into the air. . . .

My observations during my stay in the country (in the German time) gave me the opinion that the Germans are absolutely unfit to colonise, as their atrocious crimes and cold-blooded murders were committed with one object—to extinguish the native race. (p. 100)

Hendrick Fraser swore under oath:

When I got to Swakopmund I saw very many Herero prisoners of war who had been captured in the rebellion which was still going on in the country. [Note: these were prisoners captured before von Trotha's arrival.] There must have been about 600 men, women and children prisoners. They were in an enclosure on the beach, fenced in with barbed wire. The women were made to do hard labor just like the men. The sand is very deep and heavy there. The women had to load carts and trolleys, and also to draw Scotch-cart loads of goods to Nonidas [9–10 km. away] where there was a depot. The women were put in spans of eight to each Scotch-cart and were made to pull like draught animals. Many were half-starved and weak, and died of sheer exhaustion. Those who did not work well were brutally flogged with sjamboks. I even saw women knocked down with pick handles. The German soldiers did this. I personally saw six women [Herero girls] murdered by German soldiers. They were ripped open with bayonets. I saw the bodies. I was there six months, and the Hereros died daily in large numbers as a result of exhaustion, ill-treatment and exposure. They were poorly fed, and often begged me and other Cape boys for a little food. . . . The soldiers used the young Herero girls to satisfy their passions. Prisoners continued to come in while I was there; but I don't think half of them survived the treatment they received.

After six months at Swakopmund I was sent to Karibib towards the end of September 1904. [Note: von Trotha's extermination order was issued about August 1904.] There I also saw an enclosure with Hereros waiting for transport to Swakopmund. Many were dying of starvation and exhaustion. They were all thin and worn out. They were not made to work so hard at Karibib, and appeared to be less harshly treated. (p. 100)

Samuel Kariko, Herero schoolmaster and son of Under-Chief Daniel Kariko, stated:

When von Trotha left, we were advised of a circular which the new Governor, von Lindequist, had issued in which he promised to spare the lives of our people if we came in from the bush and mountains where we lived liked hunted game. We then began to come in. I went to Okambahe, near my old home, and surrendered. We then had no cattle left, and more than three-quarters of our people had perished, far more. There were only a few thousands of us left, and we were walking skeletons, with no flesh, only skin and bones. They collected us in groups and made us work for the little food we got. I was sent down with others to an island far in the south, at Luderitzbucht. There on that island were thousands of Herero and Hottentot prisoners. We had to live there. Men, women and children were all huddled together. We had no proper clothing, no blankets, and the night air on the sea was bitterly cold. The wet sea fogs drenched us and made our teeth chatter. The people died there like flies that had been poisoned. The great majority died there. The little children and the old people died first, and then the women and the weaker men. No day passed without many deaths. We begged and prayed and appealed for leave to go back to our country, which is warmer, but the Germans refused. Those men who were fit had to work during the day in the harbour and railway depots. The younger women were selected by the soldiers and taken to their camps as concubines.

Soon the great majority of the prisoners had died and then the Germans began to treat us better. A Captain von Zulow took charge, and he was more humane than the others. After being there over a year, those of us who had survived were allowed to return home.

After all was over, the survivors of our race were merely slaves. (p. 101)

Hosea Mungunda, Herero Headman at Windhoek, stated:

Those who were left after the rebellion were put into compounds and made to work for their food only. They were sent to farms, and also to the railways and elsewhere. Many were sent to Luderitzbucht and Swakopmund. Many died in captivity; and many were hanged and flogged nearly to death and died as the result of ill-treatment. Many were mere skeletons when they came in and surrendered, and they could not stand bad food and ill-treatment.

The young girls were selected and taken as concubines for the soldiers; but even the married women were assaulted and interfered with . . . [I]t was one continuous ill-treatment . . . [W]hen the railways were completed and the harbour works, we were sent out to towns and to farms to work. We were distributed and allocated to farmers, whether we liked them or not. (p. 101)

Traugott Tjienda, Headman of the Hereros of Tsumeb, who also surrendered under von Lindequist's amnesty order, testified:

I was made to work on the Otavi line which was being built. We were not paid for our work, we were regarded as prisoners. I worked for two years without pay. . . . As our people came in from the bush they were made to work at once, they were merely skin and bones, they were so thin that one could see through their bones—they looked like broomsticks. Bad as they were, they were made to work; and whether they worked or were lazy they were repeatedly sjambokked by the German overseers. The soldiers guarded us at night in a big compound made of thorn bushes. I was a kind of foreman over the labourers. I had 528 people, all Hereros, in my work party. Of these 148 died while working on the line. The Herero women were compounded with the men. They were made to do manual labour as well. They did not carry the heavy rails, but they had to load and unload wagons and trucks and to work with picks and shovels. The totals above given include women and children. . . . When our women were prisoners on the railway work they were compelled to cohabit with soldiers and white railway labourers. The fact that a woman was married was no protection. Young girls were raped and very badly used. They were taken out of the compounds into the bush and there assaulted. I don't think any of them escaped this, except the older ones. (pp. 101ff.)

Edward Lionel Pinches, an English resident of Keetmanshoop, confirmed the "native" reports:

At the time I entered the country then known as German South-West Africa in the year eighteen hundred and ninety-six the Hottentots and Damaras were divided into tribes and were living under the jurisdiction of their Chiefs. The natives were prosperous and the country was fairly well populated. Any estimation of the actual native population would be extremely difficult to give. At this time I was continuously travelling about the country, and I got a fairly accurate idea of the number of natives of the different tribes I came in contact with. On the outbreak of the Hottentot war the natives were about the same in number as when I entered the country, but on the conclusion of that war in my estimation the total native population was not more than one-fifth of its former number. The war was to all intents and purposes a war of extinction of the native races, and has been admitted to be so by Germans of high standing. This tremendous reduction of population was by no means owing to actual losses through the war, but is directly due to the treatment received by the natives during captivity. I have myself been several times in Luderitzbucht, where large numbers of Damaras were kept in confinement, and have seen them being buried by their fellows, who were little better than dead themselves, at the rate of twelve to fifteen per diem. Judging by the appearance of these natives, they were dying from sheer starvation. (p. 102)

Leslie Cruikshank Bartlet, an Englishman residing in South-West Africa, reported:

I came to German South-West Africa with the first transport during the Hottentot war in 1905. The prisoners, Hereros and Hottentots, mostly women, and all in a terribly emaciated condition, were imprisoned on an island adjoining Luderitzbucht. The mortality amongst the prisoners was excessive, funerals taking place at the rate of ten to fifteen daily. Many are said to have attempted escape by swimming, and I have seen corpses of women prisoners washed up on the beach between Luderitzbucht and the cemetery. One corpse, I remember, was that of a young woman with practically fleshless limbs whose breasts had been eaten by jackals. This I reported at the German Police Station, but on passing the same way three or four days later the body was still where I saw it first. The German soldiery spoke freely of atrocities committed by Hereros and Hottentots during the war, and seemed to take a pride in wrecking vengeance on those unfortunate women. When the railway from Luderitzbucht to Keetmanshoop was started, gangs of prisoners, mostly women scarcely able to walk from weakness and starvation, were employed as labourers. They were brutally treated. I personally saw a gang of these prisoners, all women, carrying a heavy double line of rails with iron sleepers attached on their shoulders, and unable to bear the weight they fell. One woman fell under the rails which broke her leg and held it fast. The Schachtmeister (ganger), without causing the rail to be lifted, dragged the woman from under and threw her on one side, where she died untended. The general treatment was cruel, and many instances were told to me, but that which I have stated, I personally saw. (p. 102)

Chapter Two
The Armenian Genocide

Rouben P. Adalian

Between the years 1915 and 1923 the Armenian population of Anatolia and historic West Armenia was eliminated. The Armenians had lived in the area for some three thousand years. Since 1071, when Turkish tribal armies prevailed over the Christian forces which were resisting their incursions, the Armenians had lived as subjects of various Turkish dynasties. The last and longest-lived of these dynasties were the Ottomans, who created a vast empire. In its waning days, with the empire in decline, the Ottoman leaders decided that the only way to save the Turkish state was to reduce the Christian populations. Beginning in April 1915 the Armenians of Anatolia were deported to Syria and the Armenian population of West Armenia was driven to Mesopotamia. Described as a resettlement policy, the deportations were actually genocide. When the dust finally settled after eight years of warfare and turmoil in the Middle East, the Armenians had disappeared from their homeland.

Who Committed the Genocide?

In 1915 the Ottoman Empire was governed by a triumvirate. Enver was Minister of War. Talat was Minister of the Interior. Jemal was Minister of the Navy and military governor of Syria. All were members of the Committee of Union and Progress (CUP), called Unionists for short. They were known in the West as the Young Turks. They had started out as members of a clandestine political organization which staged a revolution in 1908, replaced the ruler of the country in 1909, and finally seized power by a coup in 1913 (Ramsaur, 1957).

When World War I started, the Young Turk Party exercised near total control in the government. Party functionaries had been appointed to posts all across the empire. Unionist cells had been organized in every major town and city. Unionist officers commanded virtually all of the Ottoman army.

The cabinet was entirely beholden to the CUP. Key decisions were made by the triumvirs in consultation with their party ideologues and in conformity with overt and covert party objectives. As heads of government and leaders of the CUP, Enver, Talat, and Jemal had at their disposal immense resources of power and an arsenal of formal and informal instruments of coercion (Libaridian, 1985, pp. 37–49).

Organized in reaction to the autocratic regime of the sultan Abdul-Hamid II, the Young Turks originally advocated a platform of constitution-alism, egalitarianism, and liberalism. They attributed the weakness of the Ottoman Empire to its retrograde system of government. They hoped to reform the state along the progressive course of the Western European countries. However, after the revolution, they were quickly disillusioned by the aggressive posture of the European powers which vied with one another for influence in the Ottoman Empire. Suspicious of British, French, and Russian colonialist motives, defeated in war by the Italians, and challenged by neighboring Greece and Bulgaria, countries which were formerly subject states of the empire, the Young Turks increasingly looked toward Germany as the model nation-state. By 1913 the advocates of the liberal program had lost out to the radical elements in the party which promoted a program of forcible Turkification.

By the time the first shots of the war were fired in August of 1914, the CUP had become a dictatorial, xenophobic, intolerant clique intent on pursuing a policy of racial exclusivity. Emboldened by their alliance with Imperial Germany, the CUP prepared to embark on a parallel course of militarism. German war materiel poured into the country, and Turkish officers trained at military schools in Germany. German army and navy officers trained the Ottoman forces, drew their battle plans, built fortifications, and when war erupted, stayed on as advisors whose influence often exceeded that of the local commanders (Sachar, 1969, pp. 5–31; Trumpener, 1968, pp. 62–107; Dinkel, 1991, pp. 77–133).

Because of the preponderance of German involvement in Ottoman military affairs, the lurking question of the degree of their involvement in either advising or permitting the deportation of the Armenians has been asked many times. Responsibility for the Armenian genocide, however, must rest with those who considered and took the decision to deport and massacre the Armenian population of the Ottoman Empire. It also rests with those who implemented the policy of the central government, and lastly with those who personally carried out the acts which extinguished Armenian society in its birthplace. In this equation the heaviest burden falls on the members of the Committee of Union and Progress. At every level of the operation against the Armenians, party functionaries relayed, received, and enforced the orders of the government. The state's responsibility to protect its citizens was disregarded by the CUP. The Ministries of the Interior and of War were charged with the task of expelling the Armenians from their homes and driving them into the Syrian desert (Dadrian, 1986). The army detailed soldiers and officers to oversee the deportation process (Toynbee, 1916, pp. 637–653; Ternon, 1981, pp. 221–239). Killing units were organized to slaughter the Armenians (Dadrian, 1989, pp. 274–277). By withholding from them the protection of the state and by exposing them to all the vagaries of nature, the Young Turk government also disposed of large numbers of Armenians through starvation (Ternon, 1981, pp. 249–260). In the absence of even minimal sanitary conditions and health care, epidemics broke out in the concentration camps and contributed to the death toll.

How Was the Genocide Committed?

The genocide of the Armenians involved a three-part plan conceived with secrecy and deliberation and implemented with organization and efficiency. The plan consisted of deportation, execution, and starvation. Each part of the plan had its specific purpose.

The most "successful" part of the plan was the deportation of the Armenian population. The Armenians in historic Armenia in the east, in Anatolia to the west, and in European Turkey were all driven from their homes. Beginning in April 1915 and continuing through the summer, the vast majority of the Armenians in the Ottoman Empire were deported. Upon the orders of the Ottoman government, often with only three days' notice, village after village, town after town was emptied of its Armenian inhabitants.

Many were moved by train (Toynbee, 1916, pp. 407–463). Others relied on horse-drawn wagons. A few farmers took their mules and were able to carry some belongings part of the way, but most Armenians walked. As more and more people were displaced, long convoys of deportees, comprising mostly women and children, formed along the roads of Anatolia and Armenia, all headed in one direction, south to the Syrian desert. Many never made it that far. Only a quarter of all deportees survived the hundreds of miles and weeks of walking. Exhaustion, exposure, and fright took a heavy toll especially on the old and the young (Hairapetian, 1984, pp. 41–145).

To minimize resistance to the deportations, the Ottoman government had taken precautionary measures. The most lethal of these measures consisted of the execution of the able-bodied men in the Armenian population. The first group in Armenian society targeted for collective execution were the men conscripted into the Turkish armies. Upon the instruction of the War Ministry, these men were disarmed, forced into labor battalions, and either worked to death or murdered (Morgenthau, 1918, p. 302; Kuper, 1986, pp. 46–47; Sachar, 1969, p. 98).

Subsequently, the older males who had stayed behind to till the fields and run the stores were summoned by the government and ordered to prepare themselves for removal from their places of habitation. Virtually all the men turned themselves over without an inkling that their government contemplated their murder. They were immediately imprisoned, many were tortured, and all of them were taken away, sometimes in chains, and felled in mass executions (Toynbee, 1916, pp. 640–641).

To assure the complete subservience of the Armenian people to the government's deportation edicts and to eliminate the possibility of protestation, prominent leaders were specially selected for swift excision from their communities (Davis, 1989, p. 51). Although the wholesale measures against the Armenians were already in the process of implementation by late April, the symbolic beginning of the Armenian genocide is dated the evening of April 24, 1915. That night, the most gifted men of letters, the most notable jurists, the most respected educators, and many others, including high-ranking clergy, were summarily arrested in Constantinople, the capital of the Ottoman Empire, sent to the interior, and never heard of again (Ternon, 1981, pp. 216–219).

The Ottoman government had made no provisions for the feeding and the housing of the hundreds of thousands of Armenian deportees on the road (Toynbee, 1916, pp. 545–569). On the contrary, local authorities went to great length to make travel an ordeal from which there was little chance of survival (Davis, 1989, pp. 69–70). At every turn Armenians were robbed of their possessions, had their loved ones held at ransom, and even had their clothing taken off their backs. Additionally, Kurdish horsemen given to marauding and kidnaping were let loose upon the helpless caravans of people (Hairapetian, 1984, p. 96; Kloian, 1985, p. 8). Apart from the sheer bedlam of their raids and the killing that accompanied it, they carried away the goods they snatched and frequently seized Armenian children and women.

The deportations were not intended to be an orderly relocation process (Walker, 1980, pp. 227–230). They were meant to drive the Armenians into the open and expose them to every conceivable abuse (Hovannisian, 1967, pp. 50–51). At remote sites along the routes traversed by the convoys of deportees, the killing units slaughtered the Armenians with sword and bayonet (Dadrian, 1989, p. 272; Walker, 1980, p. 213). In a random frenzy of butchering, they cut down persons of all ages and of both genders. These periodic attacks upon the unarmed and starving Armenians continued until they reached the Syrian desert.

The Armenians were brought to the Syrian desert for their final expiration (Walker, 1980, pp. 227–230). Tens of thousands died from exposure to the scorching heat of the summer days and the cold of the night. Men and women dying of thirst were shot for approaching the Euphrates River. Women were stripped naked, abused, and murdered. Others despairing of their fate threw themselves into the river and drowned. Mothers gave their children away to Arab bedouins to spare them from certain death. The killing units completed their task at a place called Deir el-Zor. In this final carnage, children were smashed against rocks, women were torn apart with swords, men were mutilated, others thrown into flames alive. Every cruelty was inflicted on the remnants of the Armenian people.

Why Was the Genocide Committed?

The Armenian genocide was committed to solve the "Armenian Question" in the Ottoman Empire. There were three basic reasons for the emergence of this so-called question. The first stemmed from the increasing national consciousness of the Armenians. The government's failure to guarantee security of life and property led the Armenians to seek reforms that would improve living conditions. These demands only invited resistance and intransigence from the government, which convinced many Armenians that the Ottoman regime was not interested in providing them the protection they desired (Nalbandian, 1963, pp. 67–89). Second, as the Armenians turned to the European powers in order to invite attention to their plight, the Ottomans only grew more suspicious. The designs of the Europeans on the Ottoman Empire left its government in a state of perpetual anxiety about its defense. The appeal of the Armenians to the Christian countries of Europe was viewed as seditious by the Ottomans. On earlier occasions European powers had exploited the tensions in Ottoman society to intervene on behalf of Christian populations, and the Ottomans were resolved to prevent the recurrence of such intervention by quickly suppressing expressions of social and political discontent (Dadrian, 1989, pp. 242–255). Third, the military weakness of the Ottoman Empire left it exposed to external threats and therefore made it prone to resorting to brutality as a method of containing domestic trouble, especially with disaffected non-Muslim minorities. A cycle of escalating violence against the Armenians set in by the late 1800s (Dadrian, 1989, pp. 232–242).

During the nineteenth century, the Ottomans had been forced out of southeastern Europe. Having relinquished the mostly Christian and Slavic regions of the Balkans whence the early Ottomans had created their empire, the Young Turks sought to restore the empire on new foundations. They found their justification in the concept of Pan-Turanism. They imagined conquering lands stretching into Central Asia inhabited by other Turkic-speaking peoples. Many of these Turkic peoples were living under Russian domination, and the Young Turks believed that the advancing Ottoman armies would be received as liberators (Walker, 1980, pp. 189–191). The Pan-Turanian state was going to unify all the Turkic peoples into a single empire led by the Ottoman Turks (Parla, 1985).

In this formulation, the Armenians presented an ethno-religious anomaly. They were an indigenous Christian people of the Middle East who, despite more than fourteen centuries of Muslim domination, had avoided Islamification. When the CUP began to implement its policy of Turkification, the Armenians resisted the CUP plans. For example, the Armenians had worked hard to build up the infrastructure of their communities, including an extensive network of elementary and secondary schools. Through education they hoped to preserve their culture and identity and to obtain participation in their government. The new emphasis on Turkism and the heightened suspicion of the subject nationalities was warning enough for the Armenians to redouble their effort to gain a say in at least the governance of regions with a heavy Armenian concentration (Libaridian, 1987, pp. 219–223).

In the increasing tension between the assimilationist policies of the Young Turk government and Armenian aspirations for a measure of self-government, the coincidence of resistance to Unionist policies and the beginning of World War I proved fatal for the Armenians. Since the German forces were prevailing against Russia in Europe, a second front in Asia seemed to guarantee success for the Ottomans. Confident of their strength and witness to the early military victories of the German army, the Young Turks chose to enter the war. They believed that the great conflict among the imperial powers of Europe offered the Ottoman Empire an opportunity to regain a position of dominance in the region.

The war placed the Armenians in an extremely precarious state. Tragically for them, their difficulties with the Young Turk regime were compounded by the fact that this second front against Russia would be fought in the very lands of historic Armenia where the bulk of the Armenian population lived. Straddled on both sides of the Russian-Ottoman frontier, their homeland was turned into a battlefield. Long chafing from the exploitation of Muslim overlords, the Armenians had welcomed the Russians into Transcaucasia. After nearly a century of relative peace and prosperous existence under Russian administration, the prospect of falling under the rule of the Ottomans was unthinkable for the Armenians living in Russia. While thousands of Armenian conscripts were serving on the Russian front in the war against Germany, many others volunteered to fight the Ottomans.

The fate of the Armenians was sealed in early 1915 with the defeat of the Ottoman offensive into Russian territory. The Russians not only stopped the Ottoman advance but slowly moved into Ottoman territory. The failure of the campaign was principally the fault of Enver, the Minister of War, who had taken personal command of the eastern front and chosen to fight a major battle in the dead of winter in rugged and snow-bound terrain. With his ambitions dashed, this would-be conqueror and self-styled liberator exacted vengeance from the Armenian population.

Instead of accepting responsibility for their ill-conceived invasion plans and the consequent defeat of their armies, the Young Turks put the blame on the Armenians by accusing them of collaboration with the enemy (Morgenthau, 1918, pp. 293–300). Charging the entire Armenian population with treason and sedition, they decided to kill the innocent for the actions of those who had chosen to put a stop to their planned conquests. That was the reason given by the Minister of the Interior when asked about the CUP policy of deporting the Armenians (Morgenthau, 1918, p. 327; Trumpener, 1968, pp. 207–210). The war in effect provided the opportunity to contemplate the Turkification of the Ottoman Empire in ways that exceeded legislation, intimidation, and expropriation. Under the cover of war, with no obligation to uphold international agreements and in an atmosphere of heightened tensions, the Unionists found their justification and opportunity to resort to extreme measures. The Turkish state now could be created internally. With the Armenians eradicated, one less racial grouping would be living on Ottoman territory. One less disenchanted group would have to be tolerated. The problems with the Armenians would be automatically resolved by eliminating the Armenians. In a country of twenty million people, the Armenians constituted only about 10 percent of the population. It was easily within the reach of the Ottoman government to displace and kill that many people.

For all the historical, political, and military reasons that may be cited to explain the Young Turk policy of destroying the Armenians, it must be understood that ultimately the decision to commit genocide was taken consciously. Genocide is not explained by circumstance. Mass murder is an act deliberately conceived. Decision makers can always exercise other options in dealing with serious conflicts. The real cause of genocide lies in the self-licensing of those in charge of government with irresponsibility toward human life and amorality in the conception of their social policies. Genocide is the fulfillment of absolute tyranny. In the new social order conceived by the Young Turks, there was no room for the Armenians. They had become that excess population of which tyrants are prone to dispose.

Who Were the Victims?

The Armenians were an ancient people who from the first millennium B.C. lived in a mountainous plateau in Asia Minor, a country to which they gave their name. This was their homeland. The area was absorbed as the eastern provinces of the Ottoman Empire in the sixteenth century. Two thousand years earlier the Armenians had formed one of the more durable states in the region. A series of monarchial dynasties and princely families had been at the head of the Armenian nation. Early in the fourth century, the king of Armenia accepted Christianity, making his country the first to formally recognize the new faith. Armenians developed their own culture and spoke a unique language. A distinct alphabet, a native poetry, original folk music, an authentic architectural style, and centuries-old traditions characterized their separate civilization (Lang, 1970, 1981).

The remoteness of Armenia from the centers of urban life in the ancient world kept the Armenians on the periphery of the empires of antiquity. Their distinctiveness was reinforced by the mountainous country and the harsh, long winters which discouraged new settlers. Their own armies fought off many invaders; but through the course of the centuries Armenia proved too small a country to withstand the continued menace of outside aggression. The strength of its armies was sapped. Its leaders were defeated in battle, and its kings were exiled and never returned. Increasingly exposed to invasions, the Armenians finally succumbed to the occupying forces of a new people that emerged from the east.

Persians, Greeks, Romans, Arabs, Byzantines, and Mongols, each in turn lorded over the Armenians; however, only the Turks made permanent settlements in Armenia. The seeds of a mortal conflict were planted as the Turks grew in number and periodically displaced the Armenians. Beginning from the eleventh century, towns, cities, and sometimes entire districts of Armenia were abandoned by the Armenians as they fled from the exactions of their new rulers. Unlike all the other conquerors of Armenia, the Turks never left. In time Armenia became Turkey. The genocide of 1915 brought to a brutal culmination a thousand-year struggle of the Armenian people to hold on to their homeland and of the Turks to take it away from them.

The Ottoman Turks who built an empire around the city of Constantinople after conquering it in 1453, and who eventually seized the areas of historic Armenia, developed a hierarchically organized society. Non-Muslims were relegated to second-class status and were subjected to discriminatory laws. The constant pressure on the Armenian population resulted in the further dispersion of the Armenians. Yet, despite the difficulties they endured and the disadvantages they faced, Armenian communities throughout the Ottoman Empire attained a tolerable living standard. By the nineteenth century a prosperous middle class emerged which became the envy of the Turkish population and a source of distrust for the Ottoman government (Barsoumian, 1982, pp. 171–184).

As the Armenians recovered their national confidence, they increased their demands for reforms in Armenia where conditions continued to deteriorate. The government, however, was opposed to the idea of introducing measures and policies which would have enhanced the progress of an industrious minority which already managed a sizable portion of Ottoman commerce and industry. This reluctance only contributed to the alienation of the Armenians from the Ottoman regime. The more the Armenians complained, objected, and dissented, the more the Ottoman government grew annoyed, resistant, and impatient. By refusing to introduce significant reform in its autocratic form of government, the Ottoman rulers placed the Armenian and the Turkish peoples on a collision course.

Who Was Involved?

The Armenian genocide was organized in secret but carried out in the open (Dadrian, 1989, p. 299; 1991, p. 558; 1993). The public proclamations ordering the departure of the Armenians from their homes alerted all of Ottoman society that its government had chosen a course of action specifically targeting this one minority for unusual treatment. At no time throughout its existence had the Ottoman state taken such a step against an entire population. The manner in which the deportations were carried out signaled to the rest of society that the measures were intended to yield a permanent outcome.

A policy directed against a select population requires the agencies of government to organize, command, implement, and complete the separation and isolation of this group from the rest of society. When the measures affect a population spread across a vast stretch of territory, it cannot be a matter of accident, or coincidence, that persons of the same ethnic background become the object of mistreatment.

Although the decision to proceed with genocide was taken by the CUP, the entire Ottoman state became implicated in its implementation. First, cabinet decisions were made to deport and massacre the Armenians (Dadrian, 1989, pp. 265–267). Disguised as a relocation policy, their purpose was understood by all concerned. Second, the Ottoman parliament avowedly enacted legislation legalizing the decisions of the cabinet (Dadrian, 1989, pp. 267–274). Third, the Ministry of the Interior was delegated the responsibility of overseeing the displacement, deportation, and relocation process. This Ministry in turn instructed local authorities on procedure, the timing of deportation, and the routing of the convoys of exiles (Dadrian, 1986, pp. 326–328). The Ministry of War was charged with the disarming of the Armenian population, the posting of officers and soldiers to herd the deportees into the desert, and the execution of the Armenian conscripts. The agencies in charge of transport also were inducted into service. To expedite the transfer of the Armenians of western Anatolia, the deportees were loaded on cattle cars and shipped en masse to points east by train. The telegraph service encoded and decoded the orders of the ministers and governors. The governors of the provinces relayed the orders to the district governors, who in turn entrusted the local authorities, courts, and constabularies to proceed with instructions. The chain of command which put the Armenian genocide into motion joined every link in the administration of the Ottoman state.

Orders, however, were not obeyed uniformly. A few governors down-right refused to deport the Armenians in their districts (Dadrian, 1986, pp. 326–327). Aware that some government personnel might be reluctant to sign the death warrant of the Armenian people, the CUP had made provisions to enforce its will on the entire corps of Ottoman officials. Young Turk Party members were entrusted by the center with extraordinary power in situations requiring the disciplining of local authority. Disobedient governors were removed from their posts and CUP partisans with a more reliable record were assigned to carry through the state's policies in these districts. Frequently, the most notorious among them happened to be army officers who were also ideological adherents of the CUP, a combination which gave them complete license to satisfy at the expense of the Armenians their every whim and that of the men under their command (Dadrian, 1986, pp. 311–359).

To handle the various aspects of its policy the CUP cabinet had to go so far as to set up new agencies. One of these was a secret extra-legal body called the Special Organization. Its mission was organized mass murder (Dadrian, 1989, pp. 274–277). It was mainly composed of convicted criminals released from prisons who were divided into units stationed at the critical sites along the deportation routes and near the relocation camps in Syria. Their assignment consisted solely of reducing the number of the Armenians by carrying out massacres. Sparing bullets, which were needed for the war effort, the slaughter of the Armenians frequently was carried out with medieval weaponry, scimitars and daggers. The physical proximity with which the butchering went on left a terrifying image of the Turk among those who happened to live through an attack by squads of the Special Organization.

Additionally, the government set up a Commission on Immigrants whose stated purpose was to facilitate "the resettlement" process. In fact, the commission served as an on-site committee to report on the progress of the disposal of the Armenians as they were further and further removed from the inhabitable regions of Anatolia and Syria. As for the Commission on Abandoned Goods, which impounded, logged, and auctioned off Armenian possessions, this was the government's method of disposing the immovable property of the Armenians by means that rewarded its supporters. Generally, the local CUP officials pocketed the profit. It is not known what sums might have been transferred to party coffers (Baghdjian, 1987, pp. 64–87).

The CUP orchestrated a much larger system of rewards in order to obtain the consent of the Turkish population (Baghdjian, 1987, pp. 121–

171). By implicating large numbers of people in the illegal methods of acquisition, the Young Turk government purchased the silence of the populace. Many enriched themselves by appropriating the forcibly abandoned properties of the Armenians. There was easy gain in plunder.

The same impulse motivated the Special Organization and the Kurdish tribesmen who were given license to raid the convoys of deportees. In their case, the booty included human beings as well. It was a form of enslavement limited to younger boys and girls, who, separated from their kinsmen, would be converted to Islam and either Kurdified or Turkified in language and custom. Lastly, the public auction of Armenian girls revived a form of human bondage that was, for the most part, erased elsewhere in the world. The auctioneer made money. The purchaser had a slave servant and a harem woman added to his household. This kind of brutalization scarred many Armenian women. Some, incapable of bearing the shame of giving birth out of wedlock to children conceived from rape and abuse by their Kurdish and Turkish owners, chose to forgo Armenian society after the war and remained with their Muslim families. A few were rescued and a few escaped, some taking their children with them and others fearing reprisal by abandoning them. Some Armenian women taken into harems against their will were tatooed on their arms, chest, or face, as signs of their being "owned," and as a way to discourage escape (Sanasarian, 1989, pp. 449–461).

The gender, age, occupational, and regional differences in the treatment of the Armenians reflected the varying operative value systems prevailing in Ottoman society. The Young Turk ideologues in Constantinople conceived and implemented genocide, a total destruction of Armenian society. Military officers and soldiers regarded the policy as a security measure. Others in Ottoman society saw it as a convenient way of ridding themselves of effective economic competitors, not to mention creditors. Others justified the slaughter of the Armenians as religious duty called upon by the concept of jihad or warfare against infidels or non-believers in Islam. All essentially aimed at eliminating the Armenian male population. Traditional society in the Middle East still looked upon women and children as chattel, persons lacking political personality and of transmutable ethnic identity. The cultural values of children and of females could be erased or reprogrammed. Genetic continuity was a male proposition. For many, but not the CUP, the annihilation of Armenian males would have been sufficient to block or impede the perpetuation of the Armenian people (Davis, 1989, pp. 54–63).

What Were the Outstanding Historical Forces and Trends at Work That Led to the Genocide?

The Armenian genocide was the result of the intensifying differences between two societies inhabiting the territories of a single state. One society was dominant, the other subordinate, one Muslim, the other Christian, one in the majority, the other in the minority. At its source, the conflict stemmed from two divergent views of the world. The Turks had established their state as a world empire. They had always ruled over lands and peoples they conquered. The receding of their empire from its far-flung provinces challenged their image of themselves. Virtually undefeated in war before 1700, the Ottomans lost battle after battle in the eighteenth and nineteenth centuries as their once mighty armies were no longer a match for the modern tactics and weaponry of the armies of the European states. New empires taking form on the European continent began to carve away Ottoman territory. France, England, Austria, and Russia, each in turn imposed its demands on the weakening Turkish state. By the second half of the nineteenth century, however, these European powers, soon joined by a Germany unified by Prussian arms, balanced each other out in their competition for global influence.

A new type of challenge arose forcing the Ottomans into retreating further. Whereas the Ottomans were in part successful in checking the territorial aggrandizement of their neighbors by relying on the balance of power system, the rise of nationalist movements among the subject peoples of the empire posed a different predicament. As imperial states are wont to do, the Ottomans resorted to very brutal methods of suppressing national liberation and other separatist movements. The response of the Ottomans to the uprisings in Greece, Serbia, Bulgaria, and elsewhere was mass action against the affected population. These tactics only invited European intervention and the settlement often resulted in the formation of a small autonomous state from a former Ottoman province as a way of providing a national territory to the subject people.

Unlike the Greeks, Serbians, or Bulgarians, the case of the Armenians was more complicated. They had long been ruled by the Turks and by the early twentieth century they were widely dispersed. In historic Armenia, the Armenians formed a majority of the population only in certain districts. This was due to the fact that a substantial Kurdish and Turkish population lived in these lands. When the Armenians also began to aspire to a national home, the Ottomans regarded it a far more serious threat than earlier and similar nationalist movements. They had come to regard historic Armenia as part of their permanent patrimony.

The fracturing of the status of the Armenians in the Ottoman Empire has a complicated diplomatic history to it. The Russo-Turkish War of 1877–1878 was concluded with the signing of the Treaty of San Stefano, which ceded the Russians considerable Ottoman territory. The European powers vehemently opposed the sudden expansion of Russian influence in the Balkans and the Middle East. They compelled the Russian monarch to agree to terms more favorable to the Ottomans in the Treaty of Berlin. All the European powers became signatories to this treaty. One of the terms in the Treaty of Berlin promised reforms in the so-called Armenian provinces of the Ottoman Empire. Armenians saw hope in this treaty. They thought an international covenant would have greater force in compelling the Ottomans to consider reorganizing the ramshackle administration of their remote provinces. When the European powers failed to persist in requiring the Ottoman sultan to abide by the terms of the treaty, the Armenians faced a rude awakening. They were disappointed with a government that did not keep its promises. They also realized that the powers had little interest in devoting time to the problems of the Armenians (Hovannisian, 1986b, pp. 19–41).

The fundamental issue separating Armenians and Ottomans was their individual definitions of equality. Empires are inherently unequal systems. They divide the people into the rulers and the ruled. The Islamic Empires, including the Ottoman state, compounded this system of inequality because the legal and judicial precepts of Islam also subordinated non-Muslim subjects to second-class status. Not only was the Ottoman system unequal, Ottoman society was unaccustomed to a concept of equality among men irrespective of their racial or religious background. Although laws were issued accepting the principle of equality among the various confessional groups in the Ottoman Empire, the Muslim populace remained unconvinced that they should accept these secular ideas. Instead of leading to a new adjustment in Ottoman society, these laws became the source of consternation among Muslims who believed these notions upset the established social order. The hierarchy of faiths had never been reconsidered in an Islamic society since the religion was founded in the seventh century. On the contrary, to the Muslims the combination of European states sponsoring reforms on behalf of Christian minorities and these peoples in turn aspiring for equal treatment under the law appeared a bid by the subject Christians for power over the Muslims.

Islamic law disenfranchised Christians and Jews. Their testimony was inadmissible in court, thus frequently denying them fair treatment by the justice system. Christians and Jews were also required to pay additional levies, such as a poll tax. For a peasantry eking out a living on the farm, the extra taxes often became an obligation that could not be met in a difficult year. The end result was commonly foreclosure and eviction. Disallowed from bearing arms, non-Muslims had no means of self-defense. They could protect neither their persons and families nor their property. In certain places dress codes restricting types of fabric used by the Christians helped differentiate them from the population at large, exposing them to further intimidation. At times a language restriction meant speaking a language other than Turkish at the risk of having one's tongue cut out. In many areas of the Ottoman Empire Armenians had forgotten their native language (Ye'or, 1985, pp. 51–77).

These disabilities would have been impairing under normal circumstances. In areas closer to the capital, competent governors oversaw the administration of the provinces, and Armenians flocked to these safer parts of the empire. In the remoter provinces such as the areas of historic Armenia, the hardships faced by the ordinary people were insurmountable. Avaricious officials exacted legal and illegal taxes. The justice system was hopelessly rigged. The maintenance of law and order was entrusted to men who only saw in their positions the opportunity for reckless exploitation. Extortion and bribery were the custom. In the countryside the army demanded quartering in the houses of the Armenian peasant, which made him and his family hostage. Unable to defend themselves, these people were also at the mercy of tribesmen who descended upon their villages and carried off goods, flocks, and women. With no recourse left, Armenians were being driven to desperation.

The disappointment over the failure of the European powers to intervene effectively, combined with the dismay over the delays of the Ottoman government, continued to fuel the crisis in the Armenian provinces. Some Armenians decided to take matters into their own hands. In certain parts of Armenia, during the 1880s and 1890s, individuals began arming themselves and forming bands which, for instance, resisted Kurdish incursions on Armenian villages. Others joined political organizations advocating revolutionary changes at all levels of society. They demanded equal treatment, an adequate justice system, fair taxation, and the appointment of officials prepared to act responsibly (Nalbandian, 1963, pp. 167–168).

The Ottoman authorities refused to consider the demands. In response to the rise of nationalist sentiment among the subject peoples, and other internal and external security concerns, the Ottoman sultans had been striving to centralize power in their hands and had been creating a modernized bureaucracy which would help expand the authority of the government in all areas of Ottoman society. Among the measures introduced by the sultan Abdul-Hamid was a secret police and special cavalry regiments, called in his honor the Hamidiye corps, to act both as border guards and local gendarmerie. They became his instrument for suppression. In 1894, at a time of increasing tension between the Armenian population and the Ottoman government, which also coincided with increased political activism by Armenians and inadequate efforts at intervention by some of the European powers, the sultan unleashed his forces. Over the next three years, a series of massacres were staged throughout Armenia. Anywhere between 100,000 and 300,000 persons were killed, others were wounded, robbed, thrown out of their houses, and kidnapped, and many fled the country (Bliss, 1982, pp. 368–501; Greene, 1896, pp. 185–242; Walker, 1980, pp. 156–173).

The Armenian massacres of 1894–1896 made headline news around the world. It engendered international awareness of the plight of the Armenians, and this horrendous treatment at the hands of the sultan's regiments invited condemnation of the Ottoman system (Nassibian, 1984, pp. 33–57). The European powers were compelled by public clamor in their own countries to urge the sultan to show restraint. The massacre was stopped, but nothing was done to punish the perpetrators or to remedy the damage.

This cycle of violence against the Armenian population repeated itself in 1909 in the province of Adana, a region along the Mediterranean coast densely settled by Armenians, where again the Armenian neighborhoods were raided and burned. The estimate on the number of victims runs from 10,000 to 30,000 (Walker, 1980, pp. 182–188). The Adana massacre coincided with an event known as the Hamidian counterrevolution. The Young Turks had achieved political prominence by staging a military revolution in 1908. They had compelled the sultan Abdul-Hamid to restore the Ottoman Constitution, which he himself had issued in 1876 and soon after suspended. The sultan was suspected of having plotted to recover his autocratic powers by dislodging the Young Turks from Constantinople. In the ensuing climate of tension and suspicion the Adana massacre erupted. The Young Turks blamed the Hamidian supporters of igniting strife in order to embarrass the progressive forces in Ottoman society, but the Young Turks themselves were also implicated in the atrocities. It augured badly for the Armenians. The Adana massacre demonstrated that even in a power struggle within Turkish society, the Armenians could be scapegoated by the disaffected and made the object of violence. In this context, Enver's embarrassment at his defeat in early 1915 and the government's casting of blame on the Armenians had a precedent. In this chain of events, the genocide of 1915 was the final, and mortal, blow dealt the Armenians by their Ottoman masters (Libaridian, 1987, pp. 203–235).

What Was the Long-Range Impact of the Genocide on the Victim Group?

The Armenians in the Ottoman Empire never achieved equality and were never guaranteed security of life and property. They entered the Ottoman Empire as a subject people and left it as a murdered or exiled population. It is estimated that the Armenian genocide resulted in the death of over a million people. Beyond the demographic demise of the Armenians in the larger part of historic Armenia, the Armenian genocide brought to a conclusion the transfer of the Armenian homeland to the Turkish people. The Young Turks had planned not only to deprive the Armenians of life and property, but also conspired to deny to the Armenians the possibility of ever recovering their dignity and liberty in their own country.

Whole communities and towns were wiped off the map. The massive loss in population threatened the very existence of the Armenian people. Hardly a family was left intact. The survivors consisted mostly of orphans, widows, and widowers. The Armenian nation was saved only through the direct delivery of American relief aid to the "starving Armenians." Millions of dollars were collected in the United States to feed and house the destitute Armenians, both in the Middle East and in Russia where tens of thousands took refuge. Without this kind of humanitarian assistance, the survival of the Armenians as a people would have been in jeopardy. Hundreds of thousands eventually received some sort of aid, be it food, clothing, shelter, employment, resettlement, or emigration to the United States and elsewhere.

The tremendous difficulty faced by the Armenians in recovering from the devastating impact of the genocide had much to do with the fact that they, as a collectivity, had been robbed of all their wealth. Their fixed assets of course were abandoned and no reparations were collected on any of their property which was confiscated. As deportees, Armenians were unable to carry with them anything beside some clothing or bedding. All the businesses were lost. All the farms were left untended. Schools, churches, hospitals, orphanages, monasteries, graveyards, and other communal holdings became state property. The genocide left the Armenians penniless.

Those who returned to reclaim their homes and properties after the end of World War I were only driven out again by the Nationalist Turks who rose to power and took charge of Turkey (Kerr, 1973, pp. 214–254). For the Armenians, the only choice was reconciliation with their status as exiles and resettlement wherever they could find a means of earning a living. With the inability to recongregate as a people in their homeland, the Armenians dispersed to the four corners of the world (Adalian, 1989, pp. 81–114).

Lastly, the genocide shattered the historical bond of the Armenian people with their homeland. The record of their millennial existence in that country was turned to dust. Libraries, archives, registries, the entire recorded memory of the Armenians as accumulated in their country was lost for all time.

What Were the Responses to This Particular Genocide?

The horror story of the Armenian genocide shocked the world at the time. The Allies threatened to hold the Young Turks responsible for the massacres (Dadrian, 1989, p. 262). The warning had no effect. The Allies were preoccupied with the war in Europe and could not commit resources to deliver the Armenians from their fate. Locally, however, humanitarian intervention by individual Turks, Kurds, and Arabs saved many lives (Hovannisian, 1992, pp. 173–207). While some Turks robbed their Armenian neighbors, others helped by hiding them in safe dwellings. While some Kurds willingly participated in the massacres, others guided groups of Armenians through the mountain passes to refuge on the Russian side. Finally, while some Arabs only saw the Armenians as victims, others shared their food.

Among the first people to see the deplorable condition of the mass of the Armenians were the American missionaries and diplomats stationed in Turkey. Their appeals to their government, the religious institutions in the United States, and the general public were the earliest of the active responses to the predicament of genocide. They strove to deliver aid even during the war (Sachar, 1969, p. 343).

After the war, the European nations were little disposed to help the Armenians as they themselves were trying to recover from their losses. Nevertheless, Britain and France, which had occupied Ottoman territory in the

Middle East, were more strongly positioned to influence the political situation in the region. Neither chose to do so on behalf of the Armenians. Their interest in retaining control of these lands also conflicted with the wider goals of Woodrow Wilson in establishing a stable world order. The American president's laudable policies were welcomed by the peoples of Europe and Asia, such as the Poles, Czechs, Arabs, and Indians, who saw in his principles for international reconciliation the possibility of attaining their national independence. He too, however, was unable to deliver more than words. The United States Congress was disinclined to involve the United States in foreign lands. Consequently, many territorial issues were solved through the pure exercise of might. Diplomacy had little chance of extending help to the Armenian refugees.

For the Turks, the failure of diplomacy provided opportunity to regroup under new leadership and to begin their own national effort at building a new state upon the ruins of the Ottoman Empire. With Mustafa Kemal at their head, the Nationalist Turks forged a new government and secured the boundaries of modern-day Turkey. Their policy of national consolidation excluded despised minorities (Dadrian, 1989, pp. 327–333). The Armenians, the weakest element, headed the list. By 1923, when the Republic of Turkey was formally recognized as a sovereign state the Armenians remaining in the territories of that state, with the exception of those in Constantinople, had been driven out. For many survivors of the deportations who had returned to their former homes, this was their second expulsion (Kinross, 1964, pp. 203–204).

Before the Turkish borders were finally sealed and the Armenians conclusively denied the right to their former homes, the absence of moral resolve in Turkish governmental circles to confront the consequences of the Armenian genocide was made abundantly clear. The postwar government proved reluctant to put on trial the Young Turk officials suspected of organizing the massacres. Only upon the insistence of the Allies were a series of trials initiated. Some dramatic evidence was given in testimony and verdicts were handed down explicitly charging those found guilty of pursuing a course of action resulting in the destruction of the Armenian population. Even so, popular sentiment in Turkish society did not support the punishment of the guilty, and the government chose to forgo the sentences of the court. The triumvirs, Talat, Enver, and Jemal, were condemned to death, but their trials were held in absentia since they had fled the country and their extradition was not a matter of priority (Dadrian, 1989, pp. 221–334).

Under these circumstances no legal recourse to justice remained open. A clandestine Armenian group called Nemesis decided to mete out punishment to the accused individuals. The principal figures in the Young Turk Party, such as Talat and Jemal, who conceived and implemented the genocide were assassinated. All of them had fled Turkey, since their enemies included more than just Armenians. They also had much to account to the Turkish people for having taken them into a war which they lost so disastrously. Although the acts of retribution against Talat and some of the others had a profound emotional effect on the Armenians, politically they were insignificant. The Armenians were never compensated for their losses (Derogy, 1990).

Is There Agreement or Disagreement among Scholars as to the Interpretation of This Particular Genocide (e.g., Preconditions, Implementation, Ramifications)?

Two schools of thought have emerged over the years. Scholars who study the Armenian genocide look at the phenomenon as either an exceptionally catastrophic occurrence coincident to a global conflict such as World War I (Fein, 1979, pp. 10–18; Horowitz, 1982, pp. 46–51) or as the final chapter in the peculiar fate of the Armenians as a people who lost their independence many centuries earlier (Kuper, 1981, pp. 101–119; Walker, 1980, pp. 169, 236–237).

All agree that the preconditions to the genocide were highly consistent with other examples where a dominant group targets a minority. They also agree on the structural inequalities of Ottoman society and how it disadvantaged the Armenians. They differ on their interpretation of the causes and consequences of Armenian nationalism. Some think that the appearance of political organization among the Armenians can be regarded as the critical breaking point. Others see these developments as inevitable and entirely consistent with global trends and not particular to the Armenians. Two questions are often debated: whether the massacres during the reign of Abdul-Hamid were sufficiently precedental to be regarded as the beginning of the Armenian catastrophe; or whether the Young Turks aggravated conditions in ways that exceeded the designs of Abdul-Hamid (Kuper, 1981, pp. 101–119; Horowitz, 1982, pp. 46–51).

In the implementation of the genocide, one thing is clear. The massacres were episodic and affected select communities. The genocide was directed practically against everyone. The sultan's policy did not aim for the extermination of the Armenians, rather it was brutal punishment for aspiring to gain charge of their political destiny. As many scholars have pointed out, at one time the Ottoman system extended a considerable measure of security to its minorities. Although for the most part they were excluded from government and at a disadvantage in holding large-scale property, Christians and Jews were allowed to practice their faiths and distinguish themselves in commerce and finance. Therefore, it was not in the interest of the sultan to dismantle his imperial inheritance. His objective remained the continuance of his autocratic power and his rule over the lands bequeathed him by his conquering forebears.

Those studying the Young Turks have pointed out that the CUP organized its committees and conducted its activities outside this system. They were opponents of imperial autocracy. Their own political radicalism also meant that they were predisposed to think in exclusionary terms. Some of these scholars contend that the Young Turk period can be seen as a transitional phase in Turkish society where the pluralistic construct of the Ottoman system was violently smashed and the ground was prepared for the emergence of a state based on ethnic singularism (Ahmed, 1982, pp. 418–425; Staub, 1989, pp. 173–187; Melson, 1986, pp. 61–84).

Perhaps the issue debated most frequently revolves around the matter of postgenocidal responsibility. There is a wide divergence of opinion on the question whether modern Turkey is liable to the Armenians for their losses, or whether it is absolved of such liability because the crime was committed under the jurisdiction of prior state authorities (Libaridian, 1985, pp. 211–227). The Turkish government dismisses all such claims since it denies that the policies implemented in 1915 constitute genocide. Some in the academic community are supportive of the Turkish position (Gürün, 1985). On the other hand, that stance raises a more complex problem. Who exactly should be held responsible for genocide: the government, the state, society? If governments put the blame on prior regimes, all they have done is merely certify the former policy by disregarding the consequences of genocide. The reluctance by a successor state to shoulder responsibility is only another form of reaping the benefits of mass murder.

Do People Care about This Genocide Today? If So, How Is That Concern Manifested? If Not, Why Not?

For a period of about fifty years the world fell into an apathetic silence over the Armenian genocide. Its results had been so grievous for the Armenians and the failure of the international community to redress the consequent problems was so thoroughgoing that the world virtually ignored the Armenian genocide. With the consolidation of Communist rule in Russia and of Nationalist rule in Turkey, the chapter on the Armenians was more or less considered closed. People wanted to forget about the Great War and its misery. As for the Armenians, they were too few, too widely dispersed, and too preoccupied with their own survival to know how to respond.

The concern over the fate of the Armenians manifested mostly in literature as various authors wrote about the massacres and memorialized the rare instances of resistance (Lepsius, 1987; Gibbons, 1916; Werfel, 1934). After a life of struggle, upon reaching retirement age, Armenians also began to write down their memoirs. Slowly a small corpus of literature emerged documenting in personal accounts the genocide and its consequences for individuals, their families, and communities (Hovannisian, 1978; Totten, 1991). This body of work began to serve as evidence for the study of the Armenian genocide. In the 1960s, as archives holding vast collections of diplomatic correspondence on the deportations and massacres were opened, a significant amount of contemporaneous documentation also became available (Hovannisian, 1978; Beylerian, 1983; Ohandjanian, 1988; Adalian, 1991–1994). This further encouraged research in the subject. Interest in the Armenian genocide has since been growing as more researchers, writers, and educators examine the evidence and attempt to understand what happened in 1915.

Commensurate to this interest, however, has been a phenomenon growing at an even faster pace. This is the denial of the Armenian genocide. For many Turks the reminder of the Ottoman past is offensive. The Turkish government's stated policy has been a complete denial (Foreign Policy Institute, 1982). The denial ranges beyond the question of political responsibility. This type of denial questions the very historical fact of the occurrence of genocide, and even of atrocities. A whole body of revisionist historiography has been generated to explain, to excuse, or to dismiss the Armenian genocide (Hovannisian, 1986c, pp. 111–133; Dobkin, 1986, pp. 97–109; Adalian, 1992, pp. 85–105). Some authors have gone so far as to put the blame for the genocide on the Armenians themselves, describing the deportations and massacres as self-inflicted, since, they say, the deportations were only countermeasures taken by the Ottoman government against a disobedient and disloyal population (Uras, 1988, pp. 855–886; Gürün, 1985). Such arguments do not convince serious scholars (Guroian, 1986, pp. 135–

152; Smith, 1989, pp. 1–38). Others regretably are more prepared to listen to revisionist argumentation (Shaw and Shaw, 1977, pp. 314–317; McCarthy, 1983, pp. 47–81, 117–130). These kinds of debates fail to address, however, the central questions about the Young Turk policy toward the Armenian population: Was every Armenian, young and old, man or woman, disloyal? How does one explain the deportation of Armenians from places that were nowhere near the war zones, if removing them from high-risk areas was the purpose of the policy? And always, one must ask about the treatment of children. What chance did they stand of surviving deportation, starvation, and dehydration in the desert?

What Does This Genocide Teach Us If We Wish to Protect Others from Such Horrors?

The lessons of genocide are as many as its victims. Although ultimately it is the exercise of political power in the absence of moral restraint that explains the occurrence of genocide, the demographic status of a people is demonstrated by the Armenian genocide to be a significant factor in the perpetration of genocide. A dispersed people juridically designated by a state as a minority, both in the numerical and political sense of the word, is extremely vulnerable to abusive policy. It lacks the capacity for any coordinated action to respond to, or resist, genocidal measures. It is evident that a government inclined to engage in the extermination of a minority can only be restrained by pressures and sanctions imposed by greater powers.

Geography was no less a contributing factor in exposing the Armenians to genocide. A people inhabiting a remote part of the world is all the more at the mercy of a brutal government, especially if it is questioning the policies of the state. Since exposure is the principal foil of crime, the more hidden from view a people lives the more likely it is to be repressed. Of all the places where the Armenians in the Ottoman Empire might have hampered the war effort, if indeed they were a seditious population, the most likely spot would have been the capital city. Yet the government spared most of the Armenians in Constantinople because many foreigners lived there, and they would have been alarmed to witness mass deportations. That singular exception underscores the importance and the high likelihood of successfully monitoring the living conditions of an endangered population.

That exception also points to another lesson which is specially pronounced in the Armenian case. Since many foreign communities had a presence in Constantinople, getting the word out to the rest of the world would not have been difficult with such corroboration. Thereby the Armenians in this one city remained in a protected enclave. This principle applies no less to the international status extended an entire people, as the European powers once did for the Armenians. Their interest in the Armenians acted as a partial restraint on the Ottoman government. The sudden alteration of the international order by global conflict left the Armenians wholly exposed. Whatever the level of international protection extended to an endangered minority, the withdrawal of those guarantees, tenuous as they might be, only acts as an inducement for genocide. Denying opportunity to a criminal regime is critical for the prevention of genocide.

The experience of the Armenian people in the period after the genocide teaches another important lesson. Unless the consequences of genocide are addressed in the immediate aftermath of the event, the element of time very soon puts survivors at a serious disadvantage. Without the attention of the international community, without the intervention of major states seeking to stabilize the affected region, without the swift apprehension of the guilty, and without the full exposure of the evidence, the victims stand no chance of recovering from their losses. In the absence of a response and of universal condemnation, a genocide becomes legitimized. The Ottoman government after the war never gave a full accounting of what happened to the Armenians, and the successor state of Turkey chose to bury the matter entirely (Adalian, 1991, pp. 99–104).

Though all too frequently unwilling to take concerted action to save populations clearly in danger of annihilation, whether through monitoring and reporting systems, whether through political or military intervention, whether through the activation of legal and economic sanctions, the international community is far better equipped to respond to genocidal crisis than ever before. When the Armenian genocide occurred there was no alarm and there was no rescue. Without alarm there can be no rescue, and that is the least that the Armenian experience teaches.

Eyewitness Accounts
The Armenian Genocide

Eyewitness and survivor accounts of the Armenian massacres were audiotaped and videotaped more than a half century after the events. That means the recorded testimony was provided by persons in their seventies and eighties who were reflecting upon a life which took a sudden turn when they were still children or very young adults. Hence the problem of the great length of time passed since the events of 1915 and the fact that those events were seen through the eyes of children who were looking at the world from their very narrow frames of reference needs to be kept in mind when dealing with testimony of this type. Certainly children have the greatest difficulty giving an accurate measure of time. Therefore, the episodes from their personal narratives occur at approximated intervals. Their memory, for instance, preserves the first names of numerous acquaintances, but last names are less frequently known.

A contrast to these limitations is the accuracy, with virtually all survivors, in their depiction of the geography and the topography which was the setting of their life's most tragic period. Because they were deported, knowledge of where they originated and the places they saw and stopped along the way and the spots they reached at the end of their journeys became vital information not only for their physical and emotional survival, but also for their ability to reconnect with other survivors of the communities from which they were separated. Most interesting, however, and useful for the documentary record it turns out, was indeed their very limited sense of the world around them. Whereas an adult would have attempted to understand the events he witnessed in terms of his community and society, children describe their experiences strictly from within the confines of their immediate family and circle of friends. As such, therefore, they preserve a sense of greater pathos undiluted by either fatalism or drama. Most seem to have retained their horror of genocide through their inability to offer any larger suggestion than their very incomprehension at what happened and why.

Helen Tatarian's account is an exceptionally rare one because it describes a massacre of Armenians which happened in 1909. When these records were created, very few survivors were old enough to have lived through occurrences of massacres earlier than 1915. The details of her account are also a valuable contrast to the pattern of the 1915 genocide. The Adana massacre is characterized by random mob action occurring within the perimeter of the city. Government forces are described as a party which simply stayed out of the way and, in this case, provided safe conduct where foreigners, specifically Americans, were concerned. More importantly, she verifies the significance of the protection provided by the missionary, and other third-party, presence. During the genocide none of these factors came into play. The missionaries were unable to protect their parishioners. The government was an active participant in the dislocation and the execution of the Armenian population. Lastly, with the exception of some towns in the farthest eastern reaches of Anatolia, little killing occurred within the towns. The other survivors, who relate the events of 1915 and after, all testify to a consistent pattern of separation, deportation, and subsequent mass executions in places away from urban centers.

Sarkis Agojian records the treatment of the adult male population which was never deported in 1915. He testifies that they were arrested, tortured, and murdered very early in the process. The deportations, as he recalls, occurred after the segment of the Armenian population capable of resistance was eliminated. Lastly, his memory preserves with a powerful poignancy the trauma of Armenian children who were spared deportation and starvation by adoption into Turkish families. The deafening silence at his last glimpse of his mother and the shattering news of her death capture the maddening grief that seized their young lives, and which marked them for all their years.

Takouhi Levonian gives an eyewitness account of an actual episode of wholesale slaughter in 1915. Her description of the physical cruelties inflicted upon the Armenian population is especially riveting. Her description of the kinds of privations endured is no less powerful. Her testimony incontrovertibly underscores the extreme vulnerability of the Armenian young female population. It would appear that the treatment they received was most abusive. The horrific sadism practiced by the perpetrators of the Armenian genocide is hereto testified in this single account.

Yevnig Adrouni's story redeems humanity through a personal narrative of survival and rescue. Too young to be mistreated sexually, her exploits are testament to the spirit of an alert child who would not submit to degradation. Spared physical torment she committed herself to escaping her fate. Clutching onto the last shreds of her Armenian identity, she proves to herself and her rescuers that determination and defiance can, sometimes, defeat evil. As she so vividly recounts, from the survival of a single human being springs forth the new hope of larger victories.

Helen Tatarian, native of Dertyol, born c. 1893. Audio-taped on April 17, 1977, Los Angeles, California, by Rouben Adalian. (Dertyol was a town inhabited mostly by Armenians. It is located on the Mediterranean coast in the region of Adana. Adana is also the name of the largest town in the area.)

There was a massacre in 1909. I was in school at Adana. Miss Webb and Miss Mary, two American sisters, ran the school. Miss Webb was the older, Miss Mary the younger.

In 1909 right in the month of April we suddenly heard guns being fired and saw flames rising. The houses of the Armenians were set on fire. There was a French school right next to ours. They burned it down completely.

At first the Turks killed quite a lot of people, then they stopped for a while. Eight days later they started firing their guns again. Reverend Sisak Manugian came running. "Do not be afraid children, a hog has gone wild," he said, "and they are shooting it." But it was a lie, nor had a hog gone wild. The Turks had gone wild. They were about to start again.

The son-in-law of our American missionary, Mr. Chambers, had climbed on the roof. He had climbed on the roof of our laundry room to look at what was going on in the city. They shot the man.

There was a window, a small window up high. We used to look from there to see that behind the school building there were people lying dead. The Turks were shooting the Armenians. This was a massacre specifically aimed at the Armenians.

During the fire those who managed to hide remained in hiding, those who did not hide were cut down. Just like Surpik Dudu, the poor woman who was going to her brother-in-law's house. Surpik Dudu was shot in the arm, great-grandmother Surpik Dudu. Later they had shot dead her husband and son. This woman owned fields. She was a rich woman. She used to travel on horseback. But it so happened that she was going in the direction of her relatives, her brother-in-law's house. Fortunately she was not killed.

We could not go out and we remained in hiding in the school building. We heard the sounds of guns, and from the sounds alone we were afraid. We were children. We cried, but we had no communication with anyone outside. Across from our building there lived an American, Miss Farris. The Turks burned her building so that our school would catch on fire and the children would have to run outside and thus they could kidnap the girls. The American missionary immediately notified the government. Soldiers came from the government and while putting out the fire a soldier fell and was burned inside.

Later we opened a hole in the wall. The missionaries did this. They opened a hole big enough to go through it in order to cross from our end of the block to the other end, to Mr. Chambers' house, the missionary's house. All the girls were there, two hundred and fifty, three hundred girls. We piled up in the man's house. The Turks were going to burn this house also. The man held out a surrender flag. They had poured gas and threatened to burn us in that house. We asked him: "Reverend, if the Turks forced you, would you hand us over to them?" "If they press me hard. If they insist," said the man. What could he do? Or else they would kill him too. Later we remained there for a night. There, we cried. The girls began such a weeping. The following morning, the government soldiers took us to the train station. By train we went to Mersin.

There was no fighting [in Adana between Armenians and Turks]. The Turks knew anyway which was the house of an Armenian. They went in and cut him down and shot the people inside and they took whatever was in the house. They robbed the houses and set them on fire. They entered them since it was the property of the Armenians. They also burned the churches, but I believe a considerable crowd had gathered in a French church. They did nothing there at that time. There were those who took refuge with our American missionaries also, but it was a little difficult to cross the street. If the Turks saw you, they were ready to shoot.

Sarkis Agojian, native of Chemeshgadsak, born 1906. Audiotaped on May 25, 1983, in Pasadena, California, by Donald and Lorna Miller. (Chemeshgadsak was a town inhabited by Armenians in the region of Kharpert in the western portion of historic Armenia.)

We were in school having physical education. We had lined up when the wife of our coach, Mr. Boghos, came and told her husband that the Turks had just arrested the principal, Pastor Arshag. You see, they first took the educated, the intellectuals. They took these people to a home which they had converted into a prison and tortured them in order to get them to talk. The mailman, who was Armenian, was also arrested and tortured. They pulled out his fingernails saying that while he was carrying mail he also was transporting secret letters; mail was carried in those days on horseback in large leather bags fastened to either side of the horse. He was Sarkis Mendishian. So upon the news that Pastor Arshag was arrested, they dismissed us from school and asked all of us to go home.

We went home. My father was not there. My uncle had run away. They had put a dress on my uncle's son, even though he was not young, to disguise him. My father's uncle was also in prison, for after taking the younger educated men, they also took the elderly. I was young so they used to send me to take food to him. I did this a few times. I would go in and sit with him. One day when I was taking his food, I met a lot of police who were saying that on that day we could not deliver food—that all the prisoners were going to leave. I saw them in two's, all chained together. I could not take the food, so I returned and gave the news. I told them that they were chained and they were coming this way and would pass by our house, there being no other way to leave town toward Kharpert.

By now, all the families had heard, so they were all in the streets to see their loved ones. I got on top of the roof and was yelling "uncle." There was a doctor in this procession, and when his wife saw him, she ran out to greet him, but with the butt of the rifle the police pushed her away—even though he was an elderly man. So the men marched on, leaving all the women and families crying and grieving. There was a place outside of town about twenty minutes with trees and water. There they took their names to see if anyone was missing. Then they marched them to the edge of the Euphrates and killed them. Apparently my great-uncle had some red gold [the rarest gold] with him; he gave it to the police who took it and then killed him.

Now that all the men were gone, deportation orders were issued for women and children. Our town was deported in two different groups, fifteen days apart. I wish we were in the first group because they made it all the way to Aleppo. When we were to leave our home, we left our bedding and other things with the landlord so that if we returned we would get it back. Also, we threw our rugs to the people at the public bath next door so that they would keep them for us. We said that we would get them when we returned. We are still to return!

Because we could afford it, we had rented a cart to carry some of our things. It was five hours from our town to the Euphrates River. On the way we had to pass on a bridge. We were told that one of our neighbor's boys had been killed and thrown over there. In fact, I heard some Turk boys saying to each other that there was a gold piece in the pocket of our neighbor's son. We could see the injured who had been shot, but were not yet dead.

The first village that we reached was one in which our landlord lived. We saw that the fruit was getting ripe. My brother, sister, uncle's son and daughter took some money to our landlord to see if he would save their lives, and they remained with him. I stayed with my mother, my uncle's wife, and her five-year-old grandchild. We left the village of Bederatil and went to the next town, Lelushaghen, which took us a day to reach. There was a Turk man who was taking Armenian boys away, and I said that I would go with him.

That night, I and two other boys slept at this Turkish agha's [chief's] house. In the morning my mother brought a bundle of clothes for me and left it with a Turkish woman whose husband had worked in my father's bakery and who had lived with this agha for years. I was there when she came to the house to leave my clothes. I was sitting there and I saw her, but it was as though I was in a trance; we never talked and she never kissed me. I don't know if it was because she could not bear it from sadness. I never saw again any of those clothes or anything that my mother might have left in them for me.

The deportation caravan now went on without me; they still had two hours to make it to the Euphrates River. When they got there, they were all killed. The way we heard this was that some of the police brought to the agha a pretty young girl and her brother that this Turk wanted. These [gendarmes] police told the agha that in a matter of a few minutes they wiped them all out. But this young Armenian girl told us that she saw the gendarmes force the deportees to take off their clothes and then shove them off a cliff into the Euphrates River far below. According to this girl, when it came time for my mother, she took gold from her bundle, threw it in the river, grabbed my four-year-old brother, and jumped down with the child in her arms. When I heard this, all of a sudden I began to weep. It's the feelings you know. I was about nine years old. As soon as this girl finished telling her story, the agha's son tried to distract me and those listening by calling me a *gavour* [infidel; italics added] making fun of the cross. I covered my head with the blanket and cried and cried.

Takouhi Levonian, native of Keghi, born 1900. Audiotaped on April 8, 1981, in Los Angeles, California, by Donald and Lorna Miller. (Keghi was another Armenian town in the region of Kharpert.)

When the war began, I could see and sense the men of our town gathering in groups. They were talking and looking very sad. The women used to sigh. The schools shut down and their grounds, as well as the churches, became filled with soldiers. That's how winter passed. In April, there was talk that they were going to move us out. I was 15 years old then. . . .

Between April 29 and 30 [of 1915], word came that they were going to transfer us to Kharpert. On May first, that news was confirmed and until the fourth [of May] every household began preparations by making *kete* [Armenian bread; italics added], preparing chickens, other meats, and so on. My father told my mom not to bother with any of these preparations. He said to just take our bedding on the mules and not to bother burying anything, like so many others had done who thought that they would return to them. He said that if we ever returned, he would be glad to come back to four walls. He was farsighted.

At the onset of the war he imported large amounts of oil, sugar, matches, and all the things that had to be imported. When we left [on the deportation], we distributed all this to our neighbors. They arrested only a few people from our town. The rest they left unharmed. They did not do anything to my father because he was respected by all, since he was so fair with every one—regardless of nationality. He did good equally to all.

We were the first caravan to leave with much tears and anguish since it meant separation for so many. They assigned a few soldiers to us and thus we began. We used to travel by day, and in the evenings we stopped to eat and rest. In five to six days we reached Palu. There while we were washing up, I will never, never forget, they took my father away, along with all the men down to twelve years of age. The next day our camp was filled with the Turks and Kurds of Palu, looting, dragging away whatever they could, both possessions and young women. They knocked the mules down to kill them. I was grabbing onto my six-year-old brother; my sister was holding her baby, and my two young sisters were grabbing her skirt; my mother was holding the basket of bread. There was so much confusion, and the noise of bullets shooting by us. Some people were getting shot, and the rest of us were running in the field, not knowing where to go. . . .

Then I saw with my own eyes the Turks beating a fellow named Sahag, who had hid under his wife's dress. They were beating him with hammers, axes right in front of me and his wife. He yelled to her to run away, that we are all going to die a "donkey death" [Expression meaning, "to die worthlessly, slaughtered like an animal."]. And then I saw the husband of my aunt, who was too old to have been taken previously, and he was being beaten in the head with an ax. They then threw him in the river. It finally calmed down. The Turks left some dead, took some with them, and the rest of us found each other.

At this time it was announced that anyone who would become a Turk could remain here. Otherwise, we must continue on. Many stayed. So we took off again. [We felt] much loss, that was not material loss only, but human loss. We were in tears and anguish as we left.

From Palu to Dikranagerd they tormented us a great deal. We suffered a lot. There was no water or food. Whatever my mom had in her bag, she gave us a little at a time. We walked the whole day, ten to fifteen days. No shoes remained on our feet. We finally reached Dikranagerd. There, by the water, we washed, and whatever little dry bread we had we wetted it and ate it.

Word came that the *vali* [governor; italics added] wanted from the Armenians a very pretty twelve-year-old girl. . . . So by night, they came with their lamps looking for such a girl. They found one, dragged her from the mother, saying to the weeping mother that they will return her. Later, they returned the child, in horrible condition, almost dead, and left her at her mother's knees.

The mother was weeping so badly, and, of course, the child could not make it and died. The women could not comfort her. Finally, several of the women tried to dig a hole, and with the help of one of the gendarme's guns, they buried the girl and covered her. Dikranagerd had a large wall around it, so my mother and a few other women wrote on it, "Shushan buried here."

We remained under the walls [where Shushan was buried] for two to three days. Then they made us leave again. This time they assigned to us an elderly gendarme. He had tied to his horse a large container of water and the whole way he kept giving it to children and never himself rode the horse, but allowed old women to take turns on it. We went to Mardin. He also always took us near the villages so we could buy some food, and he would not allow the villagers to sell food at expensive prices. A lot of people either died on the way or stayed behind, because they could not keep up. So by the time we reached Mardin we were a lot less in number, although still a lot. They deposited us in a large field. There they gave us food. . . . At this point my mother was not with us.

A Kurd woman came and told my sister that two horsemen were going to kidnap me. She panicked and started looking for my mom, but she was not around. So she thought of giving the baby, who was in her arms, to the Kurd woman, so that she would help me. So she disguised me, but when we turned around, the woman was gone with the baby.

Turks used to pay high prices for babies, probably the woman sold him. My poor sister, Zarouhi, went crazy. I, too, was going crazy, feeling that I was the cause. I cried and cried. We remained in Mardin for five days and never found the baby. My poor sister was lactating, and her milk was full, but there was no baby to nurse. . . .

It came time to leave, and we had to leave the baby behind with uncontrollable tears. The journey was dreadful. With no shoes on our feet, it was so painful to walk on the paths they took us on. We used to wrap cloth on them to ease the pain, but it didn't really help much. There was no water. In fact, at one stretch, for three full days, we had no water at all. The children would cry: "Water, water, water." One of the children died.

Then toward morning one day, my sister and another woman crawled out of camp to a far place and brought some water in a tin can. Finally, they dumped us next to a small river. There my mother took me to the river to wash my face which was always covered up, except for my eyes. But one of the gendarmes, having spotted my eyes, showed up and grabbed me. My mother fainted, and, acting bravely, I shook his hand loose and ran, mingling among the people. I could hear the women yelling to my mother to wake up, that I got away. As the caravan moved again, I kept watching that man, always trying to stay behind him. . . .

Yevnig Adrouni, native of Hoghe, born c. 1905. Audio-taped on August 13, 1978, by Rouben Adalian. (Hoghe was an Armenian village in the Kharpert region.)

My uncle, my cousin, the government took them away. Later they gathered the noteworthy people including my father. They took him to prison, to Kharpert. After this they began to gather the men and to take them to the place called Keghvank. That place was a slaughterhouse. I remember my uncle's wife and others used to go there. My father was still in prison at this time. They used to go there and find that their men were missing. They had taken them and killed them with axes even then.

During the time when my father was in prison, there occurred the thing called Amelie Taburie [labor battalions]. They recalled all the Armenian soldiers. They set them to work at road construction. In this way they gathered all of them, including the Armenian soldiers, and filled them in the prisons. Later, when my father was still in prison, they set fire to the prison so that the Armenians would be killed. Already they were torturing them every day. When he escaped from prison, a Kurd saw my father. He was an acquaintance. My father fled with the Kurd to our village. But his nails were pulled out and his body was black and blue. They had tortured my father continuously. He lived but a few days. He died.

This is in 1915. My mother was deported first. A Turk was going to keep us, but he proposed that we Turkify. My mother did not accept. Therefore, since I was young, they thought that if my mother was not with me, they might be able to convince me to Turkify. My mother was deported three months before the rest of us. This happened in spring. As for me, they would say: "Would the daughter of a tough infidel become a Muslim?"

They deported me also, thirsty and hungry, all the way to Deir el-Zor. They did not even allow us to drink water. Along the way they took us by very narrow roads. Many of the old people who were hungry and thirsty could not walk. They used to strike them with stones and roll them down the slope. Pregnant women, I have seen with my own eyes. . . . (I cried a lot. Whenever I go to church, the whole thing is in front of my eyes, the scene, the deportation.) They tore open the bellies of pregnant women so that the child was born. It fell free. They used to do that. I have seen such things.

There were some men. They killed them at that time. All of us, hungry, thirsty, we walked all the way to Deir el-Zor. They came, Kurds, Arabs, and carried us away from the caravan. When a piece of bread fell in my hands for the first time, I chewed it but could not swallow it because I was starved.

Along the way they did not allow us to drink water. The river was there. It flowed. They did not let us go and drink. A girl, she was thirteen, fourteen perhaps . . . we suddenly saw that the caravan was stopped there in the field. That girl came, her face scratched, bloodied, all her clothes torn. Her mother had sent her secretly in order to fetch water. There were Kurdish boys . . . all the things they have done to the poor girl. The Turkish guards caught her mother. They asked: "Who is her mother, let her come forward?" The caravan was seated. A woman moved her lips. The guards said: "This is her mother." The child was in her lap. They seized the woman and in front of our eyes, they shot her [daughter] dead, saying: "Because you did not have the right. We had forbidden you to send anyone to the river."

They used to take the little ones and carry them away. The Kurds carried me away as well. For eight years I remained lost among the Kurds, the Turks, and the Arabs. I was among the Kurds. I forgot the Armenian language, but I did not forget the Lord's Prayer. Later they used to have me tend sheep. They gave me a dog with the name of Khutto. I used to write in the dirt with my finger my name, my last name, and the name of my birthplace. I used to write the alphabet in the dirt and in this way I did not forget the Armenian letters. I did not forget the Lord's Prayer and I did not forget where I was from.

First I was with an Assyrian. They took me to Merdin. Later I was placed with Muslims to be brought up as their child, but I became ill. They returned me to the Assyrian. The Assyrians helped us a great deal. From the church the sister of the patriarch of the Assyrians took me to her house. They were poor as well. The Assyrians used to go to the road in order to break stones and make a living, and I went along with them. We used to go there to break stones. When that finished, it seems the war was ended, I said I am going to Aleppo. Instead of going to Aleppo, Kurdish tribesmen carried me away. They took me to their villages as a servant. I knew that I had relatives in Aleppo but how would I find them, how would I get there. I was among Kurds.

They took me to the place called Tersellor. Tersellor was a village of Kurds in the environs of Aleppo at the place called Musulme. I remained there tending sheep, but I had made up my mind that I would go to Aleppo. I did not know any other Armenians. There were no

Armenians. There was nobody, but I thought to myself that my cousin might be there. By night I escaped. I went down the road. I hid from the Kurds. I saw a traveler on horseback with young ones around him. They saw me.

Now the languages, Arabic, Kurdish, I spoke fluently already. They asked me: "Where are you going?" I said: "I am going to Aleppo." They looked at each other's faces. They said: "We are going to Aleppo. We will take you along." They took me with them. They were from Aleppo, but Muslims. They have villages. In the summer they go to their villages. In the winter they return to Aleppo. They took me with them, but they did not let me out of their house in Aleppo. Next door to the house I was staying in there was an Armenian girl. She was younger than I. She remembered only her name, Mary. She brought news from the outside. She is also Armenian and I am Armenian, but I acted as if I was a Kurd since I had presented myself as a Kurd to the others. I was afraid to tell the truth to that Armenian girl. She was younger than I.

One day she had fallen down the stairs and broken her foot. They took her to the hospital. At the hospital they told her: "You are Armenian." "No, my name is Fatma," she had said. I saw that she had come back. When we were taking out the garbage, I asked her: "Where were you?" She related what had taken place. "I was at the hospital." She said that they told her: "You are Armenian." She said: "At first I denied it." After talking for a while she conceded. "Yes, I only remember that we were under a tent. My father, my mother, all, they killed and they took me. Only that much I remember." They said: "Do not go. Do not be afraid. Now there are Armenians. We have an Armenia." This is at the end of 1922. After I was freed I discovered what the date was. She said: "No. I came back because they spent ten red gold pieces for my foot."

Look, God sent her for me. I believe that God sent her for me. "But I will escape," she said. "I will escape." I said: "Alright, we will escape together." We had a shoemaker who was Armenian. We did not know that he was Armenian. He was from Aintab. Now I regret very much that I did not take down his name. Eventually, through his assistance we managed to escape.

I told the girl: "Tell that boy from Aintab that there is another Armenian girl." He asked her: "Does she use a veil?" At that time I had been given a small veil since I was with a Muslim. He made me work as a servant. She said: "Yes." "Do not believe that she is Armenian," he said. The girl came and told me this. I said: "Tell him I know the Lord's Prayer." She went and told him. He said: "Anyone from another race can learn that by heart just as they learn languages." It so happened that Armenian men had attempted to rescue girls from the houses of other Arabs only to discover that they were not Armenians. I said: "Tell him that I know how to read Armenian." He said: "If she knows how to read Armenian, let her write." I wrote my name, my last name, where I was from, but I wrote in Turkish with Armenian letters. When she gave him the letter, he told her: "We will not rescue you until she is ready too. Now we believe that this girl is Armenian." If I had not known how to read and write Armenian I would not be here today. The Armenian letters saved me. This letter was handed to Nishan Der-Bedrosian, a man from Kharpert. It came into his hands and he wrote me a letter which reached me through that girl. "Try in every way to escape. . . ."

The shop of the shoemaker was close to where we lived. The first day I found that he had locked the door to the shop and left. I went the following day. He said: "You know I cannot keep the store open after a certain hour. It is against the law." Then I found the means to escape. When I was escaping, they realized that I was escaping so they locked the door with two keys. But finally I found the way. I escaped by night. A man was standing in the dark and the shoemaker had not closed his shop. They took me and we left. It was a feast day. It was Christmas Day. Apparently it was December or January, perhaps the beginning of 1923. I was free.

So this is my story. But the things which the Turks did, the massacres, I never forget. In front of our eyes . . . Haygaz . . . on his mother's knees, they butchered him. These sort of things I have seen. And I always cry. I cannot forget.

Chapter Three

Soviet Man-Made Famine in Ukraine

James E. Mace

It is now generally accepted that in 1932–1933 several million peasants—most of them Ukrainians living in Ukraine and the traditionally Cossack territories of the North Caucasus (now the Krasnodar, Stavropol, and Rostov on the Don regions of the Russian Federation)—starved to death because the government of the Soviet Union seized with unprecedented force and thoroughness the 1932 crop and foodstuffs from the agricultural population (Mace, 1984; Conquest, 1986). After over half a century of denial, in January 1990 the Communist Party of Ukraine adopted a special resolution admitting that the Ukrainian Famine had indeed occurred, cost millions of lives, had been artificially brought about by official actions, and that Stalin and his associates bore criminal responsibility for those actions (*Holod,* 1990, pp. 3–4).

The Ukrainian Famine corresponded in time with a reversal of official policies which had hitherto permitted significant self-expression of the U.S.S.R.'s non-Russian nations. During and after the Famine, non-Russian national self-assertion was labeled *bourgeois nationalism* and suppressed. The elites which had been associated with these policies were eliminated (Mace, 1983, pp. 264–301). The authorities of the period denied that a famine was taking place at the time, sought to discredit reports on the factual situation, insofar as possible prevented the starving from travelling to areas where food was available, and refused all offers of aid to the starving (Conquest, 1986; Commission on the Ukraine Famine, 1988: vi–xvv). They were assisted in this policy of denial by certain Western journalists, most notably Walter Duranty of *The New York Times* (Taylor, 1990, pp. 210–223).

In order to understand the Ukrainian Famine, a brief excursion into the preceding period is necessary. Despite their numerical strength as the second-largest of the Slavic-speaking nations, Ukrainians may be classed with what Czech scholar Myroslav Hroch (1985) designated the "small nations" of Europe. Such nations "were in subjection for such a long period that the relation of subjection took on a structural character," that is, the majority of the ruling class belonged to the ruling nation, while the subjugated nation possessed an incomplete social structure partially or entirely lacking its own ruling class (Hroch, 1985, p. 9). The Ukrainians were basically a nation of peasants, their national movement being led by a numerically small intelligentsia. As in other areas occupied by subject nations in imperial Russian and early Soviet history, the local nobility, bourgeoisie, and urban population in Ukraine were overwhelmingly Russian or Russian-speaking (Liber, 1992, pp. 12–15). In the nineteenth century Ukrainians underwent a national revival similar to that of Czechs and other "small nations," that is, romantic scholarly excursions into the local language and history along with the creation of a vernacular literature brought a spreading sense of local patriotism and national identity which in turn gave way to political aspirations and, ultimately, territorial home rule. Yet, when in 1925 Stalin wrote, "The national question is, *according to its essence,* a question of the peasantry" (Stalin, 1946–51: VII, p. 72), this held true for almost all the non-Russian peoples of the Soviet Union and certainly for Ukrainians.

The social development of Ukrainians in the Russian Empire had been retarded by extraordinarily repressive policies. In 1863, the imperial Russian government responded to what it perceived as a nascent threat of "Ukrainian separatism" by banning education and publications (except for folk songs and historical documents) in the Ukrainian language, declaring it to be a substandard variant of Russian. This ban was broadened in 1876 to eliminate the modest exemptions in the earlier measure and remained in effect until 1905 (Savchenko, 1930). After 1905, a Ukrainian language press enjoyed a brief flowering in central Ukraine, but creeping reimposition of the old prohibitions all but eliminated it within a few years. Because repressive tsarist policies had stunted the growth of social differentiation within Ukrainian society, Ukrainian activists could expect to gain mass support only among the peasantry. Consequently, when Ukrainian political parties evolved in imperial Russia at the turn of the century they assumed a revolutionary socialist character, and the form in which Ukrainian political aspirations gained majority support during the revolution of 1917 was through the agrarian socialism of the Ukrainian Party of Socialist Revolutionaries (Hermaize, 1926; Khrystiuk, 1921–1922, Vol. 1, p. 35).

After the collapse of the Russian imperial authority in 1917, the national movements which attempted to establish local governments throughout the former empire's non-Russian periphery, including the Ukrainian movement, drew most of their mass support from the village, while in the cities various groups competed more or less as they did in Russia proper.

The group which seized power in the center, Lenin's Bolsheviks, mistrusted the peasants as petty property owners and relied on forced requisitions of agricultural produce in order to keep the urban population fed. Thus, the national struggle between Russians ("Red" or "White"), and the subject peoples was at the same time a social struggle of the countryside versus the town, where even the working class was drawn from the oppressor nation or had assimilated its culture. As Ukrainian Communist spokesmen recognized as early as 1920, the Russian-speaking worker, who provided the main source of support for Soviet rule in Ukraine, sneered at the Ukrainian village and wanted nothing to do with it (Mace, 1983, pp. 68–69). During the wars that followed the Russian Revolution of 1917, a Soviet regime had been imposed on Ukraine by Russia against the will of most of Ukraine's inhabitants, an absolute majority of whom had voted in free elections for groups that supported Ukrainian self-rule (Borys, 1980, p. 170, table).

In order to overcome rural resistance to the Soviet order, in 1921 Lenin proclaimed the New Economic Policy (NEP), which ended forced procurements and allowed a private market in which agricultural producers could sell what they had produced. In 1923, in order to overcome the continued national resistance of the non-Russian countryside, Lenin proclaimed a policy of "indigenization" *(korenizatsiia)*, which attempted to give non-Russian Soviet regimes a veneer of national legitimacy by promoting the spread of the local language and culture in the cities, recruiting local people into the regime, ordering Russian officials to learn the local language, and fostering a broad range of cultural activities (Mace, 1983, pp. 87–95; Liber, 1992, pp. 33–46).

The Ukrainian Famine of 1932–1933 occurred within the context of the so-called "Stalinist Revolution from Above," a violent experiment in social transformation in which state-orchestrated paranoia about internal and external enemies was used to blame shortcomings on the machinations of class enemies. Like Naziism, Stalinism attempted to explain the world as a struggle between different categories of people, some of whom were considered inherently deleterious and whose elimination was an essential prerequisite toward the attainment of a new and better state of affairs. As a degenerated offshoot of Marxism, Stalinism attempted to explain the world by using class categories rather than the racial ones employed by the Nazis. But what Hitler and Stalin had in common was a dualistic view of human society as composed of two implacably hostile forces, the "good" force destined for victory (Aryans for Hitler and the proletariat for Stalin) which could only liberate itself and achieve its destiny by destroying utterly the forces of evil (for Hitler, Jews and Gypsies, which he considered racially polluting elements, and for Stalin, representatives of "exploiter classes").

A major difference between Stalinism and racism (like Naziism) is that racism at least knows how to define what it hates: people who look or speak differently or have different ancestors. Class warfare, however, is a sociological concept, and sociological categories are much easier to manipulate than racial ones, especially when applied in and by a state that claims, as did Stalin's, a monopoly on truth and science thanks to its correct understanding and application of a theory based on claims of holistic scienticism; that is, claims that it explains everything with the certainty of (pseudo-) scientific laws. By redefining and manipulating such notions as class enemies, enemies of the people, and objectively serving the interests of such dark forces, Stalin was able to declare practically any group or individual as worthy of destruction. This enabled Stalin to reduce Marxism, one of the great (if flawed) intellectual systems of the nineteenth century, to the level of a sanctioning ideology for perhaps the paradigmatic example of what Leo Kuper (1990) has called the genocide state.

Marxism views history as class struggle. It holds that modern capitalism is defined by the struggle between proletarians and capitalists, the former being destined to triumph over the latter and thereby create a new socialist stage of human history in which the economic exploitation of one person by another will be abolished. Independent smallholding peasants are viewed as peripheral to this struggle, a petty capitalist holdover of an earlier era. Leninists saw an inevitable process of class differentiation among peasants into three strata: the relatively wealthier *kulaks* (Ukrainian *kurkuls*) or village exploiters, the middle peasants or subsistence farmers who did not hire labor or depend on outside employment to get by, and the poor peasants, who could only make ends meet by working for others and thus were at least partially rural proletarians. The middle and poor peasants were often lumped together as the *toiling peasantry* in order to mark them off from the kulaks. However, such a division of the peasantry into such categories was arbitrary, and just who was a kulak was never defined with any precision (Lewin, 1985, pp. 121–141).

As for the national question, most varieties of Marxism reject nationalism as a species of false consciousness which reflects the interests of an exploitative bourgeois class by convincing the exploited that they owe loyalty to their capitalist-ruled nation rather than to the international working class. Orthodox Marxists believe that only internationalism can serve the interests of the working class. There have been many conflicting policy prescriptions advocated by Marxists designed to overcome nationalistic prejudices and achieve the internationalist unity of the toiling classes.

Just as nationalism can have a variety of meanings, so can internationalism. In the pre-Stalinist period, the Soviet authorities found what they considered the "correct" internationalist approach to building socialism by attempting to combat the imperial pretensions of Russians (the dominant group) and by assisting the formerly subject peoples of the Russian Empire to overcome the legacy of colonial domination by rebuilding their various national cultures and societies—under the Party's guidance, of course. This ideological prescription actually reflected political necessity: before the adoption of such a policy non-Russian peasant dissatisfaction had threatened political stability in wide areas of the new Soviet Union. But there were certainly other Marxist views of internationalism. For example, Rosa Luxemburg (1976) advocated a view often criticized as "national nihilism" when she argued that national self-determination was a chimera: it was utopian so long as capitalist exploitation survived and would be rendered irrelevant once socialism had brought about the final end of all forms of exploitation (pp. 308–314).

Once an ideology comes to power, theory becomes the stuff of practical politics, influencing and being influenced by considerations of power. Ukrainization, the Ukrainian version of indigenization, went further than elsewhere in the Soviet Union because roughly thirty million Ukrainians were several times more numerous than any other single national group. On the eve of the Famine they constituted about two-fifths of all non-Russian inhabitants of the U.S.S.R. The policies of indigenization, designed to placate the *national* aspirations of the non-Russian, overwhelmingly peasant nations, went hand-in-hand with the limited free market policies of the New Economic Policy (NEP), which were designed to satisfy the economic aspirations of both Russian and non-Russian peasants. With indigenization having legitimized national priorities among non-Russian Communists and the high politics in Moscow centering on a protracted struggle for power, during the 1920s national Communists in the constituent republics of the

U.S.S.R. accumulated a large measure of autonomy from central dictates. When at the end of the decade Joseph Stalin emerged victorious in the succession struggle, he abruptly changed course by announcing the crash collectivization of agriculture on the basis of the liquidation (that is, destruction) of the *kulaks* as a class.

Collectivization meant forcing millions of small farmers into large collective farms, which many peasants—not without reason—saw as a reinstitution of serfdom, the only difference being that the state was now taking the place of the nobleman who owned the peasants' grandparents. Forcing the majority of the population to restructure their lives in a way they did not wish to meant provoking a degree of hostility that rendered politically irrelevant concessions that had been designed to placate the non-Russian peasants on national grounds.

The changed political situation enabled Stalin to pursue four objectives toward the non-Russians. Donald Treadgold (1964) rightly has summarized them as follows: (1) the elimination of centrifugal pressures by stifling local nationalism, (2) subversion of neighboring states by having members of a given Soviet nationality conduct propaganda among their co-nationals in neighboring areas, (3) "economic and social transformation designed to destroy native society and substitute a social system susceptible of control by Moscow," and 4) the economic exploitation of non-Russian areas (pp. 297–298).

Transforming society by force far exceeds the capacity of any traditional authoritarian state. It requires the mobilization and motivation of mass constituencies who could be called upon to do the regime's will. Starting with a phony war scare in 1927 and followed by show trials designed to point out various social groups (managers and engineers held over from the old regime, academicians, people who had been associated with national or religious movements, etc.) as nests of plotters in the pay of world capitalism, a massive propaganda campaign was carried out designed to convince people that the Soviet Union was under siege by the hostile capitalist world which encircled it. Soviet society had to catch up with the capitalist West or be crushed. The crash collectivization of agriculture was portrayed as essential in order to do this.

In order to expropriate *kulaks,* enforce collectivization, and take possession of agricultural produce, the authorities mobilized anyone they could. As a self-proclaimed workers' state, it was logical that the regime would turn first to the workers and trade unions for personnel to impose its will. The entire network of officially sanctioned social organizations was mobilized. The resistance they faced was interpreted in class terms as kulak terrorism, for who but a kulak or his agent could oppose the socialist transformation of the countryside? Ultimately, any problem was blamed on "kulaks" or their "agents" and repressive policies were justified by the need to combat an enemy presence which was ever more broadly defined. The village itself became an object of official mistrust as tens of thousands of factory workers were issued revolvers and sent into villages with the power to completely reorganize life there as well as to circumvent or abolish governmental bodies on the village level. Workers were sent from factories, and sometimes a factory would be named "patron" of a given number of villages; that is, the factory would be assigned villages from which to enforce collectivization and seize food. Local "activists," that is, individuals whose position gave them an active role in officially sanctioned social and political life, would also be given these responsibilities. Special peasant "tow" *(buksyr)* brigades were organized and given the task of "taking the kulaks in tow" by ejecting those selected by the local authorities for expropriation from their houses or searching for concealed foodstuffs. The members of these brigades did not always volunteer: sometimes county or district authorities would simply call up the able-bodied men in one village to act as a tow brigade in a neighboring village. For example, a schoolteacher had no choice but to take part in the work of the local activists. At the height of the famine, when most peasants were physically incapable of work, lines in front of city stores were raided from time to time, and the unfortunates rounded up were sent to weed sugar beets (Commission, 1988, 448–449).

The essence of the collective farm system was official control over agricultural production and distribution. The state's "procurement" of agricultural produce was carried out by force such that procurements (purchases) really became forced requisitions. Since, however, the collective farm was in theory a private cooperative, not a state enterprise, the authorities assumed no responsibility for the welfare of the collective farmers. Whatever the state required came from the "first proceeds" of the harvest; that is, the state took its quota first. If there was anything left, it went first to what was needed to run the farm, such as seed reserves, and what was left over was then shared among the collective farmers according to the *labor days (trudodni)* they had earned (Jasny, 1949, pp. 64–85).

These labor days were not actual days worked. Rather, they were allocated according to complex formula designed to calculate the different values of different kinds of labor by converting all types of labor on the farm into the Marxist concept of simple labor time. Skilled workers, like a tractor driver, might earn two labor days for each day worked, while a simple farmer without any particular skill might have to work two days in order to earn one labor day. This, however, was of no consequence if there was nothing left: in that case, of course, the labor days of the collective farmers were worthless.

At the time of the famine, roughly 20 percent of the Ukrainian peasantry was still outside the collective farms. They had their own household quotas which were imposed by local authorities. If they could not meet a given quota, they were fined, and their farms searched with the aid of metal prods.

Collectivization led to a crisis in agricultural production which the regime met sometimes with force and sometimes with promises to overcome "errors" or "excesses" or "deviations" from the party's "Leninist general line." Such shortcomings were always blamed on subordinate officials, never on the policies of the Communist party and Soviet state, which were held to be infallible. The first agricultural procurement campaign after crash collectivization, that of 1930, was met, thanks to a fortunate harvest. The following year, the quota was not met in spite of considerable force which succeeded only in creating pockets of starvation. In the first half of 1932, the regime announced that there had been a crop failure in parts of the Volga Basin and Asiatic Russia and sent aid there from other regions. In May, agricultural quotas for the coming crop were lowered to about the level of what had been obtained from the 1931 crop. Various officials were denounced for having used excessive force in seizing agricultural produce and promises were made that such "distortions" of the official policy would not be tolerated in the future. Some local officials who had been particularly harsh toward peasants in their charge were publicly tried and punished. For a few weeks, even Ukraine received limited food aid.

Then, in the summer of 1932, with Ukraine on the verge of mass starvation, Stalin abruptly changed course. At a Ukrainian Communist party conference in July, amid reports that the situation in the Ukrainian countryside was growing desperate, Stalin's top assistants—Prime Minister Viacheslav Molotov and Agriculture Minister Lazar Kaganovich—announced that Ukraine's quotas for bread grain deliveries would stand at the level announced the previous May. But once the harvest was in, there simply wasn't enough grain to meet the quota. The Ukrainian authorities appealed to Moscow for an end to the grain seizures but to no avail. Throughout the fall of 1932, Stalin sent various high officials to Ukraine to supervise the local Communists. In November, bread that had been "advanced" to the collective farmers at harvest time was declared to have been illegally distributed and was therefore seized. In order to make up for shortfalls elsewhere, those farms which met their quotas were subjected to supplementary quotas of foodstuffs which had to be delivered to the state. Local officials were ordered to determine how much bread there was in every collective farm and to put it toward the quota.

On December 14, Stalin's intimate involvement in the Ukrainian Famine became clear when he called the top leaders of Ukraine, the North Caucasus, and the Western (Smolensk) District to Moscow. The meeting produced a secret decree signed by Stalin as head of the Party and Molotov as head of government. While the leader of the Western District was let off with a simple admonition to meet its quotas, the Ukrainian and North Caucasus representatives were blasted for having failed to root out Ukrainian nationalism:

> As a result of the extremely weak efforts and lack of revolutionary vigilance of a number of local Party organizations in Ukraine and the North Caucasus, in a substantial portion of these organizations counter-revolutionary elements—kulaks, former officers, Petliurists, adherents of the Kuban Rada and so forth—have been able to worm their way into the collective farms as chairmen or as influential members of their administration, bookkeepers, store managers, threshing brigade leaders, and so forth, were able to worm their way into village councils, agricultural offices, cooperatives, and attempted to direct the work of these organizations against the interests of the proletarian state and the Party's policy, attempted to organize a counterrevolutionary movement, to sabotage the grain procurements, and to sabotage the sowing, the All-Union Communist Party Central Committee and Council of Peoples Commissars of the USSR direct the Communist Party and government leadership of Ukraine and the North Caucasus to resolutely root out the counterrevolutionary elements by means of their arrest, long sentences of confinement in concentration camps, and not excluding application of the highest measure of legality [that is, execution—JM] in the most criminal cases. ("Postanova TsK VKP(b) ta RNK SRSR pro khlibozahotivli na Ukraïny, Pivnichnomu Kavkazi ta Zakhidnii oblasti"

[Decision of the All-Union Communist Party Central Committee and USSR Council of Peoples Commissars on Grain Procurements in Ukraine, the North Caucasus, and Western District], *Zoloti vorota: Al'manakh*, No. 1 (1991), p. 78.)

The decree went on to name officials on the local level who had failed to make their quotas, mentioning the officials by name and detailing which of them were to be given prison sentences and which of them were to be shot. In addition, Ukrainian officials were condemned for their "mechanistic" (that is, overzealous) implementation of Ukrainization, while Ukrainization was ordered halted in the North Caucasus (Postanova, 1991).

A week later, Stalin's representatives in Ukraine ordered the seizure of even the seed that had been put aside for spring planting. In January 1933, Stalin took direct control of the Ukrainian Communist party apparatus. His appointees, accompanied by tens of thousands of subordinates, initiated a campaign which led to the destruction of nationally self-assertive Ukrainian elites, the end of the Ukrainization policy and virtually all Ukrainian cultural self-expression, and the gradual return to Russian language in Ukraine's cities and educational institutions (Commission, 1988: xi–xvii; *Holod*, 1990, pp. 148–235).

The food seized, people began to starve. Millions died either from starvation—an agonizingly slow process in which the body literally consumes itself until the muscles of the chest can no longer lift the rib cage to inflate the lungs and the victim suffocates—or, more commonly, from diseases which in such a weakened condition the body can no longer fend off. But to report deaths from starvation or from diseases like typhus, which are associated with famine, was considered anti-Soviet. Physicians used euphemisms like vitamin or protein deficiency (which does usually accompany caloric deficiency), heart failure (because the heart stops), diarrhea (from eating plants the body cannot digest), or "exhaustion of the organism" (Gannt, 1937, pp. 147–162). Estimates of the number of victims in Ukraine range from three to eight million. According to the long-suppressed 1937 census, released only in 1991, in 1937 Ukraine had a million fewer inhabitants than in 1926, three million fewer than official estimates of the early 1930s, which were probably not far off the mark (*Vsesoiuznaia*, 1991, p. 28, table). Using these and other long suppressed figures, demographers in the former Soviet Union have calculated that, while the population of the U.S.S.R. increased from 148.7 million in 1927 to 162.5 million in 1937, during the year 1933 the population decreased by 5.9 million. Their figures further suggest that the number of victims of famine in 1933 was between 7.2 and 8.1 million (summarized in Ellman, 1991, pp. 375–379). Given that all but one or two million of these victims perished in Ukraine, the number of victims of the Ukrainian Famine would be in the range of five to seven million.

As living conditions worsened, the authorities expanded the system of hard currency stores, the *torgsin*. The name was an abbreviation for the Russian phrase, *torgovlia s inostrantsami* (trade with foreigners), because only foreigners had the right to possess precious metals and convertible currency. In exchange for food, these stores helped extract the last valuables remaining in the countryside. Often a small piece of jewelry, a gold tooth, or a concealed silver or gold coin meant the difference between life and death.

The Famine had a major long-range impact on Ukrainians. The adoption in 1932–1933 of an internal passport system from which peasants were excluded meant that the agricultural population could not leave the countryside without official permission. This meant attaching the peasantry to the land in a way not entirely different from traditional serfdom. The psychological traumatization inevitable in any situation of mass mortality was undoubtedly compounded by a policy of official denial extending to the most remote village. At the height of the famine, Stalin adopted the slogan: "Life has become better; life has become more fun," and even the starving had to repeat it. To speak openly of everyday reality meant running the risk of punishment for propagating anti-Soviet propaganda. Children were encouraged to inform on their parents, and Pavlik Morozov, a boy who had informed on his parents and was killed by villagers after the parents' subsequent arrest, was held up as a model for Soviet young people. As a result, parents became afraid to talk openly in front of their own children. While Stalin's rapid industrialization brought millions of Ukrainian peasants to Ukraine's cities, mines, and factories, the abandonment of policies promoting the use of the Ukrainian language there often meant the rapid linguistic and cultural Russification of these new workers and city dwellers.

As a result of the Famine and accompanying destruction of national elites, the Ukrainian nation was literally crushed. Their leadership (including the natural village leadership, the more prosperous and industrious peasants) was destroyed. Their language and culture, which had made significant inroads in the cities in the 1920s, was largely pushed back to the countryside whence it came. And in the countryside, about one out of every five people had perished. As a result, the development of Ukrainians as a nation was violently and traumatically set back.

The Ukrainians might never have recovered as a nation had it not been for Stalin's 1939 pact with Hitler, by which the Soviet Union annexed Western Ukraine as its share of the dismembered Polish Republic. Western Ukraine contained areas which had never been under Russian rule and were consequently the most developed and nationally conscious regions of Ukraine. The joining of Western Ukraine to the devastated central and eastern Ukrainian territories largely undermined Stalin's deconstruction of the Ukrainian nation in the 1930s, paving the way for Ukrainian independence in the 1990s.

Drawing lessons from history is always a risky business, but surely one of the principal lessons of the Ukrainian Famine has to do with the dangers of pseudo-scientific totalitarian ideologies. Such ideologies, which claim scientific validity, explain problems within a given society by blaming them on the presence of permanent enemies which by virtue of their very existence prevent the bulk of society from achieving its destiny, the good life, or otherwise solving its problems. Such enemies may be racial, national, political, or social, but however defined, such ideologies may easily be used as warrants for mass murder and genocide. The monopolies or near-monopolies of propaganda, reward, and coercion which totalitarian societies possess in turn make it possible for totalitarian regimes to attract sufficient mass participation to carry out such designs. Moreover, as George Orwell demonstrated nearly half a century ago in *1984*, the totalitarian monopoly of official expression allowed the Stalin regime to define and redefine concepts in order to radically change their meaning. Thus, in the Ukrainian case, class categories were manipulated in order to redefine national issues as class ones. Thus, the Ukrainian Famine further shows that the Fascist Right has no monopoly on genocide. Even ideologies espousing internationalism and social justice can be manipulated so as to target ethnic groups by redefining its terms to mean whatever might seem expedient at a given moment.

The refusal of even the moderate Left to perceive the full horror of Stalinism also carries lessons about the selective perception of evil. While it is understandable that one is more charitable to actions taken by regimes that profess adherence to "one's own" side of the political spectrum, civilized adherents of both the Left and the Right should realize that the most important issue of political life is not between continuity and change but between those who uphold such universal human values as the right of living people to remain among the living and those who do not recognize such a right for members of a given out-group. For those who profess humane values, the willingness to countenance the death of millions for their goals ceases to have anything in common with political progress: it is simply mass murder on an unspeakable scale.

Eyewitness Accounts
Soviet Man-Made Famine in Ukraine

Account 1

S. Lozovy, "What Happened in Hadyach County," *The Black Deeds of the Kremlin: A White Book,* ed. S. Pidhainy, et al. (Toronto and Detroit, 1953–55), I: 246–255. *The Black Deeds* is the classic collection of eyewitness accounts of the famine, compiled by the Democratic Association of Ukrainians Who Had Been Repressed by the Soviets (DOBRUS), which was associated with the Ukrainian Revolutionary Democratic Party, a socialist group formed after World War II by Ukrainians who had emigrated from Central and Eastern Ukraine.

Having received from comrade Kolotov, boss of the county seat, instructions to establish a commune, the chairman of the village soviet, Tereshko Myshchachenko, took great pains to carry them out. He gave them wide publicity and, as a further incentive, put his name first on the list of commune farmers. Another reason was comrade Gapon from the city of Orel who certainly would have been made chairman if Tereshko had failed in his "duties."

This was in 1930. The village of Kharkivtsi then numbered 780 individual farmers. Out of this number, only four followed his lead and joined the commune. It was easy for them to do so because they had never had places of their own, or else had sold their houses shortly before the instructions were received.

But this venture was still-born. Even these four, having tasted commune life for one season, turned against it and began to think of leaving it.

The authorities, aware of the fact that people were reluctant to join a commune, changed their tune and began to encourage the idea of a collective farm. With this object in view, there appeared Demen Karasyuk from the city of Tambov. He spoke a Russian-Ukrainian jargon, while his family spoke only Russian. Karasyuk appropriated the house of *seredniak* (middle peasant) Brychko and sent him to Siberia, where the poor fellow was worked to death six months later. Thus began collectivization and the liquidation of *kurkuls* (kulaks) as a class.

Rallies were held in the center of the village each day, at which communists from the county seat agitated for collectives. But people did not want to join them and said so, arguing that the government had divided the land against them. And every day GPU agents arrested two or three men.

The village soviet, seeing that people did not want to attend these rallies, hired a boy of 12 to go around with a list and ask people to sign promises that they would attend the gathering. The measure was not successful because men would hide, and their wives would sign their own names arguing that the law gave both sexes equal rights. They also caused a lot of confusion at the rallies by making a terrible noise. The GPU stopped this by sentencing Maria Treba to one year in jail.

The communists changed their tactics. The farmers were called out individually. Under threat of reprisals they were asked to sign papers agreeing to have their property nationalized.

The farmers began to sell their livestock and horses. Their unwillingness to join the collective was stimulated by the fact that people from the neighboring counties of Komyshany and Myrhorod, from villages already collectivized a year ago, came to the village begging for bread. This was an indication as to what they could expect from a collective farm and "communist socialism."

The taxes had to be paid in kind and those who paid them received additional demands, sometimes even greater than the first time, to pay with their products, especially grain.

Seeing no end to this the people began to hide their grain and potatoes if they had any left. A new arrival from the Hadyach Center, comrade Shukhman, who was commissioned to collect grain in three or four counties, gave orders to form *buksyr* (tow) brigades who had authority to manhandle every farmer until he gave all his grain to the state. These brigades were supplied with special tools made in advance in some factory to facilitate the "grain hunt." These were steel rods about 5/8 inch in diameter, three to ten feet long, with one end sharpened to a point and the other equipped with an oval-shaped handle. Some had a kind of drill on the end instead of a point. The *buksyrs* would attack piles of straw, first of all sticking their rods into it to see if sacks of grain were hidden in it. The other tool was used to drill in the gardens and other likely places. The grain when found was, of course, confiscated and the owner was forbidden to remain in Ukraine and was sent to Russia (Solovky, Siberia, etc.). The collective farmers did not hide the grain they received for their labor days (*trudodni*) because there was very little of it.

In October 1932, comrades Shukhman and Kolotov organized a "Red Column." Commandeering about 60 farm wagons, they filled them with toughs and sent them to the villages. Coming to a village, the toughs would scatter, go to the houses of the collective farmers and ask how much grain each had, pretending this was only for registration purposes. When the information was in hand, teams would come up to each house and the grain would be taken away. When all the farmers had been robbed of their grain, the wagons would be decorated with banners and slogans which proclaimed that the farmers had voluntarily, and in an organized manner, given their grain to the state.

This red column passed through villages to be observed, but it was always under GPU protection. When guards were absent, the columns would run into the woods or be robbed by former prisoners who escaped. Such columns took their toll from all the neighboring villages.

It should be observed here that the communists robbed people not only of grain but also of potatoes and any other thing that could be eaten. In some cases farmers were ordered to thresh the straw when the records showed a yield to have been poor. Combatting the communist menace, farmers would leave some grain in the straw by breaking the teeth in the cylinder of the threshing machine. Sometimes they succeeded in concealing up to 30% of grain which remained unthreshed in the straw. They hoped to thresh out this grain later, and thus save themselves and their families. But cases when farmers, in desperation, burned the straw together with their sheds were common.

Searches and arrests led people to despair. The indignation reached its culminating point on November 21, 1932, when great unrest in the village made the village soviet and all the *buksyrs* flee to the county seat for protection. The collective flew to pieces in half an hour. It was exclusively the work of women. They took their horses and cattle home, and the next day went to the approximate location of their former fields because all the field boundaries were destroyed.

The communists were prompt in checking the incipient rebellion. They arrived in force in GPU cars the next night, arrested five persons and ordered that all collective farm property be returned. This order was carried out.

A stranger was now the chairman of the village soviet. Nobody knew where he came from, though he had a Ukrainian name, Boyko. He began to continue the work of his worthy predecessor, paying special attention to the Ukrainian movement for independence. "This is the work of our arch-enemy, Petlyura," he said. Then he tried to find out who had served in Petlyura's army.

Alarmed by the prospect of inevitable doom which was approaching, the people carried off one night all the grain from the collective farm stores, covering their tracks with pepper to protect themselves from detection by GPU hunting dogs. Some went to the forest to gather acorns, but this practice was soon stopped by Boyko, who declared the woods to be state property. It was forbidden to go there.

It was impossible to grind grain in the mill because the government grain quotas were not fulfilled. The farmers constructed hand mills and stampers. Boyko issued an order for the immediate arrest of the man who had built these machines, O. Khrynenko, but he was warned in time and ran away to the Donbas (industrial region of the Donets River Basin). His wife was thrown out of the house, and it was locked by the GPU. Then she was tortured to reveal the whereabouts of her husband and where he had hidden some gold coins. She gave them 230 rubles in gold but did not know where her husband was and died in their hands.

The former chairman of the village soviet, Myshchachenko, sold his house to buy liquor. Then he took a house from Petro Yarosh and, with the assistance of Boyko, managed to have the Yarosh family exiled to the region of Sverdlovsk where all eight family members died from hard labor and ill treatment. Another case was that of F. Shobar, who did the same thing with the brothers Mykola and Stepan Nedvyha. One of them escaped and the other perished in Siberia together with his family of ten.

A week or so later the GPU arrested the following families: Borobavko—5 persons, V. Brychko—7 persons, Ostap Ilchenko—5

persons, Nykyfor and Zakhar Koronivsky—3 persons, O. Perepadya—
4 persons, K. Riznyk—7 persons, Shyka—4 persons, Taras Elesey—6
persons, Vasyukno—4 persons, and others. All of them received life
terms with hard labor and were sent 280 miles north of Sverdlovsk. In
1942, 5 of them returned and said that all the others had died from
hard labor and scurvy. They were lucky to get forged papers and escaped to Donbas, where they worked in the mines. (During their terms)
they had not stayed long in any one place, because as soon as they
cleared a patch in the forest and built barracks and other buildings,
they were sent to another place in the wilderness 18 to 24 miles away
where the same thing was repeated. The direction was always further
north. Their address was Sverdlovsk 5, Letter G.

"There are no *kurkuls* now and presumably no Petlyura partisans,
and we can build up our collective farm in peace," said Boyko. "But
you should keep in mind that there are many *sub-kurkuls* whom we
have to watch and, if they are going to harm our Soviet government, we
will send them after the others." He again held meetings urging people
to join the collective farm. The government took away grain and meat
for taxes. There were no cows or sheep in the village.

In the evening of November 2, an unknown group of farmers attacked a *buksyr* brigade. Makar Verba was killed, and three men ran
away. The next day the GPU confiscated all the shotguns in the village.
The attackers were not caught. Boyko then threatened that the Soviet
Red Army would come and wipe out all the farmers.

The people were terrified. It was hard to find a farmer who had not
served a jail term. Practically all joined the collective farm now; only
twelve swore that they would not do it and did not until 1941. But
these were all women and children whose husbands were in exile in
Siberia.

After the fall of 1932, it became customary to go around and beg
for bread or food from neighbors. These beggars were usually children
and old people.

A new *buksyr* brigade appeared in the village, more cruel than the
first one.

In the spring of 1933 one third of the people in the village were
starving. The others had a little food and ate once a day to keep from
swelling. To save themselves and their families from starvation, men
began to offer their properties for sale or in exchange for food. Some

went to Kharkiv, Kiev or Poltava (major cities of Ukraine) to buy a little food and came back disappointed. Those cities were no better than Hadyach. Then they went to Moscow, Stalingrad, Voronezh and Orel (cities in Russia) where food could be obtained. But the GPU soon found this out and the people were searched on the trains, food confiscated, and they themselves were charged with speculation. Then an order was issued that no farmer would be allowed to travel by train without a permit from the county soviet executive.

In March 1933 all the people from the collective farm went to the authorities, asking for bread. They were not even allowed to enter the courtyard.

On March 28, 1933, we were shocked by the news that Myron Yemets and his wife, Maria, had become cannibals. Having cut off their children's heads, they salted them away for meat. The neighbors smelled meat frying in the smoke coming from their chimney and, noticing the absence of children, went into the house. When they asked about the children, the parents began to weep and told the whole story. The perpetrators of this act said that they would have children again. Otherwise, they would die in great pain and that would be the end of the family.

Chairman Boyko arrested them himself, and about six hours later the GPU began to question them. "Who has so cunningly persuaded you to do this, *kurkuls*, near-*kurkuls* or Petlyura henchmen? You know that this is the work of our enemies to cast dishonor upon our country, the Soviet Union, the most advanced country in the world. You have to tell us who did it!" Hoping to save themselves in this way, the accused pointed to Pavlo Lytvynenko, who was supposed to have said: "If you have nothing to eat, butcher the children and eat them!" Lytvynenko was arrested and shot as an example to the others. Myron and Maria were sentenced to ten years in prison. However, they were shot about three months later because even the Soviet government was ashamed to let them live.

At the end of March or the beginning of April, a big department store was opened in Hadyach on Poltavska Street, by the park, across the street from Lenin's monument. It was called *Torgsin*. Stocked very well even with goods from abroad, it had one fault, that of selling only for platinum, gold, silver or precious stones. The prices were: For 10 gold rubles one could buy there 17 pounds of bread, 22 pounds of buckwheat cereal, 6²/3 pounds of millet and 10 herrings.

As soon as people learned about this, all who had any gold or silver flocked to the city. There was a line eight abreast and 1/3 mile long in front of the store. There were always 50–70 people who could not get in before the store closed for the day. They spent their nights on the sidewalk disregarding cold, storm or rain. Thefts were very common, but most died from hunger or stomach cramps after eating too much and too greedily the food they bought. The corpses were removed every morning by a GPU truck.

I also stood in line with my mother. There I saw with my own eyes ten dead bodies thrown on the truck like so many logs and, in addition, three men that were still alive. The dead were hauled to Hlyboky Yar (Deep Ravine) and dumped there.

None of the clerks in this store were Ukrainians and the store belonged to the state.

A month later, in April, this store was broken into and robbed. Half an hour before the opening an alarm was sounded that the store had been robbed at daybreak. The militia with dogs began to search the people waiting in line. All who were a little stronger, had little or no swelling and, perhaps, some gold, were arrested and taken to the building of the country executive committee which was quite close and had a large basement. The prisoners were searched and the gold coins or any other valuables they might have had were confiscated. Other GPU agents without dogs did the same.

One woman, Maria Bovt, had a gold "ship" which had been awarded her husband during the Russo-Japanese War for his bravery in saving a Russian ship. She was also arrested during this investigation and was sent to work at construction projects in Komsomolsk on the Amur River near the Pacific Ocean. All trace of her vanished. The ship must have been taken to swell the Russian treasury or went into the pocket of some GPU agent. Two weeks later, it was discovered that the real culprits had been the clerks in collusion with the militia. They were not punished because they had false documents prepared in advance, and they escaped arrest. This explanation was given out by comrades Shukhman and Kolotov.

The department store had its good and bad sides. The Russians robbed the people of practically all the gold they had. On the other hand, it saved many people's lives because 6–11 pounds of grain often saved one from starving to death. Those who had no gold for food died like flies or went to the cemeteries in search of corpses.

The most critical point was reached just before harvest. More and more people starved to death each day. Everything was eaten that could be swallowed: dogs, cats, frogs, mice, birds, grass, but mostly thistles, which were delicious if the plants were about 15 inches high and cleaned of spines. Many people went to graze and often died in the "grazing fields."

When rye ears began to fill out and were at least half full, the danger of death from starvation receded. The people cut ears of grain in the fields, dried them and, rubbing them down, they ate the precious green grains.

The communists now began to combat "the grain barber menace," that is, people who cut off ears of grain with scissors. Mounted guards on watchtowers protected the grain from the "barbers." One of these watchmen, Fanasiy Hursky, killed a fellow who dared to "steal government property." But sometimes the "barbers" struck back. Some of them sawed through the props under the tower of Ivan Palchenkov when he was asleep. When the wind blew, the tower toppled down, and Ivan was killed.

In the spring of 1933, 138 people died in the village of Kharkivtsi. In comparison with some places this was very good. A great many people died from diseases caused by hunger, especially dysentery. There was only one child born at that time in the whole administrative unit to which Kharkivtsi belonged.

The 1940–1941 school year saw no beginners at all, while previously there had been about 25 each year. The new school principal, a communist, saw the implication, and to save face made a first grade out of children a year younger if they were a little better developed than others. The same thing happened in neighboring villages.

The orphans who survived the famine were taken to a children's home in the village. They were well cared for and most of them grew up properly and reached maturity in the years 1939–1941. The boys raised in these homes when inducted into the army in 1941 were the first to desert with arms and go back to avenge themselves on the communists in their home villages, who deserved punishment.

Account 2

Case History SW34, U.S. Commission on the Ukraine Famine, *Report to Congress* (Washington, 1988), pp. 385–393. The interview was conducted as an oral life history in 1987 by Sue Ellen Webber and translated by Darian Diachok under the auspices of this commission.

Question: Please state your year of birth.
Answer: 1922.
Q: Where were you born?
A: In Stavyshche, in Kiev Province.
Q: In which district?
A: The Stavyshche District.
Q: Where did you live during the 1920s and the 1930s?
A: In Stavyshche.
Q: What was your parents' profession?
A: My father worked in a bank, and my mother worked as a saleslady in a store.
Q: I see. So they weren't peasants, is that correct?
A: No, they weren't.
Q: And you had said you were born in. . . .
A: 1922.
Q: Do you remember anything from the NEP period?
A: Well, I might have been, oh, about seven or eight years old at the time. People lived well then. But this was only for a few years. Then people were milked dry. Every single drop was wrung out of them.
Q: What can you recall about collectivization?
A: I only remember that they took away horses, farming implements, tools. Everything was taken from people against their will. And then they shoved you into a collective farm.
Q: And what social category were you given, given the fact that your family wasn't a peasant family, how were you designated?
A: Well, I come from the peasant class, but I'm not a peasant. It was a painful experience looking at all that was going on, seeing how the people were being uprooted and scattered about, how the dying were being brought in. At the time I lived close to the hospital. People were being driven in from villages near and far, as well as from Stavyshche, my native village. People were even bringing in their own children, who were already swollen. They would come to spend the night. And they would spend the night, and then they would be. . . .

Close by, there was a park belonging to the hospital. It was quite a large park. There were yellow acacias planted in the center of the park and fenced off. Well, this is right where the cemetery was. Enormous open pits were dug and the doctors carried on stretchers the bodies of those who had died and tossed them into the pits. The process would be repeated each day until the open pit was filled and covered over with dirt shoveled over it. I know the earth over the pits has settled quite a bit since that time. But today you can still locate the exact burial spot, right by the cemetery. This was the hospital morgue where they took patients who had died. Later, they didn't bother with the morgue anymore, but took the corpses straight to the open pits on stretchers. Often nurses carried as many as ten children on stretchers and tossed them into the pit.

Q: When did people begin to die?

A: The precise time? When spring came. People were wandering about the gardens and hoping to come upon something left behind in the gardens; they would dig and dig, and examine every clump of earth. If they came upon a smelly old potato, they would clean it and take the starchy residue. They would also dry and grind acacia blossoms. Linden leaves would also be dried and made into ersatz pancakes. People dug up all sorts of roots. It was terrible, absolutely terrible. People scattered all over; they wandered here and there. Sometimes, they'd spot some small creature in the water, like a turtle and eat it as food. It was terrible. People were reduced to this state. I was right there. Some of the starving were in such a bad way that they had begun to stink already. Their feet would swell up; their wounds would open and fester. It was terrible. You would see them walking about, just walking and walking, and one would drop, and then another, and so on it went.

Q: How many were there in your family?

A: Well, there were four children, my mother, father, and grandmother, who was already quite old.

Q: And how did you survive?

A: How I survived? I'll tell you. We always had a supply of pickled cabbage, which we would prepare for the winter, as well as a supply of onions and potatoes. And that's all we had. This was the common practice. In villages, there were various ways to prepare provisions. Some people had had all their provisions, all their potato crop, seized, and they themselves had been thrown out of their houses. That's all that I remember, because I was still small then. It all began in 1929, and at that time I was only seven years old. And I can recall how they would deport people, people who never returned. And where they exiled these people, I can't say. Everything that they had was destroyed.

Q: Was there a church in your village?

A: We had three churches, in fact. One of them was called the Rozkishna Church. It belonged to a rather large town of over ten thousand inhabitants. The town was located on the other side of a dam and could be reached by taking the bridge. But for some reason Rozkishna church was on our side. I recall going past it in 1931 when the cross was being taken down. But I was not an actual witness to the dismantling of the bells. Apparently, they needed the metal to make weapons. During the dismantling, a band of the women assembled at the church to protest what was going on. The militia was called; the women were roughed up, hit over the head. The next day, activists arrived at night and quietly cut down the bells.

The church was converted into a grain storage building. They would bring grain from Zhazhkiv, eighteen miles away from our village, which was once part of Kiev Region, but which is now part of Cherkasy Region. And that's one of the places from where they were trucking the grain out. They had an enormous grain elevator there, and day and night they transported the grain from there, grain collected from the collective farms. Day and night!

This was all done at the MTS, the Machine-Tractor Station. And everywhere there were placards with the inscriptions, MORE GRAIN!, and other similar exhortations. More grain for the government. They literally pumped the grain out of the countryside, and all for the use of the government. In the spring the Party sent in Komsomol members, who walked about the villages with pikes to which small scoops were attached. The Komsomol members searched literally everywhere to find hidden grain. They looked especially in places like hay piles in barns. They dug everywhere. And if they happened to find some grain that someone had hidden away, well, that was pretty much the end of him. He would never see the light of day again. That's how it was.

Q: And who exactly were these Komsomol members? Whose children were they?

A: The Komsomol members? Well, there were some Ukrainians among them, that's true. But the vast majority were sent from Moscow. At one point, the so-called 10,000-ers had been sent; there were supposed to have been ten thousand of them sent. Later, the government realized that this number was not enough, so it brought in the so-called 25,000-ers. And it was these groups that confiscated the grain all over the countryside. And if you happened to be a member of the Komsomol, you were forced to do these things, too. But the possibility was always open to you, that if you did find hidden grain, you could fail to report it, or you pretend you hadn't seen anything.

Q: Did the Committees of Non-Wealthy Peasants exist at this time?

A: Non-Wealthy Peasants? Yes, there were such committees, in fact, pretty much all over the countryside; but they were quickly suppressed. Even though I was quite young, I remember that during the SVU (in 1930), they were branded as "enemies of the people." I myself was also considered "an enemy of the people." They took away my father in 1937.

Q: Why was he taken away?

A: Why? Well, he had been branded an "enemy of the people," and they took him away in 1937. And they also took away one of my father's brothers, and another brother, as well. And to this day, we don't know what happened to them. And when my mother went to inquire as to my father's whereabouts at the militia, they told her that he had been sentenced to ten years without the right of correspondence. It was common knowledge that this meant he had been shot. Most likely, his body is somewhere in Vinnytsia. So, the four of us were left. Yurii was the youngest, just six months old at the time. And that was how my mother was left to fend for herself. Many of the other women were sent off to Kazakhstan. It was common practice for wives of the men that had been sentenced to be sent for five years to Kazakhstan to pick cotton, or to perform similar tasks. Five years! My own Godmother was sent there and actually returned. But this was during the war. After the war, my mother came here for a visit, and told us that it became standard practice to tell the wives whose husbands had been sentenced without the right of correspondence: "Your husband was killed in 1945." This was the standard line they gave everyone during the Khrushchev era.

Q: Do you recall how many people died of hunger during the Famine? What was the percentage?

A: In our village, you mean?

Q: Yes. Would you say it was about a half of the villagers?

A: Well, there was a village not far away from us called Krasenivka, which had a population of about ten thousand. It was a rather large village. They had to put up a black flag at one end of the village, and another one at the other end which indicated that absolutely no one had survived, not even a dog, or cat. The houses were all overgrown with goosefoot and other weeds. And our village? Well, what can I tell you? About ten percent of our village died of hunger. It was terrifying. Utterly terrifying.

Q: Were you yourself repressed during collectivization?

A: Well, in the beginning, you know, we had our own house, which later became my uncle's house. They evicted us and told us that they needed our house as part of the new collective farm, and they made an office out of my uncle's house. And they also confiscated ninety percent of everything we had. They took the land together with the house and all our belongings. We had had this garden there—and we lost all of this.

Q: And they didn't tell you anything?

A: At that point, they took whatever they wanted to, since technically these things were no longer ours. They would walk all over our fields, probing the latter with the sharp pikes. The pike was jammed into the ground and pulled up. If any grains of wheat were picked up, the conclusion was that grain was being hidden from the state. The men with the pikes were everywhere.

Q: Were you going to school at the time? And if so, was it a Ukrainian school?

A: Yes, it was. In our school, whenever any of the children mentioned the famine, they were corrected by the teachers. They were told that there was no famine, simply a year of difficulties. They confiscated all that we had and designated the year as one of difficulties!

Not far from us was a cemetery. There were many beautifully made crosses and memorials there. This was during the famine. Every night there were two or three graves dug up. Wealthy people had been buried there, and, naturally, there were valuables in the caskets—a ring perhaps, a watch, or earring. The robbers were caught: a man by the name of Abramovich and his son. The father had forced the son into it. Well, they had been trying to break into a tomb—the rich people had all been buried in tombs. The valuables buried with them were just waiting to be taken. Nothing was done to prevent theft. The entire site was ruined and everything of value was taken.

Well, when someone like a priest was buried, a gold cross was often placed in his casket. During the famine hundreds of graves were

unearthed. On one occasion, they caught the father who had been forcing his son to steal. They crawled into the tomb with a candle . . . and
they managed to get in carrying a candle, and the two were caught. The
father was placed in custody . . . the boy was crying; his classmates were
asking him about it.

During the famine they used to give us tea and a small piece of
bread at school. The tea was made in the following fashion. It was simply overcooked sugar and some coloring. And that was our tea. A lot of
children did not go to school; they were no longer able to, because they
had already reached the stage where their bodies had swelled. A large
number of children died.

A few of the villagers had planted potatoes in the spring, but they
had to do the plowing with shovels, because by this time, all the horses
had died and no implements were left. They dug the earth with shovels
and planted the potatoes. But the problem was that anyone could easily figure out where it was that you planted the potatoes, and the next
day, usually at night, someone would come and dig up what you had
planted. The field would again be barren. That's what went on. So, as a
result, people would try to cover their tracks by raking over the newly
sowed ground dig. We used to plant small potato cuttings which were
little more than peels. Well, we planted these in our garden, and the
potatoes grew beautifully. Something so simple, it could only have come
from God. It was just a potato peel with some eyes on it. We planted
the peels and got perfectly good potatoes that way. That's how we did
it.

The greatest number of deaths from starvation actually occurred
when the wheat-ears had matured. People began to steal the wheat-
ears. They were starving, you understand, and all at once the wheat-
ears were available. And when the people began eating great quantities
of wheat-ears, they died even more rapidly, because their intestines would
rupture. That's when the greatest number of corpses began appearing.

Q: And what did they do with the corpses?

A: What indeed! Well, they went looking for them; they collected
the corpses and dumped them into pits. And if the authorities happened to come across someone who was somehow managing to stay
relatively healthy, well, they gave him the job of watching over the pit
that they had dug out to make sure that it wasn't used by anyone else.

Q: Are you aware of any cases of cannibalism?

A: I heard of instances, but had never witnessed anything personally. But everyone talked about it. We had our own newspaper, *The Red Collectivist*. The newspaper mentioned that someone had been apprehended in connection with the discovery of barrels of salted meat. I can't recall the entire episode. Rumors were circulating involving the activists. There were Ukrainians among them, and there may have been others as well. They were the real activists, you know. They were involved in dekulakization, and they used to go drinking in the gardens. In fact, they didn't do much of anything else, except when it came time to dekulakize someone, they'd come and confiscate everything, throwing the children out, like unwanted puppies, into the courtyard. And this was in the dead of winter. The head of the household would go the village Soviet and request help for his seven children, and the activists would tell him something like, "Get out of here, and take those little mongrels with you!" That's how it was. And no one would help these people out. And so they would just die. . . .

Q: Who was the head of the village Soviet at the time?

A: The head of the village Soviet? A man by the name of Makharynsky. I've forgotten his first name. And later they took him away as well. I don't know what the cause of that was.

Q: And what sort of man was he? Can you describe him?

A: What kind of man? Well, he did whatever they ordered him to do.

Q: I see, a bureaucrat.

A: Whatever the bureaucracy told him to do, he'd do. You know, he himself didn't actually participate in the dirty work of dekulakization; and whenever they told him to pump the grain out of a particular village, he would send in the activists, the so-called 10,000-ers, and later the 25,000-ers sent by Moscow. And these were all foreigners, outsiders.

The famine existed only in Ukraine. There were a lot of people, a lot of people who wanted to go to Russia. People figured they could go there with the shirt on their backs and sell it for bread. On their way back everything they were carrying would be confiscated. And they would be arrested and sentenced. I myself know of several people who went there. You see, Russia was some distance away from us. The people who lived closer did try to go, but the ones who made it never returned with anything. Everything they managed to get was confiscated. By this time, the passport system had already been introduced. According to this system, you would be arrested and in great difficulties if you happened to be somewhere for nine days without reporting. So, whatever you did, you would invariably find yourself in hot water.

Q: Did you leave the village during the famine?

A: My father was still around. I remember once we bought some coffee. The so-called coffee had actually been made out of barley. It was just over-roasted barley. Well, since there was nothing to eat, we were told to mix some of this and some of that into this coffee. This mixture was awfully bitter! Yecch!

Q: Do you remember how the famine came to an end?

A: How the famine ended? Well, they began to provide a little something for the people; people began to go to the collective farms for soup. But as far as to how the famine actually ended? Well, it happened gradually, in stages. How can I explain? Well, the thing is that it never really completely ended. That's the way it is over there. People were no longer dying en masse, but in a sense the famine still continued. In fact, it recurred in 1947. Once again there was a great famine in Ukraine. My mother recounted how there was a great migration to the cities. Life was a bit better in the cities. But even in the cities, people were dying of hunger.

Q: Did a lot of people try to get to Donbas during the famine?

A: A lot of people fled to Donbas. They got jobs in the mines, but they weren't permitted to register as residents there. In our village there was a man by the name of Kruk. He had been involved in the revolution and was supposed to have shot some Communists. In schools, this fellow was always mentioned as a "bandit." When the Germans came, he returned to the village from Donbas, where he had been the director of a mine there. And he had also been a Party member. And he also provided papers to people who needed them to enable them to get on with their lives. The older villagers immediately recognized Kruk upon his arrival. I didn't know him personally. They shouted that Kruk had arrived, but what happened to him after that, I can't say.

Q: What sort of people joined the Party in your village?

A: There were very few Party members in our village.

Q: Well, what sort of people were the Party members?

A: What sort? There was a man by the name of Pokotylo who shot himself during the famine. I believe he was in the District Party Committee, but I don't know what his rank was. I just know that he was a

Communist and that he shot himself. There was another by the name of Nahornyi who also shot himself. This all happened during the famine. These Communists committed suicide during the famine, as did Mykola Khvyliovy, the writer, and Skrypnyk. Others committed suicide, too, because they saw what was actually going on. At one time they had embraced Lenin's slogans that Ukraine would be allowed to separate from the Soviet Union if it chose to. They believed the slogans, or at least I suppose they did. But later, when they understood the truth, they shot themselves. They had to. And that's how it was with our Party members.

And then came the Party purges. They were directed from Moscow. Party purges. And these were public spectacles. There was a building in our village that served as a club. And this is where the proclamations were made. When the Party purge began, they zeroed in on this fellow named Hrynchenko. They started in on him, tagging him with all sorts of accusations—that he had pumped out insufficient quantities of grain, that there was too little of this and too little of that. Although there was already nothing at all left to pump out, and they were still accusing him of falling short. "Too little!" they shouted at him.

By 1934 they were already giving out 250 grams for one labor day. This is about half a pound of bread a day. But you really had to work to earn this ration. This was a very difficult life, but people began to manage. They planted potatoes and different varieties of pumpkins, beets, and other staples. But during the famine, a group of Soviet ruffians would come through the villages and would even pull out whatever people happened to be baking in the oven. In the markets, they would even confiscate and destroy such items as beans in jars. It was terrible. Well, this is what I myself know and saw.

Q: How did people rebuild their lives after the famine?

A: Slowly. Before collectivization, there were still large barns around the countryside, but all these were burned as firewood. Whoever had fences for keeping in domestic livestock, these were burned also because people didn't have anything to keep themselves warm. The only housing that was left were so-called "houses on chicken legs." Reconstruction was simply awful. It was repulsive just to look at these buildings. It's probably the same way today. They say that there have been some changes, some minor changes made, that some sidewalks have been added, that electrical lines have been added, and that sort of thing. . . .

Q: Did people ever talk about the famine after it was over?

A: They talked about it constantly. If I knew you well, then I would feel free to talk about it; but if I didn't know you well, I wouldn't feel comfortable talking. I would be afraid of your denouncing me to the NKVD. There were so-called Judases who were capable of turning you in. Whatever you would say, they would immediately report it, and you would be in for some real trouble.

Q: You were only eleven years old during the famine?

A: Yes.

Q: But did you hear the adults talking about the political affairs of the day? Did you know at the time who Skrypnyk was? Kaganovich? What was being said about these political figures?

A: We all knew! Kaganovich, Molotov. Except that at that time no one could speak openly about these matters. We couldn't speak openly. Let me tell you about this little song that we had from that period. I can still remember this song from my school days.

During the famine, they sent this fellow, Postyshev, as secretary to Ukraine. And then there was this other fellow, Kossior, who was Polish. He was in the Politburo. So you can see for yourself what lovely songs we had to sing as we starved:

Hey, our harvest knows no limits or measures.
It grows, ripens, and even spills over onto the earth,
Boundless over the fields; while the patrolling pioneers
Come out to guard the ripening wheat-ears of grain.

And now here's the refrain:

We've hardened our song in the kiln's fires
And carry it aloft like a banner, offering it to you;
And in this way, Comrade Postyshev, we are submitting
Our report of the work we've done.

I remember the song as if it were yesterday. We had a very beautiful park in our village, with a stream flowing by. A gorgeous park. And in all the parks, there were loud-speakers placed, as part of this radio network, which was itself linked to the post office. And in these parks, you could always hear songs in Russian being sung, one song in particular:

James E. Mace

> Swiftly as birds, one after another,
> Fly over our Soviet homeland
> The joyous refrains of town and country:
> Our burdens have lightened
> Our lives have gladdened.

They broadcast this song while people were dying in the famine. "Our lives have gladdened." I can recall this song from my school years, when they were teaching the children to sing *The Patrolling Pioneer.* What kind of a country is this in which they keep bread from the people for the sake of a "better life?" They themselves sang, "The joyous refrains of town and country." And this song would play every day, ten times a day, and as you listened to the song, everywhere all around you people are screaming, and starving to death, while the song played on: *"Our burdens have lightened."*

Q: And what were you thinking?

A: What could I think?! All I could think of was where could I get some food. I didn't think anything. They let the Ukrainians have it because they had wanted to separate from Russia. That's what I think. The Ukrainian nation is still paying for that even up to this very day.

Q: Would you like to add anything to what you've said?

A: What is there that I could add? As long as you have Communism there, you will have this endless agony there. They can always institute another policy similar to NEP; they can always try something like that again. From what I hear, they want to give the people a greater share, a greater share of land as well—the primary reason being that the private plots of land yield more crops per acre than the collective farms. But people aren't going to fall for this. First of all, they don't have the implements with which to farm private land; and, secondly, let's say, if a man does work his field, and he seeds it and plants something—potatoes, for example—then they'll tell him to pay his taxes. And regardless whether or not something grows or doesn't grow in your garden, you have to come up with the payment. People don't want this system and aren't going to be taken in by it. And as long as this system continues to exist over there, then that's how it will be over there.

Q: Thank you very much indeed for this most interesting testimony.

A: I was quite young, but I saw a great deal. In fact, I can recall the events of those times better than I can recall what I did yesterday.

Q: Oh, yes.

A: It was all so horrible.

Account 3

Vasyl' Pakharenko, "Holodnyi 33–yi," *Molod' Cherkash-chyny,* July 18–24, 1988; trans. Vera Kaczmarskyj, *Soviet Ukrainian Affairs,* Autumn 1988, pp. 14–15. The author is a schoolteacher in the city of Cherkassy, a regional capital in Ukraine.

Recently I was leafing through a thick notebook filled with eyewitness accounts. I had jotted them down at various times and different villages. They are simple narratives (I tried to record them verbatim). A surrealistic tragedy unfolds behind these words. . . .

Here is Iaryna Larionivna Tiutiunyk's account of the death of her neighbor's 6-year-old son, Myt'io. (Iaryna was born in 1905 in the village of Subotiv in the Chyhyrin region): "He was on his way to the kindergarten one morning, where the collective farm was distributing a serving of millet meal, the size of a matchbox. And he dropped by, begging—Auntie, give me a piece of bread. I am so hungry. I didn't give him any because I was mad at him for eating the greens I had planted in the garden. To the day I die I will not forgive myself for begrudging the child a piece of bread. In the evening, on our way home from work, we found him sitting right in the middle of the footpath—dead. He was probably returning from the kindergarten, had got tired, sat down, and died."

Antonina Oleksandrivna Polishchuk (born in 1925). She lived in the village of Buzhanka in the Lysians'kyi raion: "In 1933, our mother pretended to sew some dolls for children, filling them with grain, so that they would not take away all the grain from us. But they found the grain even there and seized it. They took our ox away . . . and killed it, taking the meat for themselves. . . .

"Our father died from hunger, as did my 14-year-old brother, Vasia, and my twin sisters, Katia and Dunia (born in 1927). We ate only weeds and drank water. The corpses were carted out to the cemeteries on big carts. They pushed 300 bodies into one hole. . . ."

Tetiana Iakivna Vdovychenko (born in 1911) lived in the same village. "It happened that they took people who were still alive and would throw them into the common graves. This happened with

Khotyna Revenko. When they came to her house, she was still alive. They started dragging her to the cart by her feet. 'Where are you pulling me to? Give me a beet. I am hungry, I still want to live.' She was young, not yet thirty.

"'You think we are going to come back for you tomorrow?' growled the men in response, pulling her onto the cart by her feet. They brought her to the gravesite and threw her inside. She did not fall on her back, but propped up in a sitting position, her back against the side. They poked at her head and she finally fell back.

"Motria Vdovychenko was also taken to the gravesite and buried alive with her two children (who were also still living). Such incidents were frequent."

Denys Mykytovych Lebid' (born in 1914) from Iablunivka in Lysians'kyi raion: "I was transported to the gravesite and thrown into the common grave, but they did not cover it up that day. My friend Iaremii Stavenko was passing by and pulled me out."

Stepanida Hryhorivna (born in 1905) from the village of Zhab'ianka in the region by the same name: "In 1933, my neighbor lured my daughter to her house, killed her with a knife and ate her. My daughter was all of 6 years old at the time. When the beast was seized and taken to the raion [to be imprisoned], she kept taking out slices of meat and eating them, saying 'Umm, how tasty. Had I known, I would have killed her earlier.' The police could not tolerate this any longer and shot her right there on the road. . . ."

Account 4

Oleksander Mishchenko, *Bezkrovna viina* (Kiev, 1991), pp. 48–49. The author, a member of the Union of Writers of Ukraine, collected 42 accounts in the Poltava region in 1990. The following account is that of Petro Ivanovych Bilous, born 1909 in the village of Andriiky, which was formed from four farmsteads (*khutirs*) including the Andreiko farmstead, in the Poltava region.

In 1932–1933 the people were terrified. They no longer slept nights but sat in their houses and waited for the brigades to come for bread. In order to survive, some tried to hide some produce somewhere. For example, at Laryvon Andreiko's house the brigade leader found some buried potatoes and beneath them a few poods of wheat. Then they crawled in the attic where there were flowerpots, cast-iron pots, and jars. And in every jar and pot there were beans, dried apples, ground millet, or crab-apples, all covered with charcoal to hide it. They found it all the same. They took it down from the attic and poured it all in one sack. They found a little cask of cheese. They ate his sauerkraut and I ate some, too, because I was hungry. Old man Laryvon was left with nothing. He survived somehow, but his wife died. In our family both mother and father perished. Mother died when the rye was already being harvested. She went to look at how they were pouring it. Even though the rye was ripe, they wouldn't allow anyone to cut an ear. Even in their own garden. My brother was already married then. He went to live with his wife's family at Marfyna Andreiko's house. They had a cow, and he survived there. Another brother went around to the small farming communities (*khutirs*) and begged. And I was already near death, so swollen that I couldn't get out of bed, but someone remembered about my army requalification. And I was taken to the hospital. I stayed there a month and got better. I returned home. The house stood empty. All there was were the four walls. I didn't think about that then. All I thought about was going somewhere in order to earn a piece of bread and not die. But in the village there was no place to go. The dead lay in the shadows, in kitchen gardens under a tree; the people wandered sluggishly, apathetically, dazed, and no one even buried the dead. Over there across the gully lived Kateryna Andreiko. She lost four daughters, and she also gave up her spirit to God, but her two sons, luckily, survived. One was already married, and his younger brother stayed with him. Andrii Vasyl'ovych Andreiko lost two boys and five daughters. The daughters were little, school-age. Andrii Vasyl'ovych from time to time served as chairman of the collective farm, and then they dismissed him, and then he died. His wife, too. Not only did our own people die but even outsiders who had been sent in. There was starvation in every house. At my wife's, thanks to the fact that her father had a cow, nobody died. But everybody was swollen: her mother, father, and brother. She was given a little bread in the collective farm—she didn't eat it herself but brought it home. And that's how she saved her immediate family. At Odarka Andreiko's house, not far from here, the father died, two brothers, and the sisters Mariika, Nastia, and Mylia. Odarka was already married then. She buried them in a pit. She worked on the burial detachment. Nobody made her. She came home and buried them herself. She buried Mariika, she buried Nastia, she buried her father. Before he died, her father asked for a piece of bread: "Give me some, my child, if only some crumbs, because I'm dying." She didn't have any to give him. There just wasn't any bread at all.

Chapter Four
Soviet Deportation of Whole Nations: A Genocidal Process

Lyman H. Legters

The informing principles of Bolshevik revolutionary thinking, before it degenerated into cynical manipulation, included several elements salient to the deportations of whole nations during World War II. Everything in the experience of Russian Social Democrats fed their expectation of determined resistance to their revolutionary program and predisposed them to the exercise of vigorous and even brutal pursuit of their aims, most particularly during the early stages of consolidation of power. Lacking precedent, in Russia or elsewhere, for the inauguration of a socialist order, they also had resort to any measures deemed necessary to get on with the building of a socialist society. Given that this was rightly seen as a total reconstruction of the social order, they recognized few if any limitations on the social engineering their program required. Finally, they possessed flexible ideological justifications for any and all measures their revolutionary program seemed to dictate.

Seen in this light, Bolshevism was a singularly ambitious project. Initially, it was almost touchingly optimistic about the possibility of wholesale social reconstruction but also quick to anathematize obstacles as products of counterrevolutionary forces. Such considerations as the widespread desire for national autonomy, for example, could not be allowed to hinder the optimal expansion of socialist jurisdiction, endorsement of the principle of self-determination notwithstanding. Nor was the historical socialist commitment to democratic procedure and individual rights permitted to impede the radical measures on which the ruling Communist party had fastened. Conscious that Russia was not "ready" in a conventional Marxian sense for socialist revolution, the Bolsheviks perceived their task as requiring them to surmount exceptional difficulties, thereby justifying in their eyes the resort to policies and practices of equally exceptional severity in the implementation of their program.

The sanguine approach to social engineering combined with a ruthlessness of execution enabled the new rulers to tackle and attempt to change social circumstances that most governments would treat as givens. One consequence was a willingness to move people around, either voluntarily or coercively, in actions that one might term "demographic intervention." Although the Soviet state exercised increasing degrees of supervision over the entire economy as Stalin's consolidation of dictatorial power proceeded, it is important that we not exaggerate the extent to which population movements occurred as features of an overweening central direction. As Robert A. Lewis (1971) has noted, most mixing of Russians with other nationalities ensued because of outmigration of surplus agricultural population from Russia proper. "Forced migrations are not unknown in the U.S.S.R., but in the aggregate they have not played an important role in mixing populations. Most migration in the U.S.S.R. is not centrally directed or subsidized" (p. 159). What is important in the present context, however, is the willingness to intervene.

Official encouragement of migration was not invariably malign, of course. In the early postrevolutionary years, the Bolsheviks were genuinely concerned about eradicating the endemic popular anti-Semitism that had disfigured the Russian Empire. However, they eventually concluded that the solution lay in supplying the Jewish population with a territorial base, the element that they alone among the Soviet nationalities lacked. As a result, the poorly conceived but well-intentioned Birobidzhan scheme was launched. By setting aside an autonomous region in the Far East for Jewish resettlement, the leadership hoped to encourage voluntary Jewish migration and therewith the establishment of a center of Jewish culture with the same limited autonomy enjoyed by other ethnic groups. The intended migration was uncoerced, and did not occur to any appreciable extent, but the benevolence of the scheme is not entirely obscured by the recognition that the state had other political and strategic aims in mind as well.[1]

Demographic manipulation has been evident in other ways, of course, oftentimes involving coercion and even brutality. A glaring case was the exile of thousands of peasants branded as "kulaks" from their homes, especially from Ukraine, in the course of the collectivization campaign starting at the end of the 1920s. This "resettlement" plan often resulted in people being incarcerated in prison camps and was conducted with unspeakable ferocity (Mace, 1983). Stalin's Russification policy encouraged Russian settlement in other republics, resulting in the dilution of patterns of ethnic cohesion and loyalty. A parallel policy resulted in the removal of segments of the local population. The penal system evidently played its part here too, for Solzhenitsyn (1978) has recorded the disproportionate incidence of minority nationalities in the prison camps. Aleksander Nekrich (1978) cites other similar instances:

> As far back as the early 1930s, Chinese and Koreans were resettled from the Far East and were also removed from the central regions of Russia. Some of them were openly accused of being Japanese agents. Later, in 1939–41, trainloads of "hostile class elements" rolled eastward from the newly annexed Baltic countries, the Western Ukraine, West Byelorussia, Northern Bukovina, and Bessarabia. (pp. 98–99)

It would be easy to cite additional examples of Stalin's demographic highhandedness and recount horror stories about the manner in which expulsions were conducted. A conspicuous case, and one that invites comparison with the later deportations of whole nations, occurred as a prelude to the German invasions in 1941. Thousands of citizens of the newly Soviet-occupied Baltic republics were deported eastward in an obvious attempt to weaken national identity in those states. Solzhenitsyn (1978) notes that this episode fails to satisfy formal criteria of "deportation of whole nations," but "their best people were removed" (p. 390). As with the Polish removals after the country's partition between Germany and the Soviet Union, this program begins to smack of genocide—in the sense that the integrity of a national group was placed in jeopardy. Although the deportations, vicious as they were in cost of human life, did not progress to the point of actually destroying whole groups or denying them continued viability as national groups, it is certainly permissible to speak of such practices as genocidal in their implications.

The foregoing cases should suffice as precedents for what has come to be accepted as a narrower range of demographic interventions, namely the deportation of whole nationalities during World War II. More particularly, the early Chinese and Korean removals, undertaken as a kind of strategic prophylaxis, point directly to the case of the German population in the Soviet Union. The latter was not only another instance of prophylaxis but also constituted the first full-scale deportation of an important ethnic community.

On June 22, 1941 Hitler launched his attack on the Soviet Union. By November his forces had occupied the Ukraine and by the following June they had reached the Crimea. Soviet citizens of German extraction lived in their own villages and settlements in both areas. Already in August 1941, the Presidium of the Supreme Court had issued its decree on resettlement of the Volga Germans, followed shortly by the formal abolition of the Volga German Autonomous region. The decree opens with the flimsy pretext for deportation:

> According to reliable reports by military authorities, there are in the Volga province among its German population thousands and ten-thousands of diversionists and spies who, upon a signal from Germany, are to commit acts of sabotage in the areas occupied by the Volga Germans. None of the Germans living in the Volga district has informed the Soviet authorities of the presence of such a large number of diversionists and spies among the Volga Germans; consequently, the German population on the Volga is concealing in its midst existing enemies of the Soviet people and the Soviet Power. . . . [I]n order to forestall undesirable consequences . . . and to avoid bloodshed, the Presidium of the Supreme Soviet has found it necessary to resettle the entire German population of the district to other areas. . . . (Koch, 1977, p. 284)

The decree formally applied to just under half of the Soviet citizens of German nationality—those that belonged to the Volga province. But the same banishment had struck Germans in the Crimea even sooner and a few months later it was imposed on German communities of the North Caucasus. No exemptions were made for Volga Germans belonging to the Communist party (not even officials) or for families of those serving in the armed forces. The deportations were carried out in an extremely brutal manner by systematically separating males from their families and scattering all of the victims to mines, factories, labor camps, and kolkhozes (collective farms) in Central Asia and Siberia. "In their consigned locations, they lived under constant surveillance and close restrictions for more than fourteen years before being released" (Koch, 1977, p. 287).[2] It was also that long before the deportation was acknowledged in the Soviet press.

Rehabilitation did come finally to the Germans and other deported nationalities in an amnesty decree of the Supreme Soviet in 1955. Although Khrushchev omitted them in his 1956 enumeration of Stalin's crimes, a resolution of the Supreme Soviet in 1964 repudiated the deportation decree. It did nothing, however, to encourage the Germans to return to their homes or to restore to them the autonomous region of an earlier time. Some have apparently found their way back to their ancestral homes, but the community has been broken decisively and the people, widely distributed as they are through other Soviet regions, no longer have access to the bonds of language and culture necessary to the preservation of group identity. (The announcement in 1992 that the Volga Republic would be reinstated is somewhat hollow in light of the large intervening emigration.)

The case of the Volga (and other) Germans was exceptional, not only in that it came earlier than the others chronologically, but also because it rested, like the American internment of Japanese citizens, on an expectation of disloyalty. The other seven deportations of whole nationalities occurred after the invading forces had occupied substantial Soviet territory and were based, however speciously, on charges of actual collaboration and treason. In light of eventual postwar admissions after Stalin's death that the deportations were improper and, in fact, undertaken on the strength of false accusations, Walter Kolarz's observation has particular pertinence:

> The liquidation of the republics [those in which the victim populations predominated] was a warning to all other non-Russian peoples, many of whom might have found themselves in the same position had their loyalty to Russia been put to the same test as that of the Volga Germans, Crimean Tartars, and Kalmyks. Had the USSR been invaded by Japan, the Autonomous Republics of the Yakuts and Buryato-Mongols might have suffered the fate of the Crimean and Kalmyk Republics; had it been Turkey, a similar doom might have been the lot of the Azerbaidzhani Turks. (Quoted in Conquest, 1970, pp. 10–11)

The seven peoples deported during the war were: Balkars, Chechens, Crimean Tatars, Ingushi, Karachai, Kalmyks, and Meskhetians. The deportations began with the Karachai and the Kalmyks near the end of 1943, continued in the first half of 1944 with Chechens, Ingushi, and Balkars, and culminated in the removal of the Crimean Tatars in the middle of that year. The Meskhetians were not mentioned in Khrushchev's secret speech to the Twentieth Party Congress, and for a long time their fate was unknown in the west, but their removal took place toward the end of 1944. (Khrushchev also failed to mention the segments of other people—Kurds, Crimean Greeks, Armenians, Khemshils, and Kabardines—that were deported in the same period, apparently as a preventive [i.e., prophylactic] rather than punitive measure.)

The deportations were not acknowledged publicly at the time; but in 1946 *Izvestia* published the decree that had abolished the Chechen-Ingush and the Crimean Autonomous Republics and contained the specious justification for the move (which were also applicable to the Kalmyk Republic, the Karachai Autonomous Province, and the truncation of the Kabardino-Balkar Republic):

> During the Great Patriotic War, when the peoples of the USSR were heroically defending the honour and independence of the Fatherland in the struggle against the German-Fascist invaders, many Chechens and Crimean Tatars, at the instigation of German agents, joined volunteer units organized by the Germans and, together with German troops, engaged in armed struggle against units of the Red Army; also at the bidding of the Germans they formed diversionary bands for the struggle against Soviet authority in the rear; meanwhile the main mass of the population of the Chechen-Ingush and Crimean ASSRs took no counteraction against these betrayers of the Fatherland. (Quoted in Nekrich, 1978, pp. 91–92)

It is, of course, undeniable that the invading Germans found willing collaborators among Soviet citizens. But for deep disagreements within Nazi ranks about the correct way to treat conquered populations, the extent of collaboration would doubtless have been even greater.[3] However, as postwar admissions made clear, there was no basis for singling out the particular nationalities of the Crimea and Caucasus for deportation. In his pathbreaking examination of the Stalin era, Roy Medvedev (1972) reflected pointedly on this rank injustice:

> More than five million people were deported. Set down in wartime conditions in sparsely populated, undeveloped districts of Kazakhstan, Siberia, and Central Asia, hundreds of thousands died of hunger, cold, and disease. The Crimean Tartars, for example, lost about half their people, mostly old folks and children. Aside from the loss of life and the damage to morale, whose results are felt to this day, these deportations did serious economic damage to the districts from which the disgraced peoples were torn away.

The pretext was treason. Some portion of some of these nationalities collaborated with the fascist enemy. The same was true of the Russians, Ukrainians, and other Soviet nationalities. . . . [A] "Russian Liberation Army" was created in Germany under Vlasov. Divisions of White Cossacks fought against the Red Army. In the Ukraine the followers of Bandera and Mel'nikov battled Soviet partisans. The Nazi forces included an SS division called Galichina and many other national legions, such as the Georgian and Latvian. (pp. 491–492)[4]

While thus underscoring the arbitrariness of Stalin's treatment of the deported peoples, Medvedev also called attention to the murderous way in which the removals were carried out and the equally devastating conditions inflicted on these peoples at their destinations. With minor variations from one group to another, the pattern was fairly uniform. Military units appeared in towns and villages announcing the "transfer" (the term preferred by Soviet officialdom over deportation) and gave the local population only a short time to assemble with very limited allowances for supplies and belongings. They were herded into trains and sent, in the most crowded and primitive conditions, hundreds of miles to their widely dispersed destinations. There is no way to be sure of the loss of life during the roundup and journey: it has been estimated that the Buddhist Kalmyks may have lost two-fifths of their number by the end of the first year of resettlement. Like the Germans before them, the deported peoples of 1943/44 were widely dispersed throughout the Urals, Central Asia, and Siberia. Except for the Meskhetians (who were not accused of any treason), the deportees lived under rigid supervision in their places of exile, working in mines, factories, and agriculture. Accounts of their eastward journey resemble those of the trains bound for Hitler's death camps; and descriptions of their circumstances in exile, extending well beyond the war years incidentally, are akin to those of the Gulag.[5] There can be no certainty about the consequent mortality, but estimates of losses among the five Caucasian peoples, for the period 1939–1959 but adjusted for deaths from military action, range from 9% for the Ingush to 30% of the Karachai (Nekrich, 1978, p. 138). It is estimated that 46% of the deported Crimean Tatars died in the first year and a half (Conquest, 1970, p. 107). (For a more detailed treatment of mortality, see R. J. Rummel's [1990] *Lethal Politics: Soviet Genocide and Mass Murder Since 1917* [New Brunswick, NJ: Transaction Press] and M. Maksudov [1981] "Losses Suffered by the Population of the USSR 1918–

1958" in Roy Medvedev's (ed.) [1981] *Samizdat Register II*, pp. 220–254 [New York: W.W. Norton & Co.])

The evidence does not suggest that killing as such was the purpose of Stalin's deportations. The staggering loss of life was "incidental" to the removals, a function of the incredibly primitive manner in which the program was carried out. Since the national groups involved did not in fact lose their identity or viability as national groups, apart perhaps from those for whom the homeland was an irreplaceable element of group identity, we cannot properly speak of a completed genocide, only of a process that was genocidal in its potentiality.

In the areas vacated by the deportees, their belongings were looted and their homes seized, by either neighbors or newcomers. Others, particularly Russians, were encouraged to fill the vacuums where the deported peoples had lived. Extraordinary measures were taken to wipe out any record of the exiles: place-names were changed, literary materials in their languages were destroyed, and history was rewritten as if those peoples had never existed— in the same way that many Old Bolsheviks had become unpersons. The assumption was quite plain that the victims would not return.

In their new places of residence, as might be expected, some individuals overcame huge obstacles to gain education or training and find more advantageous niches in the social order of their new homes. By and large, however, opportunities for improvement of status were rare; most subsisted in conditions of hardship. More crucial, probably, for the preservation of ethnic identity, even where members of a group resided in close proximity to each other, was the absence of institutional sustenance for the group's culture. Schooling was provided in the new locations but without reference to the language or cultural integrity of the deported group. The fabric of culture, as embodied in newspapers, literature, arts and crafts, museums, and scholarship, had been demolished in the former homeland without being replaced in the new places of residence. Thus, ethnic identity was as untended as individual welfare, and it mattered little whether the deportation was viewed, officially, as preventive or punitive as far as the survival of distinctive culture was concerned. Apart from whatever adjustment exiles could make to new conditions of life, there was no relief until 1956.

Nikita Khrushchev's famous address to the Twentieth Party Congress in 1956 denounced Stalin's cult of personality and listed a lengthy inventory of crimes, including the deportation of whole nationalities. Although the reforms associated with Khrushchev were brief in duration and limited in extent, the so-called secret speech inaugurated a period of significant change for the deported peoples. However, his failure to mention the Volga Germans, the Crimean Tatars, and the Meskhetians foreshadowed the very checkered and uneven course of restitution that followed.

The Party Congress took place in February and before 1956 was over several developments had occurred. Already before the Congress convened, some of the special restrictions had been lifted from certain classes of deportees but, although increasing numbers were clandestinely finding their way back to their original homes, central authorities were still not considering repatriation. With the abrogation of remaining "special settlement" restrictions by the Presidium of the Supreme Soviet just a month after Khrushchev's speech, an effort was launched to persuade resettled groups to accept recruitment for work elsewhere in the country. Since repatriation was by this time under discussion, the diversion, unsuccessful though it was, reflected official fears of ethnic clashes should the exiles return home. Nevertheless, after discussion and debate within the party, the Central Committee issued a decree in November "On the Restoration of the National Autonomy of the Kalmyk, Karachai, Balkar, Chechen, and Ingush Peoples." In January 1957, the Presidium of the Supreme Soviet decreed the restoration of the Chechen-Ingush A.S.S.R., the formation of a Kalmyk Autonomous Region within the Russian Republic, and the reorganization of both the Kabardino-Balkar A.S.S.R. and the Karachai-Cherkess Autonomous Region. Repatriation was to be orderly within fixed time limits and voluntary as far as the exiles were concerned. But there still was no mention of Volga Germans, Crimean Tatars, or Meskhetians (Conquest, 1970).

Leaving aside these unexplained omissions, there are two aspects of the new situation that deserve attention. It must not be forgotten, as we observe the much more radical changes of recent times, what a dramatic departure Khrushchev's speech and the ensuing repatriation were. After a dozen or more years of governmental inaction on their behalf and of systematic repression of attention to their plight, the deported peoples were abruptly relieved of the onus contained in Stalin's wild charges of treason and were able for the first time to contemplate a legal return to their homelands.

At the same time, it must be clear what a limited redress of grievances this change represented. It was a rehabilitation, in the same sense that certain of the Old Bolsheviks were rehabilitated from time to time; and it was a gesture of conciliation, a lifting of restrictions unjustly imposed in the first place. But there was nothing restitutive about it—no attempt to restore these peoples' former condition or to compensate for interim hardship, still less to atone for a massive loss of life. Upon their return home, many of the deportees had difficulty finding suitable housing or employment and were sometimes resettled in less desirable parts of their homelands, thus facing constant reminders of the advantages still enjoyed by interlopers. There were undoubtedly many among the returning exiles who reconciled themselves to this minimal sort of restoration by the regime, just as some of their number had accepted and accommodated to exile. But it is impossible not to see a connection between the inadequate redress and the rebellious stance taken up by the Chechens in particular vis-à-vis Boris Yeltsin and the Russians in 1991 (*Guardian Weekly,* November 17, 1991, p. 13).

If the repatriated groups remained restive and disgruntled in some indeterminate measure, the situation was incomparably worse for the three neglected peoples. The Crimean Tatars have won the greater attention, within the Soviet Union and without, because their resistance was the most fully organized and because they had the most prominent defenders. From 1956 onward, the Crimean Tatar movement grew spontaneously, starting in Uzbekistan—the primary resettlement location—and spreading to the entire diaspora, expressing itself mainly in pleading petitions for repatriation. Such activity, not to mention the more demonstrative efforts of the 1960s, was greeted by repression, their more prominent leaders being subjected to trial and imprisonment (Mustafa Dzhemilev, for instance) or psychiatric punishment (General Grigorenko). Once the Crimean Tatar movement linked up with the nationwide human rights movement, the dissident *Chronicle of Current Events* (a running underground account, eventually repressed, of official transgressions) was filled with information about the Crimean Tatar cause.

In 1967, even before the movement reached its highest level of protest, two decrees seemed to promise some relief. The first simply rescinded the charge of treason and the second released the Tatars from special settlement restrictions. The latter also encouraged the exiles to think they might return to the Crimea, though the regime was busy with additional measures that would make that impossible. From 1967 to 1978, some 15,000 Tatars succeeded in returning legally to the Crimea, less than 2 percent of the Tatar population. Frustration intensified the protests by and in behalf of the Crimean Tatars, resulting in turn in more vigorous repression and, finally in the later 1970s, actual deportations of the repatriated, along with a ban on further resettlement (Alexeyeva, 1985).

The Meskhetians, much less numerous (especially after the loss of life resulting from their assigned labor in the irrigation of Gulistan), fell victim to ethnic ambiguity. They are divided among themselves in regard to whether they should be called Turks or Georgians. Furthermore, during years of Turkish rule they had adopted Islam and other Turkish characteristics. In order to relieve them of their exile status without returning them to Meskhetia, the regime declared them to be Azerbaidzhanis and allowed them to resettle in that republic or in Kabardino-Balkaria. Many of them did resettle but chiefly to be closer to their ancestral home. Like the Crimean Tatars, the continuing frustration of their wishes led to protest, petitions, and demonstrations—of course, on a much smaller scale—with the same accompanying repression. Some Meskhetians were prepared to emigrate to Turkey if their grievances were not addressed, but that impulse was also frustrated by the regime (Alexeyeva, 1985).

The Volga Germans, relieved of special settlement restrictions sooner than other deportees, had the charge of wartime treason lifted only in 1964. Thereafter, the Germans, by now scattered widely throughout the Soviet agrarian sector, began to agitate politely for a return to their homeland and for restoration of their autonomous republic. The official line, by way of response, was that they had taken root in the parts of the country in which they found themselves. By the 1970s, their appeals greeted by growing repression, the Soviet Germans turned increasingly to emigration (to West and East Germany) as a solution. Throughout that decade and into the next, a modest but steady stream of emigres left the U.S.S.R., but denials of permission far outnumbered permissions (Alexeyeva, 1985).

Although details are lacking, it is certain that the deported nations of the Soviet Union benefited from the general relaxation of the Gorbachev era, along with other Soviet citizens. But it was only late in 1989 that a specific measure was applied to their special circumstances. On November 14, the Supreme Council of the U.S.S.R. adopted a declaration "On the Recognition as Unlawful and Criminal of the Repressive Acts against the Peoples Forced into Violent Resettlement and on the Guarantee of Their Rights." This declaration mentioned all eight of the deported nations, adding "Koreans, Greeks, Kurds, and other peoples." It concludes: "The Supreme Council of the USSR thinks it necessary to adopt appropriate legislative acts for unconditional restoration of the rights of all Soviet peoples—the victims of the repression" (quoted in Sheremet, 1990, p. 94).[6] Given the turmoil that gripped the entire Soviet Union and its successor governments, it is impossible to assess the degree to which this, the first forthright admission embracing all of the deported nations, will produce genuine restitution.

Although the term "genocide" began to be used by the deported peoples, especially the Crimean Tatars in their campaigns for restoration, I have used the term sparingly to this point because of certain ambiguities in its application to this aspect of Soviet history. The focus on entire nations (or nationalities) as victims does of course call the term to mind, but its applicability remains suspended conceptually somewhere between cruel and murderous acts on the one hand and effective national destruction on the other.

There is certainly no doubt that the deportations were murderous in their execution and that the conditions of exile were scarcely less so. But loss of life, even when deliberately occasioned, is not a defining feature of genocide. It is a conceptual fallacy that because an episode is particularly horrible, it is ipso facto a genocide. With the U.N. definition of genocide in mind, it is possible to conceive of a genocide that kills nobody (universal sterilization of a social group) or of one that kills only a select few (the priesthood and learned lay leadership of a religious group). Conversely, one can imagine large-scale random killing of the members of a particular group that would leave the group intact in its communal and cultural integrity and thus not count as a genocide.

Since that last consideration seems to be pivotal in determining that a genocide has occurred, the way is open in the case of the deported peoples of the U.S.S.R. for the aforementioned ambiguity. All of the nations in question attached importance to their homelands and to the degree of autonomy their territories had enjoyed. But a particular political status would not seem vital to a people's ethnic or communal integrity, and it seems plain that certain of the nations regarded ancestral terrain as more essential than did certain others. The Crimean Tatars, for instance, have found it all but impossible to consider group survival apart from the homeland, whereas other peoples proved more adaptable to resettlement. Reportedly, the Koreans, though not one of the "whole nations," accommodated to new surroundings. A goodly portion of the Soviet Germans also did so, presumably in part because they were already well distributed outside the Volga region. Among the repatriated nationalities, the Ingush were more readily reconciled than their Chechen cousins in the same republic. Although such fine distinctions may seem like hairsplitting, they do bear on a verdict of genocide.

There can be little doubt that the lethal nature of the initial deportation coupled with prolonged confinement under the special settlement regimen would, if not interrupted but carried to the program's logical conclusion, have amounted to genocide for the eight nations in exile. The victims were widely dispersed and without means for the preservation of their respective cultures and group identity. It is also at least arguable that permanent removal from ancestral homelands might, for some groups, have resulted in a completed genocide—though there are obvious difficulties with an argument that labels a uniform policy and resulting practices as a genocide for one people but not for another. In any event, if the core meaning of genocide is to be preserved, we must be wary of a loose or too sweeping application of the term.

It may clarify matters somewhat to adopt the vantage point of 1989 and the aforementioned declaration of the Supreme Council of the USSR and ask: Which if any of the eight nations, even if given appropriate restitution, had no possibility of reconstituting itself as an integral cultural community having definite continuity with its own history? It may be that the combination of dispersal and emigration of Soviet Germans has gone so far that even the restoration of homelands and political autonomy would not suffice. It may also be that the dissolution of the Soviet Union will preclude the implementation of the policies needed by several of these peoples for effective survival. However, the balance sheet would be incomplete if we failed to note the positive effect of persecution, on the Crimean Tatars and Meskhetian for example, in generating a resistance movement that is itself an instrument of cultural survival and national regeneration.

What seems then to be indisputable is that the eight deported peoples were subjected to policies and practices that were *genocidal* (by the nature of their foreseeable outcomes) even if they did not eventuate in actual *genocides*. That distinction does nothing to exculpate Stalin and his fellow perpetrators, but it acknowledges the absence of an ultimate destruction.

Eyewitness Accounts
Soviet Deportation of Whole Nations

The oral accounts included here come from an extremely fragmentary corpus of material available in English. These excerpts emphasize mainly the sheer brutality of the forced migration of the several Soviet nations and, by implication at least, the kafkaesque quality of the program as it appeared to its victims. They also disclose something of the frustration experienced by victims, some more than others, as they tried to reclaim their homes after the deportations had been officially admitted (first in Khruschev's secret speech to the Twentieth Party Congress in February 1956) and after restitution had presumably become accepted policy. As it happens, the extracts presented here are very uneven in their representation of the several deported nations, but this failing is unimportant in the sense that all the deportations and resettlements were conducted with the same brutality and disregard for human life. Differences only appeared later in the unevenness of corrective measures accorded the deported nations.

We can be certain that there is a vast body of oral testimony yet to be discovered. When a comparative relaxation of control was introduced by Khrushchev, permitting publication of Solzhenitsyn's novel *One Day in the Life of Ivan Denisovich*, Soviet journals and publishing houses were inundated with stories and memoirs of life in the prison camps. The outpouring was so dramatic that the regime was moved to clamp down once again out of fear that the thaw had gone too far. Much of the material generated at that time may eventually come to light again, and some of it will surely illuminate the plight of the deported nations. Underground publications (*samizdat*) in the ensuing years down to the 1980s also contained relevant material, accessible in the several *samizdat* archival collections but not in English. The *Chronicle of Current Events* and *A Chronicle of Human Rights* indicate an enormous body of oral testimony awaiting publication, but they were mentioned in those sources more often as reports than as verbatim accounts.

Now, as the deported nations are regaining the measure of autonomy that they lost (and possibly more than they ever had before), it is inevitable that they will generate a body of literature chronicling their hardships and loss of life during settlement.

This first piece of testimony comes from an Estonian woman evacuated from her homeland during the German invasion of the U.S.S.R., illustrating not a deportation of a whole nation per se but rather the confusion and helplessness that would later be characteristic of those wholesale deportations. It comes from Michael R. Marrus' *The Unwanted: European Refugees in the Twentieth Century* (New York: Oxford University Press, 1985).

Everything was on fire and we didn't know where to run. Father, an old soldier who had already been through one war, was wearing two suits, one on top of the other, with a short fur jacket on top of the lot. . . . He had a little money, which he had saved over the previous year. He gave each of his children a few hundred rubles, in case we would be separated, and we hid the money in our belts. We got onto a train which we discovered was going to the front, so we got off and boarded another train. . . .

The following account comes from a Volga German soldier who was on active duty when news reached him by chance that his family and people had been deported. This excerpt is from Fred G. Koch's *The Volga Germans.* University Park: Pennsylvania State University Press, 1977, p. 288

While our company was halted for a rest period in a Russian village one day I learned of the deportation of my family and the entire colonial population through an unusual coincidence. A resident of this community, upon overhearing several of us conversing in German, approached our little group out of curiosity to learn who we were. When told we were Volga Germans, he was quite surprised; then he informed us of the mass evacuation of our people, and that several families from this community in which we had halted already were enroute to the Volga to occupy our homes—homes completely furnished, farmyards with domestic animals and machinery, potatoes to dig and cabbages to harvest—in fact, everything to start life new there.

We were shocked and could not believe this stranger. Yet, he roused a nauseating uneasiness in all of us, and so we wrote home at once. After two months, our letters were returned "Adresat Vybil"—Addressee Moved. Only one person in our group received a reply. It was from his sister who was married to a Russian, and therefore permitted to remain in her village.

The following is from an appeal by the Crimean Tatar people, addressed to the Presidium of the Soviet Communist Party. It contains an account of the actual deportation as experienced by Tenzila Ibraimova, a woman living by then in Tashkent. It is from Aleksander M. Nekrich's *The Punished Peoples.* New York: W.W. Norton & Co., 1978, pp. 110–111.

We were deported from the village of Adzhiatman in Freidorfskii district on May 18, 1944. The deportation was carried out with great brutality. At 3:00 in the morning, when the children were fast asleep,

the soldiers came in and demanded that we gather ourselves together
and leave in five minutes. We were not allowed to take any food or
other things with us. We were treated so rudely that we thought we
were going to be taken out and shot. Having been driven out of the
village we were held for twenty-four hours without food; we were starving but were not allowed to go fetch something to eat from home. The
crying of the hungry children became continuous. My husband was
fighting at the front, and I had the three children.

Finally we were put in trucks and driven to Yevpatoria. There we
were crowded like cattle into freight cars full to overflowing. The trains
carried us for twenty-four days until we reached the station of Zerabulak
in Samarkand region, from which we were shipped to the Pravda *kolkhoz*
in Khatyrchinskii district.

Another account of the deportation of the Crimean Tatars was given in
1957 at a hearing before the Central Committee of the Communist Party
by Shamil Aliadin, a Crimean Tatar writer and veteran of the war. This is
from Aleksander M. Nekrich's *The Punished Peoples.* New York: W.W. Norton
& Co., 1978, p. 111.

And now allow us to present a true picture of the deportation of the
Tatars from the Crimea, which, in our view, may not as yet be completely clear to the members of the Presidium.

At 2:00 in the morning of May 17, 1944, Tatar homes were suddenly broken into by NKVD agents and NKVD troops armed with
automatics. They dragged sleeping women, children, and old people
from their beds and, shoving automatics in their ribs, ordered them to
be out of their homes within ten minutes. Without giving them a chance
to collect themselves, they forced these residents out into the street,
where trucks picked them up and drove them to railroad stations. They
were loaded into cattle cars and shipped off to remote regions of Siberia, the Urals, and Central Asia.

People were not allowed to get dressed properly. They were forbidden to take clothes, money, or other things with them. The agents and
armed troops swept through these homes, taking these people's valuables, money, and anything they liked, all the while calling the Tatars
"swine," "scum," "damned traitors," and so on.

These people left their homes naked and hungry and traveled that way for a month; in the locked, stifling freight cars, people began to die from hunger and illness. The NKVD troops would seize the corpses and throw them out of the freight car windows.

There was no order or discipline in the journey. Trains destined for Uzbekistan were sent to Siberia or the Altai region. But the bulk of the population ended up in Uzbekistan.

Tenzila Ibraimova also provided the following description of life in the Tatar special settlements after deportation. It is from Aleksander M. Nekrich's *The Punished Peoples*. New York: W.W. Norton & Co., 1978, pp. 116–117.

We were forced to repair our own individual tents. We worked and we starved. Many were so weak from hunger they could not stay on their feet. From our village they deported thirty families, and of these only five families, themselves stricken with losses, survived. In the surviving families only one or two remained, the rest having perished from hunger and disease.

My cousin Manube Sheikislamova and her eight children were deported with us, but her husband had been in the Soviet Army from the very first days of the war and was lost. And the family of this fallen soldier perished in penal exile in Uzbekistan from starvation; only one daughter, named Pera, survived, crippled by the horrors and hunger she had experienced.

Our men were at the front and there was no one who could bury the dead. Sometimes the bodies lay among us for several days.

Adzhigulsum Adzhimambetova's husband had been seized by the fascists. She was left with these children, one girl and two boys. Her family starved just as ours did. No one gave them either material or moral support. As a result the daughter died of starvation to begin with, and then the two sons, both the same day. The mother was so weak with hunger she could not move. Then the owner of the house threw the two little infant corpses out onto the street, on the edge of an irrigation canal. Some Crimean Tatar children dug little graves and buried the unfortunate little ones. How can I speak of this? I can hardly even bear to remember it. Tell me, why were such horrors permitted?

Aleksei Y. Kosterin was an uncompromising advocate of the deported peoples. The following is one of many eulogies presented at his funeral in November

1968 by members of groups he had defended. This one is by Khalid Dudaevich Oshaev, a writer from the Chechen-Ingush ASSR. This excerpt is from George Saunders (ed.), *Samizdat: Voices of the Soviet Opposition.* New York: Monad Press, 1974, pp. 314–317.

Dear Comrades! We can only admire the example of the life and death of Aleksei Yevgrafovich. I would like to end my earthly existence as he did and wish that you would see me off as warmly as you have my friend.

Of all those present, I perhaps am the oldest. Aleksei Yevgrafovich and I were bound together by a friendship which lasted fifty years. In 1918, he was sent from the city of Baku to the city of Grozny with a group a sixty workers, half of whom were sailors, in order to strengthen Soviet and party work. He was sent by one of the twenty-six Baku commissars, by Ivan Fioletov. I first became acquainted with Kosterin after the hundred-days battle which ended November 1918. This acquaintance soon developed into a very warm friendship which continued until the end of his days—for fifty years.

What I will say about him briefly is what my entire fifty years of experience has confirmed. He was a brave, inflexible Leninist fighter. He was that way on the first day we met and he was that way until he died. I'll cite a few examples from our youth together.

In February 1919, the city of Grozny was occupied by Denikin's forces. At that time, Aleksei was laid up with typhus, and although he was so weak that he could have been blown over by a strong breeze, he left with the rest for the Chechen territory. More than 5,000 men moved out at that time—Bolsheviks, Soviet workers from Grozny, Red Army members, and rank-and-file workers. From their ranks, a strong partisan detachment was organized in the Chechen mountains. Yevgrafovich was appointed assistant commander of the detachment's operations division. While working in this post, he took part in many partisan skirmishes with the Whites. And at the time when the Whites occupied half of the Ukraine and all of South Russia and when they were approaching Tula, in the Chechen mountains, there was a small speck of territory still held by the Soviets. Here, the red flag was still flying. Surrounded by the raging sea of the Denikin forces, the Chechen partisans and the Russian partisan detachment defended this flag and repelled the enemy which was pressing on them from all sides. Aleksei

Yevgrafovich led the military operations of the Russian partisan detachment at this time. I well remember the great battle which took place at the Vozdvizhensky settlement on January 31, 1920. A White detachment with 1200 bayonets and sabers surrounded a partisan detachment which had about 300 bayonets and which was serving as an outpost at the entrance to the Argun River Canyon.

The detachment fought from early morning until late in the evening. It seemed as though its fate was decided. But the mountaineers struck at the White forces from the south. A breach was made in the ring of White troops. And the Red fighters who were still alive passed out through it, carrying their wounded (around forty) and their thirty-three dead. The entire operations was commanded by N. F. Gikalo, Sultan Dudaev, and Ingush, who perished in this battle, and A. Ye. Kosterin. The latter was seriously wounded in the battle (the bridge of his nose was shot off), but that did not put him out of action. The detachment retreated into what was formerly the czarist fortress of Shata. Eyewitnesses told me that when the detachment entered the gate of the fortress Aleksei Yevgrafovich was in the vanguard. His head was bound with a bloody rag, and on his feet instead of boots were dirty *onoochas* [cloth wrappings] wound with twine. And the detachment was singing as it marched along. This was the young Kosterin.

Soviet power was soon consolidated in the Northern Caucasus. Aleksei Yevgrafovich was appointed Chechen military commissar. Later he worked in the city of Vladikavkaz in Kabardia. He began to write essays and stories. It was at this time he wrote his first book—*In the Mountains of the Caucasus* (1919–1920). After that Aleksei was a member of our so-called Persian Red Army which was booting the English out of Persia. Aleksei Yevgrafovich and I maintained continuous and lively contact until 1937.

In 1937, I was sucked into the black vortex of Stalinism. I was sent to Kolyma in 1940 to serve a ten-year term. While I was there I found out that Aleksei was also near the Arctic Circle in the camps on the Nera River. It was virtually impossible for a prisoner in one of Stalin's camps to communicate with a prisoner in another. For attempting to do this one could be thrown in the camp punishment cell. But all the same I sent Aleksei two letters and received one from him.

In 1957, my people, the Chechen-Ingush, returned from exile in Central Asia to our small homeland. I found out that Aleksei was in

Moscow. The bonds of our friendship were quickly renewed and were to be maintained right up to the present tragic day.

The Crimean Tatars love and respect Aleksei Yevgrafovich as a man who bravely and courageously called for a return to Leninist norms on the nationalities question in relation to the long-suffering Crimean Tatar people. So too, Aleksei proved to be a devoted friend of national minorities, a genuine fighter, and an internationalist during the first year after the Chechen-Ingush people had returned to their homeland. He wrote a letter about the Chechens and Ingush which circulated among these peoples with lightening speed. In this letter he called upon the party and the government to devote attention to the disastrous situation of the mountain peoples who had returned to their native land. But N. S. Khrushchev, who was leader at that time, not only failed to heed the cry from this Russian writer's heart, but began the persecution campaign which ultimately led to Kosterin's heart attack.

We have said farewell forever to Aleksei Yevgrafovich today. Next to his body, Pyotr Grigorevich Grigorenko—the friend and comrade in arms of our beloved deceased—made a courageous speech. It is a speech I will never forget because it vividly depicted Aleksei Yevgrafovich's personality as a Communist, a human being, an internationalist, and a fighter for human rights and justice. He said that the urn containing Aleksei Yevgrafovich's ashes will be taken to the Crimea and given to the Crimean Tatar people after a new life has been restored to them, when they have been allowed to return to the land of their ancestors and the *Crimean Autonomous Soviet Socialist Republic* has been reestablished.

When I heard this I thought: "You know, the urn should have been given to us the *Chechen-Ingush* people." But later I understood that the suffering of the Crimean Tatars has been immeasurably greater than ours; and it became clear to me that our Aleksei was right about this. The urn holding his ashes should be given only to the Crimean Tatars. Their suffering and their courageous struggle has given them the right to be the keepers of the ashes of this person beloved by all national minorities.

Comrades! The Crimean ASSR was created by a decree signed by Lenin, and I believe that sooner or later the cause and the will of Lenin will triumph on this question. The Crimean Tatar people will return to their fair homeland and will build there a glorious Communist future based on close friendship with all the peoples living in the Crimea. I believe that the Leninist foundations of nationalities policy, which were trampled underfoot by Stalin, will be restored. And if I live until that joyous time, I, as a Chechen who has tasted the bitterness of being exiled from my native land and the bitterness of inequality, will come without fail to the Crimea to rejoice with the Crimean Tatar people. Then, all of us, his friends, will recall the deceased. We will again shed tears over his ashes and again speak well of his name.

May there be eternal praise to the memory of this fighter for Leninist justice and humanity!

Mustafa Dzhemilev, a Crimean Tatar who fought vigorously for the return of his people to the Crimea, was persecuted and repeatedly imprisoned for his efforts. The report includes an appeal on his behalf by his mother. In it she refers to the deportations. This piece is from *The Chronicle of Current Events,* September 30, 1975, volume 37, p. 4.

The threat of a new trumped-charge against Dzhemilev gave rise to protests and appeals for him to be helped.

On 17 June A.D. Sakharov appealed to UN Secretary-General, Amnesty International and leaders of Moslem nations, calling on them to save Dzhemilev: ". . . He is being threatened with a new prison sentence, possibly with death, for he is seriously ill and has declared a hunger strike." He recalled that in 1973 international support had saved Andrei Amalrik.

Pyotr Grigorevich Grigorenko and Zinaida Mikhailovna Grigorenko issued a protest against the unlawful persecution of Dzhemilev.

Mustafa's mother, Makhfure Mustafayeva-Dzhemileva has appealed to the UN Committee for International Women's Year. She writes:

> . . . A fourth sentence is hanging over my son's head. His guilt consists entirely of his love for our long-suffering nation. Mustafa was a year old when soldiers broke into our house early on the morning of 18 May (1944) and ordered me: "Get your children together and be ready to leave the house in 20 minutes." My five children were asleep and the sixth lay under my heart. They pushed us into railway goods wagons and took us away. . . .

People were dying in the wagons. . . . God saved my children. . . . We were thrown out into a wilderness. In two years, we
were driven from one place to another, six times. All my brother-
in-law's family died.

My Mustafa grew up in the midst of all this suffering. Having
grown up, he campaigned for our return to the Crimea, the homeland of our people. For this, he is being held in prisons and camps.

Help me, a mother, in my fight for the release of my son.

On 9 July 18 Muscovites issued a declaration, "Mustafa Dzhemilev
is threatened with a new prison term." The declaration told the story of
how Dzhemilev had been persecuted on various charges, though "in
essence because of his constant, unremitting demands that the Crimean
Tatar nation should be given back its expropriated homeland." The
declaration states: "A number of cases are already known where the
Soviet investigation and court authorities begin a "case" against someone and repeatedly sentence him, not for crimes committed by him,
but as a kind of preventive measure.

In February 1956, Nikita Khrushchev delivered his famous Secret Speech
to a closed session of the Twentieth Party Congress of the Communist party
of the Soviet Union (CPSU). Part of his expose of Stalin's crimes was devoted to the deported nationalities. This excerpt is from *The Anti-Stalin
Campaign and International Communism.* New York: Columbia University
Press, 1956, pp. 56–58.

Comrades, let us reach for some other facts. The Soviet Union is justly
considered as a model of a multinational state because we have in practice assured the equality and friendship of all nations which live in our
great fatherland.

All the more monstrous are the acts whose initiator was Stalin and
which are crude violations of the basic Leninist principles of the nationality policy of the Soviet State. We refer to the mass deportations
from their native places of whole nations, together with all Communists and Komsomols without any exception; this deportation action
was not dictated by any military considerations.

Thus, already at the end of 1943, when there occurred a permanent break-through at the fronts of the great patriotic war in favour of

the Soviet Union, a decision was taken and executed concerning the deportation of all the Karachai from the lands on which they lived. In the same period at the end of December 1943, the same lot befell the whole population of the Autonomous Kalmyk Republic. In March 1944 all the Chechen and Ingush people were deported and the Chechen-Ingush Autonomous Republic was liquidated.

In April 1944, all Balkars were deported to faraway places from the territory of the Kabardine-Balkar Autonomous Republic and the Republic itself was renamed Autonomous Kabardine Republic. The Ukrainians avoided meeting this fate only because there were too many of them and there was no place to which to deport them. Otherwise, he would have deported them also. [Laughter and animation in the hall.]

Not only a Marxist-Leninist but also no man of common sense can grasp how it is possible to make whole nations responsible for inimical activity, including women, children, old people, Communists and Komsomols, to use mass repression against them, and to expose them to misery and suffering for the hostile acts of individual persons and groups of persons.

Chapter Five
Holocaust: The Jews

Donald L. Niewyk

The Nazi slaughter of the Jews during World War II gave the world the idea of genocide. The Nazis themselves did not use the term, nor was this the first such mass murder. But the Holocaust—the systematic extermination of between five and six million Jews through shootings, gassings, and forced labor—was a catastrophe on a massive scale. It was, moreover, closely related to broader Nazi racial policies that led to the murder of very large numbers of Gypsies, Russian and Polish prisoners of war, East European slave laborers, and Germans who were physically disabled or mentally retarded.

Perpetrators

Following Hitler's seizure of power in Germany in 1933, the Nazi state pursued policies designed to isolate and pauperize the 600,000 German Jews. The goal, more or less openly acknowledged, was to make the Jews despair of their future in Germany and emigrate, which many of them did. Violent attacks on Jews were uncommon, and Jews were sent to concentration camps only if they had been prominent in anti-Nazi parties. The exception to these rules was the "Crystal Night" pogrom of November 9, 1938, when Nazi thugs physically attacked thousands of Jews and sent them to concentration camps; they were released only after promising to leave Germany. These actions were clearly the work of virulent anti-Semites in the Nazi party, supported by government officials who found pogroms useful in advancing economic objectives. Most ordinary Germans ignored these atrocities out of indifference to the Jews or a sense of powerlessness to help them.

These policies aimed at forcing Jewish emigration held for more than a year after World War II began. While many Jews in the part of Poland conquered by Germany in 1939 were mistreated, the Nazi bureaucracy made plans to expel them and all other Jews in German lands farther to the east or else to the Indian Ocean island of Madagascar. Only when Hitler invaded the Soviet Union in 1941 did emigration give way to extermination. Believing that the German people would not understand such a ghastly policy, the Nazis carried out the genocide of the Jews in secrecy and under cover of war. Accordingly, responsibility for mass murder was placed in the hands of the SS, Hitler's special guard of policemen and soldiers that had grown into the central agency of terror in Nazi-dominated Europe. Some of its officers were convinced anti-Semites who accepted the view that the Jews were Germany's most dangerous enemies. All of them were convinced Nazis who were sworn to obey orders without question.

Genocide was too vast a process for the SS alone. The German army cooperated in the roundup of victims. Volunteers from the conquered Eastern countries served as auxiliary police and as guards in the camps out of sympathy with the Nazis or the desire to escape some worse fate at German hands. Occasionally local mobs in the Baltic states and Ukraine massacred their Jewish neighbors, with German encouragement. However, none of these other groups was dedicated to the systematic slaughter of every single Jew in Europe. The Holocaust was masterminded and implemented by Hitler's elite guard, the SS.

Genocide: Policies and Procedures

As SS leaders prepared to participate in Hitler's invasion of the U.S.S.R. in June 1941, they created four mobile killing squads called *Einsatzgruppen* for the purpose of liquidating Jews, Polish and Soviet intellectuals, and Communist party officials. The 3,000 members of these four squads shot and buried in mass graves between one and two million Jews during the course of the war on the Eastern Front, but their methods were considered slow and inefficient if all eleven million European Jews were to die. Hence, Hermann Goering placed the formulation of what was to become the Nazis' "Final solution to the Jewish problem" in the hands of Reinhard Heydrich, the most powerful SS leader after Heinrich Himmler. Heydrich's plan was approved at a conference of top Nazi officials held in the Berlin suburb of Wannsee in January 1942. It called for concentrating all the Jews under Nazi control in Eastern European ghettos where those capable of doing slave labor for the Third Reich would be worked to death. Those that could not work or who were not needed would be sent to special camps for immediate extermination.

Existence for the Jews in ghettos and their nearby forced labor camps defies description. Overcrowded, overworked, and underfed, they could hope only that producing for the Nazi war machine would buy enough time to save at least a remnant of the Jewish people. That hope combined with the Nazi policy of holding all the Jews of the ghetto collectively responsible for any attempt at opposition or escape kept Jewish resistance to a minimum. In 1944 the SS shut down the last of the ghettos and sent their piteous remnants to camps in Germany or else to the extermination centers.

The six extermination centers, all of them situated on what had been Polish territory, ended the lives of three million Jews. Four of them—Chelmno, Belzec, Sobibor, and Treblinka—were strictly killing centers where victims were gassed immediately following their arrival. The Nazis already possessed the technical expertise, having employed poison gas to kill more then 70,000 incurably ill Germans in a "euthanasia" program between 1939 and 1941. The remaining two extermination centers—Auschwitz and Majdanek—were both killing and slave labor camps. In them the able-bodied were selected for work in various military industries; the rest were consigned to the gas chambers or firing squads. To be selected for work often meant only a brief reprieve, since conditions were atrocious. As the SS saw it, the victims were to die eventually anyway, and there was no reason to spare them when a steady stream of replacements kept arriving. Hence tens of thousands were literally worked to death. Others were subjected to grotesque and painful medical experiments. Survival depended on almost superhuman determination to live and often on the good fortune of securing jobs in camp kitchens, offices, or medical wards.

Auschwitz was the last of the extermination centers to be shut down as Soviet forces overran Poland late in 1944. The SS drove the survivors of the various camps to Germany where they were dumped in already overcrowded concentration camps and their outlying slave labor centers. Deprived of even the most elementary needs in the last days of the war, thousands died of malnutrition, tuberculosis, typhus, and other diseases. The liberating Allied armies found the camps littered with unburied corpses, and many of those still alive were too far gone to be saved. Of the approximately 200,000 Jews who survived, the majority attempted to return to their former homes while the remainder entered European displaced persons' camps and applied for permission to enter Palestine, the United States, or some other place of permanent refuge.

Why the Jews?

Answering this question requires an understanding of Adolf Hitler, the undeniable author of the Holocaust. His anti-Semitism dates from his youth
in Austria before World War I, where Jew-baiting was advanced by the politicians he admired and the tabloids he read. If the psychohistorians are to be
believed, it may have been more deeply rooted in some early personal trauma
(Binion, 1976; Waite, 1977).

Whatever its sources, Hitler's Judeophobia comprised all the well-es-
tablished and virtually universal stereotypes. Jews were corrupt and preda-
tory materialists, devoid of patriotism and feelings for others. They advocated subversive ideas such as liberalism, Marxism, and cultural modernism.
Hitler adopted this hackneyed litany in its most extreme, social Darwinian
form that interpreted history as a struggle between superior and inferior
races. By the time he began his political career in postwar Munich, he was a
convinced anti-Semite.

Doubtless Hitler's anti-Semitism, and that of many of his followers,
was intensified by the Bolshevik revolution in Russia, Germany's defeat in
World War I, and the abortive Spartacus Revolt by German Communists in
1919. Then Hitler and his fledgling Nazi party began associating the Jews
with the alleged "stab in the back" of the German army, the liberal Weimar
Republic established in Germany after the defeat, and the Communist menace. Anti-Semitism was always one of his central teachings. Occasionally
Hitler called for the emigration or deportation of the Jews, but more often
he blamed problems on a Jewish world conspiracy without specifying a cure
beyond inviting Germans to support his movement. Moreover, the Nazi
party tended to use anti-Jewish propaganda opportunistically, playing it up
or down depending on the responses it received. Hence no one could know
exactly what Hitler and his party planned to do with the Jews, and it cannot
be said that the large minority of Germans who came to support him after
1930 deliberately endorsed violent anti-Semitism. Today it is far clearer
than it was at the time that genocide was implicit in Hitler's ideology.

That genocidal impulse became explicit as part of events surrounding
Operation Barbarossa, the attack on the U.S.S.R. in 1941. No one knows
exactly when the decision to kill all the European Jews (and not just those
targeted by the *Einsatzgruppen*) was made or how it came about. It may
have been formulated at the same time as the planning for the attack in the
expectation that the war would provide a perfect cover for mass murder.
Equally plausible is the argument that the decision was reached in the eu-

phoric atmosphere of Germany's initial victories on the Eastern Front, promising, as they seemed to at the time, rapid and total triumph. Yet another
possibility is that genocide was the Nazi response to stiffening resistance by
the Soviets after their disastrous routs in the early months of fighting, and
to the growing realization that there was no longer any likelihood of deporting millions of European Jews abroad. What is clear, however, is that the
extermination of the Jews was closely bound up with Hitler's increasingly
barbaric campaign against what he called "Judeo-bolshevism."

The Victims

Although the Third Reich targeted all the Jews in Nazi-dominated Europe,
their fate varied with local conditions. Jews were most vulnerable where
German officials managed affairs directly, and did so from the beginning of
the Holocaust; where the Jewish communities were large and unassimilated;
and where indigenous anti-Semitism encouraged some degree of cooperation with the murderers.

All three of these elements combined to decimate the Jews of Poland,
the western U.S.S.R., and the Baltic states. There Nazi rule was most openly
brutal. First under the guns of the *Einsatzgruppen* and then in ghettos and
labor and extermination camps, Jews from these areas died in numbers
amounting to three quarters of the total Holocaust casualties. Very few survived. Direct German control over Serbia, the Protectorate of Bohemia-
Moravia, and part of Greece meant that their Jews were deported to Poland
and subjected to similar atrocities. Such was also the fate of the remaining
German and Austrian Jewish communities. Only small numbers of German Jews who were of mixed race, living in mixed marriages, highly decorated war veterans, or prominent persons were spared. Hungary came under direct German rule only in March 1944, following which the SS, aided
by Hungarian officials, swallowed up more than half of the large Jewish
population. Doubtless the losses in Hungary would have been even greater
had the Nazis taken control earlier.

Unlike Hungary, Germany's other Eastern European allies—Romania,
Bulgaria, Slovakia, and Croatia—retained some measure of independence
to the end of the war. Slovakia and Croatia, both satellites created by Nazi
Germany, willingly established their own forced labor camps for some of
the Jews and sent the rest to the extermination centers. Romania and Bulgaria, however, refused to comply with some Nazi demands. Neither was a
German creation, and both were fiercely jealous of their national rights.

Bulgaria confiscated the property of many native-born Jews and set some of them to forced labor, but it would not hand them over to the Germans. It did, however, deport Jews from lands newly acquired from Greece and Yugoslavia. In Romania, where (unlike Bulgaria) there was considerable anti-Semitism, tens of thousands of Jews in the newly reconquered provinces of Bessarabia and Northern Bukovina were murdered in pogroms or else deported across the Dniester River to be finished off by the *Einsatzgruppen* or at Auschwitz. And yet, the majority of Bulgarian and Romanian Jews survived the Holocaust.

The Jews of Western Europe, remote from the killing fields and the intense anti-Semitism of Eastern Europe, lost about 40 percent of their numbers to the Nazis. The SS gave priority to exterminating the Jews of the east, and the war ended before it could finish its work in the west. There, too, the pace of extermination varied with local conditions. Three quarters of the Dutch Jews perished in the Holocaust because they were numerous, heavily concentrated in one place (Amsterdam), led by passive community officials, and had little opportunity to escape or hide in that heavily populated country. French Jews, too, perished as a result of collaboration with the Nazis by the Vichy regime. And yet, only about 20 percent of them died in the Holocaust because their smaller numbers, highly dispersed in a large country, facilitated resistance and concealment. At the opposite extreme, almost all the very small Danish Jewish community was transported the short distance by boat to Sweden by Danes who had no sympathy with anti-Semitism. The Italians, too, although German allies, were not racists. Only after Mussolini's fall and the German takeover of the country were about 16 percent of the Italian Jews sent to their deaths, and the retreating Nazis had to do the job themselves. Hence resistance to the occupiers by local officials and private individuals saved lives in certain circumstances. The fate of the different Jewish communities was determined by various concatenations of local attitudes, opportunities for flight or concealment, the size and location of the Jewish populations, and the nature of Nazi rule in the several countries (Fein, 1979).

Participants and Bystanders

Direct participation in the Holocaust by SS officials, *Einsatzgruppen* personnel, and camp guards was required of relatively small numbers. Indirect involvement by police, civil servants, private businessmen who profited from slave labor, and the like was considerably broader. Moreover, news of the exterminations rapidly leaked out of Eastern Europe in 1942, enmeshing much of the world in the catastrophe.

German police and government bureaucrats who defined, identified, assembled, and deported the Jews to the east were rarely fanatical Nazis or anti-Semites. They were careerists and efficient professionals, dedicated to following instructions and improvising solutions to problems in the spirit of their superiors. Amorality was encouraged by specialization; each department and individual was accountable for only one small segment of the program, diffusing personal responsibility. Ordinary Germans who had nothing to do with the Holocaust might hear rumors of crimes against the Jews in Eastern Europe, but they were preoccupied with staying alive and making ends meet in an increasingly disastrous wartime situation. The Jews quite literally were out of sight and out of mind.

In occupied Western Europe the Nazis were stretched thin and depended heavily on local authorities to deliver the Jews for deportation. Especially in France and Holland such assistance was widespread, encouraged by careerism and fears of reprisals. Small minorities in all the West European countries risked their lives to hide Jews or help them escape to neutral havens. Tens of thousands were saved as a result. Equally small minorities of Nazi sympathizers turned Jews and their helpers in to the authorities. The vast majority, however, were as apathetic and self-absorbed as most Germans.

Neutral countries such as Switzerland, Sweden, Spain, and Turkey accepted limited numbers of refugees, but none wanted to antagonize Hitler while his armies seemed invincible. Once the tide turned against him, however, they became more willing to aid the Jews. The Vatican also held to its traditional neutrality. Pope Pius XII kept silent about the Holocaust, evidently fearing German reprisals and hoping to enhance his role as a mediator. Individual Catholic clerics and laymen, however, did intervene on behalf of the Jews, notably in France, Hungary, and Slovakia.

The nations allied against Hitler reacted to the genocide of the Jews in diverse ways. The Soviet Union gave refuge to large numbers of Eastern European Jews who had fled before the Wehrmacht, but it acknowledged no special Nazi program to kill the Jews. In contrast, Great Britain and the United States warned the Germans and their allies that they would be called to account for their acts of genocide. Could more have been done? It has been charged that Jewish lives could have been saved if President Roosevelt had not waited until 1944 to establish the War Refugee Board; if Germany and its satellites had been pressed to release their Jews; if the Allied air forces had bombed Auschwitz and its rail approaches in 1944; and if negotiations with the Nazis to ransom the Jews had been pursued (Wyman, 1984). That the measures were not taken may be explained by indifference or even covert anti-Semitism among Allied leaders. Or it may be argued that the Allies' single-minded preoccupation with the military side of the war was responsible. As they saw it, the best way to help all the victims of fascism was to press for the quickest possible victory. Nor will everyone agree that such measures would have altered the outcome in any significant way. No one should underestimate Nazi determination to exterminate the Jews, regardless of disruptions of the killing centers and promises held out in negotiations.

The Burden of History

A number of historical trends combined to make the Holocaust possible: anti-Semitism, racism, social Darwinism, extreme nationalism, totalitarianism, industrialism, and the nature of modern war. The absence of any one of these trends would have made the genocide of the Jews unlikely.

Anti-Semitism has a long history in most of Europe, not just in Germany. Traditional anti-Semitism arose out of Christian rejection of the Jews as deicides and deliberate misbelievers. Once it had generated pogroms, but in modern times it inspired contempt for the Jews by providing an explanation for their alleged materialism. Having rejected the saving grace of Jesus, so the argument went, they had lost their ethical standards in the pursuit of physical wealth and materialistic philosophies. Religiously based Judeophobia partially merged with newer criticisms of the Jews' role in the modern economy. Having been emancipated from special laws and restrictions only in the nineteenth century, the Jews were still concentrated in a few highly visible economic sectors such as banking, publishing, and the metal and clothing trades. This made them convenient targets for the victims of industrialization, some of whom blamed the Jews for depressions, bankruptcies, and unemployment. At the same time the Jews' support for liberal political movements that had advocated Jewish emancipation generated anti-Semitism among conservative foes of individualism and representative government. The prominence of Jewish intellectuals like Karl Marx and Leon Trotsky in the European socialist movements sparked criticisms of Jews for sacrificing patriotism to internationalism.

Although anti-Semitism was widespread before World War I, it was not a central issue. Most Judeophobes advocated solving the "Jewish problem" through assimilation or the restoration of special laws for the Jews, not through violent action. Only in backward Russia were there pogroms against the Jews. Racism, which implied that Jews were incapable of changing their ways, and social Darwinism, some forms of which predicted inevitable struggle between nations and races, gained adherents before 1914. But even their most radical exponents limited themselves to advocating Jewish emigration, and they were marginal figures without much influence.

World War I changed that. Anti-Semitism became entwined in the outraged nationalism of defeated Germany and in the quest for national identity in new states like Poland and Hungary and would-be states like Ukraine and Croatia. Demagogues such as Adolf Hitler in Germany associated the Jews with economic hard times and the foreign oppressors. The growth of threatening Communist movements, some of them led by Jews, added grist to the anti-Jewish mill. Hitler, who had become a racial anti-Semite and social Darwinist as a young man in Vienna before 1914, advocated total solutions to Germany's staggering economic and political problems. Once in power his totalitarian Third Reich enforced the "leadership principle" of absolute obedience to authority. Like Lenin, Hitler had learned totalitarianism from total war between 1914 and 1918. Then the belligerents had employed political centralization, economic regimentation, and thought control to mobilize all national resources in a terrible war of attrition. The Third Reich would use them to destroy domestic rivals, to mobilize the German economy for aggressive war, and ultimately to exterminate the Jews.

All of these historical trends came together in 1941 with Hitler's war against the Soviet Union. Having identified the Jews with communism, the dictator's crusade against "Judeo-bolshevism" provided both cover and justification for genocide. In Hitler's name highly specialized bureaucrats used the latest industrial technology to make war on the Jews as part of the larger national struggle for survival. The techniques of mass slaughter developed in World War I were brought to new levels of perfection, only this time poison gas would be reserved for noncombatants.

Post-Holocaust Victim Responses

Studies of Holocaust survivors have shown that virtually all suffered to some degree from a "survivor syndrome" that included acute anxiety, cognitive and memory disorders, depression, withdrawal, and hypochondria. Some became clinical cases, but most learned to live with their trauma and rebuild old lives or start new ones (Berger, 1988).

Nazi genocide decimated the once-thriving Jewish communities of Eastern Europe. Hundreds of thousands of Holocaust survivors, fearing communism and renewed outbreaks of anti-Semitism, would not or could not return to their former homes. Stranded in displaced persons' camps in Germany and Austria, virtually all expected to emigrate to Palestine or the United States. The American government, however, limited the entry of refugees and placed heavy pressure on Great Britain to admit large numbers of Jews to Palestine. When Britain chose instead to honor its promises to the Arab majority limiting Jewish immigration, guerilla uprisings by militant Zionists and international pressure forced it to withdraw. The Jewish state that emerged from the partition of Palestine by the United Nations might eventually have come into being anyway, but the creation of Israel in 1949 was greatly facilitated by the need to find a home for large numbers of Holocaust survivors and by the widespread sympathy for Zionism engendered by Hitler's murderous actions.

The genocide of the Jews also had a major impact on Jewish religious thought. For Judaism, God's covenant with the ancient Israelites bound Him and the Jewish people to the end of time. History was viewed as the expression of God's will, working out a divine plan in which the Jews occupied a special place. Judaism conceived of God as merciful, loving, and omnipotent. How, then, could the dehumanization and mass murder of God's people be explained?

For some Jewish scholars this question could not be confronted without challenging traditional Judaism. After Auschwitz, they reasoned, faith in the redeeming God of the covenant, an omnipotent and merciful deity, was no longer possible. Nor did they find it credible any longer to regard the Jews as His chosen people. Just where this reappraisal was leading remained unclear, and other Jewish theologians rushed to the defense of continuity with covenantal Judaism. One such response was to reaffirm orthodoxy by placing the Holocaust within the tradition that heard God's commanding voice in catastrophes such as the destruction of the First and Second Temples. Judaism endured then, and Jews must not hand Hitler a posthumous victory by losing faith as a result of his policies. A second approach embraced the traditional covenant by distinguishing between God's work and man's. God, for reasons that would become evident at the end of time, voluntarily placed restraints on Himself in order to make history possible. Hence the genocide of the Jews was man's responsibility, not God's. A third line of thought accepted that the covenant had been shattered in the

Holocaust but held out the possibility of renewing it by returning to the quest for redemption and redefining tradition by living authentically religious lives (Roth and Berenbaum, 1989, pp. 259–370). In all these viewpoints the impact of genocide on Judaism and on the Jews' sense of their place in the world was unmistakable.

Other Post-Holocaust Responses

Among Christian thinkers the Holocaust induced a profound reappraisal of the traditional view of the Jews as living examples of what happens to those who reject Jesus. It is unlikely that those who advanced this view ever intended it to culminate in violence against the Jews, nor would it have done so by itself. And yet, there was no explaining away the contributions made by Christian anti-Semitism to the climate of opinion that made the genocide of the Jews possible in the European heartland of ostensibly Christian Western civilization.

Protestant theologians demanded a critical reappraisal of traditional Christian teachings of contempt for Judaism. They called for a reinterpretation of church Christology and eschatology to affirm the authenticity of the religion of the Jews and Christianity's vital roots in Judaism. The Catholic Church faced up to Christian Judeophobia during the reforming pontificate of John XXIII. One of the key documents that emerged from the Second Vatican Council in 1965 recognized the common patrimony of Christianity and Judaism and denounced "hatred, persecutions, and displays of anti-Semitism, directed at Jews at any time and by anyone." German church scholars of both denominations confronted the lamentable failure of German Christians to stand up for the Jews under Hitler.

Germans as a whole, however, were slow to absorb the implications of the genocide of the Jews. Although a few called it an Allied fabrication, most repressed it and the whole memory of the now-discredited regime that had brought about their downfall. Although the new West German government in 1952 agreed to pay reparations to Jewish survivors, the West German courts were reluctant to pick up prosecutions of war criminals where the Allied jurists left off in 1949. German consciousness of the Holocaust arose principally during the 1960s when a new generation began asking uncomfortable questions, primed by the sensational 1961 trial of SS lieutenant Colonel Adolf Eichmann in Jerusalem. Since that time critical examinations of the Holocaust and the regime that brought it about have entered the media and the school and university curricula. Perhaps the most concrete expression of Germany's reaction to the human rights abuses of the Nazis is its asylum law, one of the most liberal in the world, that has made Germany a haven for political refugees from many lands.

The Eichmann trial also caused the Holocaust to have a delayed impact on American Jewry. Before then, little attention was paid to survivors and GI liberators of the concentration camps. The effects of the trial were intensified by the Six Day War of 1967, which raised the specter of a second Holocaust annihilating the state of Israel. These events strengthened the Jews' sense of solidarity with Israel and encouraged them to encounter the agony of their coreligionists under Hitler as a means of intensifying their Jewish identity. For some American Jews that suffering imposed a special obligation to become involved in all forms of civil rights movements.

Elsewhere the genocide of European Jewry had a much smaller impact. Austrians, who had welcomed Hitler in 1938 and perpetrated anti-Semitic outrages, hid behind the cloak of having been passive objects of Nazi aggression. Eastern Europeans, and especially Poles, saw themselves as victims of Nazism on the same level as the Jews. Until recently that view was reinforced by the refusal of Communist governments to acknowledge that the Jews had been singled out for annihilation by the Nazis.

Debates about the Holocaust

Did Hitler order the extermination of the Jews? For a group of historians referred to as "intentionalists" the answer is obvious. Hitler had hated the Jews for so long and with such intensity that he required only the opportunity to act upon his murderous intentions. The intentionalists concede that no written "Führer order" for the Holocaust has ever been found, but they aver that such an order probably would have been given orally. Supporting the intentionalist position is the testimony of surviving SS officers that the "final solution" was presented to them as "the Führer's wish." Opposing this interpretation is the "functionalist" view that genocide came about when lower-level state and party officials improvised increasingly harsh methods of dealing with huge numbers of unwanted Eastern European Jews who could no longer just be "dumped" someplace. This approach to the Holocaust is part of a larger functionalist analysis of the Third Reich that sees it as less a finely tuned totalitarian system than a chaos of rival agencies that constantly fought for power. Everyone sought to get ahead by initiating programs that would gain the Führer's approval. Hence the functionalists do not exonerate Hitler, but rather attempt to show that his personal initiative was not always necessary to draw out what was latent in his thinking. If the functionalists are correct, genocide depended heavily on the evolution of the war and on the automatic functioning of the Nazi bureaucracy (Niewyk, 1992, pp. 9–53).

Some Holocaust scholars have faulted the Jews for failing to offer armed resistance to the Germans (Hilberg, 1985, pp. 1030–1044) or cooperating with them to some degree (Arendt, 1964). Other scholars have disputed this reasoning, stressing instead the Jews' almost total vulnerability to their tormentors and demanding a broader definition of resistance. Recent research has demonstrated that armed resistance by small bands of brave Jewish fighters was more common than previously supposed. But most Jews lacked opportunities to resist. Not only did they usually lack arms, but they had trouble escaping from ghettos or hiding out among gentiles when the Nazis imposed terrible reprisals on the families of all concerned (Krakowski, 1984). Hence critics of negative evaluations of Jews in the Holocaust prefer a definition of resistance that embraces all efforts to keep Jews alive. These included measures to make Jews economically useful to the Germans, to smuggle food into the ghettos and Jews out of Nazi-dominated territory, and to provide the victims with morale-building cultural and social support (Bauer, 1979, pp. 26–40).

The Holocaust Today

The Holocaust is perhaps the one genocide of which every educated person has heard. Especially in Israel and the United States its memory is kept alive by schools, the mass media, and the observance of national days of remembrance. A network of Holocaust memorial centers educates the public at large, although they often come under pressure from groups that would vulgarize the genocide of the Jews by placing it at the service of their political agendas.

German consciousness of this genocide recently helped spark what has come to be called the "historians' debate." Conservative German historians suggested that their countrymen are much too mindful of past Nazi crimes. It is time, they said, to regard the Holocaust as one of many genocidal acts around the world and pay closer attention to more positive episodes in German history. They were strongly attacked by scholars who stressed the uniqueness of the Holocaust and the need for Germans to confront their heavy historical responsibility for it. It remains to be seen whether and how Germans' preoccupation with reunification will affect their receptivity to neo-conservative revisionism.

Austrians were shaken out of their historical amnesia by the recent scandal over their president, Kurt Waldheim. Although he was no war criminal, Waldheim clumsily attempted to cover up his youthful service in Hitler's armed forces; once revealed, it called attention to Austria's role in the atrocities of the Third Reich. Similarly, the recent trial in France of Klaus Barbie, the Gestapo "butcher of Lyon" who excelled in deporting French Jews to Auschwitz, raised uncomfortable questions about French complicity in Nazi crimes against the Jews. In Eastern Europe, however, the post-Communist revival of nationalism seems ill suited to any similar reconsideration of the Holocaust.

Lessons of the Holocaust

German history dramatizes the insidious nature of racial prejudice. Many Germans were prejudiced in varying degrees, but only a minority wanted or expected actual violence against the Jews. Although the Nazis were deliberately vague about the practical implications of their anti-Semitism, they were sufficiently bold in their propaganda against the Jews that anyone supporting Hitler had at least to condone his Judeophobia. Moderate anti-Semitism made that possible and helped deliver the German nation into the hands of history's most malicious leader. The Holocaust demonstrates that there is no safe level of racism. On the contrary, it teaches that any agenda that places economic and political concerns above human rights has the potential to result in disaster.

Once the genocide of the Jews began, there was little that outsiders could do to rescue them. Earlier, however, many of the victims might have been saved had other countries opened their doors to Jewish refugees. The time to aid the targets of racial bigotry is before their situation becomes untenable.

Those who were called upon to carry out the extermination process found that the modern state has effective ways of securing obedience and cooperation. Although the threat of coercion and reprisal was always present, compliance was more commonly assured by assigning each person only a single, highly specialized function, often not particularly significant in itself. Overall responsibility rested with someone else, and ultimately with Hitler. Unable and unwilling to answer for anything but their little spheres, well-educated and cultured individuals effectively placed themselves at the service of barbarism. Their participation made possible the bureaucratic organization of modern technology for mass extermination, this genocide's most characteristic feature. It challenges us to develop sufficient moral sensitivity to take responsibility as individuals for all our fellow human beings.

Eyewitness Accounts
Holocaust: The Jews

Although the Germans kept careful records of their genocide of the Jews, not all of those records survived the downfall of the Third Reich, and in any event they could never view events from the standpoint of the victims. Hence oral histories of the Holocaust are indispensable sources. Fortunately, interviews of survivors and witnesses have been conducted in many countries. These interviews cover a wide range of topics, including Jewish life before the Holocaust, Nazi policies toward the Jews in many countries, ghettoization, slave labor, resistance, successful and unsuccessful attempts at escape, liberation, and efforts to start over. Naturally Jewish survivors living in North America, Western Europe, and Israel are most heavily represented.

Among the first scholars to interview Holocaust survivors was the American psychologist David P. Boder. During the summer of 1946, he wire-recorded interviews with seventy displaced persons, many of them Jews, at camps in France, Italy, Germany, and Switzerland. Eight of the interviews were translated and published in book form under the title *I Did Not Interview the Dead*. The interview that follows was conducted by Boder, but was not included in that volume.

The Holocaust can never be encapsulated in a single person's recollections. However, this interview with Nechama Epstein reveals a remarkable breadth of experiences, including survival in ghettos, slave labor camps, and extermination centers. Made soon after World War II ended, it has the advantages of freshness and immediacy. Epstein begins her story in 1941 when the eighteen-year-old native of Warsaw and her family were herded into the city's ghetto together with 350,000 other Jews. [Note: This interview is housed in the David Boder Collection at the Simon Wiesenthal Center in Los Angeles, CA. Acquisition # 81–992, spools 95, 96, pp. 104A/2593–2668.]

> Epstein: When the ghettos began, among us began a great fight of hunger. . . . We began selling everything, the jewelry. . . . We finished at the last at the featherbed. . . .

Question: Who bought it?

Ep: People who were smuggling. They had. They were earning. Christians bought it. . . . And then we could already see that it was very bad. We had nothing to sell any more. Eight people were living on a kilo [2.2 lbs.] of beets a day. . . . With water. And every day, day by day, there remained less strength. We did not have any more strength to walk. My brother's four-year-old child did not have anything to eat. He was begging for a small baked potato. There was none to give him. . . . And thus it lasted a year's time. Until . . . the first burned offering in my home was my father who, talking and walking, said he is fading from hunger, and died. My father was sixty years old. . . . When my father died, there began among us a still greater hunger. A kilo of bread cost twenty zlotys. . . . Every day there were other dead, small children, bigger children, older people. All died of a hunger death.

Qn: What was done with the dead?

Ep: The dead were taken . . . if one fell on the street . . . a paper was taken. He was covered. A stone was put on top, and thus he lay until. . . . There was not enough time to collect the dead. . . . And then people drove around with small carts. There were no funeral coaches any more, nothing. People drove around with small carts, collected the dead, loaded them up, took them to the cemetery, and buried them— women, men, children, everybody in one grave. . . . And we. . . . It had broken out, the first deportation that was in the year 1942. . . . I do not remember the exact month. In the beginning of winter [*sic.* Between September 5 and 12, 1942. Ed.] There came down a whole . . . a few thousand Germans had come down, with weapons, with machine guns, with cannons, and they . . . made a blockade. They surrounded from one end of the street to the other. . . . They began to chase the people out of the houses. . . . It was terrible. Many ran into the gates. They [the Germans] saw small children. They grabbed them by the legs and knocked them against the walls. . . . The mothers saw what is being done to their children. They threw themselves out of windows. . . . They went into a hospital, a Jewish hospital. . . . And they began taking out all the sick that were there. . . .

Qn: Did you see it yourself?

Ep: Yes. . . . I was being led to the rail terminal. . . . The sick began jumping out the windows. So they [the Germans] ran on the roofs with machine guns and shot down at the sick. And all were shot. And we were led away to the rail terminal. There I was the whole night. That night was a terrible one. . . .

Qn: What sort of a building was it [the rail terminal]? . . .

Ep: A school was there at one time. . . . Then a depot was made there, and the Jews of the ghetto were all concentrated there. They were led in there, and there they were a night, two nights. They led a railroad siding to the street, and in trains [Jews were] transported to Treblinka. . . . At night Germans came in, threw hand grenades. At the people. . . . There were loud screams. We had no place to go out. One lay on top of the other; we had to . . . eh . . . relieve ourselves on the spot. . . . It was a frightful experience to live through that night. . . . In the morning they began to chase us out. "Alle aus!" . . . And they began to arrange in rows of five mothers with children, men, everybody together. And who-ever could not . . . walk straight, he was immediately shot on the spot. . . . We got into the railroad cars. Two hundred persons were packed into one railroad car. Riding in these wagons everyone saw death before the eyes at any instance. We lay one on top of the other. One pinched pieces from another. We were tearing pieces.

Qn: Why?

Ep: Because everybody wanted to save oneself. Everybody wanted to catch air. One lay suffocating on top of another. . . . We could do nothing to help ourselves. And then real death began. . . . After we had traveled for four hours, it became terribly hot. But so fast did the train travel that there was nothing. . . . We began thinking, the youths, what should we do. The mothers were telling their children they should save themselves, they should jump. Maybe in spite of all they will remain alive.

Qn: Were the doors open?

Ep: Closed, everything! There was a small window with bars.

Qn: Then how could one jump?

Ep: Many had along with them files, knives, hammers. . . . There had begun a great thirst. It became terribly hot. Everybody undressed. . . . There were small children who began to cry terribly. "Water!" . . . So we started banging on the doors. The Germans should give water. . . . We were screaming. So they began to shoot inside, from all four sides.

Qn: On the stations?

Ep: Not on the sta . . . while traveling. They were sitting on the roofs . . . where one steps down, on the steps, Germans were sitting. . . .

And they began to shoot inside. When they began to shoot inside, very many people were killed. I was sitting and looking how one gets hit by a bullet, another one gets hit by a bullet. I, too, expected to get hit in a moment. . . . And I saved myself by hiding under the dead. I lay down underneath the dead. The dead lay on top of me. The blood of the killed was flowing over me. . . . There lay a little girl of four years. She was calling to me, "Give me a little bit of water. Save me." And I could do nothing. Mothers were giving the children urine to drink. . . .

Qn: Is it really true?

Ep: I saw it! I did it myself, but I could not drink it. I could not stand it any more. The lips were burned from thirst. . . . I thought this is it, I am going to die. . . . So I saw that the mother is doing it, and the child said, "Mama, but it is bitter. I cannot drink it." . . . So she said, "Drink, drink." And the child did not drink it, because it was bitter. And I myself imitated it, but I was not able to drink it, and I did not drink it. But what then? There were girders inside the railroad cars. . . . From the heat, perspiration was pouring from the girders. This we . . . one lifted the other one up. It was high up, and we licked the moisture off the girders. . . . It was very stifling. There was that little window, a tiny one, so we wanted to open it. Every time we opened it, they would shoot in. . . . And when we wanted to open it, not minding that they were shooting, we did. There were small children, and they were all suffocating. . . . We could not stand it any more.

Qn: And then?

Ep: And thus I rode all night. Early in the morning—it was about two in the morning, maybe three, just before dawn—my mother began crying very much. . . . She begged us to save ourselves. The boys took a saw and cut a hole—it [the door] was locked with a chain from the other side. . . . And we took the bars off the windows. . . . And we started to jump. No. What does "to jump" mean? One pushed out the other one. . . .

Qn: Aha. Did the Germans let them?

Ep: They did not let them. They immediately started shooting on the spot. When I jumped out I fell into a ditch. . . . And I remained lying completely unconscious. And the railroad car . . . the train passed. . . . I came to. It was at night, around three in the morning, so I . . .

Qn: And your mother herself did not jump.

Ep: No. The mother could not. With the small child she could not jump. And a woman of sixty, she could not jump. . . .

Qn: And then? . . .

Ep: I came to. I got back my thoughts, so I went to look for my brother. . . . In the meantime there arrived some sort of a Polish militia man . . . and told me that I should quickly run away from here, because the Gestapo is all around here. I will be shot here. I should run away. He told me that I had jumped near Radzin and Lukow. . . . So he told me to go to the Miedzyrzec ghetto. There is a ghetto with Jews. . . . I began to walk on foot toward Miedzyrzec. . . . When I jumped out I met a little girl. She had also jumped. She had her entire leg completely torn open. While jumping she had caught on a piece of iron, and she tore open her leg. . . . And the two of us started to walk. Yes, after getting up I went to look for my brother. I had gone about ten feet. He lay shot. He had a bullet here in the heart. . . . I could not move away from him, but that Christian [the militia man] said that I should go away quickly. The struggle for life was stronger than anything. I left my brother on the road. I do not know what happened to his bones. And I went on. I had walked with that little girl for about three hours. Dark it was. Through woods, through fields we crawled, crawled, crawled. . . .

Qn: That little girl was a stranger?

Ep: A strange little girl. I don't know at all that little girl. . . . She was about fourteen years old. . . . And the little girl with the bleeding leg . . . for terror she did not feel the pain. . . . After having walked thus for perhaps ten kilometers, the two of us remained sitting where the road leads into a forest. And we could not walk any more. The child said that she cannot walk any more. The leg hurts her. We don't know what will be. In the meantime I had heard gentiles saying that Germans prowl on this road looking for Jews. And I saw it is bad. With the child I cannot walk. So I took the child. I did not know what to do. I carried her perhaps . . . perhaps, who knows, a kilometer or two. I myself did not have any strength. I was barefoot. My shoes had remained in the railroad car, because I had undressed. I did not have the time to put anything on. I was completely naked and barefoot. And that child remained in the field. And I went away. I could not help any more at all. The child had fallen, and I could not do anything to help any more. I went away. [pause]

Qn: Go on.

Ep: I had walked thus for about twenty kilometers. I do not know myself how many kilometers I had covered. I came to the Miedzyrzec ghetto. . . . I went in. It was a day after a large deportation. So I went in. . . . Entering the ghetto, it became faint before my eyes. It was at night. I did not have anywhere to go. When arriving there, I regretted very much that I had jumped off the train, because at every step, wherever I went, shot people were lying. Broken windows, all stores looted. Terrible things happened there. . . . In that ghetto I lived eight months.

Qn: Did you . . .

Ep: . . . in deathly fear.

Qn: . . . register with the . . .

Ep: There was a Jewish Community Council. I registered with the Jewish Community Council, and I [just sat there and waited]. It was not worth it. Every four weeks there were new deportations. From the small towns all around and around Jews were brought in there. And there was a sort of an assembly depot for Jews. And from there all the Jews were being sent to Treblinka. There I lived through three terrible deportations. During the first deportation I hid in an open attic and lay there for four weeks. I lived just on raw beets. . . . I did not have anything to drink. The first snow fell then, so I made a hole in the roof and pulled in the hand a little snow. And this I licked. And this I lived on.

Qn: Were you there alone?

Ep: No. We were about . . . there were about twenty people there. There was a father with a mother with child. There were some others. . . . We had nothing to eat. Thus we lived four weeks. We found raw peas which we ate. I had pared the beets, and afterwards I gathered the rinds of the beets, because I had nothing more to eat. And thus I nourished myself for four weeks, till there was a deportation. It lasted four weeks, that deportation. After the deportation we came down from the attic. At that time a lot of Jews had also been shot. Coming down from the attic, it was a terrible thing to see. We had to . . . we were taken to work removing the dead.

Qn: Who were the SS? Germans and who else? . . .

Ep: There were a few Ukrainians, too, but not many. . . . All the streets were splashed with blood. In every ditch Jewish blood had been poured. We went down. We had nothing to eat. We started looking for something to eat so we . . .

Qn: Was there no council, no Community Council?

Ep: At the time the chairman had been taken away. The chairman
had been shot. He was taken out first. He was the first. . . . A very fine
man. He was taken out the first with the wife, with the child. They
were told to turn around, and they were shot. There were Jewish police,
too. . . . Jewish policemen. So they [the Jews of the ghetto] were shot
little by little. During each deportation ten, twenty were taken and also
transported into the railroad cars. And they were shot, sent away. Those
who escaped were shot. . . . So there was nobody to turn to. Everybody
was afraid to go out. Many were lying [in hiding] there still a few weeks
after the deportation. They did not know that it is already safe. . . .
When we came down it was sort of peaceful for about two months. For
two months time we lived on that which the Jewish Council gave to
those who were strangers [from other towns and waiting for deporta-
tion]. . . . They gave them every day a kilo of potatoes and a piece of
bread. The food was not important, because it was . . . every day we
lived in great fear. People walking in the streets were shot at.

Qn: Did you have relatives there? Did you know anyone?

Ep: Nobody. I was all alone. . . . Mine had all gone away. I had
remained all alone. I had to support myself. By how did I support myself? I carried water.

Qn: For whom?

Ep: For the Jews who lived there I carried water. And for that I
received a few pennies. And that is how I supported myself. . . . In
brief, it dragged on till winter, till the Birth of Christ.

Qn: That is when? Christmas?

Ep: Yes. Then there was a frightful night to live through. There
came down drunken Gestapo from Radzin. . . . And in the middle of
the night we were asleep in a room. There were perhaps, who knows,
thirty people altogether in that house where we were. . . . And they
entered. I was sleeping there with two little girls. These children had
also escaped from the Radzin ghetto. Two girls, little ones. One was
about eight years old, and one about six years. I was sleeping with them
in the room. There were other girls. In our room there were about
fifteen persons. In the middle of the night we hear . . . shooting. We lay
in great deathly fear. And they were knocking on our door. And I did
not know why they could not enter through the door. In the morning
I got up. I opened the door. A shot person fell into . . . my room, into
the house where we were lying. When we came in [into the other rooms]

there lay shot all who were living in those rooms. Two children with a father who were sleeping in bed, everything was shot. A man lay with his stomach completely torn open, his guts outside on the ground. And later Jewish police came in. The Germans had left, and we had to clean up the blood and all that. . . . During the second deportation I was not able to hide any more. I was led away to a synagogue. There was a large synagogue. There all the Jews were assembled. In the synagogue it was terrible. They simply came in—if they heard a cry, they shot in. They threw grenades. They beat. They struck. They did not give anything to drink. We had to relieve ourselves on the same place were we slept. I was there a whole night. I saw it was bad. I did not want to go to death. I went on fighting against it. I went over to a window. It was on the first floor. We took two towels, I and another girl. We lowered the towels from the windows, and we crawled down and escaped down into a cellar, and there we again lived through the second deportation. . . . Again we lived [there] a few months. During the last deportation I was not able to hide any more. I was led away into a transport. It was a beautiful summer day. . . . It was May Day. . . . We were loaded on railroad cars. We were led through the streets exactly like we had been driven to Treblinka. They shot at those who did not walk in line. Many people fell, children. [We were] running fast. I myself received from a German . . . a [rubber] hose over the head. I got a large bump. I did not pay attention to the pain, but I ran fast. . . .

Qn: What then?

Ep: We were put into the railroad cars. It was the same as to Treblinka, shooting. We had nothing to drink. We drove a day and a night. We were taken down to Majdanek. Many were saying that we were being taken to Treblinka, but the direction was toward Majdanek. We were taken off at the Majdanek camp. We were all lined up. There were many who were shot. They were taken down, those who were still alive. They were taken down on the square, and they were immediately shot to death. The mothers were put separately, the children separately, the men separately, the women separately. . . . Everything was separated. The women, the young women, were taken to the Majdanek camp. The men were taken to another camp. The children and the mothers were led to the crematory. All were burned. . . . We never laid eyes on them again. . . . I was in Majdanek two months. I lived through many terrible things. We had nothing to eat. We were so starved. At first we did not know yet what such a thing as a camp means. In the morning, at six in the morning, came in a German, an SS woman, and started to chase us with a large strap, beating everybody. We were lying on the beds, grieved, with great worries, thinking where the mothers were, where the fathers and the children were. We were crying. Then came in a German woman at six in the morning with a large strap and beat us over the head to go out to the inspection. At inspection it could happen that we would stand four, five hours.

Qn: Why so long?

Ep: People were being kept so long because everybody did not know yet what . . . what this was all about. Many children of about sixteen years hid in the attic. They were afraid to come out. They thought they were going to be shot. . . . And for that, that they had hidden, we stood five hours as a punishment. Later nobody hid any more. They said whoever will hide himself will be shot. And so I was in Majdanek two months.

Qn: Did you work there?

Ep: Yes. We were sent to do garden work. We were sent to carry the shit which. . . . There were no toilets there, so we carried it in buckets. We were not given anything to eat. They were hitting us over the legs. They were beating us over the heads. The food consisted of two hundred grams [seven ounces] of bread a day, and a little soup of water with [leaves of] nettles. This was the food. And I was there two months' time. The hunger there was so great that when a caldron of food was brought, we could not wait for it to be distributed, but we threw ourselves on the food, and that food would spill on the ground, and with the mud we ate it. After having been there two months, . . . they began to select the healthy, healthy children who are able to work. . . . They tested the heart. Whoever had the smallest blemish on the body did not come out [any more] from there. Only six hundred women were picked out, and I was among them. This was in . . . July. . . . I was taken away to Auschwitz. The conditions were then already a little better. Fewer were being packed into a railroad car. They were putting in already sixty to a wagon. . . . Arriving at Auschwitz, we were led into a large hall before taking us to be bathed. All the women had their hair cut off. . . .

Qn: That was the first time you had that done?

Ep: For the first time . . . just in Auschwitz. . . . So I had my hair shorn off, and they tattooed numbers on us. . . . We had very great anguish, because we had our hair cut off. How can a woman live without hair? They took us and dressed us in long pants . . .

Qn: Who cut off your hair?

Ep: Our hair was cut off by women who were working there.

Qn: Yes. What then? They cut it from the whole body?

Ep: Completely. On the body, here [she points], everywhere, everywhere, everything. . . . And we were dressed in trousers and blouses. We were terribly hungry. . . .

Qn: What did you do there? . . .

Ep: We went to work in a detail which was called the death detail. Why? This I will tell, too. . . . We went to work, the six hundred women from Majdanek. It took a month, and there remained no more than four hundred and fifty. We died out of hunger. . . . We worked carrying stones on barrows, large stones. To eat they did not give us. We were beaten terribly. There were German women who were also prisoners [i.e. prisoner foremen]. They were imprisoned for prostitution. . . . They [the prostitutes] used to beat us terribly. They said that every day they must kill three, four Jews. And food they did not give us. . . . We carried stones on . . . barrows. We carried sand, stones. We were building a highway—women! The work was very hard. We got heavily beaten with rubber hoses over the legs from those German women overseers, those who also were imprisoned, prisoners. . . . Thus I labored for three months, until I became sick. I had gotten malaria. . . . I went around for two weeks with a 41 degree fever [about 105 degree F]. I was afraid to go to the sick-ward. There was such a sick-ward. . . . I was afraid to go, because it was said that if one goes there one does not come back any more, one is taken away to the crematory. . . . I saw that I cannot stand it any more. The legs were buckling under me. Each day I got more and more beaten, because I did not work. I could not eat any more. . . . I would accumulate bread from one day to the next. I could not eat it any more. I gave it away to other girls. . . . I decided to go away to the sick-ward. . . . There were no medicines. I lay around for about four weeks without medicine. . . . There was a doctor, also a prisoner, a Jewess. . . . She was not able to help at all. She had no medicaments. None were given to her. And in this way I pulled through the crisis. . . .

Qn: And then?

Ep: I lay around in such a way for four weeks. I did not have anything to drink. . . . I pleaded for a drink of water. They did not want to
give it to me, because the water there was contaminated. It was rusty
from the pipes. If one drank that water one became still more sick. I
passed the crisis, and during that time there were three such . . . selec-
tions. They came to take sick [people] to the crematory. During each
time I lived through much deathly fear. My whole method of saving
myself was that I hid myself. Christian women were lying there, so I
climbed over to the Christians, into their beds, and there I always had
the good fortune to hide.

Qn: Did the Christian women let you?

Ep: Yes. There was a Christian woman, a very fine one. . . . She
was also very sick. She was already near death, that Christian woman.

Qn: Why was she in the concentration camp?

Ep: She was there for political causes. . . . And . . . she was not
taken. Christians were not taken to the crematory, just Jews. . . . [Ed.
note: Epstein was mistaken on this point.] They had it much better.
They received aid from the Red Cross. They received packages from
home, and we nothing. We had to look on how they ate. If there was
one, a kind one, she would occasionally give us, the sick, something.
And that is how I was going on saving myself in the sick-ward. My
sickness was very terrible to describe. Complications set in afterwards.
I had many boils on the body. I had neglected scabies. . . . And I had
nothing with which to cure myself. At one time I lay already completely dead, that the Christian women cried . . . they made an outcry
that I am already going to die. So there came up to me a doctor, and she
brought some sort of an injection, and she gave it to me.

Qn: A Jewish doctor?

Ep: Yes. . . . [Ed. note: The SS routinely used Jewish doctors to treat
fellow inmates who fell ill. This illustrates the tension that existed between the need to provide slave labor and the ultimate goal of genocide.]
After that injection I became a little stronger, and I got out of bed. I
nursed the other sick. Much strength I did not have, but I was already
able to walk around a little. Three weeks had passed. There came an
order to deliver the names of all the sick, everyone who had scabies. . . .
Then one knew that he is for sure going to his death. And I had it, too. I
was very worried, and I knew that now has come the moment that I have
to go. . . . I did not sleep at night. I could not eat, because I knew that all

my misery, all my suffering was for nothing, because now had come my
end. . . . But it was not so. The same day when they had ordered to make
the list of us, they came to that sick-ward where there were only typhus
patients, and all were taken out, the entire sick-ward. Not one remained.
It was on the night of Yom Kippur.

Qn: What was done with them?

Ep: All were taken, undressed, nude, wrapped in blankets, thrown
in the . . . truck like sheep, shut the trucks, and driven away in the
direction of the crematory. We all went and looked, so we saw how the
women [on the trucks] were singing Kol Nidrei. . . . They were singing
the Hatikvah. When they said good-bye, they said, "We are going to
death, and you take revenge for us." . . . They are still pleading to be
left. They are young. There was a girl eighteen years old, and she was
crying terribly. She said that she is still so young, she wants to live, they
should leave her, they should give her some medicine to heal her scabies. And nothing helped. They were all taken away.

Qn: How come you were not included? You also had scabies.

Ep: I was not yet in the line. . . . Everything went according to the
line. . . .

Qn: How many sick were taken?

Ep: Four hundred persons. An entire block. . . .

Qn: Could the crematory be seen burning?

Ep: Of course! When we went out at night we saw the entire sky
red [from] the glow of the fire. Blood was pouring on the sky. We saw
everything. We knew. When we went to the shower hall we saw the
clothing of the people who were not any more lying there. The clothing was still there. We recognized the clothing of the people who had
left and returned no more. . . . So that we knew. It was a hundred per
cent! We saw every night the burning crematory. And the fire was so
red it was gushing forth blood towards the sky. And we could not help
at all. Sometimes, when we would go out at night to relieve ourselves,
we saw how illuminated . . . how transports were brought with mothers and children. The children were calling to the mothers.

Qn: That was in Birkenau. [Ed. note: Birkenau was the extermination division of Auschwitz.]

Ep: It was to Birkenau that they brought huge transports from
Hungary, from Holland, from Greece, . . . from all over Europe. . . .
And all that was burned in Auschwitz. The children they burned im-

mediately, and from a certain number of people, from thousands, a hundred might be taken out, and they were brought to the camp. . . . And the rest were burned. . . . The next morning a German doctor appeared. I became very scared. All who were in the block became scared—we were all sick from malaria—because it was said that the others were taken yesterday and us they will take today. . . . In the meantime he came with a list, and called out my name and another twelve Jewish names, and to that another fifty Christian women. . . . And he said that we who are sick with malaria, who show a positive sickness—because there were positive and non-positive. . . . Because on me was made a . . . a . . . a . . .

Qn: A blood test?

Ep: . . . a blood test, and it showed that I had a positive malaria. So they told us that we were going to Majdanek, back to Majdanek. . . . I did not believe it. In the evening all of us were taken, seventy-odd people. We were put on a truck and driven to the train. Riding on the truck all of us believed that we were going to the crematory. We had thought that it will be an open truck, and we will be able to see where we are being taken to, but ultimately it turned out to be quite different. We were taken in a closed one. But [as we were driven] past the guard we heard . . . "seventy-odd prisoners for Majdanek." . . . So we already knew that we were being taken to Majdanek. . . . We were put . . . on the station, we were led into a freight car, which is used for transporting cattle. We were all put in. Among [us] were many ethnic German women who had also been imprisoned there in the camp. . . .

Qn: Because of what?

Ep: They were for prostitution.

Qn: How did they behave, those women?

Ep: Very mean. Very mean. They beat so. They hit so. One can't at all imagine.

Qn: [Fighting] among themselves?

Ep: No they beat us, us. . . . And upon coming into the railroad car they made such a little piece of a ghetto. They put us into a small part of the railroad car. . . . And for themselves they took the bigger part. And in our part we were squeezed one on top of another. We nearly crushed ourselves to death. En route two girls died. They were very weak. We had no food. And they were full of scabies. . . . They could not stand it any more. En route . . . they were taken down in the middle of the night in Majdanek, and they were dead. . . . We arrived there, eleven Jews. . . . There were no Jews any more. Because when I was there the first time there were still thirty thousand Jews. . . . A few days later we found out that there were Jews here. So one Jew sneaked away . . . and came to us. She wanted to see the Jews who had arrived. From them we learned about a most sad misfortune. . . . On the 3rd of November it was. At four in the morning there came down the entire Gestapo with many police-men, with many SS men. They surrounded the entire Majdanek camp and called out all the people. There were twenty-three thousand people.

Qn: Not only Jews, everybody. . . .

Ep: Just the Jews. All the Christians remained in the blocks. . . . The Jews were taken out and told to form rows of five. The music played very violently and . . .

Qn: Was it Jewish music?

Ep: No. Polish music. German music. . . . And the people were told to go up [to the place where] the crematory had been installed. Two days before, eighty men had been taken out. And they were told to dig very large pits. And nobody knew what these pits were for. . . . Ultimately it turned out that those pits were for the people who had dug them. . . . They went up in rows of fives, children, mothers, old, young, all went up to the fifth sector [of the camp]. Coming to the graves, there stood sentries with Tommy guns and with machine guns. And they told them all to undress. Young women flung themselves at the sentries and began to plead that he should shoot them with good aim so that they should not suffer. . . . In the head . . . not in the stomach or the leg so that they should suffer. . . . And the sentries laughed at that and said, "Yes, yes. For you such a death is too good. You have to suffer a little." And not everyone was hit by the bullet. And from them were separated three hundred women, those who had remained whom we had met. And these women had to clean up next morning all those who remained, the shot. They were doused with gasoline and were burned.

Qn: In the pits?

Ep: In the pits. And afterwards they had to take the clothes which everybody recognized from her mother from her sister, from her children. They cried with bloody tears. They had to take those clothes and sort them. And everybody was thinking, "Why did I not go together with them? Why did we remain alive?" . . .

Qn: How had they been selected?

Ep: They came to the square where they were standing and picked out the most beautiful women . . . the youngest, the healthiest women were separated. . . . And fifty-five men. . . . Those men were prisoners of war. . . .

Qn: Were they Christians or Jews?

Ep: Jews. All Jews. . . . And these Jews had remained there, these fifty-five Jews who helped us very much—[we] the women who had returned from Auschwitz. . . . We were completely non-human [i.e. de-humanized]. We looked like skeletons. And they [the fifty-five Polish-Jewish POWs] put us on our feet. They helped us very much.

Qn: What could they do?

Ep: They had . . . in the things that they sorted from the dead was very much gold, very many diamonds, whole bars of gold. This they gave away. There were Christians there. . . . And the Christians received food packages from home, from the Red Cross. So they [the Polish Jewish POWs] gave all that away, and they received pieces of bread, whatever one could. And with that they nourished us.

Qn: Tell me, you were all searched. They looked and they searched, and one had to undress. How was it possible to find gold on the dead? . . .

Ep: A Jew had it sewn in their drawers. A Jew had it in the sole of the shoes. A Jew had it concealed in the hair. On a Jew they could never . . . they searched and they searched, and they did not find. . . . With that the Jews would save themselves. They always had something on themselves. . . .

Qn: And they did not hand it over to the Gestapo?

Ep: No. It made no difference any more. Who wanted to go to the Gestapo? We knew today we live and tomorrow we die. . . . It was already all the same. At that time we were not afraid of anything any more, because we knew that our turn was coming now and now we have to perish. . . . Later, . . . when we became healthier, we were transferred to the fifth sector and we lived together in one block with these three hundred women. . . .

Qn: You had recovered from the scabies?

Ep: Yes, I became cured, because these men took from the Christians salves which they received from the Red Cross, stole it from them and brought to us. . . .

Qn: Why did they bring you over there? . . . To Majdanek, these who had positive malaria?

Ep: Because they . . . it was [just] a whim on their part. Thirty thousand they burned and thirteen they led to life. . . . That is how it was being done by them. . . . And I had the luck that I was among these thirteen, and that I had been taken out. . . . And we could not believe it ourselves. . . . And we were in Majdanek also thinking any day we will be burned. There are no Jews. To the crematory we saw them bringing every day other . . . children, women. . . . They were brought and immediately burned, from Lublin, from all over, from the entire Lublin region. Christians. . . .

Qn: They were not gassed?

Ep: Gassed first and then burned. If there was no gas, they [the SS] would shoot and then burn [them]. We even heard shots, too, because it was very near. . . . And we were there together with them and we lived together with them. The women told us about those tragedies. It was so frightful. They cried so terribly that it was. . . . They would just repeat, "Are there still Jews in the world?" We thought there were no more Jews, only we few have remained. We thought that they have already exterminated all the Jews from Europe, from all Poland. And we told them there is still a camp in Auschwitz, they are still burning Jews every day. . . .

Qn: And then?

Ep: After having been eight months in Majdanek, the second time, an order came: These women, the three hundred, the women survivors of the action, must go to Auschwitz. And we, the thirteen of whom had remained eleven, go someplace else, because we have been tattooed, and they [are] not. They began crying very much. . . . Two days later we were led out to Plaszow. . . . Near Cracow, a [forced labor] camp. . . . They had added yet three hundred women from Radom. . . . There were little children, too. Pregnant women were there, and they led us away to Plaszow. Arriving in Plaszow, they took away the small children. They took away the pregnant women. There was a famous hill. They were taken to the top and undressed nude. There were no crematories. They were shot, and afterwards we carried boards and made a fire, and they were all burned.

Qn: You yourself carried the . . .

Ep: Yes, I carried the board! We carried the boards, and we saw how they shot them. If anyone had gold teeth, they pulled the teeth out.

Qn: You saw that yourself?

Ep: Saw myself. I had afterwards still worse [experiences]. Before leaving Plaszow. . . . It was on the Jewish cemetery. Where the cemetery was once . . . they made a camp. . . . We walked on the tombstones. With the tombstones they made streets. They [the SS] shot people every day at first. A Jew was pushing a barrow with stones. He struggled. So he [the guard] did not like the way he pushed it. He was instantly shot. . . .

Qn: And then?

Ep: While in Plaszow, a transport was brought with small children from Krasnik. I was all alone. I had it very hard, but I remedied it a little. I went to scrub floors in the blocks. People who had [something] gave me a little piece of bread to eat. When they brought the children I took a great liking to a little girl. That little girl was from Krasnik. Her name was Chaykele Wasserman.

Qn: How come children were brought without mothers?

Ep: The mothers had been. . . . It was like this. They had liquidated the camp. The Russians were approaching Krasnik, so they liquidated the camp. And that child's mother had escaped, and she was shot. And that child had come alone, without a mother, to the lager. And many children—they were all without mothers, because the mothers were immediately taken away. And the children separately. And the children were . . . they did not have enough time to take along the mothers. They grabbed the children and ran with them. And the children were brought to Plaszow. I took that little girl. I was with that little girl for four months. That child was very dear to me. I loved it very much. That child could not go anyplace without me. I was thinking I shall live through this war. I will be very happy with such a pretty and smart little girl, because it had hurt me very much that I had lost my brother's children. And I cheered myself up a little with that child. . . .

Qn: What did the child do there all day in the camp?

Ep: The child did nothing. The child went around . . . on the street. It was not even called to inspection. Sometimes it went to inspection, and sometimes not. . . . After a time they [the guards] came and took away from us all the children, without exception. And that child was very clever. She had a very clever head on her.

Qn: How old was she?

Ep: She was eight years old. . . . She hid in a latrine, that is in a privy. . . . All the children were taken away. People came and told me to go there, Chaykele is calling me, she cannot crawl out from the hole. And I went and pulled out the child. The child stank very badly. I . . . washed her up, dressed her in other clothes, and brought her to the block. And that child . . .

Qn: You have to excuse me. When a child hides in a latrine . . . did the other people know when they went to the latrine. . . .

Ep: No. When inspection was over [and] the children were taken away, women went to the latrine. This was a women's latrine. So the child began yelling they should call me and I should take her out. . . . And I was instantly called, and I pulled the child out. When I pulled her out she was overjoyed with me, and she said she was a very clever little girl. "Now I shall already remain alive." You see? . . . But, alas, it was not so. After a time we were . . . The Russians were approaching Plaszow . . . and we were again dragged away. I was the second time taken to Auschwitz. . . . We arrived in the middle of the night.

Qn: And the child with you?

Ep: The child I took along. What will be, will be. I kept the child with me. We came there at night. All night long the child did not sleep. She did not want to eat anything. She just kept asking me, "Does gas hurt?" . . . If not, [then] she is not afraid. But I cried very much. I said, "Go, you little silly one. There is a children's home. There you will be." She says, "Yes, a children's home! You see, there is the crematory, it burns. There they will burn me." It was very painful for me. I could not stand it. I could not sleep. But suddenly the child fell asleep in my arms. I left the child lying on the ground and went over to some man who worked there in the shower-bath, and I pleaded with him. I lied to him. I said it was my sister's child, and he should see to help me save the child. So he said, "You know what? Tomorrow morning you will all be undressed nude, and you will all be led before the doctor. He will make such a selection. And the child . . . you will hide in your rags when you will undress." And that child was very clever. She did not even take off the shoes. She hid in the rags. And I was waiting thus—it was in the morning—till the evening, till the child will come out. And in the evening I saw the child all dressed up. . . . When they took away all the children . . . the child got out from under the rags and came to me. The German doctor had left, and the child came to me.

Qn: And who . . . how did she wash herself and everything?

Ep: In the shower-bath there were Jewish women, there where the bath was. She was washed. Clothes there were very plentiful, from the many children [who] had been burned there, thousands, hundreds of thousands of children. She had been dressed very nicely. And the child came to me with great joy. "See," she says, "again I have remained alive. I shall again remain alive."

Qn: And how . . . you too were left [alive]?

Ep: I bathed and was sent out. . . . They beat badly. We were chased out. I waited. It was a huge transport of a few thousand people, so I waited till the last. Everybody had gone to the camp, to the block and I waited for the child to come out. . . . And together with the child I left for the block. . . . While being in the block, not long, a short time, three days, it was very bad. It was cold. They chased us out bare to inspection. There was nothing to eat. . . . The cold was so cutting, one could get sick. And the child, too, had to go to inspections. . . . The child was counted as a grown-up person, but that child had much grief. She was not numbered. . . . [Ed. Note: Only those who were to be kept alive were tattooed.] After the three days there came a doctor. . . . And he again selected women to be sent to Germany. I was taken away. And that child cried very much. When she saw that I was being taken, she cried very much and screamed, "You are leaving me. Who will be my mother now?" But, alas, I could not help any. I could do nothing with the German. I went away and left the child. . . .

Qn: Did you ask them . . . they should . . .

Ep: I asked, so he said, "If you want to go to the crematory, you can go with the child. And if not, then go away from the child." . . .

Qn: And so you don't know what happened to the child.

Ep: I don't know anything [about] what happened to the child. I know only one thing: I left. The child said good-bye to me, and I was led away to Bergen-Belsen. . . . Arriving in Bergen-Belsen, there reigned a terrible hunger. People were dying . . .

Qn: Do you remember in which month, in what year? . . .

Ep: The last month. In the year 1944, in winter. . . . I was in Bergen-Belsen three months. The hunger was so great—a terror. We went to the garbage heap and picked the peels from the turnips that were cooked in the kitchen. And if one chanced to grab a turnip. . . . I was very daring. I did everything. I fought strongly to stay alive. So I got out through the gate, where they were shooting, and grabbed a turnip. And a minute later they shot a girl who grabbed a turnip. I ran into the block.

Qn: Did the turnip lay outside the gate?

Ep: No. Outside the gate there was located the kitchen . . . with . . . with wires so one would not be able to get near. . . . So I opened the gate and go in. I risked it. I knew that the moment I grab it the bullet may hit me, but the hunger was stronger than [the fear of] death. . . . And I went and brought such a turnip. I returned to the block. People, corpses, dead ones, assaulted me, that I should give them [some] too. I shared it with them. We rejoiced. We finished the meal and went to sleep. After having been [there] three months, a German came again, and again selected Jews. I did not know where to [turn]. But I only wanted to go on, on. It always seemed to me here it is no good, there it will be better. And again I traveled. They collected two hundred Hungarian women, three hundred Polish women, and we were led away to Aschersleben. . . .

Qn: What was there?

Ep: There was an airplane factory. . . . There everything had been bombed. . . . There was a camp commander, a very mean one. There were foreigners. . . . Prisoners of war . . . Dutch, French, Yugoslavian. [Ed. note: After about two months the camp was evacuated on foot as American forces approached.]

Qn: Where did you go?

Ep: Very terrible was the road. On the way many were shot, those who couldn't walk. We didn't get [anything] to eat. They dragged us from one village to another, from one town to another. We covered sixty, seventy kilometers a day.

Qn: How many people were you?

Ep: Five hundred. . . . Only women. Two hundred fell en route. . . . I stood and looked how the camp commander took out his revolver, and [to each] one who couldn't walk he said, "Come with me," took aside and shot her. . . . We endured all that till they dragged us as far as Theresienstadt. . . . [Ed. note: Theresienstadt was the model Nazi ghetto, in Czechoslovakia, about 260 km. from Aschersleben.] Arriving in Theresienstadt we were completely in tatters. From the blankets we had to cover ourselves with, we made socks, we dressed ourselves. We were very dirty. . . . We were badly treated. We were beaten. They screamed at us. "Accursed swines! You are filthy. What sort of a people are you?" . . . We were thinking how would they look if they were on our level. . . . There were only Jews, many Jews from Germany. There were very many old women who were mixed [intermarried], Germans and Jews. They had Jewish sons, SS men. . . . They were serving Hitler, and she was Jewish; the husband was a German. And that is the reason they remained alive. All old, grey women, and all the children with mothers had been transported to Auschwitz before. . . . There was very little food. And the Germans prepared a large crematory. They had heard that the front is again approaching. They prepared a large crematory, but they did not have enough time to do it. . . . [Ed. note: Theresienstadt was liberated on May 8, 1945.] We heard the Russian tanks were here. And we didn't believe it ourselves. We went out, whoever was able. There were a lot of sick who couldn't go. We went out with great joy, with much crying. . . .

Qn: And then?

Ep: But now there began a real death. People who had been starved for so many years. . . . The Russians had opened all the German storehouses, all the German stores, and they said, "Take whatever you want." People who had been badly starved, they shouldn't have eaten. . . . And the people began to eat, to eat too much, greedily. . . . Hundreds of people fell a day. After the liberation, two, three days after the liberation, there had fallen very many people. In about a month half of the camp had fallen. And nothing could be done about it . . . there were full stables, full with dead. People crawled over the dead. It stank terribly. There was raging a severe typhus. And I, too, got sick. I lay four weeks in the hospital. . . .

* * *

Epstein recovered from typhus and returned to Warsaw where she married and made preparations to emigrate to Palestine.

Chapter Six
Holocaust: The Gypsies*

Sybil Milton

The mass murder of between one-quarter and one-half million Roma and Sinti (Gypsies) during the Holocaust has been underrepresented in current historiography about Nazi genocide. Instead, suspicion, prejudice, and stereotypes have continued to dominate historical literature about this subject.[1] Thus, Yehuda Bauer's suggestion that "the Nazis simply did not have a policy regarding the Gypsies" and that therefore Nazi persecution of Gypsies was fundamentally different from that of Jews is erroneous. Similarly, Hans-Joachim Döring's contention that Nazi policy was motivated by a combination of crime control and military security considerations or Bernhard Streck's classification of the killing of Roma and Sinti in Auschwitz-Birkenau for epidemiological and public health reasons is equally fallacious.[2] To be sure, the "Jewish Question" loomed larger than the "Gypsy Plague" in Nazi ideology, since Roma and Sinti were socially marginal whereas Jews were increasingly assimilated in German society and culture; the Gypsies were also far fewer in number, representing about 0.05 percent of the 1933 German population. Nevertheless, there is a striking parallelism between the ideology and process of extermination for Jews and Gypsies. Despite the similarity and simultaneity of persecution, the disparity between the vast quantity of secondary literature about Nazi Judeophobia and the limited number of studies about the fate of Roma and Sinti has inevitably influenced current historical analyses, in which Gypsies are at most an afterthought.[3]

It is clear that the persecution of Roma and Sinti on racial grounds preceded the Nazi assumption of power. Under the Second Empire and the Weimar Republic, the states of Baden, Bavaria, Bremen, Hesse, and Prussia had developed laws discriminating against Gypsies and established legal ste-

*©1994 "Chapter Six. Holocaust: The Gypsies," by Sybil Milton.
This essay is a revised and expanded version of a paper presented at the 1991 annual meeting of the German Studies Association, Los Angeles.

reotypes defining them as vagabonds, asocials, criminals, and racially inferior aliens. Already in 1899, Bavaria had established an "Information Agency on Gypsies" (*Nachrichtendienst in Bezug auf die Zigeuner*) that collected genealogical data, photographs, and fingerprints of Gypsies above the age of six.[4] Although under Article 108 of the Weimar constitution, Gypsies received full and equal citizenship rights, they were nevertheless vulnerable to discriminatory legislation. The Bavarian law for "Combatting Gypsies, Vagabonds, and the Work Shy" (*Gesetz zur Bekämpfung von Zigeuner, Landfahrern und Arbeitsscheuen*) of 16 July 1926 mandated registration of all domiciled and migratory Gypsies with the police, local registry offices, and labor exchanges. A similar Prussian decree from 3 November 1927 resulted in the creation of special Gypsy identity cards with fingerprints and photographs for 8,000 Roma and Sinti above the age of six. During the last years of the Weimar Republic, arbitrary arrest and preventive detention of itinerant Gypsies—ostensibly for crime prevention—became routine. In April 1929, a national police commission adopted the 1926 Bavarian law as the federal norm and established a "Center for the Fight against Gypsies in Germany" with headquarters in Munich.[5] This agreement was renewed on 18 March 1933 with the proviso that any state could issue additional regulations.[6]

Clear lines of demarcation cannot be drawn between these Weimar legal precedents that stigmatized Roma and Sinti as habitual criminals, social misfits, vagabonds, and so-called asocials and the first Nazi measures after 1933. Initially, the Nazis developed parallel racial regulations against Jews, Gypsies, and the handicapped. Gypsies were included as "asocials" (an aggregate group including—but not limited to—prostitutes, beggars, shirkers, and any persons the police designated as "hooligans") in the July 1933 Law for the Prevention of Offspring with Hereditary Defects and in the November 1933 Law Against Habitual Criminals. The first law resulted in their involuntary sterilization,[7] while the second permitted their incarceration in concentration camps. The Denaturalization Law of 14 July 1933 and the Expulsion Law of 23 March 1934, initially implemented against *Ostjuden* (Eastern and Polish Jews), was also used to expel foreign and stateless Gypsies from German soil. Following passage of the 1935 Nuremberg racial laws, semi-official commentaries interpreting these laws classified Gypsies, along with Jews and Blacks, as racially distinctive minorities with "alien blood" (*artfremdes Blut*).[8] Racially mixed marriages between those of German blood and "Gypsies, Negroes, or their bastard offspring" were prohibited on 26 November 1935 in an advisory circular from the Reich Ministry of the Interior to all local registry offices for vital statistics. In the ever-escalating series of interlocking Nazi regulations implementing the Nuremberg racial laws, both Gypsies and Jews were deprived of their civil rights.[9] Racial scientists compiled the official handbooks for the interpretation of the Nuremberg laws, providing the scientific justification for the regime for the later mass murder of Jews and Gypsies.

Already in 1934, the Nazi Racial Policy Office together with the Gestapo began to compile an "asocials catalog." The Nazi police and health bureaucracies continued and expanded the systematic registration of Gypsies as potential criminals, genetically defined, that had already begun during the Weimar Republic.[10] Thus, anthropological and genealogical registration (*Rassenbiologische Gutachtung*) identified Gypsies as "racially inferior asocials and criminals of Asiatic ancestry."[11] Moreover, Nazi social policy toward Jews and Gypsies resulted in decreased expenditures for welfare; assistance to the growing number of impoverished Jews was assigned in 1933 to the *Reichsvertretung der Juden in Deutschland* (Reich Representation of German Jews)[12] and after 1939 to the *Reich-svereinigung der Juden in Deutschland* (Reich Association of Jews in Germany),[13] whereas indigent Gypsies received progressively less financial assistance from municipal authorities.[14] These same officials subsequently interned Roma and Sinti in Gypsy camps.

A March 1936 memorandum to State Secretary of the Interior Hans Pfundtner contains the first references to the preparation of a national Gypsy law (*Reichszigeunergesetz*) and to the difficulties of achieving a "total solution of the Gypsy problem on either a national or international level." The interim recommendations in this memorandum include expulsion of stateless and foreign Gypsies, restrictions on freedom of movement and on issuing licenses for Gypsies with itinerant trades (*Wandergewerbe*), increased police surveillance, sterilization of Gypsies of mixed German and Gypsy ancestry (the so-called *Mischlinge*), complete registration of all Gypsies in the Reich, and confinement in a special Gypsy reservation.[15]

In lieu of national legislation, the Central Office of Detective Forces (*Reichskriminalpolizeiamt*, or RKPA) and the Reich Ministry of Interior established in early June 1936 the Central Office to Combat the Gypsy Menace (*Zentralstelle zur Bekämpfung des Zigeunerunwesens*) in Munich, which intensified harassment, coercion, and intimidation of Gypsies by the police. This Munich office served as the headquarters of a national data bank on Gypsies and represented all German police agencies with the Interpol International Center for Fighting the Gypsy Menace in Vienna.[16]

On 6 June 1936, the Reich and Prussian Ministry of Interior issued a circular containing new directives for "Fighting the Gypsy Plague."[17] The circular also authorized the Chief of the Berlin Police to direct raids throughout Prussia to arrest all Gypsies prior to the Olympic games. Consequently, 600 Gypsies were arrested in Berlin on 16 July 1936, and marched under police guard to a sewage dump adjacent to the municipal cemetery in the Berlin suburb of Marzahn.[18] Although the presence of both sewage and graves violated Gypsy cultural tabus, Berlin-Marzahn became the largest Gypsy camp (*Zigeunelager*). It consisted of 130 caravans condemned as uninhabitable by the Reich Labor Service; the camp was guarded a detachment of Prussian uniformed police (*Schutzpolizei*). The hygienic facilities were totally inadequate; Marzahn had only three water pumps and two toilets. Overcrowding and unsanitary conditions were the norm; for example, in March 1938 city authorities reported 170 cases of communicable diseases.

The Gypsies at Berlin-Marzahn were assigned to forced labor. Further, the Reich Department of Health forced them to provide detailed data for anthropological and genealogical registration. In turn, this data provided the pretext for the denaturalization and involuntary sterilization of the imprisoned Gypsies. The Berlin-Marzahn Gypsy camp provided evidence of a growing interagency cooperation between public health officials and the police, essential for subsequent developments resulting in the deportation and mass murder of German Gypsies.[19] After 1939, the prisoners at Marzahn were compelled to work at forced labor in the Sachsenhausen stone quarries or to clear rubble from Berlin streets after Allied air raids. Most were deported to Auschwitz in 1943.

In spring 1936, the Reich Department of Health created the Racial Hygiene and Demographic Biology Research Unit (*Rassenhygienische und Bevölkerungsbiologische Forschungsstelle*), as its Department L3. Headed by Dr. Robert Ritter, the unit began systematic genealogical and genetic research in 1937.[20] Ritter and his associates worked in close cooperation with the Central Office for Reich Security (*Reichssicherheitshauptamt*, or RSHA) and the Reich Ministry of Interior. Funded by the *Deutsche Forschungsgemeinschaft*, Ritter's unit was assigned to register the approximately 30,000 Gypsies and part-Gypsies in Germany in order to provide genealogical and racial data required for formulating a new Reich Gypsy law. Ritter's group aimed to show that criminal and asocial behavior was hereditary.[21]

In 1937, the anthropologist Dr. Adolf Würth, one of Ritter's associates, described the growing parallels in Nazi policy toward Jews and Gypsies:

The Gypsy question is for us today primarily a racial question. Thus, the national socialist state will basically have to settle the Gypsy question just as it has solved the Jewish question. We have already begun. Jews and Gypsies have been placed on equal footing in marriage prohibitions in the regulations for implementing the Nuremberg laws for the Protection of German Blood. The Gypsies are not of German blood nor can they be considered related to German blood.[22]

Würth conducted genealogical and anthropological research on Gypsies in Württemberg and in 1940 supervised the first experimental deportation of 500 Roma and Sinti from the Württemberg state prison at Hohenasperg to Lublin.[23] Würth and the other practitioners of racial hygiene provided not only the intellectual infrastructure for genocide, but were also accessories in the process of mass murder. Their resesearch was utilized by the police for implementing the segregation, sterilization, and deportation of Gypsies from the Reich.

Ritter's associates included his assistant Eva Justin, a nurse who later received a doctorate in anthropology in 1944 for her research on Sinti children separated from their families and raised in "alien" surroundings at the Catholic St. Josefspflege home in Mulfingen; after her dissertation research was completed, these children were deported to Auschwitz-Birkenau, where most were killed.[24] Ritter's other colleagues included Dr. Sophie Ehrhardt, a zoologist and anthropologist, whose research focused on East Prussian Gypsies and on Jews and Gypsies in the Lodz ghetto and the Dachau and Sachsenhausen concentration camps. Ehrhardt was subsequently appointed Professor of Anthropology at Tübingen University in 1942.[25]

After 1935, municipal governments and local welfare offices pressured the German police to confine a growing number of German Gypsies in the newly created municipal *Zigeunerlager*. These gypsy camps were in essence *SS-Sonderlager:* special internment camps combining elements of protective custody concentration camps and embryonic ghettos. Usually located on the outskirts of cities, these *Zigeunerlager* were guarded by the SS, the gendarmerie, or the uniformed city police. After 1935, these camps became reserve depots for forced labor, genealogical registration, and compulsory sterilization. Between 1933 and 1939, *Zigeunerlager* were created in Cologne, Düsseldorf, Essen, Frankfurt, Hamburg, and other German cities. These camps evolved from municipal internment camps into assembly centers (*Sammellager*) for systematic deportation to concentration camps after 1939.[26]

In Frankfurt, for example, local officials—including Frankfurt Chief of Police Beckerle, Mayor Krebs, and representatives from the welfare office— expanded existing municipal anti-Gypsy ordinances in the spring of 1936. New measures included police searches of all Gypsy residences three times a week; police checks on all Gypsy identity papers to determine whether any were stateless or foreigners, vulnerable to expulsion; compulsory municipal genetic and genealogical registration; resettlement of all Roma and Sinti found within the city limits in the Frankfurt *Zigeunerlager*; prohibition on renting local campsites to Gypsies outside the municipal *Zigeunerlager;* and expelling migrant Roma and Sinti upon arrival in Frankfurt.[27]

Additional measures in Frankfurt further increased police harassment of both domiciled and migrant Gypsies. These directives included restricting the number of new trade licenses issued to itinerant Gypsies, thereby preventing or limiting their employment as knife (or scissors) grinders, horse traders, traveling salespersons, fortune-tellers, musicians, and circus performers; checking school attendance by Gypsy children, truancy to be punished by removal to municipal juvenile facilities; and compulsory registration of all Gypsies detained or arrested by the police.[28] At the Düsseldorf Höherweg camp, the Gypsies were compelled to pay six marks monthly for inferior accommodations in barracks that did not even have electricity; they were also barred from receiving either unemployment or welfare assistance. In addition, the camp commandant mandated rigid curfews, prohibited children from playing on the grounds, and banned visits and communications from non-Gypsy relatives.[29] Similar measures were implemented in other municipal Gypsy camps.

A reexamination of existing historical literature about the concentration camp system before 1939 reveals that several Sinti had already been arrested and detained in the Worms-Osthofen concentration camp in 1933 and that 400 Bavarian Gypsies were deported to Dachau in July 1936. This latter arrest occurred almost simultaneously with the arrest of Berlin Gypsies and the creation of Berlin-Marzahn. An additional 1,000 Gypsies "able to work" were arrested in raids on 13–18 June 1938 and deported to Buchenwald, Dachau, and Sachsenhausen concentration camps; women were sent to Lichtenburg concentration camp in Saxony. These 1938 arrests were authorized under an unpublished decree on "crime prevention" (*vorbeugende Verbrechensbekämpfung*) issued in December 1937. This decree extended the use of preventive arrest to all persons whose asocial behavior threatened the common good, irrespective of whether the individual had a criminal record. It was applied to migrant and unemployed Gypsies, asocials, the unemployed, habitual criminals, homeless panhandlers, beggars, and Jews previously sentenced to jail for more than thirty days (including for traffic violations). The arrests were made by the Kripo (rather than the Gestapo) and provided the expanding camp system with potential slave labor.[30]

Austrian and German Gypsies were also sent to Mauthausen and Ravensbrück prior to the outbreak of war in 1939. In summer and fall 1938, about 3,000 allegedly "work shy" Roma and Sinti from the Ostmark (incorporated Austria) were also deported to concentration camps. Thus 2,000 male Gypsies above the age of sixteen were sent to Dachau and later remanded to Buchenwald, and 1,000 female Gypsies above the age of fifteen were sent to Ravensbrück.[31] In 1939 and 1940, special internment camps at Maxglan/Leopoldskron in Salzburg and Lackenbach in Burgenland were created specifically for Roma and Sinti in the Ostmark and all German decrees and regulations against Gypsies, including genealogical and police registration, were implemented.[32]

The registration and census of Gypsies in Austria was begun in late October 1939. Similarly, a census of Gypsies was conducted in the Protectorate of Bohemia and Moravia in August 1942 after the incarceration of Gypsies in compulsory penal labor camps at Pardibice near Prague, Lety in Bohemia, and Hodonin in Moravia.

In the Netherlands, in February 1936 the Dutch Minister of Justice had already created a central Gypsy register linked to the Munich central police office and the Vienna Interpol office specializing in Gypsies. On 30 December 1937, the Police Gazette of Holland announced the opening of the Dutch Central Office for Gypsies; this office was closed in January 1939. In early 1941, a central registry for Gypsies, nomads, aliens, and the stateless was opened and implemented German anti-Gypsy measures for the arrest, internment, and deportation of Dutch Gypsies.[33]

Similarly in France, before the war in late 1939, Interior Minister Albert Sarraut specified that Gypsies be included among those without fixed domicile to be interned as security risks in the *camps de concentration.* The situation of French Gypsies did not improve with German occupation. The Commissariat for Jewish Affairs under Xavier Vallat in Vichy France also held jurisdiction over the fate of Gypsies as part of its responsibility for the administration of "measures for the maintenance of racial purity."[34] As in the case of French Jews, the Nazi plan—requiring the cooperation of the French police and civil service—for the identification, concentration, and deportation of Gypsies was not fully implemented before the Allied armies liberated France.

The literature about Gypsies in the pre-1939 German concentration camps is too fragmentary to permit valid generalizations, and we therefore still do not know why some Gypsies were sent to municipal internment camps while others were committed to concentration camps.

In 1938 and 1939, the Nazi ideological obsession with Gypsies became almost as strident and aggressive as the campaign against the Jews.[35] In August 1938, Gypsies were expelled, ostensibly as military security risks, from border zones on the left bank of the Rhine and, once war had begun, they were prohibited from "wandering" in the western areas of the Reich. In May 1938, Himmler ordered that the Munich bureau of Gypsy affairs be renamed *Reichszentrale zur Bekämpfung des Zigeun-erunwesens* (Central Office to Combat the Gypsy Nuisance) and placed within the RKPA (*Reichskriminalpolizeiamt*, Department V of the Central Office for Reich Security) in Berlin by early October 1938. Moreover, on 8 December 1938, Himmler promulgated a decree for "Fighting the Gypsy Plague," basing it on Robert Ritter's anthropological and genealogical registration (*rassenbiologische Gutachtung*).

This decree recommended "the resolution of the Gypsy question based on its essentially racial nature" (*die Regelung der Zigeunerfrage aus dem Wesen dieser Rasse heraus in Angriff zu nehmen*) and mandated that all Gypsies in the Reich above the age of six be classified into three racial groups: "Gypsies, Gypsy Mischlinge, and nomadic persons behaving as Gypsies." The guidelines for implementation published in early 1939 stipulated that the RKPA assist in "the development of a comprehensive Gypsy law prohibiting miscegenation and regulating the life of the Gypsy race in German space (*im deutschen Volksraum*)."[36] Comprehensive and systematic residential and genealogical registration of Gypsies by local police and public health authorities became mandatory and photo identity cards were to be issued to all Gypsies and part Gypsies. The implementation of Himmler's decree also resulted in the purge of several dozen Gypsy musicians from the Reich Music Chamber in the spring of 1939, thereby effectively banning their employment as musicians.[37] The radicalization of Nazi attitudes by 1940 is also evident in a report from 5 February 1940, from Senior State Attorney Dr. Meissner of the Graz Circuit Court (*Oberlandesgericht*) to the Reich Minister of Justice in Berlin, which rejected the idea of Gypsy employment as musicians in Burgenland: "The Gypsies live almost exclusively from begging and theft. Their work as musicians is simply a cover and not genuine employment."[38]

The deportation of German Gypsies began shortly after the outbreak of war in 1939. On 17 October 1939, Reinhard Heydrich issued the so-called *Festsetzungserlaß*, prohibiting all Gypsies and part-Gypsies not already interned in camps from changing their registered domiciles; this measure was essential for implementing deportations.[39] In the second half of October, Arthur Nebe, chief of the RKPA (RSHA Department V), tried to expedite the deportation of Berlin Gypsies by requesting that Eichmann "add three or four train cars of Gypsies" to the Nisko Jewish transports departing from Vienna. Eichmann cabled Berlin that the Nisko transport would include "a train car of Gypsies to be added to the first Jewish deportation from Vienna."[40] However, the failure of the Nisko resettlement scheme at the end of 1939 precluded the early expulsion of 30,000 Gypsies from the Greater German Reich to the General Government.[41] The aborted October 1939 deportation took place belatedly in mid-May 1940, when 2,800 German Gypsies were deported from seven assembly centers in the Old Reich to Lublin.[42] In Austria, the deportations to the General Government planned for the second half of August 1940 were postponed indefinitely and the Gypsies were subsequently deported to Auschwitz-Birkenau in 1943.[43] The rules concerning inclusion and exemption for Gypsies paralleled the later regulations used in Jewish transports.

The property and possessions of the deported Gypsies were confiscated and the deportees were compelled to sign release forms acknowledging the transfer of their possessions as *volks-und staatsfeindliches Vermögen* (under the Law for the Confiscation of Subversive and Enemy Property initially used for the seizure of assets of proscribed and denaturalized political opponents after July 1933).[44] The same confiscatory procedures were also employed during the earliest deportations of Jews, prior to the passage of the 11th Ordinance. The 11th Ordinance provided for automatic loss of citizenship and confiscation of property if a German Jew took up residence in a foreign country; deportation to the East (including to the *Ostland* and the General Government) counted as such a change of residence.[45] The deportation of Gypsies from Germany and Austria was again suspended in October 1940 because the General Government had protested the potential dumping of 35,000 Gypsies as well as the impending arrival of large numbers of German Jews.[46] Again in July 1941, the RSHA halted the deportation of East Prussian Gypsies, probably because of the invasion of the Soviet Union, noting that "a general and final solution of the Gypsy question cannot be achieved at this time." Instead, the RSHA proposed to construct a new *Zigeunerlager* enclosed with barbed wire in the outskirts of Königsberg.[47]

The patterns of both Gypsy and Jewish deportations reveal the evolving system of killings. Thus, as with the Jewish deportations to Lodz, the deportation of 5,000 Austrian Gypsies from transit camps at Hartburg, Fürstenfeld, Mattersburg, Roten Thurm, Lackenbach, and Oberwart from 5–9 November 1941, dovetailed with the establishment of Chelmno (Kulmhof), where these Gypsies were killed in mobile gas vans in December 1941 and January 1942.[48] Similarly, the Gypsies incarcerated in the Warsaw ghetto were deported to Treblinka in the summer of 1942.[49] By that time, the SS *Einsatzgruppen* operating in the Soviet Union and the Baltic region had already killed several thousand Gypsies alongside Jews in massacres.[50] Thus the RSHA reported in its "Situation Report USSR No. 153," that "the Gypsy problem in Simpferopol [had been] settled" in December 1941.[51] And in October 1947, Otto Ohlendorf, who had headed the *Einsatzgruppe* that operated in southern Russia and the Crimea, testified at Nuremberg that the basis for killing Gypsies and Jews in Russia had been the same.[52] In similar fashion the Reich Commissar for the Ostland in July 1942 informed the Higher SS and Police Leader in Riga that "treatment of Jews and Gypsies are to be placed on equal footing (*gleichgestellt*)."[53]

Ritter's racial research estimated that 90 percent of the German Roma and Sinti were of mixed ancestry, thus Nazi measures were directed primarily against Gypsy *Mischlinge* in Germany and Austria up to 1942. In 1942, the regime dropped the distinction between part and pure Gypsies and subjected all Gypsies to the same treatment. In 1942 and 1943, when most Gypsy deportations from the Reich occurred, the Nazis also eliminated all distinctions between the treatment of Gypsies and Jews. Thus, on 12 March 1942 new regulations placed Jews and Gypsies on equal footing for welfare payments and compulsory labor.[54]

There is suggestive evidence that Hitler may have been involved in the formal decision to kill the Gypsies. On 3 December 1942, Martin Bormann wrote a letter to Heinrich Himmler, protesting that the Reich Leader SS had exempted certain pure Gypsies from "the measures to combat the Gypsy plague" until additional research into their "language, rituals . . . , and valuable Teutonic customs" could be completed. Bormann complained that neither the public, nor the party, nor the Füher would "understand or approve." Himmler added a handwritten note on the face of the letter about preparing data on Gypsies for Hitler. The marginalia states: *"Führer. Aufstellung wer sind Zigeuner* (Führer. Information who are the Gypsies").[55] Himmler met with Hitler on 10 December 1942, and six days later, responding to Bormann's pressure and probably to Hitler's order, Himmler issued the Auschwitz decree on Gypsies, which led to their deportation to and eventual murder in Birkenau.[56]

The evidence suggests that Hitler was directly involved and informed of most killing operations, and that simultaneously the administration of policy by German officials stationed outside Germany cumulatively radicalized the implementation of central policy toward German and European Gypsies.

Already on 26 September 1942, three months before Himmler's Auschwitz decree, 200 Gypsies were transferred from Buchenwald to Auschwitz and assigned to build the new Gypsy enclosure (BIIe) at Birkenau. On 26 February 1943, the first transport of German Gypsies arrived at the newly erected Gypsy "family camp" (BIIe) in Birkenau; Gypsies from occupied Europe arrived at Auschwitz-Birkenau after 7 March 1943.[57] The pattern of deporting Gypsies as a family unit was first established during the May 1940 Hohenasperg deportations to Lublin and continued in Auschwitz. The history and fate of the Gypsies in the Birkenau *Zigeunerlager* paralleled the creation and later destruction of the so-called *Familienlager* for Theresienstadt deportees in Birkenau BIIb.[58] On 2 August 1944, the Gypsy camp at Auschwitz-Birkenau was liquidated. An earlier SS attempt to obliterate the Birkenau Gypsy camp BIIe on 16 May had failed because of armed resistance; the prisoners fought the SS with improvised knives, shovels, wooden sticks, and stones.[59] By the time Birkenau was evacuated, 13,614 Gypsies from the German Reich had died of exposure, malnutrition, disease, and brutal medical experiments, and 6,432 had been gassed; thirty-two had been shot while trying to escape. Thus, about 20,000 of the 23,000 German and Austrian Roma and Sinti deported to Auschwitz were killed there.[60] Finally, on 25 April 1943, both Jews and Gypsies were denaturalized and placed on an equal footing under the provisions of the 12th Ordinance to the Reich Citizenship Law and on 10 March 1944 a circular letter from Heinrich Himmler directed that the publication of restrictive decrees against Jews and Gypsies be discontinued as their "evacuation and isolation" had already been largely completed.[61]

Despite the growth of specialized monographs, the lacunae in Holocaust literature about Nazi policies toward Roma and Sinti are still vast.

Future research should address the need for a comprehensive and systematic handbook listing all published and unpublished Nazi laws, ordinances, and directives against German and Austrian Gypsies, as well as similar decrees in the other countries of Axis and occupied Europe. It is also important to analyze the presence and deportation of German Gypsies to ghettos in Bialystok, Cracow, Radom, Warsaw, and Lodz. Scattered entries in Adam Czerniakow's diary recorded the presence of German and Polish Gypsies in the Warsaw ghetto in April and June 1942; parallel decrees from the city and county of Warsaw confirm the incarceration of Gypsies in the Warsaw ghetto in June 1942 and their subsequent deportation to Treblinka.[62] Although fragmentary data is available, research about Roma and Sinti resistance is still negligible.

Current literature has also ignored references to the killing of Gypsies in Einsatzkommando situation reports from the occupied Soviet Union, although a more systematic analysis of this material would be relatively simple.[63] Likewise, Nazi usage and language toward Gypsies requires more organized analysis, since it seems logical that the pacification and antipartisan operations in the occupied Soviet Union and Baltic, known as *Bandenbekämpfung*, included activities against Jews, Gypsies, and communist partisans. The public language of Nazi propaganda was used both for indoctrination and intimidation, whereas the less public language of Nazi bureaucrats utilized code words and circumlocutions for deportations and killing operations. The Nazis generally described their victims in pejorative terms, transmuting objective language into terms of contempt to describe the victims that their own policies and deeds had created.[64]

Holocaust historiography during the past forty years has emphasized anti-Semitism and the Jewish fate. Despite new sources and research during the 1980s, the older interpretations are still dominant. There are still no parallel studies about the fate of Gypsies and Jews in the major German concentration camps (Bergen-Belsen, Buchenwald, Dachau, Mauthausen, Natzweiler, Ravensbrück, and Sachsenhausen), in transit camps such as Westerbork in Holland and Malines in Belgium, in killing centers at Belzec, Chelmno, Sobibor, Treblinka, and Auschwitz-Birkenau, and in the labor camps that dotted the Reich and all of occupied Europe.[65] Furthermore, there are no comparative studies about the parallel fate of German Gypsies in concentration camps and *Zigeunerlager* prior to 1939. Current literature analyzing the fate of Roma and Sinti in occupied Europe is still relatively narrow, apart from several significant works about the Netherlands and

Czechoslovakia.[66] The gaps in our knowledge about the Gypsy final solution are still vast, although significant progress has been made toward understanding the connection between Nazi ideology, German social policy, and the genocide of German and European Gypsies.

Discrimination against Sinti and Roma did not cease with the collapse of Nazi Germany in 1945. During the immediate postwar years, harassment by German and Austrian police, housing, health, and welfare authorities was common. In Germany, Gypsy registration files created during the Nazi era along with some of the police personnel were transferred to postwar successor agencies; these compromising files disappeared and were sometimes destroyed when public disclosure of their existence proved embarrassing. Thus, for example, from the early 1950s to the mid-1970s, the *Landfahrerzentrale* (Vagrant Department) of the Bavarian police retained the Gypsy records of the Nazi Central Office to Combat the Gypsy Menace headquartered after 1936 in Munich. These records disappeared and were allegedly destroyed in the 1970s, when the nascent Sinti and Roma civil rights movement initiated inquiries about them.[67]

Prior to the 1980s, few archives and scholars were interested in documenting Nazi crimes against Roma and Sinti. The fragmentation and dispersion of German records during and after World War II hampered early recognition of the importance of the partial files of Dr. Robert Ritter's Racial Hygiene and Demographic Biology Research Unit located in Professor Sophie Ehrhardt's research collection at Tübingen University; it also required several years to catalog these records after they were transferred in 1981 to the German Federal Archives in Koblenz.[68]

In addition, German bureaucrats encouraged the emphasis on Jewish victimization in Holocaust historiography, since the excesses of anti-Semitism could be blamed on the pathology of Hitler and his SS followers; whereas, the murder of German nationals in the so-called euthanasia killings and the killing of Sinti and Roma, both carried out by "ordinary" German bureaucrats, scientists, and policemen, implicated a far larger segment of the German population. Moreover, the focus on Nazi anti-Semitism also prevented discussion of how deeply the German scientific community was involved in the killing operations against Jews as well as against Gypsies and the handicapped.

And finally, German postwar restitution legislation and its implementation excluded most Sinti and Roma survivors, subjecting them to arbitrary and repetitive bureaucratic humiliations. Most Gypsy survivors were initially disqualified from receiving compensation as racial victims for imprisonment prior to the March 1943 Auschwitz decree. Although this date was later changed to December 1938, both dates excluded restitution for incarceration in early internment camps such as Marzahn or Lackenbach, ignored deportation to ghettos such as Radom or Bialystok after 1940, restricted claims for health disabilities caused by involuntary sterilization and medical experiments, and required minimum periods of involuntary detention in certain officially recognized camps and ghettos to qualify for meager settlements. Claims filed by Gypsy survivors for homes and businesses impounded at deportation were invariably disallowed, often after investigation by the same policemen who had previously arrested them in the Nazi era. Health claims for physical and psychological trauma were similarly disregarded. This failure of empathy with Gypsy survivors was rationalized using the language of Nazi stereotypes that defined the victims as "asocial and criminal." Despite minor improvements in both legislation and court decisions by the 1980s, hostile practices such as the involuntary denaturalization of many German Sinti survivors and the reduction of modest restitution settlements by deducting any prior welfare assistance established a flagrant pattern of official dissembling and hostility.[69]

Despite democratization and economic recovery, denazification in postwar Germany and Austria remained incomplete. West German political culture included widespread amnesia to the continuities of personnel in government and academia. This continuity exemplified one aspect of the collective failure to assume political responsibility for the Nazi murder of Sinti and Roma. For example, the staff of the Racial Hygiene and Demographic Biology Research Unit in Berlin-Dahlem had little difficulty in securing employment after 1945, and they eluded all penalties during postwar judicial proceedings. Robert Ritter taught criminal biology at the University of Tübingen from late 1944 to 1946 and was hired in December 1947 as a physician for children by the Frankfurt Health Office. Once again, Ritter hired Dr. Eva Justin to work with him; she was employed as a psychologist at the Frankfurt Health Office. After brief investigations, judicial proceedings against Ritter and Justin as accessories in the murder of German Gypsies were discontinued.[70] Dr. Sophie Ehrhardt continued her research and teaching as a professor of anthropology at Tübingen University, where she used the plaster casts of Gypsy heads and fingerprint data from the records of the Racial Hygiene Unit entrusted to her after the war. Judicial proceedings against her were dropped in 1985.[71] Dr. Adolf Würth became an official in the Bureau of Statistics in Baden-Württemberg from 1951 to 1970. Würth was never tried as an accessory to murder, since judicial investigations of his career were discontinued. Many perpetrators were never placed on trial; for example, the physician and anthropologist Professor Otmar Freiherr von Verschuer, who had supervised and subsidized many of Mengele's notorious experiments on Gypsy and Jewish twins at Auschwitz, was never indicted or investigated. After the war, he established the Human Genetics Institute at the University of Münster in 1951 and was appointed a professor at Münster in 1953.[72]

Postwar police careers revealed a similar lack of repercussions for involvement in the deportation and killing of Sinti and Roma. Thus, Josef Eichberger, who had been responsible for Gypsy deportations in the RSHA, became head of the "Gypsy" department of the Bavarian State Police; Leo Karsten became head of the "Migrants (*Landfahrer*) Department" of the Baden State Police in Karlsruhe; and Hans Maly, a senior officer in Department VA2 (preventive measures against asocials, prostitutes, and Gypsies) of the RSHA from January to late September 1943, was later hired as head of the Bonn Kripo after 1945. Judicial proceedings were dropped against these police.[73]

In 1969–1971, during the trial of Otto Bovensiepen, the former chief of the Berlin Gestapo from March 1941 to November 1942, the statute of limitations had expired on all crimes of the Nazi period except murder. Bovensiepen was indicted for "knowingly and with base motives assisting in the deportation and killing of at least 35,000 Berlin Jews and 252 Gypsies." The trial was suspended in 1971, since Bovensiepen had suffered a heart attack and his physician testified that he would never be able to live through the trial.[74] Recently, after a 43-month trial, the Siegen District Court sentenced Ernst August König on 24 January 1991 to life imprisonment for murders he had committed as SS Blockführer in the Gypsy camp BIIe at Auschwitz-Birkenau.[75]

Allied tribunals of the four postwar occupation armies and the successor states (the Federal Republic of Germany, the German Democratic Republic, and the Republic of Austria) tried large numbers of Nazi criminals for crimes committed during World War II; usually specific crimes against Sinti and Roma were part of larger indictments for participation in the Einsatzkommandos or crimes committed in the concentration camps.[76] Similarly, it is uncommon to find explicit acknowledgment of Sinti and Roma victims in most postwar Holocaust memorials. Their tragic fate is explicitly recognized in monuments on Museumplein in Amsterdam, at the former Gypsy camps in Salzburg and Lackenbach, in concentration camp memorials at Bergen-Belsen and Auschwitz-Birkenau, and in new memorials at the children's home in Mulfingen as well as at the sites of their deportation in Heidelberg and Wiesbaden.[77]

German unification and changes in the former Soviet bloc since 1990 have altered the political map of Europe. These changes are, however, still incomplete and it is still too early for any final analysis. Nevertheless, recent developments do show that the administration of memorials in the countries of Eastern Europe and in reunited Germany will at best transform and at worst diminish the status of most Holocaust memorials. Growing popular resentment against Jews and Gypsies, hatred of outsiders, as well as the emergence of local fascist and neo-Nazi groups also bode ill for the future of these memorials.[78]

The belated recognition of the Gypsy Holocaust is still incomplete in current historiography. During the 1980s new sources and research have produced interpretations that correct many of the old imbalances by pointing to the connections between the murder of the Jews and that of the Gypsies and the handicapped. These new analyses have, however, been unable so far to alter the older interpretation; prejudice and the habits of forty years cannot be reversed overnight.

The Gypsy Holocaust has taught us that the German health care system and the involvement of German scientists—physicians, psychiatrists, anthropologists, and geneticists—were essential to implement the mass murder of all European Gypsies alongside that of the European Jews.

These new findings also provide us with a better understanding of how Nazi policy evolved. Although there is an obvious link between policy and ideology, there was no defined corpus of Nazi ideology (even other Nazi leaders did not read Alfred Rosenberg). Instead, Nazi ideology was reflected by the writings of large numbers of people, including party functionaries, government bureaucrats, and racial scientists. In fact, policy was revealed less in ideological statements by leaders than in the day-to-day activities of middle-level management. Hitler set policy goals, but middle-level management delineated and implemented policy. Hitler was preoccupied with racial purity, and was determined to cleanse the gene pool of the German nation. He demanded the exclusion of the unfit and the alien. In cooperation with racial scientists, the Nazi party and German government bureaucrats defined the groups to be excluded. From the beginning in 1933 these

bureaucrats focused on the handicapped, Jews, and Gypsies, advancing solutions for exclusion that became progressively more radical. Before the final solution of mass murder became feasible, these bureaucrats proposed
sterilization and deportation (or emigration) as solutions. The handicapped
were thus sterilized before they were killed, and this also applied to many
Gypsies. Even during the war, Nazi functionaries continued to search for an
easy method that would make mass sterilization of Jews possible. When
emigration or expulsion was no longer feasible but before the killings commenced, the Nazis instituted the deportation of Jews and Gypsies as a means
of exclusion. Sterilization, deportation, and killings thus reflected the evolving
policy of exclusion and was applied to the handicapped, Jews, and Gypsies.

Further, party and government agencies competed for the right to implement policy. Ideologues like Julius Streicher, even Joseph Goebbels, were
"outside the loop" when the policy to kill was decided and implemented.
The killing of the handicapped was directed by the Führer Chancellery in
cooperation with racial scientists and health care functionaries. The killing
of Jews and Gypsies was directed by Reinhard Heydrich (later Ernst
Kaltenbrunner) as chief of the Security Police and SS Security Service. Under Heydrich's command, the Gestapo (political police) dealt with Jews,
and the Kripo (detective forces) dealt with Gypsies. While it is true that the
Kripo, traditionally concerned with crime prevention, tended to focus on
Gypsy mobility and supposed Gypsy crime, it deferred to racial scientists
for its guidelines on how to classify and exclude Gypsies. The delineation of
Gypsy policy thus largely devolved on Dr. Robert Ritter, a psychiatrist whose
research in racial science centered on Gypsies, and who headed the Eugenic
and Criminal Biological Research Station (*Rassenhygienische und
Kriminalbiologische Forschungsstelle*) of the Reich Health Office and later
the Criminal Biological Institute of the Security Police at Kripo headquarters. Both Gestapo and Kripo thus relied on racial scientists to define the
condemned groups. They also needed Hitler's order, or at least his authorization, to implement a policy of mass murder. In the final analysis, the
activities and records of these implementing agencies reflect policy decisions about genocide better than do public declarations, even the Führer's
speeches.

The German racial theories that served as the basis for extermination
were never rational or consistent. Thus in Germany "pure" Jews were killed,
but those of mixed ancestry were usually not included in killing operations,
because the bureaucracy chose not to alienate Germans related to Jews. In

contrast, Gypsies of mixed ancestry were the first victims, because their German relatives, usually holding low social status, posed no bureaucratic problems. And while the bureaucracy worked hard to limit the number of exempted Jews of mixed ancestry, Ritter classified 90 percent of all Gypsies as having mixed origins. Various Nazi leaders, including Heinrich Himmler, had their own favorite racial theories, but none ever inhibited the relentless bureaucratic drive toward extermination. The files of Ritter's agency provide incontrovertible documentary evidence that "pure" Roma and Sinti were registered and incarcerated, thereafter deported, and eventually killed. Our growing understanding of the Gypsy Holocaust enables us to restore the complexity of this history and perhaps this history may also provide us with a better understanding of the interaction between science and state bureaucracy with the forces of popular prejudice and racism.

Eyewitness Accounts
Holocaust: The Gypsies

A Note about Sources
The fate of the Gypsies (Roma and Sinti) in the concentration camps and killing fields of the Holocaust has been largely invisible in current historiography about Nazi genocide. Recent scholarship about the experiences of Roma and Sinti in Nazi-occupied Europe has generally been printed by an assortment of small publishers, thereby discouraging most scholars from ferreting out this diverse literature and impeding the inclusion of new data as more than an afterthought. This has resulted in a tacit conspiracy of silence about the isolation, exclusion, and systematic killing of the Gypsies, rendering much of current Holocaust scholarship deficient and obsolete.

Several reasons explain the disparity between the vast quantity of literature about Nazi persecution of the Jews and the limited number of studies about Nazi anti-Gypsy ideology and practice. Although the percentage of Gypsy mortality was approximately the same as the percentage of Jewish mortality in the Holocaust, the sheer weight of numbers of the Jewish victims captured immediate attention. Moreover, even in the 1940s, surviving sources about the fate of European Jews were far more numerous than those about Gypsies. Further, Jewish survivors published a substantial memoir literature, whereas Gypsy survivors were less articulate in print and more dependent on oral traditions. As each group of victims tended to write its own history of the Holocaust, the larger Jewish communities obviously dominated postwar historiography, whereas the less articulate communities of Gypsies remained largely silent and had no academic representation.

Although there is at present no comprehensive bibliography about the fate of Roma and Sinti during the Holocaust, the growing literature about this subject has been a by-product of the European Roma and Sinti civil rights movement since the 1980s. A substantial number of these new local and regional studies include eyewitness narratives.

The following survivor narratives were selected from this published literature. They represent typical aspects of the cumulative experiences of German and Austrian Roma and Sinti men and women between 1933 and 1945. These events include the internment of German Sinti in special municipal camps after 1935, such as the Dieselstrasse camp in Frankfurt (Jakob Müller); the May 1940 deportation from Hamburg to Lublin (Lani Rosenberg); the Belzec labor camp (Lani Rosenberg); imprisonment in Sachsenhausen, Gross Rosen, and Litomerice concentration and labor camps (Hugo Franz); medical experiments on Gypsy prisoners at Natzweiler-Struthof and Neckarelz (an unnamed Sinto from Nuremberg); daily life in the Auschwitz-Birkenau Gypsy family camp, BIIe, including the May 1944 revolt and the August 1944 liquidation (Elisabeth Guttenberger and Anna P.); the 1942 killings of Gypsies at Treblinka (Michael Chodźko); and the difficulties encountered by Roma survivors in Austria after 1945 (Maria Kohlberger, Leopoldine Papai, and Johann Breirather). Editorial insertions are marked in square brackets in the translations. All translations are by Sybil Milton.

The German Sinto, Jakob Müller, born in 1928, recounts his childhood experiences of deportation from Worms to the special municipal Gypsy internment at Dieselstrasse in Frankfurt am Main, where he was forced to live from 10 September 1940 until his family was deported to Auschwitz on 13 March 1943. His detailed description of the Dieselstrasse special camp reveals the overcrowded conditions and the special difficulties of the incarcerated Sinti children. Müller's story is published in Eva von Hase-Mihalik and Doris Kreuzkamp, *Du kriegst auch einen schönen Wohnwagen: Zwangslager für Sinti und Roma während des Nationalsozialismus in Frankfurt am Main.* [You will also get a nice wagon to live in: Involuntary internment camps for Sinti and Roma in Frankfurt under the Nazis.] (Frankfurt: Brandes and Apsel, 1990, pp. 23–27):

... No reasons were given when we were picked up in Worms. We lived in a large area with many other Sinti. After surrounding the area, they arrived in our home at Kleine Fischerweide 50, located adjacent to the Nibelungen school. Screaming "out, out, out"—we could only take the most essential items with us. We were placed on a truck that took us directly from Worms to Frankfurt. My father wasn't at home, since he was with the German air force.

In 1941, my father was dishonorably discharged from the army "for racial reasons" and he too was sent to the Frankfurt camp. We arrived at the Dieselstrasse camp in Frankfurt on 10 September 1940 and were there until we were deported to Auschwitz on 13 March 1943.

The Dieselstrasse camp was about 80 meters [ca. 240 ft.] long and 20 meters [ca. 60 ft.] wide. We were forced to live in abandoned moving vans. There were about 25 such vans and initially 150 to 180 persons were housed there. Many families with 8 to 12 members were forced to live in a space 7 meters [21 ft.] long by 2 meters [6 ft.] wide. They were forced to live in about 14 square meters [ca. 17 sq. yd.] and were crowded together in very cramped quarters.

There was always roll call in the mornings; we were counted—we were, to be sure, fenced in; there was a guard booth at the exit and four policemen on rotating shifts were always stationed there. . . .

We were allowed to attend the Riederwald school for one year, but then the local population complained about this and eventually we were seated separately in the last row of the class. Then came the Frankfurt order that forbade Gypsy children from attending schools. . . .

Lani Rosenberg, a German Sinto, describes his experiences after 1938 in Hamburg and Belzec labor camp. His father and brother were initially arrested during the June 1938 raids targeting "asocials" and deported to Sachsenhausen concentration camp; in mid-May 1940 the rest of his family was arrested and deported from Germany to Lublin [in occupied central Poland]. Rosenberg's account is excerpted from Rudko Kawczynski's essay, "Hamburg soll 'zigeunerfrei' werden" ["Hamburg will be 'free of Gypsies'"], published in Angelika Ebbinghaus, Heidrun Kaupen-Haas, Karl Heinz Roth, ed., *Heilen und Vernichten im Mustergau Hamburg: Bevölkerungs- und Gesundheitspolitik im Dritten Reich* [Healing and Killing in the Model Gau Hamburg: Reproductive and Health Policies in the Third Reich] (Hamburg, published with permission of Konkret Literatur Verlag, 1984), pp. 49–50:

The eldest in our family were arrested first. My father and older brother were arrested by the police in June 1938 at 5 A.M. In the greatest of haste, my mother asked an attorney to try to free my father and brother. Although the police had no grounds for arresting them, shrugging his shoulders the attorney reported that one couldn't do anything about it. He informed us that they had been taken to Sachsenhausen concentration camp. I wrote petitions for clemency, requesting my father's and brother's release, to Department C2 of the Reichskriminalpolizeiamt in Berlin and to the Führer. Eventually, I received a warning from the Hamburg-Eimsbüttel local police to stop annoying the Führer, or I too would also be arrested. Those Sinti that were still free were ordered not to leave the city limits. For starvation wages, I was compelled to do heavy physical labor.

On 16 May 1940, I, my mother, and all my other siblings still in Hamburg were arrested. I asked the police why we were being arrested. They replied that we were being resettled in Poland. We were assembled together with several hundred other Gypsies and brought to a shack near the harbor. Each of us received a red number painted on our skin. The transport to Poland began several days later. We were permitted to take only some of our clothing with us. All money and items of value were confiscated.

After several days travel we arrived in Poland at a place called Belzec. We were immediately received by an SS unit and were separated by age and gender. The SS took no great pains with many of the Gypsies, who were forced to dig their own graves; these Gypsies were then shot and buried. While being beaten we were forced to run to a shack. Later we had to put barbed wire around this hut. Early every morning we had to stand for roll call. Afterwards there were more beatings, we then received our tools, and were forced to run to "work" while again being beaten. The work place was located close to the Russian border. During the first three months of arrest, many of the younger children died of starvation and disease. There was no medical care. I often witnessed how Gypsies were shot, only because they tried to get some water. Once I observed that several 8–12 year old children were compelled to lie on the ground while booted SS men marched over their bodies. It is im-

possible to detail everything that I experienced during five years in the
concentration camps, since words are inadequate to report all of it. I
lost eight brothers and sisters as well as my parents under the Nazis. My
father was shot someplace near Schwerin shortly before the war
ended. . . .

Hugo Franz, head of the German Sinti organization in Düsseldorf, was a
victim of German racial persecution. Franz was born in Dresden in 1913 to
a family that had lived in Germany for three hundred years. When Franz
graduated from secondary school (*Gymnasium*), Nazi racial laws prevented
him from entering law school. He instead attended the Saxon state orches-
tral school and then formed his own band in Hamburg together with his
three brothers; after 1939 his identity papers were confiscated and he was
not permitted to accept road engagements for his band. Franz was compelled to abandon his profession as a musician and was forced to work at
the Blohm and Voss copper plant. Arrested in January 1942, he survived
subsequent imprisonment in Sachsenhausen, Gross Rosen, and Litomerice
concentration and labor camps. His experiences are published in an interview in Jörn-Erik Gutheil, and others, ed., *Einer muß überleben: Gespräche
mit Auschwitzhäftlinge 40 Jahre danach* [One of us must survive: Conversations with Auschwitz prisoners forty years later] (Düsseldorf: Der kleine
Verlag, 1984), pp. 50–52:

> At the time I was living with my parents in Hamburg. On 7 January
> 1942, I was arrested by the Gestapo at 5 in the morning. They told me
> to pack my toothbrush and other toiletries. My mother was told that I
> would be taken to a concentration camp. . . .
>
> At the police station, I had to countersign the protective custody
> order for my arrest, and I was then imprisoned for about a month until
> a transport for Oranienburg-Sachsenhausen could be consolidated.
> Beatings had already started during the transport. We wondered, "What
> will become of us, and where had we landed?" Everything was utterly
> new and strange.
>
> We stood in the grim cold in Sachsenhausen for five hours—it was
> winter—and were then delivered to the Political Department. There an
> SS Technical Sergeant informed me that since I was a Gypsy, my trans-
> fer to this concentration camp was the end of the road for me, that it
> was a one-way street with no way back out. There, for the first time in

my life, I saw shrunken heads like the ones made by headhunters, but these were Gypsy heads. They stood on a sideboard in the Political Department.

We were then taken to a barrack, where every hair on our bodies was shorn and shaven off. We were next taken to the bath, an ice cold shower. We were compelled to hand over all of our clothing and in return received prisoner uniforms—zebra uniforms. I wore size 39 shoes and was given size 43. By this time, we all looked a bit odd. The beating began when we arrived back in the barracks. There were already Sinti prisoners in this camp and I knew a few of them. They had connections to the clothing depot and arranged for me to get half-way decent clothing. A brown triangle had been sewn onto my prison uniform, because I had been classified an antisocial. [The inverted brown or beige triangle was the special marking used to identify Gypsy prisoners; it was frequently replaced by the more common black triangle for Roma and Sinti prisoners reclassified as "asocials" in the concentration camps.]

We were then separated into different work groups. We carried stones that were to be used in construction and had to move everything at double time. We had to carry hundred-weight sacks, two at a time. Anyone not able to do this had signed his own death warrant because SS guards kicked him mercilessly with their rubber boots. Out of a work commando of a hundred men, thirty to forty were often gone by the end of the day. . . .

[In mid-March 1942], we were transferred to work in a rock quarry in Gross Rosen concentration camp; we often worked until midnight on the construction of the camp. We slept four men to a blanket. The windows had not yet been installed in our barracks, and when we awoke in the morning, there was often snow on our blankets.

Our rations were a piece of bread, which had at best thirty percent flour; the rest consisted of ground chestnuts and sawdust. Afternoons turnips, evenings coffee. We had to save some of our breakfast bread for evening, and we then got one cube of margarine for sixty people. The result of this bad food was dysentery. For medicine, there was carbon or chalk tablets, and this white substance had to be taken by spoon. The result was zero, nothing whatsoever. The majority of prisoners died. A transport of five to six thousand prisoners was completely used up in eight weeks.

I, too, had typhus and at one point weighed only seventy-eight pounds. A friend managed to have me transferred to the kitchen, where I peeled potatoes. There I did not have to work as hard, and I received a half-liter more to eat per day. That's how I recovered from that disease. Otherwise typhus meant a death sentence. The crematorium could not keep up. We had mountains of ashes which were used to fertilize fields. Whenever a German prisoner died, the camp notified his relatives. These notices were of course pre-printed forms. They usually stated that the cause of death was due to a generally weakened condition or heart failure. For twenty marks, the family could receive the ashes of the deceased in an urn. . . .

At Gross Rosen, the Sinti were not housed together in a separate barracks, but you could tell who they were by their triangular marking. . . . As Gypsies, we could not be appointed to any prisoner posts. I was, however, the only Sinti who kept the barracks register for the *Lagerältesten* [camp elder]. It worked as follows: The block leader, a prisoner, received his assignment from the camp elder, who in turn reported to the SS. The SS appointed the prisoners to clean the barracks. The members of this work crew were responsible for order and cleanliness in the barracks, reporting to the block leader. The SS made it easy for themselves. If anything untoward occurred, punishments descended down the hierarchy; the SS would beat the camp elder, who in turn would beat the barracks elders, then the barracks elder would in turn beat the room elder, and then the room elder would beat the prisoners.

My block elder had been brought up in a juvenile care program, starting in special schools and homes and then in prison. Whenever he wanted to write home, I had to write these letters for him, but never received any benefits for doing this. A German prisoner could become a capo, a room elder, a block elder, or even a messenger to the Political Department. No Sinto could get any of these posts. . . .

I was in Gross Rosen until 1943 and was then transferred to a satellite camp, a chemical plant owned by BASF at Dyhrenfurth near Breslau. There were three hundred prisoners in the small camp at this factory. The factory produced poisonous gas for weapons: bombs, grenades, these were the Führer's last weapons. Many prisoners became unconscious and died while filling these weapons. We were almost blinded by our work, and tiny little pills were placed in our eyes to dilate the iris so we could continue to see. Because we worked with these weapons, we were sworn to secrecy. I was not allowed to tell any of the other prisoners anything about my work. And because I knew these secrets, I had a double sense of despair and hopelessness that the Nazis would not allow me to survive.

When Lodz was liberated by the Russians on 2 January 1945, we were evacuated and had to march seventy kilometers in wooden clogs back to Gross Rosen. Prisoners too exhausted to survive the march were shot. The main camp at Gross Rosen was filled beyond capacity, since all the satellite camps had been reassembled at the main camp. After a brief stop at Gross Rosen, we were marched to Striegau. . . . I will never forget that march. Women standing along the road threw stones and other objects at us, calling us "pigs." At Striegau we were loaded onto open freight cars, but the locomotive did not arrive and we were forced to march back to Gross Rosen through the night. Two to three hundred prisoners were crammed into a barrack normally assigned to one hundred prisoners; we stood packed together like sardines in a box.

In the middle of the night, the barracks were lit up when the camp came under attack. The Russians had probably learned that the prisoners had been evacuated, but were unaware that the prisoners had been forced to return that night. We pushed the window panes out and sought safety from the shelling outside. We saw many wounded and dead lying everywhere. The next morning the transport to Striegau was reassembled. Every hundred prisoners were placed in open freight cars, seated adjacent to grenades that were tied together. We collected snow from the edge of the train car in order to moisten our lips, since we had not received any water all day. We travelled for six days in those open freight cars from Gross Rosen via Dresden to Litomerice in Czechoslovakia; the latter camp was located four kilometers [2.4 miles] from Theresienstadt. By then, there were only thirteen prisoners left in my car.

We arrived at the camp, a former barracks already occupied by Czech and Polish prisoners. The bunk beds consisted of ten levels of boxes and since the lower tiers were already occupied, a weak prisoner could not climb that high. Our block elder from Gross Rosen arranged that we were sent to a small satellite camp called Elsabe. The prisoners worked 150 meters [490 feet] deep in subterranean mine tunnels completing tank motors for the Elsabe Company of Chemnitz. . . . After

two months there, I learned from a guard that the tunnels were mined
and would be blown up along with the prisoners to prevent these motors from falling into enemy hands. . . .

A German Sinto from Nuremberg, whose name is deleted to protect his
privacy, narrates his ordeal with phosgene gas experiments at Natzweiler-
Struthof concentration camp in the excerpt "I was a Guinea Pig," published
in Jürgen Ziegler, ed., *Mitten unter uns; Natzweiler-Struthof: Spuren eines
Konzentrationsagers* [In our midst; Natzweiler-Struthof: Traces of a concentration camp] (Hamburg, 1986, pp. 96–98; reproduced with the permission of VSA Verlag):

On 8 March 1943 our entire family was arrested. We were sent to the
Nuremberg prison and then to the concentration camp at Auschwitz.
Auschwitz was a nasty camp. We were frequently beaten and had to do
heavy labor. The death toll was high. One day, ninety volunteers were
requested for construction work in Germany. We reported since conditions couldn't be worse than here at Auschwitz.

More people reported than were selected. They took only young
men who still had some strength left. We were taken from Auschwitz to
Rothau in cattle cars. From there we traveled by truck uphill to Struthof.
Our transport was divided into two groups: forty-five men had to share
a small room with three tier bunk beds; each bed was occupied by two
men. We had to hand over all of our clothing and received only a night
shirt and wooden shoes. We lived in this room for a while. Then the
medical experiments began. By then, we regretted volunteering and
said "not one of us will come out of here alive." . . . Meanwhile we
learned that previously at Struthof, not even one women among the
ninety who had been subjected to medical experiments had survived.

One day we were informed that physicians would come to inocu-
late us. We were told that we shouldn't be afraid, since antidote shots
would also be distributed. The physicians in their white coats arrived
and we had to march past them with goose steps. I received an injection in my upper left arm. Everyone became ill with high fevers. One
person went mad hitting his head repeatedly with his wooden clogs
until he died after several days. He was not the only person to go crazy
after these experiments. At first I was spared from the high fevers. The
others couldn't eat anything because of high fevers. Several people died

in our room. When the others were improving, I had a high fever and was bathed in sweat for several days, but I survived. We were not forced to work in the camp during these medical experiments, but were isolated and prohibited from leaving our room. The experiments lasted from fall 1943 to spring 1944. After this, we were compelled to work in the camp. We had to cart away waste from the latrines. The carts had to be pulled up the mountain. . . .

One day a transport for Neckarelz was assembled. [Neckarelz contained two satellite labor camps for male prisoners from Natzweiler and existed from 21 March 1944 to late March 1945.] Everyone reported for labor. Since I didn't want to remain in Natzweiler, where I feared I would die of lethal injections or be forced to participate in phosgene gas experiments, I volunteered for Neckarelz. . . .

We were taken to Neckarelz by train and housed in a school. The school was surrounded by barbed wire. I was, however, too weak to work. When we reported for roll call, the other prisoners assisted me. I was also carried to work in the tunnels. I tried to hide whenever I could. One day a prisoner physician who occasionally visited the school informed me: "I can no longer keep your [condition] secret and will have to send you back to Natzweiler." Since I was too weak to work loading stones onto trucks in the tunnels, I was sent back to Natzweiler. I was immediately placed in a large room with perhaps 100 other prisoners, they were ill with tuberculosis. They died like flies: in front of me, behind me, and next to me. Here I met a prisoner physician to whom I owe my life. He was French. He concluded that my illness was not that severe and that he could help me. Once I was a bit better, I was moved to another room. One day, we were informed that all Gypsies in the camp had to report. We were taken to the gas chamber in Struthof. Many of us were taken to that gas chamber. Before I entered it, an SS doctor gave me an injection. . . . The interior of the gas chamber had white tiles. I had previously heard that there were gas experiments on prisoners at Struthof. One of the other prisoners said to me: "If you are sent inside, you should urinate on your handkerchief, hold it to your mouth, and lie down next to the door sill." I couldn't really imagine this, but in any case I followed those instructions. When I entered, I took a towel scrap on which I had urinated, held it firmly to my nose and mouth, and placed myself as low as possible by the door sill. After a while, the door was opened and I stumbled out. Even today, I don't know how I survived. Perhaps I was lucky, perhaps it was the injection, or maybe they had used too little gas. At any rate, I emerged from the gas chamber and reentered the camp. I stayed there until late summer 1944, when the camp was evacuated to Dachau. The Americans arrived [at Dachau] on 29 April 1945 and we were liberated. . . .

The report by Anna P., née Schopper, born in 1926 in Dortmund details her experiences in the Gypsy family compound BIIe at Auschwitz-Birkenau from mid-March 1943 to early summer 1944. It is excerpted in the published catalog of the Dortmund municipal Holocaust memorial: Günther Högl, ed., *Widerstand und Verfolgung in Dortmund, 1933–1945: Katalog zur ständigen Ausstellung des Stadtarchivs Dortmund in der Mahn- und Gedenkstätte Steinwache* (Dortmund: Wittmaack Verlag, 1992), pp. 440; reproduced with permission from the Stadtarchiv Dortmund:

I was deported to Auschwitz as a 16 year old girl together with my mother and nine brothers and sisters. The journey from Dortmund lasted several days and was horrible. We were packed together in cattle cars and received almost nothing to eat and drink. We reached Auschwitz on 14 March 1943. On arrival, we were immediately forced to hand over the few things we had been allowed to take with us; they even seized our clothing and shoes. We were shaved and tattooed; I was assigned number Z 2964. Housing consisted of barracks without windows and with very few air vents. There was barely any possibility to bathe and there was never any soap. The bathrooms—simple outhouse toilets—mocked every description. It was ghastly.

I had to work on road construction crews together with other women; we hammered the pavement level and hauled stones. Frequently, we were whipped to force us to continue working.

Provisions were catastrophic. One small loaf of bread was divided into eight portions; we had to make do with one portion bread, a small pat of margarine, and a minuscule quantity of turnip greens. For lunch we were fed turnip stock. We were always hungry and grew steadily weaker. Many died from exhaustion and illness, especially from typhus. I got sick with dysentery and felt wretched. There were no drugs. I was compelled to eat charcoal, a by-product of the wood burning stoves in the barracks and thus perhaps survived that illness.

I later worked in the kitchen and recovered a bit. Since I was able to work, I was transferred in early summer 1944 together with my sister to a munitions plant in Zwodau/ Graslitz [today respectively called Svatava and Kraslice in Czechoslovakia; the 1944 site of a subsidiary labor camp of Flossenbürg concentration camp]. It was there, totally emaciated and at the end of my strength, that I was liberated.

Elisabeth Guttenberger, a German Sintezza, was born in Stuttgart in 1926 and completed eight years of primary school there. She attributes her survival at Auschwitz to her earlier education that resulted in her assignment to a camp office. Together with four brothers and sisters, she had previously lived "in a very beautiful part of Stuttgart with many gardens and parks. My father earned his living with antiques and stringed instruments. We lived peacefully together with our neighbours." Arrested and deported to Auschwitz-Birkenau in early March 1943, she was given prisoner number Z-3991. She describes resistance by the prisoners of the Birkenau Gypsy family camp (BIIe) in mid-May 1944 and the liquidation of BIIe in early August 1944, resulting in her transfer on 1 August 1944 to Ravensbrück concentration camp. Elisabeth Guttenberger has told her story in many books, including H. G. Adler, Hermann Langbein, and Ella Lingens-Reiner, ed., *Auschwitz: Zeugnisse und Berichte* [Auschwitz: Testimony and reports], 3rd rev. exp. ed. (Frankfurt: Europäische Verlagsanstalt, 1984), 131–134. Her narrative was republished in German, Polish, and English languages in: Auschwitz-Birkenau State Museum and Documentation and Cultural Center of German Sinti and Roma, Heidelberg, ed., *Memorial Book: The Gypsies at Auschwitz-Birkenau*, 2 vols. (Munich, London, New York, and Paris: K.G. Saur, 1993), 2, pp. 1497–1503; reproduced with permission from Elisabeth Guttenberger and the Dokumentations- und Kulturzentrum Deutscher Sinti und Roma, Heidelberg. Her published account in the *Memorial Book* has been reedited by Sybil Milton to include additional material from Guttenberger's earlier published accounts:

> Gypsies, like the Jews, were persecuted for racial reasons. All Gypsies that could be found were deported to Auschwitz, without consideration for their profession or trade, whether they had fixed domiciles or not. . . . As a 17 year old girl, I was arrested . . . and taken to Auschwitz.
> . . . We were arrested in March 1943. At 6 o'clock in the morning the police came and took us away in a truck. I was then seventeen. I was deported to Auschwitz together with my parents, four brothers

and sisters, a three year old niece, my 80 year old grandmother, and many other relatives. My other grandmother came somewhat later with her daughter and nine grandchildren. . . .

The first impression I had of Auschwitz was horrible. It was already dark when we arrived. A huge tract of land, although one was able to see only the lights. We had to spend the night on the floor of a huge hall. Early the next morning we had to march into the camp. There, prisoner numbers were tattooed on our arms and our hair was cut off. The clothes, shoes, and the few things we still had with us were taken away. The Gypsy camp was in the Birkenau section, located between the men's camp and the prisoners' infirmary [*Häftlingskrankenbau*]. In this section were thirty barracks which were called blocks. One block served as the toilet for the entire camp. More than 20,000 Gypsies were kept in the rest of the barracks. The barracks had no windows, only air vents. The floor was made out of clay. In one barrack, where there was enough room for perhaps 200 people, 800 or more people were lodged. This way of housing so many people was a horrible martyrdom. My aunt walked next to me. We looked at each other and tears began to roll down our faces. . . . It was dreadful. The people sat motionless on their plank beds and just stared at us. I thought I was dreaming. I thought I was in hell.

After about fourteen days, we were divided into work gangs. With many other women, I was forced to carry heavy stones for construction work in the camp. The men were forced to build the camp road. Even old men, whether they were sick or not, had to work. . . . Everyone was used. My father was then 61. No one paid any attention to that. . . . Auschwitz was a death camp.

At that time, the construction of Birkenau had not yet been finished. The worst part was the hunger. The hygienic conditions are barely describable. There was virtually no soap or facilities for washing. When typhus broke out, the sick could not be treated, because there was no medicine. It was hell. One cannot imagine anything more horrifying. First the children died. They cried day and night for bread. Soon they all starved to death. The children who were born in Auschwitz did not live long either. The only thing the Nazis were concerned with was that the newborn were properly tattooed and registered. Most infants died several days after their births. There was no child care, no milk, no warm water, let alone powder or diapers. The older children, above the age of ten, had to carry rocks for the camp road, despite the fact that starvation caused them to die every day. . . .

In our labor brigade, we had to do everything while running. An SS *Blockführer* accompanied us by bicycle. If a woman tripped, because she was too frail, she was whipped. Many died from those beatings. The Blockführer in charge of the Gypsy camp was an SS Corporal [Ernst August] König; I never heard that he was tried or sentenced after the war. Even today, I could identify him immediately. [König was belatedly arraigned and indicted for murders he had committed in the Birkenau Gypsy camp and after a trial lasting nearly two years was sentenced to life imprisonment in January 1991 in the Siegen District Court. He subsequently committed suicide in prison after his appeal was rejected.]

Early morning roll calls were torture, standing at attention from 6 to 8 in the morning irrespective of weather. Everyone had to assemble for roll call, even the elderly, the children, and the sick. On Sunday, roll calls often lasted until noon, often standing in harsh heat without protective head covering. Many collapsed from heat prostration and infirmities.

After my first month in Auschwitz, a transport with 2,000 Russian Gypsies arrived. These poor people were in the camp for only one night. They were sent to the crematoria and gassed the next day. Everyone, however short their stay in Birkenau, asked about the chimneys that produced smoke all night and all day. They were told that people were gassed and burned there. On the evening that the Russian Gypsies were gassed, the barracks were secured and we were forced to remain in our barracks [*Blocksperre*]. At about nine that evening, trucks arrived at our compound and the Russian Gypsies were forcibly shoved aboard and driven to the crematoria. I secretly witnessed their departure.

I was also an eyewitness to another gassing operation. I had already been assigned to work in the camp clerical office and was permitted to walk outside our barracks. The so-called sick camp [*Krankenlager*] was adjacent to our barracks. Jewish and Polish male prisoners were incarcerated there. I observed two trucks driving up to their barracks and the sick were thrown on board. Many could no longer walk and were starved skeletons. A few were naked; others had only a shirt. Before the trucks departed, a few prisoners mustered enough courage to curse their murderers.

After about a half year, I was put to work in a camp clerical office. There I had to file note cards for the transport lists, and was placed in charge of the main men's register for our camp. I had to enter the death notices brought in from the infirmary. I entered thousands of names into that book. I had been in the office for just eight days when a death notice with my father's name arrived. I was paralyzed and tears streamed down my face. At that moment, the door swung open and SS Staff Sergeant Plagge stormed in and screamed, "Why is she blubbering in the corner?" I could not answer. My friend, a clerk named Lilly Weiss, said "her father died." In response Plagge said "We all have to die," and left the office. . . .

The Gypsies also tried to defend themselves against the liquidation of the Gypsy camp. That was a very tragic story. The Gypsies made weapons out of sheet metal. They sharpened the metal into knives. With these improvised weapons and clubs, they tried to defend themselves as best they could. I know an eyewitness, a Polish woman named Zita, who worked across from us and lived through the liquidation of the Gypsy camp. Later, she told me how the Gypsies hit out and defended themselves, because they knew that they were going to be gassed. The resisters were mowed down with machine guns. . . .

In 1944, about 2,000 Gypsies able to perform labor were deported from our compound; about 4,500 people were left behind. These were the elderly, the sick, and those no longer able to perform heavy labor. These people were "liquidated," as the SS called it, during the night of 31 July to 1 August 1944. Of the 30,000 Gypsies deported to Auschwitz, only about 3,000 survived. I know these figures because I worked in the camp office.

I lost about thirty of my relatives in Auschwitz. Both of my grandmothers died there. An aunt with ten children was there, only two children survived. . . . My father literally starved to death in the first few months. My older sister contracted typhus and died in 1943. Naturally, malnutrition and hunger were significant factors. Then my youngest brother died at the age of thirteen. He had to carry heavy rocks until he was an emaciated skeleton. My mother died of starvation several months afterwards. Auschwitz cannot be compared to anything else. To say, "the hell of Auschwitz" is not an exaggeration. . . .

I left the camp ill and am still sick today. I would like to remove the prisoner number tattooed on my lower left forearm. When I wear summer clothing without sleeves, I always cover this number. I have noticed that people stare at this tattooed number and often make malicious and vicious comments, thus always reminding me of the hellish camp experiences. . . .

There are few survivor reports about the killing fields of occupied Poland and the Soviet Union, where Jews and Gypsies were executed in forests, drowned in local rivers, and killed inside many ghettos, labor camps, and killing centers. Several eyewitness accounts by local residents are excerpted in Polish postwar regional publications as well as in the materials assembled by postwar Polish judicial authorities. These extracts provide us with some insight about the fate of Gypsies deported from various Polish ghettos to Treblinka or killed in Polish fields and forests. The narrative by Michael Chodźko, a former prisoner at the Treblinka labor camp, was initially published in his article "The Gypsies in Treblinka," *Rzeczpospolita* [The Republic], Lublin, no. 35, 6 September 1945) and was reproduced in Jerzy Ficowski's book, *Cyganie na polskich drogach: Wydanie trzecie poprawione i rozszerzone* [Gypsies on the Roads of Poland], 3rd rev. exp. ed. (Cracow and Wroclaw: Literary Publishing House, 1965), pp. 125–126:

In the spring of 1942, Gypsies . . . were locked up within the narrow walls of Jewish ghettos. The death penalty was threatened for leaving the ghetto and not wearing the armband with the letter Z [*Zigeuner*, Gypsy]. Until the fall of 1942, Gypsies were hauled off along with Jews to the killing centers at Majdanek, Treblinka, and others, where they were killed in the gas chambers, or else shot, and their bodies later burned. Despite the walls and barbed wire closing off the Jewish quarters, groups of Gypsies succeeded in temporarily getting outside the ghettos. The Germans sent Gypsies to the "labor camp" at Treblinka with assurances that they would like it in the camp especially organized for them in the forest. . . . They arrived in Treblinka to set up "their camp." The march was halted at the edge of the forest which was the place of execution and the grave for hundreds of thousands of people. Trustingly, the crowd sat down in a meadow; they were allowed to light a fire, over which they prepared hot meals. A few hours later the SS arrived, and the men were separated from the women and children. Their possessions and baggage were piled up in one big heap. The men were led off deeper into the forest. . . . They were forced into a pit a hundred at a time, and then machine-gunned. The Gypsies who were still alive were forced to bury those who had been shot—and who were often only wounded—before they themselves were pushed into the pit, and a hundred people more were deprived of their lives in the clatter of machine-gun fire. The bodies were covered with a shallow layer of earth. . . . When the men were taken away, the Gypsy women did not know what had happened to them, but when they heard the constant gun fire, they began to scream and wail. The Nazis at that point ceased to dissemble: they no longer spoke of a "Gypsy camp" and encouraged the soldiers to begin a brutal massacre. They seized babies from their mothers and killed the infants by bashing their heads against trees. With whips and cudgels the SS covered with blows the women who had been driven insane by the spectacle. The women threw themselves at the soldiers and tried to wrest their babies away. This scene was only brought to an end by salvos of gunfire from the surrounding SS and soldiers. The bodies of the executed women and children were later cleared by other prisoners specially brought in for that purpose; the corpses were taken to graves that had been prepared beforehand in an adjacent forest.

An Austrian Roma survivor Leopoldine Papai, then thirty-six years old, was interviewed in 1966 in her modest home on the outskirts of Vienna by Selma Steinmetz for a project of the Documentation Archives of the Austrian Resistance, Vienna. Excerpts from this interview were reprinted in Selma Steinmetz, *Österreichs Zigeuner im NS-Staat* [Austria's Gypsies under the Nazis] (Vienna, Frankfurt, and Zurich: Europa Verlag, 1966), pp. 40–41; reproduced with permission of the Dokumen-tationsarchiv des österreichischen Widerstandes, Vienna:

My father was the village blacksmith in Holzschlag. Many Gypsies lived there in 1938. And we were permanent residents, not like now [living] at the edge of town. We were then a large family with nine children; three of my brothers were already married and had many children. My married sister also had four children, when the persecutions began. Already in 1941, they took my father, three brothers, and two sisters to Sindisdorf near Pinkafeld. Two brothers and a sister were deported to Litzmannstadt [the Lodz ghetto] and were never heard from again. My parents and my other siblings were sent back home after two days and their ration cards were returned to them.

However, the SS returned in April 1943. My father was then above the age of sixty. I was still a child, only 14; my youngest sister was four years younger. We were deported in cattle cars. If our town officials had been consulted, we would certainly have been allowed to remain at home. The mayor had tears in his eyes, when we last saw him. We petitioned to be allowed to remain at home. The residents assuredly needed a blacksmith like my father. This is why we had initially been allowed to stay. But by April 1943, it was too late and no pleas would have helped. We were forced to leave.

We were sent directly to Auschwitz with a large transport and were immediately driven to heavy labor. [Steinmetz notes that the Auschwitz Calendarium of 16 April 1943 records the registration of 1,847 Austrian Gypsies arriving at Auschwitz, and that Leopoldine Papai was assigned the number Z-7706.] I had to carry 10 kg. [22 lbs.] of heavy stones. I also witnessed how Jews were sent to the gas chambers. We observed how they undressed. . . .

My parents were killed in Auschwitz, my father died of typhus. In the fall of 1944 . . . there were no longer any Gypsies in our large camp. We were told that they had all been sent to the gas chambers.

Shortly thereafter, my sister and I—together with many Jews— were sent to Ravensbrück. Many on this transport were shot, many died. After eight months, we were again deported, initially to Mauthausen and later to Bergen-Belsen. That was the worst. There was absolutely nothing to eat there and we slept on the bare ground. The British freed us in Bergen-Belsen.

There are only two of us alive out of 36 family members; my sister and I. . . . I have lung problems because of the camps and will probably never be completely healthy.

The former Austrian political prisoner Johann Breirather wrote to the Federal Association of the Austrian Resistance and the Victims of Fascism on 21 February 1961 about the fate of his foster daughter, the Roma child Sidonie Adlersburg. Sidonie Adlersburg's tragic childhood was also narrated in a popular Austrian television dramatization entitled *Requiem for Sidonie*, directed by Karin Brandauer in 1990. This text by Sidonie's foster father is preserved in the Documentation Archives of the Austrian Resistance (DÖW), file 668:

Post Neuzeug 200, Upper Austria
Neuzeug, 21 February 1961

Dear Comrades!

Our family read in the newspapers that Franz Hofer, former Gauleiter of the Tyrol, was arraigned. I would now like to record the following:

In 1933, we accepted a foster child with dark skin from the child welfare office. Ostensibly the mother had abandoned this child, but we never learned more precise information. These are the circumstances of how we obtained this child. Her name was Sidonie Adlersburg and she was presumably of Gypsy descent.

We considered her a member of our family along with our two other children. Everyone, except for racial fanatics, was fond of this child with her amusing manner.

In the fall of 1942, we were repeatedly told by the Steyr district child welfare office that our Sidonie would be sent to a children's home. We appeared several times at the child welfare office in order to keep this child. We don't want to describe those difficult times. At the end of February 1943, the child welfare office informed us that they had ostensibly located the child's mother. The mother was in Hopfgarten in the Tyrol. On 10 March 1943, a nurse from the Steyr child welfare office took Sidonie to Hopfgarten. We were not convinced that the mother had actually been found. After the collapse of the Third Reich, I became a communal official of Sierning and with American permission, telephoned Hopfgarten. I learned that Gypsies of all ages had been assembled and deported from Hopfgarten and that the children were deported last. This transport, which included our Sidonie, was sent to Auschwitz in Poland. After 1945 we learned from the Steyr district child welfare office that according to a nurse from Vienna, who had herself been a prisoner at Auschwitz, Sidonie Adlersburg was infected with typhus bacilli and had then been gassed. I will end my report here.

Comrades, I was a political prisoner during the years 1933–1934 and this fact is officially certified in document no. 243 issued to me by the Upper Austrian state government.

We are not screaming for revenge, but everyone responsible for the death of others should be held accountable before a court of law. If former Gauleiter Franz Hofer is responsible for the deportation of Gyp-

sies and people of color from all of Austria, he should be placed on trial.
I am enclosing a photograph [of Sidonie] for your documentation.

With fraternal greetings,

[signed] Johann Breirather

An official statement by the Austrian Roma, Maria Kohlberger, on 3 May 1948 at the Linz district administration [*Bezirkshauptmannschaft*] tells of her inability to work as a commercial exhibitor, her assignment to forced labor, and the death of most of her family in several concentration camps. Her statement reveals the failure of postwar restitution to Roma and Sinti Holocaust victims. Maria Kohlberger's affidavit is found in the Documentation Archives of the Austrian Resistance (DÖW), Vienna, file 13457:

> Ms. Maria Kohlberger, born on 25 March 1909 in Buch, Lower Austria, Austrian citizen, commercial exhibitor, residing at Ödt 34, Traun, records the following statement at the Linz district administration office on 3 May 1948:
>
> Until 1938, I held a license as a commercial exhibitor. With the incorporation of Austria in the German Reich, this license was rescinded, since as a descendant of Gypsies I was unable to document that I was Aryan. Since that time, I was constantly under Gestapo surveillance. I was assigned to conscript labor in the Göring armament factory, was not allowed to leave the city, and was not deported to a concentration camp, since my employers reported that I was a good worker.
>
> My mother Cäcilie Kohlberger died in Auschwitz. My brother Julius Kohlberger, together with his three children, perished at Dachau. My sister Albine Rosenfeld died together with her eight children in Litzmannstadt (Lodz), only because they were not Aryans.
>
> I suffered severe injury as a racial persecutee under the terms of the Victims Welfare Law (*Opferfürsorgegesetz*). All professional items were confiscated from my sister Albine Rosenfeld, who was also a licensed commercial exhibitor. I have never received restitution for all impounded articles related to the practice of my licensed trade. Police official Neudorfer at the police presidium in Linz can confirm these facts. I am therefore requesting under paragraph 4 of the Victims Welfare Law that all objects urgently needed to reestablish my business be returned to me. . . .

Chapter Seven
Holocaust: Disabled Peoples

Hugh Gregory Gallagher

Aktion T-4 Euthanasie: Summary of Program

In the late 1930s and throughout World War II, physicians of Germany's medical establishment, acting both with and without the acquiescence of the Nazi government, systematically killed their severely disabled and chronically mentally ill patients. These people were said by their doctors to be "useless eaters"—persons with "lives not worth living."

The officially sanctioned killing program, begun in 1939, was called "Euthanasie" although most of its victims were neither terminally ill nor in unbearable pain, nor were they anxious to die. The program's proponents advanced various arguments in its justification—compassion, eugenics, economics, racial purity. The official program was halted by Hitler in the summer of 1941, in the face of a rising wave of protests from disabled people, their families and friends, and religious officials. Even so, many doctors, acting largely on their own counsel, continued killing patients in hospitals and institutions throughout Germany.

Over the course of the official program and the unofficial so-called runaway euthanasia which followed it, more than two hundred thousand German citizens met their death at the hands of their physicians. The mass murder techniques developed in the euthanasia hospitals were later utilized against Jews.

Aktion T-4 Euthanasie: Operation—To Whom, by Whom, How, and Why?

In the fall of 1939 at the successful conclusion of the Polish campaign, Adolf Hitler signed an order that read, in toto, "Reichsleiter Bouhler and Dr. Brandt, M.D., are charged with the responsibility of enlarging the authority of certain physicians to be designated by name in such a manner that persons who, according to human judgment, are incurable can, upon a most careful diagnosis of their condition of sickness, be accorded a mercy death" (U.S. Nuremberg War Crimes Trials, November 21, 1946–August 20, 1947 [National Archives Microfilm Publications], M887, Tape 17, Doc. 630–PS).

Hitler and Brandt together worked most carefully on the wording of the order. Brandt felt that it was impossible for a doctor to say with absolute certainty that a patient was incurable, and that, therefore, a certain leeway was required. But Hitler, who distrusted doctors after the death of his mother from cancer, did not wish to give them too much leeway; he insisted upon adding, "Upon the most careful diagnosis of their (the patients') condition of sickness." Brandt gave this account in his testimony at Nuremberg. He emphasized repeatedly that the order was not an order to kill; it was instead an authorization to specifically designated physicians allowing them to act if, in their judgment after "the most careful diagnosis," the patient is "incurably sick." The physicians were given a license to kill; they were not directed to do so (Mitscherlich, 1962, p. 265).

Dr. Brandt and the chief of Hitler's Chancellery, Philip Bouhler, set to work implementing the order. Bouhler's deputy, Viktor Brack, would handle administrative details; and three other men were placed in charge of policy formulation and operation. All three were physicians: Dr. med. Herbert Linden, who held the sub-Cabinet level position of Chancellor in charge of all sanatoria and nursing homes within the Department of Interior, Professor Heyde and his deputy Professor Nitsche, who served as the chief medical experts of the euthanasia program. Heyde had held the position of Professor of Psychiatry at the University of Wurzburg and was head of the University Clinic for Nervous Diseases (Amir, 1977, p. 183). The new operation was housed in an imposing Berlin villa, address Tiergartenstrasse 4, and for this reason the program came to be known as Aktion T-4.

Three corporations were set up to handle the actual operation of the program. These were given purposely vague and misleading names:

- Allgemeine Stiftung für Anstaltwesen: The "Foundation for the Care of Institutions in the Public Interest" handled the budgetary and financial aspects of the program—the costs of which were not small.
- Reichsarbeitsgemeinschaft Heil- und Pflegeanstalten: The "National Group for Study of Sanitoria and Nursing Homes" was charged with the actual administration of the program—the National Group

developed the selection criteria, prepared the questionnaires, provided administrative support for the review committees, and actually operated the terminal "observation institutions."

- Gemeinnützige Krankentransportgesellschaft: the "Limited Company for the Transport of Invalids in the Public Interest," which
organized and operated a unique, complex system for moving tens
of thousands of the sick and helpless about the countryside.

Concurrently established, although separately administered, was the
"Reich Committee for Research on Hereditary and Constitutional Severe
Diseases." This committee was charged with "assisting the dissolution" of
mentally afflicted, severely handicapped, or "idiotic" children. The authority under which this last committee functioned was a decree issued by the
Ministry of the Interior on August 1938, which in fact predated Hitler's
euthanasia order.

Both before and after Hitler's order of September 1939, secret meetings were held across Germany. At these meetings, the leading psychiatrists,
physicians, and medical professors were carefully briefed on the new euthanasia program. Euphemisms were used to describe the program: "negative
population policies" was mass killing; "refractory therapy cases" were disabled people targeted for killing; "specialist childrens wards" were children
killing centers; and "final medical assistance" was, of course, murder. There
was never a doubt as to what was being discussed.

These men were told the euthanasia program was a part of the "break-
through campaign" necessary to obtain the new medicine of the Third Reich.
This held that medical attention and money should go, on a cost-benefit
analysis, to those who can be brought back to full productive health, while
the chronically disabled would be removed from society as, said Dr. F. Klein,
"I would remove the purulent appendix from a diseased body" (Hanauske-
Able, 1986, p. 271).

In both the minutes of the "Reich Committee for the Scientific Registration of Serious Illnesses of Hereditary or Protonic Origin"—a high-level
physician's committee which met regularly with the Reich Chancellory—
and in the reports of the briefing meetings with rank and file physicians, it
was fiercely argued that the radical modernization of therapeutic activity
cannot be achieved without, and, in fact, must go hand-in-hand with, the
elimination of these "refractory therapy cases" (Aly and Roth, 1984, p. 148).

There can be no doubt the existence and operation of the euthanasia program was general knowledge within the medical community of the wartime Reich.

* * *

Aktion T-4 officials moved quickly to institutionalize the authority Hitler had given them. They appointed between ten and fifteen doctors chosen for their "political reliability" to act as assessors. Above them were appointed review committees of chief surveyors made up of university professors of psychiatry and medicine.

An organizing conference was called in which the professors of psychiatry and the chairmen of the departments of psychiatry at the medical schools of the universities of Berlin, Heidelberg, Bonn, and Würzburg were participants. Continuing meetings of this oversight group were conducted on a quarterly basis under the direction of the professor of psychiatry at Heidelberg (Wertham, 1968, p. 168).

"The Reich Committee" oversaw the preparation of a questionnaire designed to elicit the information it regarded useful in determining which persons were "worthy of help," and which were "useless lives," candidates for "final medical assistance." An instruction leaflet was also drawn up, giving detailed directions on how the questionnaire was to be answered. Many thousands of copies were printed by the Reich Minister of the Interior. These were distributed to the long-term hospitals, sanitoria, and asylums, along with a covering letter from Dr. Conti, Chancellor of Sanatoria and Nursing Homes, saying that a form in full must be completed for each patient by the attending physician. The information was to be typewritten with three carbons. The forms should be filled out at once, explained Conti's letter, owing to "the necessity for a systematized economic plan for hospitals and nursing institutions." At the briefings, confusion had been expressed over who was to be covered by the program. This confusion was certainly not relieved by Conti's letter, the questionnaire, or the instruction pamphlet. This material does, indeed, provide a puzzling and imprecise picture of what facts were sought or for what purpose.

The pamphlet contained a list of qualifying illnesses which was so general as to be virtually all inclusive of patients in long-term care facilities. The terms "insanity," "imbecility," "paralysis," "chronic diseases," and "senile maladies" are not narrow.

There were three full questions on the patient's work, ability, and experience—more than on any other topic. There were but two questions related to genetic theory—did the patient have a twin? Did he have blood relatives of unsound mind? The twin question was easy enough to answer, but the term "unsound mind" was so general as to be meaningless. No conclusions about the genetic origins of the patients' conditions could be drawn from such sketchy information.

Speaking in medical terms, the form was a trivial business. As a witness testified at the Nuremberg "Doctors Trial," "On the basis of the questionnaires it was impossible for experts or top experts to form an exact medical opinion on the physical state of the patients" (U.S. Nuremberg War Crimes Trials, M887, Tape 17, No. 617).

The physicians of the appraisal committee reviewed the information contained in each of the questionnaires, and determined which of the patients should live and which should die. Originally, a death warrant required the approval of all members of the appraisal committee. However, as the program came into operation, a majority of two out of three or three out of four members was usually sufficient.

The decisions of the appraising physicians were gathered and forwarded to a senior expert—usually a professor and head of a medical department at one of the major universities. Final decision would be made by this senior expert. Names of the patients to be killed were then routed to Doctor Herbert Linden, who worked in conjunction with the General Patient Transport Company to arrange for the pickup and carriage of the selected patients from the nationwide array of mental institutions, nursing homes, and long-term facilities to the euthanasia institutions. There were six major euthanasia institutions. T-4 referred to them by letter. They were:

A. Grafeneck, in the Black Forest, southwest of Ulm
B. The "old jail" at Brandenberg, near the hospital at Gorden, southwest of Berlin
C. Hartheim, northwest of Linz in Austria
D. Bernberg, in central Germany
E. Hadamar, in Hesse, north of Frankfurt
F. Sonnenstein—often called "Die Sonne"—near Dresden in Saxony

Throughout the life of the program—whether death came by pill, starvation, or carbon monoxide shower—it came at the hand of a physician. It was Brack's firm and oftstated belief that, "The syringe belongs in the hand of a physician" (Lifton, 1986, p. 71).

Bouhler was insistent that a way of death be found that would be not only painless, but also imperceptible to the patient. He did not want to frighten the patients, nor make them uncomfortable. These things must be "done according to his orders, and in a dignified and not a brutal fashion" (Trials of War Criminals, I:877).

The original regulations envisioned a "conservative" program with careful review procedures. In operation, the program became a matter of killing in wholesale lots. The psychological reasons physicians were willing to participate in these killings are no doubt complex. There is, however, an aspect of the structure of the program which made it easier: There was no single point of responsibility—no place in the procedure at which it was possible to say, here is where the patient receives his death warrant; no point where it could be said, *this* physician is responsible for this patient's death.

The local practicing physician simply filled out the questionnaires as he was required to do. The members of the assessing committee simply gave their individual opinion on each case. Nothing more would happen unless the members were in substantial agreement. The senior review physician simply went along with the committee or else expressed an objection. He was expressing a medical opinion, nothing more. Neither the assessors nor the review physicians ever saw the patient. The transportation staff was involved in transporting patients—but it was no business of theirs where or why the patients were being moved. The staff which ran the centers were simply doing their jobs. Even the physician whose job it was to operate the gas chamber was not responsible for the death of the patients—after all, he played no part in their selection; he knew nothing of their cases. He was only following the procedures laid down by his superiors; carrying out the policy of his government as advised by the most eminent members of the medical profession.

Disposal of the bodies of the dead patients presented a fairly sizable logistic program. The German nation was in an all-out war posture, and it was simply not practical to clutter up the transportation system by shipping corpses all over the landscape. It was this reason, as much as public health reasons, that caused Bouhler to insist upon immediate cremation at the major centers. Permanent furnaces were constructed at some of the sites, but other hospitals relied upon an ingenious device, a portable furnace on wheels.

Some of the centers were so mechanized as to have a conveyer belt system installed to carry the corpses from the gas chamber to the oven. As a contemporary witness wrote, "The corpses enter the furnace on a conveyer belt, and the smoke from the crematorium chimney is visible for miles" (Sereny, 1974, p. 39). The ash remains of the deceased were gathered from the oven and placed in ceremonial urns and delivered to their families along with a letter of condolence. No effort was made to distinguish the ashes of one victim from another. The family receiving an urn assumed they were receiving the remains of their own loved one—the letters surely indicated as much—but they were not.

A guide was prepared, probably by one of the T-4 physicians' committees, for the use of the doctors as they were preparing the fake certificates. This helped to ensure that the cause of death assigned and the medical history of the patient were internally consistent with each other and medically sound. For example, in discussing septicemia as a cause of death in the mentally ill, it was explained that these patients frequently have boils which they scratch and, "It is most expedient to figure four days for the basic illness and five days for the resultant sepsis" (Lifton, 1986, p. 74). Doctors were warned that this diagnosis "should not be used with patients who are meticulously clean"; instead, it is "preferable for young strong patients who smear readily" (Lifton, 1986, p. 74). However, the guide warned, if septicemia is used as a cause of death for the young, it should be noted that "seven to eight days have to be allowed for the illness to take effect, since their circulation is relatively more resistant" (Lifton, 1986, p. 74).

The official, centralized euthanasia program lasted from 1939 through the summer of 1941. After two years of operation, the program's existence was widely known. The churches had raised strong and vocal objections. There had been public demonstrations in opposition to the killings. The German army was deep in the Russian campaign, and Hitler had no wish for public unrest at home. Accordingly, the Führer in a conversation with Dr. Brandt, without ceremony or discussion, verbally ordered a halt to the euthanasia program.

This did not, however, bring an end to the killing of the disabled and the insane. Physicians across Germany continued to administer "final medical treatment" to patients they considered as having "lives not worth living." The killings continued, but the decision making and the criteria used in these decisions became those of the immediate doctor, rather than the assessor committees and the review professors. The "children's campaign," by which retarded and deformed infants were put to death, proceeded unabated. The killing continued even *after* the war, as U.S. Army occupation forces discovered at Kaufbeuren and Eglfing-Haar (Gallagher, 1990, p. 250).

As the bombing of German cities increased, Brandt undertook to evacuate institutionalized patients to the countryside. Many of those evacuated also were killed by their physicians. On the eastern ramparts of Germany—in Danzig, Pomerania, and West Prussia—as well as in Poland, mentally ill patients were simply shot by the local SS and police forces. Operation *14 f 13* practiced wanton killing of the sick and disabled in the camps and elsewhere. What the Germans at the time referred to as "wild euthanasia" led to additional widespread, unorganized, and indiscriminate killing. As Dörner has said, "Unplanned groups and individuals were murdered: welfare wards, asocials, wayward children, healthy Jewish children, or those of mixed blood, homosexuals, political offenders, elderly wards of nursing homes, sick and healthy Eastern workers" (Dörner, 1967, p. 151).

It is not possible to tell with any accuracy how many disabled German citizens were put to death during the Nazi years. No reliable figures exist for the spontaneous killings.

Figures survive for the official centralized T-4 killings:

Anstalt	1940	1941	Sa
A (Graf.)	9,839	—	9,839
B (Brand.)	9,772	—	9,772
Be (Bernb.)	8,601	—	8,601
C (Linz)	9,670	8,599	18,269
D (Sonnes.)	5,943	7,777	13,720
E (Hadamar)	—	10,072	10,072
	35,224	35,049	70,273

Klee, 1983.

In the summer of 1991 unexpected verification of these figures was unearthed in the cellar of the headquarters of Stasi, the former East German secret police. The medical files of these 70,000 patients, filed alphabetically, were discovered by English scholar Michael Burleigh (Horner, 1991, p. 25).

In some of the trial documents, the figure 120,000 is given as the overall number of inmates killed in public institutions. According to Aly and Roth, this number is on the low side and does not include those who died in such separate programs as the children's operation, random euthanasia, and the so-called Brandt campaign whereby 20,000 lost their lives (Aly and Roth, 1984, p. 162). Dr. Leo Alexander, who served with the Office of the Chief of Counsel for War Crimes at Nuremberg and who performed the major study of the euthanasia program for the court, has estimated that 275,000 persons were killed (Breggin, 1979, p. 81).

The psychiatrist Fredric Wertham has looked into hospital records. He found, for example, that the Province of Brandenberg, in 1938, had 16,295 mental patients from Berlin. By 1945, there remained but 2,379 patients. In an institution called Berlin-Buch, out of 2,500 patients, 500 survived. Kaufbeuren in Bavaria had 2,000 patients at the beginning of the war, and 200 remaining at the war's end. Many mental institutions simply closed their doors because of lack of patients. In 1939, for all of Germany there were some 300,000 mental patients. In 1946, there were 40,000. This is not to say that all these persons were destroyed by the German State in the course of its euthanasia operation. After all, the general German war losses were colossal (Muller-Hill, 1988). Nevertheless, it cannot be doubted that the euthanasia program swept out entire wards, cleaned out entire hospitals. It decimated the entire German population of the severely disabled and the chronically insane.

Aktion T-4 Euthanasie: Origins in History and Thought

The Euthanasie killing program was no Nazi aberration. Rather it was the efficient application through public policy of the theories of leading scientists and philosophers in Western society.

Darwin's theories of evolution, combined with the rediscovery of Mendelian law, encouraged Victorians in the belief that the biological world could be as knowable, as predictable as Newton's physical world. Social Darwinism and the "science" of eugenics sought to apply evolutionary and genetic principles, as understood, to human society and breeding. Eugenicists believed most human characteristics to be inherited. In W. Duncan McKim's book *Heredity in Human Progress,* which was published in 1900, heredity is blamed for, among other things, "insanity, idiocy, imbecility, eccentricity, hysteria, epilepsy, the alcohol habit, the morphine habit, neuralgias, 'nervousness,' Saint Vitus's dance, infantile convulsions, stammering, squint, gout, articular rheumatism, diabetes, tuberculosis, cancer, deafness, blindness, deaf-mutism, color blindness" (Haller, 1963, p. 42). It is, he said, "the fundamental cause of human wretchedness" (Haller, 1963, p. 42).

U.S. President Theodore Roosevelt spoke for many forward-thinking

people when he said, "Someday we will realize that the prime duty, the ines-
capable duty, of the *good* citizen of the right type is to leave his or her blood
behind him in the world; and that *we have no business to permit the perpetuation of citizens of the wrong type*" (emphasis added) (Haller, 1963, p. 79).

The impact of Darwinian theory upon German thought was no less
than it had been in Britain and America. Darwin cast a long shadow over
the development of National Socialism and the Third Reich. Perhaps most
influential was the 1920 book *The Destruction of Life Devoid of Value,* written by psychiatrist Alfred Hoche and lawyer Karl Binding. These men were
professors of reputation and importance. They argued that the medical profession should participate not only in health-giving, but under certain circumstances, in death-making as well. With a carefully reasoned argument,
defining their terms precisely, their analysis concluded that certain people
should be exterminated for racial "hygienic" purposes. They argued that the
retarded, the deformed, the terminally ill, and those who were mentally
sound but who were severely damaged by disease or accident should be put
to death. They believed that the death should be painless and expertly administered—that is, by a physician. According to their reasoning, the right
to "grant death" was a natural extension of the responsibilities of the attending physician.

Binding and Hoche were widely read and vigorously discussed. One of
their readers was the young Adolf Hitler, who had read a good deal on
eugenics and Monism prior to his writing of *Mein Kampf.* Upon one occasion Hitler even allowed his name to be used in advertisements for Hoche's
books (Breggin, 1979, p. 81).

There were other books and articles on the subject. The romantic phi-
losopher Ernst Haeckel's book *The Riddle of the Universe* sold well for many
years. His disciple Heinrich Ziegler was a popular writer on such issues and
won the important Krupp literary award. The 1920 book *Moral der Kraft*
by Ernst Mann advocated that disabled war veterans kill themselves to reduce welfare costs.

An exceedingly popular movie in the Germany of the mid-1930s dealt
entirely with the issue of euthanasia for the disabled. *I Accuse* was the story
of a young woman suffering from multiple sclerosis. Her husband, a doctor,
after lengthy soul searching, in the last reel kills his wife, as a fellow physician in the next room plays softly and funereally on the piano.

Another film (title unknown) of the Nazi years illustrated the unbearable life of the insane with particularly grisly shots of defective dystonias.

This was made for the use of the medical societies. The film was widely shown to physician gatherings and was shown to the Nazi Party Meeting of 1935 by Dr. Gerhardt Wagner, leader of the medical delegation.

Although long lost, unedited footage of the original film was found in the basement of Stasi secret police headquarters in the summer of 1991 by Michael Burleigh. In the film, a "professor" posits that the "incurably mentally ill" have a "right to die." "Is it not the duty of those concerned," he asks, reasonably enough given his premise, "to help the incapable—and that means total idiots and incurable mental patients—to their right?" (Horner, 1991, p. 25).

The general devaluation of disabled lives can be seen even in Nazi schoolroom textbooks. A mathematics text *Mathematics in the Service of National Political Education* set the following problem: "If the building of a lunatic asylum costs six million marks and it costs fifteen thousand marks to build each dwelling on a housing estate, how many of the latter could be built for the price of one asylum?" Another asked how many marriage allowance loans could be given to young couples for the amount of money it costs the state to care for "the crippled, criminal, and insane" (Mitscherlich, 1962, p. 234, and Alexander, 1949, p. 39).

When the German physicians and medical professors set up T-4 Euthanasie, they were instituting a program whose principles had been widely and thoroughly discussed.

Aktion T-4 Euthanasie: Impact and Response

After the war, Dr. Karl Brandt, director of the Euthanasie program, and Viktor Brack, administrator of the program, were hanged at Nuremberg for war crimes and crimes committed against humanity. Many of the principal T-4 physicians fled or disappeared. Occasionally, one has surfaced and faced trial. These trials have been long, drawn out, unsatisfactory affairs, largely because of the unwillingness of one physician to testify against another.

Other principal physicians simply resumed their practice under assumed names. Their presence was known to their peers in the medical community, but was not reported. The rank and file of the German physicians, those who had been active in the program, and the rest who had raised no objection to it, continued the practice of medicine, albeit no longer killing their patients.

Over the half century since the T-4 program, the German medical establishment has never acknowledged, examined, or apologized for the killings. A book summarizing accurately the T-4 Euthanasie evidence accumulated in the Nuremberg trials, written by a young psychiatrist Alexander Mitscherlich, was published in 1949. It was suppressed, denounced as "irresponsible . . . lacking documentation." The book was seen as an attack upon the "inviolable honor of German medicine." One reviewer said that only a "pervert" would read such a book and called its author a "traitor to his country" (Hanauske-Able, 1986, p. 272).

The German medical establishment retains, and rightly so, much prestige in the society. German physicians have made many important contributions throughout the history of medical science. Unfortunately it has chosen to deal with the Euthanasie episode with what amounts to an across-the-board denial. Medical students have been expelled from medical schools for attempting to discuss the matter. It is reported (personal communication) that Dr. Harmut M. Hanauske-Able was no longer able to practice in Germany after publishing a 1986 article on the subject in the British medical journal *Lancet* (1986). In 1977, the courageous Margarete and Alexander Mitscherlich wrote in the foreword to their book *Die Unfähigkeit zu trauern* [The Inability to Grieve], "Today in many minds, there is a reluctance to accept the facts of history. . . . What happened in the Third Reich remains alive in our subconscious, dangerously so. It will be fatal for us to lose touch with the truth of what happened then. We must struggle to seek out the truth of that era rather than search for improved defenses to hide us from this truth."

Encouragingly, in the 1980s a new, younger generation of historians has focused their attention on the social history of the Nazi years. In the course of their studies, they have done important research on the T-4 Euthanasie program and associated killing—work which is only now being published. These historians include Ernst Klee, Goetz Aly, Harl Heinz Roth, Benno Hill, and Michael H. Kater. Their work documents the known killings and continues to uncover killings hitherto unknown. The medical killing of disabled patients was widespread indeed.

In Germany today, as in the United States, there is a lively, ongoing debate over questions of medical ethics: abortion, amniocentesis, tracking the genome, "right to die," euthanasia, disability rights. Present, like Banquo's ghost, in all these discussions is the memory, expressed or unexpressed, of the medical killings of the 1930s and 1940s.

A particularly vivid example of this took place at Rehab 88, the fifth international rehabilitation trade fair, held at Karlsruhe in 1988. The person asked to give the keynote address for the professional section of the conference was Hans Henning Atrott, president of the German Society for Humane Dying. His subject was "Active Assistance for Dying: The Final Rehabilitation." It is perhaps not surprising that organizations of disabled persons were outraged that such a talk should be given at such an occasion. They protested to the conference organizers, but to no avail. As a last resort, they broke up Atrott's lecture by bursting into the hall in their wheelchairs, dressed in garbage bags, sipping from cans labeled "cyanide," and waving signs which read, "useless lives" and "lives not worth living" (Gallagher, 1990, p. 270). Atrott found it all most unfortunate, telling the media that the protest reminded him of Nazi tactics. It was a return, he said, to "terror against different thinking" (Gallagher, 1990, p. 270).

In 1987, Pope John Paul II made a visit to West Germany. He made a pilgrimage to Münster Cathedral to pray at the tomb of Cardinal Graf von Galen, the bravest of the religious leaders to protest the T-4 killing of disabled people. Later, in a meeting with disabled people, the Pope warned that, "Human life should not be divided into that which is worth living and that which is not" ("Pope Condemns . . . ," 1988, p. 2).

Aktion T-4 Insight

Close to two hundred years ago, German doctor Christoph Huffeland wrote, "If the physician presumes to take into consideration in his work whether a life has value or not, the consequences are boundless and the physician becomes the most dangerous man in the state" (Wertham, 1968, p. 153). In T-4 Euthanasie, the physicians of Germany demonstrated just how dangerous.

Eyewitness Accounts
Holocaust: Disabled Peoples

The victims of the T-4 Euthanasie program were not aware they had been selected for "final medical assistance" until too late. Without warning, they were bundled from their hospital beds into the waiting transports, taken to the killing centers, and, quite promptly, killed. It was all most efficient, and there were few escapees. The victims were chronically mentally ill, mentally retarded, and severely disabled people, struggling to survive in time of war; it is not surprising there are no memoirs. There are, however, eyewitness accounts of what went on.

What follows are accounts by those who observed the operation of the killing program. The witnesses include three parents of disabled children, a nurse, an archbishop, and a judge.

The first three accounts are taken from testimony heard in a criminal trial of three doctors in Vienna, Austria, in 1946. Austria had been part of Germany during the Nazi years and the T-4 program took the lives of many disabled Austrians. The first witness, Leopold Widerhofer, tells how his daughter, a schizophrenic patient, survived, thanks to his efforts and those of sympathetic doctors. These doctors were taking great risks by trying to save their patients from T-4.

The two other Austrian accounts are those of parents whose infants were killed—one of the victims was a four-year-old with speech difficulties and weak leg muscles; the other, a two-year-old, also with speech difficulties. These children were not severely disabled; they were not in pain, nor were they dying. Killing them had nothing to do with euthanasia; it had a lot to do with murder.

Leo Alexander was a physician in the U.S. Army of Occupation in Germany at the end of World War II. He was one of the very first to investigate the Aktion T-4 killing program. Included here is a verbatim statement made to him, August 5, 1945, by Amalie Widmann, a nurse who went looking for her patients that had been transferred to a killing center. Nurse Widmann's concern for her patients nearly cost her her life.

The activity at the killing centers was supposed to be secret. Soon enough, the neighborhoods surrounding the hospitals figured out what was going on. The impact of the killings on the community is vividly described in a courageous letter to the Ministry of Justice written by the Bishop of Limburg. The letter, printed here, is now in the U.S. Archives. It was a part of the evidence gathered for the "Doctors Trial," one of the Nuremberg War Crimes Trials of 1946.

The killing program, complained Heinrich Himmler, head of the SS, "is a secret and yet is no longer one" (Gallagher, 1988, p. 144). It had, in fact, become something of an embarrassment. Local law officials were alarmed by the unrest and fears stirred in the community by the killing, as demonstrated in the extract printed here of an unsigned report from a provincial court to the Ministry of Justice in Berlin.

One man became the symbol of the resistance to the so-called euthanasia program. He was the Bishop of Münster, Graf von Galen, the "Lion of Münster." A man of commanding presence and unquestioned moral authority, von Galen risked his life by giving a powerful sermon decrying the killing. "Woe to humanity," he thundered from his pulpit, "Woe to the German people if God's holy command 'Thou shalt not kill' is not only transgressed but if this transgression is tolerated and carried out without punishment." Copies of the sermon were distributed undercover all over Germany—to the fury of Hitler—and had much to do with the public outcry against T-4 Euthanasie. The text of von Galen's sermon has been included in the following collection of accounts.

Testimony of Leopold Widerhofer

This testimony was presented before the Vienna District Court (Landesgericht) in the proceedings against Dr. Ernst Illing, Dr. Marianne Türk, and Dr. Erwin Jekelius, Vienna, 27 February 1946.

Source

Documentation Archives of the Austrian Resistance (DÖW), Vienna, E 18282a (photocopy of file at Landesgericht Wien Vg 4d Vr 5442/46).

A facsimile of this document is reprinted in Elisabeth Klamper, ed., *Dokumentationsarchiv des Österreichischen Widerstandes, Vienna*, vol. 19 of the series *Archives of the Holocaust* (New York and London: Garland, 1991), pp. 114–116.

The Defendants

Dr. Ernst Illing (b. 1904, Leipzig) was a physician who joined the Nazi party on 1 May 1933; he was the director of the Vienna City Psychiatric-Neurological Clinic for Children Am Spiegelgrund, 1942–1945, where he killed about 200 children. He was sentenced to death by the Vienna District Court on 18 July 1946.

Dr. Erwin Jekelius (b. 1905) was a physician and member of the Nazi party. He was director of the Vienna City Psychiatric-Neurological Clinic for Children Am Spiegelgrund, 1940–1942.

Dr. Marianne Türk (b. 1914, Vienna) was appointed physician at the Vienna City Psychiatric-Neurological Clinic for Children Am Spiegelgrund in August 1940. Together with Dr. Ernst Illing, she killed a total of 200 children (ca. 7–10 per week) under the so-called euthanasia program. She was sentenced to 10 years in prison by the Vienna District Court, 18 July 1946.

The clinic Am Spiegelgrund located in Am Steinhof, Vienna: The clinic Am Spiegelgrund, officially known as the Vienna City Psychiatric-Neurological Clinic for Children, was located on the grounds of Am Steinhof and was used as a children's ward for the children's euthanasia program.

Am Steinhof was the popular name for the Wagner von Jauregg Mental Hospital and Nursing Home of the City of Vienna. About 4,000 patients were sent from Am Steinhof to the Hartheim euthanasia killing center.

Witness Interrogation
Hallein County Court
District Court I for Criminal Cases, Vienna II

On 27 February 1946 Beginning at 11:30 A.M.

Present:

Judge: Dr. Sandri
Secretary: Dr. Vavrovsky

Criminal Case:

Against Dr. Ernst Illing, Dr. Marianne Türk, and Dr. Erwin Jekelius
regarding paragraph 134 of the Penal Code

The witness is warned to answer the questions addressed to him truthfully to the best of his knowledge and conscience, to conceal nothing and to give testimony, in such a way that, if necessary, he can affirm it under oath.

He stipulates the following personal data:

1. First and last name: Leopold Widerhofer
2. Age: 76 years old
3. Place of birth: Waya-on-the-Enns, Upper Austria
4. Religion: Roman Catholic
5. Marital status: married
6. Occupation: retired grammar school headmaster

7. Place of residence: Vienna I, Bräunerstrasse 4, currently Hallein No. 278.
8. Relationship to the defendant or to other individuals involved in the investigation: none.

My daughter, Gerta Widerhofer, was brought to the sanatorium Am Steinhof in 1933 because of schizophrenia. She remained in treatment as a psychiatric patient there.

At the beginning of August 1940, my wife and I heard a rumor during a visit to the Steinhof institution that patients at this institution were being transferred to Germany secretly at night and that they would continue to be taken away in the future. Out of concern for our daughter's life, in mid-August 1940, I personally went to see Dr. Erwin Jekelius, who was then director of the Viennese Health Office, Vienna I, Schottenring 28, in order to inquire about this. After considerable discussion, I attempted to discover whether my daughter was on the list of patients to be transferred. He denied this. I was satisfied with this.

Soon thereafter, I heard in the waiting room of the director's office of the institution, Am Steinhof, that my daughter actually was on the list, and Dr. Wilhelm Podhaisky, Vienna 109, XV Baumgartnerhöhe, showed me my daughter's file, which he had already removed to his custody in order to try to save her life. This file was taken out of the records of those individuals who were to be prepared for transport; thus Dr. Podhaisky kept her file.

Dr. Podhaisky later arranged a meeting for me with the Director, Dr. Jekelius, in the waiting room of the executive offices of Am Steinhof; this would have been at the beginning of October 1940. During the nearly one hour discussion between me and the Director, Dr. Jekelius, which Dr. Podhaisky attended on behalf of the patients, Dr. Jekelius said to me twice in the presence of Dr. Podhaisky: "Your daughter must die." He tried to justify this because her disease was incurable. To my excited demand that my daughter, if she must die, would wish to die here at Am Steinhof, rather than be carried off, Dr. Jekelius replied: "Herr Direktor, you probably understand that we cannot allow our staff doctors to be implicated." I replied: "I only know that the patients will really be killed." Dr. Jekelius never responded to this.

The transports with mentally ill patients from Am Steinhof to unknown destinations continued throughout the next weeks. During this time, the two physicians from Steinhof, Dr. Unlauf and Dr. Podhaisky, routinely tried to delay the transports and they rescued my daughter by relocating her to ward 24. When this ward was evacuated at night, they moved my daughter to convalescent ward 20.

The deportations from Steinhof stopped at the end of December 1940. My daughter is still in Am Steinhof today and her condition has improved substantially.

I would also like to add that acquaintances of mine who likewise had dependents at Am Steinhof had already received notifications written between September and November 1940 that stated, that their sick dependents, who had been transferred from Am Steinhof, had suddenly died of some disease, such as infected tonsils or pneumonia.

I would also like to state that during the subsequent months, children that were difficult to handle arrived in the vacant women's wards and that Dr. Jekelius was named director of the children's department created here.

My wife, Marie Widerhofer, never observed these matters directly, but learned of them only from my comments. She never spoke with Dr. Jekelius, nor with Dr. Podhaisky nor Dr. Umlauf. She therefore cannot testify in these proceedings based on her own observations.

Testimony of Anny Wödl

This testimony was presented before the Vienna District Court in the proceedings against Dr. Ernst Illing, Dr. Marianne Türk, and Dr. Erwin Jekelius, Vienna, 1 March 1946 [mistyped in document as 1945].

Source
DÖW E 18282 (photocopy of file Landesgericht Wien Vg 4d Vr 5442/46). A facsimile of this document is reprinted in Elisabeth Klamper, ed., *Dokumentationsarchiv des Österreichischen Widerstandes, Vienna*, vol. 19 of the series *Archives of the Holocaust* (New York and London: Garland, 1991), pp. 117–119.

Gugging
Provincial Mental Hospital and Nursing Home in Lower Austria. In 1940, more than 500 of the over 1,000 patients at Gugging were deported to the Hartheim euthanasia killing center, many of them via the Niedernhart hospital.

Witness Interrogation
Vienna District Court for criminal offenses
District Court I for Criminal Cases, Vienna II

On 1 March 1945 [*sic,* actually 1946], beginning at

Present:

Judge: Agr. Dr. Zips
Secretary: Bürgert

Criminal Case:

Against Dr. Ernst Illing et al.

The witness is warned to answer the questions addressed to him truthfully to the best of his knowledge and conscience, to conceal nothing and to give testimony, in such a way that, if necessary, he can affirm it under oath.

He stipulates the following personal data:

1. First and last name: Anny Wödl
2. Age: 43 years old
3. Place of birth: Gutenstein
4. Religion: Roman Catholic
5. Marital status: single
6. Occupation: nurse
7. Place of residence: Vienna 9, Thurngasse Nr. 5/11
8. Relationship to the defendant or to other people involved in the investigation: none.

I refer to my petition on page/lines 179 through 187 of the record, which I fully uphold and add to my testimony.

I am appending the following:

I bore a handicapped child on 24 November 1934 who had difficulties walking and talking and did not develop as he should. It turned out that he understood everything, but that he couldn't speak. Also his legs were obviously too weak to carry him, so that in essence he could not walk. The doctors couldn't really determine if he actually suffered, nor could they de-cide the cause of his condition. I put him in the institution at Gugging when he was four years old.

I was very concerned about my child when the operation against the "incurably ill, mentally ill, and elderly" began, especially since I knew the Nazi state's position in principle about these matters. When the "operations" were carried out in Vienna, there was anxiety in the population. I was determined to appeal to Berlin in order to save my child or to stop the mechanism. I have described in detail in my petition what I achieved. The only person who really wanted to help was Dr. Trub, who was employed at Ballhausplatz.

With the exception of Dr. Jekelius, I spoke to no other physicians about this matter. In any case, Dr. Jekelius was fully aware of what was happening and it was unambiguously clear from his remarks that he totally endorsed the entire operation against "life unworthy of life" and that he was prepared to act as the Nazi state demanded. I finally realized that I could not save my child after this conversation. Therefore, I wanted at least to stop my child from being carried off somewhere. I also wanted to spare the child any further pain, if it had to die. For these reasons, I begged Dr. Jekelius, that if the death of my child could not be stopped, that it be quick and painless. He promised me this. I never learned whether he himself carried out the deed, or whether he let someone else do it and in what manner. I saw my child's corpse. I was struck by the look of pain on his face.

On the whole, an individual could not do anything to stop these "actions," as is evident in my case. Most people did not dare try anything, since it was clear that it was much too dangerous. Meanwhile, the killing operations had spread to all sanitoriums and were carried out. I do not know the details. I only know what we heard when things leaked out and what also appeared in the press.

Testimony of Emma Philippovic
This testimony was presented before the Vienna District Court (Landesgericht) in the proceedings against Dr. Ernst Illing, Dr. Marianne Türk, and Dr. Erwin Jekelius, Vienna, 2 March 1946.

Source
DÖW E 18282a (photocopy of file at Landesgericht Wien, Vg 4d Vr 5442/ 46). A facsimile of this document is reprinted in Elisabeth Klamper, ed.,

Dokumentationsarchiv des Österreichischen Widerstandes, Vienna, vol. 19 of the series *Archives of the Holocaust* (New York and London: Garland, 1991), pp. 120–121.

Witness Interrogation
Vienna District Court for criminal offenses
District Court I for Criminal Cases, Vienna II

On 2 March 1946, beginning at

Present:

Judge: Agr. Dr. Zips
Secretary: Bürgert

Criminal Case:

Against Dr. Ernst Illing et al.

The witness is warned to answer the questions truthfully to the best of his knowledge and conscience, to conceal nothing and to give testimony, in such manner that, if necessary, he can affirm it under oath.

1. First and last name: Emma Philippovic
2. Age: 47 years old
3. Place of birth: Vienna
4. Religion: Jewish
5. Marital status: widowed
6. Occupation: homemaker
7. Place of residence: Vienna 5, Schönbrunnerstr.
8. Relationship to the defendant: none

I refer to my petition on page 202 of the document, which I wish to add to my testimony. My daughter displayed speech defects at the age of two. They subsequently intensified, eventually resulting in a complete inability to speak. But it then became better again. I do not know whether she would have become completely healthy.

I did not see my child after her death. But my husband, who has since died, did see her corpse and he told me that the girl was emaciated. I was told that the child had died from pneumonia. At that time, pneumonia was widespread. On the death certificate, which I have presented for examination, no cause of death is given. I suspect a violent death. I do not know who was responsible for this; I also do not know which doctor was in charge of the ward at the time. After all, as a Jew, I was not permitted to go there and visit my daughter.

Excerpt from: *Public Mental Health Practices in Germany: Sterilization and Execution of Patients Suffering from Nervous or Mental Disease*

Reported by Leo Alexander, Major, M.C., AUS. CIOS Item 24, Medical. Combined Intelligence Objectives Sub-Committee, G-2 Division, SHAEF (Rear) APO 413, p. 35, 19 August 1945.

Miss Widmann stated that the first transport of patients to a killing center left Wieslech on 19 February 1940. Among the patients were a good many who had become endeared and attached to Miss Widmann. After they had been taken to the killing center, Miss Widmann became unable to take her mind off the sad fate of these patients, and she became unable to rest day or night. She had to think about them all the time. She finally felt that it might give her ease of mind if she could actually see what happened, and she decided to visit the killing center in Grafeneck herself. So she asked for a furlough, not telling anybody what she planned to do, and she went to Grafeneck on 22 July 1940. When she got off the train at Marbach an der Lauter bei Munzingen, which is the railhead for Grafeneck, the people whom she asked for directions to Grafeneck looked at her in a peculiar way as if there was something strange or funny about her. When she finally arrived in front of the institution in Grafeneck, she found a sign reading: "Entry strictly prohibited because of danger of infection." There were heavily armed men in green uniform, obviously police about the area. Suddenly Miss Widmann felt gripped by an overwhelming feeling of anxiety and she ran away over an open field crying bitterly. She sat down and cried for a while. She then saw that she was on the premises of a stud farm. The farmer came and asked her whether he could do anything for her, and she told him that she wanted to go and see the institution in Grafeneck. The farmer then told her: "Do not go there. One must not say anything." Shortly afterwards, an SS man appeared, accompanied by other SS men, with hounds. They took her into the building, where she was brought before an official who asked her what she wanted. She said that she wanted to see some of her old patients and find out how they were. The official then stated that the patients liked it so much there that they would never want to leave again. He then interrogated her sharply about her antecedents and her connections with any group, if any. He then called up Dr. Möckel. Miss Widmann added that she felt she owed her life to Dr. Möckel because if he had not talked for her they would have killed her. The reason why she went there was because of her deep feeling of close relationship with her patients.

Excerpt from: U.S. Nuremberg War Crimes Trials, November 21, 1946–August 20, 1947. National Archives Microfilm Publications, M887, Doc. 615—PS
In August 1941 the Bishop of Limburg wrote, *inter alia*:

About 8 kilometres from Limburg in the little town of Hadamar, on a hill overlooking the town, there is an Institution which had formerly served various purposes and of late had been used as a nursing home. This Institution was renovated and furnished as a place in which, by consensus of opinion, the above-mentioned euthanasia has been systematically practised for months—approximately since February 1941. The fact is, of course, known beyond the administrative district of Wiesbaden because death certificates from the Hadamar-Moenchberg Registry are sent to the home communities.

(Moenchberg is the name of this Institution because it was a Franciscan monastery prior to its secularization in 1903.)

Several times a week buses arrive in Hadamar with a considerable number of such victims. School children of the vicinity know this vehicle and say: "There comes the murder-box again." After the arrival of the vehicle the citizens of Hadamar watch the smoke rise out of the chimney and are tortured with the ever-present thought of the poor sufferers, especially when the nauseating odours carried by the wind offend their nostrils.

The effect of the principles at work here is that children call each other names and say, "You're crazy; you'll be sent to the baking oven in Hadamar." Those who do not want to marry, or find no opportunity, say "Marry, never! Bring children into the world so they can be put into the bottling machine!" You hear old folks say, "Don't

send me to a State hospital! When the feeble-minded have been finished off, the next useless eaters whose turn will come are the old
people."

**Excerpt from: U.S. Nuremberg War Crimes Trials, November
21, 1946–August 20, 1947. National Archives Microfilm
Publications, M887, Doc. 844**
The following is an extract of a letter from the Frankfurt am Main Provincial Court of Appeal to the Ministry of Justice in December of
1939.

People living near sanatoria and convalescent homes, as well as in adjoining regions, sometimes quite distant, for example throughout the
Rhineland, are continually discussing the question whether the lives of
incurable invalids should be brought to an end. The vans which take
patients from the Institutions they occupy to transit stations and thence
to liquidation establishments are well-known to the population. I am
told that whenever they pass the children call out: "There they go again
for gassing." I hear that from one to three big omnibuses with blinds
down go through Limburg every day on their way from Weilmünster
to Hadamar, taking inmates to the Hadamar liquidation centre. The
story goes that as soon as they arrive they are stripped naked, given a
paper shirt and immediately taken to a gas-chamber, where they are
poisoned with prussic acid and an auxiliary narcotic. The corpses are
said to be transferred on a conveyor belt to an incineration chamber,
where six are put into one furnace and the ashes then packed into six
urns and sent to the relatives. The thick smoke of the incinerators is
supposed to be visible every day over Hadamar. It is also common talk
that in some cases the heads or other parts of the body are detached for
anatomical investigation. The staff employed on the work of liquidation at these Institutions is obtained from other parts of the country
and the local inhabitants will have nothing to do with them. These
employees spend their evenings in the taverns, drinking pretty heavily.
Apart from the stories told by the people about these "foreigners," there
is much anxiety over the question whether certain elderly persons who
have worked hard all their lives and may now in their old age be somewhat feeble-minded are possibly being liquidated with the rest. It is
being suggested that even old peoples' homes will soon be cleared. There

is a general feeling here, apparently, that proper legal measures should be taken to ensure that above all persons of advanced age and enfeebled mentality are not included in these proceedings.

Sermon of Clemens August Graf von Galen, Bishop of Münster, August 3, 1941

Source
Dokumente zur Euthanasie, ed. Ernst Klee, Fischer Tuschenbuch Verlag, 1985 (reprinted with permission).

Devout Christians! A pastoral message of the German bishops of June 26, 1941, which was read in all Catholic churches on July 6, says: "According to the Catholic moral code there are some commandments which need not be kept if their observance would involve great difficulties. But there are others, holy obligations of our moral consciousness which we have to fulfill even at the cost of our lives. Never, under any circumstances, may a human being kill an innocent person outside of war or in just self-defense." On July 6 I already had occasion to add to the words of this universal pastoral message the following explanation: For the past months we have heard reports from care and residential institutions for mental patients that patients who had been ill for a long time and who appear to be incurable have been removed forcibly on orders from Berlin. Relatives are being notified a short time afterwards that the corpse has been cremated and that they can claim the ashes. There is a suspicion bordering on definite knowledge that these numerous unexpected deaths among psychiatric patients are not due to natural causes but have been intentionally brought about. The philosophy behind this is the assumption that so-called unworthy lives can be terminated, innocent human beings killed if their lives have no value for the nation and the state. This is a terrible doctrine that seeks to justify the murder of innocent people and allows the killing of invalids who can no longer work, cripples, incurable patients, and the feeble elderly.

We have heard from reliable sources that lists have been made of such patients who will be removed from the care and residential institutions in the province of Westphalia and shortly afterwards killed. The first transport left the Marienthal institution near Münster in the course of the past week.

German men and women! Paragraph 211 of the criminal code is still in force. It states, "Whosoever intentionally kills a person will be punished for murder by death if he has done it with premeditation."

To protect those who intentionally kill those poor people, members of our families, from legal punishment, patients who have been designated to die are being removed from their home institutions to far-away facilities. Some illness is given as a cause of death. Since the corpse is immediately cremated neither relatives nor the criminal police can ascertain what the cause of death was. But I have been assured that neither the Ministry of the Interior nor the agency of Dr. Conti, the surgeon general, denies that a large number of psychiatric patients have been intentionally killed in Germany and will be killed in the future.

Paragraph 139 of the criminal code states, "Whosoever becomes aware of the plan for a capital offense and does not bring it to the attention of the authorities or the threatened person will be punished." When I heard of the plan to remove patients from Marienthal and to kill them, I filed the following charges by letter with the prosecutor of the court in Münster and the president of police in Münster: "According to reports a large number of patients, so-called unproductive citizens, of the provincial care institution of Marienthal near Münster have been transferred in the course of this week to the Eichberg institution to be intentionally killed as has happened in other institutions according to general belief. Since such a procedure is not only contrary to the divine and natural moral code but has to be punished by death according to paragraph 211, I herewith dutifully raise charges according to paragraph 139 of the criminal code and ask that the threatened citizens be immediately protected through prosecution of the agencies which organize the transport and the murder and that I be notified of whatever has been done." I have not received any information on intervention by the state prosecutor or the police.

I had previously lodged a protest on July 26 with the provincial administration of Westphalia which is responsible for the institutions to which patients have been entrusted for care and cure. It was in vain. I have heard that three hundred persons have been removed from the residential care Wartstein institution.

Now we have to expect that these poor defenseless patients will be murdered in due time. Why? Not because they have committed a heinous crime, not because they attacked the caregiver in a way which would have forced him to defend his own life in justified self-defense. Are these cases in which killing is allowed and even necessary, besides killing of the enemy in a just war? No, these hapless patients have to die not for any of these reasons but because they have become unworthy to live according to these opinions they are "unproductive citizens." The judgment holds that they cannot produce any goods; they are like an old machine which does not run anymore, they are like an old horse which has become lame and cannot be cured, they are like a cow which has ceased to give milk. What does one do with such an old machine? One wrecks it. What does one do with a lame horse, with unproductive cattle? No, I do not want to labor the comparison, justified and illuminating as it would be. We are not dealing with machines, or horses, or cows, whose only destiny is to serve people, to produce goods for human beings. They can be wrecked, they can be slaughtered when they can no longer serve their purpose. No, these are human beings, our fellow citizens, our brothers and sisters. Poor people, sick people, unproductive people, so what. But have they forfeited their right to live? Do you, do I have a right to live only as long as we are productive, as long as others recognize us as being productive? If the principle is established and applied that "unproductive fellow citizens" can be killed, woe to all of us when we get old and feeble. If it becomes permissible to kill unproductive people, woe to the invalids who invested and sacrificed and lost their energies and sound bones during their working careers. If unproductive fellow citizens can be eliminated by force, woe to our brave soldiers who return to their homeland severely injured, as cripples, as invalids. Once it becomes legal for people to kill "unproductive" fellow citizens—even if at presently only our poor defenseless mentally ill are concerned—then the basis is laid for murder of all unproductive people, the incurable, the invalids of war and work, of all of us when we become old and feeble.

All that is necessary is another secret decree that the procedure tested with mental patients is to include other "unproductive persons," is to be applied to patients with incurable lung disease, to the feeble elderly, the disabled workers, to severely injured veterans. Nobody would be safe anymore. Some commission can put him on the list of the "unproductive." And no police will protect him and no court prosecute his murder and punish the murderer. Who could still trust his physician?

Maybe he would report the patient as "unproductive" and would be ordered to kill him? It is inconceivable what depraved conduct, what suspicion will enter family life if this terrible doctrine is tolerated, adopted and carried out. Woe to humanity, woe to the German people if God's holy command "Thou shalt not kill" is not only transgressed but if this transgression is both tolerated and carried out without punishment.

I will give you an example of what happened today. In Marienthal there was a man about fifty-five years old, a farmer in a village in the area of Münster—I know his name—who had been suffering from episodes of mental derangement for some years and who had been brought to the Marienthal care and residential institution. He was not really a psychiatric case; he was able to receive visitors and was always happy when his relatives came. Just two weeks ago he was visited by his wife and one of his sons who was home on leave from the front. The son dotes on his father. Saying farewell was difficult, since nobody knows if the son will return and see his father again because he may be killed fighting for his fellow citizens. The son, the soldier, will certainly not see his father again, who has meanwhile been placed on the list of "unproductive" people. A relative who wanted to visit the father this week in Marienthal was sent away with the information that the patient had been transferred on orders of the Ministry for Defense. The destination was unknown but the relatives would be informed in a few days. What will this information contain? The same as in other cases? That the person died, was cremated, and that the ashes could be claimed after payment of a fee? The soldier who fights and risks his life for fellow German citizens will not see his father again on this earth because fellow German citizens in his own country have killed him.

Chapter Eight
The Indonesian Massacres

Robert Cribb

During six months from October 1965 to March 1966 approximately half a million people were killed in a series of massacres in Indonesia. The victims were largely members of the Indonesian Communist Party (PKI, Partai Komunis Indonesia), which until that time had been the largest communist party in the non-communist world. By 1965 it appeared to many observers inside and outside Indonesia that the party was well-placed to come to power after Sukarno's departure. The massacres followed an attempted coup d'etat in the Indonesian capital, Jakarta, in which the PKI was implicated, at least in the public mind, by circumstance and vigorous military propaganda, and resulted in the party's destruction. This paved the way for the accession to power of a business-oriented and military-dominated government under General Suharto.

Who Committed the Genocide?

The Indonesian killings were the work of anti-Communist army units and civilian vigilantes, drawn especially, but by no means exclusively, from religious political parties. Both groups brought to the killing a long-standing hatred of communism.

The army's hostility dated from the years of armed struggle against the Dutch (1945–1949), when communist influence had been strong both within army units and among independent irregular troops, or *lasykar*. The professional soldiers who soon struggled into the top military positions resented both party influence in the junior ranks and the independent Communist units which challenged their monopoly of armed force. Resentment had become alarm when the crypto-Communist Defense Minister Amir Syarifuddin attempted to introduce political commissars into army units in 1946. With bitter disgust, moreover, senior officers recalled the so-called Madiun Affair of 1948, when Communist army units had declared a Soviet

Republic in the East Java town of Madiun. At that time the Indonesian Republic had been reduced by Dutch offensives to a constricted area in Central and East Java and was girding itself to resist an expected final onslaught. The uprising had been a complex affair, the product at least in part of anti-Communist provocation of the Communist troops, but the incident lived on in the memories of the army leadership as proof of Communist treachery (Sundhaussen, 1982).

Religious opposition to the PKI came mainly from orthodox Islam. Although Islam was statistically the religion of just under 90 percent of the population, approximately half the Muslim population belonged to a distinctive Javanese form of the religion, often called Kejawen, which was strongly mystical and blended with pre-Islamic beliefs. Whereas the followers of Kejawen often saw little to fear in communism, pious orthodox Muslims feared that the Communists would install an atheist state, anathema to Islam, if they came to power. The Indonesian Republic had adopted belief in God, but not Islam, as one of its guiding principles in 1945, and for many Muslims even this was a barely tolerable compromise. This religious antagonism was compounded by memories of the Madiun affair, when Communist forces briefly in control of parts of East Java had massacred several hundred Muslims who resisted them. Among Indonesia's Christian communities, attitude toward the PKI were more divided: some Christians shared the Muslim anathemization of Communist atheism, while others were sympathetic to the party's goal of social justice and indeed backed the party's campaigns on land and other issues in some regions.

A third pole of opposition to the PKI came from the conservative wing of the secular Indonesian Nationalist Party (PNI, Partai Nasional Indonesia). Although sections of the PNI were sympathetic to the left, the party establishment was generally conservative, representing the interests of the entrenched bureaucratic elite. The PNI's electoral support had depended especially on the traditional loyalty of peasants to this elite, and the party was threatened more than any other by the rise of PKI support in the countryside. It, thus, provided a rallying point for civilians who were opposed to the PKI but suspicious of organized Islam.

Hostility between the army and organized Islam had been strong during the years after independence, with the army taking fifteen years to suppress a fundamentalist Muslim uprising called Darul Islam. The two, however, found themselves gradually drawn closer by their shared hostility to the prospect of the PKI coming to power. In Indonesia's only fully free elections in 1955, the Communist party had won 16.4 percent of the national vote, making it the fourth largest party, but its influence was growing rapidly and it maintained by far the best disciplined and organized party structure in the country. Sukarno drew it into his orbit as he consolidated his political power in a system he called Guided Democracy (1959–1965), declaring communism to be part of the state ideology and sponsoring a gradual penetration of state institutions by the party (Mortimer, 1974). In early 1965 it appeared likely that workers and peasants would be armed and trained to make up a "Fifth Force" alongside the army, navy, air force and police, thus creating a militia which would give the PKI direct access to armed force for the first time since the revolution.

The anti-Communist coalition was broadened by a widespread and more general hostility to the PKI. This stemmed partly from the party's energetic efforts to recruit support throughout society which saw it take sides on a wide variety of issues. For each issue that won it allies, it acquired also a set of enemies, and on some issues, such as the redistribution of farmland in East Java, social violence had reached high levels even before the massacres began (Walkin, 1969). In East Java, the PKI supported Hindu revivalists against the local Muslim establishment: in Hindu Bali, the party vigorously denounced Hinduism and disrupted religious practice (Hefner, 1990, pp. 193–215; Cribb, 1990, pp. 241–248). The immediate reason for hatred between Communists and non-Communists, therefore, varied enormously over the breadth of the Indonesian archipelago and for many years formed one of the important obstacles to better understanding the massacres as a whole.

Hostility to the party also stemmed from what were widely believed to be the circumstances of the 1965 attempted coup in Jakarta. The coup itself was an ambiguous affair which may never be fully understood. Army units from the presidential palace guard, headed by Lieutenant Colonel Untung, abducted six senior anti-Communist generals from their homes early on the morning of 1 October. This was ostensibly an attempt to thwart a rumored right-wing coup d'etat by the generals. The generals were probably to be kidnaped, intimidated and humiliated into abandoning their alleged coup plans. A clandestine bureau of the PKI was probably involved with the kidnapers, though the rest of the party, except for a few leaders, was certainly unaware of the plot. The targeted generals, however, were killed, and the kidnapers announced from Halim Air Force Base near Jakarta that a new Revolutionary Council had seized power. It is probable that the announcement was a panicked response to the botched kidnapings, but it was widely perceived in Indonesia, including by PKI members themselves, as the party's attempt to seize power (Crouch, 1978, pp. 97–134).

The coup appeared to be a cynical grab for power, upsetting the uneasy balance of Guided Democracy. The killings of the generals, moreover, were the first significant political assassinations since the chaos of the war of independence; the young daughter of another general was fatally injured in crossfire. Rumors then emerged that a number of the generals had been tortured and mutilated before death by frenzied Communist women who celebrated their achievement with an orgy involving party cadres and left-wing air force officers (for definitive disproof of these rumors, see Anderson, 1987). Word quickly spread, too, that Communists throughout the country had planned a similar fate for their other enemies and that holes had been dug in every district to accommodate the bodies of their victims. The stories of torture and mutilation, and those of the preparation of holes, have now been shown to be false, but they contributed greatly to the anti-Communist determination to kill.

How Was the Genocide Committed?

Although the motives driving the killers varied greatly, there was a common pattern to much of the killing itself. In each region, typically, news of the attempted coup in Jakarta was followed by a period of tense relative calm in which both sides attempted to assess what had happened. In most cases the killings did not begin until the arrival of anti-Communist troops from outside, though there were some exceptions to this. In strongly Muslim Aceh, in northern Sumatra, local Muslim leaders took the initiative to kill Communists within days of the coup attempt. Knowledge that the killing of Communists was sanctioned by the armed forces was enough to set the massacres off in some areas, but the army often intervened to give weapons and rudimentary training to anti-Communist vigilantes. In a few regions, the army itself conducted most of the killings, while here and there it felt obliged to dragoon unwilling local communities to help in the slaughter.

The killing was carried out mostly at night and commonly with bayonet or *parang*, the single-bladed machete of the Indonesian peasant. In some cases entire communities closely associated with the PKI were killed, but more commonly the army and vigilantes took with them blacklists of intended victims who were taken from their villages and killed nearby. The bodies were generally dumped in rivers or caves or were buried in shallow graves. The sites of some of these graves are still known locally and avoided. At times the bodies of the victims were mutilated. Some killers may have wished to avenge the alleged mutilation of the generals or to conceal the identity of the victims, but in some cases they had a more spiritual motive: in local belief, influenced by Islamic practice, to damage a body immediately before or after death is also to damage the soul, condemning it to lesser existence in the hereafter and limiting its capacity to return to earth to afflict its tormentors (Gittings, 1990).

Few of the victims offered significant resistance. The vast majority of party members were as unprepared for violent conflict as their anti-Communist enemies. Indeed, some of the victims were strikingly passive. In North Sumatra victims were reported to have formed long, compliant lines at the river bank as they waited for methodical executioners to behead them and tumble the head and body into the water. There are reports from Bali that party members went calmly to their deaths wearing white funeral clothes (Hughes, 1967, pp. 160, 181). In parts of Central Java, where the PKI had been strongest there was some attempt to set up stockades in defense of Communist villages, but this was largely futile against the army. After most of the killings were over, remnants of the PKI attempted to establish a guerrilla base in the countryside of southern East Java, but this too was soon suppressed.

Why Was the Genocide Committed?

Discussion of the reasons for the Indonesian massacres, aside from considering the motives mentioned above, has focused on the unexpected ferocity of the killings in a country whose people had something of a reputation for gentleness. Most authors have argued that the killings involved something more than the political elimination of the PKI. It is likely that the destruction of the party as a political force could have been achieved with many fewer deaths than actually occurred.

This issue raises questions of national psychology which are both difficult and delicate, and most attempts to explicate the event have not been convincing. Some scholars have suggested that the massacre represented a kind of collective running amok, *amok* being, after all, an Indonesian word. *Amok,* however, almost invariably takes place in response to apparently imminent defeat and humiliation, normally ends in the death of the amokker, and has many of the hallmarks of an indirect form of suicide (Spores, 1988). Others have suggested that the Javanese shadow puppet play, or *wayang,* portrays the characters on the left of the puppeteer as both wrong and doomed to violent destruction, and so inclined Indonesians to expect the PKI to perish in a welter of blood, but this theory fails to do justice to the complexity of *wayang* philosophy (see Anderson, 1965).

More promising is our growing knowledge of the role of the men of violence (rural and urban gangsters, enforcers, and the like) in Indonesian society and the special role that terror plays in consolidating their authority (Cribb, 1991, pp. 52–55). In the discussion below under "Who Was Involved?" however, we shall see that there are formidable obstacles to developing this line of analysis. However, first let us consider briefly who the victims were.

Who Were the Victims?

The killings were directed primarily against members and associates of the PKI and its affiliated organizations. The party claimed a membership of three million and its affiliates another twenty million, though both figures were probably exaggerated. In the course of the killings, many private quarrels were also settled and a significant number of non-Communists perished because of mistaken identity or association with Communists. In the politically charged atmosphere of the mid-1960s, however, many private quarrels had taken on a political dimension, and the distinction between private and political was correspondingly vague.

Few records of any kind were made or kept of the killings as they took place. The few foreign journalists who were in the country found access to the countryside very difficult and were in any case kept busy reporting the complex political changes taking place in national politics. Indonesians on the whole have remained reluctant to speak about the killings, except in very general terms. This reluctance probably stems both from a sense of shame at the magnitude of the massacres and an unwillingness to discuss what is still a sensitive topic in a country dominated by the military who presided over the killings in the first place.

This lack of information makes it impossible to say for certain how many people perished during the killings of 1965–1966. The death toll certainly included most of the party leadership, including the general secretary D.N. Aidit. Estimates have ranged from a low of 78,000 to a high of two million. Most scholars today accept a figure of between 200,000 and 500,000. The Indonesian government itself, which considers the killings to have been a necessary purge of Communist influence from society, has never seriously denied that the killings took place and indeed has publicly inclined to the higher figure (Cribb, 1990, p. 12). As we shall see in "Historical Forces and Trends," the Indonesian government draws some political advantage from cultivating the memory of massive killing. The intensity of the killing varied dramatically from region to region. It was most ferocious in areas where the PKI had been on the ascendant, in the countryside of Central and East Java, in Bali, and in the plantation belt of North Sumatra; it was least in the cities, and in places such as Aceh, West Sumatra, and Madura, where overwhelming community hostility to the party had made it a minor part of the political landscape.

At the time it was reported that Indonesia's substantial Chinese community were especially targeted as victims. The Chinese were and are deeply resented in Indonesia for their relative success in business since colonial times, and they were further encumbered in 1965 by their perceived association with the People's Republic of China. In 1959, however, Chinese traders had been expelled from rural areas, thus removing them from the regions where the heaviest killing took place. The PKI had been more tolerant of Indonesian Chinese than most other parties, and there were thus many Chinese among the party activists who perished, but there is no evidence that the Chinese suffered disproportionately on this occasion.

Who Was Involved?

Only in a few instances does the available information permit us to identify individual killers. This is partly because those involved often kept their identities secret by wearing masks and acting at night. But it is also a result of a strong sense of communal responsibility for the massacres. This communal responsibility rests on traditional village notions of justice in which crime was seen as committed both by and against whole communities, regardless of the individual who may have carried it out or who may be charged with avenging it. Even those whose hands were never physically bloodied have consequently felt a shared responsibility for the killings.

This sense of mass responsibility was also deliberately encouraged by the army, which aimed to ensure that it did not carry the burden of blood alone. Until the massacres were well advanced, many observers inside and outside Indonesia were uncertain whether the PKI could indeed be effectively eliminated as a political force. The army was therefore keen to recruit irrevocably to its side as many groups as possible, knowing that those who had joined in the bloodshed could never change sides. As the killing proceeded, participation became something of a test of anti-Communist credentials. Those who had made compromises with the leftist elements in Guided Democracy often felt that they could prove themselves only by joining with especial enthusiasm in the anti-Communist witch-hunt. This was especially so on the island of Bali (Soe, 1990).

Historical Forces and Trends

The massacres of 1965–1966 played a key role in the long-term destruction of political parties as a significant force in Indonesian public life. The nationalist movement during the closing decades of Dutch rule in the first half of the twentieth century had formed itself into a series of political parties and at independence it had seemed natural that one or more political parties should take the lead in determining the country's future. The resilience of local party organizations was strengthened by the self-reliance they developed during the war of independence when central control was at a minimum. At a national level, however, the parties were for the most part fragile and even coincidental alliances of politicians whose power bases lay in regional, social, ethnic, or religious groups. Only in the PKI did the party organization have a powerful base in its own right. Independent Indonesia adopted a parliamentary system in which governments were created by coalition on the floor of parliament, but this political form proved to be profoundly disappointing to many Indonesians. Coalitions were unstable, few lasting longer than a year, and politicians in general appeared to be obsessed with peddling influence and favors, rather than with determining policy in the national interest.

Sukarno's suspension of the parliamentary system and declaration of martial law in 1957, therefore, were greeted favorably by many Indonesians in the hope that an authoritarian government less beholden to sectional political interests would rule the country better. Guided Democracy's economic performance was dismal, but most observers attributed this to Sukarno's concentration on ideology and foreign affairs and to the growing influence of the PKI rather than to his authoritarian political structures. The forces who marshalled against the PKI in 1965, therefore, included many who were determined to prevent parties from ever again exercising a decisive role in Indonesian politics.

In this perspective, the massacres were less important for their elimination of one particular party than for the curse they cast on party politics in general. While believing firmly that the PKI had to be exterminated, many conservatives deeply regretted that Indonesian politics had reached such a point and they blamed the hatreds which underlay the killings not simply on the PKI but on the freedom which all parties had used to pursue their own sectional interests. In Suharto's Indonesia, therefore, the killings have become a horrible warning of what may happen if populist politics are permitted. At each carefully managed national election, when the government electoral organization, called "Golkar," wins handsomely against the two permitted alternative parties, the spectre of the violence of 1965–1966 is one of the forces which shepherd voters into support for the government.

Long-Range Impacts

The killings eliminated the PKI as a significant political force in Indonesia. The party has been formally illegal since March 1966, and aside from two or three attempts during the late 1960s to establish rural guerrilla bases on a Maoist model there has been no clear sign of any PKI activity within Indonesia since that time. The Indonesian government regularly warns the public against the "latent danger" of the party and from time to time unexplained incidents, such as fires in public buildings, have been blamed on a putative PKI underground, but it is most probable that the PKI is simply being used as a convenient scapegoat in these cases. A somewhat factionalized party-in-exile continues to exist, based originally on party members who happened to be abroad in October 1965 or who subsequently escaped the killings, and drawing more recently on exiled Indonesian dissidents, but it appears to have little impact in Indonesia itself.

The psychological impact of the killings on both survivors and perpetrators is difficult to assess. As mentioned above, Indonesian biographical writing about the killings is exceptionally sparse. In the late 1960s, a number of short stories appeared in which authors tackled various aspects of the killings (Aveling, 1975), but the topic failed to develop even as a genre in Indonesian literature. One or two anecdotes exist which describe killers who suffered horribly in later life as a consequence of their participation, but these are balanced by accounts of killers who live easily with their memories (Young, 1990, p. 80).

The memory of the killings, moreover, appears to have relatively little significance for those one might regard as survivors. This is partly because the killings appear to have been remarkably effective in eliminating those whom they targeted; that is, the active cadre of the PKI. More important, however, the relative disregard of the killings is a consequence of the fact that an even larger number of leftists were punished by detention during the years after the coup. The Indonesian government itself has put the number of detainees at one and a half million. Not all these people were held at once, and some were released after a few months, but many were kept for years and large numbers were exiled to the isolated prison island of Buru in eastern Indonesia. Virtually all shared the experience of hunger, humiliation, and mistreatment during their detention, and it appears that this experience of suffering has overshadowed for most of them the briefer and more distant terror of the killing months.

The impact of the killings is perhaps seen most strongly today in the changed religious geography of parts of Java, Timor, and North Sumatra, where an estimated 2.8 million people converted to Christianity in the years immediately after 1965. These conversions were partly a consequence of the military government's insistence that all Indonesians should profess a religion. Although some Christian vigilantes were as brutal in the killings as their Muslim counterparts, the Christian churches in general took a much more active pastoral role amongst the families of victims and were rewarded with many converts. Conversion was also perhaps a consequence of a general spiritual crisis which the appalling level of violence presented to Indonesian society.

Responses

News of the killings reached the international press soon after they began and, although the obstacles to effective reporting were formidable, a thin stream of news and feature articles (Kirk, 1966; King, 1966; [Palmos] 1966; Turner, 1966) made available to the world community the fact that a massacre of enormous proportions was under way in Indonesia. The international response was muted, partly because attention focussed on the growing power of the military in Jakarta, and partly because the non-communist world had no wish to make an issue of events it regarded favorably. Without specifically commending the Indonesian army for its actions, the world preferred not to know the details of what was happening, though *Time* magazine came close to commendation when it described the PKI's suppression as "The West's best news for years in Asia" ("Vengeance with a Smile," *Time,* 16 July, 1966, p. 26).

Leftists outside Indonesia for their part have been reluctant to investigate the details of the killing. This is probably for two reasons. First, leftist critics of the Suharto government, as well as other organizations such as churches and human rights organizations, have generally focused on what they see as its current shortcomings—restrictions on political activity, corruption, regressive development policies, and the like—rather than on what they would regard as historical crimes. Second, the left has been aware that the PKI created many enemies in Indonesian society by its vigorous espousal of contentious issues such as land reform. PKI activists were, according to circumstance, unyielding, unreasonable, and even inconsistent. Their enemies had many grudges one might regard as legitimate, even if the response was unnecessarily violent. The left, therefore, has found its analysis of the killings to be most effective when they are simply interpreted as a general "white terror" or violent conservative reaction to communism, and the precise details of each killing are not explored.

Scholarly Interpretation

No significant observer had predicted the extent of the violence in Indonesia in 1965–1966 on the basis of a scholarly understanding of Indonesian society. Nor have scholars since that time generally treated the massacres as a major event in Indonesian history. This is partly a consequence of the lack of information, but it reflects also a broader historiographical difficulty in blending the separate courses of local and national history into a single coherent narrative. Because the national significance of the killings cannot be explained without reference to local conditions, any more than the local significance can be discussed without reference to national events, the killings have had an elusive character which has militated against close analysis.

Disregard for the killings may also be related to the character of the scholarly community which studies Indonesia. At least until recently, this community tended to be dominated by scholars who had made the study of Indonesia their life's work and who brought to their studies a deep familiarity with Indonesia and an affection for its people. Perhaps because it is hard to reconcile such widespread killings with affection for Indonesians, scholars with the experience which would enable them to examine the killings in detail have tended to look for other research topics and to focus their discussion of the events of 1965 on the attempted coup of 30 September 1965. The circumstances of the coup are themselves shrouded in uncertainty, but they at least permit scholars to identify innocent parties in a way in which the killings do not permit.

Insofar as historical debate exists, it focuses on the relative responsibility of the armed forces and of the vigilantes in initiating and sustaining the killings. The left on the whole gives greater emphasis to the role of the military, the right to the vigilantes, but this disagreement has never reached the level of controversy.

Current Attitudes

Interest in the Indonesian massacres appears to have revived in recent years after two decades of neglect. A small number of previously little known personal accounts have appeared (see Eyewitness Accounts) while a recent collection of essays on the killings has attempted to restore the topic to the scholarly agenda (Cribb, 1990). The main reason for this interest appears to be a growing awareness that the survivors on both sides of the massacres are reaching old age and may soon not be able to add their testimony to our current knowledge unless what they know is recorded now. President Suharto, moreover, had his seventieth birthday in 1991 and it is widely accepted that his period of dominance in Indonesian politics is coming to an end. As scholarly assessment of his impact on Indonesia takes shape, a deeper understanding of the circumstances which brought him to power becomes increasingly important.

Lessons from the Indonesian Massacres

The Indonesian killings share with those in Cambodia an overwhelmingly political, rather than racial, orientation which distinguishes them from the other racially or ethnically motivated genocides discussed in this volume. They were an extreme example of the violence which is a part of the political process throughout much of the world. However, political motives are also not absent in many other massacres. In any case, the predominance of political considerations in the Indonesian killings reminds us that genocide does not simply occur because of racism but rather is a consequence of deep human antagonisms. The whirlwind which destroyed the Indonesian Communists sprang up with little warning out of a combination of long-term antagonisms and shorter-term hope and fears.

Eyewitness Accounts
The Indonesian Massacres

Three eyewitness accounts of the Indonesian killings are included here. As the analysis above explained, the Indonesian killings have produced remarkably few direct testimonies by survivors or participants, and the first two accounts reproduced here are unique for the detail they provide: other accounts, published and unpublished, tend to be secondhand and/or fragmentary.

The first account was written by an anonymous author who was a member of a left-wing youth organization in Kedurus, near Surabaya, the main city of East Java. The Brantas is Java's longest river and it enters the sea near Surabaya. The author makes clear that he would have become a victim himself had he been caught. The account was written in 1989, over twenty years after the events it describes.

The second account describes the killings in Kediri, also in East Java, from the point of view of a young man whose family was not on the communist side but who nonetheless viewed the fate of the PKI with concern. The author, Pipit Rochijat, describes himself throughout the account as "Kartawidjaja's Son No. 2." This is due to the fact that Indonesians are often reluctant to use personal pronouns, because this can seem forward; thus, names are commonly used as a polite substitute.

Both testimonies highlight the contrast between the clandestine nature of the actual killings and the public knowledge that they were taking place. The author of the first account witnessed the murder of his old teacher and the others only because he happened to be hiding near the secluded abattoir where the killings took place. The killers whom he watched took some care to conceal the identity of their victims but none at all to conceal the bodies, which were simply flung into the river. Pipit Rochijat, too, describes the way in which victims were often taken away to some secluded spot to be killed, yet bodies and parts of bodies were widely displayed. This phenomenon (contrasting with the public executions and the secret disposal of bodies employed by some repressive regimes) highlights the extent to which the killings were intended to create terror, as well as simply eliminating political opponents. Uncertainty about who had been killed and where and why kept the Communists and the left in general off balance, encouraging rumor and uncertainty. Unable to be sure just what the scope of the killings would be, the Communists could not judge whether it was best to fight, to flee, or to confess.

This uncertainty also emerges powerfully in the final testimony. This account is the work of an Indonesian journalist sent by his newspaper to investigate one of the last outbreaks of killing associated with the suppression of the PKI. The poverty-stricken Purwodadi region of Central Java was one of a small number of rural areas where the PKI began to develop a guerrilla strategy, and the suppression of the party's incipient military campaign was reportedly accompanied in late 1966 and early 1969 by a wave of killings of civilians by army and home guard forces. Maskun Iskandar visited the region in early 1969 at the invitation of the Indonesian army, which denied the killings had taken place. His report was published serially in the independent newspaper *Indonesia Raya*.

Iskandar's testimony is in many ways unsatisfactory. He saw no bodies, heard little testimony except from official sources, and draws no conclusions. His account leaves the reader hanging and the fact that he visited the region as a guest of the Indonesian army would seem to cast further doubt on his credibility and on the figures he cites. To a Western reader, his report seems almost inconsequential: to an Indonesian reader, however, aware of the constraints of official censorship and unofficial controls on journalism, his report leaves little doubt that a significant massacre took place. His diffident reference to the "camps of death" at Kuwu and the "left-overs" in the camps elsewhere, for instance, would give the censor little to object to, but draw the reader's attention to ominous nomenclature. He dismisses as "useless" his questions to children about their missing parents, but reports faithfully that their eyes brim with tears. He describes the sergeant known as 007 (licensed to kill) as if he disbelieves the story, but his readers will draw their own conclusions from the nickname. When he talks casually about the risk of "losing" his notes, his Indonesian readers know immediately that he is referring to the risk of confiscation by the authorities.

Maskun's report does not tell us what happened in Purwodadi, but his writing reminds us powerfully that not all victims of genocide are able to leave oral or written testimony as their memorial. There are times in human history when neither victims, nor survivors, nor perpetrators have preserved more than a fragmentary record of genocide. The victims at Purwodadi, whose fate is faintly recorded in Iskandar's account, stand for a much larger group, not only in Indonesia, whose destruction remains unrecorded.

Account 1

By the banks of the Brantas, first published in *Injustice, Persecution, Eviction: A Human Rights Update on Indonesia and East Timor* (New York: Asia Watch, 1990), pp. 87–90. Reprinted by permission of Asia Watch.

Some people spoke of Pak[1] Mataim, the bicycle-tire repairman, one of whose eyes was white. His house had been used as the local PKI secre-

tariat, and they said he was the first person in the village to be arrested.
He had been frightened out of his wits. He was taken to the police
station and later detained in Mlaten.

Mlaten? Where was there a prison in Mlaten? There wasn't. That
night I went to Mlaten to see for myself. In fact it was a warehouse that
had become a detention center. Now the building was surrounded with
a thick fence of woven bamboo, so that you couldn't see it from the
outside. The police station I passed seemed empty. I kept going south,
past the subdistrict military headquarters. It was guarded not just by
the army but by members of the Banser.[2] Banser was also guarding the
subdistrict government offices—they were everywhere.

Now every night, raids took place. Four members of my organization were arrested. They were all able to escape or perhaps they were
deliberately let go. They were asked about me, and it was clear I was
already on the list of those to be arrested. After that I no longer slept at
home at night. More often I became a wanderer on the banks of the
Brantas. I didn't have to exhaust myself finding a place to hide because
there was an abattoir, surrounded by high grasses, which was completely
deserted. My younger brothers knew about my hiding place, and one
day brought a schoolmate to see me and warn me to get out of the city.
She said I didn't need to go back to school, especially since the school was
being searched and one of the people they were looking for was me.

Politics forced my transformation from student to fisherman. There
were many other on the Brantas, fishing with nets or rods. Unfortunately for me, the fish I caught didn't bring in any money; I couldn't
sell one.

In November, the rains began to come. The river ran muddy and
fast with weeds, leaves, human limbs and headless corpses. Fishermen
vanished from the banks. I was the only one left, not to fish but to save
my life. At night it was the same as before, only now I was on my own.
One night I heard a rustling coming from the abattoir. I got closer and
lay prone in the bushes like a snail. When I heard voices, I got frightened, but I still wanted to know what was going on. A few seconds
later, I heard the engine of a car. Several Banser members got down
from a Willis jeep. Some of them wore black and carried a piece of
rattan about half a meter long in their left hands, while in the right they
carried machetes. Then came a truck which I recognized as belonging
to Pak Abu, the owner of a textile mill in Jarsongo. . . .

Among those wearing black were several people I knew. Pak Harun wore glasses, had a paunch, and always wore a black fez when he went out. He had a small mustache and dark skin. He was the number one man in Nahdatul Ulama [the national Islamic organization] in the Karangpilang subdistrict. Rejo, still young, was a member of Ansor, the Nahdatul Ulama youth wing, in Wiyung, a village to the west of Kedurus. He was large and tall, also mustached, and wore a seaweed bracelet around his right wrist. He often frequented bars.

"Is the sack ready?" Harun asked. The others said everything was ready. An oil lamp flickered over my head and forced me to lie flat, hoping that the tall grasses would obstruct their view. I didn't dare move, ignoring the ants and mosquitos.

A man was hauled off the truck, his feet and hands bound. A plump man, he was dragged around like a banana stalk. It took three people to do it. They were only ten meters in front of me when, reaching the abattoir, they untied his feet. He was wearing a white cotton shirt with brown stripes. He looked disheveled, as though he hadn't changed clothes in days. He seemed weak—maybe he hadn't been getting enough to eat. The Petromax lamp suddenly illuminated his face, and I got a shock. It was Pak Mukdar, the elementary school principal in Kedurus. His head was bare (usually he wore a fez), and his eye-glasses were gone. Weak as he was, he was forced to stand. There were a few uniformed army sergeants and other military men, but it wasn't clear what rank the others held or what unit they were from. They asked Pak Mukdar questions, and I strained my ears to hear. I just heard murmurs; it wasn't clear whether he had answered.

"If you don't answer what we ask," said one of the military, "say your last prayers. We're going to send you to meet your maker."

The old man didn't say anything. Instead, he began to sing the song so frequently sung by PKI members, the Internationale. Before he could finish, he was shoved from behind by a man in black and fell flat. Maybe he fainted. With his hands still tied, his neck was hacked by Rejo, the youth from Wiyung. He finished off the unconscious, weak old man, whose hands were still tied. My teacher—such a meaningless death, in an abattoir meant for slaughtering cattle. His head was removed and put in the sack. Then they dragged his body to the river and tossed it in. It washed away slowly in front of me. . . .

Another body was also thrown in, also headless. I couldn't count how many headless corpses passed by me. Every time, the head was put in the gunny sack. Then I heard a shout from a voice I recognized and froze; it was Pak Mataim, our bicycle repairman who I think was illiterate. He seemed very thin, and he too was dragged along like a banana stalk. He moaned, begging for mercy, for his life to be spared. They laughed, mocking him. He was terrified. The rope around his feet was taken off, leaving his hands still tied. He cried, and because he couldn't keep quiet, they plugged up his mouth with a clump of earth.

Rejo went into action, and like lightning, his machete cut through the neck of his victim, the one-eyed, powerless, bicycle repairman. His head went into the sack. Then his hands were untied, so that it looked as though he died without first being bound. At first, his headless body disappeared beneath the surface of the water, then eventually it floated up. The next person killed was a woman; I don't know who she was.

At midday when my brother came, he told of seeing a corpse caught against a tree on the edge of the river. From the clothes and certain features of his body, they discovered it was Pak Mukdar. I didn't say a word of what I'd seen. The news caused my mother to fall ill, but such news came every day from the Brantas. Our house was finally raided but I managed to slip away. Following the suggestion of a friend from school, I left the Surabaya area for Lawang, but there too the murderers were roaming around. Suheri, a young killer from the village of Bambangan, invited me to join in helping herd a young man he wanted to kill to the Purwasari forest. He was one of Suheri's own group, not a member of any organization. But Suheri wanted his wife, then a beautiful woman. He didn't get his way, though. When he went to claim his victim's spouse, the woman concerned had disappeared.

Forgive me if I don't include pictures of the places I have described here. At the very least, I hope this little account of the last moments of the many victims can become a kind of explanation for their children, wives, and even grandchildren. Because one thing is clear, not a single person has taken responsibility for all those murders, let alone officially informed the families of those killed.

Account 2

Extracted from Pipit Rochijat. "Am I PKI or non-PKI?" *Indonesia*, 40(1985), pp. 37–52. Reprinted by permission of the Cornell University Modern Indonesia Project.

The Situation during G30S 1965

Up to 1965, the [national] front was divided in two: on the one side the Communist Front, and on the other the United Nationalist-Religious Front. And their respective strengths were about evenly balanced. For some reason or other, PKI strength in the region of Kediri, Tulungagung and Blitar was especially conspicuous. Maybe there was some kind of spillover from Madiun towards Kediri.

The events of October 1, 1965, are something difficult, impossible to forget. The atmosphere was so tense, as though everyone was expecting something [catastrophic] once the takeover of power in Jakarta had been broadcast. All Kartawidjaja said to his family was: "Watch out, be very careful. Something's gone very wrong in Jakarta." Usually the doors and windows of the house were shut around 10:00 P.M., but on October 1 they were closed at 7:00. Fear seized the Kartawidjaja family, for the rumor that the PKI had made a coup and murdered the generals was already spreading. The PKI's own aggressive attitude and the way in which the generals had been killed strengthened the suspicion of PKI involvement. "Such brutal murders could only be the work of *kafirs,* i.e., the Communists," was the kind of comment that one then heard. At the same time, the Kartawidjaja family felt very thankful that General Nasution[3] had escaped with his life. The only pity was that his little daughter was beyond rescue. For almost two weeks, everything was quiet in the Kediri region. People merely stayed on the alert and tensely watchful. In State High School No. 1 too the atmosphere was very heated. Reports that it was the PKI that had gone into rebellion spread rapidly. At every opportunity the Nationalist and Religious groups vilified the students involved with the IPPI.[4] For its part, IPPI took evasive action and rejected all "accusations." They claimed to know nothing about what had happened. They said that the events in Jakarta were a matter of the Council of Generals.

About two weeks after the events of October 1, the NU[5] (especially their Ansor Youth) began to move, holding demonstrations which were joined by the *santri*[6] masses from the *pondok* and *pesantren*[7] around Kediri. They demanded the dissolution of the PKI, and that the death of each general be paid for with those of 100,000 Communists. Offices and other buildings owned by the PKI were attacked and reduced to rubble by the demonstrators. It was said that about eleven Communists died for nothing, simply because they were foolish enough to feel bound to defend PKI property. In an atmosphere of crisis suffused with so much hatred for the PKI, everything became permissible. After all, wasn't it everyone's responsibility to fight the *kafir?* And vengeance against the PKI seemed only right, since people felt that the Party had gone beyond the pale. So, the fact that only eleven Communists had [so far] died was regarded as completely inadequate. This kind of thinking also infected Kartawidjaja's Son No. 2.

Yet there was a [strange] episode which is worth mentioning here. To the east of the Kediri municipal bus station there was a certain PKI office. Actually, it was really only an ordinary house. But in front of it there was a signboard bearing all those names smelling of the PKI; from the PKI itself through the BTI,[8] Gerwani,[9] and IPPI, to the People's Youth. It so happened that when the demonstrators arrived in front of that house, they found an old man out in front getting a bit of fresh air. They asked him whether he was a member of the PKI. "No," he answered, "I'm a member of the BTI." "Same thing!" yelled a number of the demonstrators as they started beating him. He toppled over, moaning with pain. He was lucky not to be killed. But the house was demolished as a result of the rage of the masses. And, as usual, before carrying out their task, the NU masses roared "Allahu Akbar [Allah is Great]!" After this bloody demonstration, Kediri became calm once more. Only the atmosphere stayed tense. And this went on for about 3–4 weeks.

Wanted:[10] Communists

Once the mesmerizing calm had ended, the massacres began. Not only the NU masses, but also those of the PNI joined in. The army didn't get much involved. First to be raided were workers' quarters at the sugar factory. Usually at night . . . to eliminate the Communist elements. It was done like this: a particular village would be surrounded by squads of Nationalist and Religious Youth (Muslim and Christian [Protestant], for example in Pare). A mass of Ansor Youth would be brought in from the various *pondok* and *pesantren* in the Kediri region. On average, about 3,000 people would be involved. The expectation was that, with the village surrounded, no Communist elements would be able to escape.

It was pretty effective too. Each day, as Kartawidjaja's Son No. 2 went to, or returned from, State Senior High School No. 1, he always saw corpses of Communists floating in the River Brantas. The thing was that the school was located to the "kulon" (west) of the river. And usually the corpses were no longer recognizable as human. Headless. Stomachs torn open. The smell was unbelievable. To make sure they didn't sink, the carcasses were deliberately tied to, or impaled on, bamboo stakes. And the departure of corpses from the Kediri region down the Brantas achieved its golden age when bodies were stacked together on rafts over which the PKI banner proudly flew.

In those areas through which the Brantas did not wind, the corpses were, as you'd expect, buried in mass graves—as, for example, around Pare. There the Christian [Protestant] masses were very active. But then, the export of corpses down the Brantas began to bother the city of Surabaya. The rumor went round that the drinking water was filtered out of the river. And by the time they reached Surabaya, the corpses were in complete decay. After protests from Surabaya, PKI were no longer flung into the Brantas, but were disposed of in mass graves. The prepared holes were dug pretty big, and were thus capable of handling dozens of Communists at a time.

Furthermore, at one time the road leading up to Mount Klotok (to the west of Kediri city) was decorated with PKI heads.

About 1 kilometer [.6 mi.] to the north of the Ngadirejo sugar factory, you'd find a lot of houses of prostitution. Once the purge of Communist elements got under way, clients stopped coming for sexual satisfaction. The reason: most clients—and prostitutes—were too frightened, for, hanging up in front of the houses, there were a lot of male Communist genitals—like bananas hung out for sale.

Naturally, such mass killings were welcomed by the Nationalist and Religious groups. Indeed, [they felt,] the target of 100,000 Communist lives for one general's had to be achieved. It was the same for Kartawidjaja's Son No. 2 and his family. Specially when they got the word that for the Kartawidjaja family a Crocodile Hole[11] had been prepared, for use if the PKI were victorious.

This atmosphere of vengeance spread everywhere. Not merely in the outside world, but even into the schools, for example State High School No. 1. There the atmosphere was all the more ripe in that for all practical purposes the school broke down, and classes did not continue as usual. Many students did not come to school at all, like Syom, for example, a friend of Kartawidjaja's Son No. 2, who had to spend most of his time going round helping purge the Kediri region of Communist elements. Kartawidjaja's Son No. 2 saw many cases where teachers and student members of IPPI at State High School No. 1 were held up [*sic*] knife point by their Nationalist and Religious comrades. With the knives at their throats they were threatened with death. They wept, begging forgiveness and expressing regret for what they had done while members of the IPPI. In the end all the secrets came out (or maybe false confessions). Each person tried to save himself at another's expense. After all, they were human beings too, and thus still wished to enjoy life.

It was evident the the Kediri area was unsafe for Communists (strangely enough, except in one instance, they made no move to offer any resistance). So most of them tried to flee to Surabaya or sought protection at the Kediri City Kodim.[12] But even in jail they were not safe. Too many of them sought safety there, and the jail could not take them all in. In the end, the army often trucked them off to Mt. Klotok (the road there passed by State High School No. 1). Who knows what the army did with them there—what was clear was that the trucks went off fully loaded and came back empty. Furthermore, the Kodim had no objections at all if people from the Nationalist or Religious groups came to ask for [certain] Communists they needed. The Kodim was prepared to turn over Communist prisoners, provided those who needed them brought their own transportation (not including motorbikes, of course).

At State High School No. 1 student activity proceeded calmly. It was practically like long vacation except for continuing to assemble at school. On one occasion a teacher asked Syom, the friend of Kartawidjaja's Son No. 2, where he'd been all this time, never coming to school. And indeed, he had seldom showed up. He answered: "On tour [of inspection], sir." And people understood what he meant by "on tour." For aside from being an acronym of *turu kanaturu kene* (sleeping there, sleeping here), it also meant "busy eliminating Communists." Syom was one of the executioners. And the fame of an executioner was measured by the number of victims whose lives he succeeded in taking.

Usually, those Communists whom people had managed to round up were turned over to an executioner, so that he could despatch their souls to another world. Not everyone is capable of killing (though there are some exceptions). According to what a number of executioners themselves claimed (for Kartawidjaja's Son No. 2 had many friends among them), killing isn't easy. After despatching the first victim, one's body usually feels feverish and one can't sleep. But once one has sent off a lot of souls to another world, one gets used to killing. "It's just like butchering a goat," they'd claim. And the fact is that Kartawidjaja's Son No. 2 often stole out of the house, either to help guard the [local] PNI headquarters located in the home of Pak Salim (the driver of the school bus in the area around Ngadirejo) or to watch the despatch of human souls. This too made sleeping difficult. Remembering the moans of the victims as they begged for mercy, the sound of the blood bursting from the victims' bodies, or the spouting of fresh blood when a victim was beheaded. All of this pretty much made one's hair stand on end. To say nothing of the screams of a Gerwani leader as her vagina was pierced with a sharpened bamboo pole. Many of the corpses lay sprawled like chickens after decapitation.

But even though such events were pretty horrifying, the participants felt thankful to have been given the chance to join in destroying infidels. Not to mention the stories brought back by Maha, a friend of Kartawidjaja's Son No. 2, who participated in eliminating the Communists in the Pare area. He was a Christian. What he said was that the victims were taken off by truck and then set down in front of holes prepared in advance. Then their heads were lopped off with a Samurai [sword] that had been left behind by a Japanese soldier in the past. When the mission was accomplished, the holes were filled in with earth.

And among so many incidents, naturally there were a few which still remain a "beautiful" memory for Karta-widjaja's Son No. 2. For example, when the Ansor Youth surrounded a particular village to the east of the sugar factory, they went into a number of houses to clean out the Communist elements. In one house, as it happened, there were two kids living there who were listed as activists in the People's Youth. When the Ansor people knocked at the door, it was the parents of the two hunted boys who answered. "Where are your sons?" "If it's possible, please don't let my boys be killed"—such was the request of the old couple. They offered to give up their lives in their children's stead. Not merely was this offer accepted, but the exterminators also killed their two children.

Next: even though Kartawidjaja was hated by the PKI, on one occasion he told Kartawidjaja's Son No. 2 to go to the home of Pak Haryo, an employee who lived next door and was an activist in the SBG. Kartawidjaja told him to fetch Pak Haryo to the house and have him sleep there, bringing with him whatever clothes he needed. But since it was then pretty late at night, when Kartawidjaja's Son No. 2 knocked at the door, Pak Haryo's family made no response. Maybe they were afraid that it might be the Angel of Death come visiting. The next morning, Karta-widjaja came himself to pick up Pak Haryo. Subsequently he was taken by Kartawidjaja to Surabaya, to be hidden there.

Naturally, helping Communists wasn't at all in line with the ideas of Kartawidjaja's Son No. 2. So he asked: "Dad, why are you of all people protecting Pak Haryo?" "Pak Haryo doesn't know a thing, and besides it would be a shame with all his kids."

Kartawidjaja was fortunate in that he was always informed about "who and who" was to lose his life. And many Communists who had once vilified Kartawidjaja now came to his house to ask for protection. On one occasion he set aside a special space in the meeting hall where people asking for his protection could stay overnight.

All through the purges, the mosques were packed with Communist visitors. Even the Worker's Hall was specially made over into a place for Friday prayers. As a result, many people judged that the PKI people had now become *sadar* [aware: of their past errors, of Allah's truth]. And hopes for survival became increasingly widespread. And at one of these Friday prayers, Kartawidjaja was asked to make a speech in front of all the assembled worshippers. He told them that "praying isn't compulsory. Don't force people to do it. Let those who want to pray pray. And if people don't want to, then they don't have to."

Account 3

This section is a condensed version of a chapter published originally in Robert Cribb, ed., *The Indonesian Killings of 1965–1966*. Monash Papers on Southeast Asia, No. 21, published by the Centre of Southeast Asian Studies, Clayton, Victoria, Australia, 1990. Reprinted by permission.

My hair, clothes, my bag were all dusty. It was a bad road from Purwodadi to Kuwu. In a few places the asphalt could still be seen, but for the rest the road was paved only with brittle stones which crushed easily. "Hard river stones are like gold in this area,"[13] said the military man who escorted us in the jeep. We proceeded slowly, seldom meeting another vehicle. I had been told that the only public transport available was an old train which ran the 62 kilometres [39 mi.] from Semarang to Purwodadi. So here was one piece of Princen's[14] information confirmed:

communications were difficult. But was the rest true? Had there been mass killings? Were conditions in the Kuwu area tense? Now that I was on my way to the area, I had to find answers to these riddles.

Before we left Purwodadi for the Kuwu area, which had been identified in press reports as the centre of the killing, the KODIM commander gave us a briefing. PKI membership in Purwodadi was estimated at 200,000, out of a population of 700,000 in eighteen *kecamatan*.[15] Two hundred of the 285 lurah [village heads] were PKI, he told us. Out of this number, only about a thousand had been "finished off," and those were only the leaders. "If we arrested everyone who was PKI," the commander told us, "we would not know what to do with them. We do not have space to detain them and we could not simply release them because the rest of the population would not have them back." The commander of KODAM VII[16] plans to transmigrate them.

On the afternoon of 5 March I visited four of the fourteen prison camps in Purwodadi *kabupaten*.[17] I saw 987 prisoners and it would be dishonest if I were to say that they were either fat or the reverse. The camps themselves, I was told, included former store houses which the military had borrowed from local people. So there were no terrifying iron bars, but they were secure enough. Let us take Camps I and II in Kuwu as examples. Local people call them *kamp maut*, camps of death. It is not clear to me, however, just what they mean by this. Is there some connection with those reports about Kuwu being in the grip of fear? I don't know.

Stories passing from mouth to mouth tend to get bigger. This was why my editor had sent me to get firsthand accounts. Had killings taken place without due legal process? Was it true that each *desa* [village] had to supply seventy-five victims a night? Was it true, as we heard, that the victims were tied up in groups of five before being shot, struck with iron bars or slaughtered without mercy? I had no success in checking these details and I got tired of hearing the same words: "I don't know," and "perhaps." My readers, I know, want positive confirmation, not inferences from lack of information. I remembered the instructions of my editor before I left: "When you are doing this job," he said, "remember that all we are interested in is the truth. Truth may be bitter, but we are not aiming to discredit anyone or damage anyone, we have no hidden agenda, as people are inclined to allege these days."

Little children surrounded the jeep, but they did not dare come close, not like the children at the army barracks. They seemed to wonder why so many outsiders were visiting their village lately. I approached one of them and asked in low Javanese, "Do you have a sister?" He was silent. "Where is your mother?" I asked again. He remained silent, making circles in the sand with his big toe. "Is your father here?" I asked at random. The child raised his eyes. They were brimming over. Then he ran away into the narrow streets of the kampung. I deeply regretted asking those "useless" questions.

Back in my hotel, I attempted to sort my confused notes. The very figures I had written down of numbers killed seemed to be shaking. The names of villagers where the killings had taken place seemed to cry out. Perhaps the light in the room was too dim. The other guests in the hotel were all asleep; I had come back rather late. It was 8:00 P.M. when we left Purwodadi for Semarang accompanied by our military escort.

I noted once again what I had heard from an official source who wanted to remain anonymous. Three hundred prisoners, he said, had been killed in the desa Simo. Two hundred and fifty in Cerewek, two hundred in Kalisari, one hundred in Kuwu, two hundred in Tanjungsari. Was this true? "Did this really happen?" I had asked him. "It's no secret any more," he told me. "All the locals know about it. No honest man will deny it. The graves of the victims are witness to it." I asked the same questions to all those who gave me information, people who wanted to crush the PKI but did not want it done in this way. What they said was, "This kind of thing will not solve anything, not for the people who do it, not for those it is done to." When the army took me through those areas which were said to be tense, I tried to find proof. Was it true that there was a grave behind Cerewek railway station which had recently been planted with banana trees? Was there a grave in the rice fields at Banjarsari? Someone told me there were graves along the river in Tanjungsari, but our escort did not let us see any of these things. I got tired of writing down the names of villages where there were supposed to have been executions and burials. In Pakis, so my official source said, there were one hundred victims; in Grobogan fifty. Outside this area my source did not have specific information, but he named villages: Toroh, Kedungglundung, Sambongbangi, Telogo, Mbogo, Banjardowo, Plosorejo, Monggot, Gundik and so on. Could any of this be proven?

Almost the whole night long, I sorted at my notes on the Purwodadi affair. I made a simple map, marking important places, places with reported killings, reported burial places, areas where there was a majority of women. I was also told that in Cerewek, Gabus, and Sulur 70 percent of the population are widows. Some people even said that in Banjardowo it was hard to find a single adult male. Where could they have gone to? It was very late and water in the bathroom was dripping constantly. Some of my notes were hard to find. "It would be terrible to lose them," I thought. "After they took so much effort to compile." I thought of all the time I had spent, asking here and there, officials only of course, and only from the KODAM and KODIM. I had even managed to talk directly to people who took active part in crushing the PKI.

I had a lot of information about the operations in Purwodadi, right from when they began, but that would take too much space. Let us start with 5 April 1968, just under a year ago. The police in Purwodadi had just arrested Sugeng, a former PKI member who conducted raids in the area. Under interrogation, he told the police that the PKI was putting together an underground organization called the People's Liberation Army [Tentara Pembebasan Rakyat, TPR], led by Suratin, who was still at large. Level I of the TPR (equivalent to the PKI's old Comite Daerah Besar, regional committees) was based first in Semarang, at Jl Dr. Cipto 280 and 298 [a street address]. Government forces then took over these buildings and began breaking up PKI operations with increasing success. The PKI kept up its operations, but it was shadowed ever more closely and had to change its operatives frequently. When did the large-scale arrests begin?" I asked one of those involved. "27 June 1968," he answered.

Hearing that date reminded me that responsibility for operations had been transferred to KODIM 0717 Purwodadi. If I am not mistaken, the headquarters had then been in Grobogan, about four kilometres [2.4 mi.] from Purwodadi, while the investigating team had been first at Kradenan and then at Kuwu, about five kilometres [3 mi.] away. I stopped writing, and tried to remember what I had noted down about Corporal S and Sergeant S. From what I had been told, both men were much feared in Kuwu. Perhaps there was some connection with the story I heard from Kuwu residents in Semarang that the sergeant was known as Agent 007. Ian Fleming's James Bond. Licensed to kill. I was surprised people could be so loose in their use of terminology. James Bond was on the side of good, but was this man? People told me that he used to summon the authorities to a ritual meal before he went out on his operations. One time he got drunk and shouted, "I am Agent 007. I have killed hundreds of people." Fortunately an official who happened to be sitting next to him was able to stop his mouth and prevent him from saying any more.

Again I rummaged through my notes on the arrests. There was an official who told me that the arrests had gone on for a month from 27 July. When the prisoners had been collected, they took seventy-five away each night, in two lots. Later this became less and they only took away seventy-five prisoners every Saturday night. Someone walked past my room. I quickly hid the papers under the mattress and switched off the light. Then everything fell quiet again, except for the constant short cough of the night watchman. It reminded me of an incident before I had met the KODIM commander in Purwodadi the previous night, but I might come back to that. I still had not finished transcribing my notes on the arrests and killings.

According to the earliest information from Princen, two to three thousand people had been killed. This seemed very high, out of a total population of eight thousand in Purwodadi *kabupaten*.[18] So I began to count. Seventy-five people at night for, say, two months, how much would that be? Now, there are 285 *desa* in Purwodadi. There cannot have been killing in all of them, so let us assume just ten, and that the killings took place once a week, not every night. This would make 8 (weeks) × 10 (*desa*) × 75 people = 6000 people. Impossible! What if I make it just one *desa*? That is still hundreds, still mass killings. I folded up my notes. I would return them in due course to the authorities in the form of questions.

I saw no beggars in Purwodadi. They say the *kabupaten* was once full of them, but there was now no sign of them. I asked my escort. They had been pulled in during the searches, he said; there were forty-three in the camps now. Were they PKI people hiding as beggars, I wondered, or just ordinary non-communist beggars? Another thing drew my attention. There were said to be five mad people in the camp, and none had been sent to a mental hospital. Even one mad person is a lot for a small *kabupaten,* but five? Perhaps Purwodadi is an exception. It was not clear whether these people were mad when they went into the camp or whether they became mad there. I do not know.

There are fourteen women among the prisoners, perhaps Gerwani, perhaps not. I did not get a chance to ask them. But let me give details of prison camps as I know them. There are fourteen camps in Purwodadi. In the town itself, there are 411 prisoners, in Toroh fifty-one, in Gundik forty. Ah yes, and before I forget, the total includes 127 prisoners left over from the arrests in 1965. In Godong there are nine prisoners; in Kradenan two camps, the first with fifty-five, the second with sixty-seven. Fifty in Sulur, seventy-two in Grobogan. The total number of prisoners, including beggars, lunatics, and women is 987 in fourteen camps. In Wirosari there are seventy-nine prisoners, in Ngaringan sixty-four, in Tawangharjo thirty-six, in Pulokulon forty-seven, in Grubug five, in Tewoganu thirty-three, in Kedungjati one. In January there were four cases of illness, in February two. Some people said these were all recent arrivals, others called them "left-overs" (*sisa*). It was not altogether clear to me what the term *sisa* meant, so I did not pay much attention to it.

I put all my notes and the materials I had not yet transcribed back in my bag and closed it with a large question mark. I hope that an investigation team dedicated to upholding the law will open it.

Chapter Nine
Genocide in East Timor

James Dunn

Introduction

In 1975 Indonesian forces invaded the Portuguese colony of East Timor, which was then in the process of decolonization. The invasion provoked a spirited armed resistance, and during the subsequent five-year period, which was marked by bitter fighting in the interior and harsh oppression in occupied areas, the population of the territory underwent a substantial decline. So heavy was the loss of life resulting from the annexation that as recently as 1991 it was reported still significantly lower than the population estimate prior to the Indonesian invasion. In relative terms, therefore, the humanitarian costs of this act of forced integration have reached genocidal proportions, and the East Timor case is manifestly one of the most serious in modern history.

While it should not be concluded that the Indonesian authorities in Jakarta embarked on a grand plan designed to bring about the systematic destruction of the Timorese people, Indonesia's occupation strategies and the behavior of the military were bound to achieve that end. Furthermore, the large influx of Indonesian settlers into the province may, in the long run, lead to another form of genocide, that is, the destruction of the distinctive culture of East Timor. Since the invasion, the Timor case has been on the U.N. agenda, and from 1977 onward Indonesia and the international community have repeatedly been advised of the humanitarian consequences of this process of annexation and subjugation.

The international response to this very serious violation of international law has mostly been indifferent and irresolute. Indeed, the government of Indonesia, despite its heavy dependence on economic aid, clearly did not feel the need to respond to international concerns in a positive way, until the Santa Cruz massacre in November 1991. These expressions of concern were so weak in the years following the invasion that the Indonesian authorities were openly defiant of world opinion. However, the Santa

Cruz massacre sent shock waves around the world and forced the Indonesian government on the defensive, but the latter's unconvincing response nevertheless has been undeserving of the credibility it has been accorded by Jakarta's major Western friends. Thanks to accommodating reactions from officials in, among others, Washington, Paris, Tokyo, and Canberra, at the time of writing the Suharto regime had regained its determination to ignore the ongoing criticisms of its annexation of East Timor.

The Setting

The island of Timor lies at the southeastern extremity of the Indonesian Nusatenggara island group, which was named the Lesser Sundas in Dutch colonial times. In this archipelago it is located at the opposite end to the island of Bali, one of Asia's best-known tourist attractions. Following a long period of rivalry and conflict, Timor came to be divided into two almost equal parts by the Dutch and Portuguese colonial administrations. The partition began to take shape about the middle of the seventeenth century, as Portugal's colonial power in the East Indies began to weaken in the face of the more vigorous Dutch intrusion. Boundary disputes between the two colonial powers persisted until the late nineteenth century, that is until the Lisbon Convention of 1893, and the subsequent signing of the *Sentenca Arbitral* in April 1913, which demarcated the borders as they exist today. The Portuguese colony of East Timor comprised the eastern half of the island, the tiny enclave of Oecussi on the north coast of West Timor and the small island of Atauro north of Dili.

East Timor is a small country, but it is not insignificant by the standards of smallness among today's membership of the United Nations. The territory has an area of about 7,300 square miles, comparable in size as well as population with Fiji and only slightly smaller in area than Israel or the state of New Jersey. On the eve of the Indonesian invasion the Timorese population of the territory was estimated at about 680,000 people, with an annual growth rate of near 2 percent.

Portuguese navigators first reached Timor about twenty years after Columbus embarked on his epic trans-Atlantic crossing half a millennium ago. About fifty years later, their colonial rule of the area began in earnest. Therefore, for more than four centuries Portugal had been the dominant, almost exclusive, external influence in East Timor—except for a brief Japanese interregnum, from February 1942 until they surrendered to Allied forces in August 1945.

Within five years, the Dutch colony of the Netherlands East Indies was formally to become the Republic of Indonesia. Portuguese colonial rule over East Timor was restored, however, and until 1974 its colonial status was virtually ignored by the nationalist leaders of the new republic. This lack of interest persisted during the last seven years of Sukarno's presidency, when Indonesia embarked on an aggressive anti-colonial policy. Sukarno's regime vigorously asserted its own claim for the "return" of West Irian. After that objective was secured, Indonesia launched in 1962 a costly and futile confrontation of Malaysia, which Sukarno perceived as a British neo-colonial creation.

At no stage during this period did Indonesia seek to bring any real pressure to bear on the Portuguese administration in East Timor, although the Salazar regime had by that time become the chief target of the mounting campaign for decolonization. Portugal had become the only colonial power which refused to declare its colonies non-self-governing. While Dutch colonialism in West New Guinea was denounced in vitriolic terms, the more traditional form of colonial rule then being conducted by the Portuguese in neighboring East Timor scarcely rated a mention in Jakarta.

From the early sixties until 1965 there were occasional remarks by a few leading Indonesian political and military figures, hinting that East Timor's future lay with its big neighbor, but these statements were not taken further by the government of the time, and certainly never evolved into a formal claim or political campaign.[1] After 1965 the Suharto regime, which was keen to develop closer relations with the Western nations sharing its hostility to communism and to attract economic assistance from them, was anxious to show that Indonesia no longer had territorial designs on the territories adjacent to it.

This policy appeared to prevail at the highest political level in Jakarta, right up to the point of Indonesia's military intervention in East Timor, with most official statements from Jakarta emphasizing East Timor's right to self-determination.[2] Certainly, at no stage, under either Sukarno or Suharto, was a claim to East Timor ever formally made by the government in Jakarta.[3]

The idea of an East Timor nation emerged spontaneously from the Portuguese colonial experience, just as Indonesia, Malaysia, Singapore, and the north Kalimantan states were shaped by British and Dutch colonial policies and rivalry. Although the two great empires of Srivijaya and Majapahit extended Java's influence to other parts of the archipelago for a period, there is no evidence that Timorese kingdoms were ever subjugated by the Javanese.

As a political concept, the notion of a nation of East Timor, even taking into account the arbitrary division of the island, is surely no less valid than the idea of an Indonesian state.

It could be said that the Indonesian nation was itself created not by a natural historical evolution but by colonial circumstances, determined by imperial and commercial rivalry in distant Western Europe. The legitimacy of the Indonesian state, it could therefore be argued, has its roots in Dutch colonial expansion and the political consensus—and dissent—it aroused, rather than in the natural evolution of a national political culture.

* * *

In the world at large in 1974, events in East Timor aroused little interest. It was poor, undeveloped, remote, and unconnected to the global network of commercial and tourist communications. It possessed no apparent strategic value to any nation, with the possible exception of Indonesia. Its status was therefore of little consequence, in perceptions of national interest, other than to Portugal, Indonesia, and Australia. By the end of that year, the Portuguese themselves, with their empire now falling apart, had turned to Europe and were little interested in the fortunes of a distant colony of very little economic value.

Australia is East Timor's nearest Western neighbor, its Northern Territory coastline lying less than 400 miles to the south, across the Timor Sea. For some years after World War II, Canberra regarded the Portuguese colony as strategically important, but by 1962 its significance had faded in the view of the Australian political establishment. In that year it was the assessment of the Australian government that Indonesian rule over East Timor would not pose any additional external threat, and was therefore not unacceptable. Significantly, in September of 1974 Prime Minister Gough Whitlam, who was attracted to the notion that East Timor's integration with Indonesia was the best solution, conveyed that view to the Indonesian leader, President Suharto, at a meeting in Java.

Based on the strong support for decolonization and self-determination declared by Whitlam after he came into office in December 1972, the Timorese had a much more optimistic view of Australia's position. Furthermore, the idea that Australia owed a debt to East Timor because of the extensive support its forces received during their commando operation against the Japanese in 1942[4] had created an unshakeable belief that Australia would help them out in the end.

While Foreign Minister Adam Malik was prepared to countenance independence for East Timor, his views were not in fact shared by Indonesia's most powerful military leaders, who had from the very outset different plans for East Timor's future. To be fair, it was not so much a desire for additional territory that motivated them—East Timor was, in the days before the recent offshore oil discoveries, anything but an economic prize. One of their main concerns was that an independent East Timor would stimulate ambitions for independence among discontented nearby ethnic groups, such as the West Timorese and the Ambonese. Also, in the aftermath of the Vietnam War, Indonesia's military leadership was obsessed with the risk of Communist infiltration and insurgency. To the military, therefore, integration was the only acceptable solution for East Timor.

As it happened, the Australian government was in a position to head off Indonesia's designs on East Timor but did not do so. From their extensive intelligence monitoring of Indonesian military activities[5] they were aware, at its very inception, that a subversive operation had been put in place with the aim of bringing about integration.[6] Before the end of 1974 this operation was set up by a group of Indonesian generals, among them, Lieutenant General Ali Murtopo, Major General Benny Murdani, a senior intelligence officer close to the President, and Lieutenant General Yoga Sugama, then head of the intelligence services. The existence of this operation, code-named *"Operasi Komodo,"*[7] became known to U.S. and Australian intelligence agencies before the year was out. Its aim was to bring about the integration of East Timor at any cost, though preferably by non-military means. Its first activities, which included a stream of clumsy propaganda vilifying the independence movement, the open backing of Apodeti (Associacao Popular Democratica Timorense [the Timorese Popular Democratic Association], a small pro-integration group), and some thinly disguised covert intelligence actions, had the effect not of dividing the two major parties, but of bringing them together.

Thus, it was partly in reaction to this heavy-handed meddling that, early in January 1975, Fretilin[8] and UDT[9] formed a common front for independence. There is little doubt that Australia's accommodating stance, at the official level, strengthened the hands of the generals bent on the annexation of East Timor. Indeed, it is probable that the viability of this operation was predicated on the assumption that Australia would accept it.

* * *

By the end of 1974 Indonesia was waging a strident propaganda campaign against Fretilin, in particular, and all Timorese in favor of independence in general. Fretilin was a party of the left and the Indonesian military chiefs were quite paranoid about its activities. The Fretilin leaders were accused of being both Communist and anti-Indonesian, and falsified accounts of links between them, Peking, and Hanoi were circulated. In reaction to the provocative propaganda outpourings from Jakarta, the Timorese themselves became increasingly hostile toward Indonesia.

In the first couple of months after April 1974 the Portuguese were rather indifferent towards the idea of independence for East Timor, with some military officers believing that joining with Indonesia made sense for such a small and undeveloped country. One senior official believed he had a responsibility to promote the idea of integration.[10] However, the apparent popular support for independence eventually convinced Lisbon and the colonial authorities that the Timorese were simply not disposed to merge with Indonesia. They saw themselves as being different, in terms of their culture, their languages, their political traditions, and their religions.[11] The aggressive approach of the Indonesians after August 1974 merely served to strengthen the East Timorese national consciousness, impelling the two major parties to form a coalition for independence. In the event the Portuguese authorities commenced a decolonization program late in 1974, presenting the Timorese political elite with three options—full independence, continuation with Portugal under some new and more democratic arrangement, or integration with Indonesia.

The year 1975 proved to be a turbulent one for East Timor. As a result of political instability in Portugal, and the demoralization of the overseas administration, the decolonization program for Timor soon ran into difficulties. Political turmoil in Lisbon weakened the colonial power's administrative control, and the Indonesian generals heading *Operasi Komodo* exploited the deteriorating situation subtly and subversively. By mid-autumn of that year political differences had surfaced between the two major parties, and in an *Operasi Komodo* operation, guided by General Ali Murtopo himself, the Indonesians sought to divide the independence movement. Their propaganda offensive against Fretilin was intensified, while the UDT leaders were invited to Jakarta—and courted. They were lectured, sometimes by Murtopo himself, on the dangers of communist subversion, were exhorted to break the coalition with Fretilin, and were sent, at Jakarta's expense, on tours of anti-communist political centers in Asia—to South Korea, the Philippines, and Taiwan. Furthermore, fabricated evidence of links between the Fretilin leaders, on the one hand, and Peking and Hanoi, on the other, was passed on to them.

At least two of the conservative Timorese leaders, Lopes da Cruz and Mousinho, were actually recruited by Bakin, the powerful Indonesian military intelligence agency.[12] By the middle of 1975, relations between the two Timorese parties had become so tense that talks between them broke down completely. At this time, rumors were circulated by Bakin agents that Fretilin was planning a coup and encouraging UDT leaders to act hastily and rashly.[13]

Early in August 1975 General Murtopo himself informed UDT leaders, who were visiting Jakarta, that his intelligence agents had uncovered a Fretilin conspiracy to launch a coup, and he encouraged them to take pre-emptive action.[14] Days after their return, these UDT leaders, with what military support they could muster, launched an abortive coup in Dili; abortive, because within three weeks the party and its followers had been overwhelmed by Fretilin. They were defeated not because of external military intervention, but because most Timorese troops, who formed the majority of the colonial military establishment, favored the left-wing party. In this brief but intense conflict[15] the Portuguese, whose administrative apparatus had been reduced to a small number of officials and less than 100 combat troops, withdrew to the offshore island of Atauro.[16]

The Indonesian military, their plans having backfired, would have no truck with the independence movement and ignored its overtures. *Operasi Komodo*'s military commanders sought to persuade President Suharto to authorize direct military intervention, but the President, who was unenthusiastic for any moves that would prejudice Indonesia's international standing (especially in Southeast Asia and in the United States) as a nation without territorial ambitions, continued to hesitate until September when Generals Murtopo, Murdani, and Yoga Sugama (then head of Bakin) managed to secure his consent to a military operation against East Timor. They were able to assure him that the governments of greatest importance to Indonesia, among them, the United States, Japan, Australia, the Netherlands, and ASEAN [Association of Southeast Asian Nations], would accommodate a military operation to secure East Timor's integration into Indonesia.

Two weeks later, Indonesia's first major military action against East Timorese territory was launched: it was carried out as a covert operation, and involved an attack on the border village of Balibo. Its casualties were to include the five members of two television teams from Australia.[17]

Weeks before this assault, the victorious Fretilin leaders had sought to assuage Indonesian fears, and had encouraged the Portuguese to return and resume decolonization. But there was no response from the Portuguese, whose government in Lisbon was still in crisis. The Indonesian response was a series of military attacks over the border from West Timor. Antara, the official news agency, claimed that the "anti-Fretilin forces" had regrouped and were counterattacking.

With the Portuguese having failed to respond to their request to return and resume decolonization, the Indonesians attacking from the west, and the international community ignoring their plight, Fretilin's decision unilaterally to declare East Timor an independent republic was hardly surprising.

The Invasion and Its Aftermath

Having in a way provoked Fretilin's hasty decision unilaterally to declare East Timor independent, the Indonesians lost no time in mounting a full-scale invasion, an amphibious attack on the capital, Dili. The status of East Timor was therefore changed abruptly on 7 December 1975,[18] when a combined military and naval force, under the overall command of Major General Benny Murdani, moved in from the sea. From the considerable evidence accumulated over the past 15 years it is clear that the invasion and subjugation of East Timor, especially in the early stages, was carried out with scant regard for the lives, let alone rights, of the Timorese people, whose plight was virtually unknown to the outside world. Not only was the act of aggression itself a violation of the U.N. charter, but the brutal way it was carried out over a period of several years constitutes a crime against humanity.

In the very first days of the invasion, rampaging Indonesian troops engaged in an orgy of indiscriminate killing, rape, and torture. Large-scale public executions were carried out—women being included among the victims—suggesting a systematic campaign of terror. In some villages whole communities were slaughtered, except for young children.

Outraged by these atrocities, the small but determined Timorese army bitterly contested the advance of the invading forces, and in terrain ideal for guerrilla warfare they were able to inflict heavy losses on the attackers. Through the early 1980s they were able to deny the ABRI[19] effective control outside the main towns and administrative centers. The retaliation of the invading force to this stiff challenge to integration was the imposition of a harsh and oppressive occupation. In the areas under Indonesian control, serious human rights violations were a daily occurrence, forcing tens of thousands of Timorese to seek refuge behind Fretilin lines.

The invasion force, which was soon to amount to more than 30,000 troops, entered the Portuguese colony from the west, where East Timor adjoins Indonesia, and in landings at major towns on the north coast, such as Baucau and Maubara. Thousands of Timorese were killed in the first weeks of the invasion when, from all accounts, troops went on the rampage, no doubt in response to the unexpectedly determined Timorese resistance to the invasion. In Dili there were a number of public executions—including at the wharf area where more than 100 were reportedly shot, at Santa Cruz, at the Military Police barracks, and at Tasitolo, near the airport. Also, in the small towns of Maubara and Liquica and at other villages in the interior, Indonesian military units carried out public executions, numbering from 20 to more than 100 persons.

While conditions in the occupied areas were harsh and oppressive, indiscriminate killing, raping, and torture were even more widespread in the disputed areas. In their advance into the mountainous interior, especially where the advance was being hotly contested, the Indonesian forces indiscriminately killed many of the Timorese they encountered. The biggest single killing reported to the author by the Timorese driver of one of the Indonesian trucks occurred in 1975 at Lakmanan, near the western border where invading troops returning from a stiff encounter with Fretilin turned their guns on a large temporary encampment of Timorese. One of these witnesses estimated that as many as 2,000 were killed over a period of several hours.[20]

As Indonesia sought to overpower the armed resistance and to suppress opposition to integration in occupied areas, tens of thousands of Timorese were to perish through the end of 1979. During this period East Timor was virtually sealed off from the outside world. The International Red Cross, which had been present in strength until just before the invasion, did not regain access to the territory until the second half of 1979, almost four years after the invasion.[21]

Although initially it was the intention of most townsfolk to remain at their homes, the widespread killing, the torture, and the raping committed by the invading troops resulted in the flight of a large proportion of the population into the interior, to the comparative safety of the mountain districts under the control of Fretilin. However, it was in the mountainous interior of the island that the greatest loss of life was to occur in the following three years. Most of the deaths were from famine and related diseases, but it was the harsh treatment meted out by the Indonesians that prompted the Timorese to flee to the mountains.

Because of the absence of demographic records, whether kept by the invaders or by other authorities, no precise account of the human cost of the invasion and its aftermath exists. However, recent Indonesian census statistics provide evidence that it attained genocidal proportions. Before the invasion East Timor's population was about 690,000, and growing at about 2 percent. It follows that today it should be more than 950,000 people. Based on recent Indonesian statistics the population of what is now designated the 27th province of Indonesia is about 740,000 people,[22] but of this number as many as 140,000 are non-Timorese who have in recent years moved into the territory from elsewhere in Indonesia, some of them transmigrants and others opportunistic drifters. It means that, in effect, the Timorese population, sixteen years later, is 12 percent less than what it was in 1975.

The annexation of East Timor has therefore had a drastic effect on all aspects of life in the community. Before the invasion, the ethnic and cultural patterns in the territory were exceedingly complex but, aside from some special characteristics, they resembled the patterns in the nearby islands of Eastern Nusatenggara.[23] The population was essentially Austronesian in character, but with a noticeable Melanesian influence. It reflected a long procession of migrations from west, north, and east. But it would be an oversimplification to describe the territory as culturally part of Indonesia if only because of the great ethnic and cultural diversity within this sprawling archipelagic nation. To call a Timorese Indonesian is rather like calling a Kurd an Iraqi or a Tibetan Chinese, labels which are imprecise, and attract resentment. The Timorese were not, however, antagonistic towards people from other parts of the archipelago, at least before Indonesia began to meddle in the affairs of the island.[24] But in the past they had regarded the occasional visiting Indonesian fishing vessels with some suspicion. Perhaps this was because, unlike the Javanese or Buginese, the Timorese were not themselves a seafaring people and felt threatened by outsiders with these skills.

The rugged mountainous interior of East Timor provided excellent conditions for Fretilin's guerrilla campaign, but the resistance forces were not in a position to provide the basic needs of the tens of thousands of people who sought refuge within this territory. Food and medical supplies were inadequate, and the Timorese were subjected to constant air attacks (including for a short period the use of napalm). The Timorese were bombed and strafed, and once the Indonesian Air Force acquired Bronco anti-insurgency aircraft from the United States, these attacks intensified. In the two years following the invasion the Timorese leaders did manage to feed the people within their lines by developing the agricultural resources available to them in the rich valleys, but according to reports from Fretilin, in 1978 these farms were subject to air attacks by AURI[25] aircraft. According to one report, chemical substances were dropped on the crops, causing the plants to die. By 1978 the food situation behind Fretilin lines was desperate and the Timorese leaders began encouraging their people to return to Indonesian-occupied areas; the resistance forces were no longer able to feed them, nor to provide even the most basic of medical treatment.

Initially, when these "refugees" moved into occupied territory their reception was anything but humane. Some suspected Fretilin supporters were summarily executed, while many others were beaten or tortured at the slightest provocation.[26] The refugees were forced into resettlement camps, where food and medical facilities were grossly inadequate. In 1979 the first international aid workers to enter the territory reported that the basic needs of the Timorese in these centers were being seriously neglected and that thousands were dying needlessly from famine and disease.

Reports on the grim situation in East Timor began to come out of the territory as early as the end of 1976. In that year a confidential report from Catholic Church sources depicted a scene of oppression and wanton killing. Its authors suggested that in the year since the invasion as many as 60,000 Timorese might have lost their lives.[27] Was the international community aware of this very heavy loss of life and, if so, how did it react? In fact these early reports aroused very little international attention. East Timor was remote, little known, and without any strategic or economic importance, even to the colonial power. While the United Nation's itself promptly condemned the invasion and called on Indonesia to withdraw its forces, its pronouncements were mostly vague and irresolute.[28]

Here there is a more sinister aspect to this sorry tale. When the gravity of the humanitarian situation in this territory began to unfold, East Timor could easily have been made an issue of international concern by nations like the United States or Australia if their governments had chosen to do so.[29] In the seventies, however, Indonesia had begun to assume a new importance in the eyes of the major Western powers. It was large, Moslem, oil-producing, and the archipelago straddled the division between the strategically important Pacific and Indian Oceans. And the Suharto regime, despite its undemocratic character, fulfilled important political conditions—it was anti-Communist, development-oriented, and it had created a facade of stability and harmony.

Under those circumstances, the Western governments with the greatest interest in Indonesia—who were also best placed to monitor events in East Timor—chose to play down the reports, most of them emanating from Church sources in Dili, that Indonesian military operations were inflicting very heavy loss of life on the general population. In the Australian Parliament, for example, these reports were repeatedly alluded to by official sources as being unproven, or ill-founded, and exaggerated.

If the foreign missions in Jakarta were aware of just how serious the humanitarian situation was, they were careful not to disclose it in their public statements. In the case of the missions representing Australia, Canada, and the United States the extent to which their diplomats were able to report on this situation was, in the experience of this writer, diminished by the tacit support that their governments had given to integration. To accord credibility to the reports from organizations such as the Catholic Church in East Timor would have been tantamount to admitting by implication a measure of responsibility.

Some of the reports made public could not have been honestly arrived at. For example, early in 1977 one U.S. State Department official told members of Congress that only 2,000 Timorese had died as a result of the invasion. A few weeks later another U.S. official, Robert Oakley, came up with a revised figure of 10,000, which yet another official source later qualified with the comment that many of these deaths had occurred in the fighting between Fretilin and UDT.[30] Australian official responses were delivered in a similar vein. Their statements appeared to be designed to minimize the seriousness of the situation on the ground in East Timor and, in so doing, to discredit reports that Indonesian troops were responsible for widespread death and destruction. It was a blatant attempt to deflect international criticism of Indonesian actions. Thus, in 1978, when conditions in the territory were being described as nightmarish, the Australian government led by Prime Minister Fraser felt able to take the extraordinary step of recognizing de facto the annexation.[31]

By the end of 1979, however, the devastating consequences of Indonesia's military annexation of East Timor could no longer be concealed. And so, some four years after the invasion, when Indonesian authorities finally allowed a small number of international aid workers to conduct a survey of the humanitarian needs of the province, the dimensions of the tragedy began to emerge. The human misery they encountered shocked even some officials with experience in Africa and Southeast Asia. Their estimates suggested that in the preceding four years Timor had lost between a tenth and a third of its population and that 200,000 of the remainder were in appalling conditions in "resettlement camps," which one official, who had previously served in Cambodia, described as among the worst he had seen.[32]

These revelations should have shocked the world into demanding that Indonesia withdraw from the former Portuguese colony, but that did not happen. Not one of the major powers, who were later to be affronted by Argentina's seizure of the Falkland Islands or Iraq's treatment of the Kuwaitis, was prepared to press Indonesia to reconsider its seizure of the territory, and to bring any real pressure to bear on the Suharto government. The best that Washington and Canberra could come up with was to urge Indonesia to admit international humanitarian relief organizations.[33] These requests, which brought some response from Indonesia, resulted in the readmission to the province of the International Red Cross, which had been forced to leave on the eve of the invasion, in the face of Indonesia's refusal to guarantee the necessary protection.[34]

It was to be more than a decade after the invasion before Jakarta could claim to exercise administrative control over most of the island. Even today armed resistance continues, despite annual large-scale operations by Indonesian forces, who invariably outnumber the guerillas by more than ten to one.[35] Thanks to the intervention of international agencies, and the work of some dedicated Indonesians, material conditions in Timor improved markedly during the eighties. However, serious human rights abuses, mostly by the Indonesian military, have continued to occur. In all annual reports of Amnesty International, the noted human rights organization, the authorities have been accused of summary executions, "disappearances," torture, and imprisonment on the grounds of conscience.[36]

Indiscriminate killings were reported at Creras, near Viqueque in 1983, and in Dili as recently as in November 1991. The Creras incident occurred in August 1983, and was recounted to the author by a priest from the district some months later. According to this account, a party of Indonesian soldiers raped and physically abused a number of young girls of the village. The news got to a nearby Fretilin guerrilla band which carried out a night attack, killing sixteen Indonesian troops. In the following days, Indonesian forces carried out severe reprisals, killing more than 200 Timorese, including women and children.[37]

The more recent of these incidents was the killing of between 70 and more than 200 Timorese when Indonesian troops opened fire on unarmed demonstrators in Dili, near the Santa Cruz cemetery. This latest of the mass killings was the most widely reported, largely because foreign media observers were present and/or in the Dili area.[38] The Timorese were apparently about to demonstrate against Indonesia's forced integration of the territory. For two or three minutes the troops fired into the crowd, expending perhaps 1,000 rounds of ammunition and killing many of the demonstrators. From the evidence which subsequently became available,[39] it seems likely that most of the killings took place after the firing had stopped. A large number of the wounded were killed in rather crude fashion, while others were said to have been killed over the next couple of days, with their bodies being secretly disposed of.

Largely in response to the international reaction, the Indonesian government set up a Committee of Inquiry (Komisi Penjelidik Nasional), which issued its Preliminary Report on 26 December 1991. While the report acknowledged some mistakes and lack of control, it absolved the authorities, including the military command in East Timor, of any responsibility for the massacre. While several senior military officers, including the East Timor and regional commanders, were removed from their posts, they were not formally charged with any offenses. Subsequently nine junior-ranking soldiers and one policeman were to face court-martial, but the charges laid against them were of a relatively minor nature. None of the troops was charged with killing, and all received relatively light sentences. For the Timorese demonstrators, however, it was a different matter. More than a dozen trials were held and, although none was charged with carrying weapons or using violence, most received severe sentences ranging from six years to life imprisonment.[40]

The Santa Cruz massacre is significant for two key reasons. First, it occurred sixteen years after the beginning of Indonesia's military action to annex East Timor. Second, it happened at a time when the Suharto regime, and governments friendly to it, were seeking to assure the international community that the East Timor situation was settled, and no further action against Indonesia was therefore warranted. Government officials in, for example, the United States, Canada, and Australia were insisting that indiscriminate killing, and most other forms of mistreatment, had been ended by a more enlightened regional administration.

Despite international criticism and the apparent decline of guerrilla activities, the dominant role of the military in Timor remains unchallenged, although plans have been announced to make some reductions. The most recent statements of the military commander, Brigadier General Sjafei, indicate that repression of political activities hostile to integration has, if anything, been tightened, with the military still wielding power over the political and economic life of the province.[41]

Responsibility for the Genocide

There can be little doubt that direct responsibility for the killing in East Timor rests with the Indonesian military forces. From the outset, the invading forces had an opportunity to extend, in accordance with the Geneva Conventions, maximum protection to the non-combatant population. The invaders almost totally ignored these basic rights, at huge cost to Indonesia.[42] A humane and disciplined occupation would have moderated the attitudes of the Timorese themselves and the character of the resistance would have been radically different. As it turned out, the senseless killing and harsh occupation policies in general, especially under General Dading Kalbuardi, stiffened the courage, determination, and endurance of the *Falintil*, the military arm of Fretilin. Indeed, because the armed resistance was effectively isolated, and was able to attract little international support, their will to resist may have collapsed much earlier had it not been for the harsh nature of Indonesian military rule in East Timor.

From time to time, it has been alleged that many of the Timorese casualties were caused by the civil war, or later internecine conflicts. In fact, between 1,500 and 2,000 were killed in the brief civil war of August 1975,[43] but there is no evidence that tribal conflicts occurred after Indonesia's invasion. On the other hand, it is known that the resistance forces killed several hundred collaborators over a period of ten years.

This brings us to the question—who was ultimately responsible for the killing? It has been argued, especially by some apologists for the Suharto regime, that none of this killing was ordered from Jakarta and that most of the blame rests with undisciplined or impulsive troops. Following the killings at Santa Cruz cemetery, for example, officials in Washington, Canberra, and some other Western capitals responded along these lines. Yet governments cannot be absolved of responsibility so conveniently. Even if these killings were not ordered by the government of Indonesia, it remains the final responsible authority. Moreover, the government can hardly claim ignorance of human rights abuses of this nature, because they have so frequently been reported in the past, and have regularly been the subject of protests by organizations like Amnesty International and Asia Watch.

The Indonesian government's line of defense is especially facile if we consider the Santa Cruz tragedy. The Indonesian decision to set up a commission of investigation was clearly a response to international outrage, and not a spontaneous reaction to the news of the killing. In the immediate aftermath of the massacre, the reaction from Jakarta was defensive, while the military's response was dismissive, even defiant. Undoubtedly, the Indonesian authorities would have reacted differently had foreign observers not been present. It may well be that no order to kill indiscriminately has ever been issued by Jakarta—even at the highest military levels. Nevertheless, it is inconceivable that the military command has been unaware of the indiscriminate killing and summary executions perpetrated by the military during these past sixteen years. Yet there is no evidence that, until the Santa Cruz incident, any of the perpetrators were ever placed on trial or disciplined. It is impossible not to conclude, therefore, that these gross violations of fundamental human rights have been tolerated by the government of Indonesia. Certainly, within the military itself these killings had become acceptable behavior. In Indonesia military and political leadership tend to merge at the top, and therefore it follows that the top-ranking responsible authorities in Indonesia have long been aware that the behavior of the military forces in East Timor has led to the decimation of the indigenous population.

Clearly, genocide, in the form of the destruction of a significant part of a group, can occur as the result of inhumane and irresponsible actions, without a formal intention being identified. Troops can be indoctrinated with hatred in what many might accept as the normal preparation for combat; that is, the strengthening of the soldier's will to fight. In Timor, for example, in the early weeks of the fighting some of the Indonesian forces were told they were fighting Communists, who had been the subject of hatred and indiscriminate killing after 1965, because of the PKI's alleged conspiracy to overthrow the government and set up a Marxist state.[44] And ideological hatred breeds racial hatred and intolerance. The way the annexation of East Timor was carried out inevitably provoked an irreconcilable antagonism on the Timorese side. Dislike therefore was mutual, causing Indonesian troops to care little about the lives of Timorese, whose language they did not speak, and whose religion most of them did not share.

On the other hand, there is no evidence that the Indonesian government, or for that matter the military leadership, sought, as a matter of deliberate policy, to destroy the Timorese people as a race or ethnic group. Yet, it cannot escape the charge that it knew about the wanton human destruction, especially between December 1975 and 1982.

There is one aspect of intention worthy of closer scrutiny. It could be argued that when it became apparent to them that the majority of the East Timorese were opposed to integration, the Indonesian military command in the province sought to destroy the will of the people for independence. This meant destroying a key element in the Timorese identity, that is, changing their identity from that of a people seeking to shape their own political future to a radically different status, that of being a loyal component of the Indonesian state.

If they had initially aimed to achieve this end by persuasion—by winning hearts and minds, why did their invading force behave like barbarians? Why did they torture, rape, and kill indiscriminately? Was not this killing and other inhuman actions, which inevitably led to tens of thousands of deaths, part of a plan to destroy the desire for independence and the will to oppose integration?

If we accept the words of no less an authority than General Benny Murdani,[45] the principal targets of the occupation authorities for eradication were, and, for that matter, still are, the independence movement leaders and their supporters. But the government's oppressive policies ensured that the vast majority of Timorese still yearn for independence, if only a few of them are prepared to take up arms. If the Indonesian military persists with the idea that all support for independence must be eliminated, perhaps then the majority of the population is at risk.

The Timor situation highlights an important dimension of the subject of this book—cultural genocide. In Portuguese times, foreigners made up only a small percentage of the population of East Timor. The largest minority was the Chinese. The Portuguese, even if we include their military, never amounted to more than a few thousand people.

Today, outsiders, that is, people who have come from elsewhere in Indonesia since the invasion, make up about one-fifth of the population. In terms of power they are not a mere minority, but the successors to the colonial power. In fact, their presence is infinitely more pervasive and has had a far greater impact on Timorese society. From the latter's point of view, these intruders dominate virtually all aspects of the government of the province.

In the economy, as well as in government and the military, the Indonesian role is much more powerful and commanding than was the place of the Portuguese, even in the Salazar years. The Indonesian newcomers are very much the ruling class, dominating as they do the military and the civil government.[46] Thousands of transmigrants have moved into some of the best lands, in some cases displacing the indigenous inhabitants. And a flood of informal arrivals, mostly drifters seeking to exploit any economic opportunity, has swollen the populations of the main towns. This massive intrusion of outsiders, and Jakarta's efforts to change Timorese ways and attitudes, is undermining the very identity of the Timorese, the least "Indonesian" of the communities of the archipelago.

Special Characteristics of the Timor Case

The case of East Timor presents a number of distinctive elements. First and foremost it is a live issue—an issue of our time as distinct from being a lesson of history. The question is still before the United Nations, which is yet to recognize Indonesia's incorporation of the colony. However, Indonesia's influence in the world body is nevertheless increasing, not least among those governments capable of exerting the kind of influence that forced Iraq out of Kuwait, the Argentinians out of the Falklands Islands, and the Russians out of the Baltic states. Secondly, the Timor case highlights the frailty of the international resolve when it comes to the small and unimportant in the global power play. It constitutes a grim reminder of the vulnerability of small states outside the mainstream of global political and economic interests.

From Jakarta's point of view, however, while the international response has at times caused some discomfort it has evidently been relatively easy to manage. The recent Santa Cruz incident illustrates this point. The official response of countries like Australia, the United States and Japan was restrained, even non-judgmental. Most of those governments who were quick to denounce recent cases of indiscriminate killing in Iraq, Bosnia-Herzegovina, and South Africa did not use the same kind of blunt language in their responses to the shooting down of more than 100 Timorese near Dili.

On the whole, in its seizure of East Timor, Indonesia was able to exploit the prevailing Cold War context. Indeed, to an extent the Suharto regime's Western friends encouraged the annexation by accepting as credible Jakarta's alleged fears of Communist insurgency in the post-Vietnam years. Perhaps the most disturbing aspect of this case is that these crimes against humanity went virtually unchallenged at a time when acts of aggression and oppression were being challenged in almost every other part of the world.

Thirdly, the annexation of East Timor could, in fact, have been averted had Indonesia's Western friends acted responsibly in the 1974–1975 period. The Suharto regime's moves to annex the colony were carefully devised against the anticipated reactions of countries like Australia and the United States, whose intelligence agencies were familiar with the unfolding conspiracy. It is in this context that the genocide dimensions of the problem are profoundly disturbing. Most Western governments, especially those members of Indonesia's aid consortium, were aware, more than a decade before the Santa Cruz killing, of the genocidal impact of Jakarta's military operations in East Timor, that is, in the terms of Article II(c) of the Convention. The failure of the IGGI members, in particular, to take up the issue at a time when the Suharto regime was heavily dependent on Western aid was at best shameful. Ever since the anti-Communist Suharto regime came to power it has been sensitive to the concerns of major Western powers like the United States. Despite this fact, even when the extent of loss of life in East Timor became evident in the early 1980s the continued acceptability of Indonesian rule of the former Portuguese colony was never seriously questioned.

Fourthly, although the Timor case has for years been before the United Nations it still has not been effectively addressed by the international community. East Timor is arguably the only remnant of the once expansive European empires to have been annexed by its neighbor, with the virtual collusion of many of those nations who today regard themselves as being at the forefront of the international movement to promote universal respect for human rights, including the right to self-determination.

The Timor Case as a Contributor to Genocide Studies

The case of East Timor is a very significant one, as a definitive case of genocide within the terms of Article II of the Convention. First and foremost, it is an unresolved issue of our time. Unlike the Cambodian case, the violation against the people of East Timor has some classical characteristics, in the sense that it resulted from an act of aggression by the large power next door. However, it occurred within a contemporary historical framework; that is, when an extensive body of human rights principles and laws had set down protective parameters for the international community. It also occurred at a time when acts of aggression of this kind were no longer tolerated by the U.N. system, as the cases of the Falklands and Kuwait dramatically demonstrated.

On the other hand, the lesson of East Timor is that some things have not changed, despite the growing intolerance of the international community toward gross human rights violations involving mass and indiscriminate killing. The East Timorese suffered from their country's remoteness, its lack of economic and strategic importance, and, conversely, from the perceived importance of the violator, today the world's largest Islamic nation, which forms a strategically and economically important division between the Indian and Pacific Oceans. However, one of the most disturbing aspects of the case is that the perpetrators of these atrocities were in practice shielded from international scrutiny by countries like Australia and the United States which pride themselves on their commitment to human rights.

Perhaps the most disturbing aspect of the experience of East Timor is that it highlights just how difficult it is to invoke the Genocide Convention, even in circumstances where the evidence that grave violations have occurred is substantial and persistent. Indeed, the Timor case suggests that the convention is so difficult to invoke that it is perceived by the victims and others as being virtually irrelevant as an international legal protection or recourse against this monstrous form of crime. On a number of occasions at the United Nations, Timorese representatives and their supporters examined the possibility of invoking the convention before the International Court of Justice, but in each case experts cast doubt on this course of action. As for the governments of Australia and the United States, genocide is a term that has been studiously avoided, even when there have been expressions of concern at the human rights situation in Timor.

The East Timor case also brings into focus the factor of cultural genocide, which is of crucial importance when the victims of aggression are massively outnumbered, in terms of population. While this aspect is not specified in the convention, it remains extremely important, as the Timor case attests. It is very likely that deliberate "Indonesianization" of the territory, together with ongoing attempts to eliminate support for a separate Timorese state, if successful, will submerge Timorese culture and ultimately destroy it.

Eyewitness Accounts
Genocide in East Timor

Since Indonesian troops invaded East Timor some seventeen years ago, eye-witness accounts have provided mounting evidence of serious human rights violations, including indiscriminate killing. Some of them have been collected by agencies like Amnesty International and Asia Watch. However, researchers, including this writer, have encountered one problem. The informants have invariably asked that their identities not be made public. It has proved even more difficult to persuade witnesses to testify publicly. The reason is understandable enough—fear of reprisals by the Indonesian security authorities against relatives and friends in East Timor. There is simply not enough international pressure, nor presence in Timor, to discourage retaliation and victimization. We have received numerous accounts of harassment by security authorities of the relatives of Timorese activists abroad. The penalties today may be less severe than, say, five years ago, but they continue to exist in a military-dominated administration, whose determination to eradicate opposition to integration has been placed categorically on record by the military commander himself on several occasions since the Santa Cruz incident. There has been no relaxation of this kind of oppression since the November massacre, and with few foreigners now making visits to East Timor—and with a low level of interest on the part of the international community—it is not yet possible to provide witnesses of indiscriminate killings and torture with adequate protection against the revenge of the military authorities.

1. The Invasion of Dili. Etelvina Correia was interviewed by the author some months after the invasion. Following is an abbreviated version of her account.

The attack on Dili began at about 4 A.M. on 7 December. Etelvina Correia was in the Church, which is located in the waterfront area. Some time later paratroops began to land (some of them dropped into the water). At 7 A.M. she saw paratroops shoot a woman in the parish garage and later 3 women in front of the Church, although their hands were raised. The Indonesian soldiers then ordered all of the people in the vicinity of the Church to go inside. Next day, Etelvina and the others were ordered by troops to go to the wharf area. There 20 women—Chinese and Timorese—were taken out in front. Some of them had children who were weeping. The soldiers tore the children from the women who were then shot one by one, with the crowd being ordered to count after each execution. At 2 P.M. on the same day 59 men, including Chinese and Timorese, were taken to the wharf and executed in the same way. Again the witnesses were ordered at gun-point to count. They were told that these killings were in reprisal for the killing of a paratrooper near the Toko Lay shop in Dili.

2. The following consists of extracts from a letter written in November 1977 by a Catholic priest in East Timor and sent to two Dominican nuns, Sister Natalia Granada Moreira and Sister Maria Auxiliadora Hernandez. Its importance is that it was written during what was probably the worst period following the invasion. At the time East Timor was securely closed off to the outside world, and external communications with the outside world heavily censored. This letter was smuggled out by a person who carried it to Jakarta.

The War

It continues with the same fury as it had started. Fretilin continues the struggle, in spite of famine, lack of clothing, death, and a crisis in understanding and objectives which has surfaced lately. The invaders have intensified their attacks in the three classic ways—from land, sea and air.

Between 7 and 31 December 1975, and up to February 1976, in Dili harbour there were at anchor up to 23 warships which vomited intense fire towards Dili 24 hours a day. Daily 8 to 12 helicopters and 4 bombers flew reconnaissance and bombing runs near Dili. Numerous tanks and armoured vehicles roamed about the territory. The Indonesian armed forces in Timor must have surpassed 50,000 (I don't know for certain). In December last year there was heavy movement of ships in Dili, discharging war materials and disembarking troops. From last September (1977) the war was again intensified. The bombers did not stop all day. Hundreds of human beings died every day. The bodies of the victims became food for carnivorous birds (if we don't die of the war, we die of the plague), villages were completely destroyed, some tribes decimated. . . . And the war enters its third year with no promise of an early end in sight. The barbarities (understandable in the Middle Ages and justifiable in the Stone Age), the cruelties, the pillaging, the unqualified destruction of Timor, the executions without reason, in a word all the "organized" evil, has spread deep roots in Timor.

There is complete insecurity and the terror of arbitrary imprisonment is our daily bread (I am on the "persona non grata" list and any day I could disappear). Fretilin soldiers who give themselves up are disposed of—for them there is no prison. Genocide will come soon, perhaps by next December. Taking advantage of the courage of the Timorese, they are being urged to fight their brothers in the interior. It is they who march in front of the (Indonesian) battalions to intimidate the prey.

[Section on the position of the Church omitted]

The Political Situation

Indescribable. Sabotage and lies dominate the information sector. Integration is not the expression of the will of the people.

The people are controlled by the Indonesians and, given the character of the oppressor and the level of the Indonesian presence, it is a lamb being led to the slaughter. In the presence of such force there is no way to resist; liberty is a word without meaning. The proclaimed liberation is synonymous with slavery. Timor is returning to the nineteen forties and anti-Communism is an Islamic slogan meaning "iconoclasm." The reform of our customs means the setting up of cabarets and houses of prostitution. . . . In commerce the search for basic needs dominates, and blackmarket is the rule. The Chinese are easily corrupted and they themselves are instruments of commercial exploitation. To travel outside of Indonesia is a dream. Mail is censored.

. . . Please do something positive for the liberty of the Timorese people. The world ignores us and our grief . . . we are on the road to complete genocide. By the end of December the war could exterminate us. All of the youth of Timor (30 percent of the population) are in the forests: the Indonesian control only one or two kilometres beyond the villages. We ask all justice-loving people to save Timor, and we ask God to forgive the sins of the Timorese people. . . .

Timor, November 1977 [name withheld]

3. The next item consists of extracts taken from a message, written in 1977, from a Timorese father to his son in Portugal, with whose whereabouts he was not familiar. Again it is in rather general terms, but it is one of the few firsthand written accounts concerning conditions in East Timor at that time.

Tell my son that for nothing on this earth should he return to Timor. I would rather die without seeing him again than to know that he had returned to this hell. . . .

There are very few Timorese in the streets of Dili; most of them are in the forests, dead or in prison; the cost of living is extremely high and there is a need for the most basic foodstuffs. The suffering is indescribable, as may be affirmed by the Apostolic Nuncio in Jakarta who went to Dili in the middle of October to celebrate an open-air mass. The weeping, the tears, the laments of the orphans, widows and forsaken were such that the Mass had to be interrupted for a quarter of an hour before it could continue. . . .

In a desperate attempt to crush by force the armed resistance which continues to exist in most of the territory, the Jakarta authorities now have sent ten more battalions to Timor. Thus, the number of Indonesian troops engaged in fighting usually cited as being over 40,000 must now be more than 50,000. . . . The increase in military operations has once more turned Timor into a place of arms and warfare. At the present time, with the beginning of the rainy season, land operations should have diminished but the constant air raids and the launching of incendiary bombs which have been systematically punishing the rural populations continue.

4. Extract from a letter from Timor also in 1977.

A continuous, increasingly violent war rages in Timor. The group of villages in which I lived have been completely destroyed. There is not one soul there. I myself am in Dili and I have gone many days without eating. These are the effects of war. But there are people who are much worse off than I. I have been sick several times and at death's door for want of medication. The cost of living in Dili is very high and the salaries are very low. One sees no one else but Indonesian soldiers and Chinese on the streets of Dili: there are very few Timorese for the majority are either in the forest, dead or in jail. The luck of Timor is to be born in tears, to live in tears and to die in tears. It would, perhaps, be more appropriate to say that one does not cry for one has no more tears to shed, for Timor is no longer Timor: it is nothing but an oppressed worm. . . .

5. The following account was taken by Michele Turner, a well-known Australian oral historian. The subject is a former Timorese guerrilla fighter, named Laurenco, who spent much of the early years of the occupation in the eastern sector of the island. He describes conditions in a mountain area, where many Timorese lost their lives, largely through air attacks, and the consequences of famine.

Both of the following accounts are extracts from Michele Turner's *Telling: East Timor Personal Testimonies, 1942–1992* (Sydney, Australia: University of New South Wales). Reprinted with permission.

Our section in the east was the last to be attacked. In 1978 they started to come against us. At first we didn't resist, just watched the enemy, let them feel confident. Matebian Mountain is a big area and there were 160,000 of us, fighters and civilians, divided into small groups.

On 17 October 1978 some Indonesians got right to the bottom of Matebian Mountain and that's when we started to fight back. For those first two months, October and November, we were very successful and about 3,000 Indonesians died. Then they got angry and scared to come close and started to bomb us from the air. They bombed twice a day, in the morning and in the afternoon with four black planes. Their name I know now is Broncos, but we called them scorpions because they had a tail that curves up at the back like that insect. Their bombs left a big hole about two metres deep. Then they got new supersonic planes. Our people were very frightened of those because you didn't even hear they were there until they were gone. Those supersonics would zoom along the valley so fast we couldn't shoot them.

The bombing became constant, in rotation. Three supersonics came to bomb for about forty-five minutes and then went back to reload. Half an hour later the black scorpions came, and this could go on all day. In Matebian there are a lot of caves and we hid there and only moved at night.

We knew by radio from the south zone that the Indonesians had dropped four napalm bombs there. Then they dropped two of these on us. I saw all the flames and heard people shouting and screaming. I was on another mountain but I could see well; there was a close view of it, straight across. Some of us set out straight away to help those people. By foot it took half an hour to go down and up again, and by the time we got there everything was completely burnt. We saw a whole area about fifty metres square all burnt, no grass, nothing except ash. On the rocks it was a brown reddish colour and on the ground ash too, no ordinary grey ash, a sort of yellow ash, like beach sand. You couldn't see where bodies had been. There was nothing except ash and burned rocks on the whole area, but we had heard those people screaming.

We could find no bones or bodies, but people near said there were about a hundred people living there who were killed by this. Those people disappeared, they were not sheltering, we never saw them again. The population was large but people were in small groups in different places and knew where each group was. The whole population was very upset—no bodies of those people left to bury. My cousin said, "If this is what they can do there is no hope for the world."

We had no food because of all the bombing and we lost radio contact. Fretilin decided they couldn't defend the people properly any more and the population should surrender, otherwise we would all be wiped out. When they announced this decision the people cried. Falintil said they couldn't force us, but this was the best thing for all. Our leader said, "You surrender and it will be better for you to get food and it will be better for us too so we can fight freely. But this doesn't mean that the war stops. We will keep fighting for our freedom and don't forget, wherever you go outside, that we are nationalists, and if ever you have a way to help us in the bush, do it." Then Falintil gave up their responsibility for the people and everyone decided for themselves to stay or go. Also the Falintil broke up into small groups to fight as guerillas.

About 2,000 of us tried to stay in the mountains. We broke into three groups to escape and I was in one of these trying to get through the encirclement. In our group there were a few hundred, mostly fighters, only about a hundred ordinary people. We kept walking and walking. The Indonesians would drop some bombs, we would hide, then walk again. We were in a valley and the Indonesians were up higher. If they shot at us our fighters did not shoot back so that the Indonesians would think we were just a normal group of people walking to surrender. We had no food, the area we were going through was mostly rocks. The enemy burnt the trees and any food growing; the animals were dead.

6. The following is an extract from an account by an elderly Timorese woman, named Eloise, who was in Dili when the Indonesian invasion of

the capital took place in 1975. This incident was only one of a number of mass killings carried out by Indonesian troops, following their assault on Dili.

On 7 December we woke and heard this big noise of planes and saw parachutes and planes covering the light—it became dark because of them, so many. There were shots and we went inside and kept listening to more and more shooting. In the afternoon some Timorese came and told us everyone must come to surrender at headquarters. We had to get a stick and put a piece of white material on it and come. They said, "These are orders from the Indonesian people." So we went, women and children and old men and young men.

Once we got there they divided us: the women and children and old men to one side, and on the other young boys they wanted to help carry Fretilin things—they had taken over their store and there was ammunition and food there. We watched while they took all this stuff out from the storeroom. When they finished they were coming to join us, but the Indonesians said, "No, stay there!" Then they ordered us to form a line and wait.

Then an Indonesian screams an order and we hear machine guns running through [sic] the men. We see the boys and men dying right there. Some see their husbands die. We look at each other stunned. We think they are going to kill us next. All of us just turn and pick up the children and babies and run screaming, wild, everywhere.

Chapter Ten
Genocide in Bangladesh

Rounaq Jahan

Introduction

The birth of Bangladesh in 1971 was a unique phenomenon—it was the first nation-state to emerge after waging a successful liberation war against a postcolonial state. The nine-month-long liberation war in Bangladesh drew world attention because of the genocide committed by Pakistan which resulted in the killings of approximately three million people and raping of nearly a quarter million girls and women. Ten million Bengalis reportedly took refuge in India to avoid the massacre of the Pakistan army and thirty million people were displaced within the country (Loshak, 1971; Mascarenhas, 1971; Payne, 1973; Ayoob and Subrahmanyan, 1972; O'Donnell, 1984).

Written two decades after the genocide, this essay addresses the following: the historical forces that led to the genocide; the nature of the genocide—why, how, and who committed the genocide; the world response; the long-range impact of the genocide on the victims; the way the genocide is remembered today; and some lessons that can be drawn from the 1971 Bangladesh genocide.

Background to the Genocide

Though the liberation war in Bangladesh lasted only nine months, the nationalist movement that preceded the war spanned the previous two decades. Indeed, the seeds of the Bangladesh nationalist movement were planted very soon after the creation of Pakistan in 1947.

When India was partitioned on the basis of religion and the new state of Pakistan was established comprising the Muslim majority areas of India, Bengali Muslims voluntarily became a part of Pakistan. But very soon it became apparent to the Bengali Muslims that, despite their numerical majority, they were being hurt in a variety of ways: (1) their linguistic cultural identity was being threatened by the ruling elite (which was predominantly non-Bengali) in the new state; (2) they were being economically exploited; and (3) they were excluded from exercising state power (Jahan, 1972).

The nationalist movement first emerged as a struggle to defend and preserve the ethnic linguistic Bengali identity of the Bengali Muslims. Though the Bengalis comprised 54 percent of Pakistan's population, in 1948 the ruling elite declared their intention to make Urdu, which was the language of only 7 percent of the population, the sole state language. Bengali students immediately protested the decision and launched a movement which continued for the next eight years until the Pakistan constitution, adopted in 1956, recognized both Bengali and Urdu as state languages (Ahmad, 1967).

The Bengalis had to defend not only the right to practice their own language, but also other creative expressions of their culture—literature, music, dance, arts. The Pakistani ruling elite looked upon Bengali language and culture as too "Hindu leaning" and made repeated attempts to "cleanse" it from Hindu influence (Umar, 1966, 1967, 1969). First, in the 1950s, attempts were made to force Bengalis to substitute Bengali words with Arabic and Urdu words. Then, in the 1960s, state-controlled media such as television and radio banned songs written by Rabindra Nath Tagore, a Bengali Hindu, who won the Nobel prize in 1913 and whose poetry and songs were equally beloved by Bengali Hindus and Muslims.

The attacks on their language and culture alienated the Bengalis from the state-sponsored Islamic ideology of Pakistan and intensified their linguistic and ethnic identity that emphasized a more secular ideology and attitude.

The Bangladesh nationalist movement was also fueled by a sense of economic exploitation. Though jute, the major export earning commodity, was produced in Bengal, most of the economic investments took place in Pakistan. A systematic transfer of resources took place from East to West Pakistan creating a growing economic disparity and a feeling among the Bengalis that they were being treated as a colony by Pakistan (Rahman, 1968; Jahan, 1972).

In the 1950s and 1960s, a group of Bengali economists carefully documented the process of economic disparity and martialled arguments in favor of establishing a "two-economy" system. The movement toward autonomy initiated in the 1950s culminated in the famous six points program of 1966, which not only rejected the central government's right of taxation but demanded that the power to tax and establish trade and commercial relations, including the establishment of separate accounts of foreign exchange earning, be placed in the hands of the provinces.

However, it was lack of political participation and exclusion from state power that gradually drove the Bengalis from participation, to demanding autonomy, and finally to demanding self-determination (Jahan, 1972). Constituting a majority of the population, the Bengalis expected to dominate or at least share the political power in the federal government of Pakistan. But soon after the creation of Pakistan, a small civil and military bureaucratic elite held a monopoly on government power. As a result, the Bengalis had virtually no representation in that power elite (Sayeed, 1967, 1968; Jahan, 1972).

From the beginning, the Bengalis demanded democracy with free and regular elections, a parliamentary form of government, and freedom of political parties and the media. But the ruling elite in Pakistan thwarted every attempt at instituting democracy in the country (Callard, 1957; Sayeed, 1967). In 1954, a democratically elected government in East Bengal was dismissed within ninety days of taking power. A constitution was adopted in 1956 after nine years of protracted negotiations only to be abrogated within two years by a military coup. Just before the first nationally scheduled election, the military took direct control of the government in 1958. This was out of fear that the Bengalis might dominate in a democratically elected government.

The decade of the 1960s saw the military rule of General Ayub Khan. It was eventually toppled in 1969 as a result of popular mass movements in both wings (East and West) of Pakistan. However, after the fall of Ayub, the civil-military bureaucratic elite again regrouped and put General Yahya Khan, who was the commander-in-chief of the armed forces, in charge of the government. The Yahya regime acceded to a number of key demands of the Bengali nationalist movement including the holding of a free democratic national election on the basis of one man one vote. The first free democratic national elections, held in Pakistan in 1970 two decades after the birth of the country, resulted in a sweeping victory of the Bengali nationalist party, the Awami League. The election results gave the Awami League not only total control over their own province, but also a majority nationally and a right to form the federal government.

Again, though, the ruling elite in Pakistan took recourse to unconstitutional measures to prevent the Bengalis from assuming state power. On

March 1, 1971, General Yahya postponed indefinitely the scheduled March 3rd session of parliament. This, in turn, threw the country into a constitutional crisis. The Awami League responded by launching an unprecedented non-violent, non-cooperation movement which resulted in the entire administration of then East Pakistan coming to a virtual standstill. Even the Bengali civil and military officials complied with the non-cooperation movement. Indeed, the movement demonstrated that the Bengali nationalists had total allegiance and support of the Bengali population.

The Yahya regime initiated political negotiations with the Bengali nationalists but at the same time flew thousands of armed forces in from West to East Pakistan, thus consolidating preparations for a military action. On March 25, 1971, General Yahya abruptly broke off the negotiations and unleashed a massive armed strike against the population of Dhaka, the capital city. In two days of uninterrupted military operations, hundreds of ordinary citizens were killed, houses and property were destroyed, and the leader of the Awami League, Sheikh Mujibur Rahman, was arrested. The army also launched armed attacks in Chittagong, Comilla, Khulna, and other garrison cities. Simon Dring, a reporter with the *Daily Telegraph London,* and Michel Laurent, an Associated Press photographer, escaped the Pakistani dragnet, and roamed Dhaka and the countryside. On March 28 they reported that the loss of life had reached 15,000 in the countryside. On the Dhaka University campus, seventeen professors and some 200 students were killed in cold blood (Loshak, 1971, pp. 88–126).

The news of the Dhaka massacre immediately spread to the rest of the country. Instead of cowing the unarmed Bengalis into submission, which was probably the intention of the Pakistani army in initiating the brutal killings, it only inflamed nationalist sentiments. Within twenty-four hours of the armed crackdown in Dhaka, on March 26, 1971, the independence of Bangladesh was declared from the city of Chittagong. It was announced over the radio, which was controlled by the Bengali nationalists, on the behalf of the Awami League and its leader Sheikh Mujibur Rahman. The upshot of this is that a new nation was born out of what was a premeditated genocide (Jahan, 1972; Ayoob and Subhrahmanyan, 1972).

Bangladesh Genocide 1971
The genocide in Bangladesh, which started with the Pakistani military operation against unarmed citizens on the night of March 25, continued unabated for nearly nine months until the Bengali nationalists, with the help

of the Indian army, succeeded in liberating the country from Pakistani occupation forces on December 16, 1971.

The atrocities committed by the Pakistan army were widely reported by the international press during 1971 (Loshak, 1971; Mascarenhas, 1971; Schanberg, 1971; Jenkins, et al., August 2, 1971; Coggin et al., August 2, 1971).

From the eyewitness accounts documented during and immediately after the genocide in 1971 and 1972 and later published over the last twenty years, it is possible to analyze the major features of the Bangladesh genocide—why and how it was committed, who was involved in the crimes, and who the victims were.

Why Was the Genocide Committed?

The genocide in Bangladesh caught the outside observers as well as the Bengali nationalists by surprise. After all, the Bengali nationalists were not involved in any armed struggle prior to March 25, 1971. They were essentially waging a peaceful constitutional movement for democracy and autonomy. Their only crime, as Senator Edward Kennedy observed, appeared to have been to win an election (Malik, 1972). So why did the Pakistani ruling elite initiate a brutal military action?

Perhaps, the main reason behind the atrocities was to terrorize the population into submission. The military commander in charge of the Dhaka operations reportedly claimed that he would kill four million people in forty-eight hours and thus have a "final solution" of the Bengal problem. (Jahan, 1972). The Pakistani military regime calculated that since the Bengalis had no previous experience in armed struggle, they would be frightened and crushed in the face of overwhelming fire power, mass killings, and destruction.

But the atrocities created a completely opposite effect on the Bengalis. Instead of being cowed, they rose in revolt and chose the path of armed struggle to resist armed aggression. When news of the Dhaka massacre reached other cities and towns, human waves overran the police stations and distributed arms to people. But the initial armed resistance was short-lived as the Bengalis lacked substantial arms and were vastly outnumbered in terms of trained soldiers. The Pakistani army was able to recapture a majority of the towns. Not surprisingly, the process was brutal and innocent civilians were killed indiscriminately by the military.

Though the initial armed resistance failed, the Bengali nationalists were not prepared to give up the liberation struggle. Instead of direct confrontation, the liberation fighters chose the course of guerrilla warfare. Nearly 100,000 young men were given armed training within Bangladesh and India and they succeeded in virtually destroying the communication and supply lines of the Pakistani army. To retaliate against the guerrillas, the Pakistani army embarked on a strategy of destroying entire areas and populations where guerrilla actions were reported. Massive killing, looting, burning, and raping took place during these "search and destroy" operations (Coggin, Shepherd, Greenway, 1971, pp. 24–29; Jenkins, Clifton, and Steele, 1971, pp. 26–30; Malik 1972).

The reasons behind the genocide, however, were not simply to terrorize the people and punish them for resistance. There were also elements of racism in this act of genocide. The Pakistani army, consisting of mainly Punjabis and Pathans, had always looked upon the Bengalis as racially inferior—a non-martial, physically weak race, not interested or able to serve in the army (Marshall, 1959). General Ayub Khan's (1967) remarks about the Bengalis in his memoirs reflected the typical attitude of the Pakistan's civil-military power elite:

> East Bengalis . . . probably belong to the very original Indian races, . . . They have been and still are under considerable Hindu cultural and linguistic influence. . . . They have all the inhibitions of downtrodden races. . . . Their popular complexes, exclusiveness, suspicion and . . . defensive aggressiveness . . . emerge from this historical background. (p. 187)

The image of the Bengalis as a non-martial race, created by the British colonialists, was readily accepted by the Pakistani ruling elite. A policy of genocide against fellow Muslims was deliberately undertaken by the Pakistanis on the assumption of racial superiority and a desire to cleanse the Bengali Muslims of Hindu cultural linguistic influence.

How Was the Genocide Committed?

On March 25, 1971, when the Pakistani government initiated military action in Bangladesh, a number of sites and groups of people were selected as targets of attack. In Dhaka, for example, the university campus, the headquarters of the police and the Bengali para militia, slums and squatter settlements, and Hindu majority localities, all were selected as special targets. The Pakistani ruling elite believed that the leadership of the Bengali nationalist movement came from the intellectuals and students, that the Hindus and the urban lumpen proletariat were the main supporters, and that the Bengali police and army officials could be potential leaders in any armed struggle. In the first two days of army operations, hundreds of unarmed people were killed on the university campus, and in the slums and the old city where Hindus lived. (Eyewitness accounts of killings in the Dhaka university campus are included in the oral testimony that accompanies this essay.)

When the news of the Dhaka massacre spread and the independence of Bangladesh was declared on March 26, spontaneous resistance was organized in all the cities and towns of the country. The Awami League politicians, Bengali civilian administration, police, army, students, and intellectuals constituted the leadership of the resistance. This first phase of the liberation war was, however, amateurish and uncoordinated and only lasted approximately six weeks. By the middle of May, the Pakistani army was successful in bringing the cities and towns under their control though the villages remained largely "liberated" areas.

In occupying one city after another, the Pakistani army used the superiority of its fire and air power to its advantage. These operations also involved massive killings of civilians and wanton lootings and destruction of property. The leadership of the resistance (e.g., Awami League leaders, army and civilian officials, and intellectuals) generally left the scene prior to the Pakistani army's arrival. They took refuge either in India or in the villages. But, in any case, the Pakistani army engaged in indiscriminate killings and burnings in order to terrorize the population. Again, Awami Leaguers, students and intellectuals, civilian and army officers, and Hindus were selected as targets of attack (Malik, 1972). The army's campaign against the cities and towns not only led to massive civilian casualties, it also resulted in a large-scale dislocation of people. In fact, nearly ten million people—Hindus as well as Muslims—migrated to India, and approximately thirty million people from the cities took refuge in the villages. Government offices, educational institutions, and factories were virtually closed.

The second phase of the liberation war—from mid-May to September—was a period of long-term planning for both the Bengali nationalists and the Pakistani government. The Bengali nationalists set up a government-in-exile and undertook external publicity campaigns in support of their cause. They also recruited nearly one hundred thousand young men as freedom fighters who underwent military training and started guerrilla operations inside Bangladesh.

The Pakistan army essentially dug in their own strong-holds during this period with periodic operations to rural areas to punish the villagers for harboring freedom fighters. The army also engaged in large-scale looting, and raping of girls and women.

In fact, systematic and organized rape was the special weapon of war used by the Pakistan army during the second phase of the liberation struggle. While during the first phase, young able-bodied males were the victims of indiscriminate killings, during the second phase, girls and women became the special targets of Pakistani aggression. During army operations, girls and women were raped in front of close family members in order to terrorize and inflict racial slander. Girls and women were also abducted and repeatedly raped and gang-raped in special camps run by the army near army barracks. Many of the rape victims either were killed or committed suicide. Altogether, it is estimated that approximately 200,000 girls and women were raped during the 1971 genocide (Brownmiller, 1981). (An eyewitness account of the mass rape camps organized by the Pakistani army is included in the oral history account that accompanies this essay.)

All through the liberation war, able-bodied young men were suspected of being actual or potential freedom fighters. Thousands were arrested, tortured, and killed. Eventually cities and towns became bereft of young males who either took refuge in India or joined the liberation war.

During the second phase, another group of Bengali men in the rural areas—those who were coerced or bribed to collaborate with the Pakistanis—fell victim to the attacks of Bengali freedom fighters.

The third phase of the liberation struggle—from October till mid-December—saw intensified guerrilla action and finally a brief conventional war between Pakistan and the combined Indian and Bangladeshi forces which ended with the surrender of the Pakistani army on December 16, 1971 (Palit, 1972; Ayoob and Subrahmanyan, 1972). As guerrilla action increased, the Pakistani army also intensified its "search and destroy" operations. Several villages were destroyed each day during this phase.

In the last week of the war, when their defeat was virtually certain, the Pakistani government engaged in its most brutal and premeditated genocidal campaign. During this time, villages were burnt and their inhabitants were indiscriminately killed. In order to deprive the new nation of its most talented leadership, the Pakistanis had decided to kill the most respected and influential intellectuals and professionals in each city and town. Between December 12 and 14, a selected number of intellectuals and professionals were picked up from their houses and murdered. Many of their names were later found in the diary of Major General Rao Forman Ali, advisor to the Martial Law Administrator and Governor of occupied Bangladesh (Malik, 1972).

The victims of the 1971 genocide were, thus, first and foremost Bengalis. Though Hindus were especially targeted, the majority of the victims were Bengali Muslims—ordinary villagers and slum dwellers—who were caught unprepared during the Pakistani army's sweeping spree of wanton killing, rape, and destruction. As previously mentioned, the Pakistani ruling elite identified certain groups as their special enemies—students and intellectuals, Awami Leaguers and their supporters, and Bengali members of the armed forces, and the police. But many members of these targeted groups went into hiding or in exile in India after the initial attack. As a result, the overwhelming majority of the victims were defenseless ordinary poor people who stayed behind in their own houses and did not suspect that they would be killed, raped, taken to prison, and tortured simply for the crime of being born a Bengali.

The sheltered and protected life of women, provided by the Bengali Muslim cultural norm, was virtually shattered in 1971. Thousands of women were suddenly left defenseless and to fend for themselves as widows and rape victims. The rape victims were particularly vulnerable. Though they were the casualties of the war, many of them were discarded by their own families as a way to avoid shame and dishonor (Brownmiller, 1981; Jahan, 1973).

Who Committed the Genocide?

The Pakistani government—the Yahya regime—was primarily responsible for the genocide. Not only did it prevent the Awami league and Sheikh Mujibur Rahman from forming the federal government, but it opted for a military solution to a constitutional crisis. In doing so, it decided to unleash a brutal military operation in order to terrorize the Bengalis. Yahya's decision to put General Tikka Khan—who had earned the nickname of Butcher of Baluchistan for his earlier brutal suppression of Baluchi nationals in the 1960s—in charge of the military operation in Bangladesh was an overt signal of the regime's intention to launch a genocide.

When Bangladesh was liberated, the Pakistani army surrendered; and shortly thereafter, the Bangladesh government declared its intention to hold war crime trials against the Pakistan army. Specific charges, however, were only brought against 193 officers (out of the 93,000 soldiers within its ranks). Bangladesh, however, later gave up the idea of war crime trials in exchange for a negotiated settlement of outstanding issues with Pakistan. This specifically involved the return of the Bengalis held hostage in Pakistan, repatriation of the Biharis from Bangladesh to Pakistan, division of assets and liabilities, and recognition of Bangladesh (O'Donnell, 1984).

But the Pakistani military leaders were not the only culprits. The political parties, e.g., the Pakistan Peoples Party (PPP), also played an important role in instigating the army to take military action in Bangladesh. The PPP and its leader Zulfikar Ali Bhutto supported the army action all through 1971 (Bhutto, 1971; Jahan, 1973).

There were also Bengalis who collaborated with the Pakistani regime. During the second phase of the liberation struggle, the Pakistani government deliberately recruited Bengali collaborators. Many of the Islamic political groups (Muslim League and the Jamaat-e-Islami) opposed to the Awami League also collaborated with the army. Peace committees were formed in different cities and localities and under their auspices *rajakars* (armed volunteers) were raised and given arms to counter the freedom fighters. Two armed vigilante groups (Al Badr and Al-Shams) were trained, and took the lead in the arrest and killing of the intellectuals during December 12–14, 1971. Some Bengali intellectuals were also recruited to conduct propaganda in favor of the Pakistanis.

The non-Bengali residents of Bangladesh—the Biharis—were the other group of collaborators. Many of them acted as informants and also participated in riots in Dhaka and Chittagong. Biharis, however, were also victims of Bengali mob violence.

The World's Response to the Genocide
World response to the genocide can be analyzed at dual levels—official and non-official. At the official level, world response was determined by geopolitical interests and major power alignments. Officially India was sympathetic and supportive of the Bangladesh cause from the beginning. The U.S.S.R., India's major superpower ally, supported the Indian-backed cause. As a result of the U.S.S.R.'s support, all the Eastern bloc countries naturally were also supportive of Bangladesh (Jackson, 1975).

Pakistan's allies were predictably opposed to Bangladesh. Pakistan launched a propaganda campaign to deny the existence of genocide (White Paper, 1971; Bhutto, 1971). Islamic countries were generally supportive of

Pakistan. So was China. The official policy of the United States was to "tilt in favor of Pakistan" because Pakistan was used as an intermediary to open the door to China (Jackson, 1975).

At the non-official level, however, there was a great outpouring of sympathy for the Bangladesh cause worldwide because of the genocide. The Western media—particularly the U.S., British, French, and Australian—kept Bangladesh on the global agenda all through 1971. Well-known Western artists and intellectuals also came out in support of Bangladesh. George Harrison and Ravi Shankar held a Bangladesh concert. André Malraux, the noted French author, volunteered to go and fight with the Bengali freedom fighters. In the United States, citizen groups and individuals lobbied successfully with Congress to stop military aid to Pakistan. Despite the Nixon administration's official support of the Pakistani government, influential senators and congressmen (such as Frank Church and Edward Kennedy) spoke out strongly against the genocide. Members of parliament in the United Kingdom, Europe, and other Western countries were also highly critical of the Bangladesh genocide.

Both officially and unofficially, India played a critical role in mobilizing support for Bangladesh. The genocide and the resultant influx of ten million refugees in West Bengal and neighboring states created spontaneous unofficial sympathy. The press, political parties, and voluntary organizations in India pressed Mrs. Indira Gandhi, the Indian Prime Minister, to immediately intervene in Bangladesh when the Pakistani army cracked down in March 1971. The Indian government initially declined to intervene but gave moral and financial support to the Bangladesh government-in-exile as well as the freedom fighters. It also sponsored a systematic international campaign in favor of Bangladesh. And finally in December 1971, when the ground was well prepared, Bangladesh was liberated as a result of direct Indian army intervention (Jackson, 1975).

The world's sympathy for the Bangladesh people in the aftermath of the 1971 genocide was also demonstrated by the tremendous relief and rehabilitation efforts mounted by the United Nations and private voluntary organizations in Bangladesh. Even before the liberation of Bangladesh, large-scale relief efforts were undertaken by the world community to feed the refugees in the India-based camps. And during the first two years of the birth of the new nation "as many as 72 foreign relief groups, including U.N. agencies, contributed to what observers considered the largest single and most successful emergency relief endeavor of our times" (O' Donnell,

1984, p. 112). Nearly $1.3 billion of humanitarian aid was given to Bangladesh in the first two years of its existence.

Though the international community responded generously in giving humanitarian aid, there was very little support for the war crime trials that Bangladesh proposed to hold. The Indian army very quickly removed the Pakistani soldiers from Bangladesh soil to India in order to prevent any reprisals or mob violence against them. India and other friendly countries were also supportive of a negotiated package as a way to settle all outstanding issues between Pakistan and Bangladesh, including the war crimes. Though public opinion favoring war crime trials against the Pakistani army was high in Bangladesh, the Sheikh Mujib regime finally decided to forego the trials. This created a deep scar in the national psyche; indeed, the lack of a trial created a sense of betrayal and mistrust.

Long-Range Impact of the Genocide on the Victims

A major impact of the genocide was the introduction of violence in Bangladesh society, politics, and culture. Prior to 1971, Bengalis were a relatively peaceful and homogeneous community with a low level of violent crimes. They were highly faction ridden and politicized but differences and disputes were generally settled through negotiations, litigation, and peaceful mass movements. After the Pakistani armed attack, Bengalis took up arms and for the first time engaged in armed struggle. This brought a qualitative change in people's attitude to conflict resolution. Non-violent means of protest and conflict resolution were largely discarded in favor of armed violence.

The genocide, looting, burning, and rapes also brutalized the Bangladeshi society. After witnessing so much violence, the people seemed to have developed a higher degree of tolerance toward wanton violence.

The role of Bengali collaborators in perpetuating the genocide created deep division and mistrust in the otherwise homogeneous Bengali social fabric. After the birth of Bangladesh the whole country appeared to be divided between the freedom fighters and collaborators. But not all collaborators were clearly identified. For example, the members of the two vigilante groups (Al Badr and Al-Shams) were never traced and punished. As a result, the feeling that the collaborators were still at large and capable of striking again created deep fear and a certain paralysis of action particularly among the intellectuals.

In addition to these three generalized impacts—violence, brutalization, and mistrust—the genocide has had several long-term impacts on the different victim groups. The Hindu community has not felt safe again in Bangladesh, and after 1971 many of them decided not to return to Bangladesh. Furthermore, there has been a steady migration of young Hindus to India even after Bangladesh was liberated.

Students and youth, who became familiar with the use of arms, did not give them up after 1971. They started using sophisticated weapons in settling political scores. Continuous armed conflicts between rival student groups have made the college and university campuses one of the most dangerous places in the country. That has resulted in destroying the academic atmosphere and the standard of educational institutions.

The genocide and the issue of collaborators also created a deep division within the armed forces. From 1975 to 1981, the various factions of the armed forces staged numerous bloody coups and countercoups which resulted in the killing of virtually all the military leaders who participated in the liberation war.

The status of women was also altered as a result of the genocide. The sudden loss of male protection forced thousands of women to seek wage employment. For the first time, women entered occupations, e.g., public works program, rural extension work, civil administration, police, etc., which were not open to them before. Violence against women has also become more widespread and common.

Do People Care Today?

The genocide and the liberation war has been kept alive primarily through creative arts—theater, music, literature, and painting. Over the last five years, nearly two decades after the genocide was committed, many vivid eyewitness accounts of the genocide and personal diaries of 1971 have been published in Bangladesh. It is interesting to note that from 1971 to 1973, it was mostly foreigners who published eyewitness accounts of the Bangladesh genocide (Mascarenhas, 1971; Malik, 1972; Payne, 1973). Bengalis themselves did not sit down to write or collect these accounts. But a decade and a half after the events, a flood of writing on the genocide has begun to emerge, most of it coming from Bangladesh written by ordinary citizens who relate their personal experiences of the genocide. These recollections are powerful and evocative.

While the genocide and the liberation war have not been forgotten by the people of Bangladesh, the collaborators have been gradually "rehabilitated" through state patronage. Since the 1975 army coup and the overthrow of the Awami League regime, many of the collaborators who had been opposed to the Awami League joined the political parties floated by the two military leaders, Ziaur Rahman (1975–1981) and Ershad (1982–1990). The two military leaders tilted the country toward Islamic ideology, allowed religious-based parties to function, and appointed a few well-known collaborators to their cabinet. The gradual ascendance of the Islamic forces in the country became even more evident when, after the 1991 election, the Bangladesh Nationalist Party (BNP) succeeded in forming the government with the support of the fundamentalist party, Jamaat-e-Islami.

The control of state power by the collaborators of the 1971 genocide finally enraged the victims of genocide to take direct political action. They launched a mass movement to eliminate the "Killers and Collaborators of 1971." A citizens' committee was convened in 1991. It was headed by Jahanara Imam, a well-known author whose son was killed by the Pakistani army in 1971. It demanded a trial of Golam Azam, the head of the Jamaat-e-Islami party for complicity in the 1971 killings. The non-partisan civic organization galvanized the support of the intellectuals and youth. The major opposition party, the Awami League, also threw in its support. The citizen's committee organized major non-violent protests, nationwide strikes were organized, and a public trial was held where children, wives, and other relatives of victims of genocide gave testimony against the Jamaat-e-Islami party and its leader Golam Azam. The genocide and the collaborators' issue, which had gradually been sidestepped since 1975, were brought back to the center stage of the political arena in 1992.

Lessons from This Genocide

What lessons can be drawn from the 1971 Bangladesh genocide? First, once a state adopts a systematic policy of genocide against any nationality group, the nationality group, threatened with genocide, will feel stronger in the legitimacy of their claim to form their own separate state.

Second, once a policy of genocide is initiated, it is difficult to settle conflict through peaceful negotiations. The Bengalis gave up the path of constitutional struggle and political negotiations and chose the course of armed struggle after the Pakistani intention of killing several million people to arrive at a "final" solution became evident to the Bengalis.

Third, the genocide creates a deep trauma in the national psyche. It creates fear, suspicion, and mistrust. The Bengalis are suspicious of all foreign powers including India, which helped to liberate the country. Resentment against the Indian army emerged in the weeks following the liberation of the country and the Indian army was withdrawn within ninety days. There is not only constant fear of foreign aggression, there is also distrust about foreign agents and collaborators. The deep animosity between the freedom fighters and collaborators makes national consensus building efforts almost impossible. Creating a civil society in Bangladesh continues to be difficult since the issue of genocide divides the nation so deeply.

Eyewitness Accounts
Genocide in Bangladesh

The following eyewitness accounts of the 1971 genocide depict different incidents. The first two eyewitness accounts describe the mass murders committed on March 25 night on Dhaka University campus. The first account is by a survivor of the killings in one of the student dormitories (Jagannath Hall) where Hindu students lived. The second account is by a university professor who witnessed and videotaped the massacres on Dhaka University campus. The third and fourth eyewitness testimonies describe the mass rape of women by the Pakistanis. The fifth testimony describes the killings in the village of Bangabandhu Sheikh Mujibur Rahman, the leader of the nationalist movement. The last account describes the atrocities of the non-Bengali Biharis who collaborated with the Pakistan army. The testimonies are taken from two sources; one is a Bengali book entitled *1971: Terrible Experiences* (Dhaka: Jatiya Shahitya Prakasheni, 1989), which was edited by Rashid Haider and is a collection of eyewitness accounts. Sohela Nazneen translated the accounts from Bengali to English. The other source, *The Year of the Vulture* (New Delhi: Orient Longmans, 1972), is an Indian journalist's (Amita Malik) account of the genocide. In the Malik book Dhaka is spelled as Dacca, which was the spelling used in 1972.

Massacre at Jagannath Hall
This testimony is from Kali Ranjansheel's, "Jagannath Hall e-Chilam" ["I was at Jagannath Hall"], in Rashid Haider (ed.), *1971: Vayabaha Ovigayata* [1971: Terrible Experiences] Dhaka: Jatiya Shahitya Prakasheni, 1989, p. 5. It was translated by Sohela Nazneen. Reprinted with permission.

I was a student at the Dhaka University. I used to live in room number
235 (South Block) in Jagannath Hall. On the night of 25th of March I
woke up from sleep by the terrifying sound of gunfire. Sometimes the
sound of gunfire would be suppressed by the sound of bomb explosions and shell-fire. I was so terrified that I could not even think of
what I should do! After a while I thought about going to Shusil, assistant general secretary of the student's union. I crawled up the stairs very
slowly to the third floor. I found out that some students had already
taken refuge in Shusil's room, but he was not there. The students told
me to go to the roof of the building where many other students had
taken shelter but I decided (rather selfishly) to stay by myself. I crawled
to the rest rooms at the northern end of the third floor and took refuge
in there. I could see the East, the South and the West from the window.
I could see that the soldiers were searching for students with flashlights
from room to room, were taking them near the Shahid Minar (Martyr's
memorial) and then shooting them. Only the sound of gunfire and
pleas of mercy filled the air. Sometimes the Pakistanis used mortars and
were shelling the building. The tin sheds in front of assembly and some
of the rooms in North Block were set on fire. . . .

After some time about forty to fifty Pakistani soldiers came to
the South Block and broke down the door of the dining room. The
lights were turned on and they were firing at the students who took
shelter in that room. . . . When the soldiers came out they had
Priyanath (the caretaker of the student dormitory) at gunpoint, and
forced him to show the way through all the floors of the dormitory.
During this time I was not able to see them as I left the restroom by
climbing up the open window and took shelter on the sunshed of the
third floor. But I could hear the cracking sounds of bullets, the students pleading for mercy and the sound of the soldiers rummaging
and throwing things about in search of valuables. The soldiers did
not see me on the sunshed.

. . . After they left I again took refuge in the washroom. I peeked
through the window and saw that the other students' dormitory,
Salimullah Hall, was on fire. The Northern and the Eastern parts of the
city was on fire too as the North and East horizon had turned red. The
whole night the Pakistani soldiers continued their massacre and destruction. . . . Finally I heard the call for the morning prayer. . . .

. . . The curfew was announced at dawn and I thought that this

merciless killing would stop. But it continued. The soldiers started killing those who had escaped their notice during the night before.

. . . It was morning and I heard the voices of some students. I came
out of the washroom, and saw that the students were carrying a body
downstairs while soldiers with machine guns were accompanying them.
It was the dead body of Priyanath. I was ordered to help the students
and I complied. We carried bodies from the dormitory rooms and piled
them up in the field outside.

There were a few of us there—students, gardeners, two sons of the
gateskeeper and the rest were janitors. The janitors requested the Pakistanis to let them go since they were not Bengalis. After a while the
army separated the janitors from us.

. . . All the time the soldiers were cursing and swearing at us. The
soldiers said "We will see how you get free Bangladesh! Why don't you
shout *Joy Bangla* (Victory to Bengal)!" The soldiers also kicked us around.
After we had finished carrying the bodies, we were divided into groups.
They then took my group to one of the university quarters and searched
almost every room on the fourth floor and looted the valuables. Downstairs we saw dead bodies piled up, obviously victims from the night
before. They also brought down the flag of Bangladesh.

. . . After we came back, we were again ordered to carry the dead
bodies to the Shahid Minar. The soldiers had already piled up the bodies of their victims and we added others bodies to the piles. If we felt
tired and slowed down, the soldiers threatened to kill us.

. . . As my companion and I were carrying the body of Sunil (our
dormitory guard), we heard screams in female voices. We found that
the women from the nearby slums were screaming as the soldiers were
shooting at the janitors (the husbands of the women). I realized that
our turn would come too as the Pakistanis started lining up those students who were before us, and were firing at them. My companion and
I barely carried the dead body of Sunil toward a pile where I saw the
dead body of Dr. Dev [Professor of Philosophy]. I cannot explain why
I did what I did next. Maybe from pure fatigue or maybe from a desperate hope to survive!

I lay down beside the dead body of Dr. Dev while still holding
onto the corpse of Sunil. I kept waiting for the soldiers to shoot me. I
even thought that I had died. After a long time I heard women and
children crying. I opened my eyes and saw that the army had left and

the dead bodies were still lying about and women were crying. Some of the people were still alive but wounded. All I wanted to do was to get away from the field and survive.

I crawled towards the slums. First I went to the house of the electrician. I asked for water but when I asked for shelter, his wife started crying aloud and I then left and took refuge in a restroom. . . . Suddenly I heard the voice of Idu who used to sell old books. He said, "Don't be afraid. I heard you are alive, I shall escort you to safety." I went to old Dhaka city. Then I crossed the river. The boatman did not take any money. From there, I first went to Shimulia, then, Nawabganj and finally I reached my village in Barishal in the middle of April.

Horror Documentary

This testimony is from Amita Malik's *The Year of the Vulture* (New Delhi: Orient Longmans, 1972, pp. 79–83).

At the professors' funeral, Professor Rafiq-ul-Islam of the Bengali Department whispered to me, "At the television station you will find that there is a film record of the massacre of professors and students at Jagannath Hall. Ask them to show it to you."

This sounded so incredible that I did not really believe it. However, I wasted no time in asking Mr. Jamil Chowdhury, the station manager of TV, whether he did, indeed, have such a film with him. "Oh yes," he said, "but we have not shown it yet because it might have dreadful repercussions." He was, of course, referring to the fact that the Pakistani army was still very much in Dacca in prisoner-of-war camps in the Cantonment, and it would have been dangerous to show them gunning down professors and students at Dacca University. The people of Dacca had shown tremendous restraint so far, but this would have been going a bit too far. However, I had it confirmed that N.B.C. VISNEWS and other international networks had already obtained and projected the film.

"But who shot the film?" I asked in wonder. "A professor at the University of Engineering, who had a video tape-recorder and whose flat overlooks the grounds of Jagannath Hall," said Mr. Chowdhury. It was therefore by kind courtesy of Dacca TV that I sat in their small projection room on January 5 and saw for the first time what must be a unique actuality film, something for the permanent archives of world history.

The film, lasting about 20 minutes, first shows small distant figures emerging from the hall carrying the corpses of what must be the students and professors massacred in Jagannath Hall. These are clearly civilian figures in lighter clothes and, at their back, seen strutting arrogantly even at that distance, are darker clad figures, the hoodlums of the Pakistan army. The bodies are laid down in neat, orderly rows by those forced to carry them at gun-point. Then the same procession troops back to the Hall. All this time, with no other sound, one hears innocent bird-song and a lazy cow is seen grazing on the university lawns. The same civilians come out again and the pile of bodies grows.

But after the third grisly trip, the action changes. After the corpses are laid on the ground, the people carrying them are lined up. One of them probably has a pathetic inkling of what is going to happen. He falls on his knees and clings to the legs of the nearest soldier, obviously pleading for mercy. But there is no mercy. One sees guns being pointed, one hears the crackle of gunfire and the lined up figures fall one by one, like the proverbial house of cards or, if you prefer, puppets in a children's film. At this stage, the bird-song suddenly stops. The lazy cow, with calf, careers wildly across the lawn and is joined by a whale herd of cows fleeing in panic.

But the last man is still clinging pathetically to the jack-boot of the soldier at the end of the row. The solider then lifts his shoulder at an angle, so that the gun points almost perpendicularly downwards to the man at his feet, and shoots him. The pleading hands unlink from the soldier's legs and another corpse joins the slumped bodies in a row, some piled on top of the very corpses they had to carry out at gun-point, their own colleagues and friends. The soldiers prod each body with their rifles or bayonets to make sure that they are dead. A few who are still wriggling in their death agony are shot twice until they also stop wriggling.

At this stage, there is a gap, because Professor Nurul Ullah's film probably ran out and he had to load a new one. But by the time he starts filming again, nothing much has changed except that there is a fresh pile of bodies on the left. No doubt some other students and professors had been forced at gun-point to carry them out and then were executed in turn. In so far as one can count the bodies, or guess roughly at their number in what is really a continuous long-shot amateur film, there are about 50 bodies by this time. And enough, one should think.

Professor Nurul Ullah's world scoop indicated that he was a remarkable individual who through his presence of mind, the instinctive reaction of a man of science, had succeeded in shooting a film with invaluable documentary evidence regardless of the risk to his life.

I immediately arranged to trace him down and he very kindly asked me to come round to his flat. Professor Nurul Ullah is a Professor of Electricity at the University of Engineering in Dacca. I found him to be a quiet, scholarly, soft-spoken, and surprisingly young man with a charming wife. He is normally engrossed in his teaching and students. But he happened to be the proud possessor of a video tape-recorder which he bought in Japan on his way back from a year at an American university. He is perhaps the only man alive who saw the massacre on the lawns of Dacca University on the first day of the Pakistani army crack-down. He took his film at great risk to his personal life. It was fascinating to sit down in Professor Nurul Ullah's sitting room and see the film twice with him, the second time after he had shown me the bedroom window at the back of his flat which overlooked both the street along which the soldiers drove to the university and the university campus. When he realized what was happening, he slipped his microphone outside [through] the window to record the sounds of firing. The film was shot from a long distance and under impossible conditions. Professor Nurul Ullah's description of how he shot the film was as dramatic and stirring as the film itself:

> "On March 25, 1971, the day of the Pakistani crack-down, although I knew nothing about it at the time, my wife and I had just had breakfast and I was looking out of my back windows in the professors' block of flats in which I and my colleagues from the Engineering University live with our families. Our back windows overlook a street across which are the grounds of Jagannath Hall, one of the most famous halls of Dacca University. I saw an unusual sight, soldiers driving past my flat and going along the street which overlooks it, towards the entrance to the University. As curfew was on, they made announcements on loudspeakers from a jeep that people coming out on the streets would be shot. After a few minutes, I saw some people carrying out what were obviously dead

bodies from Jagannath Hall. I immediately took out my loaded video tape recorder and decided to shoot a film through the glass of the window. It was not an ideal way to do it, but I was not sure what it was all about, and what with the curfew and all the tension, we were all being very cautious. As I started shooting the film, the people carrying out the dead bodies laid them down on the grass under the supervision of Pakistani soldiers who are distinguishable in the film, because of their dark clothes, the weapons they are carrying and the way they are strutting about contrasted with the civilians in lighter clothes who are equally obviously drooping with fright.

"As soon as firing started, I carefully opened the bedroom window wide enough for me to slip my small microphone just outside the window so that I could record the sound as well. But it was not very satisfactorily done, as it was very risky. My wife now tells me that she warned me at the time: 'Are you mad, do you want to get shot too? One flash from your camera and they will kill us too.' But I don't remember her telling me, I must have been very absorbed in my shooting, and she says I took no notice of what she said.

"It so happened that a few days earlier, from the same window I had shot some footage of student demonstrators on their way to the university. I little thought it would end this way.

"Anyway, this macabre procession of students carrying out bodies and laying them down on the ground was repeated until we realized with horror that the same students were themselves being lined up to be shot. After recording this dreadful sight on my video tape-recorder, I shut it off thinking it was all over only to realize that a fresh batch of university people were again carrying out bodies from inside. By the time I got my video tape-recorder going again, I had missed this new grisly procession but you will notice in the film that the pile of bodies is higher.

"I now want to show my film all over the world, because although their faces are not identifiable from that distance in what is my amateur film, one can certainly see the difference between the soldiers and their victims, one can see the shooting and hear it, one can see on film what my wife and I actually saw with our own eyes. And that is documentary evidence of the brutality of the Pak army and their massacre of the intellectuals."

Our Mothers and Sisters

The following testimony is from M. Akhtaurzzaman Mondol's "Amader-Ma Bon" ("Our Mother and Sisters") which appears in Rashid Haider (Ed.) *1971: Terrible Experiences,* p. 197. It was translated by Sohela Nazneen. Reprinted with permission.

We started our fight to liberate Vurungamari from the Pakistani occupation forces on November 11, 1971. We started attacking from West, North and East simultaneously. The Indian air forces bombed the Pakistani stronghold on November 11 morning. On November 13 we came near the outskirts of Vurungamari, and the Indian air force intensified their air attack. On November 14 morning the guns from the Pakistani side fell silent and we entered Vurungamari with shouts of "Joy Bangla" (victory to Bangladesh). The whole town was quiet. We captured fifty to sixty Pakistani soldiers. They had no ammunition left. We found the captain of the Pakistan forces, captain Ataullah Khan, dead in the bunker. He still had his arms around a woman—both died in the bomb attack in the bunker. The woman had marks of torture all over her body. We put her in a grave.

But I still did not anticipate the terrible scene I was going to witness and we were heading toward east of Vurungamari to take up our positions. I was informed by wireless to go to the Circle Officer's office. After we reached the office, we caught glimpses of several young women through the windows of the second floor. The doors were locked, so we had to break them down. After breaking down the door of the room, where the women were kept, we were dumbfounded. We found four naked young women, who had been physically tortured, raped, and battered by the Pakistani soldiers. We immediately came out of the room and threw in four *lungis* [dresses] and four bedsheets for them to cover themselves. We tried to talk to them, but all of them were still in shock. One of them was six to seven months pregnant. One was a college student from Mymen-singh. They were taken to India for medical treatment in a car owned by the Indian army. We found many dead bodies and skeletons in the bushes along the road. Many of the skeletons had long hair and had on torn *saris* and bangles on their hands. We found sixteen other women locked up in a room at Vurungamari High School. These women were brought in for the Pakistani soldiers from nearby villages. We found evidence in the rooms of the Circle

Officers office which showed that these women were tied to the windowbars and were repeatedly raped by the Pakistani soldiers. The whole floor was covered with blood, torn pieces of clothing, and strands of long hair. . . .

The Officer's Wife

This testimony is from Amita Malik's *The Year of the Vulture*, pp. 141–42.

Another pathetic case is that of a woman of about 25. Her husband was a government officer in a subdivision and she has three children. They first took away the husband, although she cried and pleaded with them. Then they returned him half-dead, after brutal torture. Then another lot of soldiers came in at 8 or 9 A.M. and raped her in front of her husband and children. They tied up the husband and hit the children when they cried.

Then another lot of soldiers came at 2.30 P.M. and took her away. They kept her in a bunker and used to rape her every night until she became senseless. When she returned after three months, she was pregnant. The villagers were very sympathetic about her but the husband refused to take her back. When the villagers kept on pressing him to take her back, he hanged himself. She is now in an advanced stage of pregnancy and we are doing all that we can do to help her. But she is inconsolable. She keeps on asking, "But why, why did they do it? It would have been better if we had both died."

The Maulvi's Story

This testimony appears in Amita Malik's *The Year of the Vulture*, pp. 102–104.

On April 19, 1971, about 35 soldiers came to our village in a launch at about 8 A.M. A couple of days earlier, I had asked the Sheikh's father and mother to leave the village, but they refused. They said, "This is our home and we shall not go away." Soon after I heard the sound of the launch, a soldier came running and said, "Here Maulvi, stop, in which house are the father and mother of the Sheikh?" So first I brought out his father. We placed a chair for him but they made him sit on the ground. Then Sheikh Sahib's amma [mother] was brought out. She took hold of my hand and I made her sit on the chair. The soldiers then held a sten-gun against the back of the Sheikh's abba [father] and a rifle against mine. "We will kill you in 10 minutes," said a soldier looking at his watch.

Then they picked up a diary from the Sheikh's house and some medicine bottles and asked me for the keys of the house. I gave them the bunch of keys but they were so rough in trying to open the locks that the keys would not turn. So they kicked open the trunks. There was nothing much inside except five teaspoons, which they took. They saw a framed photograph and asked me whose it was. When I said it was Sheikh Sahib's, they took it down. I tried to get up at this stage but they hit me with their rifle butts and I fell down against the chair. Finally, they picked up a very old suitcase and a small wooden box and made a servant carry them to the launch.

Then they dragged me up to where the Sheikh's father was sitting and repeated, "We shall shoot you in 10 minutes." Pointing to the Sheikh's father, I asked: "What's the point of shooting him? He's an old man and a government pensioner." The soldiers replied, "Is liye, keonki wohne shaitan paida kiya hai" ["Because he has produced a devil."]. "Why shoot me, the *imam* of the mosque?" I asked. "Aap kiska imam hai? Aap vote dehtehain" ["What sort of an *imam* are you? You vote."], they replied. I said: "The party was not banned, we were allowed to vote for it. We are not leaders, we are janasadharan [the masses]. Why don't you ask the leaders?" The captain intervened to say that eight minutes were over and we would be shot in another two minutes. Just then a major came running from the launch and said we were to be let alone and not shot.

I immediately went towards the masjid (mosque) and saw about 50 villagers inside. Three boys had already been dragged out and shot. The soldiers asked me about a boy who, I said, was a krishak (cultivator). They looked at the mud on his legs and hands and let him go. Khan Sahib, the Sheikh's uncle, had a boy servant called Ershad. They asked me about him. I said he was a servant. But a Razakar *maulvi,* who had come with them from another village, said he was the Sheikh's relative, which was a lie. The boy Ershad was taken to the lineup. He asked for water but it was refused.

Another young boy had come from Dacca, where he was employed in a mill, to enquire about his father. He produced his identity card but they shot him all the same. They shot Ershad right in front of his mother. Ershad moved a little after falling down so they shot him again. Finally, the boy who had carried the boxes to the launch was shot. With the three shot earlier, a total of six innocent boys were shot by the Pakistani army without any provocation. They were all good-looking and therefore suspected to be relatives of the Sheikh.

After this, the Sheikh's father and mother were brought out of the house. Amma was almost fainting. And the house was set on fire and burnt down in front of our eyes until all that remained was the frame of the doorway which you can still see. Altonissa, the lady with the blood-stained clothes of her son, is the mother of Torab Yad Ali who was shot. They did not allow her to remove her son's body for burial, because they wanted the bodies to be exposed to public view to terrorize the villagers. They also shot Mithu, the 10-year old son of this widowed lady. She had brought him up with the greatest difficulty—they never had anything to eat except *saag-bhaat* (spinach and rice). They shot little Mithu because he had helped the Mukti Bahini. You can now ask the ladies about their narrow escape.

Shaheeda Sheikh, Sheikh Mujib's niece, then added that fortunately all the women were taken away to safety across the river to a neighbouring village three days before the Pakistani soldiers came. For months they had lived in constant terror of Razakars pouncing on them from bushes by the village pond. Beli Begum, Mujib's niece, a strikingly lovely woman, told me how she had fled from the village when seven months pregnant and walked 25 miles to safety. Pari, a girl cousin, escaped with a temperature of 104 degrees. Otherwise they would all have been killed.

Massacre at Faiz Lake

This testimony is from Abdul Gofran's "Faiz Lake-Gonohataya" ("Massacre at Faiz Lake"), which first appeared in Rashid Haider (ed.), *1971: Terrible Experiences*. It was translated by Sohela Nazneen.

I own a shop near Akbar Shah mosque in Pahartali. On November 10th, 1971, at 6. A.M. about forty to fifty Biharis came to my shop and forced me to accompany them. I had to comply as any form of resistance would have been useless against such a large number of people.

They took me to Faiz Lake. As we passed through the gates of Faiz Lake I saw that hundreds of non-Bengalis had assembled near the Pump-house and wireless colony. The Bengalis who had been brought in were tied up. They were huddled by the side of the lake which was at the north side of the Pump-house. Many of the Biharis were carrying knives, swords and other sharp instruments. The Biharis were first kicking and beating up the Bengalis brutally and then were shoving their victims towards those carrying weapons. These other group of armed Biharis were then jabbing their victims in the stomach and then severing their heads with the swords. I witnessed several groups of Bengalis being killed in such a manner. . . . When the Biharis came for me one of them took away my sweater. I then punched him and jumped into the lake. . . . I swam to the other side and hid among the bushes. . . . The Biharis came to look for me but I was fortunate and barely escaped their notice. From my hiding place I witnessed the mass murder that was taking place. Many Bengalis were killed in the manner which had been described earlier.

The massacre went on till about two o'clock in the afternoon. After they had disposed off the last Bengal victim, the Biharis brought in a group of ten to twelve Bengali men. It was evident from their gestures that they were asking the Bengalis to dig a grave for the bodies lying about. I also understood from their gestures that the Biharis were promising the group that if they completed the task they would be allowed to go free. The group complied to their wish. After the group had finished burying the bodies, they were also killed, and the Biharis went away rejoicing. There were still many dead bodies thrown around the place.

In the afternoon many Biharis and [the] Pakistani army went along that road. But the Pakistani soldiers showed no sign of remorse. They seemed rather happy and did nothing to bury the dead.

When night fell I came back to my shop but left Chittagong the next day.

Chapter Eleven
The Burundi Genocide

René Lemarchand

With the exception of Rwanda, nowhere else in Africa has so much violence killed so many people in so small a space as in Burundi in the spring and summer of 1972. Between 100,000 and 150,000 human lives were lost in one of the most appalling examples of human rights violations recorded in independent Africa. The genocidal scale of the 1972 killings makes Burundi one of the continent's grimmest laboratories for the study of ethnic violence. As much as the extent of the carnage, the element of intent is what differentiates the Burundi killings from most other instances of ethnic violence (Chalk and Jonassohn, 1990, p. 23). In fact, it is in Burundi and more recently in Rwanda that the definition of genocide contained in the United Nations Convention on the Prevention and Punishment of the Crime of Genocide—"acts committed with intent to destroy, in whole or in part, a national, ethnical, racial or religious group" (art. 2)—find its most tragically accurate illustration.

On certain basic facts concerning the killings there is widespread unanimity: whereas the victims belonged to the Hutu majority, the perpetrators of the genocide were for the most part drawn from the ruling Tutsi minority; the killings occurred in response to an abortive Hutu-led insurgency which caused thousands of deaths among innocent Tutsi civilians; the repression and subsequent massive physical elimination of Hutu civilians were largely conducted by government troops assisted by the youth wing of the ruling party; and, in the wake of the slaughter tens of thousands of Hutu men, women, and children fled the country, seeking asylum in neighboring states.

Typical of the general international indifference surrounding the genocide was the official stance of the United States during the Nixon administration, which, according to a study of the Carnegie Endowment for International Peace, revealed an extraordinary combination of "indifference, inertia and irresponsibility" (Brown et al. 1973). Not only were international reactions to the slaughter remarkably low-key, but the subsequent military and economic assistance given to the Burundi government by external third parties (China, France, North Korea) contributed in no small way to reinforce the dominant position of Tutsi elites (Lemarchand, 1974). The new cycles of violence and repression that burst upon the country in 1988, 1991, 1992, and 1993, each time causing thousands of deaths, are in part traceable to the continued monopoly of military power by the Tutsi minority.

More difficult to pin down are the historical forces that led to the genocide, and its overall impact on Hutu communities within and outside the country. Not only are there sharp disagreements between Hutu and Tutsi intellectuals about the roots of the 1972 killings, but the question is also a source of considerable discord among Western analysts. While some (mostly Hutu) are tempted to read into the killings the gruesome evidence of long-standing enmities, rooted in the precolonial past, others (mostly Tutsi) would deny altogether the existence of a deep-seated conflict between Hutu and Tutsi. Instead of looking to the past for an answer, they point to the unfortunate legacy of the divide-and-rule policies of the Belgian colonizer, the continued efforts of self-serving Hutu politicians to subvert the state, and their ability to enlist the support of external powers (notably Rwanda). Paralleling these radically divergent interpretations are entirely different estimates of the significance of the 1972 killings. For many Hutu, the slaughter is proof of irreconcilable cultural, social, and political differences between Hutu and Tutsi which can only be resolved by establishing a Hutu Republic, inspired by the Rwanda model. For most Tutsi, on the other hand, the historical ties and cultural affinities between the two groups rule out assumptions of basic enmities; tragic as the 1972 events were for both Hutu and Tutsi, they claim the killings were largely instigated by extremist elements and thus should not be seen as an insuperable obstacle in the way of social harmony.

A closer look at the historical record reveals a rather more complex situation. The roots of the Hutu-Tutsi conflict do not lie in the precolonial past (though claims that it does have contributed significantly to its persistence); as we shall see, they lie in the bitter struggle for power unleashed by the introduction of electoral processes in the years following independence. On the other hand, there is no gainsaying the fact that the traditional society contained within itself a rich potential for conflict. Given the relative size of ethnic segments—the Hutu representing anywhere from 75 to 80 percent of the population, and the Tutsi approximately 20 percent—it is easy to see why majority rule should raise fears of permanent Hutu domination among Tutsi, and why, by denying them their fair share of political power, the Tutsi should have created a sense of outrage among the Hutu.

Historical Context

In contrast with most other states in the continent, Burundi's boundaries remained virtually unchanged since its emergence as an archaic kingdom in the eighteenth century. Like Rwanda, its neighbor to the north, Burundi was once part of the German colony of East Africa, later to become a League of Nations Mandate and a United Nations Trust Territory under Belgian administration. While sharing many ethno-cultural affinities with Rwanda, including a vertical pattern of stratification in which wealth and status tended to coincide with ethnic divisions between Hutu and Tutsi, ethnic relations in Burundi were more fluid and not easily reducible to a simple Hutu-Tutsi split (Lemarchand, 1970). Hence their radically different political trajectories, with Rwanda acceding to independence as a Hutu-dominated republic, and Burundi as a constitutional monarchy under a mixed, Hutu-Tutsi government.

In the traditional Burundi society, power was the monopoly of the king and his chiefs (most of them recruited among the princes of the blood, the so-called *ganwa*); yet, with few exceptions, neither king nor chiefs were identified with the Tutsi minority. The *ganwa* elite were seen as a group apart, ethnically distinct from both Hutu and Tutsi. Moreover, family and clan distinctions among Hutu and Tutsi tended to correspond to different shades of social status, thus adding another element of complexity to the social pyramid. Especially noteworthy in this connection is the division between Tutsi-Hima and Tutsi-Banyaruguru: though both are identified as Tutsi, in the traditional pecking order the Banyaruguru ranked far above the Hima subgroup in terms of social status and wealth. In the years after independence, however, the Hima emerged as the dominant group within the army, and thus bear much of the responsibility for the 1972 massacre. To this day they stand as the social axis around which much of the country's power structure seems to revolve.

Under the impact of colonial rule a new pattern of stratification began to emerge, in which class-based cleavages tended increasingly to mirror Hutu-Tutsi differences (Gahama, 1981). By withdrawing recognition from those

Hutu notables who held influential positions at the court and in the king's estates, the colonial state significantly altered patterns of recruitment (mostly to the advantage of Tutsi elements). By imposing upon the Hutu masses a wide range of obligations, it added immeasurably to their traditional burdens; and by the selective allocation of educational opportunities to Tutsi children, it further reduced the life chances of the Hutu as a group. Even so, on the eve of independence ethnic polarization was still at an incipient stage; princely factionalism, rather than ethnic conflict, was the central characteristic of Burundi society.

Thus in contrast with what happened in Rwanda, where the sharpness of the Hutu-Tutsi cleavage led to a major revolutionary upheaval in the years immediately preceding independence, eventuating in the birth of a Hutu-dominated republic, in Burundi the Hutu-Tutsi split did not become politically significant until well after independence (1962), and then largely as a consequence of the demonstration effect of the revolution in Rwanda. Until then much of Burundi politics revolved around a thinly veiled struggle for power between two princely factions, the Bezi and the Batare, the former identified with the ruling dynasty and the latter with rival claimants to the throne. Playing one group of princes (*ganwa*) off against the other became a standard feature of Belgian colonial policies, with the Batare faction eventually emerging as the Residency's favorite partner against the Bezi. As independence finally came into view in the late 1950s, the stage was set for an increasingly polarized pattern of competition between the Parti Democrate Chrétien (PDC) and the Parti de l'Unité et du Progrès National (Uprona), associated, respectively, with Batare and Bezi politicians.

The legislative elections of 1961, a year before independence, resulted in a landslide victory for the Uprona and the appointment of its recognized leader, Prince Rwagasore, as Prime Minister designate. As the oldest son of King Mwambutsa, and a figure of immense popularity among both Hutu and Tutsi, Rwagasore stood as the embodiment of nationalist aspirations and the strongest supporter of the monarchy. His assassination on October 13, 1961, by a Greek gunman in the pay of the PDC opposition, ushered in a crisis of legitimacy from which the country has yet to recover. His death created a political void which no other leader has since been able to fill, thus setting the stage for a rapid polarization of society along ethnic lines.

The Roots of Conflict

Broadly characterized, the Hutu-Tutsi conflict is a recent phenomenon, rooted in part in the long-term processes of social change introduced by the colonial state, and in part by the rapid mobilization of ethnic identities under the pressure of electoral competition. Equally important, however, are certain specific factors and circumstances that lie in the background of the 1972 bloodbath. For the sake of clarity, they can be subsumed under the following major headings:

1. *The Demonstration Effect of the Rwanda Revolution.* Perhaps no other factor has played a more decisive role in hardening the lines of ethnic cleavage than the psychological impact of the Rwanda revolution on the collective consciousness of both Hutu and Tutsi. The proclamation of a Hutu Republic in Rwanda served as a powerful source of political inspiration for many Hutu politicians; for most Tutsi, on the other hand, the Rwanda model evoked a nightmarish vision of Hutu domination to be avoided at all costs. And with tens of thousands of Tutsi refugees from Rwanda entering the country—each with tales of horror—few were the Tutsi of Burundi who did not see the "handwriting on the wall." The Rwanda revolution carried a powerful demonstration effect on both Hutu and Tutsi, causing enormous mutual distrust between them.

2. *The Political Mobilization of Ethnic Segments.* The revolution in Rwanda happened to coincide with a major leadership crisis within the ruling Uprona party—traceable to Prince Rwagasore's untimely death—which, in turn, greatly magnified ethnic tensions within and outside the party. The intraparty struggle thus quickly spilled over into the urban arena of the capital city (Bujumbura), pitting Hutu trade unionists and politicians against young Tutsi militants for the most part affiliated with the Uprona youth wing. In the countryside, political mobilization along ethnic lines did not reach a significant scale until the legislative elections of May 1965, in which the Hutu scored a landslide victory with 23 seats out of a total of 33 in the National Assembly. The critical sequence of events, however, took place immediately after the elections, when king Mwambutsa, instead of appointing a Hutu as head of the government, turned to a princely figure and long-time protege of the court (Leopold Biha) to act as Prime Minister. Robbed of their victory at the polls, the Hutu elites reacted angrily to what they perceived as an intolerable interference in the parliamentary life of

the country. Some came to the conclusion that they had no other choice but to use violence to make good their claims to power. Anti-Tutsi violence thus inevitably led to anti-Hutu retribution. A kind of uneven *lex talionis* came to preside over acts of violence, whereby every challenge was met by retribution in kind; yet each time repressive violence came into play, the severity of the Tutsi-led repression clearly exceeded the nature of the challenge.

3. *Political Exclusion.* The continued and systematic exclusion of Hutu elements from all positions of political responsibility in the party, the government, the civil service, and the army is the key to an understanding of the horrors of 1972 (Lemarchand, 1974). Only through a combination of extraordinary luck and ruthlessness were the Tutsi elites able to assert themselves as a ruling minority. Their luck stemmed from the abortive Hutu-instigated coup of October 1965, which resulted in the physical elimination of some 34 Hutu officers, the arrest of scores of Hutu politicians, and the collapse of the monarchy. From this point on, the instruments of power were firmly in Tutsi hands, or, more accurately, in Hima hands. Their ruthlessness emerged with singular perversity during the 1972 killings. In the view of many Hutu, anti-Tutsi violence during the 1972 insurgency was not just a matter of legitimate revenge; its motivating force came from the pervasive sense of moral indignation felt by many Hutu in the face of what they perceived to be an intolerable denial of their legitimate political rights. To this day recourse to violence is viewed by many Hutu not only as the sole available alternative to the perpetuation of Tutsi hegemony, but as a morally justifiable one as well.

The 1972 Watershed

On April 29, 1972, like a bolt out of the blue, a violent Hutu-led insurrection burst upon the normally peaceful lakeside towns of Rumonge and Nyanza-Lac in the south. In a matter of hours terror was unleashed by Hutu upon Tutsi. After seizing control of the armories in Rumonge and Nyanza-Lac, the insurgents proceeded to kill every Tutsi in sight, as well as a number of Hutu who refused to join the rebels. During the first week of violence the insurgency may have claimed the lives of anywhere from 2,000 to 3,000, most of them Tutsi. At this point, in an attempt to build a political base, some of the insurgents retreated to Vugizo commune, near the provincial capital of Bururi, and proclaimed a "People's Republic." A week later government troops brought the nascent experiment to an end. By then the repression had already caused untold casualties throughout the country.

On May 30, after proclaiming martial law, the country's President, Michel Micombero, requested immediate military assistance from President Mobutu of Zaire. With Zairian paratroopers holding the airport, the Burundi army then moved in force into the countryside. What followed was not so much a repression as a hideous slaughter of Hutu civilians. The carnage went on unabated until August. By then almost every educated Hutu element was either dead or in exile.

Exactly how many died between May and August is impossible to say. Conservative estimates put the total number of victims somewhere between 100,000 and 150,000. This is considerably less than the 300,000 claimed by Hutu opponents of the regime, and far more than the 15,000 at first cited by the Burundi authorities. However much one can disagree about the scale of the massacre, that it reflects a planned annihilation is hardly in doubt. Much of the "planning," as we now realize, was the work of the Minister of Foreign Affairs at the time, Arthemon Simbananiye, assisted in his task by the Minister of Interior and Justice, Albert Shibura, and the executive secretary of the Uprona party, Andre Yanda. All three are of Hima origins; the latter two also held key positions in the army.

For many Hutu, "le plan Simbananiye" is the key to an understanding of the killings. According to this master plan, conceived long before the Hutu uprising, the aim was to provoke the Hutu into staging an uprising so as to justify a devastating repression and cleanse the country once and for all of the Hutu peril. There is in fact little evidence of any such provocation; nor is it at all clear that any such plan existed prior to the Hutu uprising. What is beyond question, however, is that Simbananiye used the "clear and present danger" posed by the Hutu insurgency as a pretext to go far beyond the immediate exigency of restoring peace and order. As the social profile of the victims clearly shows, the ultimate objective was to systematically kill all educated Hutu elements, including civil servants, university students, and school children, and in so doing eliminate for the foreseeable future any serious threat of Hutu rebellion. It is in this sense that one can indeed speak of a "Simbananiye plan."

The systematic targeting of educated Hutu elements is a point on which most observers agree. As Jeremy Greenland (1976) reported, "the government radio broadcasts encouraged the population to 'hunt down the python in the grass,' an order which was interpreted by Tutsi in the interior as license to exterminate all educated Hutu, down to the level of secondary, and in some cases even primary school children. Army units commandeered merchants' lorries and mission vehicles, and drove up to schools removing whole batches of children at a time. Tutsi pupils prepared lists of their Hutu classmates to make identification by officials more straightforward" (p. 120). In Bujumbura, Gitega, and Ngozi all "cadres" of Hutu origins—not only local civil servants but chauffeurs, clerks, and semi-skilled workers—were rounded up, taken to the nearest jail and either shot or beaten to death with rifle butts and clubs. In Bujumbura, alone, an estimated 4,000 Hutu were loaded up on trucks and taken to their graves.

Some of the most gruesome scenes took place on the premises of the Université Officielle in Bujumbura, and in secondary and technical schools. Scores of Hutu students were physically assaulted by their Tutsi classmates, and many beaten to death. In a scenario that would repeat itself again and again, groups of soldiers and members of the Uprona youth wing, the so-called Jeunesses Révolutionnaires Rwagasore (JRR), would suddenly appear in classrooms, call the Hutu students by name, and take them away. Few ever returned. Approximately one-third (120) of the Hutu students enrolled at the university disappeared in such circumstances. What few Tutsi urged restraint did so at their own peril. As Michael Hoyt (1972), then acting Deputy Chief of Mission at the U.S. Embassy, stated, "We have reliable reports that some Tutsi urging restraint in Bujumbura on the basis that the situation has gone too far are being arrested and immediately executed" (Hoyt, 1972).

Nor was the Church spared. Reporting from Bujumbura in early June, Marvine Howe (1972) noted that "12 Hutu priests are said to have been killed, and thousands of Protestant pastors, school directors and teachers" (p. 4). No sector of society was left untouched. Least of all the military. This is how Hoyt (1972) describes the extent of the purges within the army:

The death toll in the army resulting from the execution of Hutu has risen. Recent Belgian estimates point to more than 500. About 150 Hutu were executed on the night of May 22. Forty one on the night of May 27. Definition of Hutu has altered, however. Now one grand-parent is enough to result in classifying soldiers as Hutu. Using this standard some 100 Hutu were believed to be alive in the army on May 23.

How many of these were spared by the continuing slaughter is anybody's guess.

To impute genocidal intentions to all Tutsi would be both unfair and inaccurate. Whether intentions ultimately made a difference is another matter. In the countryside anti-Hutu violence stemmed from a variety of motives, some involving personal enmities, others rooted in crassly material calculations. The desire to appropriate the victims' property appears to have been a major inducement to violence. Again to quote from Greenland (1976): "In countless cases the furniture was removed from the homes of arrested Hutu, with the widows and orphans left sitting on the bare floor. The cars and lorries of wealthier Hutu became the property of those who arrested them" (p. 122).

Clearly, responsibility for the killings cannot be ascribed collectively to all Tutsi. Many paid with their lives their determination to protect Hutu elements, and the same is true of those Hutu who, during the insurgency, took it upon themselves to shelter Tutsi civilians. The key participants in the genocide were the army and the JRR, often operating hand in hand, in groups of varying size depending on the magnitude of the task that lay ahead. "In Muramvuya," according to Hoyt (1972), "the populace was thrown into near panic by the sudden arrival of nearly 1,000 JRR elements." In most instances the arrests and subsequent executions were conducted by mixed teams of army men and JRR elements consisting of a dozen individuals; and where neither group could be summoned in sufficient numbers, arms were distributed to local Tutsi males with instructions to act as surrogate paramilitary groups. In an atmosphere saturated with fear, the killing of Hutu seemed to have become part of the civic duty expected of every Tutsi citizen. A number of Tutsi refugees from Rwanda accepted the assignment with little or no hesitation. Particularly in the northern region, where refugee camps were located, much of the killing was done by Tutsi refugees, perhaps as much out of revenge as out of fear that they might once again be the target of Hutu violence.

Fear of an impending Hutu-instigated slaughter of all Tutsi elements, nurtured by lingering memories of what happened in Rwanda in 1959–1962, certainly played a crucial part in transforming the repression into a genocide. That many Tutsi perceived the Hutu attacks as posing a mortal threat to their survival, there can be no doubt; nor is there any question that many viewed the wholesale elimination of Hutu elites as the only way of dealing effectively with this clear and present danger—a kind of "final solution" to a situation that threatened their very existence as a group. In the short run, their calculation proved entirely correct: the wholesale decapitation of the Hutu elites ensured a modicum of "peace and order" for the next sixteen years. But as is now becoming increasingly clear, the long-term effects of the genocide have enormously complicated the quest for a peaceful solution of the Hutu-Tutsi question. Among the new generations of Hutu elites few are willing to forget or forgive.

The Aftermath

The essential point to note about the long-term impact of the genocide is the sense of martyrdom felt by the Hutu as a group. To this day, their collective self-image is that of a victimized community, against whom deliberate atrocities have repeatedly been committed.

The vision they have of themselves is one in which past and present are but two sides of the same coin. In the perceptions of many Hutu intellectuals, the events of 1972 are only the most recent manifestation of a long history of ethnic conflict, traceable to the precolonial past. In their minds, and in their writings, the Tutsi are invariably categorized as "Hamitic" (or "Nilotic") elements who came from the north; in keeping with their origins they brought into the country profoundly malefic influences, fundamentally alien to Hutu culture. Only through a combination of ruse and cruelty were the Tutsi able to establish their domination upon the unsuspecting Hutu. The account given by a Hutu refugee is not untypical of the manner in which history is being reconceptualized to fit the horrors of 1972: "The Tutsi are of Nilotic provenance. They came from Somalia. And then they stole our livestock, cows, chickens, domestic animals, even the birds, the fish, the trees, the banana fields. . . . They came perhaps 400 or 500 years ago . . . " (Malkki 1989, p. 147). Present-day conflicts, in short, are but the carry-over into the post-independence era of deep-seated, historically rooted ethnic antagonisms. In the minds of many Hutu, these seemingly irreducible incompatibilities leave little hope for compromise.

Thus history is increasingly being recast as myth, and in the process new identities have crystallized around the terms "Hutu" and "Tutsi." No longer are these ethnic labels relatively free of moral connotations, or socially ambivalent, as used to be the case in the traditional society; they now carry a powerful emotional load, identified as they are with entirely different social, moral, and historical connotations. For many Hutu, the Tutsi are the embodiment of moral perversity; for many Tutsi, the threat of genocide is the subliminal message inscribed in the efforts of the Hutu masses to become full participants in the political life of the country. Here the recent history of Rwanda is repeatedly invoked as an ominous precedent.

Among the Hutu the omnipresent fear of a reenactment of the 1972 bloodbath has become something of a self-fulfilling prophecy. Indeed, memories of 1972 played a critical role in the renewed outburst of ethnic violence in August 1988 in the northern communes of Ntega and Marangara: triggered by repeated provocations of local Tutsi personalities, and fueled by rumors of an impending massacre of Hutu peasants on a scale similar to what had happened in 1972, some 500 Tutsi civilians were killed by enraged Hutu elements before the army moved in and unleashed another bloody repression, resulting in the deaths of an estimated 15,000 Hutu. As in 1972, anticipation of a Tutsi genocide by the Hutu certainly played a decisive role in the "preemptive strike" against Hutu elements in 1988 (Lemarchand, 1991; Chrétien et al. 1989). The exigencies of self-preservation make it imperative for the Tutsi not only to retain control over the instruments of force but to use force whenever confronted with threats to their own survival as a minority.

Unlike what happened in 1972, the international community responded to the 1988 killings with a sense of shock. Substantial press coverage of the "events," coupled with international charges of massacre from the European Community, were instrumental in prompting the Burundi government to initiate major reforms in the wake of the 1988 slaughter. In the United States, the most significant departure from the generalized public indifference about Burundi came during the course of a congressional hearing in September 1988 that led to the passage of a nonbinding resolution by the House of Representatives. In it, the House

urged the government of Burundi to maintain and greatly increase its recent efforts at national reconciliation . . . condemned the recent violence reportedly carried out by the armed forces . . . and urged the President and the Secretary of State to conduct a comprehensive reassessment of the United States' bilateral relationship with the Government of Burundi with a view to immediate suspension of US assistance (other than humanitarian aid) unless within six months (a) an impartial enquiry has been initiated . . . (b) the Government of Burundi has taken steps to investigate and prosecute those military and administrative officials responsible for the recent atrocities . . . (c) the Government of

Burundi has made substantial progress in promoting the safe return to their homes of Burundi's refugee population. . . . (Lemarchand, 1991, p. 86)

By driving home to the Burundi authorities that their failure to heed congressional warnings would entail major costs, primarily in the form of economic assistance and international loans, the resolution did carry important consequences. And so did the strong condemnations issued by Belgium, Canada, and the European Parliament.

This is not the place for a sustained discussion of the important political reforms introduced since the passage of this resolution. Whether, as a result of these reforms significant changes will take place at the societal level with regard to the distribution of wealth, status and privilege between Hutu and Tutsi, is hard to tell. Memories of the 1972 and 1988 killings will persist for generations, and so will the mutual fears and hatreds they have instilled in the minds of the Burundi masses.

One of the more important lessons to be learned from the Burundi genocide is that unless the perpetrators of such atrocities can anticipate severe costs from the international system, they are unlikely to be deterred or forced to mend their ways. Most instructive in this respect is the contrast between the 1972 and 1988 massacres: in 1972 international reactions were conspicuously muted; the 1988 killings, though not nearly as devastating, generated a major public outcry and immediate threats of economic sanctions from the United States, Belgium, Germany, and even the World Bank. International concern, however, if it is to materialize into effective pressures, presupposes an honest and impartial coverage of mass killings by the media. Again, the relative silence of the media during the 1972 crisis is in sharp contrast with the abundant and graphically detailed accounts of the 1988 horrors in the Western press. Finally, and most importantly, nongovernmental human rights organizations can play a decisive role in alerting public opinion, as indeed happened in 1988, when Danish, Belgian, and German human rights groups launched a major press campaign to reveal to the world the agonies of Burundi. What these and other "preventive" measures cannot do, however, is erase these atrocities from the collective memories of Hutu and Tutsi. For years to come the past will indeed continue to haunt Burundi's political future, shaping its ethnic destinies in ways that are as yet impossible to predict.

Eyewitness Accounts
The Burundi Genocide

Note: Oral witness accounts of the events surrounding the 1972 genocide
are extremely scarce, in part because of the restrictions placed by the
Burundi authorities on unaccompanied travel through the countryside—
especially when the aim is to interview survivors of the genocide—and in
part because of the logistical, administrative, and political difficulties involved in gaining access to refugee camps in neighbouring states. Liisa
Malkki is one of the very few trained anthropologists to have conducted
extensive interviews with refugees in Tanzania (in Mishamo, Kigoma, and
Ujiji). The following three accounts are reproduced from her doctoral
dissertation, *Purity and Exile: Transformations in Historical-National Consciousness Among Hutu Refugees in Tanzania* (1989). All were recorded in
1987, in Mishamo (Tanzania). What is particularly noteworthy about these
oral "mythico-histories," as Malkki described them, is the manner in which
they intersperse myth and history, thereby providing the basis for a fundamental redefinition of collective identities. As Malkki (1989) points out,
"if 'history' could ever be defined as a faithful recording of facts in an
absolute reality, the Hutu constitution of history would be 'realistic.' The
Hutu history, however, went far beyond accurate recording. It represents
not only a description of the past, nor even merely an evaluation of
the past, but a subversive recasting and reinterpreting of it in fundamentally moral terms" (pp. 124–125). In short, the implication
is not that every word is pure fiction, only that reality has been filtered through the prism of an exceptionally traumatic experience. The
result is a set of collective representations that have become part and par-
cel of the vision that the refugees have of themselves and of their recent
history.

It should be noted that the names of Malkki's interviewees are not available. The key reason is that their discourse carries significant political implications which could conceivably be held against them.

Account 1
The first account is a graphic description of the atrocities committed by
Tutsi against Hutu. How much is invention, how much is a faithful rendering of reality is impossible to tell. Although some of the more nauseating
forms of torture alluded to in the text are probably made up, they reveal a

construction of social reality rooted in a horrifying experience that continues to shape the consciousness of many Hutu refugees. Recorded in Mishamo (Tanzania) in 1987.

There was a manner of cutting the stomach (of pregnant women). Everything that was found in the interior was lifted out without cutting the cord. The cadaver of the mama, the cadaver of the baby, of the future, they rotted on the road. Not even burial. The mother was obliged to eat the finger of her baby. One cut the finger, and one said to the mother: Eat! . . . Another case which I remember: they roped together opapa [a father] with his daughter, also in Bujumbura. They said: Now you can party! They were thrown into the lake. . . . My older brother, he was roped, and then he was made to roll, slide on the asphalted road behind a car. The Tutsi's intention was to equalize the population, up to 50 per cent. It was a plan. My brother's body was left in the forest. If it had been left on the road, the foreigners would have seen it, and they would have written about it. . . . The girls [Tutsi] in secondary schools . . . killed the Hutu [girls]. The Tutsi girls were given bamboos. They were made to kill by pushing the bamboo from below (from the vagina) to the mouth. It is a thing against the law of God. Our party would never do this. God must help us. During the Genocide every Tutsi had to make an action [to kill]. In the hospitals, in the Churches. . . . Even the sick were killed in the beds of the hospitals. The genocide lasted three months, from the twenty ninth of April to the end of August. But the killing was started again in 1973, above all in Bukemba. . . . In other cases a bonfire was lighted, then the legs and arms of the Hutu were tied [informant describes how the arms, tied in the back of the body, and the legs were fastened to ground, so that a circle of captives around the fire was forced to bend backwards]. Then the fire, the heat, inflates the stomach, and the stomach is ruptured. You see, with the heat much liquid develops in the stomach, and then the stomach is ruptured. For others, a barrel of water was heated, and the people were put into it. . . . For the pregnant women, the stomach was cut, and then the child who had been inside—one said to the mama: Eat your child! This embryo! One had to do it. And then, other women and children, they were put inside a house, like 200, and then the house was burned. Everything inside was burned. . . . Others utilized bamboos, pushing them from here (anus) up to here (mouth). . . . (Malkki, 1989, pp. 183–184)

Account 2

The second account brings to light a crucial aspect of the 1972 killings: the wholesale massacre of all middle-class and educated Hutu elements, down to the primary schoolchildren. It brings out the sense of deep moral indignation felt by virtually every survivor of the massacre when reflecting upon the fact that educational achievement was sufficient reason for being killed. Recorded in Mishamo (Tanzania) in 1987.

> They wanted to kill my clan because my clan was educated. The clans which were educated, cultivated, they were killed. In my clan, there were school teachers, medical assistants, agronomists . . . some evangelists, not yet priests, and two who were in the army. . . . All have been exterminated. Among those who were educated, it is I alone who remains. . . . There are many persons who leave Burundi today because one kills everyday. The pupils, the students. . . . It is because these are intellectuals—because if you do not study you do not have much *maarifa* [knowledge, information]. Many Hutu university people were killed. The government workers, they were arrested when they were in their offices, working. The others also in their places, for example an agronomist, when he was walking in the fields where he works, he was arrested. Or a veterinary technician: one finds him in his place, where he works. There were medical technicians, professors. . . . Or the artisans in the garage, or those who worked in printing houses or in the ateliers where furniture is made. They were killed there, on the spot. . . . The male missionaries and the female missionaries, who were doing their work in the Churches, in the schools as professors, or in the hospitals as doctors, they were not killed on the spot. They were killed in the prison. I think that the very first who were poured into the lake were the masculine missionaries and the feminine missionaries. . . . If you are a student, that's a reason for killing you; if you're rich, that's a reason; if you are a man who dares to say a valid word to the population, that's a reason for killing you. In short, it is a racial hate. (Malkki, 1989, pp. 193–194)

Account 3

The third account reveals the circumstances of the massacre: the helicopters hovering over bands of hapless peasants, their flight into the bush, the constant fear of being picked up by soldiers, their long march into exile, their relief upon meeting friends and relatives whom they thought had been killed, their sadness upon learning of the death of others. And then the redeeming opportunity to "talk, talk, talk about what had happened. . . ."

We heard the guns: boom! boom! boom! boom! And then there were helicopters, and when they saw a group of men on the ground, they killed them. We left home. We went into the forest and hid ourselves in the rocks. Others they took flight immediately, all the way to Tanzania, but we stayed three months in the rocks, from April until June. We put the children under the rocks, and then we looked around. If the soldiers were far, we went into the fields to find cassava, sugar cane, like that, to give to our children. . . . Then, in the night, around eight o'clock, we began the voyage (toward Tanzania) having prayed to God that he would protect us. That was the ninth of June 1972. We walked for one day and two nights. We arrived in Tanzania . . . with meat from our horses, with knives and three radios, with money in our pocket (Burundi francs). When we arrived at the frontier they said to us: "Approach, approach, dear friends!" We were fearful. We asked each other: "What? The soldiers have reached here already?" They said, "We are the soldiers of Tanzania." We did not know where the boundary was. We just walked like sheep, truly like animals. We were very tired. Our children, their feet were swollen. The Tanzanian soldiers asked, "So, what do you have?" We said, "knives and radios. . . ." Concerning the money we said nothing. The soldiers said: "Yes, approach." They said, "Sleep here on the sand first, near the lake." We slept perhaps two hours. Then they said, "Now we will take you to Kigoma." While we were going towards Kigoma, on the way, we thought it was just us who had come here, but we ended up being 150. But then the others said, "No, no, no, we want to return to Burundi. Here in Tanzania we will starve. We want to go home." So, 35 of us remained in Tanzania. But—sad to say—all those who returned were killed. When we arrived in Kigoma, oh, oh, oh! . . . we met many, many, many men, women, from all the provinces of Burundi. We even saw people from different provinces whom we had met in the Church conferences in Burundi. All of them, they were all there! We asked them, "Where is your wife?" They said, "My wife is already killed; I ran away alone." And then, "Where is the pastor of your commune?" They responded, "He, he was killed." Like this we learned the news. One said: "Many, many were killed in the area where we lived. . . ." The majority of the people came from Bururi, near the frontier. The first thing they did was talk, talk about what had happened. . . . We stayed in Kigoma for eight weeks, then the trucks came to take us to the camp. (Malkki, 1989, p. 209)

Account 4

This last account, called "Refugees from the Homeland," is borrowed from Hanne Christensen's excellent study of a Burundi refugee settlement in Tanzania, *Refugees and Pioneers: History and Field Study of a Burundian Settlement in Tanzania* (Geneva: UNRISD, 1985). Described by the author as "extracts from interviews with refugees," which were conducted in 1984, it is a composite picture of the personal traumas and sufferings many have experienced in Burundi and in exile, while at the same time conveying the sense of nostalgia felt by most refugees for their homeland.

Homeland was a beautiful place, full of gentle hills and peacefully grazing cattle. My dreams are still bound to the homeland. We left Homeland during the warfare. Our relatives were killed. My husband lost eleven brothers, I five. They were killed by guns, spears and arrows. My husband was put in jail for three months. All that time he was tied, and fellow detainees were killed in front of his eyes. He kept alive, fortunately. After the killing stopped he was released—and we fled. I had already taken flight from our homestead. We met on the way, in a hidden place just by coincidence. I had been living in the bush for one month, and we proceeded together to the host-country. Entering a foreign country as a refugee is to suffer extreme hardship. You feel lost after having left your country. Your belongings are completely separated from you. You live in fear of starvation. You are shocked because you have witnessed the execution of others, sometimes even of your relatives and friends. You are afraid that you have become invisible to God's merciful eye. You feel totally desolate. Arriving in the area of settlement, we got scared to death. It was in the middle of nowhere. Never in our lives had we seen such thick forest, inhabited only by wild animals, snakes and big, biting flies. We slept close to one another in a big bundle in the open air under the trees, surrounded by fires. During the daylight hours we cleared the forest. We were absolutely positive that we would starve, but prayed and prayed to get courage and food. (Christensen 1985, pp. 136–137)

Chapter Twelve
The Cambodian Genocide—1975–1979

Ben Kiernan

In the first few weeks after Cambodia fell to the Khmer Rouge in April 1975, the nation's cities were evacuated, hospitals emptied, schools closed, factories deserted, money and wages abolished, monasteries emptied, and libraries scattered. Freedom of the press, movement, worship, organization, association, and discussion, all completely disappeared for nearly four years. So did everyday family life. A whole nation was kidnapped, and then besieged from within. Meals had to be eaten in collective mess halls: parents ate breakfast in sittings, and if they were lucky their sons and daughters waited their turns outside. Democratic Kampuchea (DK, 1975–1979) was a prison camp state, and the 8 million prisoners served most of their time in solitary confinement. And 1.5 million of the inmates were worked, starved, and beaten to death.

Pol Pot and His Circle
The shadowy leaders of this closed country gave few clues to their personal lives. The first journalists into Democratic Kampuchea, from Yugoslavia in 1978, had to ask the Prime Minister, "Who are you, comrade Pol Pot?"[1] He was evasive (Pol Pot, 1978, pp. 20–21). New light on his social background suggests its importance for his political life. How little is explained by his personality, though, remains an anomaly.

The story began in a large, red-tiled, timber house on stilts overlooking a broad, brown river, downstream from the town of Kompong Thom. The river teemed with fish, its lush banks lined by coconut and mango trees. Behind the houses along the bank, stretched large rice fields. A small Chinese shop sold a few consumables.

On May 19, 1928, Pol Pot was born Saloth Sar, the youngest in a family of one girl and six boys. His parents owned nine hectares of riceland, three of garden-land, and six buffalo. Pol Pot's father Saloth, with two sons and adopted nephews, harvested enough rice for about twenty people. In later years the family would have been "class enemies." But few villagers thought so then. Rich or poor, everyone tilled the fields, fished the river, cooked tasty soups, raised children, propitiated local spirits and French colonial officials, or thronged Buddhist festivities in Kompong Thom's pagoda. In 1929, a French official described Kompong Thom people as "the most deeply Cambodian and the least susceptible to our influence."

But the Saloth family were Khmer peasants with a difference. They had royal connections. Pol Pot's cousin had grown up a palace dancer, becoming one of King Monivong's principal wives. At fifteen, his eldest sister Saroeung was chosen as a consort. In 1928, the eldest brother, Loth Suong, began a career in palace protocol. Pol Pot joined him in 1934, aged six.

The country boy Saloth Sar never worked a rice field, or knew much of village life. A year in the royal monastery was followed by six in an elite Catholic school. His upbringing was strict. The girl next door, Saksi Sbong, recalls that Suong "was very serious and would not gamble or allow children to play near his home" (Kiernan, 1985, p. 27). The palace compound was closeted and conservative, the old king a French puppet. Outside, Phnom Penh's 100,000 inhabitants were mostly Chinese shopkeepers and Vietnamese workers. Few Cambodian childhoods were so removed from their vernacular culture.

At 14, Pol Pot went off to high school in a bustling Khmer market town. But he missed World War II's tumultuous end in Phnom Penh. Youths forced his cousin, the new boy-king Norodom Sihanouk, to briefly declare independence from France, and Buddhist monks led Cambodian nationalists in common cause with Vietnamese communists. In 1948, while back in the capital learning carpentry, Pol Pot's life changed. He received a scholarship to study radio-electricity in Paris.

He wrote Suong occasionally, asking for money. But one day a letter arrived asking for the official biography of King Sihanouk. Suong sent back advice: Don't get involved in politics. But Pol Pot was already a member of the Cambodian section of the French Communist Party, then in its Stalinist heyday. Those who knew him then insist that "he would not have killed a chicken"; he was self-effacing, charming. He kept company with Khieu Ponnary, eight years his senior, the first Khmer woman to get the Baccalauréat. The couple chose Bastille Day for their wedding back home in 1956.

Most of Pol Pot's Paris student friends, like Khieu Samphan, Ieng Sary, and Son Sen, remain in his circle today. He had early disagreements with

Hou Yuon, later a popular Marxist intellectual, who was to be a first victim after the seizure of power in 1975. But Pol Pot stood out in his choice of a *nom de plume*: the "Original Cambodian" (*khmaer da'em*). Others preferred less racial, modernist code-names, like "Free Khmer" or "Khmer Worker." Pol Pot's scholarship ended after he failed his course three years in a row. His ship arrived home in January 1953 (Kiernan, 1985, pp. 30–32, 119–122).

The previous day, King Sihanouk had declared martial law to suppress Cambodia's independence movement, which was becoming radicalized by French colonial force. Pol Pot's closest brother, Saloth Chhay, joined the Cambodian and Vietnamese communists, and took him along. In this first contact, Vietnamese communists began teaching him, as one of them later put it, how to "work with the masses at the base, to build up the independence committees at the village level, member by member." It seemed a patronizing slight, like his failure to quickly rise to the leadership, despite overseas experience. A former Cambodian comrade claims that Pol Pot "said that everything should be done on the basis of self-reliance, independence and mastery. The Khmers should do everything on their own" (Kiernan, 1985, p. 123).

In the 1960s, a group of younger, mostly French-educated communists took over the leadership of the more orthodox (pro-Vietnamese) Workers' Party of Kampuchea, which had led the struggle against French colonialism in the 1950s. The new leadership changed the party's name to "Communist Party of Kampuchea" in 1966, and set out on their path to power by staging an uprising against Prince Norodom Sihanouk's neutralist government. After victory over Sihanouk's successor regime, that of Marshal Lon Nol, in 1975, they proclaimed the state of Democratic Kampuchea (DK), which lasted nearly four years before being overthrown by a Vietnamese invading army in 1979.

The ruling body in DK comprised the members of the Standing Committee of the Central Committee of the Communist Party of Kampuchea (CPK). The leaders with maximum national power and responsibility for the genocide were those based in Phnom Penh and not specifically responsible for a particular geographic area of the country. They were known as the party "center." As of 1992 all are still active as Khmer Rouge leaders, and their ambassador still occupies Cambodia's mission at the United Nations. They are: Saloth Sar (alias Pol Pot), Secretary General of the CPK since 1962, and Prime Minister of DK; Nuon Chea, Deputy Secretary General of the party since 1960, and President of the Representative Assembly of DK; Ieng Sary, who has ranked no. 3 in the party leadership since 1963 and was one of DK's Deputy Prime Ministers (responsible for foreign affairs); Son Sen, No. 11 in the party in 1963 and a Deputy Prime Minister of DK (for defense and security); Khieu Samphan, a party member since the 1950s who became DK's President; Ieng Thirith, wife of Ieng Sary and DK Minister of Social Action; and Yun Yat, wife of Son Sen and DK Minister of Culture. Khieu Ponnary, older sister of Ieng Thirith and childless wife of Pol Pot, was a provincial party official and President of the Women's Association of Democratic Kampuchea, but reportedly suffered insanity after 1975. (Pol Pot remarried in Thailand after his overthrow and now has two children.)

Two other figures were longtime members of Pol Pot's group. Though they held regional posts in 1975, they increasingly assumed responsibility for the implementation of genocidal policies throughout the country. Mok, No. 9 in the party in 1963, was Party Secretary of the key Southwest Zone and later Chief of the General Staff of the Khmer Rouge armed forces; and Ke Pauk, Party Secretary of the Central Zone of DK, later became Undersecretary General of the Khmer Rouge armed forces.

The Mechanics of Power

The late twentieth century saw the era of mass communications, but Democratic Kampuchea tolled a vicious silence. Internally and externally, Cambodia was sealed off. Its borders were closed, all neighboring countries militarily attacked, use of foreign languages banned, embassies and press agencies expelled, local newspapers and television shut down, radios and bicycles confiscated, mail and telephones suppressed. Worse, Cambodians had little to tell each other anyway. They quickly learned that any display of knowledge or skill, if "contaminated" by foreign influence (normal in modern societies), was a folly in Democratic Kampuchea. Human communications were reduced to daily instructions.

The CPK center, known as *Angkar Loeu* (the "high organization"), began its purges in the 1960s by assassinating party figures assumed to be too close to Vietnam's Communists. In the early 1970s, before taking power at the national level, the center organized the arrest and "disappearances" of nearly 900 Hanoi-trained Khmer Communists who had come home from North Vietnam to join the insurgency against Lon Nol's regime. They had accounted for half the party's membership in 1970. Then the center gradually exerted its totalitarian control over the population by replacing autonomous or dissident Zone administrations and Party Committees with center-backed forces commanded by loyalist Zone leaders Mok and Pauk. By 1978, purges had taken the lives of half of the members of the party's Central Committee, although there is no evidence that this body had ever officially met.

Democratic Kampuchea was initially divided into six major Zones, and 32 Regions, each of which in turn comprised districts, subdistricts, and villages. One aim of the CPK center was to build larger and larger units at the local level, abolishing village life altogether in favor of "high-level cooperatives" the size of a subdistrict. At the other end of the hierarchy, the center set about reducing the autonomy of the Zones by bringing them under its own direct control.

The most common pattern was for Mok's or Pauk's forces to undermine another Zone from below, first purging the district, subdistrict, and village committees, then Regional ones, before finally picking off the severely weakened Zone Party leadership. Another tactic was to carry out purges through the regional Security forces (*santesok*) in a direct chain of command from the center, bypassing the Zone leadership. Those arrested were taken to the nerve center of the system, the national Security service (*santebal*) prison in Phnom Penh, code-named Office S-21, now preserved as Tuol Sleng Museum of Genocide. Up to 20,000 people, mostly suspected CPK dissidents and regional officials, were tortured and killed there from 1976 to 1979. Chief of the *Santebal*, Kaing Khek Iev, alias Deuch, reported directly to Son Sen, who was the center official responsible for security.

The process began in the insurgent zones before victory. In 1973, with center backing, Mok emerged supreme in a factional battle for control of the Southwest Zone Party Committee, executing his senior and rival, Prasith, who had been No. 7 in the 1963 party hierarchy. The poorest region, renamed the Western Zone, was assigned to another rival, Chou Chet, who was eventually executed in 1978. After victory in 1976, Ke Pauk's forces carried out a violent purge of cadres loyal to his executed predecessor, Koy Thuon, in the Northern Zone, now enlarged and renamed the Central Zone. In 1977, Mok's Southwest Zone forces and administrators carried out a similar purge of the Northwest Zone, eventually arresting the Zone Party Secretary, Nhim Ros, No. 8 in the 1963 party hierarchy. On the other side of the country, Mok also took over two of the five Regions of the Eastern Zone. Finally, a May 1978 conventional military suppression campaign commanded by Son Sen, Pauk, and Mok overran the rest of the Eastern Zone and abolished its Party Committee. The Zone Secretary, So Phim, No. 4 in the party hierarchy since 1963, committed suicide.

The center's struggle for total control was complete. But it had sown the seeds of its own overthrow. Surviving officials of the Eastern Zone went into rebellion, and in late 1978 they crossed the border and requested the Vietnamese military assistance that brought Democratic Kampuchea to an end.

The Ideology of Genocide

Along with Stalinist and Maoist models, an underlying theme of the political worldview of the Pol Pot group was a concern for national and racial grandiosity. Their disagreements with Vietnamese communists in Paris in the early 1950s concerned the symbolic grandeur of the medieval Khmer temple of Angkor Wat, and their sensitivities over the small size of Cambodia's population. In their view, Cambodia did not need to learn or import anything from its neighbors. Rather, they would recover its pre-Buddhist glory by rebuilding the powerful economy of the medieval Angkor kingdom, and regain "lost territory" from Vietnam and Thailand. Democratic Kampuchea treasured the Cambodian "race," not individuals. National impurities included the foreign-educated (except for Pol Pot's Paris-educated group) and "hereditary enemies," especially Vietnamese. To return Cambodians to their imagined origins, the Pol Pot group saw the need for war, and for "secrecy as the basis" of the revolution (Boua et al., 1988, pp. 214, 220). Few of the grass-roots, pragmatic Cambodian communists could be trusted to implement such plans, which Pol Pot kept secret from them, just as he never admitted to being Saloth Sar. The Party Center, with its elite, urban background, French education, and a racial chauvinism little different from that of its predecessor the Lon Nol regime, inhabited a different ideological world from that of the more moderate, Buddhist-educated, Vietnamese-trained peasant cadre who made up the mass of the party's membership. The acknowledged lack of a political base for its program meant that tactics of "secrecy" and violence were considered necessary. These tactics were used first against suspected party dissidents, and then against the people of Cambodia as a whole. Given the sacrifices from the population that the nationalist revival required, the resistance it naturally provoked, and the regime's preparedness to forge ahead "at all costs," genocide was the result.

Who Were the Victims? Who Was Involved?

Genocide against a Religious Group

Pol Pot's government tried to eradicate Buddhism from Cambodia. Eyewitnesses testify to the Khmer Rouge massacres of monks and the forcible disrobing and persecution of survivors. Out of a total of 2,680 Buddhist monks from eight of Cambodia's 3,000 monasteries, only 70 monks were found to have survived in 1979 (Boua, 1991, p. 239). There is no reason to believe these eight monasteries were atypical. If the same death toll applied to the monks from all the other monasteries, fewer than 2,000 of Cambodia's 70,000 monks could be said to have survived.

A CPK center document dated September 1975 proclaims:

> Monks have disappeared from 90 to 95 per cent. . . . Monasteries . . . are largely abandoned. The foundation pillars of Buddhism . . . have disintegrated. In the future they will dissolve further. The political base, the economic base, *the cultural base must be uprooted.* (Boua, 1991, p. 235, emphasis added)

This clear evidence of genocidal intent was carried through. As Chanthou Boua (1991) points out, "Buddhism was eradicated from the face of the country in just one year" (p. 227). By early 1977, there were no functioning monasteries and no monks to be seen in Cambodia. In 1978, Yun Yat claimed that Buddhism was "incompatible with the revolution." The Cambodian people, she said, had "stopped believing" and monks had "left the temples." She added: "The problem gradually becomes extinguished. Hence there is no problem" (Jackson, 1989, p. 191).

Genocide against Ethnic Groups

The largest ethnic minority groups in Cambodia before 1970 were the Vietnamese, the Chinese, and the Muslim Cham. Unlike most other communist regimes, the Pol Pot regime's view of these and the country's twenty other national minorities, who had long made up over 15 percent of the Cambodian population, was virtually to deny their existence. The regime officially proclaimed that they totaled only 1 percent of the population. Statistically, they were written off.

Their physical fate was much worse. The Vietnamese community, for instance, was entirely eradicated. About half of the 450,000-strong community had been expelled by the U.S.-backed Lon Nol regime in 1970 (with several thousand killed in massacres). Over 100,000 more were driven out by the Pol Pot regime in the first year after its victory in 1975. The ones who remained in Cambodia were simply murdered.

In more than a year's research in Cambodia since 1979 it has not been possible to find a Vietnamese resident who had survived the Pol Pot years there. However, eyewitnesses from other ethnic groups, including Khmers who were married to Vietnamese, testify to the fates of their Vietnamese spouses and neighbours. This constituted a campaign of systematic racial extermination.

The Chinese under Pol Pot's regime suffered the worst disaster ever to befall any ethnic Chinese community in Southeast Asia. Of the 1975 population of 425,000, only 200,000 Chinese survived the next four years. Ethnic Chinese were nearly all urban, and they were seen by the Khmer Rouge as archetypal city dwellers, and therefore as prisoners of war. In this case they were not targeted for execution because of their race, but like other evacuated city dwellers they were made to work harder and under much more deplorable conditions than rural dwellers. The penalty for infraction of minor regulations was often death. This was systematic discrimination based on geographic or social origin.

The Chinese succumbed in particularly large numbers to hunger and to diseases like malaria. The 50 percent of them who perished is a higher proportion even than that estimated for Cambodia's city dwellers in general (about one-third).

Further, the Chinese language, like all foreign and minority languages, was banned, and so was any tolerance of a culturally and ethnically distinguishable Chinese community. That was to be destroyed "as such" (Kiernan, 1986).

The Muslim Chams numbered at least 250,000 in 1975.[2] Their distinct religion, language and culture, large villages, and autonomous networks threatened the atomized, closely supervised society that the Pol Pot leadership planned. An early 1974 Pol Pot document records the decision to "break up" the Cham people, adding: "Do not allow too many of them to concentrate in one area." Cham women were forced to cut their hair short in the Khmer style, not wear it long as was their custom; then the traditional Cham sarong was banned, as peasants were forced to wear only black pajamas; then restrictions were placed upon religious activity.

In 1975 the new Pol Pot government turned its attention to the Chams with a vengeance. Fierce rebellions broke out. On an island in the Mekong

River, the authorities attempted to collect all copies of the Koran. The villagers staged a protest demonstration, and Khmer Rouge troops fired into the crowd. The Chams then took up swords and knives and slaughtered half a dozen troops. The retaliating armed forces massacred many and pillaged their homes. They evacuated the island, and razed the village, and then turned to a neighboring village, massacring 70 percent of its inhabitants.

Soon the Pol Pot army forcibly emptied all 113 Cham villages in the country. About 100,000 Chams were massacred and the survivors were dispersed in small groups of several families. Islamic schools and religion, as well as the Cham language, were banned. Thousands of Muslims were physically forced to eat pork. Many were murdered for refusing. Of 113 Cham *hakkem*, or community leaders, only 20 survived in 1979. Only 25 of their 226 deputies survived. All but 38 of about 300 religious teachers at Cambodia's Koranic schools perished. Of more than one thousand who had made the pilgrimage to Mecca, only about thirty survived (Kiernan, 1988).

The toll goes on. The Thai minority of 20,000 was reportedly reduced to about 8,000. Only 800 families survived of the 1,800 families of the Lao ethnic minority. Of the 2,000 members of the Kola minority, "no trace . . . has been found" (Kiernan, 1990).

Genocide against a Part of the Majority National Group

Finally, of the majority Khmers, 15 percent of the rural population perished in 1975–1979, and 25 percent of the urban. Democratic Kampuchea initially divided its population into the "old citizens" (those who had lived in Khmer Rouge zones before the 1975 victory) and "new citizens," who had lived in the cities, last holdouts of the Lon Nol regime. All cities were evacuated in April 1975. The next year, however, the "new citizens" were rebaptized "deportees," and most failed to even qualify for the next category, "candidates," let alone "full rights citizens," a group to which only favored peasant families were admitted. But not even they were spared the mass murders of the 1977–1978 countrywide purges.

The most horrific slaughter was in the last six months of the regime, in the politically suspect Eastern Zone bordering Vietnam. I interviewed 87 survivors: in just 11 villages, the Khmer Rouge carried out 1,663 killings in 1978. In another community of 350 people, there were 95 executions in 1978; 705 executions occurred in another subdistrict, 1,950 in another, 400 in another. Tens of thousands of other villagers were deported to the northwest of the country. En route through Phnom Penh they were "marked" as easterners by being forced to wear a blue scarf, reminiscent of Hitler's yellow star for Jews (Kiernan, 1989a), and later eliminated en masse.

A total 1978 murder toll of over 100,000 (more than one-seventeenth of the eastern population) can safely be regarded as a minimum estimate (Kiernan, 1986a). The real figure is probably much higher.

Table 12.1 Approximate Death Tolls under Pol Pot, 1975–1979

Social group	1975 pop.	Nos. perished	%
1. "New Citizens"			
Urban Khmer	2,000,000	500,000	25
Rural Khmer	600,000	150,000	25
Chinese (all urban)	430,000	215,000	50
Vietnamese (urban)	10,000	10,000	100
Lao (rural)	10,000	4,000	40
Total New citizens	3,050,000[3]	879,000	29
2. "Base Citizens"			
Rural Khmer	4,500,000	675,000	15
(Khmer Krom	5,000	2,000	40)
Cham (all rural)	250,000	90,000	36
Vietnamese (rural)	10,000	10,000	100
Thai (rural)	20,000	8,000	40
Upland minorities	60,000	9,000	15
Total Base citizens	4,840,000	792,000	16
Cambodia	7,890,000[4]	1,671,000	21

The Historical Forces at Work

Rural conditions were better in prerevolutionary Cambodia than in neighboring countries like Vietnam or even Thailand. Land was more equitably distributed, and most peasant families owned some land. However, rural debt was common, and the number of landless tenants or sharecroppers increased from 4 percent of the farming population in 1950 to 20 percent in 1970 (Kiernan and Boua, 1982, p. 4). Thus, alongside a landowning middle peasant class, a new class of rootless, destitute rural dwellers emerged. Their position was desperate enough for them to see nothing to lose in any kind of social revolution.

The gap between town and countryside has been cited as a precondition for the Khmer Rouge's march to power. Unlike the countryside, the cities were not predominantly Khmer, but included large populations of ethnic Chinese and Vietnamese. Nor was the urban manufacturing sector very significant, producing few consumer goods for the countryside. Many peasants saw cities as seats of arbitrary, even foreign, political and economic power. But none of this explains why the Pol Pot regime turned against the peasantry in such large numbers.

Another factor was the rapid expansion of education in Cambodia in the 1960s, after long neglect of education under French colonial rule. A generation gap separated peasant parents from educated youth, who were often unable to find work after graduating from high school, and drifted into political dissidence. The Khmer Rouge in the 1960s recruited disproportionately among schoolteachers and students.

Other important factors included the increasing repression by the Sihanouk regime, which drove the grass-roots left into dissidence, enabling the French-educated Khmers of elite background, led by Pol Pot, to harness these home-grown veterans of the independence struggle to its plans for rebellion in 1967–1968; and conflict between the Vietnamese and Chinese communists over Cambodia, which gave Pol Pot's faction Chinese support and valuable maneuverability against the orthodox pro-Vietnamese Khmer communists (Kiernan, 1985). And although it was an indigenous political phenomenon, Pol Pot's regime would not have come to power without the massive economic and military destabilization of Cambodia by the United States, beginning in 1966.

On 18 March 1969, the U.S. Air Force began a secret B-52 bombardment of Vietnamese sanctuaries in rural Cambodia (Shawcross, 1979, pp. 21–23, 31). Exactly one year later, Prince Norodom Sihanouk was overthrown by the U.S.-backed general Lon Nol. The Vietnam War spilled across, Sihanouk swore revenge, and a new civil war tore Cambodia apart.

The U.S. bombing of the countryside increased from 1970 until August 15, 1973, when Congress imposed a halt. Up to 150,000 Cambodians were killed in the American bombardments. Nearly half of the 540,000 tons of bombs fell in the last six months. Hundreds of thousands of peasants fled into the cities, to escape first the bombing and then the imposition of Khmer Rouge power. In the ashes of rural Cambodia arose the CPK regime, led by Pol Pot.

Pol Pot's forces had profited greatly from the U.S. bombardment. Contemporary U.S. government documents and peasant survivors reveal that the Khmer Rouge used the bombing's devastation and massacre of civilians as recruitment propaganda, and as an excuse for their brutal, radical policies and their purge of moderate and pro-Vietnamese Khmer communists and Sihanoukists (Kiernan, 1985, 1989). By 1975 they had national power.

The Long-Range Impact on the Victim Groups

The population of Cambodia totalled around 6.5 million in 1979. The survivors thus emerged from the Pol Pot period nearly 3.5 million fewer than the 1980 population that had been projected in 1970 (Migozzi, 1973, p. 269). Not all of the difference is attributable to the Pol Pot regime; much is the result of the American war and aerial bombardment of the populated areas of Cambodia from 1969–1973, and of projected population growth that was unrealized due to instability, population displacement, and harsh living conditions throughout the 1970s. But 1.5 million deaths are attributable to the Khmer Rouge regime (Table 12.1, and Kiernan, 1990a).

After the Vietnamese overthrow of the Khmer Rouge, between 1979 and 1989 the Cambodian population increased at one of the world's fastest growth rates (Curtis, 1989, pp. 6–7), to 8.4 million, plus another half million living abroad.

The Cham Muslim population also rejuvenated itself. Fewer than 165,000 Chams may have remained inside Cambodia in 1979, but 182,256 were officially counted there in December 1982, and refugee survivors abroad brought the total population of Cambodian Chams to 195,000. Chams living in Cambodia in 1991 numbered over 200,000.

By December 1989, about 8,000 new and former Buddhist monks had been ordained in Cambodia, and they lived in about 3,000 restored *wats* [Buddhist temples] (Curtis, 1989, p. 8).

The major long-term demographic result is the preponderance of women in modern Cambodia. Women, including large numbers of widows, make up 60 to 80 percent of the adult population in various parts of the country, as well as among Cambodians abroad (Boua, 1982).

Despite significant demographic recovery, the Cambodian population remains severely affected by psychological trauma. Posttraumatic stress syndrome is a general problem, including illnesses such as psychosomatic blindness, which has been diagnosed among survivors living in the United States.

International Responses to the Genocide

In 1979, the Vietnamese army invaded Cambodia, overthrowing the Khmer Rouge regime. A new, much less repressive regime was established, with Hun Sen as Foreign Minister (later Prime Minister). Much of the country was rebuilt. Vietnamese troops withdrew in 1989, after training a new Cambodian army which then succeeded in defending the country on its own. But from 1979, most of the international community embargoed the new government and continued to recognize the "legitimacy" of the Pol Pot regime, voting for it to occupy Cambodia's U.N. seat for another twelve years. Until 1989, the Khmer Rouge flag flew over New York. As of 1992, Pol Pot's ambassador still runs Cambodia's U.N. mission there. Not a single Western country has ever voted against the right of the Khmer Rouge government-in-exile to represent its former victims in international forums.

Independent commentators often followed suit. An interesting example is British journalist William Shawcross, author of *Sideshow*, a good study of the pre-1975 U.S. intervention and wartime destruction of Cambodia. In 1979, Shawcross chose to hang the label of "genocide" on the Khmer Rouge's *opponents*. He alleged that Hanoi's invasion to topple Pol Pot meant "subtle genocide" (Shawcross, 1980) by enforced starvation, and warned of "two million dead by Christmas" (Shawcross, 1979). Fortunately, he was very wrong. In 1984, in his second book on Cambodia, *The Quality of Mercy*, Shawcross conceded that "there is no evidence that large numbers of people did . . . starve to death" at the hands of the Vietnamese or their Cambodian allies, and that "For the overwhelming majority of the Cambodian people the invasion meant freedom" (Shawcross, 1984, pp. 370, 78).

But he remains preoccupied with opponents of the Khmer Rouge. Shawcross brands them alternately as supporters of "Vietnam's cause," and as "apologists" for the Khmer Rouge—though his own preferred Cambodian leader, Norodom Sihanouk, was a Khmer Rouge ally for twenty years until 1991 (Shawcross, March 31, 1991). For instance, Shawcross asserts that on the last day of the Pol Pot regime in January 1979, Sihanouk "roundly denounced the brutality of the Khmer Rouge" (Shawcross, 1984, p. 74). In fact, Sihanouk had stated that "the people seem to be quite happy with Pol Pot," "very gay," with "more than enough to eat," and that "the conditions were good . . . so my conscience is in tranquillity."[5] Those whom Shawcross brands "leftwing skeptics" and "apologists" for the Khmer Rouge were far more critical of the Pol Pot regime.[6]

I should disclose here that Shawcross has levelled such accusations against me, for instance, calling me "unreliable." This followed his unacknowledged reproduction in the *New York Review of Books* (10 May 1984) of work by Chanthou Boua and myself, namely our translation of a document from the Pol Pot regime's Tuol Sleng prison. In the same breath, Shawcross wrote that he could "recall no one" making the analogy with a Stalinist prison, though in the very article he was using without attribution, we had indeed compared the Tuol Sleng records to "the archives of Stalinism" (Boua et al., 1980, p. 670). His memory lapse recurred in *The Quality of Mercy* (Shawcross, 1984, p. 422).

As interpreter for Shawcross in Cambodia in 1980, I had tape-recorded our conversation with an elderly Cambodian peasant woman. Shawcross badly misreported her testimony. In his *New York Review* article, and twice in *The Quality of Mercy*, he used the example of the Khmer Rouge killer of the woman's son to suggest that such people had been promoted into "positions of new authority" by the Vietnamese-backed, anti–Pol Pot, Cambodian government (Shawcross, 1984, pp. 38–39, 358–359). But the woman had clearly said the opposite, that the killer had "run away." Presented with the facts, Shawcross declined to admit this error (Shawcross, September 27, 1984).

His usual target, however, is the Australian-born journalist and filmmaker John Pilger, who for over a decade has been instrumental in drawing world attention to the crimes of the Khmer Rouge and the threat of their return. In 1991, Pilger received the coveted Richard Dimbleby Award for a lifetime of journalism, including five major documentary films about Cambodia since 1979, the last of which also won an Emmy Award. Each film had been criticized by Shawcross. On the day of Pilger's Dimbleby Award presentation, Shawcross denounced him for "anti-Americanism." (However, he did concede "the fact that since the Vietnamese invasion of 1979 the Khmer Rouge has been rebuilt, principally by China but with *Western complicity.* . . . There is now a real threat that the Khmer Rouge might come back to power" [Shawcross, March 17, 1991].[7])

Eschewing anti-Americanism, Shawcross sees international communism as solely responsible for the plight of Cambodia—regardless of anyone's actual conduct. Having realized that Hanoi could not plausibly be accused of starving Cambodians to death in a genocidal campaign, he changed tack. Exonerating the Western powers, whose diplomatic and material aid he acknowledges helped revive the Khmer Rouge, Shawcross now held Hanoi responsible: "Vietnam's conduct since its invasion of Cambodia rarely suggested that it wished to see a compromise in which the Khmer Rouge were removed as a viable force in Cambodia—which was what the ASEAN countries and their Western partners insisted was their aim" (Shawcross, 1984, pp. 356–357).

In fact, ASEAN and the West confounded Shawcross's apologetics. They insisted all along, even after Vietnam's 1989 troop withdrawal, that Pol Pot's Khmer Rouge *not* be "removed as a viable force." That is why Khmer Rouge leaders are back in Phnom Penh as I write. Shawcross's judgments of both sides in the Cambodian conflict could hardly have been more unreliable. He now takes aim at those who *do* favor ending the Khmer Rouge threat, for allegedly supporting "Vietnam's cause in Cambodia" (Shawcross, March 31, 1991).

His defense of the ASEAN states, particularly the military regimes in Thailand, ill befits a critic of apologists for the Khmer Rouge. In 1985, the Thai Foreign Minister called the Pol Pot regime's deputy prime minister, Son Sen, "a very good man." In 1991, the new military strongman in Bangkok described Pol Pot as "a nice guy," who should be treated "fairly." And Thailand's Prime Minister reassured the Pol Pot regime's President Khieu Samphan in May 1991: "Sixteen years ago, I was also accused of being a Communist and now they have picked me as Prime Minister. In any society there are always hard-liners and soft-liners, and society changes its attitude to them as time passes by."[8] None of this frank rehabilitation of genocidists provokes protest from Shawcross, in contrast to the decibel level of his twelve-year obsession with John Pilger.

The Quality of Mercy was Shawcross's critique of the aid program that helped save Cambodia from the threat of famine in 1979–1980. The book's conclusion is extraordinary: Even though the aid program "helped millions of ordinary Cambodians . . . overall its results were not a cause for great rejoicing" (Shawcross, 1984, p. 415). Perhaps hoping for Sihanouk's return to power, Shawcross apparently considered that the aid program's aims had less to do with "ordinary Cambodians."

Sharing this view, the British government (like the United States) regularly voted for the Khmer Rouge and its allies in the United Nations, and supported an international embargo on Cambodia until 1992. In 1990, the UK Charity Commission began an investigation of Oxfam, a leading force in the successful 1979–1980 aid program and a lifeline to Cambodia ever since. In May 1991, the Charity Commission criticized Oxfam for having "prosecuted with too much vigour" its public education campaign on the nature of the Pol Pot regime and the threat of its return (Cohen, May 10, 1991; and Pilger, May 17, 1991, p. 8).[9] It is unlikely many "ordinary Cambodians" would agree. But the Charity Commission obliged Oxfam to cease distributing a book, *Punishing the Poor: The International Isolation of*

Kampuchea (Mysliwiec, 1988). Its author, Eva Mysliwiec, is a U.S. relief worker who has lived in Phnom Penh since 1980, after eight years' development experience in rural Africa. Shawcross (1984), Oxfam's critic, has praised Mysliwiec as "dedicated," living frugally for three years on no pay at all: "Oxfam was fortunate to acquire Mysliwiec's services. She was the most experienced foreign aid worker in Phnom Penh. . . . She understood the regime, knew its various personalities well, and worked with them with great good humor" (pp. 394–395). Thanks to the UK Charity Commission, Mysliwiec's excellent book on Cambodia became unavailable.[10]

Varying Interpretations

Interpretations of the nature of the Pol Pot regime have varied widely and controversially, even among Marxists and neo-Marxists. Its enemy and successor regime, for instance, quickly claimed that Pol Potism had been a case of Maoism exported to Cambodia by China's leaders in the 1970s.[11] Indeed, a 1985 official Chinese publication described the Khmer Rouge rule as "the period of economic reconstruction" (Guangxi People's Publishing House, 1985).[12] And the pro-Chinese, neo-Marxist Samir Amin (1977) had initially welcomed Democratic Kampuchea, as "a correct assessment of the hierarchy of contradictions" in Cambodia, and as a model for African socialists to follow because of its "rapid disurbanization" and its economic autarchy (pp. 150, 147). Amin dismissed the claim that it was "an insignificant peasant rising." But in a 1981 reflection, Amin preferred to identify a Cambodian *combination* of Stalinist orthodoxy with what he now called "a principally peasant revolution": "The excesses, which today cannot be denied, are those which we know from the entire long history of peasant revolts. They are of the same nature and represent the same character."[13]

In 1984 the historian Michael Vickery took up this very theme as a reason to *reject* Democratic Kampuchea, because, he argued, "nationalism, populism and peasantism really won out over communism." In Vickery's (1984) view, Democratic Kampuchea was no Stalinist communist regime, but "a victorious peasant revolution, perhaps the first real one in modern times" (pp. 289–290, 66).

Samir Amin's contribution is his analysis of Cambodian society as a relatively undifferentiated peasant society, similar to others in South Asia and Africa, and quite unlike China and Vietnam with their powerful landlord classes. His sympathy with the Khmer Rouge was based on their innovativeness in adapting a communist strategy to these particular conditions. However, he later conceded, "this success itself has been the origin of the tragic difficulties," including "the well known excesses and shortcomings."[14]

But Michael Vickery (1984), in explaining the outcome of the Cambodian revolution, denies the very existence of the Stalinist vanguard attractive to Amin. He sees the Pol Pot leadership as not significantly influenced by foreign communist models, but "pulled along" by "the peasant element" (Vickery, 1984, p. 287). Vickery's approach combines an influential postwar intellectual trend in Southeast Asian historiography with a 1970s revisionist trend evident in the historiography of Hitler's Germany. I will examine each in turn.

In his pathbreaking 1955 work *Indonesian Trade and Society,* J. C. Van Leur remarked that European historians of premodern Southeast Asia tended to see the region as outsiders, "from the deck of the ship, the ramparts of the fortress, the high gallery of the trading house." Yet, Van Leur (1955) argued, at least until the nineteenth century the European impact on Southeast Asia had been minimal and superficial: "The sheen of the world religions and foreign cultural forms is a thin and flaking glaze; underneath it the whole of the old indigenous forms has continued to exist" (Van Leur, 1955, p. 95).

Vickery (forthcoming) applies this analysis to Hinduism in early Cambodian history, stressing the "Indic facade" on the indigenous culture of the pre-Angkor period. He also applies it to communism in modern times. In *Cambodia 1975–1982,* he writes that "foreign relations and influences are very nearly irrelevant to an understanding of the internal situation" (Vickery, 1984, p. xii). He later explains: "We need investigations into autonomous development rather than superficial diffusionism, a change in emphasis which has become common in most of the social sciences and has led to important advances in the last 30 years." Thus, in Vickery's (1988) view, "*the only way* to account for the apparent similarities between DK and the programme of Sendero Luminoso" (the Peruvian Maoist guerrilla movement) is as cases of "convergent social and political evolution out of similar backgrounds" (p. 17).[15] So the Cambodian and Peruvian parties' common adherence to and study of Marxism-Leninism–Mao Zedong Thought is seen as meaningless, if not a dangerously misleading "facade."

But in my view, DK ideology was not purely indigenous. It was an amalgam of various intellectual influences, including Khmer elite chauvinism, Third World nationalism, the French Revolution, Stalinism, and some aspects of Mao Zedong's "Great Leap Forward"—which DK claimed to outdo with its own "Super Great Leap Forward." The motor of the Pol Pot program was probably Khmer racist chauvinism, but it was fueled by strategies and tactics adopted from unacknowledged revolutionary models in other countries. Such syncretism is historically very common in Southeast Asia,[16] and it suggests that in an important sense the Khmer Rouge revolution was *sui generis*. The future path of the Sendero Luminoso guerrilla movement in Peru may indeed shine light on this question.

Vickery combines his argument for the primacy of the indigenous with a separate one. This is that the peasantry as a mass dominated the Cambodian revolution and took it in a direction the Pol Pot leadership could not have "either planned or expected." "It is certainly safe to assume that they did not foresee, let alone plan, the unsavoury developments of 1975–1979. They were petty bourgeois radicals overcome by peasant romanticism. . . ." (Vickery, November 1988; and Vickery, 1984). Now this argument is not unlike Hans Mommsen's analysis of Nazi Germany. Mommsen believes, for instance, that Hitler did not plan the extermination of the Jews early in his career, but that Nazi policy was formed on an *ad hoc* basis over time and under the pressure of developing circumstances. It was a case of "cumulative radicalisation." Mommsen's argument is that Hitler was no freak aberration, and that German history and society more broadly are also implicated in the genocide of the Jews.[17] Similarly, Vickery considers DK an illustration of what happens when a peasantry assumes power: "It now appears fortunate that those who predicted a predominance of agrarian nationalism over Marxism in China and Vietnam were mistaken" (Vickery, 1984, p. 290).

The Pol Pot regime, then, was made up of "middle-class intellectuals with such a romantic, idealized sympathy for the poor that they did not imagine rapid, radical restructuring of society in their favour would lead to such intolerable violence" (Vickery, November 1988, p. 14). But, Vickery (November 1988) claims, these Khmer Rouge leaders simply discovered that "it would have been impossible to hold the support of their peasant army," unless political enemies were "punished" and a departure was made from the 1917 Bolshevik model of maintaining a "normal administration" and urban "privilege" (pp. 5, 20). And when the urban populations were deported to the countryside, "the majority base peasants" of Cambodia allegedly participated "with some glee" in the persecution of those Vickery calls "their class enemies" (Vickery, 1989, p. 47). "The violence of DK was first of all because it was such a complete peasant revolution, with the victorious revolutionaries doing what peasant rebels have always wanted to do to their urban enemies" (Vickery, November 1988, p. 17). It "did not spring forth from the brains of Pol Pot or Khieu Samphan" (Vickery, 1984, p. 286).

A major problem with this analysis is lack of evidence. Vickery's (1984) *Cambodia 1975–1982* contributes much to our knowledge of the Khmer Rouge, but he did not consult peasant sources seriously. Among the ninety or more interviewees Vickery (1984) presents in his survey of Democratic Kampuchea,[18] only one is a peasant. This single interviewee hardly supports the notion of a peasant revolution, reporting "that they were fed well, but overworked and subject to 'fierce' discipline" (Vickery, 1984, p. 112). One family which Vickery describes as "half peasant–half urban," although "most of them by 1975 had long since ceased doing field work," all survived DK, but they "said that their many cousins, aunts, uncles, etc., . . . had perished, mainly of hunger and illness, although they were peasants. . . . In the opinion of the survivors, DK mismanagement had simply been so serious that not even peasants could survive" (Vickery, 1984, p. 106).

Nearly all Vickery's oral testimony in fact comes from male urban evacuees he met in refugee camps in Thailand in 1980.[19] His account of DK's Southwest Zone, which he correctly calls "the 'Pol Pot' zone *par excellence*," is based on the testimony of four former students, a former French teacher, a former Lon Nol soldier and a medic, an agricultural engineer, "a girl from the 'new' people," and "an attractive, well-educated woman of the former urban bourgeoisie" (Vickery, 1984, pp. 91, 97, 98). These ten accounts offer unconvincing documentation of a key zone in a "peasant revolution." The few inside accounts in the book include corroboration of an initial order to "kill urban evacuees indiscriminately." This order went out to both the Southwest and the Northwest Zones (Vickery, 1984, p. 98, 112). It clearly emanated from the central government—indeed from the very "brains of Pol Pot and Khieu Samphan."

This is probably the major controversy in the historiography of the Cambodian revolution: the question of central control. Anthony Barnett has argued that DK was "a highly centralized dictatorship." He also stresses its Stalinism, and its creation of "a nation of indentured labourers" (Chandler and Kiernan, 1983, pp. 211–229, esp. 213). But Serge Thion contends that it was "a bloody mess," "riddled" with factional and regional divergence, so that "the state never stood on its feet" (Chandler and Kiernan, 1983, pp. 10–33, esp. 28). "Stalin, at least, was a realist. Pol Pot . . . was and is an unimaginative idealist, a forest monk, lost in dreams" (Thion, February 1993, p. 5). David P. Chandler (1991) also follows Vickery, asserting: "Under the regime of Democratic Kampuchea (DK) a million Cambodians, or one in eight, died from warfare, starvation, overwork, misdiagnosed diseases, and executions. *Most of these deaths, however, were never intended by DK.* Instead, one Cambodian in eight fell victim to the government's utopian program of total and rapid social transformation . . ." (p. 1, emphasis added).

Barnett is closest to the truth. Despite its millenarian tone, Pol Potism was not a centrifugal or a peasant ideology but a centralizing one (Kiernan, 1983, pp. 136–211). Understating the death toll of 1.5 million, Chandler (1991) also fails to adduce evidence that the regime "never" intended "most" of the deaths, and skims the issue of how many *were* intentional. He does suggest (without citing a source) that in 1978, "perhaps a hundred thousand Eastern Zone people were killed," but is vague in attributing responsibility, and explains it as an evacuation which "degenerated into a massacre" (Chandler, 1991, p. 271), suggesting it was unintended despite the deliberate marking of victims in Phnom Penh itself (Kiernan, 1989a, 1991). The regime was able to plan such mass murders precisely because of its concentrated power. Barnett has remarked that the Khmer Rouge leadership not only succeeded in conscripting a massive labor force to turn Cambodia's landscape into a checkerboard of irrigation works: "They even communalised people's breakfasts !"[20] The regime's intent is clear, and was successful.

Chandler (1991) also overlooks the other major controversy, the case for genocide. He briefly notes the abolition of religion (Chandler, 1991, pp. 263–265), but not the ban on minority languages and cultures nor the enforced dispersal of communities, and he offers no estimates of any death toll among either monks or minorities. He concedes that "the party seems to have . . . discriminated against the Chams," whom he calls "a Muslim minority unsympathetic to the revolution"—a false imputation until the genocide began in 1975. He avers that DK, as he puts it, treated the Chinese "poorly," but that China may have helped protect them. And he notes that "a central committee directive ordered the execution of ethnic Vietnamese residents in Cambodia." Yet Chandler concludes: "By and large, the regime *discriminated against* enemies of the revolution rather than against specific ethnic or religious groups" (Chandler, 1991, pp. 285, emphasis added; p. 375 n. 36). He reveals no basis beyond DK's own for regarding these victims as "enemies of the revolution."[21]

Current Status of the Cambodian Genocide Issue

In more than a decade since Pol Pot's overthrow, many reputable legal organizations dismissed proposals to send delegations to Cambodia to investigate the crimes of the DK regime. The International Commission of Jurists, the American Bar Association, and LawAsia all refused such opportunities to report on what the U.N.'s own Special Rapporteur on genocide, Benjamin Whitaker, described in 1985 as genocide, "even under the most restricted definition."[22]

A few voluntary organizations around the world have pressed on, unaided by the major league human rights lobby. These include the U.S. Cambodia Genocide Project, which in 1980 proposed a World Court case; the Australian section of the International Commission of Jurists, which in January 1990 called for "international trials" of the Pol Pot leadership for genocide; the Minnesota Lawyers International Human Rights Committee, which in June 1990 organized a one-day mock trial of the Khmer Rouge following the procedures of the World Court, with testimony by a dozen victims of the genocide; the Washington-based lobby group, Campaign to Oppose the Return of the Khmer Rouge,[23] which has the support of 45 U.S. organizations, a former Cambodian Prime Minister, and survivors of the Khmer Rouge period; and the Oxfam-initiated NGO Forum, an international body of private voluntary agencies working in Cambodia.

Nevertheless, recent years have witnessed a progressive elimination of international diplomatic criticism of the 1975–1979 Cambodian genocide. At the first Jakarta Informal Meeting on 28 July 1988, the Indonesian chairman's final communique had noted a Southeast Asian consensus on preventing a return to "the genocidal policies and practices of the Pol Pot regime" (Vatikiotis, August 11, 1988, p. 29). But the 3 November 1989 United Nations General Assembly resolution watered this down to "the universally condemned policies and practices of the recent past." A February 1990 Australian proposal referred only to "the human rights abuses of a recent past." And the five Permanent members of the U.N. Security Council (the United States, the United Kingdom, France, the U.S.S.R. and China) emasculated this in August 1990, vaguely nodding at "the policies and practices of the past" in the Peace Plan they drew up and imposed on Cambodia in late 1991.

In June 1991, the two co-chairs of the Paris International Conference on Cambodia, Indonesia and France, accepted the Phnom Penh government's proposal that the final agreement stipulate that the new Cambodian consitution should be "consistent with the provisions of . . . the UN Convention on the Prevention and Punishment of Crimes of Genocide" (*Indochina Digest,* June 7, 1991). But the great powers rejected it, and reference to the Genocide Convention disappeared from the agreement.

However, in Western countries public pressure on governments mounted. One result was the British government's disclosure on 27 June 1991 that despite repeated denials, its elite SAS military teams had indeed trained forces allied to the Khmer Rouge, from 1983 to at least 1989.[24] The U.N. Sub-commission on Human Rights, which the previous year had quietly dropped from its agenda a draft resolution condemning the Pol Pot genocide, now changed its mind and passed a resolution noting "the duty of the international community to prevent the recurrence of genocide in Cambodia" and "to take all necessary preventive measures to avoid conditions that could create for the Cambodian people the risk of new crimes against humanity."[25] As an initiator of the resolution put it, this was the first time that the genocide was acknowledged "in an official international arena" (Jennar, September 13, 1991, p. 35). *The New York Times* then called on Washington to publish its "list of Khmer Rouge war criminals and insist on their exclusion from Cambodian political life," and for their trial before "an international tribunal for crimes against humanity" (*New York Times,* August 28, 1991). In an attempt to draw some of the fire, Pol Pot, Ieng Sary, and Mok announced that they would not stand for election, but insisted on their right to campaign for the Khmer Rouge candidates (*Indochina Digest,* August 30, 1991). It was clear that they would continue to lead the organization from the shadows.

Washington eventually decided to address the issue, but to leave the task to others. In September 1991, unnamed diplomats revealed that "Western nations want the former head of the notorious Khmer Rouge to leave his nation, quickly and quietly," and that the United States had approached China for help in ensuring this "or at a minimum, making sure he remains in a remote part of Cambodia." However, Khieu Samphan retorted that Pol Pot had no plans to leave Cambodia, and this appears to be the case (Leopold, September 22, 1991). United States pressure on China or the Khmer Rouge remained verbal; Washington's material policy involved pressure on Hanoi, "to see that Vietnam holds Hun Sen's feet to the fire."[26]

In October, U.S. Assistant Secretary of State Richard Solomon said Washington "would be absolutely delighted to see Pol Pot and the others brought to justice for the unspeakable violence of the 1970s." However, he then incorrectly blamed Prime Minister Hun Sen for the Agreement's failure to include provision for a trial. "Mr. Hun Sen had promoted the idea over the summer months of a tribunal to deal with this issue. For reasons that he would have to explain he dropped that idea at the end of the negotiations" (*Indochina Digest*, November 1, 1991). The facts show, however, that the U.S. had never supported the idea of a trial from the time it was first broached in June 1986 by the then Australian Foreign Minister Bill Hayden, and that, as we have seen, the United States and China themselves forced Hun Sen to drop the demand (Kiernan, 1991a).

In Paris on October 23, 1991, the day the final Agreement was signed, Secretary of State James Baker stated: "Cambodia and the U.S. are both signatories to the Genocide Convention and we will support efforts to bring to justice those responsible for the mass murders of the 1970s if the new Cambodian government chooses to pursue this path" (Shenon, *New York Times*, October 24, 1991, p. A16). Australia's Foreign Minister Gareth Evans, who had also previously balked at legal action against the Khmer Rouge, now said: "We would give strong support to an incoming Cambodian government to set in train such a war crimes process" (Murdoch, October 24, 1991, p. 1). If the non-Communist allies of the Khmer Rouge win the election, they may decline to establish a tribunal. The charge of genocide remains hostage to political convenience.

Eyewitness Accounts
The Cambodian Genocide—1975–1979

Oral accounts of the Cambodian experience under the Khmer Rouge regime were difficult to collect after 1975, when that regime established itself and immediately closed the country to outside visitors (except for occasional short guided tours by foreign diplomats). Along with the broadcasts of the official Democratic Kampuchea radio station, the accounts of refugees who managed to flee to Thailand, Laos, or Vietnam were nevertheless the major source of information reaching the outside world. In 1979, after the Vietnamese destruction of the Khmer Rouge regime, Cambodia was opened to journalists and researchers, and many more refugees also found their way to foreign countries. Thousands of refugees and others who remained in Cambodia have now told their stories of the 1975–1979 years, and some literate Cambodians have published books on their experience.

But relatively few have been published in English, and even fewer narrate the experiences of the Khmer peasant majority, of ethnic minorities, of women, or of children. The accounts that follow have been chosen to fill that gap.

These testimonies were collected by Ben Kiernan and Chanthou Boua in 1979 and 1980, in the immediate aftermath of the overthrow of the Khmer Rouge. Kiernan, then a graduate student in Southeast Asian History at Monash University, Melbourne, Australia, was conducting his dissertation field research on twentieth-century Cambodia. One of the interviews took place in a refugee camp in Thailand, two in a Buddhist monastery inside Thailand, one in a French provincial town, and one in a Cambodian village. The interviews were conducted in Khmer without an interpreter and in the absence of any person exercising authority over the interviewees. The conversations were tape-recorded and translated as accurately as possible by Kiernan and Boua. The details recounted are reasonably typical of hundreds of other interviews recorded by Kiernan in 1979–1980, and do not conflict with anything known from other sources about Cambodia in the 1970s, though the mass of material is for logistical reasons difficult to corroborate on all specific points.

Account 1: "The Chams Are Hopeless," by Nao Gha

Nao Gha, a minority Cham Muslim woman, was interviewed by Ben Kiernan in her village in Takeo province on August 26, 1980. The translation from the Khmer is by Ben Kiernan.

> I am 45 years old. I was born in Smong village, Smong subdistrict, Treang district, Takeo province. I first met the Khmer Rouge in 1972–73, when they came here. In 1973, they called all of us Chams to the mountains. We went to Kampot province, to Ang Krieu in Angkor Chey district. We spent a year there. They still treated us well, let us work and fend for ourselves. They spoke well to us. They called us "deported base people" [*neak moultanh phniaer*]. They did not persecute us. Our leaders were chosen from among us Chams. In 1974 they sent us back home. Everyone came back from Angkor Chey, over 100 families, but religion was no longer allowed.
>
> In 1975, after liberation, the persecution began. Some Chams came from Phnom Penh to live in a nearby Cham village. We had to work on irrigation non-stop, day and night. Killings of Khmers began in 1975.

In 1976–1977 they killed someone every one or two months, for small infringements.

Then in 1976 they dispersed the Chams. The ten villages of Chams in this area were all dispersed, for instance to Samrong, Chi Khma, and Kompong Yaul subdistricts. We were not allowed to live together. Our village was also dispersed. They burnt our village down. Four to eight families were sent out to each of eight villages. I went with five families to Kantuot village, in Tralach subdistrict. There I had to grow dry season rice, far away, and would return to the village only after seven months.

Our Cham leaders were dismissed in 1976, and replaced by Khmers. We were not allowed to speak Cham. Only the Khmer language was allowed. From 1977, they said: "There are no Vietnamese, Chinese, Javanese [Chams and Malays]—only the Khmer race. Everyone is the same."

No Cham women joined Pol Pot's revolution. A few men had but the Pol Pot regime did not trust us. They did not let us do anything; they did not let us into their kitchens. When we went to eat [in the communal mess halls established in 1976] we could only go to the tables, we weren't allowed to go into their kitchens or anything. They were afraid we would poison the food or something. They hated us. They brought up the issue of the Chams being "hopeless." Soeun, the district chief of Treang [and son-in-law of the Southwest Zone commander Mok], said this several times in meetings of people from the entire district, beginning in 1977 and also in 1978. He also said at every meeting that the Chams had "abandoned their country to others. They just shouldered their fishing nets and walked off, letting the Vietnamese take over their country." [Soeun was referring to the seventeenth-century Vietnamese takeover of the kingdom of Champa, after which many of the Chams fled central Vietnam and settled in Cambodia. On this, Nao Gha volunteered the following comment:] I don't know anything about that. It happened long ago. I don't know which generation it was when the Vietnamese invaded and they shouldered their fishing nets and ran off to live in another country. I don't know, I don't know which generation that was.

All the Chams were called "deportees," even the base people. [In Democratic Kampuchea those who had lived in the Khmer Rouge areas before the 1975 victory were called base people, or "people of the bases." They were distinguished from the urban evacuees, or "deportees."]

The Cham base people were denied this status; after being dispersed, they too were called "deportees."] The Khmers were called "full rights" and "candidate" people. We were called "minority" and were all classified as "deportees." Deportees were the most numerous, followed by candidates. The full rights people were relatives of cadres. The deportees, the candidates, and the full rights people all ate together, but lived separately and held separate meetings. They met in one place and studied politics; and the other two categories had meetings elsewhere.

1977 and 1978 were years of hard work and the greatest persecution. 1978 was the year of hardest work, night and day. We planted from 4 A.M. to 10 A.M., then ate a meal. At 1 P.M. we started again, and worked until 5 P.M., and then from 7 to 10 P.M. There was some education, for young children to learn the alphabet. It was about one hour per day, from 12 to 1 P.M.

There was not enough food, and foraging was not allowed. Rations consisted of yams and *trokuon* [a leafy Cambodian water vine]. Twice a month in 1978 we were forced [against their religious beliefs] to eat pork on pain of execution. People vomited it up. My three brothers died of starvation in 1976, 1977, and 1978. My other relatives are still alive. Of the five families with whom I went to Kantuot village, one person died of illness. In four other villages, one or two others were killed for refusing to eat pork. They were accused of being holy men [*sangkriech*] in the old society. There was starvation in Samrong subdistrict, mostly in 1977, and one or two killings. In 1978 they killed four entire families of Chinese in my village. I don't know why. Also in 1978, they killed our former Cham leaders who had joined the Khmer Rouge but had been dismissed in 1976.

Account 2: "They Did Nothing at All for the Peasants," by Thoun Cheng

Thoun Cheng, a Cambodian refugee who fled the Pol Pot regime in June 1977, was interviewed in the Khmer language by Chanthou Boua and Ben Kiernan at the Lao refugee camp at Ubon Ratchathani, northeast Thailand, on 13 and 14 March 1979. His story has been arranged in sequence by Boua and Kiernan, with occasional editorial comments in square brackets.

I was born in 1957 in the village of Banteay Chey, in Chamcar Loeu district, Kompong Cham province, Cambodia. My father was a car-

penter, but with the help of just his family, he also worked his six hectares [12.5 acres] of *chamcar* (garden farmland) growing pineapples and
bananas. My mother died when I was small; I had three older brothers.

During the 1960s, Banteay Chey was populated by about 3,200
ethnic Khmers, who mostly worked *chamcar*, and about 400 Chams,
who grew rice. There were four Buddhist *wats* and one Muslim mosque.
Land was unevenly distributed: an elderly landlord owned 30 hectares
[75 acres] in the village and an unusually large holding of 770 hectares
[1,900 acres] in other parts of the district, including one large pine-
apple plantation. Poor farmers usually owned from one to three hectares [2.5 to 7.5 acres].

I studied in primary school in the village; my education was interrupted by a three-year stay with relatives in the town of Kompong Cham,
and six months in Phnom Penh.

The overthrow of Prince Norodom Sihanouk in 1970 was greeted
with some disappointment by the villagers of Banteay Chey. I remember some of them travelling to Kompong Cham to take part in protest
demonstrations. Soon after, fighting took place in the area between
troops of the new Lon Nol Government and revolutionary Khmer Rouge
claiming loyalty to the Prince. The Lon Nol troops retreated and were
not seen in the area again.

As Banteay Chey itself was free of fighting, my relatives from
Kompong Cham, a bus driver and his family, came to live in the village
in 1970.

The war put an end to supplies of medicine to the village. Schools
were closed, too, and I never got the opportunity of a secondary education. So from 1970, I made furniture and tilled the soil with my father.

Vietnamese Communist troops began making frequent visits to
Banteay Chey. They paid for supplies that they needed and did not
mistreat villagers. We first saw indigenous Khmer Rouge troops (who
spoke like people from Kompong Cham) when they entered the village
in 1972 and left again without causing upset. They lived in the forest
and visited the village frequently over the next three years; life went on
as before. The Khmer Rouge never stayed in or recruited from Banteay
Chey and were busy fighting the Lon Nol troops all the time.

In 1973, the Vietnamese stopped coming; in the same year, the
village had to withstand three months of intense bombardment by
American B-52s. Bombs fell on Banteay Chey three to six times a day,

killing over 1,000 people, or nearly a third of the village population. Several of my family were injured. After that, there were few people left to be seen around the village, and it was quiet. Food supplies remained adequate. Later, in 1973, the Khmer Rouge temporarily occupied most of Kompong Cham City and evacuated its population to the country-side. Seventy-four people from the town came to Banteay Chey and took up a normal life there. Some of the evacuees had died of starvation and bombardment by Lon Nol planes along the way.

The Khmer Rouge victory in April 1975 and their evacuation of Phnom Penh city brought 600 more people to Banteay Chey. The new-comers were billeted with village families. Relatives of ours, a couple and their three children, and one single man, stayed in my father's house. They had set out on foot from Phnom Penh fifteen days earlier and arrived tired and hungry, although unlike some others they had not lost any of their family members along the way. [The single man, Kang Houath, was eventually to escape from Cambodia with Cheng. Houath took part in one of the interviews with Cheng in Ubon. He said that some village people along the way had given the evacuees food, and others had exchanged food for clothes and other goods offered by the Phnom Penh people. The bulk of the people travelling the roads at the time, however, were former peasants who had taken refuge in Phnom Penh during the war and had been instructed or allowed to return to their villages by the Khmer Rouge, Houath added.] In return for food and shelter, the new arrivals in Banteay Chey helped the locals in their work in the fields.

Also in April 1975, Khmer Rouge troops came to live in the vil-lage. It was not long before they began imposing a very harsh life-style on the villagers. Everybody was now obliged to work in the fields or dig reservoirs from 3 or 4 A.M. until 10 P.M. The only breaks were from noon till 1 P.M. and from 5 to 6 P.M. [This compared to an average 8-hour day worked by the *chamcar* farmers in the preceding years.] One day in ten was a rest day, as well as three days each year at the Khmer New Year festival. Land became communal.

Also from 1975, money was abolished and big houses were either demolished, and the materials used for smaller ones, or used for ad-ministration or to house troops. The banana trees in the *chamcar* were all uprooted on the orders of the Khmer Rouge and rice planted in their place. Production was high, although some land was left fallow and rations usually just consisted of rice porridge with very little meat. After the harvest each year, trucks would come at night to take away the village's rice stores to an unknown destination.

In 1975, the Khmer Rouge also began executing rich people, although they spared the elderly owner of 800 hectares [2,000 acres]. They also executed college students and former government officials, soldiers and police. I saw the bodies of many such people not far from the village. Hundreds of people also died of starvation and disease in the year after April 1975, when medical supplies were lacking.

At this time the Khmer Rouge, led by "friend Sang," claimed that they were "building Communism"; they occasionally mentioned a Communist Party, although its local (and national) members were unknown to us. The soldiers did not work in the fields but mounted an armed supervision over those who did; non-military members of the Khmer Rouge worked unarmed alongside the villagers. There were no peasant organizations formed or meetings held about work; every decision concerning the work to be done and how to do it was made by the supervisors, with no participation on the part of the workers.

There was a large number of Khmer Rouge troops in the village, in the hundreds; they lived separately from the people in a big hall which no one else was allowed to visit. I never chatted with any of the soldiers in the two and a half years I lived with them in Banteay Chey.

Everyone, including my father, disliked the Khmer Rouge in Banteay Chey—the work was simply too hard, the life-style too rigid and the food too inadequate. The Khmer Rouge occasionally claimed to be on the side of the poor, the peasants, but they did nothing at all for them. On the contrary, sometimes they said: "You were happy during the war, now is the time for you to sacrifice. Whether you live or die is not of great significance."

I managed to hide two radios buried in the ground. The batteries were precious so I listened to the radio only once or twice a month. Traditional village music was banned; the Khmer Rouge theatre troupes that visited the village about once in three months were the only form of entertainment.

In the April 1976 elections, only the very big people [i.e. the leading officials] voted in Banteay Chey. Also, by that stage, the *wats* [Buddhist pagodas] and the mosque in Banteay Chey were empty. Saffron-robed Buddhist monks were nowhere to be seen. The Muslim Chams were obliged to eat pork on the occasions it was available; some adamantly refused, and were shot.

During 1976–1977 most of the Khmer Rouge leaders in the village changed six times. More than 50 Khmer Rouge were executed in these purges. Sang's position was finally assumed by Friend Son.

Then, from January 1977, all children over about eight years of age, including people of my age [20 years], were separated from their parents, whom we were no longer allowed to see although we remained in the village. We were divided into groups consisting of young men, young women and young children, each group nominally 300-strong. The food, mostly rice and salt, was pooled and served communally. Sometimes there was *samlor* [Khmer-style soup].

The Khmer Rouge soon began attacking the Vietnamese Communists in speeches to these youth groups. These speeches were propaganda.

Also in early 1977, collective marriages, involving hundreds of mostly unwilling couples, took place for the first time. All personal property was confiscated. A new round of executions began, more wide-ranging than that of 1975 and involving anyone who could not or would not carry out work directions. Food rations were cut significantly, leading to many more deaths from starvation, as were clothing allowances. Three sets of clothes per person per year was now the rule. Groups of more than two people were forbidden to assemble.

1977 was easily the worst year of all. Many people now wanted to escape, although they knew it was very dangerous. My mind was made up when it became clear that I would remain unable to see my father and brothers. It was June 1977.

Houath, a neighbor, one other man and I took three baskets of dry rice. [Cheng did not say how this was acquired.] Avoiding everyone along the way, we headed north and east for Thailand. Laos was closer but I had heard on the radio that Laos was "building communism" too and I didn't want to go there. As it turned out, however, the four of us lost our way to Preah Vihear Province and hit the Lao border at Kompong Sralao. Although Khmer Rouge troops were thinned out because of the conflict with Vietnam, we were spotted by soldiers who fired immediately, killing two of my companions. Houath and I were separated but arrived safely in Laos, where we met up again in a local jail on the banks of the Mekong.

I noticed that the Lao soldiers behaved differently from the Khmer Rouge I knew. They asked questions first, before apprehending people they suspected, whereas the Khmer Rouge were much more inclined to shoot suspects on the spot. I also gained the impression that living conditions in Laos were considerably better than in Cambodia.

Houath and I spent a total of 37 days in two Lao jails. I was given rice to eat, much more than I had had for a long time in Banteay Chey. I was not ill-treated, but when I was told that Vientiane was being asked for instructions whether to send me back to Cambodia, I escaped with Houath, and we fled to Thailand on 8 September 1977.

I spent another ten months in a Thai jail, before being transferred to the Ubon refugee camp.

Account 3: "A City Girl in Democratic Kampuchea," by Ang Ngeck Teang

Ang Ngeck Teang, a fourteen-year-old ethnic Chinese girl from Phnom Penh, was interviewed by Ben Kiernan in Toulouse, France, on December 9, 1979. The translation from the Khmer is by Ben Kiernan.

In 1975 I was evacuated from Phnom Penh to Koh Thom. I went with my family—my mother, and my four brothers and sisters. We walked for nearly a month, past Kbal Thnal and Kien Svay, to Thmey village, Sampan subdistrict, Koh Thom district [in Kandal province]. We saw deaths and killings along the way. We saw four or five deaths on the road, and we saw Khmer Rouge shoot people taking sugar, salt and peanuts from people's warehouses. But we all arrived safely in Koh Thom, and spent a month there.

There were "base people" living there, more than us "new people." At first they did not know anything about the Khmer Rouge, they were very happy. They were nice to us refugees too, and gave us enough to eat. The Khmer Rouge gave each of us only a cup of rice and one ear of corn per day. After work, we had time to fetch crabs and mussels to eat.

Boys and girls worked separately from adults. We gathered thatch and dug dams, collectively. It was happy. At first we had no idea. We could eat, the base people gave us food, so we could all eat together. There was no food problem. And I saw or heard of no more killings there. There were no Buddhist monks to be seen in Koh Thom.

After a month we got a boat to Kompong Chhnang, then a truck to Siemreap. We went with six or eight other families of new people from Thmey village. From Siemreap city we rode ox-carts to the village of Phnom Liep. It was in Region 5, in Preah Net Preah district of Siemreap province. Most of the people there were "base people," apart from the six or eight families from Phnom Penh, and some from Battambang. There were about 500 families in all. The base people were very keen on the Khmer Rouge, and did whatever they were told, because they were afraid of death. There were no Buddhist monks.

We had to tell them what we had done in the "old society." Rank-and-file soldiers were killed, hired workers were spared. Some of the Phnom Penh people were "lazy," but the base people were used to farm work and did what they were told, so the Khmer Rouge liked them. The Phnom Penh people had never done any work, and were called lazy when asked to work. Only the children of the base people got shirts. We were not given many shirts. They told us to do what we were told: "Don't resist the line, or you won't be spared." Many were killed in my village, and most died of starvation. At first, every two days we got salted fish and *prahoc* [preserved fish], plus soap and rice. Communal eating began in 1975, and then we got meals of rice gruel ten months of the year. After work, we could forage for food. There was not much starvation in 1976.

1977 was the worst year for killings. In early 1977 some village cadres were replaced. A new cadre came from Takeo province. But the village chief, who was free to eat what he wanted, was not replaced. A person was shot for stealing ten kilograms [22 lbs.] of food, and one family of urban evacuees were executed.

In 1977 and 1978 we got nothing but gruel to eat. Production was low because of flooding; the dam broke. The locals told us that you had to plant floating rice in this area. But the Khmer Rouge wanted to try something else, and it all died. So there was nothing to eat. The locals' land and houses were all flooded out. They wandered around begging for food, even into Region 3 and Region 4. They were very skinny. In the old society, a family could get by on one hectare of land, but now under the Khmer Rouge there was nothing to eat. This was because farming was collective, or if there was enough food, it was stored away, not given to us to eat. There were eleven people in my family. None were killed, but ten died of starvation in 1977–78, and only I survived. By 1979 just over twenty families out of 500 were left in the village.

In 1977, the Khmer Rouge said: "The Vietnamese are bad, don't trust them." There were no Vietnamese in my village, but there were two or three families of Chams, who were given only fishing duties. They were happy because they could secretly keep some of the fish, while we could eat only what we were given after work.

In 1978 children were no longer allowed to live with their parents. We were all collected from three or four villages and put in a *wat.* We cried for our parents, but we were not given hard work to do. We could visit our parents once a week. Some children also ran home for brief visits, then returned. Children of base people and new people lived together. We were taught revolutionary songs by a woman from Takeo province, aged 22. She was not nice. She hated Phnom Penh people. Whatever was not tasty, we got to eat. She taught fifty or sixty of us. We learned a few things, but she did not know much of the alphabet. I still cannot read Khmer. Once I could read Chinese, but I have forgotten it all now.

When the Vietnamese approached, the Khmer Rouge ran away. They took along two families from the village. Other people from the village headed for Phnom Penh. Some of us were too sick to move, including one nephew of mine, so we stayed in a *wat.* Once, six or eight Khmer Rouge with guns cautiously came back from the forest and asked if we were well yet, and if so to come into the forest before the Vietnamese arrived.

The Vietnamese were good. If we asked them for food, they gave it. If we were sick they gave us medicine. My hand was infected, and they cured it. I stayed in Siemreap for a week, and saw the Vietnamese capture some Khmer Rouge. The Khmer Rouge were very angry; they said that when they escaped they would retake Battambang and make *prahoc* out of the people.

There was a market again in Siemreap, with people selling cakes. The Khmer Rouge had killed all the Vietnamese people, and only Khmers and Chinese were left. And Vietnamese soldiers. And Heng Samrin soldiers, who were no good Khmer. They would not let us stop to sleep on the road to Sisophon, saying that we had not asked them for permission to do so. And they searched us, and if they found something they asked, "Where did you get that from ?" We said we had bought it, but they didn't believe us. They said we had stolen it. They wanted our gold and necklaces before letting us move on. That lot only want gold, that's all.

The Vietnamese were very honest. If we had a chicken we could exchange it for soap from them. I asked them for a lift to Phnom Penh. I went via Skoun. In Phnom Penh, my elder brother found me. My house was all destroyed by the Khmer Rouge. It had been knocked down, and the television destroyed, etc. I now have no relatives in Phnom Penh.

Account 4: Peasant Boys in Democratic Kampuchea, by Sat and Mien

These are accounts of the experiences of two teenage Cambodian peasant boys (Sat and Mien) during 1975–1978. Chanthou Boua and Ben Kiernan interviewed them in a Buddhist *wat* [pagoda] near where they were tending their new master's horses, in Thailand's Surin province, on March 7, 12, and 19, 1979. The text includes every detail recounted by the boys, translated and arranged in sequence by Boua and Kiernan. Occasional points added appear in square brackets.

"They Were Killing People Every Day": Sat

I was born in 1966 in the village of Lbaeuk, Kralanh district, Siemreap province, Cambodia. The village is a long way from Siemreap town, and I have never been there. My father Kaet was a rice farmer. He had married again after my mother died. I had five brothers and sisters; I was the third oldest.

In the years 1975 and 1976, they were killing people every day. Killings took place at some distance from the village. I heard that victims were bound and then beaten to death. They were usually people found to be fishing illegally or who had failed to inform the Khmer Rouge of all their activities. Also during 1975–76, food was scarce in the village; rice porridge with banana stalks was the usual meal.

I can't remember when the Khmer Rouge first came from Oddar Meanchey Province and took rice from the people of Lbaeuk. They soon began ordering the demolition of half a dozen big houses in the village, and the building of a large number of smaller ones to house the villagers. Many of the new houses became flooded in the subsequent rainy seasons. They were built in a circle around the outskirts of the village; to provide communal dining facilities, a large "economics hall" (*kleang setakec*) was constructed in the now empty centre of the village.

The Khmer Rouge recruited a large number of volunteers in Lbaeuk, mostly youths about 20 years old. They were attracted by the much larger food rations that Khmer Rouge received, and by the fact that they did not have to work, and could kill people. On some occasions Khmer Rouge members who had committed some transgression were executed by their fellows.

The village *wat* [pagoda] was also demolished; several people were killed in an accident that occurred in the process. The large statue of Buddha from inside was thrown in a nearby stream. The local Khmer Rouge leader had given orders for this to be done, without giving a reason; he was obeyed out of fear. From that time on, monks were no longer seen around the village.

The year 1976 was worse than 1975. By now, no one in Lbaeuk dared complain or question the regime. My father was temporarily jailed by the Khmer Rouge. I don't know the reason.

In 1977, all young children no longer breastfeeding were taken from their parents and cared for permanently by female members of the Khmer Rouge. The reason given was to enable the mothers to work more effectively. Boys of my age [11] and older were taken together to a forest locality called Lbaeuk Prey. There were over 100 boys in all. Our task was to plant rice, supervised by about twenty armed Khmer Rouge in their early twenties. We worked there for five months, during which time more than twenty of us were taken away to a nearby mountain top. I never saw them again. I believe they were killed.

They were boys who had not worked hard or had missed work or played games, and had ignored three warnings to this effect. [More minor infringements of the rules, Sat says, were punished with a spell breaking rocks to make roads.] Or, they were people who didn't reply when asked what were their parents' occupations.

Morale was low among the young workers. Laughing was permitted, but there was no singing while we worked and no dancing or other entertainment afterwards. Every night there were meetings, in which we boys were urged to work harder; there were no political speeches or discussion at these meetings, and nationalism was mentioned only in the context of the Vietnamese "attempt to take over our land." There were no references to China.

Other tasks we performed were removing weeds from the rice fields and making fertilizer. The job I preferred was tending crops such as watermelons, cucumbers, and other vegetables. I was able to spend a lot of time doing this because I was ordered to. Khmer Rouge leaders on bicycles and with guns [both possessions were a sign of office] occasionally inspected my work. I was never allowed to eat any of the fruits of my labour, all of which were carted away by truck; I don't know where. The food rations I received varied from rice porridge with salt, to rice porridge with fish.

At night we were obliged to mount guard duty. I was taught how to use a gun but never considered becoming a Khmer Rouge soldier when I was older.

Many of us missed our parents badly. Some of us cried with grief at times; the Khmer Rouge would then beat them with sticks until they stopped crying. One month after commencing work at Lbaeuk Prey, we were permitted to visit our parents in Lbaeuk. Some of the parents broke into tears on seeing their sons. My father told me he had now been assigned the task of catching fish for the village communal dining hall; he was forbidden to use any of his catch for his or his wife's consumption. My brothers and sisters had all been taken elsewhere and were not at home. After this visit, which lasted several hours, I returned to Lbaeuk Prey and never saw my family again.

In late 1977, all the boys from Lbaeuk Prey were taken in trucks to Samrong in Oddar Meanchey province. As before, the workers there were all teenage boys. I do not know where the teenage girls from my village had been taken.

In Samrong we began building a road that was to go to Preah Vihear [through hundreds of kilometres of uninhabited forest]. We were told that the road would be used to transport food and supplies. We all worked at the rate of two or three metres of road per day, using locally-made buckets to shift the earth; some boys threw up the soil, while others packed it down into a road surface. By the time I left this site five months later, no vehicles had yet been seen on the road.

There was nothing enjoyable about this experience. We boys were not taught to read or write or to sing any songs; we were never shown any radios, books or magazines, although I noticed that some of the Khmer Rouge had such things.

Later we boys were taken to a place in the forest called Ken, also in Oddar Meanchey province. We were again put to work building a road. We worked from 6 A.M. to 10:30 A.M., had a short lunch break and then worked until 6 P.M., when we had another short break and a wash and then worked until 10 P.M. There were no rest days. The work was so exhausting that some of the boys fell down unconscious at the work-site.

Then, early in 1979, a Khmer Rouge leader arrived on a bicycle and announced that the Vietnamese were in Kralanh. We were told to walk to nearby Paong; when we arrived we were led towards the Thai border on foot for three or four days, carrying our own food and sleeping when tired.

I crossed into Thailand. However, one group of boys came across some Thai tanks; never having seen such things, they ran frightened back into the jungle, where they were killed by Khmer Rouge soldiers.

Now, I am not allowed to walk around or talk to people.

When I become an adult, I want to live with other people.

"The Khmer Rouge Leader Was a Kind, Easygoing Person": Mien

I was born in 1965 in the village of Samlaeng, Roang subdistrict, Preah Vihear Province, Cambodia. My parents, who were rice farmers, called me Daung.

[In early 1970, troops of the new Lon Nol regime retreated from Preah Vihear and from that point the province was under undisputed Communist control.] During the next few years, Vietnamese Communist troops passed through Samlaeng, on one occasion, provoking a lot of interest but no hostility. They didn't steal anything from or harm the villagers; after paying for what they wanted, they moved on.

Also during the war, Samlaeng was bombed "many times" [by U.S. or allied aircraft] over a long period. I don't know if any of the people were killed.

In 1975 [after the Khmer Rouge captured and evacuated Phnom Penh], a number of people arrived in Samlaeng on foot after walking from Phnom Penh. Some people had died along the way; the villagers helped the newcomers settle in to their new environment.

During 1975–76, life went on as before. My parents were happy during this period. Khmer Rouge troops lived in the village but did not cause any upset; I never heard any mention at all of any actual or suspected executions. Food supplies were adequate.

Then, in 1976, the revolution began. Its purpose was "to build up the country," I was told. The entire village was now obliged to eat in a communal dining hall. Rations were tight—usually only rice porridge. In late 1976, I heard that a Phnom Penh evacuee had disappeared from the village and was thought to have been executed. This was the only such case I knew of while living in Samlaeng.

In 1977, myself and three other village boys my age were taken away from our parents. The Khmer Rouge who escorted us away said that they would come back later to take away the other boys in the village, in groups of four at a time. I was taken to Samrong in Oddar Meanchey Province, joining a work group of about 30 boys, the oldest of whom was 17. Our job was to clear the forest for *chamcar*, or garden farmland. Each morning we got up at 4 A.M. and worked around the house we lived in, tending fruit and vegetable crops, until 6 A.M. Then we would go into the forest and work there until 10 A.M. when we ate our lunch. This consisted of a carefully rationed bowl of rice porridge, sometimes with salt, sometimes with *samlor* [Khmer-style soup]. It was not tasty but I was always hungry and would eat it all. At 6 P.M. we would stop working in the forest and return to our houses. Every night we boys were assigned a small plot of land to tend near the houses we lived in. When we finished this task to the satisfaction of the overseers we were allowed to go to sleep.

While living with my parents, I had only been accustomed to do-ing household chores, and I found it difficult to adjust to the new lifestyle. The work was not enjoyable; each boy was allocated an area of forest to clear and we worked some distance from each other. We were not taught to sing songs or dance, or to read or write. I was never allowed to visit my parents again.

Nevertheless, the leader of the Khmer Rouge where I worked was a kind, "easygoing" person who never got angry and did not physically mistreat the children. The Khmer Rouge leader was about 30 years old.

After many months at Samrong, all the boys were sent to a place called Phnom Phtol, or Phnom Seksor. There we spent a few months looking after herds of water buffaloes. In early 1979, with Vietnamese troops approaching the area, we were told to go to Paong; we crossed the border into Thailand, followed by a large number of Khmer Rouge soldiers and children, not long after.

Chapter Thirteen
Physical and Cultural Genocide of Various Indigenous Peoples

Robert K. Hitchcock
Tara M. Twedt

Introduction

The indigenous peoples in the world today have been described as "victims of progress" (Bodley, 1990) and who as people have had to face "colonization, genocide, and a constant struggle for cultural and physical survival" (Independent Commission on International Humanitarian Issues, 1987, p. xi). Indigenous peoples are small-scale societies that frequently have been dealt with harshly by the governments and citizens in the states in which they live. Some see them as being particularly vulnerable to genocidal acts because of their small group sizes, cultural distinctiveness, occupation of remote areas, and relative technological and organizational simplicity (Kuper, 1985, p. 301; Burger, 1987, p. 38; and, Amnesty International, 1992a, pp. 61–62).

Sometimes called aboriginals, native peoples, tribal peoples, Fourth World peoples, or "first nations," these populations have suffered from mistreatment, discrimination, and lack of equal opportunity in employment for centuries. This was especially true from the time of colonial expansion into Africa, Asia, the Pacific, and the New World (International Labour Office, 1953; Wolf, 1982). As Burger (1987) notes, "When the indigenous population did not encounter direct genocide, they faced instead enslavement, forced labor, and menial work" (p. 38). Over the past 500 years literally millions of indigenous peoples have had to cope with destruction of their lifeways and habitats, disease, dispossession, and exploitation (Bodley, 1990).

Substantial numbers of indigenous peoples have been the victims of gross violations of human rights. These violations have ranged from genocide to large-scale massacres of entire groups and from extrajudicial executions of individuals and torture to intentional starvation. According to one non-government organization concerned with indigenous rights, a conservative estimate of the annual deaths of indigenous peoples by violent means is around 30,000 (International Work Group for Indigenous Affairs, 1988, p. 1). In many cases worldwide, these deaths are attributable directly to state actions and to the unwillingness of non-indigenous agencies and individuals to assess the impacts of their policies on indigenous societies. A critical problem is that although international human rights standards pertaining to indigenous peoples exist, these standards frequently are ignored.

Several major factors have been responsible for the threats to the lives and well-being of indigenous peoples in the twentieth century. The first is competition for resources, the second is that a number of indigenous groups have sought self-determination in the face of efforts on the part of governments to assimilate them, and the third is the opposition on the part of some indigenous groups to the plans and policies of political elites and development agencies. Genocides of indigenous peoples occur, as Kuper (1985) notes, "in the process of struggles by ethnic or racial or religious groups for power or secession, greater autonomy, or more equality" (p. 155). Many indigenous groups have suffered from the depredations of governments, private companies, and individuals bent on taking their land and resources forcibly or through quasilegal means such as treaties and agreements (DeLoria, 1969, 1985; World Bank, 1982; Burger, 1987, 1990; Bodley, 1990; Durning, 1992, pp. 21–23; Amnesty International, 1992a, pp. 34–41).

Indigenous populations frequently have been denied the right to practice their own religions and customs and to speak their own languages by nation-states, a process described as "cultural genocide" or "ethnocide" (Kuper, 1981, pp. 31, 41; Burger, 1987, p. 31; Heinz, 1988, p. 75; Bodley, 1990, p. 40; and, Chalk and Jonnasohn, 1990, pp. 9, 23). For purposes of this chapter, ethnocide will be distinguished from genocide as it refers to the destruction of cultures rather than people *per se*. Ethnocide ultimately may have a significant impact on the well-being of indigenous societies since it sometimes results in people becoming so dispirited as to lack the desire to survive.

This essay centers on issues relating to the physical and cultural genocide of various indigenous peoples. We deal first with the question of the characteristics of indigenous peoples. Next, we focus on the issue of the definition of genocide as it relates to indigenous populations, and we examine the various typologies that have been presented which incorporate indigenous peoples as victim groups. We follow with a discussion of the contexts in which genocides of indigenous groups occur, and we conclude with some recommendations for ways in which to protect indigenous peoples from the horrors of genocide.

Who Are Indigenous Peoples?

No single agreed-upon definition of the term "indigenous peoples" exists. According to the Independent Commission on International Humanitarian Issues (1987), four elements are included in the definition: (1) pre-existence, (2) non-dominance, (3) cultural difference, and (4) self-identification as indigenous (p. 6). The term "indigenous peoples" is usually used in reference to those individuals and groups who are descendants of the original populations residing in a country. In the majority of cases they are ethnic minorities, and in general they do not control the governments of the countries where they live. The term "indigenous" sometimes applies to non-European groups residing in regions that were colonized by Europeans.

There are different approaches among analysts to the issue of defining indigenous peoples. The International Labour Office (1953) uses the phrase "tribal and indigenous peoples" (pp. 3–5), while the World Bank and the United Nations prefer "indigenous peoples" (Swepston, 1989, p. 260; Martinez Cobo, 1987; World Bank, 1991). As The World Bank's Operational Directive on Indigenous Peoples (1991) notes, no single definition is appropriate to cover the diversity present in these populations (p. 1).

Indigenous peoples generally possess ethnic, economic, religious, or linguistic characteristics that are different from the dominant groups in the societies where they exist. In many cases, they tend to have a strong sense of cultural identity and social solidarity which many group members attempt to maintain. There are instances, of course, in which indigenous peoples try to hide their identity in order to avoid poor treatment or racial prejudice. Most indigenous peoples prefer to reserve for themselves the right to determine who are and are not members of their groups.

Forty percent of the world's countries (72 of 184) contain peoples defined as indigenous. As shown in Table 13.1, there are over 350,000,000 indigenous people representing some 5,250 nations. Together, these populations comprise about 6.4 percent of the world's total population. Some of these groups are found in a number of different states. The 95,000 Bushmen, for example, are found in six countries of southern Africa (Angola, Botswana, Namibia, South Africa, Zambia, and Zimbabwe), while the Kurds of the Middle East reside in five countries (Iraq, Syria, Turkey, Iran, and the

Table 13.1 Estimated Numbers of the World's Indigenous Peoples

Region	Number of Groups	Overall Population	
North America	250	3,500,000	
Indians (Canada)		1,500,000	(633 bands)
Indians (United States)		2,000,000	(515 tribes)
Latin America and the Caribbean	800	40,000,000	
Aché (Paraguay)	400		
Mapuche (Chile)		600,000	
Miskito (Nicaragua)		75,000	
Yanomami (Brazil, Venezuela)		15,000	
Former Soviet Union	135	40,000,000	
Saami (Russia)		2,000	
China and Japan	56	67,000,000	
Ainu (Hokkaido, Japan)		26,000	
Shui (Guizhou, China)		280,000	
The Pacific	750	2,000,000	
Papuans (New Guinea)		1,300,000	
South Asia	700	70,000,000	
Adivasis (India)		63,000,000	
Tribals (Bangladesh)		1,200,000	
Southeast Asia	500	30,000,000	
Orang Asli (Malaysia)		71,000	
Penan (Borneo)		20,000	
Thailand Hill Tribes		484,000	
Australia and New Zealand	100	550,000	
Aboriginals		300,000	
Maaori (New Zealand)		250,000	
Africa	2,000	50,000,000	
Batwa (Pygmies)		200,000	(7 countries, central)
Bushmen (San)		95,000	(6 countries, southern)
Eyle (Somalia)	450		
Hadza (Tanzania)	1,000		
Maasai (Tanzania/Kenya)		500,000	
Tuareg (Tamacheq)		3,000,000	(5 countries, west)
Grand total	5,290	357,000,000	

Note: Data obtained from a map entitled "Earliest Residents," *The World Monitor* 6(3): 11 (1993) as well as Burger (1990), IWGIA (1992); Durning (1992); and Hitchcock (1993).

former Soviet Union). Inuit are found in the United States, Canada, Greenland, and the former Soviet north. Indigenous peoples represent the majorities in several states, as is the case in Papua, New Guinea (87 percent); Bolivia (77 percent); and Guatemala (55 percent).

Particular problems arise in defining people as indigenous in Africa and Asia. In many parts of Africa, it is difficult to determine antecedence since a variety of populations have moved in and out of local areas over time. Most African countries are multiethnic entities that contain a sizable number of different societies. Nigeria, for example, has at least 160 ethnic groups within its borders. African governments are often reluctant to disclose what percentage of their population is indigenous, taking the position, as Botswana has recently, that all the people in the country (with the exceptions of Europeans and Asians) are indigenous. Individual Africans, on the other hand, frequently identify themselves as members of specific tribal or ethnic groups which they tend to see as indigenous. Even if some people claim to be indigenous, the countries where they live may not recognize them as aboriginal. The government of India, for example, maintains on the one hand that there are no indigenous groups within the country, but on the other hand designates tens of millions of its citizens as "tribals" (Adivasis, "Scheduled Tribes").

African and Asian countries tend to take one of two different positions on the issue of indigenous populations: (1) they claim that there are no indigenous peoples whatsoever within their boundaries, or (2) they state that all groups in the country are indigenous (Martinez Cobo, 1987, p. 5; Sanders, 1989, pp. 417–418). Some countries, such as Botswana, prefer not to differentiate specific groups as targets of assistance, in part because they do not wish to be seen as practicing a kind of *apartheid* or separation on the basis of ethnic identification, as seen in neighboring South Africa. On the other hand, a number of states do not want to admit to having indigenous peoples because they do not want to have to respond to queries or submit to investigations by the United Nations and other agencies on behalf of indigenous peoples. Some of them, such as Tanzania, also do not want to meet the demands of indigenous populations for compensation or rights to blocks of land and resources.

Indigenous peoples are united in their desire to maintain their identities and to seek better standards of living and fair treatment. In some cases, these desires have led to efforts on their part to resist the attempts of states or other groups to change them. Some ethnic groups have been successful in their attempts to seek self-determination and sovereignty, as seen, for example, in the case of the people of Eritrea, which became Africa's newest nation in mid-1993.

While there is tremendous diversity among the world's indigenous peoples, they have a number of socioeconomic features in common. Many indigenous peoples have strong ties to the land and its resources. Their economies are subsistence-oriented, although many of them do engage in market activities and raise cash through sales of goods and services. Some indigenous peoples derive a significant portion of their diet and material requirements from hunting and gathering. Others are pastoralists who graze their domestic animals in savannas, deserts, temperate zones, and mountain environments. The vast majority of indigenous peoples are farmers who not only raise crops but also engage in various off-farm activities and rural and urban wage sector employment. Although many of these groups occupy remote areas, they are not isolated.

Some analysts suggest that contemporary indigenous groups are among the world's most disadvantaged populations (Heinz, 1988; Bodley, 1990). A large percentage of the world's indigenous people live below the poverty line. In Namibia, for example, three out of four Bushmen are poverty-stricken, while 95 percent of the Semang of Malaysia have incomes below $200 per year. Infant mortality rates among them tend to be high while health and nutritional standards generally are low. Unemployment rates are high, with some Native American groups having 50–70 percent of their populations without a job. Most indigenous peoples do not own land, and most groups have experienced dispossession or reductions in their ancestral territories. Educational and literacy levels are generally low, although some groups, such as Australian Aborigines, Mohawks, and Ju/'hoansi Bushmen in Namibia have started schools with curricula geared to their specific needs.

Racism is a fact of life for indigenous peoples throughout the world. They are usually at the bottom of the socioeconomic scale of the countries where they live, and they are marginalized politically and legally. Indigenous groups have had difficulty getting redress for crimes committed against them, and they have often been treated negatively by courts when they have been charged with illegal activities. Often, the sentences that they receive are more severe than is the case for non-indigenous individuals. Members of indigenous communities tend to be overrepresented in the prisons of states such as Australia and Canada. Sometimes charges against indigenous groups are trumped up in order to remove them from lands which others want, as was the case with the Triqui Indians in Mexico in 1984–1985 and with the Penan in Malaysia in 1988–1989. Indigenous leaders argue that they have paid a terrible price for their interaction with non-indigenous societies.

Genocide among Indigenous Peoples

Many researchers, human rights workers, and journalists have deemed the ways in which indigenous peoples have been dealt with in the twentieth century to be genocide (Lewis, 1969, 1974, 1976; Munzel, 1973, 1985; Arens, 1976, 1978; Souindola, 1981; Clay, 1984; Mey, 1984; Steingraber, 1986; Morris and Churchill, 1987; Legters, 1988; Barta, 1987; Tatz, 1991; Churchill, 1991; Jaimes, 1992; Totten and Parsons, n.d.). It is clear from a critical review of the literature on indigenous peoples that most writers use a fairly broad definition of the concept of genocide. While some researchers see genocide as a set of acts committed with the intent to destroy groups in whole or in part, as defined by the United Nations Convention on the Prevention and Punishment of the Crime of Genocide, others extend the concept to include such actions as intentional prevention of ethnic groups from practicing their traditional customs; forced resettlement; denial of access to food relief, health assistance, and development funds; and destruction of the habitats utilized by indigenous populations.

Sometimes victim groups label actions as genocidal in order to bring about greater condemnation of the agencies responsible for mistreating them. Describing all negative actions affecting indigenous groups as genocidal in intent or practice is problematic since such a strategy potentially could limit action against perpetrators. Defining genocide too narrowly, on the other hand, could have the effect of allowing authorities to overlook actions which are destructive and which eventually could result in the extinction of indigenous populations. As Totten and Parsons (n.d.) point out, if we are to develop sound conventions and warning systems to prevent genocide from occurring, then we need to have a comprehensive understanding of what does and does not constitute genocide (p. 3).

Genocide, in the eyes of a number of social scientists, is the deliberate and systematic destruction of a racial, political, social, religious, or cultural group by the state (Horowitz, 1980; Chalk and Jonassohn, 1990). One problem with this approach, however, is that it may not cover those acts that are committed by individuals or groups considered separate from the state (e.g., settlers and miners in the Amazon, or private companies involved in the implementation of development projects). Clearly, in order to cover the diversity existing in cases of annihilation of indigenous peoples, it is necessary to use a definition which incorporates the full array of target groups and perpetrators and which specifies intent.

Fein (1990) defines genocide as "sustained purposeful action by a perpetrator to physically destroy a collectivity directly or indirectly, through interdiction of the biological and social reproduction of group members, sustained regardless of the surrender or lack of threat offered by the victim" (p. 24). This definition is useful in that it excludes single massacres and accidental deaths. It includes mass or selective murders that are aimed at physically destroying group members selected on the basis of their being part of a collectivity. At the same time, it implies that the perpetrator is an organized agency or unit but does not specify whether the actions of the perpetrator were authorized specifically by the state.

It is important to note that genocide is by no means a simple or unified phenomenon. Genocide represents systematic efforts to destroy collectivities, many of which are minorities. Cases of physical genocide include those in which the killing of members of a collectivity threatens the survival of the group as a whole. In practice, however, genocidal acts usually do not result in total annihilation of the population. Groups which have been subjected to genocidal treatment often end up being victimized in other ways as well; they are sometimes raped, enslaved, deprived of their property, and forcibly removed to new places. Some groups have died out as a result of indirect impacts of genocide, including starvation and disease.

Chalk and Jonassohn (1990) use the term "genocidal massacre" in reference to those cases in which a combination of genocide and ethnocide was employed (p. 26). In these instances, "There is no intent to kill the entire victim group, but its disappearance is intended" (Chalk and Jonassohn, 1990, p. 26). The distinction between physical and cultural genocide is by no means clear-cut. According to Chalk and Jonassohn (1990) assimilation policies on the part of the United States, combined with differential legal treatment of Indians, had major impacts on the well-being of Native Americans (pp. 195–203). In America, Australia, South Africa, and other settler societies, most indigenous peoples suffered and died from disease, starvation, and related physical and cultural stresses (Wolf, 1982; Barta, 1987; Bodley, 1990, pp. 38–41, 78–93; Tatz, 1991).

While the U.S. government generally did not openly espouse extermination policies, it did engage throughout its history in cultural modification programs that led to the destruction of Indian societies. It is not surprising, therefore, that Native American writers tend to describe American government policy as genocidal in intent (see, for example, DeLoria, 1969; DeLoria, 1985; Churchill, 1991). Most non–Native Americans would reject the suggestion that they are part of a genocidal society (for a discussion of this concept, see Barta, 1987, pp. 237–240). The fact is, though, that while the U.S. government employed ethnocide as its major indigenous peoples' policy, it was always ready to resort to genocide if it was deemed desirable (DeLoria, 1969; DeLoria, 1985; Legters, 1988; Chalk and Jonassohn, 1990, p. 203; Jaimes, 1992). Examples of genocidal actions against Native American populations include the massacres of over 200 Minnecojou and Hunkpapa Sioux at Wounded Knee in 1890 and the systematic extrajudicial killings of dozens of Oglala Lakota in and around the Pine Ridge Reservation in South Dakota in the 1970s (Weyler, 1982; Matthiessen, 1983; Crow Dog and Erdoes, 1990, pp. 115–116).

Forced relocation, education of Native American children in Euro-American concepts rather than Native American ones, destruction of the subsistence economies of indigenous groups, and imposition of new forms of sociopolitical organization all were implemented by American governmental agencies. It was not until 1924 that Native Americans even received U.S. citizenship rights, and it was another decade before the government lifted its ban in Native Americans' practice of their traditional religious activities (Amnesty International, 1992b, p. 7). Native Americans in America today are still seeking religious freedoms, which have been compromised by a series of court decisions.

Cultural genocide takes place under conditions of state imposition of educational programs, modernization efforts, and nation building. Throughout the world, indigenous peoples have been coerced or cajoled into giving up their cultural traditions. Sometimes this is done in the name of "national reconciliation" after decolonization. States as diverse as Turkey, Somalia, and Russia have required their citizens to learn national languages. Even countries with positive human rights records, such as Botswana, have implemented programs aimed at getting indigenous populations to settle down and take part in a national education system which fails to instruct indigenous students in their own customs and languages (Hitchcock, 1993). Ethnocide also occurs in situations where non-native religious organizations promote their views and seek actively to discourage the practice of indigenous traditions. It is important to note, however, that although ethnocidal policies are practiced widely, they have not necessarily led to cultural disintegration. A cultural resurgence or a kind of ethnogenesis process is occurring among a sizable number of indigenous peoples (Burger, 1990; Bodley, 1990, pp. 152–178; Durning, 1992, pp. 37–46).

Genocides of indigenous peoples in the twentieth century have occurred in a number of different contexts, ranging from ones in which there is competition over resources and land to multiethnic settings with socioeconomic stratification and cleavages among the various groups. In the past, a significant proportion of the genocides of indigenous peoples occurred during the course of colonial expansion, a process seen in the twentieth century primarily in the movements of settlers, companies, and government agencies into frontier zones. The expansion of miners and settlers into the interior of Brazil, for example, led to the destruction of a number of indigenous groups, some of whom were killed by Indian agents of the government's Indian protection agency (Davis, 1977; Price, 1989). Invasions of Yanomami land by miners, with the complicity of the government and the army, has resulted in killings and environmental devastation (American Anthropological Association, 1991; Albert, 1992). Indian agents, settlers, and miners have also been responsible for both purposeful and accidental introduction of diseases which had terrible impacts on tribal populations.

"Indigenous peoples are killed simply for who they are," according to Maya human rights activist and anthropologist, Victor Montejo (n.d., p. 2). Indigenous peoples increasingly are protesting the human rights abuses they suffer at the hands of governments, development agencies, and multinational corporations. They note that they face many forms of persecution. Organized political killings and "disappearances" of indigenous leaders and members of opposition groups are common in countries such as Guatemala and Peru (Carmack, 1988; Manz, 1988; Amnesty International, 1992a). In South and Southeast Asia, the Amazon Basin, the Middle East, Africa, and the Pacific, entire communities of indigenous peoples have been massacred (Anti-Slavery Society, 1984; Burger, 1987; IWGIA, 1988, 1991, 1992; Gurr and Scaritt, 1989; Tatz, 1991).

In Brazil, more than eighty Indian tribes that came in contact with the national society were destroyed between 1900 and 1957, and the indigenous population dropped from approximately a million to less than 200,000 (Davis, 1977, p. 5). Worldwide, in 1984, some 200,000 indigenous peoples lost their lives (Clay, 1984 p. 1). As Clay (1984) notes, "There probably have been more genocides, ethnocides, and extinctions of tribal and ethnic groups in this century than any in history" (p. 1). From the standpoint of indigenous peoples' survival, the twentieth century has been brutal.

Indigenous peoples have been the victims of genocidal and ethnocidal acts in part because of the ways in which they have been represented by dominant societies. In many cases, members of indigenous communities have been described as "primitives," "subhuman," "savages," "vermin," or "nuisances." They have been subjected to these and other negative stereotypes for generations. The images of indigenous peoples have reinforced the tendencies on the part of governments to establish destructive and oppressive racial policies. Efforts on the part of states to vilify indigenous groups are frequently preconditions for genocidal action. This is especially true in those situations where states are concerned about the possibility of indigenous groups supporting opposition movements, as has been the case in Guatemala and Somalia (Menchu, 1984; Carmack, 1988; Manz, 1988; Africa Watch, 1990).

It is extremely difficult to obtain reliable information on genocidal actions and/or outright genocides of indigenous peoples. There are several reasons for this. First of all, most contemporary indigenous groups that are victimized tend to be located in remote places or in conflict zones where it is difficult to gain access. Second, most governments and agencies that come in contact with indigenous groups tend to downplay or deny the severity of their treatment of those peoples. Third, many of the indigenous groups that have been the victims of genocidal acts have members who do not read or write; consequently, written records of what happened to them are rare. Fourth, members of indigenous groups speak their own languages but not necessarily national languages which people doing interviews tend to speak; the result is that translation becomes something of a problem. Not surprisingly, there are relatively few first-person accounts of genocide of various indigenous peoples (Totten, 1991, pp. 311–319).

In the twentieth century, indigenous groups have disappeared at an unprecedented rate (Clay, 1984, p. 1; Durning, 1992, p. 9). This loss of cultural diversity is a product of both physical and cultural extinction. Table 13.2 contains a summary of twentieth-century cases of physical genocide of various indigenous peoples. The reports from which the data is drawn include the *Urgent Action Bulletins* (UAB) of the non-government organization Survival International, published sources, and personal communications. It is evident from the data presented here that a variety of indigenous peoples in a number of different countries have been the victims of geno-

Table 13.2 Twentieth-Century Cases of Genocide of Indigenous Peoples

Group Name	Country	Date(s)	Reference(s)
South America			
Aché	Paraguay	1966–76	Munzel (1973); Arens (1976, 1978); UAB (1988a)
Arara	Brazil	1992	UAB (1992a)
Cuiva	Colombia	1967–71	Arcand (1972)
Mapuche	Chile	1986	UAB (1986a)
Nambiquara	Brazil	1986–87	Price (1989)
Nunak	Colombia	1991	UAB (1991a)
Paez	Colombia	1991	UAB (1992b)
Pai Tavytere	Paraguay	1990–91	Grumberg (1991)
Ticuna	Brazil	1988	UAB (1988b)
Waorani	Ecuador	1986–92	UAB (1987a, 1990a, 1992c)
Yanomami	Brazil	1988–89, 1993	AAA (1991); Ramos Albert (1991, 1992)
Central America			
Indians	Guatemala	1968–93	UAB (1987b); Menchu (1984); Carmack (1988); Amnesty Intl. (1992a)
Indians	El Salvador	1980–92	Chapin (1986)
Miskito	Nicaragua	1981–86	Dodds (1986); U.S. State Department (1986); Dunbar Ortiz (1986)
Africa			
Barabaig	Tanzania	1990–92	UAB (1990b); Lane (1993)
Bubi	Equatorial Guinea	1969–79	Kuper (1985:133–134)
Bushmen	Angola	1980–88	Souindola (1981)
Dinka	Sudan	1992–93	Sudan Human Rights Org. (n.d.)
Herero	Namibia	1904–07	Bridgman (1981)
Hutu	Burundi	1972, 1988	Lemarchand (1992)
Isaak	Somalia	1988–89	Africa Watch (1990)
Karimojong	Uganda	1979–86	Dyson-Hudson (pers. comm.)
Nuba	Sudan	1991–92	UAB (1992d)
Tuareg	Mali, Niger	1988–90	Mezhoud (1992)
Tyua	Zimbabwe	1982–83	Hitchcock files
Asia			
Agta	Philippines	1988	Fay (1987); Headlands (n.d.)
Armenians	Turkey	1915–18	Adalian (1991); Dadrian (1986)
Atta	Philippines	1987	Fay (1987); UAB (1987c)
Auyu	West Papua, Indonesia	1989	UAB (1991b)
Cham	Kampuchea	1975–79	Kiernan (1991)
Dani	Papua, New Guinea	1988	UAB (1988c)
Higaonan	Philippines	1988	UAB (1988d)
H'mong	Laos	1979–86	Morris and Churchill (1987)
Kurds	Iraq	1987–present	Middle East Watch and PHR (1993); Saeedpour (1992)
Nasioi	Bougainville, Papua N.G.	1990–91	IWGIA (1991)
Penan	Sarawak, Malaysia	1986–89	UAB (1986b, 1987d, 1989a, b)
Tamil	Sri Lanka	1983–86	Amnesty International (1986)
Tribals	Chittagong Hill Tracts, Bangladesh	1977–present	Anti-Slavery Society (1984); Chowdhury (1989); Chittagong Hill Tracts Commission (1991)

cidal actions. Indigenous hunter-gatherers, who Kuper (1981) sees as victimized groups that are perpetually at risk, have been particularly hard hit (p. 158). The treatment of foraging societies is extremely difficult to monitor, in part because they tend to be mobile and often reside in out-of-the-way places. Because of the tendency of hunter-gatherers to have fewer links with the larger society and their small numbers, the plight of these groups often goes unnoticed (Kuper, 1981, p. 158; Kuper, 1985, pp. 201–202; Hitchcock, 1985, pp. 457–459).

Typologies of Genocide Relating to Indigenous Peoples

Researchers have presented a number of typologies of genocide which include categories relevant to indigenous peoples as victim groups (Dadrian, 1975; Kuper, 1981, pp. 46–54, 88, 158; Kuper, 1984, pp. 32–33; Kuper, 1985, pp. 151, 200–202, 211–212; Smith, 1987, pp. 23–25, 30–32; Chalk and Jonassohn, 1990, pp. 22–29, 195–222, 412–414; Fein, 1990, pp. 28–30, 79–91). Of five categories of genocide identified by Dadrian (1975), one of them, which he called utilitarian genocide, was aimed at obtaining control of economic resources. Examples of this kind of genocide include the Ache of Paraguay and the Indians of Brazil (Dadrian, 1975).

Smith (1987) sees genocide as an aspect of (1) war, and (2) development, and he notes that in the past it appeared in a variety of contexts, including conquest, religious persecution, and colonial domination. Smith (1987) distinguishes five different types of genocide, one of which he also calls utilitarian genocide (pp. 23–25). This kind of genocide, according to Smith (1987), occurred especially in the sixteenth- to nineteenth-century period when colonial societies came in contact with indigenous peoples in the Americas, Australia, Tasmania, and Africa (p. 23). It has continued in the twentieth century as the Indians of Paraguay, Brazil, and Peru have been destroyed, as Smith (1987) puts it, "out of cold calculation of gain, and, in some cases, sadistic pleasure" (p. 23). The basic objectives of twentieth-century genocides of indigenous peoples have been, according to Smith (1987), Indian land and resources and labor (p. 25).

Like some other analysts of genocide, Smith (1987) rejects the hypotheses of population surplus and political crisis as being primary causes of the destruction of indigenous peoples, arguing instead that "They are being killed because of a combination of ethnocentrism and simple greed" (p. 25). He goes on to suggest that the basic motivation behind utilitarian genocide is that some people must die "so that others might live well" (Smith,

1987, p. 25). Smith adds that one of the reasons that this kind of genocide claims fewer lives today than in the past is because earlier genocides were so effective and contemporary indigenous populations are so small (Smith, 1987, p. 25). In Smith's view, genocidal actions against indigenous peoples are not simply accidental or unpremeditated events but are acts done purposely to achieve economic objectives.

Chalk and Jonassohn (1990) classify genocides according to the motives behind them (p. 29). They distinguish four types of genocide which they see as being done (1) to eliminate a real or potential threat, (2) to spread terror among real or potential enemies, (3) to acquire economic wealth, and (4) to implement a belief, theory, or ideology. The genocide most relevant to indigenous peoples is that aimed at acquiring economic wealth. That said, genocides also occur in order to terrorize indigenous peoples into subservience (Chalk and Jonassohn, 1990, pp. 29, 36–37). Substantial numbers of killings of indigenous peoples occurred in the context of European expansion into the Americas, Africa, and the Pacific and were a result of campaigns by frontier settlers. Sometimes these actions were opposed by governments, but, as Chalk and Jonassohn (1990) note, efforts to protect indigenous peoples were feeble at best (pp. 36–37).

An equivalent category to the utilitarian genocide suggested by Dadrian (1975) and Smith (1987) and that of genocide aimed at acquiring economic wealth suggested by Chalk and Jonassohn (1990) is what Fein (1984) refers to as developmental genocide (pp. 8–9). This kind of genocide generally is preceded by the movement of development agencies, governmental organizations, or individuals into frontier zones where indigenous groups reside and make their living. There was significant variation in the ways in which encroaching individuals and agencies dealt with resident groups. In some cases the outsiders attempted to negotiate with local people; in other cases, they took their land and resources away from them without their permission; and in still other cases they tried to annihilate them (Fein, 1984, p. 8; Bodley, 1990, pp. 24–93).

Harff (1984) and Gurr and Harff (1992) differentiate between genocides and politicides, the former referring to extreme repression aimed at destroying groups defined on the basis of their membership in particular ethnic, religious, national, or racial groups, and the latter referring to victims defined in terms of their political position (e.g., classes or political organizations opposed to the state or dominant group). Politicides, they contend, are more numerous and just as deadly as genocides (Gurr and

Harff, 1992, p. 169). Worldwide, a number of indigenous peoples are caught up in conflicts between governments and local insurgent organizations. Of the 105 armed conflicts ongoing in 1992, 74 were between states and people within their borders (Durning, 1992, p. 14). Some indigenous groups, such as the Bushmen of Namibia and Angola, have been described as some of the most heavily militarized people in the world in the sense that they have had a large proportion of the adult male population trained as soldiers and used in counterinsurgency operations (Gordon, 1992, p. 2). In South America, Asia, the Pacific, and Africa, many of the instances of genocide of indigenous peoples have occurred in the context of armed conflicts in which either the government forces or the opposition groups or both have targeted local people for their support of one side or the other or solely for being in the region where military actions occur.

It is possible to distinguish specific types of genocide involving indigenous populations. The first type, which can be termed *socioeconomic genocide,* comes about in the context of colonization or exploitation of resources in areas occupied by indigenous groups. The perpetrators of socioeconomic genocide range from government organizations established ostensibly to assist indigenous peoples to settlers who receive subsidies from the state and from large landowners to peasant farmers. Multilateral development banks such as the World Bank and the Inter-American Development Bank have been responsible for the destruction of indigenous populations through funding projects in the Chittagong Hills of Bangladesh (Anti-Slavery Society, 1984; Chittagong Hill Tracts Commission, 1991), the Kalahari Desert region of Botswana (Hitchcock, 1993), and the islands of Sumatra, East Timor, Sulawesi, and Kalimantan of Indonesia where the Transmigration Program, a large-scale resettlement effort, is being implemented (Burger, 1987, pp. 142–147; Bodley, 1990, p. 92). Survival International, the Environmental Defense Fund, the Natural Resources Defense Council, and other non-government organizations have attacked the World Bank in particular for its failure to undertake comprehensive social and environmental impact assessments and to implement adequate compensation and resettlement programs.

A second type of genocide in which indigenous peoples are victims is *retributive genocide,* in which actions are taken against collectivities that are perceived as threats or as representing opposition to state ideology and interests. This kind of genocide occurs in contexts in which (1) there is civil conflict, or (2) there are challenges to the legitimacy and authority of a dominant class or group. Indigenous peoples in a number of countries have been the victims of retributive genocide in the twentieth century, including the Hereros of Namibia, the Maya of Guatemala, the Nuba of Sudan, the Kurds of Iraq, the Nagas of India, and various tribal groups in the Philippines and Papua New Guinea. Data on these and other cases has been provided by governments, non-government organizations, opposition groups, anthropologists, and indigenous people themselves. This information has sometimes resulted in further investigations into the treatment of indigenous groups (see, for example, Anti-Slavery Society, 1984; American Anthropological Association, 1991). The problem, however, is that the findings of these investigations have not always led to improvements in the situations facing indigenous populations.

It is useful, as Kuper (1984) points out, to draw a distinction between "domestic" genocides, those arising from internal divisions within a society, and genocides resulting from international warfare (p. 32). The majority of cases of genocides among indigenous peoples fall into the category of domestic genocides. Chalk and Jonassohn (1990) note that it is new states or regimes which are trying to impose ideological conformity that are especially likely to commit genocide (p. 18). Fein (1984) points out that the structural relationships most conducive to genocide are ones based in ethnic stratification in which state power is not constrained effectively by internal or external checks (p. 6). The victims of genocide are often ones not fully incorporated into the state system, middleman minorities, or opposition groups.

Protection of Indigenous People and Prosecution of Perpetrators
Human rights organizations have argued that specific cases of genocide should be followed up on and prosecuted to the fullest extent of the law. This can be done in part through the application of archaeological and forensic techniques aimed at determining the causes of death and identities of individuals, as was done, for example, in the case of the Kurds killed during the Anfal Campaign of the Iraqi government and army in 1988 (Middle East Watch and Physicians for Human Rights, 1988). The evidence for genocide should be presented at a newly created permanent international tribunal which can try cases of human rights violations.

Organizations established at the national level to provide assistance to indigenous peoples have been relatively unsuccessful in ensuring the long-term survival of the people they are charged with protecting. The National Foundation for the Indian (FUNAI) in Brazil, for example, has engaged in pacification programs and has facilitated the process whereby Indians have been removed from their lands (Davis, 1977; Bodley, 1990, pp. 67, 85; Albert, 1992). In the Philippines, the tribal peoples' agency known as the Presidential Assistant on National Minorities (PANAMIN) has been involved in carrying out resettlement programs that have had devastating effects on indigenous peoples. FUNAI, PANAMIN, and other national indigenous peoples' organizations have sometimes worked closely with international development agencies and multinational corporations in their efforts to establish projects that have had deleterious social and environmental impacts. Some of these projects have been accompanied by the intentional killings of indigenous residents of the areas being developed (Bodley, 1990, p. 173; Survival International, 1990b, 1991b, 1992c). Responses of indigenous groups to intensified pressure and genocidal actions have ranged from peaceful protests and appeals to governments and human rights agencies for help to the establishment of grassroots political movements and armed resistance (Burger, 1987; Bodley, 1990; Durning, 1992).

Given the prevailing attitudes toward indigenous peoples, it is not surprising that in the vast majority of instances the people responsible for killing them were never brought to justice. Very few cases of human rights violations against indigenous people by agents of governments have resulted in punishment of the offenders. According to Amnesty International (1992a), the phenomenon of impunity, or tacit protection from prosecution, is one of the crucial factors contributing to the continuing pattern of genocidal acts and human rights violations against indigenous peoples (p. 71). After several centuries of genocide, it was only in the latter part of the 1980s that the Brazilian government actually brought federal charges of genocide against individuals. In 1988, five men were accused of intending to "exterminate or eliminate an ethnic group or race" for their murder of a number of Xacriaba Indians (Chalk and Jonassohn, 1990, p. 414). Other countries in South America (Colombia, Bolivia) and Southeast Asia (Malaysia) are also considering trying people for these crimes.

Agents of governments accused of genocide of indigenous peoples have been quick to deny the charges. When accused of genocidal acts against the Ache Indians of Paraguay, the country's Defense Minister argued that, by definition, genocide was not perpetrated. In doing so, he made the assertion that:

Although there are victims and victimizer, there is not the third element necessary to establish the crime of genocide—that is "intent." Therefore, as there is no "intent," one cannot speak of genocide. (Lewis, 1976, p. 63)

A similar defense was presented by the Permanent Representative of Brazil to the United Nations in 1969, who argued that crimes committed against Brazilian indigenous populations could not be seen as genocide because (1) they never eliminated Indians as an ethnic or cultural group, and (2) the actions were committed for "exclusively economic reasons" and therefore lacked "the special malice or motivation necessary" to be characterized as genocide. (United Nations Human Rights Communication No. 478, 29 September, 1969, cited in Kuper, 1984, p. 33). Taken to its logical extreme, this argument would mean that practically none of the actions against indigenous peoples that are obviously genocidal in nature could be described as genocide.

Over the past several decades, efforts have been made by a wide variety of agencies, groups, and individuals to promote the interests of indigenous peoples and to educate the public about their situations (Sanders, 1989; Swepston, 1989; Burger, 1990; Bodley, 1990, pp. 174–207). These efforts have included the documentation of human rights abuses, working directly with people whose rights have been violated to try to obtain legal redress, bringing pressure to bear on governments and agencies involved in activities deleterious to indigenous peoples, and providing funds and technical assistance to indigenous groups seeking to improve their lives. The work of these organizations has been constrained by lack of funds and political support.

The activities of indigenous peoples' rights organizations have not been without controversy. In the 1970s, for example, the London-based nongovernment organization Survival International stated that the government of Paraguay had committed genocide against the Aché Indians (Munzel, 1973; Arens, 1976; Survival International, 1988a, 1993). These allegations were rejected not only by the governments of Paraguay, the United States, Britain, and West Germany, but also by Cultural Survival, an American indigenous peoples' support organization (Maybury-Lewis and Howe, 1980). The denial of the occurrence of genocide of indigenous groups was based in part upon a definitional question relating to whether or not there had been a "planned or conscious effort on the part of the government of Paraguay to exterminate, molest, or harm the Ache Indians in any way" (Survival International, 1993, p. 5). Clearly, definitional issues are of major importance in the discussions concerning physical and cultural genocide. Equally as clear is the fact that the protection of indigenous groups from genocide would be enhanced if there were greater cooperation and coordination among the various organizations involved with indigenous peoples' welfare.

What the Genocides of Indigenous Peoples Have Taught Us

Many countries have made rhetorical commitments to enforce laws with respect to freedom of association, access to fair and impartial judicial procedures, and elimination of discriminatory treatment of minorities. In practice, however, numerous countries have engaged in repressive actions against their citizens. Most states, along with the United Nations, have been reluctant to criticize individual nations for their actions on the pretense that this would constitute a violation of sovereignty. They have also tended to accept government denials of genocides at face value. As a result, genocidal actions continue.

In the twentieth century dozens of indigenous peoples have been the victims of physical and cultural genocide. The lack of teeth behind the rhetorical commitment to the protection of indigenous peoples' rights has been, and continues to be, a tremendous problem. If the gross violations of human rights of indigenous peoples are to be stopped, then efforts must be made to enforce existing international human rights law and to impose sanctions on those countries, institutions, agencies, and individuals responsible for genocidal actions. Attempts must also be made to develop genocide early warning systems and to determine the preconditions for genocide (Kuper, 1985, pp. 218–219; Chalk and Jonassohn, 1990, p. 4).

A lesson learned from the experiences of indigenous peoples harmed by development projects is that detailed social and environmental impact assessments and careful consultations with local people must be carried out prior to the implementation of any projects. It is also evident that development agencies must provide for the legal protection of the lives and assets of people affected by projects. Failure to do so should result in the cutting off of all financial support for those agencies.

The protection of indigenous peoples from genocide at the international level has generally been ineffective. Few cases of genocide against indigenous peoples have been brought before the Commission on Human Rights of the United Nations. Those who have brought complaints to the

United Nations have learned that the international agency does not provide redress for alleged human rights violations. In addition, they have discovered that the United Nations does not have the capacity or, according to some, the commitment, to provide direct protection from perpetrators of human rights abuses. Thus, one of the lessons gleaned from the experiences of indigenous groups is that the United Nations must improve its performance in the human rights arena. A second lesson is that humanitarian intervention can and should be considered in cases of genocides and gross human rights violations. If this is to be effective, however, substantial efforts will need to be made to gain detailed knowledge of the situation on the ground before such interventions are attempted.

The failure to prevent genocide of indigenous peoples is the result of a combination of factors, including government inaction, bureaucratic inefficiency, lack of enforcement of international human rights law, racism, and outright greed. Experience has taught us that genocide cannot be prevented unless the perpetrators perceive that the costs of their actions will outweigh the benefits. Without efforts to document cases of genocide and to impose penalties on those governments and agencies responsible, killings and disappearances will be commonplace occurrences not just for indigenous groups but for many of the world's peoples.

Eyewitness Accounts
Physical and Cultural Genocide of Various Indigenous Peoples

It has proved to be exceptionally difficult to obtain reliable and detailed information on genocides of indigenous peoples. This is particularly true when it comes to locating first-person accounts of genocides involving such groups. One reason for this situation is that many contemporary indigenous groups who have been subjected to genocidal treatment tend to live in out-of-the-way places which are often inaccessible for environmental or political reasons. Documentation of genocidal events against indigenous communities is also rare since those groups residing in remote locations tend to be illiterate or have limited exposure to educational opportunities. Concomitantly, language proficiency of individuals visiting indigenous communities is often limited at best.

Gathering data on genocides of indigenous peoples is also difficult because in many cases the gross violations of human rights are ongoing. Individuals are reluctant to talk for fear of reprisals. It is not uncommon for people to express deep concern that those responsible for the genocidal acts would retaliate against them and their families for their having revealed what transpired. They therefore are often unwilling to provide information such as their names, identities of relatives, places of residence, and any other data that could be used to determine who they are.

During the course of interviews of indigenous people who have been the victims of atrocities, a number of them address the topic of violence only indirectly or in careful terms. Some of them emphasize that they find it extremely difficult to put into words all that had happened. They describe their experiences in culturally appropriate ways, which means that one has to be reasonably familiar with the languages and cultures of the societies of which they have been a part in order to get at the full meaning of what they are saying.

One of the difficulties faced by anthropologists and others investigating genocidal acts is that most of the existing accounts are not from indigenous groups but rather come from the government, the military, or other agencies who have come in contact with those groups. Fortunately, indigenous peoples themselves are recording their experiences and telling their stories more often now than has been the case in the past. This is sometimes done in autobiographical form, as is the case with Nobel Prize recipient Rigoberta Menchu, a Guatemalan Quiche Indian woman who has described the suffering of her family and Indian peoples generally in a country that has expended considerable energy oppressing its indigenous populations.

One type of oral testimony obtained from indigenous peoples consists of statements made to investigators, some of whom are human rights workers such as those from Africa Watch, Survival International, or Cultural Survival. An advantage of these oral histories is that they sometimes are obtained not long after the genocidal events occurred, thus ensuring that the effects of gradual memory loss are minimized and reducing the chances that subsequent reports have influences on individual perceptions.

Another type of oral testimony on genocides of indigenous peoples is that obtained during the course of interviews designed to get other kinds of information such as life histories of individuals. In these cases, the genocide is not the object of the discussion and is only alluded to in passing. Once genocidal actions are mentioned, additional details are sought. The difficulty in these situations is that so little is known of the general context in which the genocide occurred that it is not easy to ask appropriate and detailed questions. Under these kinds of conditions, it is hard to assess the efficacy of the testimony provided.

Clearly, there is a tremendous need to obtain additional first-person accounts of genocides of various indigenous peoples. Having more detailed information on genocides will facilitate the process whereby genocide early warning systems can be developed. Analysis of the case material can also contribute to a better understanding of the conditions under which genocides of indigenous peoples occur.

The oral testimonies presented here have been chosen to illustrate the types of information available on genocides of various indigenous peoples. The accounts are drawn from Guatemala, Somalia, and Zimbabwe. The first account is taken from the autobiography of Rigoberta Menchu (*I, Rigoberta Menchu, An Indian Woman of Guatemala*, edited and introduced by Elisabeth Burgos-Debray and translated by Ann Wright. London: Verso Editions, 1984). The second set of first-person accounts is drawn from a report by Africa Watch (*Somalia, A Government at War with Its Own People: Testimonies about the Killings and Conflict in the North*. Washington, D.C. and New York: Africa Watch, 1990). The third oral testimony is one obtained by Robert Hitchcock from a Tyua Bushman man in western Zimbabwe in June 1989.

Account 1: The Indians of Guatemala by Rigoberta Menchu

Rigoberta Menchu is a 36-year-old Quiche Indian woman from the village of Chimel in the province of El Quiche in Guatemala. Like other Indians of her country, Ms. Menchu was a victim of genocidal actions which resulted in the deaths of her mother, father, and brother. Her book describes these and related events in strong detail, and it illustrates some of the ways in which indigenous peoples in Guatemala responded to the pressures exerted upon them.

Guatemala, as Burger (1987) has noted, is a country where the political persecution of indigenous peoples is unparalleled in the contemporary world (p. 76). The treatment of Indians in this Central American country has been decried by indigenous peoples' groups, human rights organizations, and anthropologists and other social scientists (Independent Commission on International Humanitarian Issues, 1987, pp. 84–87; Burger, 1987, pp. 76–85; Carmack, 1988; Manz, 1988; Amnesty International, 1992a, pp. 11–13, 20–22, 43–44). Tens of thousands of Indians, the vast majority of them non-combatants, have been killed during the course of counter-insurgency operations of the Guatemalan military beginning in the 1960s and 1970s and continuing to the present. Leaders of grassroots Indian groups, labor organizers, and critics of Guatemalan government policy have disappeared in substantial numbers over the past thirty years (Manz, 1988, p. 30; Amnesty International, 1992a, p. 12). As a result of the repressive policies, hundreds of thousands of Guatemalan Indians were displaced, many of them ending up in refugee camps in other countries (Manz, 1988).

Rigoberta Menchu was a witness to many of these events. In her book, she writes of genocidal massacres such as the one at Panzos, Alta Verapaz, which resulted in the deaths of over 100 Indians. She describes in avid detail the murderous actions of the Guatemalan army and its supporters and the vilification of Indians by the government. Her discussion provides insights into the ways in which Indians were repressed in Guatemala, and it illustrates how indigenous peoples can become the victims of state policies.

I was ashamed to stay safely in my village and not think about the others. So I decided to leave. My father knew and he said: "Where you are going, you may not have control over your life. You can be killed at any time. You could be killed tomorrow, the day after tomorrow, or anytime."

But before that, under Kjell,[1] there was a massacre of 106 peasants in Panzos, an area of Coban. It was the 29th of May, 1978. Panzos is a town where they discovered oil and began throwing peasants off their land. But since the peasants didn't know where to go, they all came down in an organised fashion with their leaders. They were Keckchi Indians and the army massacred them as if they were killing birds—men, women and children died. Blood ran in the main square in Panzos. We felt this was a direct attack on us. It was as if they'd murdered us, as if we were being tortured when they killed those people. It all came out in the newspapers. But nobody paid much attention, they were more interested in the government which had just come to power. So the story died. Nobody was interested in the death of all those peasants. The CUC condemned this act, and that's when it was recognized under the name of Comite Unidad Campesina, as an organisation defending peasants' rights. Our objectives were: a fair wage from the landowners; respect for our communities; the decent treatment we deserve as people, not animals; respect for our religion, our customs, and our culture. Many villages in El Quiche were unable to perform their ceremonies because they were persecuted or because they were called subversives and communists. The CUC championed these rights. It came out into the open. Then the repression against it began. We held a huge demonstration to herald the CUC with the participation of Indian men, women and children, although the CUC also recognizes that it is not only Indians who are exploited in Guatemala but our poor ladino companeros as well. The CUC defends all peasants, Indians and ladinos. And within the framework of the organisation, we began having contacts between ladinos and Indians.

So the CUC comes into the open; it calls strikes, demonstrations and demands for a fair wage. We obtained a wage of 3.20 quetzals. That was the bare minimum, really. For a family which has to feed none or ten children 3.20 is not a fair wage. The finca owners said yes. They signed an agreement to pay a minimum wage of 3.20 quetzals. They agreed. It was a victory for us obtaining 3.20 but, in practice, the landowners didn't pay that. They kept on paying their peones the same: 1.20 quetzals. What the landowners actually did was to supervise the work more closely, raise the work quotas and, at the same time, charge for every tiny error the peasants make. Now we couldn't let even the tiniest fly alight on a leaf, or walk on it, because we'd have to pay for the plant. This was very hard for the peasants. We kept up our demands but we didn't know how to act. It was a bitter blow when our first companeros fell. But we carried on working.

It was in 1978, when Lucas Garcia[2] came to power with a lust for killing, that the repression really began in El Quiche. It was like a piece of rag in his hands. He set up military bases in many of the villages and there were rapes, tortures, kidnappings. And massacres. The villages of Chajul, Cotzal and Nebaj suffered massacres as the repression fell on them again. It fell above all on the Indian population. Every day new clandestine cemeteries, as they call them, would appear in different parts of the country. That is, they'd kidnap people from a village, torture them, and then some thirty bodies would appear in one place. On a hillside for example. Then they'd tell the people to go and get their relatives there. But they didn't dare look for the bodies because they knew they'll be taken away too. So the bodies just stayed there. Then what they did was dig a pit for the bodies and put them all in: so it was a secret cemetery. . . .

On 9 September 1979 my brother was kidnapped. It was a Sunday, and he'd gone down to another village—he worked in other villages as well as his own. His name was Petrocinio Menchu Tum—Tum is my mother's name. Well, my brother had a job to do. He was very fond of organising work. So he went round organising in various places, and the army discovered him and kidnapped him. After 9 September my mother and the rest of us began to worry. At that time—and I still thank God they didn't kill all of us—my mother nonetheless went to the authorities to enquire after him. If they kill me because of my son, she said, let them kill me. I wasn't there at the time; I was in Huehuetenango when my brother was captured. They say that the day he fell, my mother was at home and my other brothers were not far away. Mother went into the village to find out where her son was, but nobody could give her any news of his whereabouts. However, he had been betrayed by someone in the community. As I said before, there are people who'll turn their hand to anything when you least expect it. Out of pure necessity, often they'll sell their own brothers. This man from the community had been a companero, a person who'd always collaborated and who had been in agreement with us. But, they offered him fifteen quetzals—that's to say fifteen dollars—to turn my brother in, and so he did. The army didn't know who he was. That day my brother was going to another village with a girl when they caught him. The girl and her mother followed along after him. From the first moment they tied his hands behind his back, they started to drive him along with kicks. My brother fell, he couldn't protect his face. The first part of him to begin to bleed was his face. They took him over rough ground where there were stones, fallen tree trunks. He walked about two kilometres [1.2 mi.] being kicked and hit all the time. Then they started to threaten the girl and her mother. They were risking their lives by following my brother and finding out where he was being taken. Apparently they said to them: "Do you want us to do the same to you, do you want us to rape you right here?" That's what this thug of a soldier said. And he told the senora that if they didn't go away they'd be tortured just like he was going to be because he was a communist and a subversive, and subversives deserved to be punished and to die.

When we reached the village there were many people who'd been there since early morning: children, women, men. Minutes later, the army was surrounding the people who were there to watch. There were machines, armoured cars, jeeps, all kinds of weapons. Helicopters started to fly over the village so that the guerrilla fighters wouldn't come. That's what they were afraid of. The officer opened the meeting. I remember he started by saying that a group of guerrillas they'd caught were about to arrive and that they were going to suffer a little punishment. A little punishment, because there were greater punishments, he said, but you'll see the punishment they get. And that's for being communists! For being Cubans, for being subversives! And if you get mixed up with communists and subversives, you'll get the same treatment as these subversives you'll be seeing in a little while. My mother was just about 100 per cent certain her son would be amongst those being brought in. I was still not sure, though, because I knew my brother wasn't a criminal and didn't deserve such punishments.

Well, a few minutes later three army lorries came into the village. One went a little ahead, the middle one carried the tortured people and the third one brought up the rear. They guarded them very closely, even with armoured cars. The lorry with the tortured came in. They started to take them out one by one. They were all wearing army uniforms. But their faces were monstrously disfigured, unrecognisable. My mother went closer to the lorry to see if she could recognise her son. Each of the tortured had different wounds on the face. I mean, their faces all looked different. But my mother recognized her son, my little brother, among them. They put them in a line. Some of them were very nearly, half dead, or they were nearly in their last agony, and others, you could see that they were; you could see that very well indeed. My brother was very badly tortured, he could hardly stand up. All the tortured had no nails and they had cut off part of the soles of their feet. They were barefoot. They forced them to walk and put them in a line. They fell down at once. They picked them up again. There was a squadron of soldiers there ready to do exactly what the officer ordered. And the officer carried on with his rigmarole, saying that we had to be satisfied with our lands, we had to be satisfied with eating bread and chile, but we mustn't let ourselves be led astray by communist ideas. Saying that all the people had access to everything, that they were content. If I remember right, he must have repeated the word "communist" a hundred times. He started off with the Soviet Union, Cuba, Nicaragua; he said that the same communists from the Soviet Union had moved on to Cuba and then Nicaragua and that now they were in Guatemala.

And that those Cubans would die a death like that of these tortured people. Every time he paused in his speech, they forced the tortured up with kicks and blows from their weapons.

No-one could leave the meeting. Everyone was weeping. I, I don't know, every time I tell this story, I can't hold back my tears, for me it's a reality I can't forget, even though it's not easy to tell of it. My mother was weeping; she was looking at her son. My brother scarcely recognized us. Or perhaps. . . . My mother said he did, that he could still smile at her, but I, well, I didn't see that. They were monstrous. They were all fat, fat, fat. They were all swollen up, all wounded. When I drew closer to them, I saw that their clothes were damp. Damp from the moisture oozing out of their bodies. Somewhere around half-way through the speech, it would be about an hour and a half, two hours on, the captain made the squad of soldiers take the clothes off the tortured people, saying that it was so that everyone could see for themselves what their punishment had been and realize that if we got mixed up in communism, in terrorism, we'd be punished the same way. Threatening the people like that, they wanted to force us to do just as they said. They couldn't simply take the clothes off the tortured men, so the soldiers brought scissors and cut the clothes apart from the feet up and took the clothes off the tortured bodies. They all had the marks of different tortures. The captain devoted himself to explaining each of the different tortures. This is perforation with needles, he'd say, this is a wire burn. He went on like that explaining each torture and describing each tortured man. There were three people who looked like bladders. I mean, they were inflated, although they had no wounds on their bodies. But they were inflated, inflated. And the officer said, that's from something we put in them that hurts them. The important thing is that they should know that it hurts and that the people should know it's no easy thing to have that done to your body.

After he'd finished talking the officer ordered the squad to take away those who'd been "punished," naked and swollen as they were. The dragged them along, they could no longer walk. Dragged them along to this place, where they lined them up all together within sight of everyone. The officer called to the worst of his criminals—the Kaibiles,[3] who wear different clothes from other soldiers. They're the ones with the most training, the most power. Well, he called the Kaibiles and they poured petrol over each of the tortured. The captain said,

"This isn't the last of their punishments, there's another one yet. This is what we've done with all the subversives we catch, because they have to die by violence. And if this doesn't teach you a lesson, this is what'll happen to you too. The problem is that the Indians let themselves be led by the communists." He was trying to convince the people but at the same time he was insulting them by what he said. Anyway, they lined up the tortured and poured petrol on them; and then the soldiers set fire to each one of them. Many of them begged for mercy. They looked half dead when they were lined up there, but when the bodies began to burn they began to plead for mercy. Some of them screamed, many of them leapt but uttered no sound—of course, that was because their breathing was cut off. But—and to me this was incredible—many of the people had weapons with them, the ones who'd been on their way to work had machetes, others had nothing in their hands, but when they saw the army setting fire to the victims, everyone wanted to strike back, to risk their lives doing it, despite all the soldiers' arms. . . . Faced with its own cowardice, the army itself realized that the whole people were prepared to fight. You could see that even the children were enraged, but they didn't know how to express their rage.

Well, the officer quickly gave the order for the squad to withdraw. They all fell back holding their weapons up and shouting slogans as if it were a celebration. They were happy! They roared with laughter and cried, "Long live the Fatherland! Long live Guatemala! Long live our President! Long live the army, long live Lucas!" The people raised their weapons and rushed at the army, but they drew back at once, because there was the risk of a massacre. The army had all kinds of arms, even planes flying overhead. Anyway, if there'd been a confrontation with the army, the people would have been massacred. But nobody thought about death. I didn't think that I might die, I just wanted to do something, even kill a soldier. At that moment I wanted to show my aggression. Many people hurried off for water to put out the fires, but no-one fetched it in time. It needed lots of people to carry the water—the water supply is in one particular place and everyone goes there for it— but it was a long way off and nothing could be done. The bodies were twitching about. Although the fire had gone out, the bodies kept twitching. It was a frightful thing for me to accept that. You know, it wasn't just my brother's life. It was many lives, and you don't think that the grief is just for yourself but for all the relatives of the others: God knows if they found relatives of theirs there or not! Anyway, they were Indians, our brothers. And what you think is that Indians are already being killed off by malnutrition, and when our parents can hardly give us enough to live on, and make such sacrifices so that we can grow up, then they burn us alive like that.

Account 2: The Isaaks of Somalia

In 1988 the army of the government of Somalia attacked villages in the northern part of the country with the aim of destroying members of the Isaak clan, one of several clans in Somalia which they blamed for participating in rebellious actions against the state. The justification for these acts was state security.

The Somalia case illustrates a kind of "autogenocide" not unlike that in Cambodia perpetrated by the Khmer Rouge. The genocidal actions in Somalia, like those in Cambodia, were aimed specifically at exterminating members of one's own ethnic group (Africa Watch, 1990, pp. 1–2). Prior to the outbreak of fighting in northern Somalia, members of the Isaak clan disappeared, some of the hands of the Somalia National Security Service and paramilitary forces whose task was to root out dissent.

An estimated 50,000 to 60,000 people, the majority of them Isaaks, died during the 1980s, most of them in the period between 1988 and early 1990. Civilians were targeted along with suspected insurgents. The Somalia government forces carried out sweeps of both urban and rural areas, and both massacres and extrajudicial executions occurred. Camel and goat-keeping pastoral nomads were victimized by the Somalia government because of the perception that they were providing economic support to the insurgents. The following oral testimonies were obtained from several people in the months following the 1988 attacks by Africa Watch and in 1990 by Robert Hitchcock.

The first oral testimony is from a woman named Monda Ahmed Yusuf, who lived in the Tuurta Turwa district of Burao in northern Somalia. She was interviewed by Africa Watch in London, England, on July 2, 1989.

Shelling with long-range weapons started on Sunday. It hit a neighbor's house, the Abdirahman family of seven people. Six of them died instantaneously. The only survivor was a little girl who had been sent to fetch sugar. The mother had just had a baby.

They were after civilians. Their scouts would direct them to those areas where civilians were concentrated and then that spot would be shelled. On Monday, the shelling intensified. Two houses behind ours belonging to my uncle were hit. Luckily, one was empty as the family had congregated in the other house. It hit that house too and his daughter, niece and sister-in-law were wounded. Our side was particularly targeted as it was one of the areas the SNM entered when they first came into town. When the bombing started, the sight of the dying, the wounded and the collapse of houses was too much to bear.

The second testimony was that of Khadija Sugal, who described how government forces intentionally separated Isaak clanspeople from non-Isaaks.

As soon as the fighting broke out, the government used loudspeakers to sort the civilians out into Darood and Isaak. They would shout, "Who is from Galkayo? Mogadishu? Las Anod? Garoe?" [Non-Isaak territory]. They appealed to the non-Isaaks to leave so they could burn the town and all those who remained behind. Most of the people from these towns left; the government provided them with transportation.

The artillery shelling began immediately after the non-Isaaks had been evacuated. Everything seemed to collapse or to be on fire. Whole areas of Burao seemed to be lit up with gunfire. Our suffering until then seemed of no significance compared to the impact of the shelling. The effect of the shelling is indescribable. The shock made people sick—many pregnant women went into early labor and, without any medical help, gave birth to premature babies. The shelling forced everyone, even the wounded and the very old, to flee.

On Tuesday, the aerial bombardment began. The smoke was overwhelming. You choked, and it felt as if you were inhaling poison. It left a sharp pain in your throat and burned your eyes. After Tuesday, the city seemed to be burning. There was smoke everywhere. By Wednesday, we became desperate. I left home without even a head scarf, with only one shoe on. I headed east with some other women. There were so many dead people spread out on the road; it seemed as if someone had laid a giant cloth on the ground.

Among the dead are: My brother, Suleiman, in his 30s, killed by soldiers as he fled; Mohamoud Jama "Ogleh," my children's grandfather, shot by soldiers. A friend of mine, Khadija Haji Abdi, a woman in her 50s, died when a bomb hit her home and the house collapsed on her.

The third testimony is that of Ismail Dualeh Mohamed, a seaman who was interviewed by Africa Watch in Cardiff on July 6, 1989:

If they [Somali government forces] had made any distinctions between SNM[4] fighters and civilians, there wouldn't have been so many casualties and there wouldn't have been so much suffering. What they wanted, to put it simply, was to wipe us out. A hail of bullets came at you from every direction. As we fled Burao, my wife was hit by a bullet and badly wounded. My mother-in-law died when a bomb hit their house. My mother's niece was also killed. So many people have died in this war, including so many members of my own extended family. Only God can count the numbers.

The fourth oral testimony on Somalia is that of Jama Osman Samater, who had been a political prisoner from 1982 through 1988:

I had just come out from the mosque from Friday prayers when I heard the news of the SNM attack on Burao. It was lunchtime. At 2:30 a whistle blew, announcing a curfew. I went home. The next morning I learned that many businessmen and elders had been arrested. I saw soldiers herding people into cars. They were confiscating all vehicles, including taxis, because when the SNM attacked Burao, taxi drivers had helped the SNM. When they couldn't find the keys quickly enough, they punctured the tires and broke the windows. I understood immediately the gravity of the situation. The soldiers were looting food and medicines from the shops and loading them on to cars. The Gulwadayaal[5] were assisting the soldiers.

As a former political prisoner, I was in danger of being re-arrested. I had to disguise myself. I went into the back of our shop, shaved my head and dressed as a nomad. As I left, I saw two other men arrested. They were "Guun," and Abdillahi Khalif, "Ku Cadeeye," both elders. I don't know what happened to them.

I went towards my house. As I was about to board the bus, one of our shop assistants told me not to go home. Soldiers had just come to the shop looking for me and they must be on their way to the house. I went to hide at a neighbor's. That night, soldiers and NSS[6] officers went to my house. They took all valuables. One of my little sons screamed "faqash" at them and they slapped him across the ears. We learned later that his eardrum burst. I stayed a second night at a neighbor's house. Then, a friend and I hid ourselves in a big rubbish bin on the outskirts of Hargeisa for an entire day. The next night, the SNM attacked Hargeisa and we came back to town. On our way back, we passed a house near a military checkpoint belonging to Yusuf Elmi Samatar and saw soldiers and a tank on the move. We learned that 18 civilians, who had fled the city center and taken shelter there, had been killed. They were robbed of everything and some of the women were raped.

We stayed in Hargeisa until June 8. My wife, mother, six children, two sisters and their children gathered in one house. After a few days, the shelling started. It was relentless. They shelled homes, even when no one was in the house. The objective was to ensure that no one escaped alive and no house left to stand. Volleys of artillery were being fired from every direction. There was burning everywhere. In front of my sister's house, a wooden house was hit and eight people, mostly women and children, perished. The shock was so overwhelming that we soon lost any sense of fear.

I realized that my suffering in prison was nothing compared to this. In prison, my pain had affected just me. Here everyone was a victim. The shelling did not discriminate. There were even dead animals, dogs and goats, everywhere. The first dead bodies I saw were two or three traders of Asian origin who had lived in Somalia for generations. I went to hide in a mosque. I couldn't walk fast as there were so many dead bodies on the road.

The fifth testimony is that of Khadra Muhumed Abdi, who spoke to Africa Watch in London on June 2, 1989:

On the Friday, I came to our hotel (Oriental Hotel), unaware, at the time, of the SNM attack on Burao. I learned that businessmen and elders were being rounded up. As a former political prisoner, I was nervous. NSS officers came to look for me. I escaped through a back door and hid in a store next door. Later, I asked a young boy to fetch me a taxi and I went to hide in my aunt's house in Dumbuluq district. I was afraid to go home for fear that they would be waiting for me.

The morning after the SNM attack on Hargeisa, I could see our district, Radio Station area, burning. It seemed as if the whole city was on fire. The government was going around with loudspeakers saying that "Four lice-ridden bandits on a suicide mission entered the town and we have now driven them away." They insisted that everything was back to normal and urged people to return to their homes. Unfortunately, many people believed them and were killed.

It was clear that the war was going on whatever the government said. I could not run because of the disability in my leg. [She limps in one leg.] My mother and my two children joined us on the third day of the fighting. A part of our house had collapsed and they tried to hide in the undamaged section. They left when it was no longer safe to stay there. A neighbor gave them shelter but the children had no milk and food was scarce.

We stayed another twelve days in my aunt's house. Soldiers came and took everything we had. What they couldn't take with them, such as trunks, they destroyed. When he sensed our tension, one of them turned around and said to me, "If I hear one word out of you, I will make you carry the heads of your children after I have cut them off." Fortunately, I made the two boys (one was a year and 3 months and the other was two years and 3 months) wear dresses, so they thought they were girls. If they had recognized them as boys, they would have shot them at once. We knew of so many boys, including babies, who had been killed. A neighbor of my aunt's, known as "Cirro," had five sons and two nephews in the house. Because of their ages, he wouldn't let them out of the house. When they ran out of food, he went to buy it himself. When he came back, all seven boys were dead—their throats slit. In that same neighborhood, in a house belonging to Abdillahi Ibrahim Aden, soldiers heard them listening to the BBC. They killed four boys with bazookas.

The shelling wouldn't cease, so we hid in another house. We tried to escape between the compounds of the 24th and the 11th sector of the army. We went to the dry-river bed, about 100 of us, but were driven away by soldiers. Then we tried to escape through a place called Meegaga but turned back when we saw soldiers again. Everyone then just fled—escaping in whatever way they could. I couldn't walk fast, let alone run, because of my foot. One of my cousins and I got lost. We hid in a hut and were found by another cousin who had come to look for us. I couldn't go on. My leg hurt too much. My cousins found a donkey cart for me. We reached Qool'Aday after three days. We found thousands of other people there. I had no idea what had happened to my children and mother.

The final testimony is that of Abdi Mohamed, who Robert Hitchcock interviewed in London in July 1990. Mr. Mohamed had gone to visit relatives in the countrywide southeast of Burao in Toghdeer Region. His relatives, who were nomads, had been attacked from the air, their camp bombed and strafed by Somali government planes. They had also found their main water points poisoned, and most of their camels had died from thirst. His testimony indicates the degree to which pastoral nomads were victimized by the Somali government.

Several months before the army attacked Burao [May 27, 1988], I went to see my children who had been staying in the area outside Ainabo. Two of my sons had been arrested by soldiers and accused of being members of the Somali National Movement. The soldiers said that they and other nomads were giving food to the SNM. They beat them very badly in prison but my sons told the soldiers nothing. When they got out they sent word to me in Burao to join them. As I travelled there, I saw many *barkad* [water reservoirs] that had been blown up by the army. One of the soldiers on the truck said that the army destroyed the reservoirs to punish the Isaaks for helping the SNM. They also killed the camels and cattle of people so that they had to move in to the cities to get food. Land mines were placed around the *barkad* to keep people away.

When I got to my sons' camp I found that some of my relatives had been killed. They were shot by the army after some soldiers were hurt by a mine on one of the roads. At night I could hear explosions and gunshots. In the morning we would sometimes find the bodies of people and livestock in camps that had been destroyed by the soldiers. Some of the bodies were burned. I will never forget the smell.

There were so many people killed, nearly all of them Isaaks. The government in Mogadishu wanted to destroy the Isaaks ever since 1982 when a state of emergency was declared.

Account 3: The Tyua of Western Zimbabwe

The Tyua Bushmen of western Zimbabwe and northeastern Botswana are an agropastoral and fishing people who are former foragers. Numbering approximately 1,000 in the Tsholotsho and Bulalima Mangwe Districts in western Zimbabwe and 6,000 in northern Botswana, the Tyua were affected by dispossession as a result of land being set aside for white settlers, the establishment of national parks and game reserves, the imposition of hunting laws which prevented them from obtaining wildlife legally, and forced resettlement into "protected villages" during the Zimbabwean War of Independence (1965–1980). Today many Tyua work on the farms and ranches of other people, including Tswana, Kalanga, and Ndebele and they sell handicrafts, meat, salt, and beer to earn extra income.

In the early 1980s, after Zimbabwe achieved its independence, tensions continued to be felt, particularly in Matabeleland, where one of the major groups of freedom fighters, the Zimbabwe African Peoples Liberation Army, the military wing of the Zimbabwe African Peoples Union (ZAPU), had its primary base of support. Some of the former guerrillas felt that they had not been treated appropriately by the new government, and tensions erupted into conflict in late 1980 and early 1981. Some of the former guerrillas returned to the bush and began what turned into a low-level insurgency. Beginning in 1982 and continuing into the mid-1980s, the Zimbabwe government carried out counterinsurgency operations against what they termed "dissidents." These operations included military attacks on villagers in western Zimbabwe, kidnappings of suspected terrorists, torture and murder of detainees, committing a wide range of atrocities against the civilian population, and restriction of the movement of food into the area.

The man who described some of these and other events occurring in the 1982–1985 period was an elderly Tyua who had been imprisoned during the Zimbabwe war for independence. Subsequently, he was detained by the new government on suspicion of having supported the dissidents. The interview was conducted by Robert Hitchcock in Tsholotsho, Zimbabwe, on June 26, 1989. The man requested that his name not be used.

I was living in western Tsholotsho just south of Hwange.[7] I used to live in the game reserve but we were forced to leave by the whites. My father hunted elephants there but he was arrested and put in prison. I helped my mother and brothers and sisters by collecting salt at Sua. But then the war came[8] and the Selous Scouts[9] came to our village and beat us up. My brother was shot as we watched. They kept saying, "You are Bushmen. You should not support the black people."[10] I was glad when Smith[11] lost the war and we got a new government. I voted in the elections. I thought that everything would be good with a new government. The Bushmen would be treated like other people, not flogged with sticks like we were by the white farmers.

Then the killings began. At first it was white people, part of Smith's army, who came to Tsholotsho and shot people. I saw my best friend taken away by the soldiers in a truck. I never saw him again. Many people were taken away. The soldiers came at night. Sometimes they shot people in their beds. They were after Ndebele and Bushmen. They called us dissidents. But we were just people trying to make a living.

At that time the drought was very bad. There were no crops in the fields, and the wild fruits were very few. Even elands[12] were dying in the bush. Then the government said we could not get food. They stopped the trucks from coming to the stores. We were very hungry, and children and old people died of starvation. People even ate their skin blankets and shoes.

It was then that the soldiers in red hats[13] came to my village. They said that we should send women to help them carry water. Later we learned that the women had been raped. Two of the women from our village were shot by the soldiers. The army people would come to Tsholotsho and say that we were dissidents. They pointed to people and they were taken away. Later we heard they had been killed and their bodies dumped into old mines. There were many places where the bodies were left. We would sometimes find them when we were looking for lost cattle.

My close friend Khunou was arrested by the soldiers. They said that he had robbed stores and stolen cattle. I told them that he was innocent, but they said, "He is just a Bushman. Bushmen are animals." That night they shot him. His wife and children fled to Botswana after the soldiers burned their houses and killed their chickens.

I was arrested by the soldiers in red hats and taken to an army base. They did not give us food or water. They tortured me by putting my head in water and hitting me on the backside. They kept calling me a "dumb Bushman." Some of the people in the camp with me died from the beatings.

Many innocent people died because of the army. We were just trying to make a living like we always have. But they felt we were just Bushmen. I wondered then why I voted for this government.

Chapter Fourteen
The Rwanda Genocide

René Lemarchand

Since April 1994 Rwanda has become a synonym for one of the worst genocides of the twentieth century. An estimated half a million people, mostly Tutsi, were killed in the course of a carnage that claimed twice as many victims in one month as the Bosnian civil war in two years. To this must be added almost as many deaths caused by military engagements, cholera, dysentery, famine, and sheer human exhaustion.

As much as the appalling scale of the bloodletting, it is the element of planned annihilation that gives the Rwanda killings their genocidal quality. The parallel with the 1972 genocide in Burundi immediately comes to mind. Although the threats to the ruling ethnocracies—the Hutu in Rwanda, the Tutsi in Burundi—came from identifiable groups of armed opponents, in the end entire civilian communities became the targets of ethnic cleansing (e.g., large-scale ethnic massacres)—the Hutu in Burundi, the Tutsi in Rwanda. In both states the enemy was demonized, made the incarnation of evil, and dealt with accordingly; in both instances the killings were planned and orchestrated from above and owed little or nothing to a supposedly spontaneous outburst of anger from below.

Where Rwanda differs from Burundi is not just that the "rebels" happen to be Tutsi, but that they are Tutsi refugees, or sons of refugees, who were driven out of the country in the wake of the 1959–62 Hutu-led revolution. Few would have imagined that thirty years later the sons of the refugee diaspora in Uganda would form the nucleus of a Tutsi-dominated politico-military organization—the Front Patriotique Rawndais (FPR)—that would successfully fight its way back into the country and defeat an army three times its size. Fewer still would have anticipated the price of their victory. Between the FPR invasion on October 1, 1990, and the fall of the capital (Kigali) on July 4, 1994, the killings wiped out one-tenth of Rwanda's population of seven million.

Seen in the broader context of twentieth-century genocides, the Rwanda tragedy underscores the universality—one might say the "normality"—of African phenomena. The logic that set in motion the infernal machine of the Rwanda killings is indeed no less "rational" than that which presided over the extermination of millions of human beings in Hitler's Germany or Pol Pot's Cambodia. The implication, lucidly stated by Helen Fein (1994), is worth bearing in mind: "Genocide is preventable because it is usually a rational act: that is, the perpetrators calculate the likelihood of success, given their values and objectives" (p. 5).

Mythologies

It is imperative to explode the myths surrounding the Rwanda genocide. Contrary to the image conveyed by the media, there is nothing in the historical record to suggest a kind of tribal meltdown rooted in "deep seated antagonisms" or "longstanding atavistic hatreds." Nor is there any evidence in support of the "spontaneous action from below" thesis. From this perspective, the killings are largely reducible to a collective outburst of blind fury set off by the shooting down of President Habyalimana's plane on April 6, 1994. However widespread, both views are travesties of reality. What they mask is the political manipulation that lies behind the systematic massacre of innocent civilians.

It is not my intention to dispose of one myth by promulgating another—the fantasy of a precolonial society where Hutu and Tutsi lived in an eternally blissful harmony. Precolonial Rwanda was unquestionably one of the most centralized and rigidly stratified societies in the Great Lakes region. Representing approximately 85 percent of a total population estimated at two million at the turn of the century, the Hutu peasants were clearly at the bottom of the heap, socially, economically, and politically; but if power, status, and wealth were generally in Tutsi hands, not every Tutsi was powerful and wealthy.

Inequality was inscribed in the differential treatment accorded to each group, and within each group. Nonetheless, Hutu and Tutsi shared the same language and culture, the same clan names, and the same customs, and the symbols of kingship served as a powerful unifying bond between them. Nor was conflict necessarily more intense or frequent between Hutu and Tutsi than between Tutsi and Tutsi. Much of the historical evidence suggests precisely the opposite.[1]

Although the potential for conflict existed long before the advent of

European rule, it was the Belgian colonial state that provided the crucible within which ethnic identities were reshaped and mythologized. The result was to drastically alter the norms and texture of traditional Rwanda society. It was the colonial state that destroyed the countervailing mechanisms built around the different categories of chiefs and subchiefs, thus adding significantly to the oppressiveness of Tutsi rule. It was the colonial state that insisted that each individual carry an identity card specifying his/her ethnic background, a practice perpetuated until 1994, when "tribal cards" often spelled the difference between life and death; and it was with the blessings of the colonial state that Christian missionaries began to speculate about the "Hamitic" origins of the kingdom, drawing attention to the distinctively Ethiopian features, and hence the foreign origins, of the Tutsi "caste" (Linden, 1977). Indirect rule, synonymous with Tutsi rule, found added legitimacy in the Hamitic lucubrations of Christian clerics, and they eventually provided the ideological ballast of the Hutu revolution, before reappearing in 1994 in the form of a violently anti-Tutsi propaganda.

The Legacy of Revolution

After decades of unrelenting support of Tutsi rule, Belgian policies underwent a radical shift in the mid-1950s.[2] Partly in response to pressure from the U.N. Trusteeship Council, and partly as a result of the arrival in Rwanda of a new generation of Catholic missionaries, imbued with the ideals of Christian Democracy, a sustained effort was made to extend educational opportunities to an increasing number of Hutu elements. This radical policy shift provoked immediate resistance from the custodians of Tutsi supremacy—that is, chiefs, subchiefs, and Tutsi intellectuals generally—while prompting educated Hutu elements to press their claims for social reform upon the trusteeship authorities.

Ethnic violence suddenly erupted in November 1959, in the form of a Hutu jacquerie directed against Tutsi chiefs. Hundreds of people were killed on both sides of the ethnic fault line. Though quickly brought under control by the intervention of Belgian troops, the rural uprising marked the first phase of a revolutionary process culminating in January 1961 with a Hutu-led, Belgian-assisted coup that formally abolished the monarchy and led to the proclamation of a de facto republican regime under Hutu rule. By the time Rwanda acceded to independence on July 1, 1962, some 200,000 Tutsi had been forced into exile, the majority seeking asylum in Uganda, Burundi, and Zaire. Not until 32 years and a million deaths later would the destiny of Rwanda be once again entrusted to Tutsi hands. The Hutu revolution constitutes a critical element in the background of the genocide: by forcibly displacing from their homeland tens of thousands of Tutsi—now in a homeless limbo and determined to go back to their country, by force if necessary—the revolution planted the seeds of the refugee-warrior militancy that led to the creation of the FPR in 1990.[3] By the same token, to the extent that the Hutu revolution came to be identified with a "democratic," "antifeudal" mass movement, its enemies could only be described in opposite terms, as feudal counterrevolutionaries bent upon restoring minority rule. It is not by accident that during the killings the Tutsi were collectively identified by Hutu ideologues with the "Feudo-Hamitic" enemy.

The Ideology of Genocide

The root cause of the Rwanda genocide lies in the extent to which collective identities have been mythologized and manipulated for political advantage. Today Hutu and Tutsi are not just ethnic labels; they are social categories that carry an enormous emotional charge. Tutsi are seen by many Hutu as culturally alien to Rwanda, their presence traceable to "Hamitic invaders from the north" who used ruse and cunning—gifts of cattle and beautiful women—to enslave the unsuspecting Hutu agriculturalists. Only the Hutu—that is the Bantu people, as distinct from the Hamites—qualify as authentic Rwandans. That such portrayals are at odds with every shred of evidence available is immaterial. The point is that they are critical elements in the cognitive map of Hutu ideologues. The Hamitic frame of reference is central to an understanding of the ideology of genocide. This is where the legacy of missionary historiography—evolving from speculation about cultural affinities between Hamites and Coptic Christianity to politicized dogma about the Ethiopian origins of the Tutsi—contributed a distinctly racist edge to the discourse of Hutu politicians.

Already the ideological stock-in-trade of Hutu revolutionaries in the 1950s, official references to the Hamitic peril gained renewed salience in the wake of the FPR invasion. The attack on Kagitumba on October 1, 1990, suddenly gave ominous credibility to the image of the Tutsi as an alien invader: did they not invade the country from the north, like their forefathers, this time with arms and ammunition provided by Uganda? Is it not the case that many of the soldiers who were enlisted in the ranks of the FPR were born in Uganda and that its leaders had close ties with President Museveni of Uganda, whose Hima origins are sufficient proof of his Hamitic sympathies? And, with characteristic cunning, did they not try to dupe President Juvenal Habyalimana into accepting the Arusha accords, which, if implemented, would have posed a mortal threat to the democratic heritage of the Hutu revolution?

What emerges from the incitements to violence distilled by Radio Mille Collines and other vectors of Hutu propaganda is an image of the Tutsi as both alien and clever—not unlike the image of the Jew in Nazi propaganda. His alienness disqualifies him as a member of the national community; his cleverness turns him into a permanent threat to the unsuspecting Hutu. Nothing short of physical liquidation can deal with such danger.

The Road to Apocalypse

With the birth of several opposition parties in 1991 a whole new set of actors entered the political arena, adding an entirely new dimension to the security threats posed by the FPR invasion. For the first time since the Hutu revolution of 1959 the circumstances were ripe for a strategic alliance between the enemies from within and those from without.

Predictably, this convergence of external and internal threats generated intense fears within the ruling party, the Mouvement Révolutionnaire National pour le Développement (MRND). At stake was not just the monopoly of power exercised by the party leadership, or even the structure of Hutu domination, but the political survival of a regime entirely controlled by northern Hutu elements. It is worth remembering in this connection that during much of the First Republic (1962–1973) power lay in the hands of Hutu politicians from the south-central regions; not until the coup of July 1973, instigated by Major-General Juvenal Habyalimana, and the proclamation of the Second Republic (1973–1994), did the northerners emerge as the dominant force in the government, the administration, the party, and the army.

Given the nature of their ethno-regional underpinnings, and shared resentment of northern Hutu rule, it is hardly surprising that the three major opposition parties—the ethnically mixed Parti Libéral (PL), the Parti Social-Démocrate (PSD), and the Mouvement Démocratique Républicain (MDR)—should have been perceived by MRND hard-liners as potential allies of the FPR, and therefore as presumptive traitors—the PL because of its mixed Hutu-Tutsi membership, the PSD and MDR because they drew much of their support from the Hutu masses of the south-central regions.

In this three-cornered politico-military struggle the Tutsi civilian populations became political pawns. Courted by the PL, solicited for cash and food (and sometimes threatened) by the FPR, thoroughly distrusted by the MRND, a good many Tutsi ended up joining hands with the FPR because they felt they had no other option. Official suspicions that every Tutsi, by ethnic definition, harbored pro-FPR sympathies created the conditions of a self-fulfilling prophecy. The wholesale slaughter of hundreds of Bagogwe (a Tutsi subgroup) in northern Rwanda in January 1991, followed by the cold-blooded murder of thousands of Tutsi civilians in the Bugesera region in March 1992, set a pattern of localized ethnic cleansing that went on almost uninterruptedly in the months preceding the genocide.

Anti-Tutsi violence increased in proportion to the magnitude of the threats posed by the FPR, but also as a result of the organizational steps taken to counter such threats. Reference must be made here to the massive recruitment and training of Hutu militias. Known in Kinyarwanda as *interhamwe* ("those who stand together"), they were ostensibly organized to protect civilians against FPR attacks; their real function, however, was to serve as a paramilitary force trained to provide auxiliary slaughterhouse support to the police, the gendarmerie, and the regular army. While the *interhamwe* came to be identified with the MRND, another group, the *impunza mugambi* ("the single-minded ones"), linked up with an even more fanatically anti-Tutsi party, the Coalition pour la Défense de la République (CDR). On the eve of the genocide the militias claimed a total membership of 50,000.

By 1992 the institutional apparatus of genocide was already in place. It involved four distinctive levels of activity or sets of actors:

a. the so-called *akazu* ("little house" in Kinyarwanda): consisting of Habyalimana's wife Agathe, his three-brothers-in-law (Protais Zigiranyirazo, Seraphim Rwakumba, and Elie Sagatwa), and a sprinkling of trusted advisers, this core group was directly responsible for planning and orchestrating the genocide;

b. the rural organizers: recruited among communal and prefectoral personnel, such as préfets, sous-préfets, bourgmestres, conseillers communaux, and numbering anywhere from three to five hundred, they supplied the middle-level cadres in charge of engineering and supervising the killings in the communes;

c. the militias (*interhamwe*): often operating in tandem with the police and the gendarmerie, they formed the ground-level operatives in charge of doing the actual killing. Many also played a key role in "persuading" (at gunpoint) Hutu civilians to kill their Tutsi neighbors. Although the term came to designate a variety of self-appointed killers, the core group has been described as "forming up to 1 or 2 percent of the population; they killed out of conviction; they were trained to kill, often smoked hashish and are thought to have killed between 200–300 people each" (Physicians for Human Rights, 1994, p. 11);

d. the presidential guard: numbering approximately 6,000, and recruited exclusively among northerners, they were trained specifically to assist civilian death squads. The systematic killing of opposition figures, Hutu and Tutsi, in the days immediately following the crash of the presidential plane on April 6, 1994, was essentially the work of the presidential guard.

The sociological profile of the killers reflects the diversity of their social and institutional ties. Especially noteworthy, however, is the number of intellectuals and professional people who participated in the slaughter. Despite many exceptions to the rule, one cannot fail to notice the number of journalists, medical doctors, agronomists, teachers, university lecturers, and even priests who were identified by survivors as accomplices in the massacre of innocent civilians. At the other end of the social spectrum were the hundreds and thousands of landless Hutu peasants and unemployed city youth whose prime motivation for killing was to steal their victims' property, their land, their furniture, their radio, or what little cash they happened to carry.

What set in motion the wheels of this infernal machine was complex, a sequence of events that began with the Arusha (Tanzania) conference (June 1992–August 1993) and ended with the shooting down of President Habyalimana's plane on April 6, 1994.

Although compromise was the very essence of the power-sharing formula hammered out at Arusha—whereby the FPR would have as many seats in the transitional government and legislature as the MRND and would contribute 40 percent of the troops and 50 percent of the officer corps to the new Rwandan army—for the hard-liners within the party and the *akazu* this was tantamount to betrayal. By instigating ethnic violence on a substantial scale in several localities, MRND/CDR extremists had every intention to derail the peace process. The wanton killing of innocent civilians thus became the quickest way of eliminating all basis for compromise with the FPR.

The decisive event that played directly into the hands of the extremists and sounded the death knell of the Arusha accords, however, was the assassination of Burundi President Melchior Ndadaye on October 21, 1993. As the first popularly elected Hutu president in the history of Burundi, his election brought to a close 28 years of Tutsi hegemony, and this after a transition widely described by outside observers as "exemplary" (Lemarchand, 1994). His death at the hands of an all-Tutsi army sent an immediate and powerful message to the Hutu of Rwanda: "You simply cannot trust the Tutsi!" With Ndadaye's death vanished what few glimmers of hope remained that Arusha might pave the way for a lasting compromise with the FPR.

Whether Habyalimana, under tremendous pressure from MNRD extremists, still hoped that Arusha could provide the basis for an orderly transition is hard to tell; that many in his entourage perceived him as an obstacle to genocide (and the imputation of his death to the FPR as justification for it) is highly probable, however. This is where the shooting down of Habyalimana's plane on April 6—on a return flight from a regional summit in Dar es Salaam, where broad agreement was reached on the security measures necessary to ensure implementation of the Arusha accords—seems consistent with the overall strategy of Hutu extremists within and outside the *akazu*. Despite the lack of solid evidence in support of an *akazu*-sponsored plot, it is easy to see the logic that might have prompted such a move. Not only did Habyalimana's death remove once and for all the specter of Arusha, but by making it unmistakably clear that "it was the FPR that did it," the same extremists could now point to their "dastardly crime" as justification for genocidal retribution.

Descent into Hell

In Kigali the killing of opposition figures, Hutu and Tutsi, began a few hours after the crash, on the basis of pre-established lists. The first to be targeted were moderate Hutu politicians affiliated with the MDR (Mouvement Démocratique Républicain) and PSD (Parti Social-Démocrate), and the Tutsi leadership and rank and file of the PL, including its president, Lando Ndasingwa. At this stage little attention was paid to ethnic criteria. Anyone suspected of FPR sympathies was seen as a traitor. Included in this category were the prime minister, Agathe Uwilingiyimana, the president of the Constitutional Court, the minister of Labor and Social Affairs, and countless other lower-ranking officials.

Opposition figures were disposed of in a matter of hours. Doing away with hundreds of thousands of Tutsi civilians—and thousands of Hutu in the Gitarama and Butare prefecture—proved a more difficult undertaking. Where local authorities refused to yield to the murderous injunctions coming from Kigali (as in Butare, where the préfet managed to keep things relatively peaceful for ten days after the slaughter began in Kigali), they were the first to be killed when the *interhamwe* showed up.

Forty-eight hours after the crash the carnage began to spread through the countryside, causing thousands of panic-stricken Tutsi to flee their homes. Some were sheltered by Hutu neighbors, others tried to flee to FPR-controlled areas, others still sought refuge in churches or went into hiding in neighboring swamps. The worst massacres occurred in churches and mission compounds, as in Nyamata, Musha, Karubamba. In Musha, 40 kilometers north of the capital, where some 1,200 Tutsi had sought refuge, the militias went to work at 8:00 a.m. on April 8; not until the evening was the "job" (*akazi*) done.

Throughout the carnage "the militias were exhorted by the privately-owned Radio Mille Collines, which continued to broadcast messages like 'the enemy is out there—go get him!' and 'The graves are only half full!'" (Richburg, 1994, p. 4). In a number of localities Hutu were ordered by the militias to kill their Tutsi neighbors; failure to comply meant a death warrant for themselves and their families.

The methods used by the militias are described with clinical precision in a report by Physicians for Human Rights (1994): "The *interhamwe* used the following methods of killing: machetes, massues (clubs studded with nails), small axes, knives, grenades, guns, fragmentation grenades, beatings to death, amputations with exsanguination, buried alive, drowned, or raped and killed later. Many victims had both their achilles tendons cut with machetes as they ran away, to immobilize them so that they could be finished off later" (p. 11).

Although the killings have stopped, the country bears countless traces of its recent agonies. Some of the wounds inflicted by ethnic hatreds may never heal. Meanwhile, the legacy of genocide casts a long shadow on the capacity of Rwanda society to rise again from its own ashes. Not only does it raise obvious questions about the chances of peaceful coexistence at home, it also impels one to wonder whether the two million Hutu refugees currently living in neighboring territories have any inclination to exchange the insecurities and hardships of life in exile for the fragile guarantees of a "fresh start" in their homeland.

Eyewitness Accounts
The Rwanda Genocide

Unlike the events surrounding the 1972 genocide in Burundi, a number of eyewitness accounts of the horrors surrounding the Rwanda genocide are available from a variety of sources. Journalists, human rights activists, members of the clergy, and others have collected a rich harvest of first-hand testimonies. Nowhere, however, are the human dimensions of the cataclysm conveyed in more chilling detail than in the London-based African Rights publication *Rwanda: Death, Despair and Defiance* by Rakiya Omaar (1994). Except for account 3, excerpted from a July 1994 report by Physicians for Human Rights (UK), *Rwanda 1994: A Report of the Genocide*, all of the testimonies below are drawn from the African Rights report.

Account 1

The following account brings out the critical role played by local government authorities—bourgmestres, communal counselors, préfets and sous-préfets —in organizing the killings in the countryside. It draws from the testimonies of Antoine Mugambira, from the Kivu commune (Gikongoro prefecture), and Francois Nzeyimana, from the Muganza commune, also in Gikongoro:

> We were attacked by interhamwe, CDR [the Coalition pour la Défense de la République], MDR-Power [Hutu hardliners in the MDR] and MRND [the Mouvement Révolutionnaire National pour le Développement]. Among those who led the attack were a certain Mukama, a soldier, together with the bourgmestre of the commune Kivu. They set fire to houses, destroyed our property and ate our cows. We fled to Muganza parish. When we arrived there we met many other people from Muganza. . . . We were with white nuns who said, "Fight those people because they are killers." The second day they came back with four soldiers, reservists from Ngara and two from Nyabimata. They shot at us and left us with fourteen wounded and six dead. That was on Saturday. On Sunday, we fled again, to Cyahinda. Soldiers shot at us. Interhamwe too. We fought them one day, the day we arrived there.
>
> Two of my children were killed, Nkusi and Muhire. I know the killer. He was a soldier, Mukama. He had a gun; he is the one who shot many people. They would shoot at a hundred or two hundred

people. . . . It is all former soldiers who killed us. Those who fell over were beaten up with clubs or hacked to death.

In the night we decided to flee to Burundi. On the Mubuga side we saw many dead bodies, for example children on top of their dead mothers . . . When we arrived in a place called Kukibuga, in a market place called Kugisenyi, we saw more than three hundred people who had been killed with their children. They were piled up. (African Rights [1994] *Rwanda: Death, Despair and Defiance*, pp. 366–367)

With other peasants we fled together at Muganza and we put up some fight against the killers by throwing stones at them but later they brought guns and shot indiscriminately. So many people were killed. Some fled to Cyahinda but there was burning and killing, so some are dead.

The killers included the bourgmestre called Juvenal Muhitira, helped by some local police. One of the policemen was called Mukama, another one called Ngenzi and others who were armed. Others who killed my parents were gendarmes who were supposed to be protecting them. They were led by Damien Biniga who was the sous-préfet. I saw more than fifteen dead bodies in all when I took my brother to the parish. We tried to take the worst off for treatment but the white doctors and nurses had fled themselves. When we went to the Nahihi commune, the local people threw spears and stones at us. The gendarmes drove us into the forest and many people were killed. We were about four hundred people when we entered the forest but only forty-five got out. (African Rights (1994) *Rwanda: Death, Despair and Defiance*, pp. 367–368)

Account 2

Nothing is more revealing of the extent of the moral breakdown engendered by the genocide than the wholesale desecration of churches. More people have been killed in churches and church compounds than in any other site. Among many others, the churches of Ntamara, Nyarabuye, the Centre Christus in Kigali, became the scene of incredible cruelties. The first testimony, by Josianne Mukeshimana, a fifteen-year-old schoolgirl, recounts what happened in Ntamara; the second, by a thirteen-year-old girl named Makuramanzi, describes the scene after she survived the massacre at Nyamata:

The day after the President died, houses started burning in our commune. Refugees began streaming in from other areas. We panicked as we saw interhamwe following people everywhere. The second day we left home and went to look for protection in the church of Ntamara. But we were not to find any protection in the church.

About five days after we had been there, there was an attack against the church. When we saw them coming, we closed the doors. They broke the doors down and tore down some of the bricks in the back wall. They threw a few grenades through the holes where the bricks had been. But most people who died were killed by machetes. When they came in, they were obviously furious that we had closed the doors. So they really macheted the refugees. The attackers were interhamwe but they were not from our sector. They were ordinary villagers from somewhere else. They surrounded the church to knock down anyone who escaped.

In a fury those inside really desecrated the church, destroying the statues. They told us: "We are destroying your church!" People could not leave. But it was also intolerable to remain in one's position as the macheting continued. So like the mad, people ran up and down inside the church. All around you, people were being killed and wounded.

Eventually I decided to drop down among the dead. I raised my head slightly; an interhamwe hurled a brick at me. It hit me just on top of my eye. My face became covered with blood which was useful in making them think I was even more dead. I tried to stop breathing so they would really believe that I was dead. The macheting continued all round me.

Once they thought most people were dead, they paid more attention to looting the dead. Most of them left. But one of them was not satisfied with his loot. He remained in the church. . . . He came to search my pockets and discovered that I was alive. He threatened to kill me unless I paid him. I said I had no money. He took my watch. In the meantime the other attackers were calling out to him, warning him that he might be killed if he delays any longer. He left. (African Rights [1994] *Rwanda: Death, Despair and Defiance*, pp. 488–489)

I tried to get up but it was in vain. I was very weak from my injuries and there were so many bodies everywhere that you could hardly move. A few children, perhaps because they were unaware of the dangers, stood up. I called one of the children to help me. She was a girl of about nine. She replied that she could not help me because they had cut off her arms. I struggled and managed to sit up. But what I could not do was to stand up. I tried and tried but just could not do it. Finally I saw a young woman I knew, a neighbor. I called out to her. At first she did not answer. I insisted and finally she responded. When I looked closely I saw she too had had her arms cut off.

By now I don't know if what I am feeling and seeing is real life or a nightmare. I asked her if it was real life. She tried to get someone else to help me but could not find anyone. Eventually I forced myself to get up and out of the church. When I got out I got so scared that I returned to the church in spite of the dead bodies. I spent the night there with all the corpses around me. (African Rights [1994] *Rwanda: Death, Despair and Defiance*, p, 3)

Account 3

Next to churches, hospitals became a prime target for the massacre of civilians. The search for, and subsequent killing, of wounded survivors of previous massacres were frequent occurrences at the Centre Hospitalier in Kigali, at the Caraes Psychiatric Hospital at Ndera, and the Butare Hospital. On April 23 militias and soldiers from the Rwandan army killed 170 patients and medical personnel at the Butare Hospital. Dr. Claude-Emile Rowagoneza was present at the hospital when the massacre began on April 21. This is his testimony:

The massacres were delayed until April 20th. That day everyone was asked to stay at home except those working in the hospital. Medical staff were transported to the hospital. Nurses had to walk and many were stopped at the check point, asked to show their identity cards and killed if they were Tutsi. There were 35 doctors at the hospital of which four were Tutsi. Because of the danger all four Tutsi stayed at the hospital as did some nurses. Drs. Jean-Bosco Rugira and Jean-Claude Kanangire are known to have been killed, and the fate of Dr. Isidore Kanangare who was hiding in the hospital and may have been evacuated by the French, is unknown.

In mid-May injured soldiers from the Kanombe barracks started being brought to Butare Hospital and no more civilians were being admitted. They also started deciding who were Tutsi on the basis of their features, looking at the nose, height and fingers because the identity cards were no longer accurate. Some of the doctors at the hospital risked their lives by helping threatened staff by hiding and feeding them. . . .

When the patients' wounds had healed some of the doctors—the 'bad' doctors—expelled the Tutsi even though everyone knew they would be killed outside. At night the interhamwe and the soldiers came in but these doctors were colluding willingly. If people refused to go they were taken out at night. They could be seen being killed by the interhamwe waiting at the gates. Later the prime minister came down to Butare— apparently the educated people in Butare asked him to come, and while here he had a meeting with medical staff. They all said peace had returned and told the patients that it was safe to return home. They wanted those who were remaining here to go. Those who did were then killed. . . .

No one knew who my family were. We had good neighbors who said my family were Hutu. My wife was taken twice by interhamwe but neighbors insisted that she was Hutu. We have a six-month-old daughter. My sister, mother and father fled to Burundi but all my aunts and uncles and in-laws were killed except for my mother-in-law. In other words more than 40 of my relatives were killed.

I spent my time hiding in a toilet at the hospital. Eventually I left the hospital and stayed with another friendly Hutu doctor who took me to another Hutu friend who hid me in his toilet. . . . On July 2nd, there was general panic as the FPR arrived. That night I moved from his friend's house to my own home. (Physicians for Human Rights [1994] *Rwanda 1994: A Report of the Genocide*, pp. 27–28)

Account 4

Attempts by the perpetrators of genocide to dehumanize their victims took many forms. Particularly horrible were the methods used to force members of the same family to kill their immediate relatives. The following account, by a 24-year-old Tutsi, Venuste Hakizamungu, tells how he was forced by a group of interhamwe to kill his own brother, Theoneste Ruykwirwa, suspected of FPR sympathies:

When the killings started our family was not aware that Tutsi were the target. Therefore we had had no time to plan our escape. Trouble began in another part of our sector, at Nyagasambu, but soon spread to our cellule. In both cellules people were chased by interhamwe who had been brought in from Bugesera. They assembled everyone in a group. When it came to our family, Hutu residents from both cellules tried to pass us off as Hutu by saying that "there was no tutsiship in our family." Those neighbors who we thought were trying to defend us told us to escape to a neighboring village. We left. We realized later that they were not trying to defend us. There was pressure on them to kill us and they did not want to kill us themselves. So they sent us to be killed to another village. . . .

My brother Theoneste went to the nearest village. But the people there refused to kill him. . . . The next day he came home and went straightaway to a roadblock surrounded by interhamwe. He told them to kill him themselves and end the story there. These interhamwe brought him back to the house. They told us that he had to be killed in order to prove that the whole family were not agents of the FPR. They left him in the house, knowing that he would not try to escape. During this time messages were coming in every hour, urging our family to kill Theoneste. The whole family was threatened with death unless we killed Theoneste. He begged us to kill him, saying that the only alternative was death for the whole family and a very cruel death for him. . . .

After these four days about twenty interhamwe, armed with machetes, hoes, spears and bows and arrows, came to the house. They stood over me and said: "Kill him!" Theoneste got up and spoke to me. "I fear being killed by a machete; so please go ahead and kill me but use a small hoe." He himself brought the hoe and handed it to me. I hit him on the head. I kept hitting him on the head but he would not die. It was agonizing. Finally I took the machete he dreaded in order to finish him off quickly. The interhamwe were there during the whole time, supervising what they called "work." When Theoneste was dead they left. The next day I buried him. And I escaped immediately afterwards. (African Rights [1994] *Rwanda: Death, Despair and Defiance*, pp. 344–345)

Account 5

The rape of women and girls constitutes yet another form of dehumanization. Many of the victims were subsequently killed. One of the few survivors is a seventeen-year old girl named Louise. This is how she described her ordeal:

They came back for me. They were three delinquents. As they came towards me, they were discussing how they were going to kill me. But then one of the thugs recognized me, saying "but she is the daughter of so and so. He is a rich man." They said I should give them money since my father is well off. I confessed I had no money. They continued to discuss ways of killing me.

Then one of them suggested that they should rape me instead. The three of them raped me in turns. Each having finished, he walked away. As the last one finished a new group of interhamwe arrived. They ordered the man who raped me last to rape me again. He refused. Then they threatened to burn both of us alive unless he raped me again. So he raped me again.

When he was through, the new group of interhamwe beat me up. Then they said, "OK let's go. We want to show you where you are going to go." They threw me into the pit latrine. The man who pushed me pushed me so hard that instead of falling in I fell across. He dragged me back by the legs and I fell in upright, on top of my aunt. I could still hear the thugs talking. One of them said I might still be alive and suggested throwing a grenade in. Another commented, "Don't waste your grenade. A kid thrown that deep cannot be alive." They left.

I tried to climb out. But I had bled so much I was feeling dizzy. I felt I had no strength left in me. I kept falling down. Finally I collapsed. . . . When somebody came to take me out of the pit, I didn't know who it was. I realized I was out of the pit when I regained consciousness. I saw a soldier standing next to me. . . . (African Rights [1994] *Rwanda: Death, Despair and Defiance*, p. 425)

Afterword
Genocide in Bosnia-Herzegovina?

Steven L. Burg

Has genocide occurred in Bosnia-Herzegovina? In this essay, I answer this question from the perspective of a specialist in the politics of the former Yugoslavia and a student of the politics surrounding the war in Bosnia-Herzegovina. Because I am not a specialist on genocide as an analytical concept or historical phenomenon, I turn first to the meaning of the question itself. I then turn to problems of context and evidence.

By "context" I refer to the broader political significance of the decision to define certain events as genocide. The determination of genocide is a highly politicized process. This is especially true of instances in which, as in Bosnia-Herzegovina, the ability of the parties involved to achieve their political goals is still in doubt and the determination of genocide can be expected to affect their ability to achieve them. It is not my intention here to polemicize with those who hold differing views on this question. My own views have changed more than once as the result of both the process of preparing this essay and the information that became available during late 1995 and early 1996 in the wake of the cease-fire and deployment of international troops to Bosnia-Herzegovina. I am acutely aware, therefore, that honest differences of interpretation are possible and that a definitive answer to the question may be many years of inquiry away. My purposes are, instead, to raise a number of concerns arising out of my commitment to scholarly inquiry as a mode of analysis and to underscore the importance of two interrelated obligations of scholars in the highly charged conditions that presently characterize inquiry into events in Bosnia-Herzegovina.

First, I believe that scholars must not allow the determination of genocide to become politicized. Second, and more important, they must not allow the determination of genocide to politicize and distort the nature of scholarship itself.

The determination of genocide depends, of course, on one's definition of the phenomenon and the criteria used to determine whether the phenomenon exists. Totten and Parsons' discussion (1995) of Raphael Lemkin's definition of the general phenomenon and the more narrow legal definition of the U.N. Genocide Convention suggests that the term can be applied to a very broad range of acts, but it seems clear that the Convention emphasizes violence and killing against persons. Intention to exterminate the target people is central to the definition (Sellers, 1995). The scope or magnitude required for such acts to be considered genocide is, however, undefined. In fact, the term "in whole or in part" that features prominently in the U.N. Convention leaves open the question of threshold and clearly suggests that small-scale acts of the type specified therein might qualify as genocide. This is at the same time both empirically problematic and morally laudable: It is problematic because it invites use of the label "genocide" to describe events that, in light of common sense, do not seem to qualify. In this way, it invites devaluation of the concept. To include destruction of "a part" of a people is at the same time laudable because to limit the phenomenon to the destruction of whole peoples might license their destruction by parts. The relative weight given to the whole and its parts is central to the process of determining genocide in Bosnia-Herzegovina, as the magnitude of apparent violations is quite different among the three warring parties.

Application of the U.N. definition to events in Bosnia-Herzegovina also raises the question of distinguishing between acts of war and genocide. Warfare often involves the destruction of peoples "in part." The fact that Bosnia is a case of ethnic war makes this distinction even more difficult to put into operation. The centrality of intent in definitions of genocide makes it difficult to distinguish between actions intended to achieve the central military-political goal of ethnic warfare—the establishment of exclusive power and control by one group over a targeted territory—and actions intended to achieve the destruction of a targeted group. Ethnic war has its origins in ethno-nationalist ideologies of exclusion, which legitimate and encourage the expulsion of ethnic aliens. This is not to argue that ethnic war always results in genocide. But it is to argue that the use of violence, intimidation and terror to achieve ethnic exclusivity as a means to a larger political-military end is likely to cross an unspecified threshold of genocide. This is especially the case when a target group resists giving up the land that is in dispute. The argument that actions specified in the Genocide Convention were the unintended consequence of resistance to implementation of an ideology that otherwise called "only" for expulsion is surely no defense against the charge of genocide. Criteria by which this threshold can be specified on the basis of behaviors alone, without necessarily having to enter into a debate over intent, are essential to the determination of genocide under conditions of interethnic warfare.

Helen Fein has developed a paradigm for achieving precisely this goal (Fein, 1993a, pp. 37–38). She identifies five conditions that distinguish genocide from other forms of warfare:

1. There is a sustained attack, or continuity of attacks, by the perpetrator to physically destroy group members.
2. The perpetrator is a collective or organized actor or a commander of organized actors.
3. The victims are selected because they are members of a group.
4. The victims are defenseless or are killed regardless of whether they surrendered or resisted.
5. The destruction of group members is undertaken with intent to kill and the murder is sanctioned by the perpetrators.

Fein developed this paradigm to distinguish between war crimes and genocide in Afghanistan and Vietnam, but it provides extremely useful guidance for evaluating the evidence in Bosnia-Herzegovina. Fein also identifies two conditions that reinforce genocide: the absence of sanctions against killing, or the failure to enforce them, and the presence of ideologies and beliefs legitimating genocide.

It is important to note that Fein does not suggest that the existence of a legitimating ideology constitutes evidence of genocide itself. It is the specific pattern of behaviors that constitute such evidence. Reference to ideology is an important means by which to *account* for genocide. The absence of sanctions against killing, or the failure to enforce them, represents another such means. But such a failure also represents a useful principle upon which to attribute responsibility for the actions in question.

The evidence in Bosnia-Herzegovina is incomplete as this is being written. Third-party actors (nongovernmental organizations, interested governments, and multinational organizations) have accumulated enormous amounts of first-hand information and eyewitness testimonies (e.g., Helsinki Watch, 1992–1933, and U.N., 1996). Large numbers of testimonies have been collected over a period of years that chronicle events from the beginning of the war in 1992 right up to the last stages of the fighting before the cease-fire in 1995. Journalists have provided additional details of events, although their accounts must be used with a great deal of caution. With the deployment of an international military force to keep the peace in December 1995, it has become possible for local and international actors to investigate allegations and pursue physical evidence in a manner that has not been possible up to now. In recent months, therefore, substantial new physical evidence of apparent violations has been discovered. It seems almost certain now that the quality and quantity of evidence of the type necessary to support the argument that genocide has occurred will increase. This is likely to strengthen the case for genocide and may even result in the discovery of evidence that implicates additional actors.

The full extent of the events in Bosnia-Herzegovina may never be known. Evidence of the genocide that took place during World War II was, literally, still being unearthed as the crisis in Bosnia unfolded (e.g., *Oslobodjenje*, 1990). That genocide was carried out by Croats, with the participation of some Muslim forces, against Serbs and Jews in the Independent State of Croatia, a fascist state allied with the Nazis that encompassed the territory of Bosnia-Herzegovina. Local media coverage of the discovery of the remains of victims of genocide in World War II may have contributed to the escalation of group fears and nationalist emotions. In the present case, the pursuit of such physical evidence is likely to go on for as long as peace is maintained in the country. The discovery of evidence with respect to intent and participation, however, is a different story.

The great powers probably control a significant amount of information relevant to this issue, gathered through intelligence sources such as electronic eavesdropping and aerial or satellite surveillance. However, they reveal such information only when it serves their narrowly defined interests (Zumach, 1996). It is almost certainly the case that information gathered through such means that contradicts the interpretation of events supported by these governments will never see the light of day. Information that supports their views may very well become public in the form of evidence submitted in connection with future prosecutions before the High Tribunal in the Hague. The most likely public sources of information about intent, though, will probably come from the testimony of the participants themselves—in court, in the media, and through memoir publications. Both the

7

recent BBC documentary, *Death of Yugoslavia*, and the published memoirs of such Yugoslav leaders as General Kadijevic and Borisav Jovic (Jovic, 1995) are relevant in this respect.

Despite the limitations inherent in these uncertainties, the mounting evidence that is available suggests that the killing, rapes, and other abuses against the Muslim civilian population carried out as part of the Serb effort to establish control and impose a nationalist regime over much of Bosnia-Herzegovina fit the definition of genocide contained in the U.N. Genocide Convention, and fulfill the conditions identified by Fein as distinguishing genocide from war crimes. Available evidence makes it clear that Serb forces carried out sustained or continuous attacks against the Muslim civilian population from the beginning of the war in 1992 right through the takeover of the Srebrenica enclave in July 1995 before the imposition of a cease-fire. It appears unquestionably to be the case that the victims of killings were selected because they were Muslims, that in the overwhelming proportion of cases they were defenseless, and that the killing was intentional.

With respect to the nature of the perpetrator (Fein's second criterion), it is clear that Serb paramilitary units constitute "a collective or organized actor" and played a major role in the killing. There is also some fragmentary evidence that high-level Serbian military commanders and political leaders authorized activities defined in the Convention as genocide. Bosnian Serb military commander Ratko Mladic, for example, is alleged by some witnesses to have overseen the mass killing of innocent civilians following the battle for Srebrenica in 1995 (O'Connor, 1996, pp. A1, A9). The killings in Srebrenica, when considered part of a sustained pattern of such actions, constitute genocide.

Stronger evidence of the direct authorization of such acts by Serb military and political leaders would strengthen the case for genocide and, perhaps, introduce reliable evidence of intent. Nonetheless, even in the absence of such evidence, it is certainly the case that, once widespread media coverage of this issue began in the summer of 1992 with revelations about Serb-run detention camps, it was impossible for Serb leaders not to have been aware of the violations that were occurring in the field. Their failure to act to stop them constitutes what Fein calls a "reinforcing condition" for genocide. It also constitutes a basis on which to argue for the culpability of Serbian authorities who had the power to stop such activities.

In the present case, evidence concerning the relationship between Belgrade (Serbian President Slobodan Milosevic) and the Bosnian Serb leadership (Radovan Karadzic and Ratko Mladic) is mixed. They appear, for example, repeatedly to have been working at cross-purposes with respect to military-political strategy and Western efforts to negotiate an end to the fighting. However, Vojislav Seselj, the extremist paramilitary leader whose organization carried out much of the killing in Bosnia-Herzegovina, and Borisav Jovic reported in interviews included in the documentary *Death of Yugoslavia* that Milosevic did exercise such control. As a specialist in Yugoslav politics, I believe that Milosevic did have the power to stop such acts—if not by political means, certainly by use of force. But, as a scholar, I know that belief alone is not enough. Additional evidence must be compiled—the most likely source being testimonies secured as part of the proceedings of the War Crimes Tribunal—to demonstrate that Milosevic, or the Belgrade leadership more generally, either directed these activities or had the power to stop them if they are to be included in a charge of genocide.

Because the definition of genocide is not linked to a numerical or proportional quota, activities carried out by other forces in the course of the war also call out for consideration as acts of genocide. The Serb population of Bosnia-Herzegovina was subjected to brutal treatment at the hands of Croat and Muslim forces from the very beginning of the war. Serb civilians were expelled from Croat- and Muslim-held territories or forced into labor battalions, and Serb villages were burned. Muslim irregular forces committed atrocities against Serbs as they overran villages in Eastern Bosnia early in the war (U.N., 1993a). The Croats complained of war crimes committed against them by the Muslims in connection with their battles for control of central Bosnia in 1993 (U.N., 1993b and 1993c). The case for war crimes on the part of both Croat and Muslim perpetrators thus seems strong. The evaluative criteria suggested by Fein provide useful guidelines for determining whether actions by Croats and Muslims can also be considered genocide.

The criterion of continuity seems most important in this respect. Reports of Croatian abuses against Serbs seem to be less numerous than those against Muslims, and do not form a continuous pattern of behavior. This is the result, of course, of the fact that Serb-Croat fighting was limited very largely to the opening and closing phases of the war. In the final months before the end of the fighting in 1995, when Croat (and Muslim) forces seized large amounts of Serb-populated territory, Serb civilians fled in the face of the arrival of Croat (and Muslim) forces out of fear of attack. The fact that Croatian forces abused the numerically few, mostly elderly Serbs who chose to remain behind may, perhaps, be indicative of what might

have happened had the Serb population stayed. But such incidents, as reprehensible as they may be, do not qualify as genocide. It is probably more
appropriate to speak of specific "genocidal massacres" or other acts "not
part of a continuous genocide but . . . committed by an authority or other
organized group against a particular ethnic or other distinguishable group
. . . on the basis of their identity alone" (Fein, 1993a, p. 33) rather than
genocide with respect to Croat abuse of Serbs.

   Croat abuses of the Muslim population in Bosnia-Herzegovina do form
a pattern of sustained, continuous activity, at least for the relatively short
period of Croat-Muslim combat in 1993—that is, up to the American-
brokered establishment of a Muslim-Croat Federation early in 1994. Croat
actions during their war against the Muslims in central Bosnia in 1993
fulfill all the criteria established by Fein. Organized Croat forces carried out
expulsions, internment, killing, and atrocities against Muslim civilians who
were victimized because they were Muslims. These actions appear to warrant description as genocide even though they are on a much smaller scale
than those carried out by the Serbs and they end abruptly with the conclusion of the Muslim-Croat political alliance. The distinction between Croat-
perpetrated genocide against Muslims and Croat war crimes against Serbs
may, in the final analysis, reflect little more than the differing sequences and
timing of combat between Croats and Muslims on the one hand, and Croats
and Serbs on the other. It seems, however, that this is a relevant distinction.

   Muslim forces committed violations similar to those of the Croats during the period of the Croat-Muslim war of 1993. There is also evidence of
persistent abuses of Serb civilians. But third-party reports do not suggest
sustained, continuous attacks of the kind that would subject the Muslim
leadership to charges of genocide. The Bosnian government formally disavowed the most egregious offenders, even if they did so belatedly or without enthusiasm. The actual intent of Muslim forces is not so clear, especially
in light of the "genocidal massacres" they inflicted upon Serb villages in
Eastern Bosnia throughout the war and on Croatian villages in central Bosnia.
Indeed, the absence of Muslim-perpetrated genocide may in the end have
more to do with the relative weakness of Muslim forces in the war, their
inability to control territories not populated by Muslims, and the resultant
lack of opportunity to perpetrate genocide than a lack of intent. Because
our emphasis here is on the patterns of conduct, however, these doubts
about intent are less important for our argument than they might be for an
argument focused on the moral standing of each party to this war. Thus, in

the case of the Muslim forces, it is probably more appropriate to speak of specific "genocidal massacres" and war crimes, rather than genocide.

The determination of genocide cannot be divorced entirely from questions about intent and responsibility. The case for intent is often made by referring to a political or racist ideology that encourages and legitimates destruction of the "other." Evidence of the existence of such an ideology among the Serbs is often used to buttress the case for genocide by Serbs against the Muslims (e.g., Cigar, 1995). But few, if any, attempts have been made to explore Croatian views on the question of Bosnia and the Muslims prior to the outbreak of the war. Is the presence or absence of such an ideology a crucial test? Fein clearly does not think so, for she defines the existence of "ideologies or beliefs legitimating genocide" as one of the two "reinforcing conditions" for genocide rather than one of her criteria for determining whether genocide has taken place.

One of the difficulties involved in determining the nature of Croat actions in 1993 (and Muslim actions more generally) is the virtual absence of critical third-party inquiry into the questions surrounding them. The relative lack of attention to violations committed by Croatian forces reflects the politicization of popular and, much more troubling, scholarly treatment of the war and the issues surrounding it. The charge of genocide is a powerful political weapon. The war in Bosnia-Herzegovina has been fought not only on the battlefield, but in the mass media and the halls of public discourse in the West, including in academia. It is, of course, appropriate to draw attention to evidence of genocide, and it is the responsibility of moral actors to oppose or prevent it where possible. But much of the concern with genocide in Bosnia-Herzegovina appears to be rooted in political rather than moral motives. Appeals for Western intervention on behalf of the Bosnian Muslims have relied on moral imperatives as a substitute for clearly perceived geopolitical or strategic interests in the region. The moral imperative to shine the light of publicity and debate on possible cases of genocide appears not to be as powerful in the case of those acts committed by the Croats and practically nonexistent in the case of the Muslims.

To be identified as the perpetrators of genocide is to be delegitimated politically in most of Western public opinion, and among almost all Western policymakers. The geopolitical and material interests of an alleged perpetrator, usually the focus of attempts by mediators to understand and resolve conflict, are far less relevant factors in the policy considerations of third parties. It becomes far more difficult for policymakers to accommodate such interests in the face of popular moral indignation, even as part of an effort to end the fighting and accompanying abuses. Hence, the political "costs" of being identified as the perpetrator of genocide can be enormous. In the present case, therefore, strenuous efforts have been made by all potential targets of the accusation of genocide to refute and, if possible, avoid the charge.

Of course, the charge of genocide can be equally "inconvenient" for a third party, including even a great power such as the United States. To acknowledge that genocide has occurred is to activate the moral imperatives noted above and to stimulate public awareness of the issue. As a result, the need for political leaders sensitive to public opinion "to do something" mounts—even in the absence of traditionally conceived strategic interests. The charge of genocide constrains the ability of a leadership to align itself militarily and politically with an alleged perpetrator or to make efforts to address the underlying clash of interests between alleged perpetrators and victims without seeming to condone or ratify genocide, even when to do so might put an end to the conflict and the killing. For precisely these reasons, the United States has been reluctant to acknowledge officially that genocide has occurred, on the part of either the Serbs or the Croats.

Governments are not the only actors to shape their reactions to genocide in Bosnia-Herzegovina in ways to suit their other interests. One of the most troubling aspects of these efforts is an apparent effort by scholars, journalists, and publicists to use the evidence of genocide by Serbs to attack and devalue the entire nation, to use the differences in the scale of Croat violations to deny or excuse their genocidal acts against Serbs and their genocide against Muslims in this war, and, most troubling of all, to use the outrage generated by the events of this war as license to rewrite the history of the last one (for a similar argument, see Kohl, 1996). As Helen Fein has demonstrated, most perpetrators of genocide are "repeat offenders" (Fein, 1993b). The likelihood that this may prove true in Bosnia, as well, appears very high. Thus, both Western governments and the governments of the states directly involved in the war in Bosnia-Herzegovina, having failed to prevent the present tragedy, still face the task of preventing the repetition, or even escalation, of genocidal behavior in Bosnia-Herzegovina. If responsible governments are to act responsibly, their publics must be educated about the issues. Specialists on genocide and on the history, politics, and culture of Bosnia-Herzegovina (and the rest of the former Yugoslavia, as well) must work together to provide an honest accounting of the origins and history of genocide and genocidal actions in the region as a means of putting an end to the conflicts that led to them. They must also actively oppose efforts by those who seek to perpetuate conflict by transporting it from the battlefield to the journals, monographs, and other arenas of what should be scholarly discourse.

There are numerous difficulties involved in applying the concept of genocide to the events in Bosnia-Herzegovina. Three parties have been engaged in what amounts to a war of each against all. The behaviors of each must be subjected to careful investigation using consistent criteria. New evidence is still coming to light almost every day. Hence, it is not surprising that honest differences of interpretation, rooted in the complexities of the evidence itself rather than in the political agendas of those who interpret it, are possible.

Notes and References

Introduction

Note

*What has been delineated here in regard to the definition of genocide is, quite obviously, a synopsis of a complex issue. For more detailed discussions, see the following: Bauer, 1984; Chalk, 1989, pp. 149–160; Chalk and Jonassohn, 1988, pp. 39–46; Chalk and Jonassohn, 1990, pp. 8–27; Charny, 1988a, pp. 20–38; Charny, 1988b, pp. 1–19; Dadrian, 1975; Drost, 1959; Fein, 1978, p. 271–293; Fein, 1984; 1990; Horowitz, 1980, pp. 9–22; Kuper, 1981, pp. 19–39; Kuper, 1985, pp. 8–22; Legters, 1984, pp. 60–66; Savon, 1972; Staub, 1989; Whitaker, 1985.

References

Bauer, Yehuda (1975). *Guide to Unpublished Materials of the Holocaust Period* (vol. 111). Jerusalem: Yad Vashem.

——— (1984). "The Place of the Holocaust in Contemporary History." In Jonathan Frankel (ed.), *Studies in Contemporary Jewry* (vol. 1). Bloomington: Indiana University Press.

Berger, Julian (1987). *Report from the Frontier: The State of the World's Indigenous Peoples.* London and New Jersey: Zed Books, Ltd.

Chalk, Frank (1989). "Definitions of Genocide and Their Implications for Prediction and Prevention." *Holocaust and Genocide Studies,* 4(2): 149–160.

Chalk, Frank, and Kurt Jonassohn (1988). "The History and Sociology of Genocidal Killings," pp. 39–58. In Israel Charny (ed.), *Genocide: A Critical Bibliographic Review.* London: Mansell Publishing.

——— (1990). *The History and Sociology of Genocide: Analyses and Case Studies.* New Haven: Yale University Press.

Charny, Israel W. (April 1993). Editorial comment. *Internet on the Holocaust and Genocide,* Issue 43, p. 3.

——— (1982). *How Can We Commit the Unthinkable?: Genocide, the Human Cancer.* In collaboration with Chanan Rapaport. Boulder, CO: Westview Press.

——— (1988a). "Intervention and Prevention of Genocide," pp. 20–38. In Israel Charny (ed.) *Genocide: A Critical Bibliographic Review.* New York: Facts on File.

——— (1988b). "The Study of Genocide," pp. 1–19. In Israel Charny (ed.), *Genocide: A Critical Bibliographic Review.* New York: Facts on File.

——— (ed.) (1984). *Toward the Understanding and Prevention of Genocide: Proceedings of the International Conference on the Holocaust and Genocide.* Boulder, CO, and London: Westview Press.

Dadrian, Vahakn N. (Fall 1975). "A Typology of Genocide." *International Review of Modern Sociology,* 5, 201–212.

Drost, Pieter (1959). *The Crime of State* (vol. 2). Leyden: A.W. Sythoff.

Dunn, James (1983). *Timor: A People Betrayed.* Milton, Queensland: Jacaranda Press.

Fein, Helen (1978). "A Formula for Genocide: Comparison of Turkish Genocide (1915) and German Holocaust (1939–1945)." *Comparative Studies in Sociology*, 1, 271–293.

———— (1984). "Scenarios of Genocide: Models of Genocide and Critical Responses," pp. 3–31. In Israel W. Charny (ed.), *Toward the Understanding and Prevention of Genocide: Proceedings of the International Conference on the Holocaust and Genocide*. Boulder, CO, and London: Westview Press.

———— (1990). "Genocide: A Sociological Perspective." *Current Sociology*, 38(1): 1–126.

Hawk, David (1988). "The Cambodian Genocide," pp. 137–154. In Israel W. Charny (ed.), *Genocide: A Critical Bibliographic Review*. New York: Facts on File.

Horowitz, Irving Louis (1980). *Taking Lives: Genocide and State Power*. New Brunswick, NJ: Transaction Publishers.

Hovannisian, Richard G. (1973). "Introduction," pp. xix–xxv. In Stanley E. Kerr, *The Lions of Marash: Personal Experiences with American Near East Relief, 1919–1922*. Albany: State University of New York Press.

Howard, Ephraim M., and Yoche Howard (1984). "From Theory to Application: Proposal for an Applied Science Approach to a Genocide Early Warning System," pp. 324–329. In Israel W. Charny (ed.), *Toward the Understanding and Prevention of Genocide: Proceedings of the International Conference on the Holocaust and Genocide*. Boulder, CO, and London: Westview Press.

Kuper, Leo (1981). *Genocide: Its Political Use in the Twentieth Century*. New Haven: Yale University Press.

———— (1985). *The Prevention of Genocide*. New Haven: Yale University Press.

Legters, Lyman H. (1984). "The Soviet Gulag: Is It Genocidal?" pp. 60–66. In Israel W. Charny (ed.), *Toward the Understanding and Prevention of Genocide: Proceedings of the International Conference on the Holocaust and Genocide*. Boulder, CO, and London: Westview Press.

Lemkin, Raphael (1944). *Axis Rule in Occupied Europe: Laws of Occupation, Analysis of Government, and Proposals for Redress*. Washington, D.C.: Carnegie Foundation for International Peace. [Reprint, New York: Howard Fertig, 1973.]

Parsons, William S., and Samuel Totten (1991a). "Teaching about Genocide." Special Issue of *Social Education*, 55(2).

———— (1991b). "Teaching and Learning about Genocide: Questions of Content, Rationale, and Methodology." *Social Education*, 55(2): 85–90.

Rupesinghe, Kumar, and Michiko Kuroda (1992). *Early Warning and Conflict Resolution*. New York: St. Martin's Press.

Savon, Herve (1972). *Du cannibalisme au genocide*. Paris: Hachette.

Smith, Roger (1987). "Human Destructiveness and Politics: The Twentieth Century as an Age of Genocide," pp. 21–39. In Isidor Wallimann and Michael Dobkowski, (eds.), *Genocide and the Modern Age: Etiology and Case Studies of Mass Death*. Westport, CT: Greenwood Press.

Staub, Ervin (1989). *The Roots of Evil: The Origins of Genocide and Other Group Violence*. New York: Cambridge University Press.

Totten, Samuel (1991a). "Educating about Genocide: Curricula and Inservice Training," pp. 194–225. In Israel W. Charny (ed.), *Genocide: A Critical Bibliographic Review* (vol. 2). London: Mansell Publishers; and New York: Facts on File.

———— (1991b). "First-Person Accounts of Genocidal Acts," pp. 321–362. In Israel W. Charny (ed.), *Genocide: A Critical Bibliographic Review* (vol. 2). London: Mansell Publishers; and New York: Facts on File.

———— (1991c). *First-Person Accounts of Genocidal Acts Committed in the Twentieth Century: An Annotated Bibliography*. Westport, CT: Greenwood Press.

———— (1987). "The Personal Face of Genocide: Words of Witnesses in the Classroom." Special issue of *Social Science Record* ("Genocide: Issues, Approaches, Resources"), 24(2): 63–67.

Tyrnauer, Gabrielle (1986). "Scholars, Gypsies, and the Holocaust." In Joanne Grumet (ed.), *Papers from the Sixth and Seventh Annual Meetings, Gypsy Lore Society, North American Chapter*. New York: Gypsy Lore Society.

Whitaker, Ben (1985). *Revised and Updated Report on the Question of the Prevention and Punishment of the Crime of Genocide*. 62 pp. (E/CN.4/Sub.2/1985/6, 2 July 1985).

Wiseberg, Laurie, and Harry Scoble (1981). "Recent Trends in the Expanding Universe of NGOs Dedicated to the Protection of Human Rights," pp. 229–260. In Ved P. Nanda, James R. Scaritt, and George W. Shepherd, Jr. (eds.), *Global Human Rights: Public Policies, Comparative Measures, and NGO Strategies*. Boulder, CO: Westview Press.

Chapter One
Genocide of the Hereros

Notes

1. For a more detailed consideration of the Hereros' genocide see Jon Bridgman, *The Revolt of the Hereros* (Berkeley: University of California Press, 1981); or Horst Drechsler, *"Let Us Die Fighting,"* translated by Bernd Zöllner (London: Zed Press, 1980). This work was originally published as *Südwestafrika unter deutscher Kolonialherrschaft* (Berlin: Akademie-Verlag, 1966).

2. Drechsler, *"Let Us Die Fighting,"* p. 55, no. 8, for a discussion of the various population estimates, which in fact went as high as 100,000 or more.

3. Cf. Bridgman, *Hereros*, Ch. 1, for a fuller discussion of the tribal peoples of South-West Africa at this time.

4. Helmut Bley, *Kolonialherrschaft und Sozialstruktur in Deutsch-Südwestafrika* (Hamburg: Leibniz-Verlag, 1968), pp. 160ff., for a more detailed analysis.

5. Theodor Leutwein, *Elf Jahre Gouverneur in Deutsch-Südwestafrika* (Berlin: E. S. Mittler, 1906), p. 559, Leutwein said that the government had not issued the ordinance out of any love of the natives, but rather to preserve the life and possessions of those whites who were living among the natives.

6. See Wellington, *South-West Africa*, pp. 198ff., and Drechsler, *"Let Us Die Fighting"* pp. 118ff.; the Hereros named each year according to the most significant event which occurred during its course, and the year 1903 was named "ojovuronde juviuego," which meant the year of traders and fraud.

7. For the most perceptive analysis of Leutwein's attitude, see Bley, *Kolonialherrschaft*.

8. This passage was contained in a message from Missionary Elger to the Rhenish Missionary Society; see also Drechsler, *"Let Us Die Fighting,"* p. 145; Jon Swan, "The Final Solution in South-West Africa," *MHQ: The Quarterly Journal of Military History* 3:3 (1991): 46.

9. Bridgman, *Hereros*, p. 65, notes that Paul Rohrbach, the colonial propagandist, is generally credited with this expression.

10. Subchief Daniel Kariko testified later that the war was aimed exclusively at German men.

11. Maherero actually sent messages to several tribes seeking alliances against the Germans, cf. Imp. Col. Off. File No. 2114, pp. 21ff., 23; Leutwein, *Jahre*, p. 468; Drechsler, *"Let Us Die Fighting,"* p. 143.

12. Maherero's judgment here was correct, the Rhenish Missionary Society or at least some of its members did plead the native cause in the German press, cf. Drechsler, *"Let Us Die Fighting,"* p. 140.

13. Wellington, *South-West Africa*, p. 148, reports on the Herero treatment of a Hottentot prisoner which apparently was typical: first the Hereros cut off his ears, then his nose, and lips, and finally they slit his throat.

14. Swan, *MHQ*, p. 51; Great Britain, *Atrocities, and Breaches of the Rules of War, in Africa* in *The Sessional Papers of the House of Lords*, vols. 5 & 6 (London: H.M. Stationery Office, 1916), pp. 74–80, shows the German army poisoned wells in South-West Africa to hinder the British invasion in 1915, and implies that this had been done in earlier wars.

15. Also see Drechsler, *"Let Us Die Fighting,"* pp. 214ff.

16. Cf. George Crothers, *The German Elections of 1907* (London: P.S. King & Son, Ltd., 1941), for a detailed account of this unusual election.

17. This article can be found in *Zeitschrift für Ethnologie*, 80:2(1955):200ff.

References

Andersson, Charles (1856). *Lake Ngami; or Exploration and Discovery During Four Years' Wanderings in the Wilds of South-Western Africa.* New York: Harper & Brothers.

Bley, Helmut (1968). *Kolonialherrschaft und Sozialstruktur in Deutsch Südwestafrika, 1894–1914.* Hamburg: Leibniz-Verlag.

Bridgman, Jon (1981). *The Revolt of the Hereros.* Berkeley: University of California Press.

Bülow, Bernhard von (1930–1931). *Denkwürdigkeiten.* 4 vols. Berlin: Ullstein.

Crothers, George (1941). *The German Elections of 1907.* London: P.S. King & Son, Ltd.

Drechsler, Horst (1980). *"Let Us Die Fighting."* London: Zed Press. [Translated by Bernd Zöllner.] [Originally published (1966) under the title *Südwestafrika unter deutscher Kolonialherrschaft.* Berlin: Akademie-Verlag.]

Epstein, Klaus (1959). "Erzberger and the German Colonial Scandals, 1905–1910." *English Historical Review,* 74(293): 637–663.

Great Britain (1916). *German Atrocities, and Breaches of the Rules of War, in Africa* in *The Sessional Papers of the House of Lords.* Vols. 5 & 6. London: H.M. Stationery Office.

Great Britain (1918). *Report on the Natives of South-West Africa and their Treatment by Germany* in *The Sessional Papers of the House of Lords.* Vol. 13. London: H.M. Stationery Office.

Imperial Colonial Office Files, nos. 2111, 2114, 2119, 2140. [Archival Records.]

Kriegsgeschichtliche Abteilung, Grosser Generalstab, Armée Prussia (1906–1907). *Die Kämpfe der deutschen Truppen in Südwestafrika.* 2 vols. Berlin: E. S. Mittler.

Leutwein, Theodor (1908). *Elf Jahre Gouverneur in Deutsch-Südwestafrika.* Berlin: E. S. Mittler.

Poewe, Karla (1985). *The Namibian Herero: A History of Their Psychosocial Disintegration and Survival.* Lewiston, NY: The Edwin Mellen Press.

Schlosser, Katesa (1955). "Der Herero im Britisch-Betschuana-Protektorat und ein Besuch in einer ihrer Siedlungen: Newe-le-tau." *Zeitschrift für Ethnologie,* 80(2): 200–218.

Schwabe, Kurd (1904). *Mit Schwert und Pflug in Deutsch-Südwestafrika.* Berlin: E. S. Mittler.

Swan, Jon (1991). "The Final Solution in South-West Africa." *MHQ: The Quarterly Journal of Military History,* 3(3): 36–55.

Wellington, John H. (1967). *South-West Africa and Its Human Issues.* Oxford: Oxford University Press.

Chapter Two
The Armenian Genocide

References

Adalian, Rouben P. (1989). "The Historical Evolution of the Armenian Diasporas." *Journal of Modern Hellenism,* 6: 81–114.

———— (1991). "The Armenian Genocide: Context and Legacy." *Social Education,* 55(2): 99–104.

———— (ed.) (1991–1994). *The Armenian Genocide in the U.S. Archives 1915–1918.* Alexandria, Virginia and Cambridge, United Kingdom: Chadwyck-Healey, Inc.

———— (1992). "The Armenian Genocide: Revisionism and Denial," pp. 85–105. In Michael N. Dobkowski and Isidor Wallimann (eds.), *Genocide in Our Time: An Annotated Bibliography with Analytical Introductions.* Ann Arbor, MI: The Pierian Press.

Ahmed, Feroz (1982). "Unionist Relations with the Greek, Armenian, and Jewish Communities of the Ottoman Empire, 1908–1914," pp. 387–434. In Benjamin Braude and Bernard Lewis (eds.), *Christians and Jews in the Ottoman Empire, Volume I, The Central Lands.* New York and London: Holmes & Meier Inc.

Baghdjian, Kevork K. (1987). *La confiscation, par le gouvernement turc, des biens arméniens . . . dits "abandonnés."* Montreal: Payette & Simms Inc.

Barsoumian, Hagop (1982). "The Dual Role of the Amira Class within the Ottoman Government and the Armenian Millet (1750–1850)," pp. 171–184. In Benjamin Braude and Bernard Lewis (eds.), *Christians and Jews in the Ottoman Empire, Volume I, The Central Lands.* New York and London: Holmes & Meier Publishers Inc.

Beylerian, Arthur (1983). *Les grande puissances l'empire Ottoman et les arméniens dans les Archives Françaises (1914–1918): recueil de documents.* Paris: Publications de la Sorbonne.

Bliss, Edwin M. (1982). *Turkey and the Armenian Atrocities.* Fresno: Meshag Publishers. [Originally published in 1896.]

Braude, Benjamin, and Bernard Lewis (eds.) (1982). *Christians and Jews in the Ottoman Empire, Volume I, The Central Lands.* New York and London: Holmes & Meier Publishers Inc.

Dadrian, Vahakn N. (1986). "The Naim-Andonian Documents on the World War I Destruction of Ottoman Armenians: The Anatomy of a Genocide." *International Journal of Middle East Studies,* 18(3): 311–360.

——— (1989). "Genocide as a Problem of National and International Law: The World War I Armenian Case and Its Contemporary Legal Ramifications." *Yale Journal of International Law,* 14(2): 221–334.

——— (1991). "The Documentation of the World War I Armenian Massacres in the Proceedings of the Turkish Military Tribunal." *International Journal of Middle East Studies,* 23(4): 549–576.

——— (1993). "The Secret Young-Turk Ittihadist Conference and the Decisions for the World War I Genocide of the Armenians." *Holocaust and Genocide Studies,* 7(2): 173–201.

Davis, Leslie A. (1989). *The Slaughterhouse Province: An American Diplomat's Report on the Armenian Genocide, 1915–1917.* New Rochelle, NY: Aristide D. Caratzas, Publisher. [Introduction by Susan K. Blair.]

Derogy, Jacques (1990). *Resistance and Revenge: The Armenian Assassination of the Turkish Leaders Responsible for the 1915 Massacres and Deportations.* New Brunswick, NJ: Transaction Publishers.

Dinkel, Christoph (1991). "German Officers and the Armenian Genocide," *Armenian Review,* 44(1): 77–133.

Dobkin, Marjorie Housepian (1986). "What Genocide? What Holocaust? News from Turkey, 1915–1923: A Case Study," pp. 97–109. In Hovannisian (ed.), *The Armenian Genocide in Perspective.* New Brunswick, NJ: Transaction Books.

Fein, Helen (1979). *Accounting for Genocide: National Responses and Jewish Victimization during the Holocaust.* New York: The Free Press.

Foreign Policy Institute (1982). *The Armenian Issue in Nine Questions and Answers.* Ankara: Author.

Gibbons, Herbert Adams (1916). *The Blackest Page of Modern History. Events in Armenia in 1915. The Facts and the Responsibilities.* New York and London: G.P. Putnam's Sons.

Greene, Frederick Davis (1896). *Armenian Massacres and Turkish Tyranny.* Philadelphia & Chicago: International Publishing Co.

Guroian, Vigen (1986). "Collective Responsibility and Official Excuse Making: The Case of the Turkish Genocide of the Armenian," pp. 135–152. In Hovannisian (ed.), *The Armenian Genocide in Perspective.* New Brunswick, NJ: Transaction Books.

Gürün, Kâmuran (1985). *The Armenian File: The Myth of Innocence Exposed.* London, and Nicosia, Istanbul: K. Rustem & Bros. and Weidenfeld and Nicolson Ltd.

Hairapetian, Armen (1984). "'Race Problems' and the Armenian Genocide: The State Department File," and "Documents: The State Department File." *Armenian Review,* 37(1): 41–145.

Horowitz, Irving Louis (1982). *Taking Lives: Genocide and State Power.* New Brunswick, NJ: Transaction Books.

Hovannisian, Richard G. (1967). *Armenia on the Road to Independence 1918.* Berkeley: University of California Press.

——— (1978). *The Armenian Holocaust: A Bibliography Relating to the Deportations, Massacres, and Dispersion of the Armenian People, 1915–1923.* Cambridge, MA: National Association for Armenian Studies and Research.

——— (ed.) (1986a). *The Armenian Genocide in Perspective.* New Brunswick, NJ: Transaction Books.

——— (1986b). "The Historical Dimensions of the Armenian Question, 1878–1923," pp. 19–41. In Richard Hovannisian (ed.), *The Armenian Genocide in Perspective.* New Brunswick, NJ: Transaction Books.

——— (1986c). "The Armenian Genocide and Patterns of Denial," pp. 111–133. In Richard

Hovannisian (ed.), *The Armenian Genocide in Perspective.* New Brunswick, NJ: Transaction Books.

────── (1992)."Intervention and Shades of Altruism during the Armenian Genocide," pp. 173–207. In Richard Hovannisian (ed.), *The Armenian Genocide: History, Politics, Ethics.* New York: St. Martin's Press.

Kerr, Stanley E. (1973). *The Lions of Marash: Personal Experiences with American Near East Relief, 1919–1922.* Albany: State University of New York Press.

Kinross, Lord (1964). *Ataturk: The Birth of a Nation.* London: Weidenfeld and Nicolson, 1964.

Kloian, Richard D. (1985). *The Armenian Genocide: News Accounts from the American Press: 1915–1922.* Berkeley: Anto Printing.

Kuper, Leo (1981). *Genocide: Its Political Use in the Twentieth Century.* New York: Penguin.

────── (1986). "The Turkish Genocide of Armenians, 1915–1917," pp. 43–59. In Richard Hovannisian (ed.), *The Armenian Genocide in Perspective.* New Brunswick, NJ: Transaction Books.

Lang, David Marshall (1970). *Armenia: Cradle of Civilization.* London: George Allen & Unwin.

────── (1981). *The Armenians: A People in Exile.* London: George Allen & Unwin.

Lepsius, Johannes (1987). *Rapport secret sur les massacres d'Arménie (1915–1916).* Paris: Edition Payot.

Libaridian, Gerard (1985). "The Ideology of the Young Turk Movement," pp. 37–49. In Gerard Libaridian (ed.), *A Crime of Silence, The Armenian Genocide: Permanent Peoples' Tribunal.* London: Zed Books.

────── (1987). "The Ultimate Repression: The Genocide of the Armenians, 1915–1917," pp. 203–235. In Isidor Wallimann and Michael N. Dobkowski (eds.), *Genocide and the Modern Age: Etiology and Case Studies of Mass Death.* Westport, CT: Greenwood Press.

McCarthy, Justin (1983). *Muslims and Minorities: The Population of Ottoman Anatolia and the End of the Empire.* New York and London: New York University Press.

Melson, Robert (1986). "Provocation or Nationalism: A Critical Inquiry into the Armenian Genocide of 1915," pp. 61–84. In Richard Hovannisian (ed.), *The Armenian Genocide in Perspective.* New Brunswick, NJ: Transaction Books.

Miller, Donald E., and Lorna Touryan Miller (1993). *Survivors: An Oral History of the Armenian Genocide.* Berkeley: University of California Press.

Morgenthau, Henry (1918). *Ambassador Morgenthau's Story.* Garden City, NY: Doubleday, Page and Co. [Reprinted in 1975 by New Age Publishers in Plandome, NY.]

Nalbandian, Louise (1963). *The Armenian Revolutionary Movement.* Berkeley: University of California Press.

Nassibian, Akaby (1984). *Britain and the Armenian Question 1915–1923.* New York: St. Martin's Press.

Ohandjanian, Artem (ed.) (1988). *The Armenian Genocide, Volume 2, Documentation.* Munich: Institute für armenische Fragen.

Parla, Taha (1985). *The Social and Political Thought of Ziya Gökalp 1876–1924.* Leiden: E.J. Brill.

Ramsaur, Jr., Ernest Edmondson (1957). *The Young Turks: Prelude to the Revolution of 1908.* New York: Russell & Russell.

Sachar, Howard M. (1969). *The Emergence of the Middle East 1914–1924.* New York: Alfred A. Knopf.

Sanasarian, Eliz (1989). "Gender Distinction in the Genocide Process: A Preliminary Study of the Armenian Case," *Holocaust and Genocide Studies,* 4 (4): 449–461.

Shaw, Stanford J., and Ezel Kural Shaw (1977). *History of the Ottoman Empire and Modern Turkey, Volume 2, Reform, Revolution, and Republic: The Rise of Modern Turkey 1808–1975.* New York: Cambridge University Press.

Smith, Roger (1989). "Genocide and Denial: the Armenian Case and Its Implications," *Armenian Review* 42(1): 1–38.

Staub, Ervin (1989). *The Roots of Evil: The Origins of Genocide and Other Group Violence.* New York: Cambridge University Press.

Ternon, Yves (1981). *The Armenians: History of a Genocide.* Delmar, NY: Caravan Books.

Totten, Samuel (1991). "The Ottoman Genocide of the Armenians," pp. 7–43. In Samuel Totten (ed.), *First-Person Accounts of Genocidal Acts Committed in the Twentieth Century: An Annotated Bibliography.* Westport, CT: Greenwood Press.

440 Notes and References

Toynbee, Arnold J. (ed.) (1916). *The Treatment of Armenians in the Ottoman Empire, 1915–1916*. London: Sir Joseph Causton and Sons, Limited. [Preface by Viscount Bryce.] [Reprint, Beirut, Lebanon: G. Doniguian & Sons, 1979.]

Trumpener, Ulrich (1968). *Germany and the Ottoman Empire 1914–1918*. Princeton, NJ: Princeton University Press. [Reprinted in 1989 by Caravan books in Delmar, NY.]

Uras, Esat (1988). *The Armenians in History and the Armenian Question*. Istanbul: Foundation for the Establishment and Promotion of Centers for Historical Research and Documentation, and Istanbul Research Center.

Walker, Christopher J. (1980). *Armenia: The Survival of a Nation*. New York: St. Martin's Press.

Werfel, Franz (1934). *The Forty Days of Musa Dagh*. New York: The Modern Library.

Ye'or, Bat [Y. Masriya, pseud.] (1985). *The Dhimmi: Jews and Christians Under Islam*. Teaneck, NJ: Fairleigh Dickinson University Press.

Chapter Three
Soviet Man-Made Famine in Ukraine

References

Borys, Jurij (1980). *The Sovietization of Ukraine 1917–1923: The Communist Doctrine and Practice of National Self-Determination*. Edmonton: Canadian Institute of Ukrainian Studies.

Commission on the Ukraine Famine (1988). *Report to Congress*. Washington, D.C.: U.S. Government Printing Office.

Conquest, Robert (1986). *The Harvest of Sorrow: Soviet Collectivization and the Terror-Famine*. New York & Oxford: Oxford University Press.

Ellman, Michael (1991). "A Note of the Number of 1933 Famine Victims," *Soviet Studies*, 43(2): 375–379.

Gannt, William Horsley (1937). *Russian Medicine*. New York: Harper & Brothers.

Hermaize, Osyp (1926). *Narysy z istorii revoliutsiinoho rukhu na Ukraïni* [Sketches from the History of the Revolutionary Movement in Ukraine]. Kharkiv: Knyhospilka.

Holod 1932–1933 rokiv na Ukraïni: Ochyma istorykiv, movoiu dokumentiv [The Famine of 1932–1933 in Ukraine: In the Eyes of Historians and in the Language of the Documents]. (1990). Kiev: Vydavnytstvo politychnoï literatury.

Hroch, Myroslav (1985). *Social Conditions of National Revival in Europe. A Comparative Analysis of the Social Composition of Patriotic Groups Among the Smaller European Nations*. Cambridge, London, New York: Cambridge University Press.

Jasny, Naum (1949). *The Socialized Agriculture of the USSR: Plans and Performance*. Stanford, CA: Stanford University Press.

Khrystiuk, Pavlo (1921–1922). *Zamitky i materiialy do istoriï ukraïns'koï revoliutsiï, 1917–1920* [Notes and Materials on the History of the Ukrainian Revolution, 1919–1920]. Prague: Ukraïns'kyi sociologychnyi instytut. 4 volumes.

Kuper, Leo (1990). "The Genocidal State: An Overview," pp. 19–52. In Pierre L. van den Berghe (ed.), *State Violence and Ethnicity*. Niwot: University of Colorado Press.

Lewin, Moshe (1985). *The Making of the Soviet System: Essays in the Social History of Interwar Russia*. New York: Pantheon.

Liber, George O. (1992). *Soviet Nationality Policy, Urban Growth and Identity Change in the Ukrainian SSR, 1923–1934*. Cambridge and New York: Cambridge University Press.

Luxemburg, Rosa (1976). *The National Question: Selected Writings*. Ed. Horace B. Davis. Ann Arbor, MI: Books on Demand.

Mace, James E. (1983). *Communism and the Dilemmas of National Liberation: National Communism in Soviet Ukraine, 1918–1933*. Cambridge: Harvard University Press.

——— (1984). "The Man-Made Famine of 1933 in the Soviet Ukraine: What Happened and Why," pp. 67–83. In Israel W. Charny (ed.), *Toward the Understanding and Prevention of Genocide*. Boulder, CO, and London: Westview Press.

"Postanova TsK VKP(b) ta RNK SRSR pro khlibozahotivli na Ukraïny, Pivnichnomu Kavkazi ta Zakhidnii oblasti" [Decision of the All-Union Communist Party Central Committee and USSR Council of Peoples Commissars on Grain Procurements in Ukraine, the North

Caucasus, and Western District], *Zoloti vorota: Al'manakh*, No. 1 (1991), pp. 78–79.
Savchenko, Fedir (1930). *Zaborone ukraïnstvo 1876 r.* [The Suppression of Ukrainian Activities in 1876]. Kharkiv and Kiev: Derzhavne vydavnytstvo Ukraïny.
Stalin, I. (1946–1951). *Sochineniia* [Works]. Moscow: Gospolitizdat. 14 volumes.
Taylor, S.J. (1990). *Stalin's Apologist: Walter Duranty, the New York Times's Man in Moscow.* New York and Oxford: Oxford University Press.
Treadgold, Donald (1964). *Twentieth Century Russia.* 2nd ed. Chicago: Rand McNally.
Vsesoiuznaia perepis' naseleniia 1937 g.: Kratkie itogi [All-Union Population Census of 1937: Summary]. (1991). Moscow: Institut istorii SSSR.

Chapter Four
Soviet Deportation of Whole Nations: A Genocidal Process

Notes

1. For a full account, see Zvi Y. Gitelman's (1972), *Jewish Nationality and Soviet Politics.* Princeton, NJ: Princeton University Press. See especially Chapter VII.
2. Chapter 14 in Fred C. Koch's (1977) *The Volga Germans* (University Park: Pennsylvania State University Press) provides a detailed account and quotes the decree more fully.
3. For a detailed account of the German side of the story, see Alexander Dallin (1981) *German Rule in Russia, 1941–1945* (Boulder, CO: Westview Press).
4. It is not clear what the basis is for the five million figure, but it presumably includes all deportations, not just the removals of whole nations.
5. The foregoing is based on more detailed descriptions in Nekrich's (1978) *The Punished Peoples* (New York: Norton). See Solzhenitsyn's (1978) *The Gulag Archipelago,* Volume III (New York: Harper & Row) for conditions that greeted many of the deportees in the Gulag.
6. The most recent indications are mixed with respect to relations between the former exiles and central authority. The Tatars now have an autonomous republic, Tatarstan, but along with other small national groups are discussing independent status. The Chechen success in defying Moscow has evidently stimulated such discussion, for example among the Ingush. See Abraham Brumberg's (January 30, 1992) "The Road to Minsk," *The New York Review of Books*, p. 26.

References

Alexeyeva, Ludmilla (1985). *Soviet Dissent.* Middletown, CT: Wesleyan University Press.
Brumberg, Abraham (January 30, 1992). "The Road to Minsk." *The New York Review of Books,* p. 26.
Conquest, Robert (1970). *The Nation Killers: The Soviet Deportation of Nationalities.* New York: Macmillan.
Dallin, Alexander (1981). *German Rule in Russia, 1941–1945.* Boulder, CO: Westview Press.
Gitelman, Zvi Y. (1972). *Jewish Nationality and Soviet Politics.* Princeton, NJ: Princeton University Press.
Guardian Weekly (November 17, 1991), p. 13.
Koch, Fred C. (1977). *The Volga Germans.* University Park: Pennsylvania State University Press.
Lewis, Robert A. (1971). "The Mixing of Russians and Soviet Nationalities and its Demographic Impact." In Edward Allworth (ed.), *Soviet Nationality Problems.* New York: Columbia University Press.
Mace, James (1983). *Communism and the Dilemmas of National Liberation: National Communism in Soviet Ukraine, 1918–1933.* Cambridge, MA: Harvard Series in Ukrainian Studies.
Medvedev, Roy A. (1972). *Let History Judge.* New York: Alfred A. Knopf.
——— (ed.) (1981). *Samizdat Register II.* New York: W.W. Norton & Co.
Nekrich, Aleksander (1978). *The Punished Peoples: The Deportation and Tragic Fate of Soviet Minorities at the End of the Second War War.* New York: W.W. Norton & Co.
Sheremet, Konstantin (May/June 1990). "Law and Social Change in the USSR of the 1990s," *Society,* p. 94.
Solzhenitsyn, Aleksander I. (1978). *The Gulag Archipelago,* Vol. III. New York: Harper & Row.

Chapter Five
Holocaust: The Jews

References

Arendt, Hannah (1964). *Eichmann in Jerusalem: A Report on the Banality of Evil* (rev. ed.). New York: The Viking Press.

Bauer, Yehuda (1979). *The Jewish Emergence from Powerlessness.* Toronto: University of Toronto Press.

Berger, Leslie (1988). "The Long-Term Psychological Consequences of the Holocaust on the Survivors and Their Offspring," pp. 175–221. In Randolph L. Braham (ed.), *The Psychological Perspectives of the Holocaust and of Its Aftermath.* Boulder, CO: Social Science Monographs.

Binion, Rudolph (1976). *Hitler among the Germans.* New York: Elsevier.

Davies, Norman (1982). *God's Playground: A History of Poland.* New York: Columbia University Press.

Fein, Helen (1979). *Accounting for Genocide: National Responses and Jewish Victimization during the Holocaust.* New York: The Free Press.

Gutman, Yisrael, and Krakowski, Shmuel (1986). *Unequal Victims: Poles and Jews during World War Two.* New York: Holocaust Library.

Hilberg, Raul (1985). *The Destruction of the European Jews.* New York: Holmes and Meier.

Krakowski, Shmuel (1984). *The War of the Doomed: Jewish Armed Resistance in Poland, 1942–1944* (O. Blaustein, trans.). New York: Holmes and Meir.

Lukas, Richard C. (1986). *The Forgotten Holocaust: The Poles under German Occupation, 1939–1944.* Lexington: University Press of Kentucky.

Niewyk, Donald L. (1992). *The Holocaust: Problems and Perspectives of Interpretation.* Lexington, MA: D.C. Heath.

Roth, John K., and Michael Berenbaum (1989). *Holocaust: Religious and Philosophical Implications.* New York: Paragon House.

Waite, Robert G.L. (1977). *The Psychopathic God, Adolf Hitler.* New York: Basic Books.

Wyman, David (1984). *The Abandonment of the Jews: America and the Holocaust, 1941–1945.* New York: Pantheon.

Eyewitness Accounts
References

Boder, David (1949). *I Did Not Interview the Dead.* Urbana: University of Illinois Press.

Chapter Six
Holocaust: The Gypsies

Notes

1. For a discussion of Gypsies in Holocaust historiography, see Sybil Milton, "The Context of the Holocaust," *German Studies Review* 13 (1990): 269–283; *idem,* "Gypsies and the Holocaust," *The History Teacher* 24, no. 4 (August 1991): 375–387; and Correspondence, *ibid* 25, no. 4 (August 1992): 515–521. For a discussion of postwar trends in German historical literature about Roma and Sinti, see Michael Zimmermann, *Verfolgt, vertrieben, vernichtet: Die nationalsozialistische Vernichtungspolitik gegen Sinti und Roma* (Essen: Klartext, 1989), pp. 87–98; and Kirsten Martins-Heuß, *Zur mythischen Figur des Zigeuners in der deutschen Zigeunerforschung* (Frankfurt: Haag and Herchen, 1983).

2. Yehuda Bauer, "Holocaust and Genocide: Some Comparisons," in Peter Hayes, ed., *Lessons and Legacies: The Meaning of the Holocaust in a Changing World* (Evanston, IL: Northwestern University Press, 1991), p. 42; *idem,* "Jews, Gypsies, Slavs: Policies of the Third Reich," *UNESCO Yearbook on Peace and Conflict Studies 1985* (Paris, 1987), 73–100; *idem,* "Gypsies," *Encyclopedia of the Holocaust,* 4 vols. (New York and London:

Macmillan, 1990), 2: 634–638; Hans-Joachim Döring, *Die Zigeuner im nationalsozialistischen Staat*, Kriminologische Schriftenreihe, vol. 12 (Hamburg: Deutsche Kriminalogische Gesellschaft, 1964), pp. 19ff. and 193; Bernhard Streck, "Nationalsozialistische Methoden zur Lösung der 'Zigeunerfrage,'" *Politische Didaktik: Zeitschrift für Theorie und Praxis des Unterrichts* 1 (1981): 26–37; and *idem*, "Die nationalsozialistischen Methoden zur 'Lösung des Ziegeunerproblems,'" *Tribüne: Zeitschrift zum Verständnis des Judentums* 20, no. 78 (1981): 53–77. Two excellent critiques of Streck's misinterpretations and unambiguous use of Nazi stereotypes and linguistic usage are: Joachim S. Hohmann, "Ihnen geschah Unrecht: Zigeunerverfolgung in Deutschland," *ibid.* 21, no. 82 (1982): 100–113; and Romani Rose, "Die neuen Generation und die alte Ideologie: Zigeunerforschung—wie gehabt?," *ibid.* 21, no. 81 (1982): 88–107.

3.   The most recent examples are Leni Yahil, *The Holocaust: The Fate of European Jewry* (New York and Oxford: Oxford University Press, 1990); and Richard Breitman, *The Architect of Genocide: Himmler and the Final Solution* (New York: Knopf, 1991).

4.   See Ludwig Eiber, ed., *"Ich wußte, es wird schlimm": Die Verfolgung der Sinti und Roma in München, 1933–1945* (Munich: Buchendorfer Verlag, 1993), pp. 14–16. For the development of police and psychiatric registration practices in the late nineteenth and early twentieth centuries, see Susanne Regener, "Ausgegrenzt: Die optische Inventarisierung der Menschen im Polizeiwesen und in der Psychiatrie," *Fotogeschichte* 10, no. 38 (1990): 23–38.

5.   See Eiber, *Die Verfolgung der Sinti und Roma in München*, pp. 40–45; Zimmermann, *Verfolgt, vertrieben, vernichtet*; and Joachim S. Hohmann, *Geschichte der Zigeunerverfolgung in Deutschland* (Frankfurt and New York: Campus, 1988).

6.   Karola Fings and Frank Sparing, *Nur wenige kamen zurück: Sinti und Roma im Nationalsozialismus* (Cologne: Landesverband Deutscher Sinti und Roma NRW and El-De-Haus, 1990), p. 3.

7.   Gisela Bock, *Zwangssterilisation im Nationalsozialismus: Studien zur Rassenpolitik und Frauenpolitik* (Opladen: Westdeutscher Verlag, 1986), pp. 361–368 and 452–456. See Theresia Seible, "Sintezza und Zigeunerin," in *Opfer und Täterinnen: Frauenbiographien des Nationalsozialismus*, ed., Angelika Ebbinghaus (Nördlingen: Greno-Delphi Politik, 1987), pp. 302–316.

8.   Wilhelm Stuckart and Hans Globke, *Kommentare zur deutschen Rassengesetzgebung* (Munich and Berlin: C. H. Beck'sche Verlagsbuchhandlung, 1936), p. 153; Arthur Gütt, Herbert Linden, and Franz Massfeller, *Blutschutz- und Ehegesundheitsgesetz*, 2nd ed. (Munich: J. F. Lehmanns Verlag, 1937), pp. 16, 21, 150, and 226.

9.   The *Reichsbürgergesetz* of 17 September 1935 reduced Jews and Gypsies to second class citizens because of their "alien blood," and in 1942 the 12th decree to the *Reichsbürgergesetz* resulted in most German Roma and Sinti being declared stateless. Jews and Gypsies above the age of 20 also lost the right to vote in Reichstag elections on 7 March 1936. See Joseph Walk, ed., *Das Sonderrecht für die Juden im NS-Staat: Eine Sammlung der gesetzlichen Maßnahmen und Richtlinien—Inhalt und Bedeutung* (Heidelberg and Karlsruhe: C.F. Müller Juristischer Verlag, 1981), no. 127, p. 156. Similarly neither Jews nor Gypsies were permitted to vote in the 10 April 1938 plebiscite on the incorporation of Austria; this directive was issued in Vienna on 23 March 1938, ten days after the incorporation of Austria. See Dokumentationsarchiv des österreichischen Widerstandes, Vienna [hereafter DÖW], file 11151.

10.   See Franz Calvelli-Adorno, "Die rassische Verfolgung der Zigeuner vor dem 1. März 1943," *Rechtsprechung zum Wiedergutmachungsrecht* 12 (Dec. 1961): 121–142; and Joachim S. Hohmann, *Robert Ritter und die Erben der Kriminalbiologie: "Zigeunerforschung" im Nationalsozialismus und in Westdeutschland im Zeichen des Rassismus* (Frankfurt, Bern, New York, and Paris: Peter Lang, 1991).

11.   See Heinrich Wilhelm Kranz, "Zigeuner, wie sie wirklich sind," *Neues Volk* 5, no. 9 (Sept. 1937): 21–27. Heinrich Wilhelm Kranz (1897–1945), an ophthalmologist, had joined both the Nazi Party and Nazi Physicians' League prior to 1933. After his appointment to teach race science (*Rassenkunde*) at Giessen, he obtained in 1938 the newly created chair for race science at Giessen University. He became the rector of Giessen in 1940. In Giessen

he also headed the Race Political Office of the Gau Hessen-Nassau. In 1940–1941, together with Siegfried Koller, he published their three-volume *Die Gemeinschaftsunfähigen*, advocating sterilization, marriage prohibition, and compulsory internment in labor camps for "asocials." For biographical data on Kranz, see Berlin Document Center: Heinrich Wilhelm Kranz file; Michael H. Kater, *Doctors under Hitler* (Chapel Hill and London: University of North Carolina Press, 1989), pp. 115–119; Benno Müller-Hill, *Murderous Science: Elimination by Scientific Selection of Jews, Gypsies, and Others; Germany, 1933–1945,* trans. George R. Fraser (Oxford: Oxford University Press, 1988), note 73 on p. 181; and Hohmann, *Geschichte der Zigeunerverfolgung,* pp. 115–121. For the antecedents of Nazi practice and ideology toward Gypsies, see *ibid.,* pp. 48–84. For a brief history of Ritter's office in the *Reichsgesundheitsamt,* see *Bundesgesundheitsblatt* 32 (March 1989), special issue "Das Reichsgesundheitsamt, 1933–1945: Eine Ausstellung."

12. The *Reichsvertretung der Juden in Deutschland* (Reich Representation of German Jews) was created in 1933, and served as the federal umbrella organization established by Jewish organizations in Germany to represent the Jewish community vis-à-vis the German government; part of its name was changed under the Nuremberg racial laws of 1935 from "of German Jews *(der deutschen Juden)"* to "of Jews in Germany *(der Juden in Deutschland)."* In February 1939, following the dissolution of all remaining individual Jewish organizations in Germany, the *Reichsvertretung* was formally replaced by the unified *Reichsvereinigung.*

13. The *Reichsvereinigung der Juden in Deutschland* (Reich Association of Jews in Germany) was the compulsory association of all Jews in Germany after 1939.

14. Bundesarchiv Koblenz [hereafter BAK], R36, files 1022 and 1023: Fürsorge für Juden und Zigeuner. The institutionalized handicapped faced similar deteriorating conditions, see Angelika Ebbinghaus, "Kostensenkung, 'Aktives Therapie' und Vernichtung," in *Heilen und Vernichten im Mustergau Hamburg: Bevölkerungs- und Gesundheitspolitik im Dritten Reich,* ed. Angelika Ebbinghaus, Heidrun Kaupen-Haas, and Karl Heinz Roth (Hamburg: Konkret Literatur Verlag, 1984), pp. 136–146.

15. BAK, R18/5644, pp. 215–227, containing cover letter and six-page memorandum from Oberregierungsrat Zindel to Staatssekretär Pfundtner, "Gedanken über den Aufbau des Reichszigeunergesetzes," 4 March 1936. The document states: "Auf Grund aller bisherigen Erfahrungen muß jedenfalls vorweg festgestellt werden, daß eine *restlose Lösung* des Zigeunerproblems weder in einem einzelnen Staate noch international in absehbarer Zeit möglich sein wird" (emphasis in the original). Reproduced in facsimile in Henry Friedlander and Sybil Milton, ed., *Bundesarchiv of the Federal Republic of Germany, Koblenz and Freiburg,* vol. 20 of *Archives of the Holocaust* (New York and London: Garland, 1993), 20, pp. 100–106.

16. Runderlaß des Reichs- und Preußischen Ministers des Innern betr. "Bekämpfung der Zigeunerplage," 5 June 1936 (III C II 20, N. 8/36), in *Ministerialblatt für die Preußische Innere Verwaltung* 1, no. 27 (17 June 1936): 783. Reproduced in facsimile in Eva von Hase-Mihalik and Doris Kreuzkamp, *Du kriegst auch einen schönen Wohnwagen: Zwangslager für Sinti und Roma während des Nationalsozialismus in Frankfurt am Main* (Frankfurt: Brandes and Apsel, 1990), pp. 43–44.

17. Staatsanwaltschaft [hereafter StA] Hamburg, Verfahren 2200 Js 2/84: Reich- und Preußisches Ministerium des Innern, Runderlaß betr. "Bekämpfung der Zigeunerplage," 6 June 1936 (III C II 20, N. 10/36); published in *Ministerialblatt für die Preußische Innere Verwaltung* 1, no. 27 (17 June 1936): 785. Reproduced in facsimile in Hase-Mihalik and Kreuzkamp, *Wohnwagen,* pp. 44–45.

18. See Ute Bruckner-Boroujerdi and Wolfgang Wippermann, "Das 'Zigeunerlager' Berlin-Marzahn, 1936–1945: Zur Geschichte und Funktion eines nationalsozialistischen Zwangslagers," *Pogrom* 18, no. 130 (June 1987): 77–80.

19. BAK, ZSg 142/3: Report about the Gypsy Camp Marzahn, 1 Sept. 1936, and report by G. Stein, "Untersuchungen im Zigeunerlager Marzahn," Frankfurt, 26 Oct. 1936.

20. See Hans Reiter, *Das Reichsgesundheitsamt 1933–1939: Sechs Jahre nationalsozialistische Führung* (Berlin: Julius Springer Verlag, 1939), pp. 356–358. See also the special issue "Das Reichsgesundheitsamt, 1933–1945: Eine Ausstellung,"

Bundesgesundheitsblatt 32 (March 1989): 13–30; and *Feinderklärung und Prävention: Kriminalbiologie, Zigeunerforschung und Asozialenpolitik*, vol. 6 of *Beiträge zur nationalsozialistischen Gesundheits- und Sozialpolitik* (Berlin: Rotbuch Verlag, 1988).

21. Robert Ritter, "Die Bestandsaufnahme der Zigeuner und Zigeunermischlinge in Deutschland," *Der Öffentliche Gesundheitsdienst* 6, no. 21 (5 February 1941): 477–489; *idem*, "Die Aufgaben der Kriminalbiologie und der kriminalbiologischen Bevölkerungsforschung," *Kriminalistik* 15, no. 4 (April 1941): 1–4; and *idem*, "Primitivität und Kriminalität," *Monatsschrift für Kriminalbiologie und Strafrechtsreform* 31, no. 9 (1940): 197–210. See also BAK, R73/14005, containing Ritter's reports and correspondence with the Deutsche Forschungsgemeinschaft; and BAK, ZSg 149/22, similar Ritter material in the Hermann Arnold Collection.

22. Adolf Würth, "Bemerkungen zur Zigeunerfrage und Zigeunerforschung in Deutschland," *Verhandlungen der deutschen Gesellschaft für Rassenforschung, Sonderheft des Anthropologischen Anzeiger Stuttgart* 9 (1937–1938): 92.

23. Müller-Hill, *Murderous Science*, pp. 143–149.

24. See Reimar Gilsenbach, "Wie Lolitschai zur Doktorwürde kam," in *Beiträge zur nationalsozialistischen Gesundheits- und Sozialpolitik* 6 (Berlin, 1988): pp. 101–134; Johannes Meister, "Schicksale der 'Zigeunerkinder' aus der St. Josefspflege in Mulfingen," *Württembergisch Franken Jahrbuch* (1984): 197–229; and *ibid.*, "Die 'Zigeunerkinder' von der St. Josefspflege in Mulfingen," *1999: Zeitschrift für Sozialgeschichte des 20 und 21. Jahrhunderts* 2, no. 2 (April 1987): 14–51. See also Eva Justin, "Die Rom-Zigeuner," *Neues Volk* 11, no. 5 (1943): 21–24; and Justin's dissertation, *Lebensschicksale artfremd erzogener Zigeunerkinder und ihrer Nachkommen*, vol. 57, no. 4 of the series *Veröffentlichungen aus dem Gebiete des Volksgesundheitsdienstes* (Berlin: Richard Schoetz, 1944).

25. Sophie Ehrhardt, "Zigeuner und Zigeunermischlinge in Ostpreußen," *Volk und Rasse: Zeitschrift des Reichsausschusses für Volksgesundheit und der Deutschen Gesellschaft für Rassenhygiene* 17 (1942): 52–57. Zentrale Stelle der Landesjustizverwaltungen, Ludwigsburg [hereafter ZStL], 415 AR 314/81, vol. 1, pp. 110–131 (Ehrhardt) and vol. 2, pp. 332–346 (Würth): Ermittlungsverfahren der StA Stuttart gg. Sophie Ehrhardt und Adolf Würth; these interrogations are reproduced in facsimile in Henry Friedlander and Sybil Milton, ed., *Zentrale Stelle der Landesjustizverwaltungen, Ludwigsburg*, vol. 22 of *Archives of the Holocaust* (New York and London: Garland, 1993), 22, pp. 315–348. See also Benigna Schönhagen, ed., *Nationalsozialismus in Tübingen: Vorbei und Vergessen* (Tübingen: Stadt Tübingen-Kulturamt, 1992), pp. 107, 110–111, 292, and 316–317.

26. For Cologne, see Karola Fings and Frank Sparing, "Das Zigeuner-Lager in Köln-Bickendorf, 1935–1958," *1999: Zeitschrift für Sozialgeschichte des 20 und 21. Jahrhunderts* 6, no. 3 (July 1991): 11–40. For Düsseldorf, see Angela Genger, ed., *Verfolgung und Widerstand in Düsseldorf, 1933–1945* (Düsseldorf: Landeshauptstadt Düsseldorf, 1990), pp. 126–133; and Karola Fings and Frank Sparing, *"Zt. Zigeunerlager": Die Verfolgung der Düsseldorfer Sinti und Roma im Nationalsozialismus* (Cologne: Volksblatt Verlag, 1992). For Essen and Gelsenkirchen, see Michael Zimmermann, "Von der Diskriminierung zum 'Familienlager' Auschwitz: Die nationalsozialistische Zigeunerverfolgung," *Dachauer Hefte* 5 (1989): 87–114; and *idem*, *Verfolgt, vertrieben, vernichtet*, pp. 18–22. For Frankfurt, see Wolfgang Wippermann, *Die nationalsozialistische Zigeunerverfolgung*, vol. 2 of the four part study *Leben in Frankfurt zur NS-Zeit* (Frankfurt: Stadt Frankfurt am Main—Amt für Volksbildung/Volkshochschule, 1986); Die Grünen im Landtag Hessen, Lothar Bembenek, and Frank Schwalba-Hoth, ed., *Hessen hinter Stacheldraht; Verdrängt und Vergessen: KZs, Lager, Außenkommandos* (Frankfurt: Eichborn Verlag, 1984), pp. 153–168; and Hase-Mihalik and Kreuzkamp, *Wohnwagen*. For Hamburg, see Rudko Kawczynski, "Hamburg soll 'zigeunerfrei' werden," in Ebbinghaus and others, *Heilen und Vernichten im Mustergau Hamburg*, pp. 45–53.

27. Stadtarchiv Frankfurt, Mag. Akte (Stadtkanzlei) 2203, vol. 1: Minutes of the Frankfurt City Council, 20 March 1936, concerning "Maßnahmen gegen das Zigeunerunwesen."

28. Hase-Mihalik and Kreuzkamp, *Wohnwagen*, p. 42.

29. Fings and Sparing, *Die Verfolgung der Düsseldorfer Sinti und Roma*, pp. 36–37.

30. StA Hamburg, 2200 Js 2/84: Decree of the Reich and Prussian Ministry of the Interior concerning "Vorbeugende Verbrechensbekämpfung durch die Polizei," 14 December 1937, and "Richtlinien," 4 April 1938. For the raids against so-called asocials, see Wolfgang Ayaß, "'Ein Gebot der nationalen Abeitsdisziplin': Die Aktion 'Arbeitsscheu Reich' 1938," *Beiträge zur nationalsozialistischen Gesundheits- und Sozialpolitik* 6 (Berlin, 1988): 43–74. For a survey of the concentration camp system, see Henry Friedlander, "The Nazi Concentration Camps," in *Human Responses to the Holocaust,* ed. Michael Ryan (New York and Toronto: Edwin Mellen Press, 1981), pp. 33–69; and Falk Pingel, *Häftlinge unter SS-Herrschaft: Widerstand, Selbstbehauptung und Vernichtung im Konzentrationslager* (Hamburg: Hoffmann and Campe, 1978). On camps for women, see Sybil Milton, "Women and the Holocaust: The Case of German and German-Jewish Women," in *When Biology Became Destiny: Women in Weimar and Nazi Germany,* ed. Renate Bridenthal, Atina Grossman, and Marion Kaplan (New York: Monthly Review Press, 1984), pp. 297–333, esp. pp. 305–307. For the 1933 imprisonment of several Sinti in Worms-Osthofen concentration camp, see Michail Krausnick, ed., *"Da wollten wir frei sein!": Eine Sinti-Familie erzählt* (Weinheim and Basel: Beltz and Gelberg, 1993), p. 73.

31. The persecution of Gypsies in incorporated Austria is relatively well documented. See Selma Steinmetz, *Österreichs Zigeuner im NS-Staat* (Vienna, Frankfurt, and Zurich: Europa Verlag, 1966); Erika Thurner, *Nationalsozialismus und Zigeuner in Österreich* (Vienna and Salzburg: Geyer Edition, 1983); and Andreas Maislinger, "'Zigeuneranhaltelager und Arbeitserziehungslager' Weyer: Ergänzung einer Ortschronik," *Pogrom* 18, no. 137 (1987): 33–36.

32. Dokumentationsarchiv des österreichischen Widerstandes, ed., *Widerstand und Verfolgung in Salzburg 1934–1945,* 2 vols. (Vienna and Salzburg: Österreichischer Bundesverlag and Universitätsverlag Anton Pustet, 1991), 2: 474–521; and Elisabeth Klamper, "Persecution and Annihilation of Roma and Sinti in Austria, 1938–1945," *Journal of the Gypsy Lore Society* 5, vol. 3, no. 2 (1993): 55–65.

33. B.A. Sijes, and others, *Vervolging van Zigeuners in Nederland, 1940–1945* (the Hague: Martinus Nijhoff, 1979).

34. See Michael R. Marrus and Roger O. Paxton, *Vichy France and the Jews* (New York: Basic Books, 1981), pp. 366–368.

35. See, for example, "Fahrendes Volk: Die Bekämpfung der Zigeunerplage auf neuen Wegen," *NS-Rechtsspiegel* (Munich), 21 February 1939, facsimile in Sybil Milton and Roland Klemig, ed., *Bildarchiv preussischer Kulturbesitz,* vol. 1 of *Archives of the Holocaust* (New York: Garland, 1990), part 1, figs. 150–151; "Die Zigeuner als asoziale Bevölkerungsgruppe," *Deutsches Ärzteblatt* 69 (1939): 246–247; and "Die Zigeunerfrage in der Ostmark," *Neues Volk* 6, no. 9 (September 1938): 22–27. See also DÖW, file 4942: Oberstaatsanwalt Dr. Meissner, Oberlandesgericht Graz, report to Reichjustizminister, 5 February 1940.

36. Runderlaß des Reichsführer SS und Chef der Deutschen Polizei im Ministerium des Innern, 8 December 1938, betr. "Bekämpfung der Zigeunerplage," *Ministerialblatt des Reichs- und Preußischen Ministeriums des Innern* 51 (1938): 2105–2110. See also "Ausführungsanweisung des Reichskriminalpolizeiamts," 1 March 1939, published in *Deutsches Kriminalpolizeiblatt* 12, special issue (20 March 1939).

37. See National Archives and Records Administration, Washington, Microfilm Publication T-70, reel 109, frames 3632755–6: Peter Raabe's remarks as President of the Reich Music Chamber published in *Amtliche Mitteilungen der Reichsmusikkammer,* 1 May 1939. The lists of expelled Gypsy musicians were published between February and December 1940. See *ibid.* frames 3632796–8, containing the list published on 15 February 1940. This material is cited in Alan E. Steinweis' *Art, Ideology and Economics in Nazi Germany: The Reich Chambers of Music, Theater, and the Visual Arts* (Chapel Hill and London: University of North Carolina Press, 1993), pp. 126–127, 132, and 205.

38. Nuremberg Doc. NG-684, copy in DÖW, file 4942.

39. StA Hamburg, Verfahren 2200 Js 2/84: RSHA Schnellbrief to Kripo(leit)stellen, 17 Oct. 1939.

40. ZStL, Slg. CSSR, vol. 148, pp. 55–57, and vol. 332, pp. 289–300, 306. Some of these documents are reproduced in facsimile in Henry Friedlander and Sybil Milton, ed., *Zentrale*

Stelle der Landesjustizverwaltungen, Ludwigsburg, vol. 22 of *Archives of the Holocaust* (New York and London: Garland, 1993), 22, pp. 71–78. See also Jonny Moser, "Nisko: The First Experiment in Deportation," *Simon Wiesenthal Center Annual 2* (1985): 1–30.

41. BAK, R18/5644, pp. 229–230: Letter from Leonardo Conti, Secretary of State for Health in the Reich Ministry of Interior, to the Central Office of the Security Police, Kripo headquarters, and the Reich Health Department, Berlin, 24 January 1940. The letter states:

> *It is known that the lives of Gypsies and part Gypsies is to be regulated by a Gypsy law (Zigeunergesetz). Moreover, the mixing of Gypsy with German blood is to be resisted and if necessary, this could be legally achieved by creating a statutory basis for the sterilization of part Gypsies (Zigeunermischlinge). These questions were already in a state of flux before the war started. The war has apparently suddenly created a new situation, since the possibility of expelling Gypsies to the General Government is available. Certainly, such an expulsion appears to have particular advantages at the moment. However, in my opinion, the implementation of such a plan would mean that because it is expedient to do this at the moment, a genuine radicalization would not be achieved. I firmly believe, now as before, that the final solution of the Gypsy problem (endgültige Lösung der Zigeunerproblems) can only be achieved through the sterilization of full and part Gypsies. . . . I think that the time for a legal resolution of these problems is over, and that we must immediately try to sterilize the Gypsies and part Gypsies as a special measure, using analogous precedents. . . . Once sterilization is completed and these people are rendered biologically harmless, it is of no great consequence whether they are expelled or used as labor on the home front.*

42. Hessisches Hauptstaatsarchiv, Wiesbaden [hereafter HHStA], 407/863. See also Milton, "Gypsies and the Holocaust," 380–381; Zimmermann, *Verfolgt, vertrieben, vernichtet*, 43–50; Hans Buchheim, "Die Zigeunerdeportation vom Mai 1940," in *Gutachten des Instituts für Zeitgeschichte*, 2 vols. (Munich, 1958), 1: 51ff.; and Michael Krausnick, *Abfahrt Karlsruhe 16.5.1940: Die Deportation der Karlsruher Sinti und Roma; ein unterschlagenes Kapitel aus der Geschichte unserer Stadt* (Karlsruhe: Verband der Sinti und Roma Karlsruhe e.V., 1991). The May 1940 deportation was linked to Reinhard Heydrich's instructions to chiefs of police and district governors in Germany in the so-called *Umsiedlungserlaß* of 27 April 1940 for the "resettlement, arrest, and deportation of Gypsies above the age of 17 from western and northwestern border zones." See BAK, R58/473: Richtlinien für die Umsiedlung von Zigeunern, Berlin, 27 April 1940.

43. See DÖW, file E18518: letter from Kripostelle Salzburg to the Reichsstatthalter Provincial President Dr. Reitter, Salzburg, 5 July 1940. The Gypsies were to be imprisoned in a special camp until deportation; there they would be registered and given medical examinations.

44. United States Holocaust Memorial Museum Archives, Record Group 7, Washington, Fojn-Felczer collection: Ruling (*Feststellung*) of the Reich Ministry of Interior, Berlin, 26 Jan. 1943, that Gypsies transferred to concentration camps on orders of the Reich Leader SS were defined as enemies of the Reich and, consequently, their property and possessions could be seized.

45. See Henry Friedlander, "The Deportation of the German Jews: Postwar German Trials of Nazi Criminals," *Leo Baeck Institute Yearbook* 29 (1984): 212.

46. Werner Präg and Wolfgang Jakobmeyer, ed., *Das Diensttagebuch des deutschen Generalgouverneurs in Polen, 1939–1945* (Stuttgart: Deutsche Verlagsanstalt, 1975), pp. 93, 146–147 (4 March 1940), 158 (5 April 1940), and 262 (31 July 1940). See also Friedlander, "Deportation of German Jews," 209.

47. StA Hamburg, Verfahren 2200 Js 2/84: RSHA Rundschreiben to Kripoleitstelle Königsberg, 22 July 1941. The fate of one East Prussian Sinti family deported to the Bialystok ghetto is detailed in Amanda Dambrowski, "Das Schicksal einer vertriebenen ostpreußischen Sinti-Familie im NS-Staat," *Pogrom* 12, nos. 80–81 (March–April 1981): 72–75.

48. See Jerzy Ficowski, *Cyganie na Polskich Drogach* (Cracow and Wroclaw: Wydawnictwo Literackie, 1985), pp. 129–151; Lucjan Dobroszycki, ed., *The Chronicles of the Lodz Ghetto, 1941–1944* (New Haven and London: Yale University Press, 1984), pp. 82, 85, 96,

101, and 107; Antoni Galinski, "Nazi Camp for Gypsies," 16 pp. mimeographed paper presented at a conference of the Main Commission for the Investigation of Nazi and Stalinist Crimes in Poland (Warsaw, April 1983); and DÖW, files 11293, 11477, and 18518. See also, Hanno Loewy and Gerhard Schoenberner, *"Unser einziger Weg ist Arbeit": Das Getto in Lodz, 1940–1944* (Frankfurt and Vienna: Löcker Verlag, 1990), pp. 186–87.

49. Raul Hilberg, Stanislaw Staron, Josef Kermisz, ed., *The Warsaw Diary of Adam Czerniakow: Prelude to Doom* (New York: Stein and Day, 1979), pp. 346–347, 351, 364–368, and 375. See the decree of the Warsaw police president "Mit den Juden auch die Zigeuner hinter Mauern," *Nowy Kurier Warszawski* no. 131 (5 June 1942); and Michal Chodzko, "Zigeuner in Treblinka," *Rzeczpospolita* (Lublin), no. 35 (6 September 1944), translated and excerpted in Tilman Zülch, ed., *In Auschwitz vergast, bis heute verfolgt: Zur Situation der Roma (Zigeuner) in Deutschland und Europa* (Reinbek bei Hamburg: Rowohlt, 1979), pp. 101–103. See also Yad Vashem, Jerusalem, E 39: Elias Rosenberg, "Das Todeslager Treblinka" (11 pp. typescript, written en route to Palestine, n.d. [1946?]), pp. 6–7. Rosenberg describes the arrival of two Roma transports in Treblinka in late November 1942 and records their defiance on the way to the gas chambers, thus necessitating the use of additional German SS and Ukrainian guards.

50. For one example, see the published judgment (sentenced to life imprisonment) against SS Lieutenant Colonel (*Obersturmbannführer*) Albert Rapp (chief of Sonderkommando 7a of Einsatzgruppe B) for killing Jews, Gypsies, and the handicapped; Landgericht Essen, 29 March 1965, 29 Ks 1/64, in *Justiz und NS-Verbrechen: Sammlung deutscher Strafurteile wegen nationalsozialistischer Tötungsverbrechen*, ed. Adelheid L. Rüter-Ehlermann and C. F. Rüter, 22 vols. (Amsterdam: University Press Amsterdam, 1968–1981), 20: no. 588, pp. 732 and 754ff. See also, ZStL, Sammlung UdSSR, vol. 245 Ac, p. 318: Extract from a 1945 Soviet report concerning the town of Elgawa, occupied on 30 June 1941, which notes that 6,000 Jews were killed; 44 institutionalized psychiatric patients were shot on 2 September 1941 and an additional 440 psychiatric patients were shot and buried in a nearby forest on 8 January 1942; and 280 Gypsies were shot and killed on 27–28 May 1942.

51. Nuremberg Doc. NO-3278: "Ereignismeldungen UdSSR 153," 9 January 1942.

52. *Trials of War Criminals before the Nuremberg Military Tribunals under Control Council Law No. 10* [Green series], 14 vols. (Washington: Government Printing Office, 1950–1952), 4: 286.

53. Yivo Institute, New York: Berlin Collection, Occ E 3–61: Reich Ministry for the Occupied Eastern Territories to Reichskommissar Ostland, 11 June 1942.

54. StA Hamburg, Verfahren 2200 Js 2/84: Anordnung des Reichsarbeitsministers betr: die Beschäftigung von Zigeuner, 13 March 1942. The parallel law for Jews was "die Verordnung über die Beschäftigung von Juden," 3 October 1941, *Reichsgesetzblatt* 1: 675, and "die Verordnung zur Durchführung der Verordnung über die Beschäftigung von Juden," 31 October 1941, *ibid.* 1: 681.

55. BAK, R19/180.

56. StA Hamburg, Verfahren 2200 Js 2/84: RSHA Schnellbrief betr: Einweisung von Zigeunermischlinge, Rom-Zigeunern und balkanischen Zigeunern in ein Konzentrationslager, 29 January 1943. The text of the 16 December 1942 unpublished decree has been lost, but the date of that December law is found in the first sentence of the 29 January 1943 Schnellbrief. Professor Richard Breitman, American University, kindly provided the information about the Himmler meeting with Hitler.

57. Danuta Czech, *Kalendarium der Ereignisse im Konzentrationslager Auschwitz-Birkenau 1939–1945* (Reinbek bei Hamburg: Rowohlt, 1989), p. 423.

58. See Milton, "The Context of the Holocaust," 275; and HHStA, 407/863: Richtlinien für die Umsiedlung von Zigeunern, Berlin, 27 April 1940.

59. Auschwitz-Birkenau State Museum and Documentation and Cultural Center of German Sinti and Roma, Heidelberg, ed., *Memorial Book: The Gypsies at Auschwitz-Birkenau*, 2 vols. (Munich, London, New York, and Paris: K. G. Saur, 1993), 2: 1547; and Czech, 774. See Elisabeth Guttenberger testimony, pp. 254–258.

60. See Benno Müller-Hill, *Tödliche Wissenschaft: Die Aussonderung von Juden, Zigeunern*

und Geisteskranken, 1933–1945 (Reinbek bei Hamburg: Rowohlt, 1984), pp. 68ff.

61. Walk, no. 480 on p. 397. See above, notes 9, 44, and 45. See also *Trials of War Criminals before the Nuremberg Military Tribunals under Control Council Law No. 10* [Green Series], 3: 713 (Nuremberg document PS 664). In 1943, German neighbors denounced the few remaining Sinti families living in Berlin-Karlshorst, see Reimar Gilsenbach, "Wie Alfred Lora den Wiesengrund überlebte: Aus der Geschichte einer deutschen Sinti-Familie," *Pogrom* 21, no. 151 (January–February 1990): 13–18.

62. See above, note 49.

63. See Helmut Krausnick and Hans-Heinrich Wilhelm, *Die Truppe des Weltanschauungskrieges: Die Einsatzgruppen der Sicherheitspolizei und des SD 1938–1942* (Stuttgart: Deutsche Verlags-Anstalt, 1981).

64. See Henry Friedlander, "The Manipulation of Language," in *The Holocaust: Ideology, Bureaucracy, and Genocide*, ed. Henry Friedlander and Sybil Milton (Millwood, NY: Kraus International Publications, 1980), 103–113.

65. The first special study on Gypsy labor assignments in concentration camps is Romani Rose and Walter Weiss, *Sinti und Roma im Dritten Reich: Das Programm der Vernichtung durch Arbeit* (Göttingen: Lamuv, 1991).

66. See Donald Kenrick and Grattan Puxton, *Sinti und Roma: Die Vernichtung eines Volkes im NS-Staat*, trans. Astrid Stegelmann (Göttingen and Vienna, 1981). Although dated, this useful study is European in scope. There are few comprehensive accounts for occupied Europe. For Belgium, see José Gotovitch, "Quelques donnes relatives l'extermination des tsiganes de Belgique," *Cahiers d'histoire de la seconde guerre mondiale* 4 (Brussels, 1976): 161–180. For Czechoslovakia, see Ctibor Necas, *Nad osudem ceskych a slovenskych Cikanu* (Brno, 1981); and idem, "Die tschechischen und slowakischen Roma im Dritten Reich," *Pogrom* 12, nos. 80–81 (March–April 1981): 62–64. For occupied and Vichy France, see Jacques Sigot, *Un camp pour les Tsiganes . . . et les autres: Montreuil-Bellay, 1940–1945* (Bordeaux: Wallada, 1983); and Uwe Knödler, "Saliers 1942–1944: Ein Romalager im besetzten Frankreich," *Pogrom* 20, no. 146 (May 1989): 39–40. For the Netherlands, see B.A. Sijes and others, *Vervolging van Zigeuners in Nederland 1940–1945*; and Leo Lucassen, *"En men Noemde hen Zigeuners"*: *De Geschiedenis van Kaldarasch, Ursari, Lowara en Sinti in Nederland, 1750–1944* (Amsterdam and the Hague: Stichting beheer IISG-SDU, 1990). For Poland, see Jerzy Ficowski, *Cyganie na Polskich Drogach*, 129–151; and idem, *Cyganie w Polsce: Dzieje i Obyczaje* (Warsaw: Wydawnictwo Interpress, 1989). See also David Crowe and John Kolsti, ed., *The Gypsies of Eastern Europe* (Armonk, NY, and London: M. E. Sharpe, 1991).

67. See Eiber, 10–11 and 132–36; and Thurner, appendix XXVIII, facsimile of 29 September 1948 notice from the Austrian Federal Ministry of the Interior to all police departments recommending expulsion for "the increasing Gypsy nuisance."

68. See Eiber, 136–138; Romani Rose, *Bürgerrechte für Sinti und Roma: Das Buch zum Rassismus in Deutschland* (Heidelberg: Zentralrat deutscher Sinti und Roma, 1987), 122–130; and Josef Henke, "Quellenschicksale und Bewertungsfragen: Archivische Probleme bei der Überlieferungsbildung zur Verfolgung der Sinti und Roma im Dritten Reich," *Vierteljahrshefte für Zeitgeschichte* 41, no. 1 (1993): 61–77.

69. See Rose, 46–67; Arnold Spitta, "Entschädigung für Zigeuner?: Geschichte eines Vorurteils," in *Wiedergutmachung in der Bundesrepublik Deutschland*, ed., Ludolf Herbst and Constantin Goschler (Munich: Oldenbourg, 1989), 385–401; Christian Pross, *Wiedergutmachung: Der Kleinkrieg gegen die Opfer* (Frankfurt: Athenäum, 1988); and Ingo Müller, *Hitler's Justice: The Courts of the Third Reich*, trans. Deborah Lucas Schneider (Cambridge, MA: Harvard University Press, 1991), 261–269. See also the script for the film by Katrin Seybold and Melanie Spitta, *Das falsche Wort: Wiedergutmachung an Zigeunern (Sinti) in Deutschland?* (Munich: Katrin Seybold Film Productions, 1980). For Austria, see Brigitte Bailer-Galanda, "Verfolgt und vergessen: Die Diskriminierung einzelner Opfergruppen durch die Opferfürsorgegesetzgebung," *Dokumentationsarchiv des österreichischen Widerstandes Jahrbuch* (1992): 16–20.

70. ZStL, 415 AR 55/82: StA Frankfurt, Verfahren gg. Robert Ritter u.a., 55 (3) Js 5582/48 (discontinued 28 August 1950); *ibid.*, 402 AR 116/61: StA Frankfurt, Verfahren gg. Eva

Justin u.a., 4 Js 220/59 (discontinued 27 April 1961); *ibid.*, 415 AR 930/61: StA Frankfurt, Verfahren gg. Eva Justin, 4 Js 220/59 (discontinued 12 December 1960).

71. ZStL, 415 AR 314/81: StA Stuttgart, Verfahren gg. Sophie Ehrhardt u.a., 7 (19) Js 928/81 (discontinued 29 January 1982, reinstituted 15 March 1982, discontinued 21 November 1985).

72. Christian Pross and Götz Aly, ed., *The Value of the Human Being: Medicine in Nazi Germany, 1918–1945*, trans. Marc Iwand (Berlin: Ärztekammer Berlin and Edition Hentrich, 1991), p. 38.

73. ZStL, 414 AR-Z 196/59: StA Frankenthal, Verfahren gg. Leo Karsten, 9 Js 686/57 abd 9 Js 153/59 (discontinued 30 July 1960); *ibid.*, 415 AR 930/61: StA Cologne, Verfahren Hans Maly u.a., 24 Js 429/61, 24 Ks 1/64 (discontinued 13 May 1970).

74. StA Berlin, Verfahren gg. Otto Bovensiepen u.a., 1 Js 9/65; microfilm of the indictment at the Leo Baeck Institute Archives, New York.

75. *Memorial Book: The Gypsies at Auschwitz-Birkenau*, 2: 1643. König committed suicide in prison.

76. Rose, 130–134; Henry Friedlander, "The Judiciary and Nazi Crimes in Postwar Germany," *Simon Wiesenthal Center Annual* 1 (1984): 27–44; Jürgen Weber and Peter Steinbach, ed., *Vergangenheitsbewältigung durch Strafverfahren?: NS-Prozesse in der Bundesrepublik Deutschland* (Munich: Günter Olzog Verlag, 1984); and Heiner Lichtenstein, *Im Namen des Volkes?: Eine persönliche Bilanz der NS-Prozesse* (Cologne: Bund, 1984). For Austria, see Karl Marschall, *Volksgerichtsbarkeit und Verfolgung von nationalsozialistischen Gewaltverbrechen in Österreich: Eine Dokumentation*, 2nd ed. (Vienna: Bundesministerium für Justiz, 1987).

77. Sybil Milton (text) and Ira Nowinski (photographs), *In Fitting Memory: The Art and Politics of Holocaust Memorials* (Detroit: Wayne State University Press, 1991).

78. See *Pogrom* 21, no. 154 (July–August 1990): 11–30, containing articles on Roma in Bulgaria, Czechoslovakia, Hungary, Romania, and the former German Democratic Republic.

Chapter Seven
Holocaust: Disabled Peoples

References

Alexander, Leo (1976). *Public Mental Health Practices in Germany: Sterilization and Execution of Patients Suffering from Nervous or Mental Disease*. Combined Intelligence Objectives Subcommittee, G2 Division, SHAEF (Rear) APO 413. U.S. National Archives.

Alexander, Leo, M.D. (July 14, 1949). "Medical Science Under Dictatorship." *New England Journal of Medicine* 241(2), 39–47.

Aly, Goetz, and Heinz Roth (1984). "The Legalization of Mercy Killings in Medical and Nursing Institutions in Nazi Germany from 1938 until 1941." *International Journal of Law and Psychiatry*, 7(2): 145–163.

Amir, Amnon (1977). *Euthanasia in Nazi Germany*. Unpublished doctoral dissertation. Albany: State University of New York Press.

Breggin, Peter Roger (January 1979). "The Psychiatric Holocaust." *Penthouse*, 81–84.

Dörner, Klaus (April 1967). Nationalsozialismus und Lebensvernichtung, *Vierteljahrshefte für Zeitgeschichte*, 15, 2, 122–152.

Gallagher, Hugh G. (1990). *By Trust Betrayed: Patients, Physicians, and the License to Kill in the Third Reich*. New York: Henry Holt.

Haller, Mark H. (1963). *Eugenics: Hereditarian Attitudes in American Thought*. New Brunswick, NJ: Rutgers University Press.

Hanauske-Able, Hartmut M. (August 1986). "Politics and Medicine: From Nazi Holocaust to Nuclear Holocaust: A Lesson to Learn?" *The Lancet*, 8501(2), 271–273.

Horner, Rosalie (September 26, 1991). "Opened Files Detail Nazi Program to Kill 'Defectives.'" *St. Louis Post Dispatch*, 25.

Kater, Michael H. (1987). "The Burden of the Past: Problems of a Modern Historiography of Physicians and Medicine in Nazi Germany." *German Studies Review*, 10(1), 31–56.

Klee, Ernst (1983). *"Euthanasie" im NS-Staat, Die "Vernichtung lebensunwerten Lebens."* Frankfurt: S. Fischer.

Lifton, Robert Jay (1986). *The Nazi Doctors: Medical Killing and the Psychology of Genocide.* New York: Basic Books.

Mitscherlich, Alexander (1962). *The Death Doctors.* Trans. James Cleugh [originally published in 1949]. London: Elek Books.

Muller-Hill, Benno (1988). *Murderous Science.* Oxford: Oxford University Press.

"Pope Condemns World War II Treatment of Handicapped" (1988, June 27). *New York Daily News,* p. 2.

Sereny, Gitta (1974). *Into That Darkness: From Mercy Killing to Mass Murder.* New York: McGraw-Hill.

Trials of War Criminals Before the Nuremberg Military Tribunals Under Control Council Law No. 10, Nuremberg, October 1946–April 1947 Volumes I and II. Washington, D.C.: U.S. Government Printing Office.

U.S. Nuremberg War Crimes Trials, November 21, 1946–August 20, 1947. National Archives Microfilm Publications, M887.

Wertham, Fredric (1968). *A Sign for Cain: An Exploration of Human Violence.* London: Robert Hale, Ltd.

Chapter Eight
The Indonesian Massacres

References

Anderson, Benedict (1965). *Mythology and the Tolerance of the Javanese.* Ithaca, NY: Cornell University Modern Indonesia Project.

——— (1987). "How Did the Generals Die?" *Indonesia,* 43: 109–134.

Aveling, Harry (1975). *Gestapu: Indonesian Short Stories on the Abortive Communist Coup of 30th September 1965.* Honolulu: University of Hawaii Southeast Asian Studies Working Paper, no. 6.

Cribb, Robert (1990). *The Indonesian Killings of 1965–1966: Studies from Java and Bali.* Clayton, Victoria, Australia: Monash University Centre of Southeast Asian Studies.

——— (1991). *Gangsters and Revolutionaries: The Jakarta People's Militia and the Indonesian Revolution, 1945–1949.* Sydney: Allen & Unwin.

Crouch, Harold (1978). *The Army and Politics in Indonesia.* Ithaca, NY: Cornell University Press.

Gittings, John (September 23, 1990). "The Black Hole of Bali." *Guardian Weekly,* p. 22.

Hefner, Robert W. (1990). *The Political Economy of Mountain Java.* Berkeley: University of California Press.

Hughes, John (1967). *Indonesian Upheaval.* New York: McKay.

King, Seth (May 8, 1966). "The Great Purge in Indonesia." *New York Times Magazine,* p. 89.

Kirk, Donald (February 25, 1966). "The Struggle for Power in Indonesia." *The Reporter,* p. 38.

Mortimer, Rex (1974). *Indonesian Communism Under Sukarno: Ideology and Politics, 1959–1965.* Ithaca, NY: Cornell University Press.

[Palmos, Frank] (August 20, 1966). "One Million Dead?" *The Economist,* pp. 727–728.

Soe Hok Gie (1990). "The Mass Killing in Bali," pp. 252–258. In Robert Cribb (ed.), *The Indonesian Killings of 1965–1966. Studies from Java and Bali.*

Spores, John (1988). *Running Amok: An Historical Inquiry.* Athens: Ohio University Center for International Studies.

Sundhaussen, Ulf (1982). *The Road to Power: Indonesian Military Politics 1965–1967.* Kuala Lumpur: Oxford University Press.

Turner, Nicholas (April 7, 1966). "Indonesian Killings May Exceed 300,000." *The Guardian.*

Walkin, Jacob (1969). "The Moslem-Communist Confrontation in East Java, 1964–1965." *Orbis,* 13(3): 822–847.

Young, Kenneth R. (1990). "Local and National Influences in the Violence of 1965," pp. 63–99. In Robert Cribb (ed.), *The Indonesian Killings of 1965–1966: Studies from Java and Bali.*

Eyewitness Accounts

Notes

1. Pak: an honorific meaning "father," used to address older men.
2. One of the Muslim viligante groups active in East Java.
3. General A. H. Nasution was at the time Chief of Staff of the Armed Forces and Minister of Defense. When the Untung group attacked his home on the morning of October 1, the general's daughter was killed by a stray bullet.
4. The League of Indonesian High School Students, affiliated with the PKI.
5. Nahdatul Ulama, the main Muslim political party.
6. Orthodox Muslims.
7. Islamic dormitories and schools.
8. The Indonesian Peasants' Front, affiliated with the PKI.
9. The Indonesian Women's Front, affiliated with the PKI.
10. The word "wanted" is in English in the original text.
11. Lubang Buaya (Crocodile Hole) was the name for the area, within the Halim Perdanakusumah Air Base perimeter, where the bodies of the assassinated generals were disposed of (down a disused well).
12. District Military Command.
13. The collection of river stones for the paving of roads was one of the traditional obligations laid on the rural population in Java.
14. H. J. Princen, an Indonesian of Dutch descent, was and is a major human rights activist who pursued humanitarian issues both under Sukarno's Guided Democracy and under Suharto's New Order. It was he who broke news of the alleged massacres in Purwodadi.
15. District; an administrative division.
16. The regional military command for Central Java.
17. Regency; the administrative division above *kecamatan*.
18. Eight thousand is, of course, far too low. Earlier Iskandar gives the *kabupaten* population as 700,000.

Chapter Nine
Genocide in East Timor

Notes

1. Curiously, the strongest argument for such an outcome was advanced in 1966 by an American academic, Professor Donald Weatherbee, who concluded that "In a sense Portuguese Timor is a trust territory, the Portuguese holding it in trust for Indonesia" [*Portuguese Timor: An Indonesian Dilemma*, Asian Survey, December 1966].
2. In June 1974, in contrast to most of his colleagues (who studiously avoided uttering the word "independence," Foreign Minister Adam Malik generously assured the Timorese of Indonesia's support for East Timor's independence. In a letter to Jose Ramos Horta, a Fretilin [Frente Revolutionaria de Timor-Leste Independente—the Revolutionary Front for an Independent Timor] leader, Malik wrote, *inter alia;* "The independence of every country is the right of every nation, with no exception for the people in Timor."
3. In 1957, for example, Indonesia told the UN First Committee, in a reference to Timor: "Indonesia has no claim to any territories which had not been part of the former Netherlands East Indies. No one should suggest otherwise or advance dangerous theories in that respect."
4. Within weeks of Pearl Harbor, Australian and some Dutch forces, ignoring the protests of the Portuguese—at that time neutral—had landed in East Timor. The Timorese gave the Australians extraordinary support until their withdrawal a year later. The Japanese then imposed a harsh occupation on the local population, which cost perhaps as many as 70,000 Timorese lives.
5. Under a special agreement (UKUSA), this intelligence surveillance was shared with the

United States and formed the basis of key Defense Intelligence Agency (DIA) briefings prepared for the Administration in Washington.

6. The Australian relationship was not as important to Indonesia as were its links with the United States, Japan, or the Netherlands, but a firm Australian stand on the decolonization rights of the Timorese, would certainly have influenced the policies of the other states, and reinforced Suharto's misgivings about military intervention.

7. Named after the dragon, or giant lizard, on the nearby island of Alor.

8. Frente Revolucionaria de Timor-Leste Independente—the Revolutionary Front for an Independent East Timor.

9. Uniao Democrata de Timor—the Timorese Democratic Union.

10. Based on remarks made to the writer by Major Metello, a senior representative of the Armed Forces Movement.

11. East Timor is predominantly Roman Catholic.

12. Based on talks in 1975 with two of those present at the meeting, Mousinho and Martins.

13. An example of the provocative disinformation role of Bakin at this point was the deliberate circulation of a story by *Operasi Komodo* agents that a number of Vietnamese officers had been smuggled in to Timor, and that they were training a Fretilin military force.

14. In fact, at the time most Fretilin leaders were out of the country, so it was an unlikely eventuality.

15. The humanitarian consequences of this civil war were assessed by the International Red Cross and an Australian Council for Overseas Aid (ACFOA) mission, of which I was the leader, with the former insisting that the total loss of life was about 1,500.

16. For an account of the withdrawal see Chapter 11 of *Missao Impossivel? Descolonizacao de Timor* by Mario Lemos Pires, the Portuguese governor at that time.

17. There is now ample evidence that these newsmen were shot by Indonesian troops, at least three of them having been executed some time after the force entered the village.

18. As an indication of Western complicity U.S. intelligence was informed in Jakarta by their Indonesian opposite numbers that the attack would take place on 6 December. However, American officials in Jakarta were shocked to discover that President Ford and Dr. Kissinger would be in the Indonesian capital on that day, and their hosts obligingly delayed the attack 24 hours.

19. *Angkatan Bersenjata Republik Indonesia*, Indonesian Armed Forces.

20. The Indonesian Army often used Timorese drivers, because of their familiarity with the difficult, and sometimes dangerous, road conditions in the interior.

21. The International Red Cross (ICRC) team, under the leadership of Andre Pasquier, was forced to withdraw before the invasion when Indonesia refused to respect its neutrality.

22. In fact, in October 1989 Governor Carrascalao, in a briefing to visiting journalists, gave a much lower total figure—659,000 which, he said, was growing at 2.63 percent annually. If this figure was correct, it gives an indication of the pace of immigration from elsewhere in Indonesia.

23. I have chosen deliberately to use the past tense, because the great upheaval caused by the invasion, especially the resettlement programs, has clearly had a significant impact on cultural and settlement patterns.

24. However, their attitudes were to an extent influenced by the hostility toward Javanese which was prevalent in Indonesian Timor, especially after the widespread killings in 1965–1966.

25. *Angkatan Udara Republik Indonesia*, Air Force of the Republic of Indonesia.

26. See *East Timor: Violations of Human Rights* (Amnesty International, London 1985).

27. A copy of this report, *Notes on East Timor*, is held by the writer.

28. A General Assembly resolution was followed by Security Council Resolution 384 (22 December 1975) which was unanimously agreed to, a rare achievement at that time.

29. Of Indonesia's major trading and aid-donor partners—the United States, Japan, West Germany, Australia, and the Netherlands—only the last-mentioned showed concern at the government level.

30. Testimony of Robert Oakley in "Human Rights in East Timor and the Question of the Use of U.S. Equipment by the Indonesian Armed Forces, before Subcommittees of the Com-

mittee on International Relations, House of Representatives, 95th Congress, 28 March 1977." And letter from Edward C. Ingraham, Department of State, 13 May 1977.

31. East Timor had by that time been designated Indonesia's 27th province. Canberra waited only until 1979 before according *de jure* status to its recognition.

32. The confidential report to which the author was given access stated that, of the 200,000, about 10 percent were in such bad shape that they could not be saved.

33. In fairness, it should be noted that Australia was a major provider of financial backing for the International Red Cross mission's operations.

34. Indonesia imposed strict conditions on the admission of the ICRC which limited its effectiveness. For example, for some years it was denied the right to carry out tracing activities. Moreover, most of its work was carried out by the Indonesian Red Cross, which was largely under military direction.

35. In fact, the last of these operations, *Operasi Senjum*, involving some 10,000 troops was carried out in the central mountain area in the middle of last November.

36. See in particular the annual reports published by Amnesty International, especially *East Timor: Violations of Human Rights* (London: Amnesty International, 1985). Also see the publications of Asia Watch, especially its detailed accounts of the circumstances of the Santa Cruz massacre in Dili in November 1991.

37. Based on an interview in 1984 of a priest from the Viqueque district. See also p. 142, John Taylor, *Indonesia's Forgotten War* (Zed Press, London 1990).

38. For accounts of this incident, see the Asia Watch Report, *East Timor: The November 12 Massacre and Its Aftermath* vol. 3, no. 26, 12 December 1991, the report by Amnesty International, *East Timor: After the Massacre* London, 21 November 1991, and the special report, *Death in Dili*, in the quarterly *Inside Indonesia*, no. 29 (Melbourne, Victoria).

39. Based on reports from Timorese who witnessed the killings or were in the vicinity at the time.

40. See *East Timor: The Courts-Martial* (Asia Watch, June 23, 1992).

41. It is noteworthy that while the Portuguese control was exercised by a military force rarely exceeding 1,000 men, the Indonesian military presence has ranged from between about 10,000 (at the present time) and more than 40,000 shortly after the invasion.

42. The spirited Timorese resistance took a heavy toll on Indonesian lives, as many as 20,000 reportedly having been killed since 1975.

43. Based on the assessment of the International Red Cross Mission, as conveyed to the writer some weeks after the civil war had ended.

44. The slaughter of more than half a million "communists," including their families, in the aftermath of the 1965 *Gestapu* affair, most of them by the army, was perhaps the bloodiest episode in Indonesia's history.

45. In a speech to Timorese officials in Dili, in February 1990, Murdani warned that those who still sought to form a separate state "will be crushed by ABRI. ABRI may fail the first time, so it will try for a second time, and for a third time." In a reference to Fretilin and its sympathizers he said: "We will crush them all . . . to safeguard the unity of Indonesian territory."

46. The governor, Mario Carrascalao, is of course a Timorese but, although he tries to be assertive and to do something for the rights of his people, real power rests in the hands of his "military advisers" and some technocrat specialists from Jakarta.

Chapter Ten
Genocide in Bangladesh

References

Ahmad, Kamruddin (1967). *A Social History of East Pakistan*. Dhaka: Crescent Book Store.

Ayoob, Mohammad, and K. Subrahmanyan (1972). *The Liberation War*. New Delhi: S. Chand and Company.

Bhutto, Zulfikar Ali (1971). *The Great Tragedy*. Karachi: Pakistan Peoples Party.

Brownmiller, Susan (1981). *Against Our Will: Men, Women, and Rape*. New York: Simon and Schuster.

Callard, Keith (1957). *Pakistan: A Political Study.* New York: Macmillan.

Coggin, Dan, James Shepherd, and David Greenway (August 2, 1971). "Pakistan: The Ravaging of Golden Bengal." *Time,* pp. 24–29.

Government of Pakistan (1972). *Summary of the White Paper on the Crisis in East Pakistan.* Islamabad: Governor of Pakistan.

Jackson, Robert (1975). *South Asia Crisis: India, Pakistan and Bangladesh.* London: Chatto and Windus.

Jahan, Rounaq (1972). *Pakistan: Failure in National Integration.* New York: Columbia University Press.

———— (1980). "Reflections on the National Liberation Movement, pp. 34–64. In Rounaq Jahan (ed.), *Bangladesh Politics: Problems and Issues.* Dhaka: University Press, Ltd.

———— (Summer 1973). "Elite in Crisis: The Failure of Mujib-Yahya-Bhutto Negotiations." *Orbis,* 17(2): 575–597.

———— (1973). "Women in Bangladesh," pp. 5–30. In Ruby Rohrlich-Leavitt (ed.), *Women Cross-Culturally: Change and Challenge.* The Hague: Mouton Publishers.

Jenkins, Loren, Tony Clifton, and Richard Steele (August 2, 1971). "Bengal: The Murder of a People." *Newsweek,* pp. 26–30.

Khan, Ayoob (1967). *Friends Not Masters.* London: Oxford University Press.

Loshak, David (1971). *Pakistan Crisis.* New York: McGraw-Hill.

Malik, Amita (1972). *The Year of the Vulture.* New Delhi: Orient Longman.

Marshall, Charles B. (1959). "Reflections on a Revolution in Pakistan." *Foreign Affairs,* 37(2): 247–256.

Mascarenhas, Anthony (1971). *The Rape of Bangladesh.* New Delhi: Vikas Publication.

O'Donnell, Charles Peter (1984). *Bangladesh.* Boulder, CO: Westview Press.

Palit, Major-General D.K. Palit (1972). *The Lightening Campaign: Indo-Pakistan War.* New York: Compton Press.

Payne, Robert P. (1973). *Massacre.* New York: Macmillan.

Rahman, Anisur (1968). *East and West Pakistan: A Problem in the Political Economy of Regional Planning.* Cambridge, MA: Center for International Affairs, Harvard University.

Sayeed, Sk. B. (1967). *The Political System of Pakistan.* Boston: Houghton Mifflin.

———— (1968). *Pakistan: The Formative Phase.* London: Oxford University Press.

Schanberg, Sidney (October 1971). "Pakistan Divided." *Foreign Affairs,* 50(1): 125–135.

(n.a.) (August 9, 1971). "Pakistan's Agony." *Time Magazine,* pp. 24–29.

Umar, Badruddin (1966). *Sampradaikata* [Communalism]. Dhaka: Janamaitri Publications.

———— (1967). *Sanskriti Sankat* [Crisis in Culture]. Dhaka: Granthana.

———— (1969). *Sanskritite Sampradaikata* [Communalism in Culture]. Dhaka: Granthana.

Chapter Eleven
The Burundi Genocide
References

Brown, Michael, Gary Freeman, and Kay Miller (1973). *Passing-By: The United States and Genocide in Burundi,* 1972. New York: The Carnegie Endowment for International Peace.

Chalk, Frank, and Kurt Jonassohn (1990). *The History and Sociology of Genocide: Analysis and Case Studies.* New Haven and London: Yale University Press.

Chretien, Jean-Pierre, André Guichaoua, and Gabriel Le Jeune (1989). *La Crise d'aout 1988 au Burundi.* Paris: Karthala.

Christensen, Hanne (1985). *Refugees and Pioneers: History and Field Study of a Burundian Settlement in Tanzania.* Geneva: United Nations Research Institute for Social Development.

Gahama, Joseph (1981). *Le Burundi sous administration belge.* Paris: Karthala.

Greenland, Jeremy (1976). "Ethnic Discrimination in Rwanda and Burundi," pp. 95–134. In Willem A. Veenhoven (ed.), *Case Studies on Human Rights and Fundamental Freedoms: A World Survey,* vol. 4. The Hague: Martinus Nijhoff.

Howe, Marvine (June 11, 1972). "Slaughter in Burundi," *The New York Times,* pp. 1, 4.

Hoyt, Michael (1972). Messages Concerning the Burundi Massacres to and from the American Embassy in Bujumbura, April 29–August 29, 1972. (Unpublished materials, available from Northwestern University Library)

Lemarchand, René (1970). Rwanda and Burundi. London: Pall Mall Press.

——— (1974). Selective Genocide in Burundi. London: Minority Rights Group.

——— (1992). "Burundi: The Politics of Ethnic Amnesia," pp. 70–86. In Helen Fein (ed.), Genocide Watch. New Haven and London: Yale University Press.

Malkki, Liisa (1989). "Purity and Exile: Transformations in Historical-National Consciousness Among Hutu Refugees in Tanzania" (dissertation, forthcoming, University of Chicago Press).

Chapter Twelve
The Cambodian Genocide—1975–1979

Notes

1. Interview of Comrade Pol Pot . . . to the Delegation of Yugoslav Journalists in Visit to Democratic Kampuchea, 1978. In his reply to this question, Pol Pot made no mention of his real name (Saloth Sar), or of his education in the palace compound in Phnom Penh, falsely claiming to have "been a monk for two years in the countryside" (pp. 20–21).

2. Michael Vickery denies that the Chams suffered genocide. He does so on a statistical basis, asserting that the toll was closer to 20,000 than 100,000. He says that I underestimate the number of survivors, and that "there had never been 250,000 [Chams] to begin with," but only about 191,000 in 1975 (Vickery, 1990, pp. 32–33). As I have shown, his figures are quite wrong (Kiernan, 1990a). Among other errors, the latter is based on a speculated pre-1975 Cham population growth rate that is far too low: for 1936–1955, for instance, far lower than my suggested 2.7% annual growth rate. The 1955 count of adult male Chams (Angkor, 30 June 1956), a minimum figure of which Vickery is unaware (Vickery, 1990, p. 33), indicates a 1955 Cham population of 150,000 and thus points precisely to a growth rate of at least 2.7% since 1936. Use of accepted national growth rates from 1955 to 1970, and of the 1970–1975 national growth rate of 2.46% (Kiernan, 1990a, p. 38), gives a 1975 Cham population of over 248,000.

3. A New Zealander working for an international agency carrying out a census of Phnom Penh's population, whom I met there in February 1975, told me that the population of Phnom Penh at that time was 1.8 million. My estimate of the number of "new people" at 3,050,000 is based on this figure plus an estimate of 1.25 million for the population of other towns and rural areas then under the control of Lon Nol's Khmer Republic. This second figure is comprised as follows: Battambang province's population in 1968 was 685,000 (Migozzi, 1973, p. 228); for 1975 I have estimated 700,000, both in rural areas and the swollen towns of Battambang, Sisophon, Nimit, Poipet, Pailin, and Maung Russei. The twelve other Cambodian urban centers under Lon Nol control in 1975 had totalled 231,000 inhabitants in 1968 (Migozzi, 1973, p. 228), but population increase as well as rural refugee influx greatly increased these numbers by 1975. For instance, Kompong Thom in 1968 had 14,000 inhabitants, but the figure rose to 60,000 in 1974 (a 76% increase); Kompong Chhnang had 19,000 in 1968, and 50,000 in 1975 (a 62% increase). An average increase of 50% from 1968 to 1975 would give nearly 350,000. I have estimated the rural population controlled by Lon Nol's regime outside Battambang (mostly in Kandal province) at another 200,000 people. With about 400,000 rural Khmers in Battambang, these comprised the 600,000 rural Khmer "new citizens."

4. For the evidence for the April 1975 national population of 7.894 million (which I have rounded down to 7.89 million here), see Kiernan, 1990a. The 1970 population was estimated at 7.363 million by Jacques Migozzi (1973, pp. 226, 212). A mid-1974 U.N. estimate, corroborated by an independent Western statistician then working with the Cambodian government, put the population at 7.89 million (W. J. Sampson, Economist, 26 March 1977). In a radio broadcast on 21 March 1976, the Pol Pot government gave its own count of the population as 7,735,279. For Vickery's unsustainable "guess" (his word) at only 7.1

million for 1975, see Vickery, 1984, p. 185. The number of survivors in 1979 is thought to have been 6.2 to 6.7 million.

5. Transcript of Sihanouk's Beijing press conference, 7 January 1979. In it Sihanouk said nothing at all about "Khmer Rouge brutality." He referred only vaguely to "violations of human rights," and said he hoped "that the horrible things they say outside Cambodia . . . have not happened." He gushed with praise for the Khmer Rouge regime: "The whole country [was] well-fed . . . the conditions were good. . . . Our people . . . had more than enough to eat. And suppose there is a regime of terror. How could they laugh? How could they sing? And how could they be gay? And they are very gay. . . . I saw the people. . . . The people were happy, so my conscience is in tranquillity. . . . It seems [there was] better social justice . . . I confess that the people seem to be quite happy with Pol Pot." Shawcross considers this a "denunciation" of the Khmer Rouge.

6. See Shawcross's letter to the *Observer*, 31 March 1991, my reply of 2 June 1991, and my "Why's Kampuchea Gone to Pot ?" *Nation Review* (Melbourne), 17 November 1978. Elsewhere I have reviewed the mythology and double standards pervading Shawcross's book, *The Quality of Mercy*. Ben Kiernan, "William Shawcross, Declining Cambodia," *Bulletin of Concerned Asian Scholars*, 18, 1, 1986, pp. 56–63.

7. Emphasis added. See Pilger's reply, and a letter from Martha Gellhorn, in the *Observer*, 24 March, 1991.

8. Quoted in Reuter, Melbourne *Age*, 3 September 1985; Senator Bob Kerrey, testimony before the U.S. Senate Foreign Relations Committee, 11 April 1991; "Pol Pot's Plans for Cambodia," *Economist*, 5 October 1991, p. 25; "Khmer factions pleased with Anand," Bangkok *Nation*, 10 May 1991.

9. I am grateful to Paul Donovan for drawing my attention to this issue.

10. Following the Charity Commission Inquirer's "unacceptable" finding on the "tone and content of some parts and particularly the prescriptive sections" of *Punishing the Poor,* Oxfam "decided that we should not reprint it or further distribute it ourselves." *Oxfam Team Briefing*, no. 13, November 14, 1991.

11. For a presentation of this case, see Vladimir Simonov, *Kampuchea: Crimes of Maoists and Their Rout*, Moscow: Novosti, 1979, p. 21: "Each act of the Kampuchean tragedy was staged according to a Chinese blueprint."

12. I am grateful to Penny Edwards for her translation of this material.

13. Samir Amin, paper presented under the title "The Lesson of Cambodia" at the "Conference on Kampuchea," Tokyo, May 31–June 3, 1981, pp. 4, 8–9, where he credits the Khmer Rouge with "the honour of having defined a strategy of anti-imperialist struggle," and then claims that "the revolution had been carried out by the peasants themselves." On page 15, Amin credits "Stalin, who in his time was a better Marxist than his successors." Amin's paper presents the Chinese government's view of the world at that time.

14. See note 13 above.

15. Emphasis added.

16. For some examples of Southeast Asian cultural eclecticism, see Jayne Susan Werner, *Peasant Politics and Religious Sectarianism: Peasant and Priest in the Cao Dai in Viet Nam*, New Haven, Yale University Southeast Asia Studies Council Monograph No. 23, 1981; and David Mitchell, "Communists, Mystics, and Sukarnoism," *Dissent*, Autumn 1968, pp. 28–32.

17. For a summary of this argument, see Richard J. Evans's 1989 *In Hitler's Shadow*. New York: Pantheon, pp. 74–76, and references cited.

18. Vickery (1984) states in his preface: "I have made no attempt to count the number of people with whom I talked. . . . Interested readers can do that for themselves" (p. xi). I counted 92 interviewees, including 17 teachers, 13 former students, 6 former Khmer Rouge, 4 people described as "bourgeois," "intellectual," or "elite," 3 "businessmen," 3 engineers and a doctor, 7 former Lon Nol officers and 3 soldiers, 6 carpenters, a radio mechanic, a truck driver, and 12 others of back-grounds clearly identified as urban. The remainder are unidentifiable by background. Vickery concedes that "bourgeois refugees . . . have provided most of the information used here" (p. 85).

19. Nine of Vickery's 90-plus informants are identified as female. See Vickery's (November 1988) "Violence in Democratic Kampuchea," p. 17.

20. Anthony Barnett, remarks at the August 1981 Chiangmai colloquium on Cambodia that led
     to the book, David P. Chandler and Ben Kiernan, 1983; see his chapter, "Democratic
     Kampuchea: A Highly Centralized Dictatorship," pp. 212–229.
21. In 1984 Chandler wrote: "Unfortunately, the imposition of foreign control, however humili-
     ating it is, particularly to people serving in the government itself, does not seem to arouse
     emotions as intense as the possibility that 'Pol Pot' might at some stage return to power"
     (Chandler, 1985, p. 182).
22. Report to the Economic and Social Council, 2 July 1985, 4/SUB, 2/1985/6, at 10 n. 17.
     "We agree with that assessment," the U.S. State Department conceded in 1989.
23. Campaign to Oppose Return of the Khmer Rouge, 100 Maryland Ave. N.E., Washington,
     D.C. 20002.
24. See John Pilger, "West Conceals Record on Khmer Aid," Sydney Morning Herald, August
     1, 1991, and "Culpable in Cambodia," New Statesman and Society, September 27, 1991.
     A report by Asia Watch and Physicians for Human Rights notes that "China and the United
     Kingdom are, or have been, involved in training Cambodian resistance factions in the use
     of mines and explosives against civilian as well as miliary targets." Land Mines in Cambo-
     dia: The Coward's War, New York, September 1991, see pp. 25–27, 59.
25. Quoted from "1991/8 Situation in Cambodia," Resolution passed by UN Subcommission
     on Human Rights, August 23, 1991, in Raoul Jennar (September 13, 1991) "The Cambo-
     dian Gamble."
26. U.S. Deputy Assistant Secretary of State for East Asian Affairs Kenneth Quinn, address to
     the Global Business Forum, Georgetown Club, Washington, D.C., September 16, 1991.
     Quoted in John Pilger, "Organized Forgetting," New Statesman and Society, November 1,
     1991, pp. 10–11.

References

Amin, Samir (1977). Imperialism and Unequal Development. Sussex, UK: Harvester Press.
Boua, Chanthou (January–February 1982). "Women in Today's Cambodia," New Left Review,
    No. 131, pp. 45–61.
——— (1991). "Genocide of a Religious Group: Pol Pot and Cambodia's Buddhist Monks," pp.
    227–240. In P. T. Bushnell, V. Schlapentokh, C. Vanderpool, and J. Sundram (eds.), State-
    Organized Terror: The Case of Violent Internal Repression. Boulder, CO: Westview Press.
Boua, Chanthou, et al. (May 2, 1980). "Bureaucracy of Death: Documents from Inside Pol Pot's
    Torture Machine," New Statesman, pp. 669–676.
Boua, Chanthou, David P. Chandler, and Ben Kiernan (eds.) (1988). Pol Pot Plans the Future:
    Confidential Leadership Documents from Democratic Kampuchea, 1976–77. Monograph
    No. 33. New Haven: Yale University Southeast Asia Studies Council.
Chandler, David P. (1991). The Tragedy of Cambodian History. New Haven: Yale University Press.
——— (1985). "Cambodia in 1984: Historical Patterns Reasserted?" pp. 177–186. Southeast
    Asian Affairs 1985. Singapore: Heinemann.
Chandler, David P., and Ben Kiernan (eds.) (1983). Revolution and Its Aftermath in Kampuchea: Eight
    Essays. Monograph No. 25. New Haven: Yale University Southeast Asia Studies Council.
Cohen, Nick (May 10, 1991). "Oxfam Activities Censured as too Political." Independent.
Curtis, Grant (1989). Cambodia: A Country Profile. Stockholm: Swedish International Develop-
    ment Authority.
Evans, Richard J. (1989). In Hitler's Shadow. New York: Pantheon.
Gellhorn, Martha (March 24, 1991). "No Trouble with Pilger" (Letter to the Editor). Observer, p. 54.
Guangxi People's Publishing House (1985). Cambodia.
Jackson, Karl (ed.) (1989). Cambodia 1975–1978: Rendezvous with Death. Princeton, NJ:
    Princeton University Press.
Indochina Digest (June 7, 1991), No. 91–23.
——— (August 30, 1991), No. 91–35.
——— (November 1, 1991), No. 91–44.
Jennar, Raoul (1991). The Cambodian Gamble, Jodoigne, Belgium: European Center for Far
    Eastern Research, pp. 35–36.

Kiernan, Ben (1983). "Wild Chickens, Farm Chickens, and Cormorants: Kampuchea's Eastern Zone under Pol Pot," pp. 136–211. In Chandler and Kiernan (eds.), *Revolution and Its Aftermath in Kampuchea: Eight Essays*. New Haven: Yale University Southeast Asia Studies Council.

——— (1985). *How Pol Pot Came to Power: A History of Communism in Kampuchea, 1930–1975*. London: Verso.

——— (1985b). "Kampuchea and Stalinism," pp. 232–250. In Colin Mackerras and Nick Knight (eds.), *Marxism in Asia*. London: Croom Helm.

——— (1986). "Kampuchea's Ethnic Chinese Under Pol Pot: A Case of Systematic Social Discrimination," *Journal of Contemporary Asia*, 16(1): 18–29.

——— (1986a). *Cambodia: Eastern Zone Massacres*. New York: Columbia University, Centre for the Study of Human Rights, Documentation Series No.1.

——— (1988). "Orphans of Genocide: The Cham Muslims of Kampuchea under Pol Pot," *Bulletin of Concerned Asian Scholars*, 20(4): 2–33.

——— (Winter 1989). "The American Bombardment of Kampuchea, 1969–1973," *Vietnam Generation*, 1(1): 4–41.

——— (February 17, 1989a). "Blue Scarf/Yellow Star: A Lesson in Genocide," *Boston Globe*, p. 13.

——— (1990). "The Survival of Cambodia's Ethnic Minorities." *Cultural Survival*, 14(3): 64–66.

——— (1990a). "The Genocide in Cambodia, 1975–1979." *Bulletin of Concerned Asian Scholars*, 22(2): 35–40.

——— (1991). "Genocidal Targeting: Two Groups of Victims in Pol Pot's Cambodia," pp. 207–226. In P.T. Bushnell et al. (eds.), *State-Organized Terror: the Case of Violent Internal Repression*. Boulder, CO: Westview Press.

——— (1991a). "Deferring Peace in Cambodia: Regional Rapprochement, Superpower Obstruction," pp. 59–82. In George W. Breslauer et al. (eds.), *Beyond the Cold War*. Berkeley, CA.: Institute of International Studies, University of California.

——— (1992). "The Cambodian Crisis, 1990–1992: The UN Plan, the Khmer Rouge, and the State of Cambodia." *Bulletin of Concerned Asian Scholars*, 24(2): 3–23.

——— (ed.) (1993). *Genocide and Democracy in Cambodia: The Khmer Rouge, the U.N., and the International Community*. New Haven: Yale University Southeast Asia Studies Council.

Kiernan, Ben, and Chanthou Boua (eds.) (1982). *Peasants and Politics in Kampuchea, 1942–1981*. London: Zed Books; New York: M.E. Sharpe.

Leopold, Evelyn (September 22, 1991). "Western Nations Want Former Cambodian Leader to Leave Country." Reuter, UN (NYC).

Migozzi, Jacques (1973). *Cambodge: faits et problèmes de population*. Paris: CNRS.

Mitchell, David (Autumn 1968). "Communists, Mystics, and Sukarnoism." *Dissent:* 28–32.

Murdoch, Lindsay (October 24, 1991). "Evans Backs Pol Pot Trial," *Melbourne Age*, p. 1.

Mysliwiec, Eva (1988). *Punishing the Poor: The International Isolation of Kampuchea*. Oxford: Oxfam.

New York Times (August 28, 1991). "Sighted in Cambodia: Peace" (An Editorial). *New York Times*, p. A20.

Pilger, John (May 17, 1991). "In Defence of Oxfam." *New Statesman and Society*, p. 8.

Pol Pot (1978). *Interview of Comrade Pol Pot . . . to the Delegation of Yugoslav Journalists in Visit to Democratic Kampuchea*. Phnom Penh: March 1978.

Shawcross, William (September 26, 1979). *Sunday Telegraph*.

——— (1979). *Sideshow: Kissinger, Nixon and the Destruction of Cambodia*. New York: Pocket Books.

——— (January 24, 1980). "The End of Cambodia." *New York Review of Books*, 26(21 and 22): 25–30.

——— (1984). *The Quality of Mercy: Cambodia, Holocaust and Modern Conscience*. London: André Deutsch.

——— (September 27, 1984) "An Exchange on Cambodia." *New York Review of Books*, XXXL(14): 63–65.

———(March 17, 1991). "The Trouble with John Pilger." *Observer* (London), p. 20.

——— (March 31, 1991). "Shawcross and Pilger: Now for Round Two." *Observer* (London), p. 25.

Shenon, Philip (October 24, 1991). "Cambodian Factions Sign Peace Pact." *New York Times*, p. A16.

Simonov, Vladimir (1979). *Kampuchea: Crimes of Maoists and Their Rout*. Moscow: Novosti.

Thion, Serge (1993). "Genocide as a Political Commodity." In Ben Kiernan (ed.), *Genocide and Democracy in Cambodia: The Khmer Rouge, the U.N., and the International Community*. New Haven: Yale University Southeast Asia Studies Council. [Originally presented as a paper at the Yale Law School symposium on "Genocide and Democracy in Cambodia," February 21–22, 1992.]

Van Leur, J. C. (1955). *Indonesian Trade and Society*. The Hague: W. Van Hoeve.

Vatikiotis, Michael (August 11, 1988). "Smiles and Soft Words." *Far Eastern Economic Review*, pp. 28–29.

Vickery, Michael (1989). "Cambodia (Kampuchea): History, Tragedy and Uncertain Future." *Bulletin of Concerned Asian Scholars*, 21(2–4): 35–58.

———— (Forthcoming). *Cambodia Before Angkor*. Clayton, Australia: Monash Centre of Southeast Asian Studies.

———— (1984). *Cambodia 1975–1982*. Boston: South End.

———— (1990). "Comments on Cham Population Figures." *Bulletin of Concerned Asian Scholars*, 22(1): 31–33.

———— (November 1988). "Violence in Democratic Kampuchea: Some Problems of Explanation." Paper distributed at a conference on State-Organized Terror: The Case of Violent Internal Repression, Michigan State University.

Werner, Jane Susan (1981). *Peasant Politics and Religious Sectarianism: Peasant and Priest in the Lao Doi in Viet Nam*. New Haven: Yale University Southeast Asia Studies Council Monograph No. 23.

Chapter Thirteen
Physical and Cultural Genocide of Various Indigenous Peoples

References

Adalian, Rouben (1991). "The Armenian Genocide: Context and Legacy." *Social Education* 55(2): 99–104.

Africa Watch (1990). *Somalia, A Government at War With Its Own People: Testimonies about the Killings and Conflict in the North*. Washington, D.C.: Human Rights Watch (Africa Watch).

Albert, Bruce (1992). "Indian Lands, Environmental Policy and Military Geopolitics in the Development of the Brazilian Amazon: The Case of the Yanomami." *Development and Change* 23(1): 35–70.

American Anthropological Association (1991). *Report of the Special Commission to Investigate the Situation of the Brazilian Yanomami, June 1991*. Washington, D.C.: American Anthropological Association.

Amnesty International (1992a). *Human Rights Violations against the Indigenous Peoples of the Americas*. New York: Amnesty International.

———— (1992b). *United States of America: Human Rights and American Indians*. New York: Amnesty International.

Anti-Slavery Society (1984). *The Chittagong Hill Tracts: Militarization, Oppression, and the Hill Tribes*. London: Anti-Slavery Society.

Arens, Richard (1978). "Death Camps in Paraguay." *American Indian Journal* 4(2): 2–13.

———— (ed.) (1976). *Genocide in Paraguay*. Philadelphia: Temple University Press.

Barta, Tony (1987). "Relations of Genocide: Land and Lives in the Colonization of Australia." In Isidor Walliman and Michael N. Dobkowski (eds.), *Genocide and the Modern Age: Etiology and Case Studies of Mass Death*, pp. 237–25l. Westport, CT: Greenwood Press.

Bodley, John H. (1990). *Victims of Progress*. Third Edition. Mountain View, CA: Mayfield Publishing Company.

Bridgman, J. M. (1981). *The Revolt of the Hereros.* Berkeley and Los Angeles: University of California Press.

Burger, Julian (1987). *Report from the Frontier: The State of the World's Indigenous Peoples.* London: Zed Press.

———— (1990). *The Gaia Atlas of First Peoples: A Future for the Indigenous World.* New York and London: Anchor Books (Doubleday).

Carmack, Robert, M. (ed.) (1988). *Harvest of Violence: The Maya Indians and the Guatemalan Crisis.* Norman: University of Oklahoma Press.

Chalk, Frank, and Kurt Jonassohn (1990). *The History and Sociology of Genocide: Analyses and Case Studies.* New Haven: Yale University Press.

Chapin, Mac (1986). "The 500,000 Invisible Indians of El Salvador." *Cultural Survival Quarterly* 13(3): 11–16.

Chittagong Hill Tracts Commission (1991). *Life Is Not Ours: Land and Human Rights in the Chittagong Hill Tracts, Bangladesh. Report of the Chittagong Hill Tracts Commission.* Copenhagen and London: International Work Group for Indigenous Affairs and Anti-Slavery International.

Chowdhury, Akram H. (1989). "Self-Determination, the Chittagong, and Bangladesh." In David P. Forsythe (ed.), *Human Rights and Development: International Views,* pp. 292–301. New York: St. Martin's Press.

Churchill, Ward (1991). "Genocide in Arizona? The 'Navajo-Hopi Land Dispute' in Perspective." In Ward L. Churchill (ed.), *Critical Issues in Native North America, Volume II,* pp. 104–146. Copenhagen, Denmark: International Work Group for Indigenous Affairs.

Clay, Jason (1984). "Genocide in the Age of Enlightenment." *Cultural Survival Quarterly* 12(3): 1.

Crow Dog, Mary, and Richard Erdoes (1990). *Lakota Woman.* New York: Grove Weidenfeld.

Dadrian, Vahakn N. (1975). "A Typology of Genocide." *International Review of Modern Sociology* 5(2): 201–212.

———— (1986). "The Naim-Andonian Documents of the World War I Destruction of Ottoman Armenians: The Anatomy of a Genocide." *International Journal of Middle Eastern Studies* 18(3): 311–360.

Davis, Shelton (1977). *Victims of the Miracle: Development and the Indians of Brazil.* Cambridge: Cambridge University Press.

DeLoria, Vine, Jr. (1969). *Custer Died for Your Sins.* New York: Macmillan.

———— (ed.) (1985). *American Indian Policy in the Twentieth Century.* Norman: University of Oklahoma Press.

Dodds, David (1986). "Miskito and Sumo Refugees: Caught in Conflict in Honduras." *Cultural Survival Quarterly* 13(3): 3–6.

Drechsler, Horst (1980). *Let Us Die Fighting: The Struggle of the Herero and the Nama against German Imperialism.* London: Zed Press.

Dunbar Ortiz, Roxanne (1986). "The Miskito Indians of Nicaragua." *Minority Rights Group Report 79.* London: Minority Rights Group.

Durning, Alan (1992). "Guardians of the Land: Indigenous Peoples and the Health of the Earth." *Worldwatch Paper 112.* Washington, D.C.: Worldwatch Institute.

Fay, Chip (1987). *Counter-Insurgency and Tribal Peoples in the Philippines.* Washington, D.C.: Survival International USA.

Fein, Helen (1984). "Scenarios of Genocide: Models of Genocide and Critical Responses." In Israel W. Charney (ed.), *Toward the Understanding and Prevention of Genocide: Proceedings of the International Conference on the Holocaust and Genocide,* pp. 3–31. Boulder, CO: Westview Press.

———— (1990). "Genocide: A Sociological Perspective." *Current Sociology* 38(1): 1–126.

———— (1992). "Introduction." In Helen Fein (ed.), *Genocide Watch,* pp. 1–14. New Haven: Yale University Press.

Gordon, Robert G. (1992). *The Bushman Myth: The Making of a Namibian Underclass.* Boulder, CO: Westview Press.

Gurr, Ted Robert, and James R. Scaritt (1989). "Minorities Rights at Risk: A Global Survey." *Human Rights Quarterly* 11(3): 375–405.

Gurr, Ted Robert, and Barbara Harff (1992). "The Rights of Collectivities: Principles and Proce-
    dures in Measuring the Human Rights Status of Communal and Political Groups." In Tho-
    mas B. Jabine and Richard P. Claude (eds.), *Human Rights and Statistics: Getting the
    Record Straight*, pp. 159–187. Philadelphia: University of Pennsylvania Press.
Harff, Barbara (1984). *Genocide and Human Rights: International Legal and Political Issues*. Den-
    ver, CO: Graduate School of International Studies, University of Denver.
Headland, Thomas N., and Janet D. Headland (n.d.). "Limitation of Human Rights, Land Exclu-
    sion, and Tribal Extinction: The Agta Negritos of the Philippines." Unpublished Manuscript.
Heinz, Wolfgang (1988). *Indigenous Populations, Ethnic Minorities, and Human Rights*. Berlin:
    Quorum Verlag.
Hitchcock, Robert K. (1985). "The Plight of Indigenous Peoples." *Social Education* 49(6): 457–
    462.
——— (1993). *Kalahari Communities: Indigenous Peoples, Politics, and the Environment in
    Southern Africa*. Copenhagen, Denmark: International Work Group for Indigenous Affairs.
Horowitz, Irving Louis (1980). *Taking Lives: Genocide and State Power*. New Brunswick, NJ:
    Transaction Books.
Independent Commission on International Humanitarian Issues (1987). *Indigenous Peoples: A
    Global Quest for Justice*. London: Zed Press.
International Labour Office (1953). *Indigenous Peoples: Living and Working Conditions of Ab-
    original Populations in Independent Countries*. Geneva: International Labour Office.
International Work Group for Indigenous Affairs (1988). *IWGIA Yearbook 1987: Indigenous
    Peoples and Development*. Copenhagen, Denmark: International Work Group for Indig-
    enous Affairs.
——— (1991). "Bougainville: Actual Situation." *IWGIA Newsletter* 91(2): 3–6.
——— (1992). *IWGIA Yearbook*. Copenhagen, Denmark: International Work Group for Indig-
    enous Affairs.
Jaimes, M. Annette (1992). "Introduction: Sand Creek, The Morning After." In M. Annette
    Jaimes (ed.), *The State of Native America: Genocide, Colonization, and Resistance*, pp. 1–
    12. Boston: South End Press.
Kiernan, Ben (1991). "The Nature of the Genocide in Cambodia (Kampuchea)." *Social Education*
    55(2): 114–115.
Kuper, Leo (1981). *Genocide: Its Political Use in the Twentieth Century*. New Haven: Yale Univer-
    sity Press.
——— (1984). "Types of Genocide and Mass Murder." In Israel W. Charny (ed.), *Toward the
    Understanding and Prevention of Genocide: Proceedings of the International Conference
    on the Holocaust and Genocide*, pp. 32–47. Boulder, CO: Westview Press.
——— (1985). *The Prevention of Genocide*. New Haven: Yale University Press.
Legters, Lyman H. (1988). "The American Genocide." *Policy Studies Journal* 16(4): 768–777.
Lemarchand, René (1992). "Burundi: The Politics of Ethnic Amnesia." In Helen Fein (ed.), *Geno-
    cide Watch*, pp. 70–86. New Haven: Yale University Press.
Lewis, Norman (February 23, 1969). "Genocide—From Fire and Sword to Arsenic and Bullet,
    Civilization Has Sent Six Million Indians to Extinction." *Sunday Times Magazine* [London].
——— (1974). *Genocide: A Documentary Report on the Conditions of Indian Peoples*. Berkeley,
    CA: Indigena and the American Friends of Brazil.
——— (1976). "The Camp at Cecilio Baez." In Richard Arens (ed.), *Genocide in Paraguay*, pp.
    58–68. Philadelphia: Temple University Press.
Manz, Beatriz (1988). *Refugees of a Hidden War: The Aftermath of Counterinsurgency in Guate-
    mala*. Albany: State University of New York Press.
Martinez Cobo, Jose R. (1987). *Study of the Problem of Discrimination against Indigenous Popu-
    lations. Volume V: Conclusions, Proposals, and Recommendations*. New York: United Na-
    tions.
Matthiessen, Peter (1983). *In the Spirit of Crazy Horse*. New York: Viking.
Maybury-Lewis, David, and James Howe (1980). *The Indian Peoples of Paraguay: Their Plight
    and Their Prospects*. Cambridge, MA: Cultural Survival Inc.
Menchu, Rigoberta (1984). *I, Rigoberta Menchu, An Indian Woman of Guatemala*. Edited and
    introduced by Elisabeth Burgos-Debray, translated by Ann Wright. London: Verso Editions.

Mey, Wolfgang, (ed.) (1984). *Genocide in the Chittagong Hill Tracts.* IWGIA Document No. 51. Copenhagen, Denmark: International Work Group for Indigenous Affairs.

Mezhoud, Salem (1992). "Murder of a Romantic Myth: The Tuareg and Their Survival." *Anti-Slavery Reporter* 13(8): 106–110.

Middle East Watch and Physicians for Human Rights (1993). *The Anfal Campaign in Iraqi Kurdistan: The Destruction of Koreme.* New York and Washington: Middle East Watch and Physicians for Human Rights .

Montejo, Victor (n.d.). "Testimony of Violence in Guatemala: A Mayan Indian Account." In C. Patrick Morris and Robert K. Hitchcock (eds.), *International Human Rights and Indigenous Peoples.*

Morris, Glenn T., and Ward Churchill (1987). "Between a Rock and a Hard Place—Left-Wing Revolution, Right-Wing Reaction and the Destruction of Indigenous People." *Cultural Survival Quarterly* 11(3): 17–24.

Munzel, Mark (1973). *The Ache Indians: Genocide in Paraguay.* IWGIA Document No. II. Copenhagen, Denmark: International Work Group for Indigenous Affairs.

——— (1985). "The Manhunts: Ache Indians in Paraguay." In Willem A. Veenhoven et al. (eds.), *Case Studies on Human Rights and Fundamental Freedoms: A World Survey, Volume 4,* pp. 351–403. The Hague: Nijhoff.

Price, David (1989). *Before the Bulldozer: The Nambiquara Indians and the World Bank.* Cabin John, MD: Seven Locks Press.

Saeedpour, Vera Beaudin (1992). "Establishing State Motives for Genocide: Iraq and the Kurds." In Helen Fein (ed.), *Genocide Watch,* pp. 59–69. New Haven: Yale University Press.

Sanders, Douglas (1989). "The UN Working Group on Indigenous Populations." *Human Rights Quarterly* 11(3): 406–433.

Smith, Roger W. (1987). "Human Destructiveness and Politics: The Twentieth Century As An Age of Genocide." In Isidor Walliman and Michael N. Dobkowski (eds.), *Genocide and the Modern Age: Etiology and Case Studies of Mass Death,* pp. 18–34. Westport, CT: Greenwood Press.

Souindola, Simao (1981). "Angola: Genocide of the Bosquimanos." *IWGIA Newsletter* 31–32, 66–68.

State Department (1986). *Dispossessed: The Miskito Indians in Nicaragua.* U.S. State Department Publication 9478. Washington, D.C.: U.S. Government Printing Office.

Steingraber, Sandra (1986). "Ethiopia's Policy of Genocide Against the Anuak of Gambella." *Cultural Survival Quarterly* 10(3): 53–56.

Survival International (October, 1986a). *Chile: Army Shoots Up Indian Villages. Guatemala: Renewed Threat at Santiago Atitlan.* Urgent Action Bulletin Double Update, UAB/CHI/1a, UAB/GUA/2a. London: Survival International.

——— (June 1986b). *Sarawak: Drowning the Longhouses.* Urgent Action Bulletin, UAB/Mal/1. London: Survival International.

——— (August 1987a). *Ecuador: Indians Kill Bishop As Oil Companies Invade.* Urgent Action Bulletin UAB/ECU/2. London: Survival International.

——— (June 1987b). *Guatemala: Indians of Santiago Atitlan Threatened with Death.* Urgent Action Bulletin UAB/GUA/2b. London: Survival International.

——— (June 1987c). *Philippines: Military Attacks on Tribal Filipinos Continue.* Urgent Action Bulletin, UAB/PHIL/4b. London: Survival International.

——— (July 1987d). *Malaysia: Tribal Blockade Halts Logging in Sarawak.* Urgent Action Bulletin, UAB/MAL/2. London: Survival International.

——— (September 1988a). *Paraguay: World Bank Project Threatens Forest Indians.* Urgent Action Bulletin, UAB/PGY/2. London: Survival International.

——— (April 1988b). *Brazil: Ticuna Massacre.* Urgent Action Bulletin, UAB/BRZ/11. London: Survival International.

——— (August 1988c). *Indonesia: Transmigration Threat to New Guinea Highlands.* Urgent Action Bulletin, UAB/INDO/2b. London: Survival International.

——— (October 1988d). *Philippines: Tribals Shelled and Bombed for Defending Their Lands.* Urgent Action Bulletin, UAB/PHIL/5. London: Survival International.

——— (September 1989a). *Malaysia: Sarawak Natives Fear Fact-finding Mission Will Ignore Their Rights.* Urgent Action Bulletin, UAB/MAL/2c. London: Survival International.

—— (February 1989b). *Malaysia: Sarawak Natives Arrested for Defending Their Forests.* Urgent Action Bulletin, UAB/MAL/2b. London: Survival International.

—— (March 1990a). *Ecuador: Oil Companies Force 700 Waorani off Their Land.* Urgent Action Bulletin, UAB/ECU/2a. London: Survival International.

—— (January 1990b). *Tanzania: Wheat Farms Engulf the Land of the Barabaig.* Urgent Action Bulletin, UAB/TAN/1. London: Survival International.

—— (August 1991a). *Colombia: Flu Threatens to Wipe Out the Nukak.* Urgent Action Bulletin. London: Survival International.

—— (April 1991b). *Indonesia: Paper Companies to Fell Tribal Forests.* Urgent Action Bulletin. London: Survival International.

—— (May 1992a). *Brazil: Arara Indians Face Extinction.* Urgent Action Bulletin. London: Survival International.

—— (January 1992b). *Colombia: Indians Massacred in Brutal Attack.* Urgent Action Bulletin. London: Survival International.

—— (July 1992c). *Ecuador: Dallas Oil Company to Invade Waorani Land.* Urgent Action Bulletin. London: Survival International.

—— (January 1992d). *Sudan: Sudanese Tribes Devastated.* Urgent Action Bulletin. London: Survival International.

—— (1993). *The Denial of Genocide.* London: Survival International.

Sweptson, Lee (1989). "Indigenous and Tribal Peoples and International Law: Recent Developments." *Current Anthropology* 30(2): 259–264.

Tatz, Colin (1991). "Australia's Genocide: They Soon Forget Their Offspring." *Social Education* 55(2): 97–98.

Totten, Samuel (1991). *First-Person Accounts of Genocidal Acts Committed in the Twentieth Century.* Westport, CT: Greenwood Press.

Totten, Samuel, and William S. Parsons (n.d.). "Confronting Genocide and Ethnocide of Indigenous Peoples: Issues of Intervention and Prevention." In C. Patrick Morris and Robert K. Hitchcock (eds.), *International Human Rights and Indigenous Peoples.*

Weyler, Rex (1982). *Blood of the Land: The Government and Corporate War against the American Indian Movement.* New York: Vintage Books.

Wolf, Eric (1982). *Europe and the People without History.* Berkeley and Los Angeles: University of California Press.

World Bank (1982). *Tribal Peoples and Economic Development.* Washington, D.C.: World Bank.

—— (1991). "Operational Directive 4.20: Indigenous Peoples." *The World Bank Operational Manual.* Washington, D.C.: World Bank.

Eyewitness Accounts

Notes

1. General Kjell Eugenio Laugerud Garcia, who became president of Guatemala in 1974 after the election of Christian Democrat Efrain Riios Montt was stolen by the military.
2. General Romeo Lucas Garcia, who was elected president of Guatemala in 1978.
3. Guatemalan special forces, part of the military which had received special training in counterinsurgency techniques and methods of torture (see Montejo, n.d.).
4. The Somali National Movement, an opposition organization composed mainly of Isaaks, one of several Somali clans, that was formed to fight the government forces of President Siad Barre in northern Somalia.
5. The Gulwadayaal, also known as Victory Pioneers, were paramilitary forces, established in the early 1970s, who worked directly for President Siad Barre. They had extraordinary legal authority over and above the Somali police and could charge people with crimes and make arrests.
6. National Security Service, the national security organization of the government of the Somali Democratic Republic.
7. Hwange, formerly Wankie National Park, the largest national park in Zimbabwe.
8. The Zimbabwe war for independence, which lasted from 1965 to 1980. The time period he is referring to is the mid- to late 1970s.
9. Elite troops of the Rhodesian military.

10. The black people they were referring to belonged to the Zimbabwe African National Union, ZANU, which was made up of Ndebele, Kalanga, Tonga, and other groups and was headed by Joshua Nkomo.
11. Ian Smith, the Prime Minister of Rhodesia.
12. *Taurotragus oryx*, large antelopes that move in herds up to about 50 animals each and which are highly prized by Bushmen for food because of their high fat content.
13. The members of the Fifth Brigade, a North Korea-trained military unit that was under the Prime Minister's office rather than the regular Zimbabwe Army. It was this brigade which was said to have been responsible for the killings of as many as 20,000 people in western Zimbabwe in 1982–1983.

Chapter Fourteen
The Rwanda Genocide
Notes
1. See Claudine Vidal (1991). *Sociologie des Passions* (Cote D'Ivoire, Rwanda). Paris: Karthala.
2. See René Lemarchand (1970). *Rwanda and Burundi*. London: Pall Mall.
3. See Filip Reyntjens (1993). *L'Afrique des Grands Lacs en Crise*. Paris: Karthala.

References

Fein, Helen (1994). "Patrons, Prevention and Punishment of Genocide: Observations on Bosnia and Rwanda," p. 5. In Helen Fein (ed.), *The Prevention of Genocide: Rwanda and Yugoslavia Reconsidered*, A Working Paper of the Institute for the Study of Genocide. New York: The Institute for the Study of Genocide.
Lemarchand, René (1994). *Burundi: Ethnocide as Discourse and Practice*. Washington, D.C., and Oxford: Woodrow Wilson Center Press and Oxford University Press.
Linden, Ian (1977). *Church and Revolution in Rwanda*. Manchester: Manchester University Press.
Physicians for Human Rights (1994). *Rwanda 1994: A Report of the Genocide*. London: Author, p. 11 (Typescript).
Richburg, Keith (May 9, 1994). "In Rwanda, 'Highly Organized' Slaughter," *International Herald Tribune*, p. 4.

Afterword
Genocide in Bosnia-Herzegovina?
References

Cigar, Norman, 1995. *Genocide in Bosnia*. College Station, TX: Texas A&M University Press.
"Death of Yugoslavia," 1995, Autumn. Brian Lapping Associates, Ltd, for BBC Television.
Fein, Helen, 1993a. "Discriminating Genocide from War Crimes: Vietnam and Afghanistan Reexamined" *Denver Journal of International Law and Policy* 22, no. 1 (Fall), pp. 29–62.
Fein, Helen, 1993b. "Accounting for Genocide after 1945: Theories and Some Findings" *International Journal on Group Rights* 1, pp. 79–106.
Helsinki Watch, 1992–1993. *War Crimes in Bosnia-Hercegovina* 2 vols. New York: Human Rights Watch.
Jovic, Borisav, 1995. *Poslednji dani SFRJ* ("The Last Days of the SFRY"). Belgrade. Politika.
Kohl, Phillip, 1996. "Trappings of State, Ethnic Stereotyping, and the Rewriting of History: The Responsibilities of Intellectuals in the Construction of Nationalist Discourses" (mimeo).
Kurtovic, M., 1990. December 25. "Salt in the Wound." *Oslobodjenje* [Sarajevo], p. 5.
O'Connor, Mike. April 3, 1996. "In Bosnia Field, Disturbed Dirt at Suspect Site." *The New York Times*, pp. A1, A9.
Sellers, Patricia Viseur, 1995. "Gender, the Genocide Convention and the Tribunal on the Former Yugoslavia," *The ISG Newsletter* 15 (Fall), pp. 1–3.

Totten, Samuel, and William S. Parsons. 1995. "Introduction" in *Genocide in the Twentieth Century*, Totten, Parsons, and Israel W. Charny, ed. New York: Garland Publishing, pp. xi–lvi

U.N., 1993a. United Nations Security Council, document number S/25835, Annex ("Memorandum on War Crimes and Genocide in Eastern Bosnia (Communes of Bratunac, Skelani and Srebrenica) Committed Against the Serbian Population from April 1992 to April 1993). June 2, 1993.

U.N., 1993b. United Nations Security Council, document number S/26454, Annex ("Report on War Crimes and Grave Breaches of Geneva Conventions Committed by BiH Army and Muslim Paramilitary Forces Against the Croatian Civilian Population in Central Bosnia and Northern Herzegovina"). September 16, 1993.

U.N., 1993c. United Nations Security Council, document number S/26617 ("Letter Dated 21 October 1993 from the Permanent Representative of Croatia to the United Nations Addressed to the President of the Security Council"). October 23, 1993.

U.N., 1996. United Nations Economic and Social Council. Commission on Human Rights, document number E/CN.4/1996/9 ("Situation of human rights in the territory of the former Yugoslavia") (August 22). (electronic mail edition) This is the final periodic report submitted by Tadeusz Mazowiecki as Special Rapporteur. Annex 2 contains a complete bibliography of all the reports submitted by Mr. Mazowiecki.

Zumach, Andreas, 1996. "Evidence Withheld," *Tribunal* 2 (January/February), pp. 2–3.

Contributors

Rouben P. Adalian is Director of the Office of Research and Analysis at the Armenian Assembly of America. He is also an adjunct professor in international affairs at George Washington University and Georgetown University in Washington, D.C. He compiled and edited *The Armenian Genocide in the U.S. Archives 1915–1918* (Chadwyck-Healy, Inc., 1991–1994), a 37,000-page collection of documentation reproduced on microfiche, along with a guide and an index. Adalian is also the author of "The Armenian Genocide: Revisionism and Denial."

Jon Bridgman received his Ph.D. from Stanford in 1961 and is currently Professor of History at the University of Washington where he teaches classes in modern European history. He is the author of *The Revolt of the Hereros* (Berkeley: University of California Press, 1981) and more recently *The End of the Holocaust—The Liberation of the Camps* (Portland, OR: Areopagetea Press, 1990).

Steven L. Burg is Professor of Politics at Brandeis University. Professor Burg received his Ph.D. in political science from the University of Chicago (1980) and an earlier M.A. in Russian Area Studies. Professor Burg is the author of *Conflict and Cohesion in Socialist Yugoslavia* (Princeton, 1983) and *War or Peace? Nationalism, Democracy and American Foreign Policy in Post-Communist Europe* (New York University Press, 1996). He is co-author, with the late Roy Macridis, of *Introduction to Comparative Politics: Regimes and Regime Change* (HarperCollins, 1991) and, with Paul S. Shoup, of *The War in Bosnia-Herzegovina: Domestic and International Dimensions* (M.E. Sharpe, forthcoming). Professor Burg is the author of numerous articles on Soviet, Yugoslav, and post-Yugoslav politics and on ethnic conflict. He served as co-chair, with Paul Shoup, of the February 1993 International Workshop on Peace in Bosnia-Herzegovina, co-sponsored by the International Research and Exchanges Board (IREX) and the Woodrow Wilson International Center for Scholars in Washington, D.C. He is presently serving as the principal consultant to the project on the South Balkans of the Center for Preventive Action of the Council on Foreign Relations in New York.

Robert Cribb is Senior Lecturer in Southeast Asian history at the University of Queensland in Brisbane, Australia. He is the editor of *The Indonesian Killings of 1965–1966: Studies from Java and Bali* (Clayton, Victoria, Australia: Monash University Centre of Southeast Asian Studies, 1990).

James Dunn has degrees in political science and Asian studies from Melbourne University and the Australian National University. Initially, he served as a defense analyst specializing in Asian affairs, then as Australian Consul to Portuguese Timor, and finally as a diplomat in Western and Eastern Europe. He went to Timor in 1974, as a member of a two-man fact-finding mission sent by the Australian government; and again in 1975, at the beginning of Indonesia's military intervention, as leader of an aid mission. For ten years prior to his retirement he was senior foreign affairs advisor to the Australian Parliament, with a specialization in Eastern Europe, Southeast Asia, and human rights issues. He is the author of *Timor: A People Betrayed* (Brisbane: Jacaranda-Wiley, 1983).

Hugh Gregory Gallagher is the author of *By Trust Betrayed: Patients, Physicians and the License to Kill in the Third Reich* (Henry Holt, 1990). A second edition of his biography *FDR's Splendid Deception* has been issued by Vandamere Press. His paper, "'Slapping up Spastics': Euthanasie?" was presented at the first International Conference on the Holocaust sponsored by the United States Holocaust Memorial Museum. Gallagher is a polio quadriplegic and has used a wheelchair for 40 years. He lives in Cabin John, Maryland.

Robert K. Hitchcock is an associate professor of anthropology and the coordinator of African Studies at the University of Nebraska, Lincoln. He has worked on rural development and human rights issues among indigenous peoples in southern and eastern Africa since 1975. In 1983–1984 he was the Planning Advisor and Research Manager on the National Refugee Commission, government of Somalia, and worked with refugees from the Ogaden War in Ethiopia. In 1988, 1989, 1990, and 1992 he conducted evaluations of development and resource managment projects and conservation policies in Zimbabwe, Botswana, and Namibia, the latter of which have had negative effects on the well-being of indigenous peoples. A member of the U.S. Commission for Human Rights of the American Anthropological Association, he is the editor of *International Human Rights and Indigenous Peoples* (with C. Patrick Morris) (forthcoming). He has written numerous articles on the status of indigenous peoples, including one for the *Internet on the Holocaust and Genocide*.

Rounaq Jahan is currently affiliated with the Southern Asian Institute at Columbia University as a senior research scholar. She was a professor of political science at Dhaka University, Bangladesh, from 1970–1993. Jahan received her Ph.D. in political science from Harvard University in 1970 and did postdoctoral research at Columbia, Chicago, Harvard, Boston, and Bergen. Her publications include *Pakistan: Failure in National Integration* (New York: Columbia University Press, 1972), and *Bangladesh Politics: Problems and Issues* (Dhaka: University Press Ltd., 1980). Jahan also worked for the United Nations for many years. She was Coordinator of the Women's Program at the United Nations Asia-Pacific Development Centre in Kuala Lumpur, Malaysia (1982–1984) and Head of the Rural Women's Employment Program at the International Labour Organization in Geneva, Switzerland (1985–1989).

Ben Kiernan, who was born in Melbourne, Australia, is Associate Professor of History and Director of the Cambodian Genocide Program at Yale University. He is the author of *How Pol Pot Came to Power* (London: Verso, 1985), and two other works on the Khmer Rouge, and co-author of *Peasants and Politics in Kampuchea, 1942–1981* (London: Zed, 1982). He edited *Genocide and Democracy in Cambodia* (Yale Southeast Asia Council, 1993), and co-edited *Revolution and Its Aftermath in Kampuchea* and *Pol Pot Plans the Future* (Yale Southeast Asia Council, 1983 and 1988). Kiernan has also published more than thirty scholarly articles on Southeast Asian history. His writing has been translated into eight languages. His most recent work, *The Pol Pot Regime,* is a social and political history of Cambodia from 1975 to 1979 (New Haven, CT: Yale University Press, 1996).

Lyman H. Legters, Professor Emeritus of Russian and East European Studies at the University of Washington, is currently Senior Fellow at the Wil–

liam O. Douglas Institute. In the latter capacity, he edited *Western Society after the Holocaust,* and is now Project Director of the Institute's program *States and Societies in East-Central Europe.* He has authored numerous chapters on Soviet events with genocidal implications and has argued, in a recent book, *Native Americans and Public Policy,* for the inclusion of the American Indian experience within the rubric of modern genocide.

René Lemarchand is professor emeritus at the University of Florida (Gainesville) and is serving as the USAID Regional Consultant for West Africa on issues of governance and democratization, in Abidjan (Cote d'Ivoire). He has written extensively on the former Belgian territories (Zaire, Rwanda, and Burundi) and on Chad. His work, *Rwanda and Burundi* (London and New York: Pall Mall and Praeger, 1971), received the Melville Herskovits Award from the African Studies Association in 1971. He is the author of *Selective Genocide in Burundi* (London: Minority Rights Group, 1973) and of several other pieces dealing with ethnic conflicts in Burundi, including *Burundi: Ethnocide as Discourse and Practice* (Cambridge University Press, 1994).

James E. Mace received his B.A. from Oklahoma State University in 1973, his M.A. (1978) and Ph.D. (1981) in East European History from the University of Michigan. Dr. Mace has been a research associate of the Harvard Ukrainian Research Institute (1981–1986), Executive Director of the U.S. Commission on the Ukraine Famine (1986–1990), Senior Research Fellow at the Harriman Institute of Columbia University (1990–1991), Research Fellow in the Ukrainian Research Program of the University of Illinois at Urbana-Champaign (1992–1993), a Supervising Research Fellow in the Institute of Ethnic and Political Studies of the National Academy of Sciences of Ukraine in Kyïv (1993–present), and has been named Director of the newly organized Ukrainian People's Institute of Genocide Studies, also in Kyïv. Among his publications are *Communism and the Dilemmas of National Liberation: National Communism in Soviet Ukraine, 1918–1933* (Harvard, 1983); "Famine and Nationalism in Soviet Ukraine," *Problems of Communism,* May–June 1984; "Genocide in the U.S.S.R." in *Genocide: A Critical Bibliographical Review* (London: Mansell & Facts on File, 1988); and with Leonid Heretz he compiled and edited *The Oral History Project of the Commission on the Ukraine Famine* (3 vols.: Government Printing Office, 1990).

Sybil Milton received her B.A. at Barnard College (1962), and her M.A. (1963) and Ph.D. (1971) in modern German history at Stanford University. After teaching at Stanford University, she was affiliated with the Commission for the History of Parliamentary Parties in Bonn and the Historical Commission in Berlin. From 1974 to 1984, Dr. Milton was Director of Archives at the Leo Baeck Institute in New York. She has been affiliated with the United States Memorial Museum since 1986 and is currently Senior Historian of the United States Holocaust Museum Research Institute in Washington, D.C.

For the past twelve years Dr. Milton's research has focused on Nazi Germany and the Holocaust. She co-edited and contributed to *The Holocaust: Ideology, Bureaucracy, and Genocide* (1980) and *Genocide: Critical Issues of the Holocaust* (1983); she was co-author of *Art of the Holocaust* (1981), which received the National Jewish Book Award in Visual Arts, 1982. She has published a number of important articles on various aspects of the Holocaust, including "The Expulsion of Polish Jews from Germany, 1938," in *Leo Baeck Institute Yearbook* (1984); "Women and the Holocaust," in *When Biology Became Destiny: Women in Weimar and Nazi Germany* (1984); "The Artist in Exile, Internment, and Hiding, 1933–1944," in *Art and Exile: Felix Nussbaum, 1904–1944* (1985); "Images of the Holocaust," in *Holocaust and Genocide Studies: An International Journal* (1986); and "Argument oder Illustration: Die Bedeutung von Fotodokumenten als Quelle," *Fotogeschichte* 8, no. 28 (1988): 60–90. Dr. Milton has served as co-editor of the *Simon Wiesenthal Center Annual*, vols. 1–7 (1984–90). She is series co-editor of the Garland project *Archives of the Holocaust*; twenty-three of twenty-six volumes have been published. Her recent articles have concerned the fate of Roma and Sinti in Nazi Germany, 1933–1945, and occupied Europe, 1940–1945; and the problem of memorials and memory in Germany and Austria.

Her most recent book is *In Fitting Memory: The Art and Politics of Holocaust Memorials*, published by Wayne State University, 1991. She is currently preparing a volume for University of North Carolina Press on photography of Nazi Germany and the Holocaust as historical evidence.

She was awarded a second prize in the 1992 American Association of Museums publications competition for her development of an artifact poster set with teachers' manual for the United States Holocaust Memorial Museum. She was elected to membership in the New York Academy of Science in 1990, and serves on the advisory council of the Wannsee Villa and Topography of Terror memorials in Berlin and also on the International Experts Commission of the Mauthausen Memorial Museum.

Donald L. Niewyk is a professor of modern European history at Southern Methodist University. A specialist in the history of anti-Semitism, he is the author of *Socialist, Antisemite, and Jew* (Baton Rouge: Louisiana State University Press, 1971), *The Jews in Weimar Germany* (Lexington, MA: D.C. Heath, 1980), and most recently *The Holocaust: Problems and Perspectives of Interpretation* (Lexington, MA: D.C. Heath, 1992).

Tara M. Twedt is a graduate student in anthropology at the University of Nebraska, Lincoln. Currently, she is attending the University of Chile in Santiago on a Rotary Scholarship. She has worked for the Mexican-American Legal Defense Foundation and Educational Fund (MALDEF) in Washington, D.C. and Los Angeles and for the Mexican-American Commission of the State of Nebraska. Her interests are in human rights, grassroots development strategies, and the politics of international anti-drug policies.

Leslie J. Worley received his Ph.D. from the University of Washington. He is a lecturer in history at the University of Washington and teaches classes in ancient and European military history. He is the author of *Hippeis: The Cavalry of Ancient Greece* (Boulder, CO: Westview Press, 1993).

About the Editors

Israel W. Charny is Executive Director of the Institute on the Holocaust and Genocide, Jerusalem. He is the author of *How Can We Commit the Unthinkable: Genocide, The Human Cancer* (Boulder, CO, and London: Westview Press, 1982); editor with Shamai Davidson of the *Book on the International Conference on the Holocaust and Genocide* (1983); editor of *Toward the Understanding and Prevention of Genocide* (1984); editor of *Genocide: A Critical Bibliographic Review* (1988), *Genocide: A Critical Bibliographic Review*, Volume 2 (1991), *Genocide: A Critical Bibliographic Review*, Volume 3 (1994), and a forthcoming Volume 4 in the series; and editor of the book by the late Shami Davidson, *Holding on to Humanity: The Message of Holocaust Survivors: The Shamai Davidson Papers* (1992).

He is also Professor of Psychology and Family Therapy and Director of the Program of Advanced Studies in Integrative Psychotherapy of the Department of Psychology and Martin Buber Center at the Hebrew University of Jerusalem.

He has been devoted to the study of the Holocaust and genocide since the mid-1960s. He is committed to the ideal that an understanding of the processes which brought about the unbearable evil of the Holocaust be joined with the age-old Jewish tradition of contributing to the greater ethical development of human civilization, and that a unique memorial to the Holocaust be forged in the development of new concepts of prevention of genocide to any and all peoples. His first publication on the subject, which appeared in *Jewish Education* in 1968, was "Teaching the Violence of the Holocaust: A Challenge to Educating Potential Future Oppressors and Victims for Nonviolence."

William S. Parsons is the former Director of Education and now Chief of Staff for the United States Holocaust Memorial Museum, in Washington, D.C. He is the author of the study guide *Everyone's Not Here: Families of the*

Armenian Genocide (Armenian Assembly of America, 1989), and co-author of the text *Facing History and Ourselves: Holocaust and Human Behavior* (Intentional Publications, Inc., 1982), the sourcebook *The African Meeting House* in Boston (Museum of Afro-American History, 1990), and "State Developed Teacher Guides and Curriculum on Genocide and/or the Holocaust: A Succinct Review and Critique" in *Inquiry in Social Studies: Curriculum, Research, and Instruction* (North Carolina Council for the Social Studies). He also co-edited the special issue "Teaching about Genocide" in *Social Education* (National Council for the Social Studies) and the special issue "African American History: Beyond Heroes" in *Social Education* (National Council for the Social Studies).

Samuel Totten is Professor of Curriculum and Instruction at the University of Arkansas at Fayetteville. He is also a member of the Council of the Institute on the Holocaust and Genocide (Jerusalem, Israel), and an Associate of the Centre for Comparative Genocide Studies (Sydney, New South Wales, Australia). He is the compiler/editor of *First-Person Accounts of Genocidal Acts Committed in the Twentieth Century: An Annotated Bibliography* (Greenwood Press, 1991). Among the essays on genocide he has published are "Educating about Genocide: Curricula and Inservice" in *Genocide: A Critical Bibliographic Review,* Volume II (Mansell and Facts on File, 1991), and "Non-Governmental Organizations Working on the Issue of Genocide" in *Genocide: A Critical Bibliographic Review,* Volume III (Transaction Publishers, 1994). He is currently co-editing a book entitled *Teaching the Holocaust: Critical Essays* (Allyn and Bacon Publishers, forthcoming).

Index

phosgene gas experiments, 196–197
policies and procedures, 137–138
responses after, 146–147
survivors of, 138
as unique event, xiii–xiv
victim responses after, 144–146
victims of, 140–141
Hon Yuon, 336
Hovannisian, Richard, xxiii
Hoyt, Michael, 324
Hroch, Myroslav, 78–79
Huffeland, Christoph, 220
Hun Sen, 345, 356
Hungary, 140
Hunter-gatherers, indigenous, 384
Hutu majority, 317–319
Hutu Republic, 318
Hutus, 327, 383, 408–422

I, Rigoberta Menchu, An Indian Woman of Guatemala, 393
I Accuse (movie), 217
I Did Not Interview the Dead, 150
Ibos, first-person testimonies of, xxiv
Ieng Sary, 337, 355
Ieng Thirith, 337
Illing, Ernst, 222
Imam, Jahanara, 304
Imperial Colonial Office, German, 26
Imperialism, German, 22
Impunity, phenomenon of, 388
Independent Commission on International Humanitarian Issues, 374
India, 376
Bangladesh and, 301–302
partitioning of, 291
Indians
estimated numbers of, 375
in United States, 379–380
Indigenous hunter-gatherers, 384
Indigenous people, genocide of, xxvi, 378–407
eyewitness accounts, 391–407
gathering data on, 391–392
lessons from, 390–391
oral testimony on, 392–393
pattern to, 239–240
twentieth-century cases of, 383
typologies of, 384–387
Indigenous peoples, 372–374
annual deaths of, 373
characteristics of, 374–378
defining, 374

estimated numbers of, 375
protection of, 387–390
racism for, 377
rights organizations of, 389–390
socioeconomic features of, 377
Indonesia, 386
Chinese in, 242
Christianity in, 245
invasion of East Timor, 264–290
Islam in, 237
Republic of, 266
United Nations and, 274
Indonesian Committee of Inquiry (Komisi Penjelidik Nasional), 277, 279
Indonesian Communist Party, 236–263
Indonesian genocide, 236–263
current attitudes toward, 247
death toll, 241–242
eyewitness accounts, 247–263
first-person testimonies of, xxiv, xxv
lessons from, 247
long-range impacts of, 244–245
perpetrators of, 236–239
reasons for, 240–241
responses to, 245–246
scholarly interpretation of, 246–247
victims of, 241–242
Indonesian Killings of 1965–1966, The, 258
Indonesian military intelligence agency, Bakin, 270
Indonesian nation, 267
Indonesian Nationalist Party, 237
Indonesian Trade and Society (Van Leur), 350
"Indonesianization," 283
"Information Agency on Gypsies," 172
Inguishi, deportations of, 117
Injustice, Persecution, Eviction: A Human Rights Update on Indonesia and East Timor, 249
International Alert: Standing International Forum on Ethnic Conflict, Genocide and Human Rights (IA), xxx
International Commission of Jurists, 354
International Work Group for Indigenous Affairs (IWGIA), xxx
Internationalism, 82, 143
Interpol International Center for Fighting the Gypsy Menace, 173
Inuit, 376
Isaaks of Somalia, 383, 400–405
Iskandar, Maskun, 249
Islam, 52
in Indonesia, 237
Islamic Empires, 54